ISBN: 960 - 86862 - 9 - 6

Copyright ©2004: Ministry of Press and Mass Media
Secrtetariat General of Information

This book has been prepared by the Laboratory of Political
Communication at the University of Athens
Co - ordinator: Professor **A - J. D. Metaxas**, Director of the Laboratory

In preparing the book, we have been greatly helped by the suggestions and assistance of Professor
Ch. Chryssanthakis and Associate Professor M. Spourdalakis.

Editor: Anthony J. Bacaloumis, Laboratory of Political Communication, University of Athens.

Language editing: Helga Stefansson

Secretarial assistance: Konstantinos Bassios

Edition Art Directors: Giannis Bazakas, Thanasis Kirianakis

Priting - Production: KORYFI PUBLICATIONS S.A.

The cover illustration is a part of the painting "Likofos" (Twilight) by **P. Tetsis**
(National Gallery collection)

Preface

"About Greece" contains useful information on contemporary Greece. The aim of this volume is not to praise the country but rather to present an objective overview. Moreover, this is a precondition for the involvement of the Laboratory of Political Communication of the University of Athens. For each topic we relied upon authors who we knew would be able to present a justified analysis. We thank all of them warmly, for their collaboration and for the quality of their contribution.

I am grateful to the General Secretariat of Information, and notably its diligent staff, whose co-operation was impeccable.

To the extent to which the cover illustration of this volume had to reveal something immediate and complete about the country, I believe the choice of the work of Panagiotis Tetsis was the best possible one. I wish to express my gratitude both to the painter and the National Gallery for permitting us to use a part of this painting, "Likofos" (Twilight).

My colleagues at the University of Athens, Associate Professor in Political Sociology Michalis Spourdalakis, and Professor in Public Law Charalambos Chrysanthakis contributed their expertise during every stage of the project. Both I thank them.

I would also like to thank all those individuals who graciously took the time to provide us with comments on the first edition.

Finally, my thanks are due to Anthony Bacaloumis, educationalist - research fellow at the Laboratory of Political Communication at the University of Athens, for his invaluable assistance in coordinating the entire project as well as editing.

Professor A-J. D. Metaxas
Director of the Laboratory of Political Communication
at the University of Athens

TABLE OF CONTENTS

THE COUNTRY

GEOGRAPHICAL REGIONS

PREFECTURE BOUNDARIES
⊙ PREFECTURE CAPITAL

HELLENIC REPUBLIC

Member of EU - Euro zone participant -
Member of NATO
Form of Government: Parliamentary
Democracy
Prime Minister: Kostas Karamanlis
Area: 131,944 sq km (51,458 sq mi)
Population: 10.3 million
Capital city: Athens (3.7 million)
Language: Greek
Religion: 98% Greek Orthodox,
1.3% Muslim, 0.7% other
GDP per head: US$12,450 (2002)
Annual growth: 4% (2002)
Inflation: 2.6% (2002)

HDI Rank (UN Human Development Indicator):
24th out of 175 countries (2003)
Major products/industries: tourism, shipping, food and
tobacco processing, textiles, chemicals, metal products,
petroleum products
Major trading partners: Germany, Italy, France, UK, USA
Average life expectancy: 78.1 years
Adult literacy rate (% age 15 and above): 97.3

THE COUNTRY

Natural Features

Greece, officially known as the Hellenic Republic, lies at the south-eastern edge of Europe. In the north, it shares borders with Albania, the Former Yugoslav Republic of Macedonia (FYROM) and Bulgaria and to the east with Turkey. The territory extends to 131,957 sq. km and the country consists of a peninsula and over 2.000 islands.

Though a relatively small country, Greece boasts an astonishing variety of landscapes -from the legendary mountains of Olympus, Pindos and Parnassos to miles of pristine coastline. Indeed, due to the large number of islands,

Greece has a particularly long coastline (15,021 km), the most extensive among all Mediterranean countries.

The climate is mostly dry and temperate, though it snows in the mountains and in the north. Northern Macedonia and northern Epirus have a climate similar to the Balkans, with freezing winters and very hot, humid summers, while the Attica region, the Cyclades, the Dodecanese, Crete and Central and Eastern Peloponnese have a more typically Mediterranean climate with hot, dry summers and milder winters.

Greece has been divided traditionally into the following geographical regions:

- The **Attica region** (Athens metropolitan area)

Almost half of the Greek population lives in the Attica basin (3,756,607 persons according to the 2001 census-provisional data). Athens, the capital of the country and its main administrative centre, is built in the Attica region. Ministries, all the higher courts, the head offices of most banks, insurance companies, other businesses and a large part of Greek industry headquarters are concentrated in the capital area. Moreover, Athens attracts visitors from many parts of the world who are coming to visit the Acropolis, the city's and country's symbol, other archaeological sites and the National Archaeological Museum.

- **Mainland Hellas** (excluding the capital area)

Delphi, the most famous oracle of Antiquity, lies in this region, at the heart of Greece. Running through central Greece is the rugged Pindos massif, with a peak of 2,637 m (Mt. Smolikas).

- **The Peloponnese**

The Peloponnese is the southernmost part of continental Greece. Many great cities of the antiquity, such as Mycenae, Sparta and Olympia, the birthplace of the Olympic Games are located in this region. Also, there is the Byzantine city of Mystras. This fertile region enjoys a temperate climate, ideal for growing olivetrees and grapes.

- **Epirus**

Epirus constitutes the north-western part of continental Greece and is bordered in the north by Albania and in the south by Central Greece. The region is almost entirely mountainous and the high Pindos massif forms the region's eastern boundary separating it from Macedonia and Thessaly. The main pole of attraction is in the northern part of the region, named Vikos National Park, which contains waterfalls, gorges, rivers, picturesque villages and dense forests.

- **Thessaly**

Thessaly lies in the middle-upper part of continental Greece. The island complex of the Northern Sporades is included in the area. The plain of Thessaly, surrounded by several mountains, the most famous of which is Mount Olympus, the highest mountain in Greece (2,917 m.), is its main geographical feature.

• **Macedonia**

Macedonia is the largest of the ten geographical regions of Greece. The region is bordered in the south by the Aegean Sea and by Thessaly, in the east by western Thrace, in the west by Epirus and in the north by Bulgaria, Albania and the Former Yugoslav Republic of Macedonia (FYROM). It contains the self-governing, monastic area of Mount Athos and Thessaloniki, the northern "co-capital" of Greece. The landscape is quite varied, since Western and Eastern Macedonia are, in general, mountainous with the exception of certain sizeable, fertile valleys. Central Macedonia contains the plain of Thessaloniki, the second largest in the country.

• **Thrace**

This region constitutes the north-eastern part of continental Greece. It is distinguished from Macedonia to the west by the river Nestos, from Turkey (Eastern Thrace) to the east and north-west by the river Evros, from Bulgaria to the north by the mountain range Rodopi and in the south by the sea. The climate can be characterised as intermediate in the type between the Mediterranean and the Mid-European. The Evros delta, where many rare species find refuge due to the favourable ecology conditions, is the main pole of attraction of the area.

• **The Aegean islands**

The Archipelago of the Aegean is made up by hundreds of islands and islets. All the islands are mountainous or hilly and they enjoy a warm climate.

Concerning the rainfall, the climate of the region is the driest in Greece, with the islands of the eastern Aegean and the Dodecanese being the most humid.

• **Crete**

Crete is the largest Greek island. As for the landscape, the island lacks any noteworthy plains, essentially mountainous. It is worth noting that the southern shoreline of Crete is the warmest area in Greece.

• **The Ionian Islands**

This region forms the smallest geographical area in Greece and consists of seven main islands, which are strung along the west coast of Greece. The islands have a mild and relatively humid climate and the rainfall rate is considerably high. As a result, the vegetation is abundant and combines elements of the tropical flora with forests reminiscent of North Europe. The islands retain significant influences from Mediterranean Europe.

Flora and fauna

Greece is endowed with a variety of flora unrivalled in Europe (some 5,500 species of flora have been identified), being particularly rich in unique plant species.

The wild flowers create spectacular views, among them, anemones, gladioli, cyclamens, irises, tulips, lilies and many more. Especially during spring, all hillsides are carpeted with flowers, which seem to sprout even from the rocks. As for the forests, the most extensive ones are found in northern Greece, in the mountains of Thrace, Macedonia and Epirus. Furthermore, the islands in the northern and eastern Aegean and similarly those of the Ionian Sea, are, to a large extent, covered with pines, aspen, as well as other forest trees. In total, the country has over 200 species of tree and large shrub and its forests consist, primarily, of conifers with deciduous trees such as beeches and chestnuts coming second.

Numerous protected areas exist in Greece, as the country has been committed to their protection through international conventions. Its national parks include Olympus (on the borders of Thessaly and Macedonia), Parnassos and Iti (central Greece), Prespes and Vikos-Aoos (Epirus), Parnitha (Attica) and Samaria (Crete). There are also 11 Wetlands, 51 preserved natural monuments, 113 important bird sanctuaries and 300 Corinne biotopes.

Moreover, 900 species of fauna live in Greece. The country is a refuge for many endangered species, which are protected through specific action pro-grammes, implemented by the authorities, aiming at the management and protection of bio-diversity. Among the protected species are the Mediterranean sea turtle (Caretta -caretta) and the monk seal (Monachus - monachus). The former finds home in the waters of Zakynthos and Cefallonia, whereas the latter is found in the Aegean and the Ionian Seas. The dense forests and rocky outcrops of the Dadia Forest River (upstream on the Evros River) in Thrace, as well as the wetlands at the Evros delta, are shelter to the largest range of birds of prey in Europe. Lake Mikri Prespa, in Macedonia, has the richest colony of fish-eating birds in Europe, including cormorants, ibises, egrets and herons. Moreover, the brown bear - Europe's largest land mammal- survives in the Pindos massif and in the mountains along the borders with Albania, FYROM and Bulgaria. Finally, the northern forests are home to wildcat, marten, roe deer, occasionally wolf and lynx, whereas jackals, wild goats and hedgehogs live in the south.

HISTORY
OF MODERN GREECE

A HISTORY OF MODERN GREECE

By Petmezas, S.

The Greek Enlightenment and the Hellenic National Revival

The rise of the Ottoman Empire brought together, for the last time, south-eastern Europe, the Black Sea, and the Middle East into a single political realm governed by the law of Islam and the Decrees of the Sultans. The real material benefits of a pacified and unified larger imperial economy and society in the 14th-18th centuries were soon obliterated by a number of factors. These included: military haemorrhage; fiscal pressure; authoritarian and cruel rule; absence of any coherent state policy to support the active commercial and productive classes and last, but not least, complete exclusion of the non-Muslim majority of the population in the Balkans and Asia Minor from the body politic. During that period, the European world underwent the experiences of the Renaissance, Humanism and Reformation. It reached the era of Enlightenment, a new phase of social and intellectual development. Individuality was fully recognised as the pivotal value of the modern world. Science was completely dissociated from dogmatic theology and the pursuit of progress and happiness was legitimised as a potentially possible and desirable goal. The peoples of south-eastern Europe, with the exception of a small minority of the non-Muslim elite, did not participate in or even have knowledge of these intellectual developments.

Greek-Orthodox Christians, as any other non-Muslim religious community in the Ottoman Empire, constituted a corporate body which has a kind of protection from the Ottoman administrative system, but was also seen as intrinsically inferior and subjugated to it. The Greek-Orthodox "Romeoi" were led and represented by their spiritual leader: the Patriarch of Constantinople or, on a local level, by their bishops in each diocese. The peoples in south-eastern Europe construed their group- and self-identity mainly through their religious affiliation.

"The massacre of Chios", by E. Delacroix, 1822-24

Since the local Balkan aristocracies had been almost completely annihilated, no paramount Christian elite was left to dominate the social and political sphere. Locally notable families, Church prelates, and the richest merchants and financiers in the big cities substituted themselves for the extinct aristocrats as political intermediaries and social leaders. Since the end of the 17th century, the Phanariots, a small number of rich and well-educated families that served as official translators for the Sublime Porte and Admiralty and later as rulers in the Danubian principalities rose to the top of this dominant group. At the level of local self-government, this corporate socio-political structure delegated authority in religious, familial and even civil affairs to the Greek-Orthodox elite and institutions. Nevertheless, this power system was as authoritarian and patrimonial as the one operating at the top of the empire.

The second half of the 18th century witnessed a whole range of developments in the Ottoman Europe. Successive defeats at the hands of the Russian and the Austrian armies had made it clear that the once formidable Muslim Empire was about to collapse. The old Christian elite was now less inclined to accept Ottoman domination unquestioningly. These external threats were combined with a unique process of political and state-financial fragmentation of power and decentralisation that was felt in literally all Ottoman provinces. Furthermore, there was a powerful drive towards the trans-

formation of the land tenure system and the subsequent deterioration of the position of the peasants, especially the non-Muslims. The state of oppressive anarchy and economic deprivation suffered by a large part of the peasant and urban strata made them less reluctant to challenge openly the rule of their lords. Finally, new opportunities for enrichment through trade with the European economies were given to many Balkan and Anatolian merchants and craftsmen, almost exclusively non-Muslim, and mainly Greek-Orthodox. These formed a new Diaspora of merchants, ship-owners and artisans in Europe, which was closely related to the old Greek merchant Diaspora in the Middle East and the Black Sea. This new and dynamic social group challenged the dominant position of the old Phanariot, Church and civil aristocracy in the Greek-Orthodox community.

Even though many of these men, merchants, notables, Church and civil magistrates were not of Greek descent, they considered themselves Greek-Orthodox "Romeoi". They used Greek as their commercial, cultural or administrative language and they would be the first to espouse the cause of the Hellenic national revival. Close commercial or educational relations with the enlightened western and central Europe exposed them, along with the Phanariots and their administrative and commercial subordinates and employees, to the influence of the late 18th century Enlight-

enment. There was a new group of intellectuals, teachers and authors, many of
whom were clergymen and most of
whom had studied in Italy or in Germany. Throughout the 18th century they
had become acquainted with the latest
European intellectual development and
had the ambition to participate in it and
"transmit" its achievements to their
cultural kin. The Greek Enlightenment
proved to be a powerful intellectual
surge, which almost entirely reconfig-
ured, in less than a century, the personal
self-perception and the collective world-
view of the leading Greek-Orthodox
elite.

Until the French Revolution, the
most timid versions of central-European
Enlightenment were echoed and various
projects for a Greek-Orthodox enlight-

ened Monarchy were conceived among
the highest spheres of the Church and
Phanariot magistrates. The French revolutionary example and, later, the French
military presence in Dalmatia, Egypt and
the Ionian Islands radically changed the
political and the intellectual agenda. The
French message of liberation was propagated by men such as Rigas of Velestino
(1757-1797) - who produced a precise
Greek version of the 1793 French Constitution - and Adamantios Koraes (1748-
1833), the celebrated scholar who was
universally respected in Greece. Some
of the best educated young men, the
most active patriots and the bravest military leaders (brigands or local militiamen) espoused this radical message
along with a more coherent view of
their identity. They saw themselves no
more as Greek-Orthodox "Romeoi", but
as "Hellenes", heirs of the republican
and enlightened tradition of classical
Hellas. The new Hellenic identity was
not meant to be based upon ethnic or
religious characteristics but upon participation in the common republican and
democratic body politic and the adoption of the enlightened classical intellectual tradition. Official ecclesiastical censure, obscurantist preaching, political
persecution, and finally the reactionary
diplomacy of the Holy Alliance and the
military might of the Ottomans ham-
pered the process. However, in less than
a quarter of a century, a rational revolutionary and republican project was
conceived and won the adherence of

Rigas Feraios, by A. Kriezis

Adamantios Koraes

revolt was propagated among the peasant and urban population. Some of the most respected and fervent patriots like Adamantios Koraes and Ioannis Kapodistrias (1776-1831), former Russian deputy Minister of Foreign Affairs however, felt that any revolutionary movement would be premature.

The Hellenic War of Independence and the Revolutionary Republic (1821-1832)

The most important political figures of the Greek-Orthodox community did falter. Furthermore the political situation in Restoration Europe was negative. In spite of this, a revolt instigated by the *Philiki Etaireia* broke out, first in Moldavia in February 1821 and then in March 1821 in many parts of mainland Greece from the Peloponnese to Macedonia. Patriotic activists who were strongly influenced

the youngest and most active members of all social groups. Secret societies, the most important and influential being the *Philiki Etaireia*, were formed and the idea of an imminent and necessary

Painting by Th.Vryzakis, inspired from the legendary beginnings of the Greek War of Independence at 25th March 1821, detail

by the European liberal and nationalist movement initially led it. From the very beginning the revolutionary authorities adopted a liberal republican discourse and the first Constitutions of the young Hellenic State (1822, 1823, 1827) clearly drew upon the ideas of the American and the French Revolutions. The identification of revived Hellenism, democracy, and national sovereignty propagated by these men found an impressive response not only in the country itself but in Europe as well. A large movement of solidarity sprung up among European intellectuals and liberals, who thought that the Greek Revolution was both the champion of European liberalism in an era of Aristocratic Restoration and the sublime revival of the purest classical matrix of Democracy and Enlightenment. The Philhellenic movement actively supported the Greek Revolution and the great romantic English poet Lord George Gordon Byron (who died in Messolonghi in 1824) is only the most symbolic figure among a large number of European Philhellenes who fought and died "so that Greece might still be free".

It is true that the large number of fighting militiamen, sailors, peasants, and other commoners had only a confused and rudimentary view of the democratic and liberal project of the *Philiki Etaireia*. They still however adopted its call for an independent Hellenic Republic and a Constitution that would guarantee their political and so-

cial emancipation, which meant freedom and land for all. These ideals, although ill understood, mobilised the great majority of the Greek-Orthodox population in mainland Greece and galvanised them to undertake an almost desperate fight against the Ottoman armies. It is estimated that in twelve years of fighting, the population of southern Greece decreased from 940,000 to 753,000. In the large urban centres of the Empire, from Constantinople to Smyrna and Larissa, the Greek-Orthodox population and clergy suffered enormously from the extortions of the undisciplined Janissaries that the Sublime Porte had let loose. The Patriarch Gregory V himself, the same man who had condemned the Greek Revolution, was hanged by the Janissary mob along with many Greek notables of Constantinople who had also been hostile to the revolt. Thus, in spite of the resolute condemnation of this revolt, as well as of any previous one by the Patriarch and the Holy Synod, the revolutionary War acquired a religious connotation due to the massive, cruel and blind Ottoman repression. This attitude forced the Greek-Orthodox population as a whole to identify itself with the revolutionaries and with their radical cause.

Within the first two years, the revolution was crushed everywhere except in the Peloponnese, central Greece, Crete, and some of the Aegean Islands such as Samos. The Ottoman armies committed ferocious atrocities but were unable to overcome Greek resistance in those areas. Even the intervention of the modernised Egyptian army that resulted in the desolation of the countryside and large-scale massacres in Crete and the Peloponnese proved unable to suppress the revolt. In the meantime, the view of conservative European Powers concerning to the necessary subjugation of the Greek revolt was undermined. Influenced by the liberal European Philhellenic movement and public opinion, the governments of Great Britain, France and Russia tried to reach an agreement that would ensure an autonomous status for Greece in the Ottoman Empire. The Sublime Porte refused any compromise and thus forced the intervention of the allied fleets of the three European powers. The destruction of the Ottoman and Egyptian power in the naval battle

of Navarino (1827) bent the Ottomans to reason. Over the next few years fighting continued, but it was only a matter of time before Greece was recognised as an independent sovereign kingdom.

During the War of Independence rival factions of provincial notables and military chiefs undermined all efforts at the implementation of the meritorious, efficient and centralised administration of the political, financial and military system. They had been brought up in and had adopted the manners of the late corrupt, decentralised and patrimonial Ottoman administration. After 1823 civil strife was almost endemic. In response, the Third National Assembly in Trezina (1827) chose Count Ioannis Kapodistrias from Corfu, a charismatic and internationally respected personality, as governor of the Greek Republic. It was hoped that he would be able to overcome the fragmentation of central power and impose the necessary re-

The Old Parliament building in Athens

Ioannis Kapodistrias (1776-1831),
oil painting by D. Tsokos

forms. This proved to be impossible for him because he did not command the required military and financial resources. His projects for an extensive land distribution program, for the establishment of a modernised and centralised administrative, financial, judicial, ecclesiastical, educational, and military system were never implemented. He was assassinated in September 1831, and the civil conflict that followed came to an end only when the "Three Protective Powers" (Great Britain, France and Russia) selected and imposed a young German prince as King of Greece. It was Otto of the House of Wittelsbach, son of Ludwig, King of Bavaria. The institution of an absolute Monarchy instead of a

Republic was the price Greeks had to pay for their inability to accept compromises. It was at the same time the guarantee offered to the conservative powers of the Holy Alliance that Greece would not prove an example to the peoples of Restoration Europe. But the Monarchy was also the key-institution through which the protective powers, and especially Great Britain, exercised their influence upon the Greek government and interfered in national politics. As a result, the dynasties and theirs entourages identified themselves with the agents that curtailed smooth institutional development.

Furthermore, only a fragment of Greece, the poorest and economically less developed south, was liberated: in total 47.516 km^2 and 753.400 inhabitants, overwhelmingly Greek-Orthodox except for two small communities of Roman-Catholic Greeks and Greek Jews (Romaniotes). A larger percentage of Greeks still lived in the Ottoman Empire in Thessaly, Epirus, Macedonia, Thrace, Crete, Cyprus and the other islands, and in parts of Asia Minor. Consequently, from the very beginning all Greeks, living either in the Kingdom of Greece, or in the Ottoman Empire, or in the Septinsular Republic (under British protection since 1814) considered the new independent state just the first step towards the unification of all Hellenes in a sovereign constitutional polity. A powerful, if somewhat utopian (in view of the paucity of Greece's resources and the declared opposition of all European powers), irredentist movement was created. It would dominate Greek politics until the inter-war period.

From Absolutist to Constitutional Monarchy (1832-1862)

Otto was still a minor when he was elected King of Greece and thus his father chose a tripartite Regency to rule in his name. In the following years a flood of Bavarian military and civil officials came to implement a policy of power centralisation, institutional modernisation and social reconfiguration. Mainly idealistic Philhellenes and Greek intellectuals assisted them, most from large urban centres outside the frontiers of the small independent Greece. Foreign and insensitive to the particularities of the country's social and political life, they were soon regarded as "arrogant intruders". They monopolised the administration and deprived local notables and military chiefs (who lacked the credentials and knowledge necessary for a career in the new bureaucratic administration) of all political influence and power. The Bavarian Regency and its successive governments followed the policy already initiated by Kapodistrias, but this time they commanded the necessary military and diplomatic support to impose their will. A new central and local administration, a regular army, and judicial and education systems along central European standards were imposed. The Church was soon forced to cut itself off the administration of the Patriarch and it was put under the complete control of the royal prerogative. In 1837, the Univer-

September 3, 1843: a revolt forces the King to grant a Constitution

sity of Athens opened its gates. It was the first such institution in south-eastern Europe and the Middle East. In spite of continuous factional strife among Bavarian bureaucrats, Philhellenic and Greek officials, and local notables and military chiefs, the centralised administration and its institutions proved solid enough and survived.

Unfortunately the new political structures, those of an absolutist German monarchy, were far from the initial project of the constitutional Republic conceived during the Greek War of Independence. The demand for a Constitution and for the distribution of the former Ottoman landed estates (already under effective control by the peasants) by the state quickly became a powerful driving force and led, on September 3, 1843, to a revolt that forced the King to grant a Constitution. The elected National Assembly worked out the 1844 Constitution in line with the other conservative constitutional charters of Europe. According to this Constitution, the elected Parliament shared its legislative power with the Monarch and the Senate, whose members were chosen by the Monarch himself. The latter had the power to choose his ministers. In spite of its conservative character, this Constitution established the independence of Justice and guaranteed all human and civil rights. Due to the predominance of small peasant ownership, suffrage was almost universal. Since 1844, Greece became a constitutional

state whose main problem remained the distance between the modernity of its institutions and the relatively archaic nature of its economic and social structure. Representative institutions and almost universal suffrage were crippled by lawlessness and political clientelism in the countryside and, in the long-term, by the lack of funds that could have permitted the creation of the infrastructure necessary for the grandiose program of institutional and social modernisation.

The Wittelsbach era was one of slow economic development and of politics dominated by three parties which were nothing more than confederated factions of local notables and potent military chiefs. Each political party was influenced and sponsored by one of the three Protective Powers that in this way exerted an unusually decisive influence on the domestic and foreign policy of Greece. In spite of this, a vivid intellectual life sprung up in the few large cities. The educational system grew rapidly, numerous books were printed, newspapers were published and, in less than a generation, a new well-educated public was created. The political system was rapidly growing obsolete.

A very strong patriotic sentiment had built up during the long and bloody War of Independence. Since the majority of Greeks still lived unhappily along with the other subjugated Christian populations under the authoritarian Ottoman rule, every diplomatic crisis of the Eastern Question and every revolt, however insignificant, mobilised Greek citizenry and became an important domestic issue. The successive revolts in Crete, Epirus, Thessaly and Macedonia initiated strong movements of solidarity and led to demands for Greek military assistance. The National Question thus dominated and haunted Greek politics until the inter-war period. Most Greeks as a consequence resented an active policy of support for the integrity of the Ottoman Empire, led by the major European powers.

Otto proved to be a fervent patriot but could not distance himself from daily party politics and soon tried to impose his will upon all government matters. He was thus credited with the few successes and all the failures of the young state. After a brief period of popularity during the Crimean War, when British and French troops occupied Athens and Piraeus to prevent Greece from taking part in the war, Otto chose to fully assume the reins of the state. The dysfunctionality of the institutional system had alienated the younger generation of notables and politicians and the growing middle classes, who were better educated than their forefathers. The strong liberal movement made its presence clear during the last years of Otto's rule and led

to two military revolts (in January and October 1862) that were strongly supported by large numbers of dissatisfied citizens and officials.

The Establishment of a Liberal Parliamentary Regime and Economic Development (1862-1893)

The short period of anarchy and civil turbulence that followed the October 1862 revolution ended with the election of a new King, George I of the Danish Glucksburg House. The government of Great Britain strongly supported this choice and, once satisfied with the advantageous solution to the crisis, bent to the old and obstinate demand of the population of the Septinsular Republic, then officially under its protection, to unite with Greece. The Union took place in March 1864, and the Heptane-

"The Parliament of the Greeks", a parliamentary session at the end of 19th century, with Charilaos Trikoupis at the podium. Oil painting by N. Orlof (Athens, 1930)

sian representatives took part in the deliberations of the National Assembly that passed the new liberal Constitution of 1864. The executive and the legislative powers were now totally separate. A one-chamber parliament was elected with universal male (until 1945) suffrage. Human rights and civil liberties were guaranteed and meticulously guarded against state arbitrariness.

The King's exclusive right to choose the ministers of his government and the strong tendency of every royal government to interfere in the elections for parliament, soon led to bitter political strife that ended with the imposition of the "principle of parliamentarism". Since 1875, the head of the Greek State asks the political leader who enjoys the majority in Parliament to form a government and this leader and all his ministers are responsible to parliament. In the final quarter of the 19th century political life was dominated by a stable two-party political system led by influential political figures such as the liberal Charilaos Trikoupis and the democrats Alexander Koumoundouros and Theodore Deliyannis. Trikoupis governed throughout most of the 1880-1895 period and associated himself with the very broad modernising reforms of the Greek administration, justice, army and education systems.

Institutional maturity was associated with rapid economic growth, initiated in the late 1860s by the foundation of the first mechanised mills and factories in Piraeus, Hermoupolis and other Greek cities. Meanwhile, new banks were founded and the prosperous Greek Diaspora started investing in independent Greece. The export of currants, olive oil, tobacco and other products of intensive arboriculture financed the rapidly increasing imports of wheat and manufactures. The incorporation of Thessaly and the Epirotan province of Arta fuelled the growing anticipation of a still more rapid economic growth in the Kingdom in 1881. The extensive plains of Thessaly were seen as the future Greek granary that would alleviate the need for wheat imports and save money for investment in more productive sectors of the economy. Unfortunately, the sharecropping system in use in the extensive and archaic Thessalian and Epirotan large farms (tsiflikia) owned by rich merchants and financiers of the Greek Diaspora tended to restrict production to subsistence level. Trikoupis, a staunch liberal, led a policy favouring absentee landowners, most of whom were members of the wealthy Greek Diaspora. On the other hand, he alienated the newly liberated Greek sharecroppers and opened the way for intense political and social unrest in Thessaly and Arta. Economically, the incorporation of these provinces proved much more a liability than an asset for the emerging Greek industry.

Apart from bureaucratic modernisation, Trikoupis envisaged and obstinately followed a policy of expensive public works: railroads; highways; ports; and lighthouses. In order to obtain the funds

Charilaos Trikoupis, Prime Minister 1882-1885, 1887-1890

necessary, he engaged Greece in a large program of public borrowing in the international capital market. The unexpected diplomatic crisis of 1885-1886 and the heavy military expenses initiated by the growing rivalry with the new Bulgarian state over Macedonia and Thrace weighed further upon the Greek budget. Since the epic Cretan revolt of 1866-1869, every new crisis of the Eastern Question (1875-1881, 1885-1886, and 1896-1897) inflated public expenses to even higher levels. In spite of the imposition of new indirect taxes, public receipts never covered the growing expenses and new loans were arranged to pay the interests of past loans. Finally, in December 1893, unable to find new loans, Trikoupis was obliged to cease servicing the Greek public debt, causing a unanimous international negative reaction.

Economic and Political Crisis (1893-1909)

The budgetary crisis was combined with a devastating agricultural crisis due to the imposition, in 1893, of protective tariffs on Greek agricultural exports by France. These tariffs literally closed the French market to currants and were the cause of a long-term income crisis that affected most peasants in southern Greece. The acute economic and financial difficulties exacerbated the social friction caused by heavy indirect taxation and the "Agrarian Question" in Thessaly. The most visible symptom of the adverse results of the chronic income crisis in the agrarian sector was the rapidly growing transatlantic emigration that literally drove away, mainly to the USA, a very large number of Greek peasants. The annual rate of demographic growth, which was as high as 1.5% in the 19th century, was halved, during the 1896-1920 period, to 0.8%.

This was only one reason for the pessimistic mood in Greece at that time. The severe ethnic strife in Macedonia and Crete weighed heavily upon the intellectual and moral climate, leading to the formation of aggressive nationalist private societies, like the *Ethniki Etaireia*, which called for active military intervention on behalf of their "oppressed national kin" in Crete and Macedonia. The Cretan revolt that broke out in 1896 had a dramatic effect on public opinion in Greece. The bungling management by the Deliyannis government of the diplomatic crisis which followed, forced Greece into a war with the Ottoman Empire that it was not prepared for and secretly wished to avoid. The intervention of the Great Powers helped the country transform a military disaster into a diplomatic draw. Greece paid a heavy financial indemnity to the Ottomans, but Crete became an autonomous principality under Ottoman suzerainty with a Christian governor chosen by the Greek government. Prince George of Greece was appointed as its first governor and since then Crete was all but officially united with Greece.

The foreign creditors of Greece were those who really profited from the outcome of the Greek-Ottoman War of 1897. During peace negotiations, the Greek government consented to the creation of an International Financial Committee (IFC) that would have the power to control Greek revenues from specific tariffs and monopolies. The IFC would ensure the servicing of the public debt and exert the right to inspect Greek finances for many years. Contrary to what was thought at the time, the IFC, which lasted until the end of the Second World War, had a beneficial influence on Greek finances since it helped Greece put public expenses in order and rationalise the use of revenues.

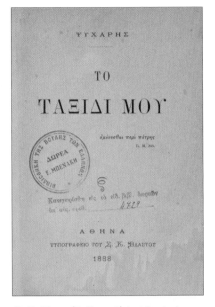

"To Taxidi mou (My Voyage"), by J. Psycharis (1854-1929). An emblematic edition for the supporters of "Demotike"

The Greek military defeat was nevertheless perceived as a symptom of national decay and as a strong omen of forthcoming national disasters. Many sought solutions in issues they considered to be the source of national regeneration, like religion or language. The so-called "language question" sharply divided Greek intellectuals. The more conservative ones maintained that katharevousa, a "purified" artificial version of Greek conceived by scholars like Koraes in the early 19th century, should remain the only language in use in Greek education and administration. On the other hand, the younger radicals believed that Modern Greek *demotike*, the "popular" vernacular language, should be substituted for the inanimate *katharevousa* at all levels. Some supporters of demotike were romantic nationalists, who believed that the Greek language constituted the basic element of Greek national identity. They also saw it as an animated medium for the transmission of the "eternal" spirit of Hellenic tradition. The other supporter of were socialists who believed that the use of the vernacular would assist the education and enlightenment of popular classes. The intellectual and the political realm split into two bitterly opposed groups and, only after many intellectual mutations, educational reforms and political reconfigurations, did this controversial issue close in 1976 when a mild version of the Demotike was officially accepted as the standard language.

The development of the national conflict in Ottoman Macedonia was the most urgent subject of concern for the Greek state and public opinion. The "Schism" of the Bulgarian Exarchate, that is, the arbitrary secession of the Bulgarian dioceses from the Greek-Orthodox Patriarchate of Constantinople in 1871, and the Berlin Treaty that concluded the war between Russia and the Ottoman Empire in 1878, had planted the seeds of later imperialist interventions and national conflicts and wars in the Balkans. Greeks, Bulgarians, Serbs, and Albanians were opposed in a fight for ecclesiastical, educational, and finally military control of the Ottoman provinces in Europe. Christian villagers, poor sharecroppers, small-owners and shepherds, were soon compelled to choose their ecclesiastical and educational affiliation under the pressure of militias of irregulars armed by all the parties concerned. The Bulgarian komitadji bands were the first to exert this kind of armed propaganda and were successful until the reckless Ilinden uprising in 1903, which ended in bloodshed perpetrated by the Ottoman army. This defeat led to internal friction among the Bulgarian nationalists and later to a series of intrigues and bloody retaliations between the "supremacists", who were unconditionally loyal to the Bulgarian national cause, and the "federalists", who were considering the possibility of an autonomous Slav-Macedonian national entity. The cautious Greek policy was much more successful in expanding the influence of its national educational system in Macedonia and later in ensuring, with the use of armed militias, the security of those villages that opted for the Patriarchate and against the Bulgarian Exarchate. When the "Young-Turk Revolution" won power in 1908, Greeks and Serbs were in an advantageous position in Macedonia at the expense of Bulgaria.

The Young-Turk military revolt had promised the re-institution of the Ottoman Constitution of 1875 and the end of all political, national, and religious oppression in the Ottoman realm. After a short period of inter-communal fraternity and great liberal and national expectations of all the nationalities in the Ottoman empire, the aggressive Turkish nationalism of the Young-Turk leaders and their centralising policy alienated not only the Christian nationalities but also the Albanian and Arab nationalists. The Greeks of the Ottoman Empire and the affluent Greek Diaspora soon understand that there was little room for them in the new Young Turk nationalist order.

In Greece, the Young-Turk revolution was seen as the last in a series of national humiliations, since a reinvigorated Turkey might have invalidated any hope for the liberation of those Greek provinces that were still under Ottoman rule. Growing dissatisfaction with the political parties, distrust of the dynasty and a sense of moral decline led a group of young officers to follow the Young-Turk example. They formed a "Military League" which called for the reorganisation and modernisation of the Greek Army and Navy, the dismissal of royal princes from any post of military authority and, finally, the reform and "moral sanitation" of the political system. The hesitant reaction of the government precipitated the military coup in August 1909 that was supported by the public who were tired of the perceived government inability to solve the urgent national and social problems and irritated by the continuous royal interference in politics. Soon a young Cretan liberal,

Eleutherios Venizelos (1864-1936), was invited to form a government and to organise the election for a National Assembly that would amend the Constitution of 1864.

Contrary to the opinion of contemporaries, Greece was not in decline at the beginning of the 20th century. The extraordinary growth of the Greek merchant marine, the relative reinvigoration of Greek light industry, the taming of the agricultural income crisis and the expanding remittances coming from Greek emigrants, sailors, and employees of the affluent Greek Diaspora boosted the economy. This helped the drachma reach parity with the golden franc in 1904, and financed a huge program of rearmament. The Venizelos government in 1911 was standing on a very firm base.

Venizelos and the Last Phase of National Unification (1909-1924)

The amended Constitution of 1911, proposed by Venizelos and his followers, protected civil liberties to a greater extent and enhanced the independence of justice and public administration from partisan politics. Furthermore, Venizelos embraced a policy of institutional modernisation and reform of the central and local administration, justice, and educational systems. New specialised ministries were created; policies of rational legal modernisation and a limited state intervention in the economy were adopted. More urgently, the army and navy were better armed and modernised, while an active diplomatic campaign succeeded in extremis to incorporate Greece into the hurried alliance of Balkan states against the Ottoman Empire.

The Balkan alliance of Greece, Serbia, Montenegro, and Bulgaria proved strong enough to win the first Balkan War (1912) against the Ottoman Empire. It was however, unable to reach an agreement concerning the partition of the liberated provinces whose Christian populations were ethnically mixed. The Bulgarian government, overconfident of its military superiority, decided to launch a surprise attack against its former allies, Greece and Serbia. This was a grave miscalculation that led to the second Balkan War, which proved to be a victory for Greece and its allies. During the two Balkan Wars (1912-1913) Greece had doubled its territory and population. However, it had also incorporated for the first time an ethnically mixed population of Christian Slavs and Vlachs, Albanians, Turks, Roms and Pomak Muslims as well as Sepheradin Jews, while a large number of Greeks still remained outside the country's frontiers.

Meanwhile the division of Europe into two camps in the coming World War influenced Greek politics as well. The liberal and modernising Venizelos, representative of the now overconfident urban bourgeoisie and of the wealthy Greek Diaspora, was a staunch propo-

Eleftherios Venizelos, Prime Minister 1910-1915, 1917-1920, 1928-1932

nent of Greek participation in the war on the side of the Western allies. The old political elite, which felt betrayed by the 1909 coup and resented the accelerated reforms brought about by the Venizelos governments, found its champion in the person of the new King Constantine I (1868-1922), the popular commander-in-chief of the Greek army during the victorious Balkan Wars. Constantine, who had studied at the Prussian military academy and was married to a princess of the Prussian Royal House, was known for his pro-German feelings and his strong conservative views. Since active participation in the war on the side of the Triple alliance was impossible, he opted for strict neutrality and found unexpected allies in the pacifist Greek Socialist movement. The conservative small-owner peasantry and petty-bourgeoisie of the old Kingdom avidly supported his policy while Venizelos, a strong supporter of Land Reform, was especially popular among the sharecroppers and landless peasants of Thessaly as well as among all the newly liberated provinces. But it was among unredeemed Greeks, both poor peasants and the opulent bourgeoisie that Venizelos was popular to the point of inspiring a real personality cult. Greece was thus rigidly divided on the important issue of participation in the new war and no compromise was sought. There was also a socio-political cleavage between the authoritarian conservative and the liberal modernising perspectives in Greek society. This so-called "National Dissension" (*ethnikos dichasmos*) between liberals and conservatives, Venizelists and anti-Venizelists, Royalists and Republicans, lasted until well into the Second World War.

The King attempted to impose his policy and forced Venizelos, who had just won the August 1915 elections, to resign from his post as Prime Minister in October 1915. A few months later a "Revolutionary government" led by Venizelos was formed in Thessaloniki. National dissension had taken the form of a low-intensity civil war. In June 1917, the Venizelists occupied Athens, ousted Constantine and put his second son Alexander in his place. Greece was one of the victors of the First World War and almost had the opportunity to implement its more ambitious hopes of national unification. The Treaties of Neuilly (1919) and Sevres (1920) were a personal triumph for Venizelos. Western Thrace, which had been under Bulgarian rule since 1912, was incorporated into Greece along with Ottoman Eastern Thrace, with the exception of Constantinople. The region of Smyrna, inhabited in part by Greeks, was under a Greek protectorate and would be allowed, after a period of five years, to decide in a referendum on its future union with Greece. Venizelos was also obliged to make concessions. The self-declared autonomous province of Northern Epirus, disputed since 1912, was to be incorporated into Albania. International treaties ratified the status of the Dodecanese islands, under Italian rule since 1911, and of Cyprus, ruled by Great Britain since 1878 and officially annexed in 1914, as legitimately under the sovereignty of these European powers. The price Greece had to pay for this triumph was active participation in all the post-war military operations of its allies in the Crimea (1919) and Asia Minor (1919-1922).

This price proved too high for a country that had lost its internal ethnic homogeneity, was sharply divided politically, and had a population tired of

Refugees from
Asia Minor

constant warfare since 1912. In hindsight it is not surprising that Venizelos lost the November 1920 elections. King Alexander had died in an accident a month before the elections and the new Anti-Venizelist government imposed his father, the old King Constantine, as his successor. To curb the Turkish national resistance, led by the brilliant general Mustafa Kemal Ataturk, to the implementation of the Treaties of Sevres, the Greek army, with open British support, launched an unsuccessful attack against Ankara in the summer of 1920. Greece was rapidly isolated from its former allies, who did not trust Constantine and had, with the exception of Great Britain, already come to an understanding with the Kemalists. Tired from ten long years of fighting, the Greek army succumbed to the massive Turkish attack in August 1922. The Greek-Orthodox and Armenian population of Asia Minor that had

openly taken the part of Greece paid a heavy penalty in lives lost and properties destroyed. The millenary Hellenic presence in Asia Minor ended in bloodshed and destruction and forced emigration, an event that has since then haunted collective memory in Greece and has been called the "Asia Minor disaster".

In the Treaty of Lausanne (July 1923), negotiated by Venizelos himself, Greece was forced to accept the conditions of the victorious young Turkish Republic. Asia Minor, Eastern Thrace and the islands of Imvros and Tenedos were conceded to Turkey. All Greek-Orthodox populations in Turkey and all Muslim populations in Greece were to be *forcibly* "exchanged". This harsh final clause, in combination with a comparable provision included in the Treaty of Neuilly (1919), which arranged a *voluntary* "exchange of populations" between

Greece and Bulgaria, led to the complete reconfiguration of the ethnological characteristics of the countries concerned. Not only Greeks but also Turkish-speaking Christians of inner Anatolia were forced to leave their ancestral lands, while Cretan and other Greek-speaking Muslims of Greece followed Turkish Muslims and moved in the opposite direction. Only the Turkish and Pomak Muslims of Eastern Thrace remained in Greece as the counterpart of the large Greek-Orthodox population of Constantinople that was allowed to remain in Turkey. The Treaty guaranteed the rights of both minorities to unprejudiced justice, free exercise of their religion, education in their national language and, of course, enjoyment of all civil rights and full security of their life and property. Seventy-five years later the Muslim community of Greece continues to live in its ancestral lands enjoying all the rights of Greek citizenry and all the additional rights granted by the Lausanne Treaty. On the contrary, the Greek community of Istanbul gradually dwindled under the continuous and undisguised discriminatory measures of successive Turkish governments.

The Second Hellenic Republic (1924-1935)

The army, which evacuated Asia Minor and returned to Greece, was agitated about what it considered high treason by the royal government. The Venizelist officers easily took power and once again,

forced King Constantine to leave the country. Soon afterwards, a Venizelist military court condemned six former ministers and generals to death for their role in the Anatolian campaign, thus exasperating partisan feelings. The radical factions in the Venizelist camp were influential and, in March 1924, the National Assembly declared Greece a Republic. A few weeks later the decision was ratified by a referendum. The young Republic, consecrated in the Constitution of 1927, was extremely fragile not only because it faced the adamant repudiation of the strong royalist minority but also because the republican camp itself, in the absence of Venizelos, was internally divided into various opposing factions.

An impoverished country was overburdened by more than one and a quarter million of destitute refugees who arrived from Asia Minor and the Balkans, relative to the only 420 thousand Muslims and Slavs who forcibly or voluntarily left the country. As a result, Greece was again transformed into a nationally homogenous country, although inter-communal relations were strained since the refugees and the indigenous peasants were competing for land while, in the industrial sector, refugees offered a miserably low paid working force. It took a generation before refugees were fully assimilated into Greek society, a major achievement in itself given the paucity of financial resources.

Land reform took a radical turn and became a sweeping movement transforming Greece into a country of small-owners and permanently binding the former sharecroppers to the Venizelist side. The newly annexed provinces of northern Greece had large plains but were poorly equipped and urgently needed funds for large-scale land improvement and drainage. More funds were needed for the establishment of the refugees in the cities. As a consequence, Greek efforts to achieve the socio-economic integration of refugees through large-scale public works and rapid economic recovery depended heavily on foreign loans that were partly arranged under the auspices of the League of Nations. The important institutional and economic reforms of the early inter-war period were largely imposed by the international community and had a positive long-term effects on the modernisation and development of the Greek economy.

Nevertheless, in the short-term, the economic and social situation in the 1920s was characterised by extremely severe and widespread economic misery and social insecurity. The abrupt end of transatlantic emigration that had earlier proved to be an indispensable security valve for the overpopulated agrarian sector exacerbated this situation. Social unrest and widespread discontent with the functioning of political institutions, combined with explosive international diplomatic disputes, opened the way to violent political con-

A. Papanastasiou, Prime Minister 1924-25

troversies and to a coup by general Pangalos (1925-1926). Only the return of Venizelos, who won a sweeping victory in the 1928 elections, temporarily stabilised the political climate and cultivated high hopes once again.

During his last term in office, Venizelos took some impressive and long lasting steps in securing positive and constructive relations with Kemalist Turkey, easing the climate of diplomatic confrontation in the Balkans and trying to provide a real boost to the ailing Greek economy. The world economic crisis that was only felt in Greece in 1931 swept his efforts away. Every European economy tried to close itself in a protective autarchic shell and Greece was no exception. As a result of this introverted international context, a notable industrial development was observed however, since the country's economic structure was strongly dependant on international commercial and monetary flows, the standard of living stagnated. The growing labour movement and the fear of increasing communist influence among workers led Venizelos and his successors to take measures severely curtailing civil liberties.

The Venizelos government lost the 1932 elections and, for the first time since 1922, a royalist government led by P.Tsaldaris was in office. Economic austerity, political instability, and social unrest marked the years that followed. Venizelos sought self-exiled in Paris, leaving the political arena empty of his dominating presence. In the inter-war period both Venizelists and Anti-Venizelists had been reduced to internally disintegrating blocs of politicians and military conspirators creating intrigues, forming secret political and military leagues and preparing military coups. The ultimate Venizelist coup in March 1935 proved to be a disaster and general Kondylis, a former Venizelist officer turned into a royalist, had no difficulty in bringing it down.

The End of the Republic and the Royal Dictatorship of Metaxas (1935-1941)

In the few months after the abortive Venizelist coup, rapid political develop-ments followed. The royalists in power radically eradicated the army of all Venizelist and democratic officers. King George II (1890-1947), unlike his father, returned as a final resort of social and political stability. By that time a large part of the urban bourgeoisie, that had once been the resolute advocate of Venizelos, scared off by bitter social unrest and by the fictitious "Communist danger", had become unconditional supporters of the royalist conservative order. Finally, in August 1936, the Prime Minister John Metaxas (1871-1941) revoked the Constitution with the active support of the King and imposed a dictatorship (1936-1941). Overall political and ideological oppression took on new excessively harsh forms, especially against political, social, and ethnic groups. Inane propaganda and stiff but ludicrous censorship were introduced into Greek political and intellectual life.

Metaxas' inspiration came from the Italian Fascist dictatorship however, lacking the enabling social strata and socio-political ideology upon which to found a fully operative Fascist regime, he settled for an authoritarian and ruthless personal dictatorship with a surplus of Fascist rituals and kitsch. Communists and socialists were savagely persecuted, tortured and internally exiled. All liberal and democratic politicians, scholars and writers who dared to question the "Supreme Leader" and his deeds were equally, though less inhumanely, maltreated.

The Second World War,
Resistance and Civil War
(1940-1949)

The Metaxas Dictatorship, closely monitored by King George and his British patrons, tried to keep Greece out of the Second World War, but the Italian Fascist government chose Greece as its easy victim. An aggressive policy of provocation reached its peak in August 1940, when an Italian submarine torpedoed a Greek destroyer that was harboured in the port of Tinos, where it was participating in religious festivities. Finally, in October 28, 1940, Mussolini presented a humiliating ultimatum which Metaxas had no choice but to reject. The Italian dictator gravely miscalculated his actions and, after six months of fierce fighting, the Greek army had occupied the greater part of south Albania, a country under Italian rule since early 1939.

In April 6, 1941, Hitler decided to help his ailing ally and invaded Yugoslavia and Greece. The Greek army could not match the Germans, who were superior in numbers and equipment, capitulated in April 24, 1941. In Crete, the Greek and British forces, with the active participation of the local population, fought a last and desperate battle in May 1941. The Nazis won a Pyrrhic victory and lost the shining lights of their airborne power. The impending attack against the Soviet Union was delayed for a few fateful months.

The King, the Greek government and what was left of the Greek Army, Navy and Air force followed the retreating British in Egypt and continued fighting until the final victory of the allies. Recruits were drawn from the Greek Diaspora and from those young men that continued to break away from Greece. The country itself was occupied for the first time since the Ottoman period and distributed as spoils to the victors. Thrace and Eastern Macedonia were under Bulgarian occupation. The rest of Greece was under Italian rule while the Germans occupied Athens, Thessaloniki and the rest of Macedonia, the greater part of Crete and the Greek-Turkish frontier. The Bulgarians and the Italians tried to dismember Greece and, in order to do that, they supported separatist movements of small ethnic groups living near the frontier. Thus the Italians used the minuscule group of Muslim Albanian Tchams on the Epirotan frontier and unsuccessfully tried to form a Vlach Legion in the Pindus Mountain range. The Bulgarian threat was much more serious, because it used excessive physical brutality and entailed forcible population movements. Many Greeks were driven out of Bulgarian-occupied eastern Macedonia and replaced by Bulgarian immigrants. Slav-speaking Greek citizens were incited or forced to declare themselves as Bulgarians. When verbal solicitations did not suffice, brute force was used in German and Italian occupied northern Greek provinces.

The first year of occupation was extremely harsh since the Nazi admin-

The liberation of Athens, October 12, 1944

istration had confiscated all alimentary stock in a country that was deficient in basic foodstuffs and unable, due to the allied naval blockade, to import the necessary food. The winter of 1942 was a period of famine for the urban populations. The poorer, the feebler and the unprotected, maybe as many as 250 thousand, starved to death in the streets of this European capital. A whole year passed before an agreement, sponsored by the Swedish Red Cross, permitted the importation of basic foodstuffs. In spite of the desperate economic situation of the country, the collaborationist government was forced to loan huge sums of money to Germany. This money was never paid back.

The Greek resistance was organised within the first months of the occupation. The left-wing National Liberation Front (EAM), the most important of all the resistance organisations, was founded in September 27, 1941. The resistance movement began to take on massive proportions in 1942. Armed groups were formed such as the EAM-sponsored ELAS, EDES, EKKA, etc. Massive protests and rallies in March 1943 were strong enough to annul the German plans to forcibly conscript Greek workers into German factories. Sabotage and armed attacks were growing in spite of the fact that Nazi retaliation to any act of resistance was brutal, savage and far out of any proportion. The male populations of the small town of Calavryta and of numerous villages like Komeno, Kleisoura, Distomo etc., were inhumanely slain in such blind retaliation operations. That did not stop the armed resistance groups from managing to control, by 1944, a large part of the mountainous countryside.

The ultimate horror was the almost complete extermination of the Jews of Greece. Since the beginning of the 16th century, Thessaloniki had an important Sephardic Jewish community and was one of the most important centres of Jewish culture in the Mediterranean. Its population was expatriated and exterminated by the Nazis. The same was true for most of the other ancient communities, like those of Corfu, Jannina, etc. In Thrace and eastern Macedonia, the Bulgarians, who had protected their own national Jewish community, closely collaborated with the Nazis. Only those Jews who participated in the armed resistance or those living in large population centres (as in Athens) were to some degree spared. Some small communities (Zante, Katerini and Volos) were successfully evacuated and saved with the help of the Church, resistance groups or local officials. Others were saved by their Christian neighbours. Nevertheless, the final toll was incredibly heavy: more than 58,800 Greek Jews (82% of their total number) were exterminated.

Greece suffered a heavy penalty during the war in human lives lost and economic destruction. Total demographic losses are estimated at 687,000 dead, to which some 60,000 un-born should be added. The Greek economic and transport infrastructure was destroyed by fighting, bombing, sabotage and pillage. But the worst was yet to come. Even since 1943 it was evident that the resistance groups were divided along political lines and armed clashes occurred. In 1944, the British and the Greek royal government were contemplating an armed confrontation with the left-wing resistance organisation EAM that had, by

then, been embraced by the majority of Greeks.

In October 1944 Athens was free again and the Greek and British armies were welcomed by an overjoyed nation. Unfortunately, very soon thereafter, a bitter antagonism became apparent between the leftist resistance organisation EAM, which was almost completely dominating the countryside and most of the big cities, and the British-backed royal government. Despite efforts at compromise on both sides, armed conflict broke out in Athens on December 3, 1944. After a month of fierce street fighting EAM, which never used its full power, and the Greek government reached an agreement in Varkiza (in February 1945), the implementation of which was guaranteed by the British government. The settlement provided for the disarming of the resistance groups, the "democratisation" of the Greek armed forces, police and administration, and the unobstructed preparation of a fair referendum on the monarchy as well as elections.

None of the articles of this agreement were effectively and fully implemented, except for the partial disarmament and demobilisation of the largest part of the left-wing resistance groups. The old Venizelist liberals were used and abused by the King and his conservative followers while in the countryside the white terrorism of the royalists exacerbated political passions. The left-wing opposition was slowly pushed towards civil war or political marginalisation. The Communist Party, under its old leader Zachariadis, who had returned from Dachau, assumed the role of the major opposition force but was unable to follow a comprehensive and steady political strategy. Its major mistake was to call for abstention from elections precipitated in March 1946. Thus, the Communists marginalised themselves in the political arena. The continued provocation and humiliation of former resistance fighters, the reconstruction of an authoritarian administration and army, the complete dominance of royalist and extreme-right wing political forces on the non-communist side, all led the left-wing opposition to the civil war that began in late October 1946.

The civil war was as destructive in lives and economic resources as the previous war, and even more bitter. It was part of the larger Cold War raging all over Europe and it retarded the normal democratic political evolution in Greece for thirty years. The USA had taken over, from decrepit Great Britain, the role of the sponsor of the royalist governments. The Communist revolt take an and in August 1949. A large number of its members and sympathisers have been self-exiled in Eastern Europe.

The "Incomplete" Parliamentary Regime and its Collapse (1950-1974)

After the end of the Civil War, the Communist party was banned, its leftist substitute (EDA) suffered strong political discrimination and the various post-Venizelist liberal centrist parties, which had supported the royalist side in the Civil War, were suspected of republican proclivities. The King was now in complete control over the army and high administration and thus dominated the political system. Greek public administration, justice, education, and the army were led and in their higher echelons, staffed by the same individuals who had served under Metaxas or even under the collaborationist governments. They were resolute royalists, anti-Communists, conservatives with anti-parliamentarian and authoritarian beliefs.

After a short-term liberal interlude (1950-1951), a strong conservative government lead by Papagos came to office. Successive right-wing governments lasted until 1963. Strongly influenced by the King and his powerful entourage, these governments were responsible for the setting up of a "lame" parliamentary system, biased against a large part of Greek citizenry. The Army, truly Royal, totally escaped political control while its officers were forming secret and less than secret leagues closely knit with groups of obscure politicians and ultra-conservative civil administrators who thought themselves the true protectors of the King, the Faith and the Country. Effective power was slipping away from the institutions.

In spite of the harsh political climate, and after a period of economic recon-

Elias Iliou, political leader of the left party EDA

struction, the Greek economy began to exhibit high growth rates. These were associated with a rapid productivity growth, massive rural depopulation, rapid expansion of the Greek Merchant Marine and a real increase in the share of industry in the GDP. The governments led by the young premier Constantine Karamanlis were instrumental in this rapid process of growth that was certainly connected to the rapid amelioration of the international economic environment, the modernisation of the country's transport and communication system, and the growing integration of Greece into western European structures. In 1952 Greece became a full member of NATO and, later, signed an Association Agreement with the European Common Market (Treaty of Athens, July 1961).

Rapid growth continued unimpeded until the 1970s and permitted Greece to catch up in part with other economically advanced European economies and become able to join the European Union in 1981. This rapid economic development was not without its bleak side since, between 1960 and 1972, a large part of the agricultural population that left the countryside was not absorbed by the urban economy and was forced to emigrate to those European countries which needed extra labour.

The social and political environment of the sixties was no less tumultuous. Karamanlis followed an independent policy that was not always favourably received by the royal entourage while, at the same time, he had to compete against the growing influence of the left. The fear of a leftist victory in the 1961 elections led to gerrymandering and electoral fraud that adulterated the final results, although the precise responsibility of every individual actor has not yet been established.

Very soon a nation-wide outrage mobilised large sectors of the Greek citizenry against the government. The movement was headed by George Papandreou, the elderly leader of the "Union of the Centre", a loose confederation of old liberal Venizelists and dissatisfied conservatives, who finally succeeded in toppling the government. George Papandreou, who triumphed in the February 1964 elections, had been able to garner considerable support

George Papandreou, Prime Minister 1963-1965

what they considered the only solution for political instability and for democracy in general, that is, a dictatorship. A group of colonels won the race against the King's generals and staged a coup on April 21, 1967, a month before the projected elections. The colonels were unknown to all except to the royal conspirators. The eclipsed King tried to regain control of the situation, staged an unsuccessful amateurish coup in December 1967, and when he was beaten, he left the country.

The military junta followed the steps of all previous dictators, adopting a policy of spendthrift economic paternalism, authoritarian brutality, imprisonment of liberal and leftwing politicians and intellectuals, and censorship. The dictator Papadopoulos himself became infamous for the ridiculously excessive language he used. A growing popular discontent became manifest in 1972 through continuous student protests that led to massive and peaceful demonstrations in November 1973, when the dictatorship tried to legitimise itself through a controlled and limited transfer of power to old conservative politicians. The army was called in to "restore" order

from liberal and leftist voters who were discontent with the authoritarian royal governments and had been wrongly perceived by the young King Constantine II as the main threat to his dynasty. Time and again the young and obstinate monarch openly disavowed the Prime minister, while his personal entourage undermined the cohesion of the elected government. The split of the Union of the Centre brought Papandreou's government down in July 1965 but proved unable to stop his growing popularity.

The political climate was poisoned by actions of the unofficial nexus of power under royal protection and beyond the control of the legal government. This and other smaller secret right-wing extremist leagues had increasingly been pursuing their own aims since 1961. They intimidated political opponents, discriminated against the centrist and leftist parties, and would soon seize the opportunity to implement

in Athens, which it did leaving more than forty citizens dead. A week later Papadopoulos was ousted by brigadier Ioannidis, his chief of Military Police and the last stronghold of power in Athens.

The new dictatorship was totally isolated internationally as well as in the country itself. Its only memorable action was the disastrous decision to use the Greek contingent in Cyprus in order to stage a coup against Archbishop Makarios, the President of Cyprus. Cyprus had won its independence in 1960, after an obstinate struggle against the British colonial authorities. Archbishop Makarios had accepted independence as a second best solution after full union with Greece. According to the 1960 Zurich Treaty, Greece, Turkey and Great Britain were the collective guarantors of the smooth functioning of the Cypriot Constitution and the country's security. Britain had sovereign rights on its two bases on the island, while Greece and Turkey had two small, armed contingents. The two communities lived side by side and relations were fair until 1964. Deteriorating inter-community relations influenced Greek-Turkish relations negatively. Cyprus' neutrality was poorly accepted by the USA, whose policy aimed at incorporating Cyprus into NATO, possibly ensuring a peaceful partition of the island between its two allies, Greece and Turkey. George Papandreou and Archbishop Makarios were strongly against this outcome and successfully blocked it in 1964. Later, the Greek military junta used a nationalist rhetoric to cover up its lack of decisiveness during the 1968 Greek-Turkish crisis. Finally, on July 15, 1974, a coup was staged. The Greek army contingent and the Greek-Cypriot militia were busy chasing their internal enemy when, on July 20, the Turkish army invaded the unguarded island, pretending to unilaterally fulfil its role as guarantor of the security of the Turkish Cypriot community. After the immediate collapse of the dictatorship and the restoration of democracy, a truce was negotiated and an agreement of the three guaranteeing powers was sought in vain. The Turkish army, which had total superiority in numbers and equipment on the island, violated the truce and engaged in a second round of military operations on August 15, 1974. It thus reached its true aim to divide the island clearly into two ethnically cleansed areas. The fighting and the voluntary brutality of the Turkish army chased more than 200.000 Greek - Cypriots away from their homes in the north of the island. The majority of the Turkish-Cypriots, urged by their communal leadership, abandoned their houses later on and moved north to the Turkish-occupied areas. Since that time, Turkey has illegally occupied the northern part of the island and has since engineered an extensive policy of colonisation by Turkish citizens with the intention of making the ethnic separation of the island permanent. Nicosia is a physically divided capital, the last in Europe after the fall of the Berlin Wall. The Turkish-Cypriot

Konstantinos Karamanlis, Prime Minister 1955-1963, 1974-1980, President of the Hellenic Republic 1980-1985, 1990-1995

also for war. The national disaster caused by the dictatorship was a natural conclusion of the extreme-right wing culture, which, in close identification with the monarchy, had dominated Greek political and intellectual life since 1935. The monarchy and its anti-parliamentary political entourage had both clearly lost their legitimisation along with any anti-liberal and anti-socialist rhetoric.

Constantine Karamanlis, self-exiled in Paris since 1963, was summoned to form a government and put into order to the mess the dictators had left behind. His second period of office (1974-1980) is linked with the impeccable referendum that restored a Greek Republic. His government took credit for securing further economic development, consolidating democratic institutions, legalising the Communist party, ending political discrimination against the Left and, finally, resolving the famous "language question" by legalising the use of a mixed Demotike in education and administration. On January 1, 1981 Greece became the tenth member of the European Common Market. Since then, its population has shown the highest percentages of identification with a future federal Union, which is the avowed aim of all political parties from the liberal conservatives of Nea Democratia to the Socialists and the non-communist Left.

economy controls the most fertile areas of the island, but extensive mismanagement and corruption has reduced it to the status of an underdeveloped country, while the Greek-Cypriot economy has been growing rapidly. Disappointed by the lack of political freedom and economic opportunities, many Turkish-Cypriots have emigrated to the UK. The Republic of Cyprus is among the ten countries newly accepted into the European Union.

The Third Hellenic Republic Since 1974

The disastrous coup in Cyprus demonstrated beyond any doubt the incapacity of the military dictatorship to prepare Greece not only for peace but

Since 1981 the Socialist Party, led by its leader Andreas Papandreou (1919-1996), won successive electoral victories and dominated Greek political life, with the exception of a short-term interlude (1990-1993). Papandreou's greatest achievements were to build a welfare state, to modernise the education system and to put a definitive end to all forms of political and social discrimination that had persisted until the late 1970s. Finally, with the concurrence of the leadership of all Greek political parties, he put a definitive end to the symbolic legacy of the civil war.

Greece was not well prepared for the rapid dislocation of the cold war military and diplomatic blocs. Given the uneasy relationship with its eastern neighbour, military ally and potential danger, the country felt like an isolated island of the European Union until the dramatic events of the 1990s. Economic misery, political instability, low or high-intensity civil wars to the north and east, from the Balkans to the Caucasus, suddenly demonstrated to all Greeks the value and fragility of democratic institutions, intercommunal tolerance and economic af-

Andreas Papandreou, Prime Minister 1981-1989, 1993-1996

fluence. A country of emigrants, Greece has turned into a country of immigration, legal or clandestine. Once considering themselves immune from xenophobic intolerance, Greeks have now to adapt themselves to their new environment and accept the fact that they no longer live on a "European" island.

GOVERNMENT & POLITICS

CONSTITUTIONAL STRUCTURE

By Chryssanthakis, Ch.

The State is structured by the Constitution. The Constitution of Greece is the fundamental Charter of the State. It has been voted by the Fifth Revisional Assembly and enforced in 1975. It was amended once, in 1986 and then, recently, in 2001 by the Greek Parliament. It includes the main rules concerning the structure of the State, the exercise of its powers by the authorities as well as a list of human rights.

The Hellenic Republic is a Parliamentary Republic. The exercise of all its powers is based on sovereignty of the people as well as the rule of law. All powers are derived from the people and exist for the people and the Nation. They are exercised as specified by the Constitution.

The powers of the State are the following three: legislative, executive and judicial. The legislative power is exercised by the Parliament and the President of the Republic. Executive power is exercised by the President of the Republic and the Government. The judicial power is vested in the courts of law, the decisions of which are executed in the name of the people.

Legislative power

Legislative power is exercised by the Parliament as well as by the President of

The parliamentary assembly

the Republic. The members of the Parliament vote in the laws of the State. Then the President of the Republic promulgates and publishes them within a month of the voting date. The President of the Republic has the authority to send back a bill voted by the Parliament, if he considers that the bill is unconstitutional. The above said bill is introduced to the plenary sitting of the Parliament. If it is voted again by the absolute majority of the total number of the members of the Parliament, the President of the Republic is obliged to publish it within ten days of the second vote.

The Parliament ("House of Deputies") consists of its members, the number of which can not be below two hundred (200) or exceed three hundred (300) according to the relevant law. Today's Parliament consists of three hundred Deputies.

The members of the Parliament represent not only the State but also the Nation as a whole. The Deputies elect the Standing Committee, according to the Parliament Code of Standing Orders.

The members of Parliament are elected through direct, universal, secret and simultaneous ballot by citizens who have legal right to vote. 'That is, they must be over eighteen years of age and legally capable of voting. The above said political right can not be infringed except in cases of legal incapacity or irrevocable criminal conviction. The exercise of this right is compulsory. This means that voting is not only a constitutional right

Anna Psarouda Benaki.
The President of the Greek Assembly

but also a (constitutional) obligation of the Greek citizen.

The candidates for the election must be Greek Citizens, at least twenty-five (25) years of age as well as legally capable of voting. The Members of the Parliament are elected for a term of four years.

Parliament convenes in regular session on the first Monday of October of each year, unless it has been convened earlier by the President of the Republic. The regular session can not be shorter than five months.

Parliament is authorised to vote on bills and law proposals as well as to exercise control over the Government. It exercises its legislative authority either in plenary session or in (two) sections or in the standing parliamentary commissions and makes a resolution by a majority of not less than two - fifths of its members. But only the plenary session is competent to debate and vote on bills concerning the exercise and protection of the constitutional rights of the individual, on bills and proposals on the authentic interpretation of the law, as well as every issue expressly covered by the Constitution or for which a special majority is required. The Parliament in plenary session exercises control on Government as a whole or on each member of it as to issues concerning State policy. The Standing Orders of Parliament may provide the exercise of parliamentary control by the Section, which is established when Parliament is in recess, as well as by the standing parliamentary committee.

Executive power
The President of the Republic

The President of the Republic is the co-ordinator of the three powers of the State. He is also ex *officio* the Head of the executive authorities of the State, which are, however, directed by the Government. He is authorised to exercise the powers, which are conferred upon him by the Constitution as well as by the laws of the State.

A person can be elected as President, if he or she has been a Greek citizen for at least five years, has a Greek father or mother, is at least forty years of age and is legally capable of voting. He is

Konstantinos Stephanopoulos, *President of the Hellenic Republic 1995-2000, 2000-today*

elected by the Parliament through a secret ballot in a special session, for a five years term that can be renewed once more.

The President is empowered to:
- represent the State internationally, to conclude or to enter into treaties of peace, alliance, economic co-operation and participation in international organisations or unions. However agreements concerning trade, taxation, economic co-operation and participation in international organisations or unions and any other providing concessions which either must be regulated by law or overburden the Greeks as individuals, are not applicable without prior ratification by a law,
- declare war,

- appoint the staff of the Presidency of the Republic,
- appoint and dismiss Prime Minister and, on his recommendation, the members of the Government,
- dissolve Parliament,
- convene Parliament,
- promulgate and publish the laws passed by the Parliament,
- issue decrees,
- apply the laws of the State or, under legal authorisation, regulate matters specified by the law,
- issue acts of legislative content under extraordinary and unforeseeable circumstances. These acts must be submitted to Parliament for ratification within a period of forty days since the time they have been issued or since the House of Deputies has been assembled. Otherwise they lose their force,
- proclaim referenda on crucial national or social issues,
- address messages to the Nation in exceptional circumstances,

- confer ranks to the members of Armed Forces which are commanded by the Government,
- appoint and dismiss the public officials,
- confer decorations as they are specified by the law,
- commute the sentences of the convicted because of crimes,
- publish the decisions of the Parliament, concerning the application of martial law

The office of the President is incompatible with any other office or position in the public or private sector.

The Government

The Government, *stricto sensu*, consists of the Prime Minister and the Senior Ministers, who are the Head of the Ministries of the State. In a boarder sense, it consists of the above officials as well as of the Alternate Ministers, the Ministers without portfolio and the Under-secretaries of the State. The members of the Government must have the qualifi-

The government Cabinet (Council of Ministers)

cations of the Deputies.

The Ministries (Departments) of the State are the following:

(a) Ministry of the Prime Minister
(b) Ministry of Foreign Affairs
(c) Ministry of National Defence
(d) Ministry of National Economy and Finance
(e) Ministry of Interior, Public Affairs and Decentralisation
(f) Ministry of Environment, Town Planning and Public Works
(g) Ministry of Justice
(h) Ministry of Education and Religious Affairs
(i) Ministry of Rural Development and Food

(j) Ministry of Culture
(k) Ministry of Development, Industry, Research and Technology, Commerce and Tourism
(l) Ministry of Employment and Social Protection
(m) Ministry of Health and Welfare
(n) Ministry of Transports and Communication
(o) Ministry of Public Order
(p) Ministry of Macedonia and Thrace
(q) Ministry of Aegean and Insular Policy
(r) Ministry of Press and Mass Media
(s) Ministry of Merchant Marine

Each Minister exercises the powers specified by law.

Government and Parliament

The Government must enjoy the confidence of the Parliament. The Government is obliged to request a vote of confidence by the members of Parliament within fifteen days from the date the Prime Minister is sworn in. The Government has the same discretionary power at any other time of its term too. Parliament is also authorised to withdraw its confidence from the Government as a whole or from one of its members. Such a decision requires a motion of censure signed by at least one - sixth (:50) of the Deputies and an absolute majority of the total number of them. The absolute majority of the members of the Parliament present must approve the motion, which, in any case, can not be less than two - fifths of the total number of Deputies.

Kostas Karamanlis, Prime Minister since 2004

The Council of State

Judical power

The judicial power is vested in three categories of courts with civil, criminal and administrative jurisdiction. These courts are composed from one or more judges who enjoy functional and personal independence. That means that the judge is obliged to apply only the Constitution and the laws of the State and not any other kind of order, even if it comes from a judge of superior rank. The judgements must be specifically and thoroughly reasoned and pronounced in a public sitting.

Civil and Criminal Courts

The civil and criminal courts are the Courts of Justice, the Courts of First Instance, the Courts of Appeal and the Supreme Court (Areios Pagos). They are composed of regular judges. They have general jurisdiction on all private disputes as well as in criminal cases. In case of major criminal cases, the composition of criminal court also includes a jury of citizens.

The charges against members or ex members of the Government are reviewed by the Special Court of article 86 of the Constitution. This court is also a criminal court that has special jurisdiction.

Administrative Courts

Administrative Courts have jurisdiction on administrative disputes between the State and the citizens or moral persons because of illegal or improper exercise of the State powers. Such courts are the Courts of First Instance, the Courts of Appeal, the Council of State and the Comptrollers Council. The Court for suits against judicial functionaries is a Court with special jurisdiction. Disputes concerning all kinds of remuneration and pensions judicial functionaries shall also be tried by the above said court.

Special High Court

Special High Court is composed of the Presidents of the Council of State, Supreme Court and Comptrollers Court, four members of the Council of State and four members of the Supreme Court chosen by lot for a two - year term. In cases concerning the below said powers (c) and (d) the composition of the Court includes two professors of the Law Schools of the country. The sittings of the Court are presided by the President of either the Supreme Court or the Council of State depending on their seniority.

The Special High Court is competent for the judgement of:

(a) objections concerning the parliamentary elections

(b) applications concerning the verification of the validity of a referendum

(c) the settlement of any conflict between:

(ca) the courts and administrative authorities or

(cb) the Comptrollers Court and the other courts

(cc) the Council of State and administrative, civil and criminal courts

(d) the settlement of controversies on the (un)constitutionality of a law or on the interpretation of a law provision, when the Council of State, the Supreme Court and the Comptrollers Court have pronounced conflicting judgements.

(e) the settlement of controversies on the designation of a rule of international law as generally acknowledged.

As far as the control of constitutionality of laws is concerned, Greece has adopted not the system of the "single constitutional jurisdiction" but the "system of diffusion". All the courts of the State have the power to review the constitutionality or the unconstitutionality of the applicable law provision. If such a provision is declared as unconstitutional, it is not applied. However, it is not annulled. The power for annulment belongs only to the Special High Court under the referred conditions. This court has the power to extinguish a legislative act irrevocably and *erga omnes* from the date of the publication of its judgement or from the date specified by it.

The Areios Pagos

POLITICAL SYSTEM AND ELECTIONS

By Christos Lyrintzis - Elias Nikolakopoulos

1. The Third Republic

The restoration of democracy in July 1974 signalled a turning point in Modern Greek political history. The military regime that had ruled the country since 1967 collapsed in the midst of an international crisis caused by the dictatorship's own policy over Cyprus. A transitional period began with the formation of a "national unity" government under Constantine Karamanlis who had played a prominent role as Prime Minister during the late fifties and early sixties. Three major decisions were taken by the "national unity" government: First, to organise free parliamentary elections for the election of a constitutional assembly; second, to organise a referendum on the question of the monarchy and third, to legalise the Communist party (KKE), which had been illegal since its formation.

Parliamentary elections were held in November 1974 with the participation of four major political parties. The right wing of the political spectrum was represented by the newly formed New Democracy party (ND) founded by Karamanlis in September 1974. The political Centre was occupied by the revival of the old centre (i.e. the Centre Union party) under the new label Centre Union-New Forces (EKND). The traditional left was represented by an al-liance under the label United Left (E. A.). It was an alliance comprising the Communist party (KKE), the KKE Esoterikou - which emerged after a split in 1968 that led to the formation of the Euro - communist left under the label KKE esoterikou (interior) - and the remnants of the old EDA party (that is the party which represented the Greek Left before 1967 when the KKE was illegal). The fourth group to contest the 1974 election was an entirely new party, the Panhellenic Socialist Movement (PASOK), founded by Andreas Papandreou, son of George Papandreou, the ex prime minister (1963-65) and prominent politician of the Centre and leader of the Centre Union party during the 1961- 67 period.

The November 1974 election gave an easy victory to N.D. party which received 54.4 per cent of the vote and an overwhelming majority of the seats in parliament (216 out of 300). The Centre Union was confined to 20.4 per cent and 61 seats, a percentage that seriously weakened the role of the main opposition party. PASOK received 13.6 per cent of the vote and 15 seats. Finally, the communist left received 9.5 per cent and 8 seats. In December 1974 a referendum resulted in a decisive vote against the monarchy (69.2 per cent opted for a Presidential Republic) thus ending a constitutional question that had caused significant problems since 1915. The parliamentary assembly drafted a new constitution providing for a President elected by parliament. The President was to have important prerogatives although the presidency was not designed according to the French model but it was closer to its Italian or German counterpart. In June 1975 Constantine Tsatsos a prominent member of the old political class and a close collaborator of Constantine Karamanlis was elected by parliament as President of the Republic for a five year term.

According to the 1975 Constitution the political system is a parliamentary democracy with the Prime Minister and the cabinet at the top of the executive. Following the lines of the Westminster model, the government needs a majority in the three hundred - seat parliament. Elections take place every four years and the leader of the political party that enjoys a majority in parliament forms a government which must receive a vote of confidence. For the first time in Greek politics special provision was made in the Constitution for the role of the political parties, their free functioning and their financing by the state.

The third Greek Republic was born and Karamanlis handled the transition to democracy with remarkable calm and determination and there can be little doubt that political developments during the seventies bear his seal. The new political system was based on an institutional setting that could guarantee

stable government, mainly through the alteration of two parties in power, while the presidency was designed as a safety valve controlling long-term political developments.

The November 1977 elections, held one year earlier than scheduled, redressed the balance of power between the major political parties. The N.D. retained its parliamentary majority with 171 seats but its share of the vote decreased from 54.4% to 41.8%. The party's decline was partly due to the emergence of an extreme right wing party (Ethniki Parataxis-National Front) which attracted a part of its electorate (6.3% of the total vote and 5 seats). The Centre, that is the Union of Democratic Forces - EDIK party (a new label for the Centre Union - New Forces party), collapsed to 12 per cent of the vote and 16 seats, a performance that marked the beginning of the end for the Greek Centre. The main beneficiary of the election was PASOK which doubled its vote and became the second largest party in parliament, with 25.3 per cent of the vote had 93 MP's, most of them newcomers in Greek politics. The KKE and the KKE interior contested the election independently and it was the KKE with 9.4 per cent and 11 seats that emerged as the dominant group, whereas the KKE interior, in alliance with four minor parties of the Greek center- left, received only 2.7 per cent and 2 seats in parliament. There can be little doubt, however, that it was PASOK and its leader Andreas

The Act of Accession in the EEC is signed by Konstantinos Karamanlis at Zappeion Megaron, Athens, (May 28, 1979)

Papandreou that emerged as the rising political force.

The 1977-81 period was marked by the gradual fragmentation and the eventual disintegration of the Centre (EDIK). At the same time, the N.D. party gradually absorbed the most important part of the National Front, while at the same time the party expanded towards the Centre by incorporating prominent politicians of EDIK and other Centre parties (among the latter Constantine Mitsotakis who was to become leader of the party and prime minister). Thus, by 1981 the Greek party system had acquired a tripartite configuration that was to last throughout the eighties. The late seventies were marked by Greece's re-entry in NATO's military arm and by the

signing in May 1979 of the treaty confirming Greece's accession to the EEC. In fact, integration into the European Union was a major objective of Karamanlis' policies as well as a strategic movement defining the overall orientation of the country's foreign policy. Moreover, it was a decision guaranteeing the country's new democratic institutions, and at the same time advancing its defence position in view of Greece's tense relations with Turkey. Thus, Greece became the tenth member of the European Union although the terms of the agreement were under heavy attack by both PASOK and the KKE. Karamanlis decided to abandon parliamentary politics and to seek election as President of the Republic. Indeed, in April 1980 he was elected as President of the Republic. His successor to the leadership of the N.D. party, though an experienced politician (George Rallis), was not a statesman of Karamanlis' calibre. This fact further weakened the party's position vis-a-vis the rising PASOK.

2. Greece in the eighties.

During the period between 1977 and 1981, PASOK managed to establish itself as a rising and convincing new political force. The party capitalised on the ability and charisma of its leader and offered the Greek electorate a radical programme which during its first years characterised PASOK as a left-wing party. As the 1981 elections approached, PASOK cultivated the image of a moderate and pragmatic party thus establishing a centre-left political identity. The October 1981 elections corroborated the trends that were already visible in 1977. PASOK's victory was accompanied by the confirmation of the tripartite structure of the Greek party system. PASOK received 48.1 per cent of the vote winning 172 seats in parliament, while N.D saw its share of the vote decrease to 35.9 per cent and only 115 seats. The centre parties were devastated and won no parliamentary representation, whereas the KKE slightly increased its power (10.9% of the vote and 13 seats). The new three-bloc configuration would last until the early nineties. It is important to note that this is the main cleavage in

Greek political life and all political antagonisms refer to it. This division goes back to the first decades of the century. The monarchy and the People's party were in acute conflict with the Centre, which was led by Eleftherios Venizelos. The left has always been identified with the Communist party (KKE).

PASOK's rise to power was a significant event for the relatively young Third Republic. It demonstrated that the new political system could survive the crucial test, that is the alteration in power. The change was remarkably smooth and the presence of two strong political parties was a guarantee for the functioning of democratic institutions. Moreover, PASOK's presence in office proved very important at the symbolic level, as it signified the vindication of the left after decades of almost uninterrupted right wing rule and at the same time the definitive heeling of the scars of the civil war.

Andreas Papandreou, Prime Minister 1981-1989, 1993-1996

PASOK and Andreas Papandreou dominated the political scene during the eighties. Irrespective of the manner in which one may assess PASOK's performance, there can be little doubt that the PASOK government introduced several changes, especially in the field of social policy and public administration. In the foreign policy affairs, PASOK soon abandoned its anti-EEC and anti-NATO stance and followed a moderate and realistic policy. The party's options and policies had the approval of the electorate, which was reconfirmed in the June 1985 elections. The pre-electoral campaign was marked by PASOK's decision not to support Karamanlis for a second term as President of the Republic. Instead, PASOK nominated its own candidate, Christos Sartzetakis, a prominent judge, who was eventually elected President with the help of the votes of the communist MPs. It was the first time that the communist votes were used to obtain a major decision in the Greek parliament. The new Parliament abolished the few prerogatives of the President - namely the right to dissolve parliament. PASOK maintained its electoral majority with 45.8 per cent of the vote and 161 seats. The N.D. party, under the new leadership of Constantine Mitsotakis increased its share of the vote to 40.8 per cent and 126 seats in parliament while the KKE's strength slightly decreased (9.9% and 12 seats).

The June 1989 election confirmed the decline of PASOK and the rise of the N.D. party. However, it was not an electoral disaster as many had anticipated: PASOK received 39.1 per cent of the vote and 125 seats thus maintaining the core of its electorate. N.D. received 44.3 per cent of the vote and 145 seats; yet, due to the new electoral system no party had an absolute majority of the seats in parliament. The alliance between N.D. and "Synaspismos", - that is the alliance of the left comprising the KKE and the KKE interior - was unexpected and formally marked the end of the long conflict between left and right in Greek politics. Moreover, this unorthodox alliance signalled the first post war entry of a communist party in government.

Constantine Mitsotakis, the leader of the N.D. party withdrew his support from the coalition and thus new elections were held in November 1989. PASOK, although still on the defensive, slightly increased its share of the vote (40.7 per cent compared to 39.1 per cent in June). N.D gained a 1.9 per cent increase in its vote and three additional parliamentary seats, but did not manage to achieve its goal of an independent parliamentary majority. In contrast, N.D.'s coalition partner, the Synaspismos, suffered a considerable setback losing over 2 per cent of its vote and a quarter of its parliamentary seats. It is interesting to note that in June Synaspismos had achieved the highest percentage for the left in a post dictatorship election, whereas in November it was the lowest apart from 1974. Obviously,

Constantine Mitsotakis, Prime Minister 1990-1993

ernor of the Bank of Greece. The main task of this "grand coalition" was to stabilise the economy. Indeed, the Zolotas cabinet tried to promote a consensual approach to economic and other problems, a task that proved very difficult as it was often impossible for the three partners to agree on major issues. Hence the failure to pass important legislation on crucial subjects as tax evasion and pollution. The initial idea behind this all-party government was to last until April 1990 when parliament was due to elect a new President of the Republic. In fact the parliament failed to obtain the necessary majority for the election of the President (180 votes) and consequently it was dissolved and new elections were scheduled for April 1990. The Greek electorate had to vote for the third time in less than a year and it was hoped that this time a parliamentary majority would emerge.

The April 1990 elections, therefore, were again dominated by the same dilemma as the previous one: single party government or coalition rule. N.D. achieved a slight rise in support, which gave her a marginal majority in parliament. (46.9 per cent of the vote and 150 seats, which became 151 after the inclusion of the one DE.ANA. M.P to the party's parliamentary group) PASOK's power slightly decreased compared to November 1989, while the Synaspismos maintained almost the same percentage as in the previous election (10.6% and 21 seats). The first task of the new parlia-

the co-operation with the right was not acceptable to a considerable part of the Synaspismos voters as many of them had strong memories of the post war persecution and of the anti-Communist policies during the fifties. Thus, the Synaspismos was the main if not the only loser in the November 1989 elections.

The November 1989 elections did not produce a parliamentary majority and consequently a new coalition government was needed. After protracted negotiations, the three major parties agreed to participate in an "ecoumeniki" that is an all-party government under Xenophon Zolotas the respected ex-gov-ment was to elect a new President of the Republic: Following the N.D.'s proposal, Constantine Karamanlis was elected for the second time President of the Republic.

The 1989/90 elections registered the emergence of two new political forces. The Ecology-Alternatives party following the model of the German Greens managed to win one seat in both the November and April election. The Ecologists, however, did not manage to acquire strong roots in Greek party politics and in the next election they would lose their parliamentary representation. (The change of the electoral law in November 1990 played a crucial role in this failure). Equally important was the presence of independent Muslim candidates in Western Thrace. The Muslim minority had been formerly represented by Muslim MPs belonging to the two major parties. Last but not least, the 1989/90 elections showed that the Greek political system was unable and/or ill prepared to adopt coalition government. Greek political culture is dominated by the antagonism between left and right and the related conflict between the two major parties. Consequently, it is very difficult to restructure the political system and certainly the simple change of the electoral law was not a sufficient condition to create substantial change. Nevertheless, the experience of the 1989/90 period eventually did reduce the level of fanaticism and polarization.

3. The New Context in the Nineties

The New Democracy government under Constantine Mitsotakis tried to implement a moderate neo-liberal programme whose major objective was to stabilize the ailing economy. The government's plans met considerable reaction on the part of the trade unions, but despite the increased number of strikes the government was able to proceed with its policies. The major problem emerged in the field of foreign affairs as a result of the creation of new states in the area of the former state of Yugoslavia. The so-called "Macedonian issue" concerned the official name of the former Yugoslavian Republic of Macedonia. This question caused a serious split in the government's ranks, with the Foreign Minister Antonis Samaras advocating a hard line. In other words, hr did not accept the name Macedonia or any other label that would include the term Macedonia as the official name of the new state - while Mitsotakis represented a more compromising stance. In April 1992 Mitsotakis accepted the resgnation of Samaras, for he was afraid that the minister's intransigent hard line could cause serious problems to Greece's foreign policy. Samaras left the N.D. party in October 1992 and in June 1993 he announced the creation of a new party the "Politiki Anixi - POL. AN." (Political Spring). In September more MP's defected from N.D. to POL. AN. and Mitsotakis was finally obliged to call for early elections. The new elections were scheduled to take place in October 1993. Samaras presented himself and his party as a new modernizing force seeking to renew Greek politics and fighting against the political establishment, that is against Mitsotakis and Papandreou.

The October 1993 elections were conducted under a new electoral law. Given the experience of the 1989/90 period, the new electoral law voted in November 1990, was designed to secure parliamentary majority. Moreover, the new electoral law introduced, for the first time in Greek politics, a 3 per cent threshold; any party failing to receive at least 3 per cent of the national vote would not be entitled to any parliamentary representation. There were considerable signs, however, that this time the electorate was frustrated with party fights, while public opinion polls registered disenchantment with the political leaders and rising rates of cynicism and political apathy. The problems of the national economy and the austerity measures taken to stabilize the economic system caused pessimism rather than optimism. Finally, it must be noted that the left fought the 1993 election divided: In 1991, the KKE abandoned the Synaspismos, leaving the Euro-communist and reformist left to carry on with the Synaspismos. It was not simply a split of Synaspismos but also a split within the KKE as several leading and popular KKE members left their party

and remained in the Synaspismos. Under the influence of the developments in the communist and post-communist world, the KKE decided not only to maintain its old label but also to insist on its hard line past by presenting an anti-European image.

PASOK won easily the election with 46.9 per cent of the vote and 170 seats in parliament. The N.D. party was clearly defeated (39.3% of the vote and 111 seats) and this led to Mitsotakis resignation and the election of Miltiades Evert as the new leader. Samaras' party, the Politiki Anixi, received 4.9 per cent of the vote and 10 seats. The Synaspismos failed to obtain more than 3% and thus had no parliamentary representation, whereas the KKE received 4.5 per cent and 9 seats in parliament. The electoral result was a vindication for Andreas Papandreou, who, despite his poor health, staged a triumphant return to power. In 1995, one year and a half after the 1993 election, Karamanlis' second term as President of the Republic expired, thus ending a long career in Greek politics. Karamanlis had no right to seek a third term and PASOK with the help of the Politiki Anixi votes supported the candidacy of Kostis Stefanopoulos, an ex leading member of the N.D. party and leader until 1994 of the small and relatively unsuccessful DIANA party. (DIANA was formed by Stefanopoulos in 1995 when he left N.D.). Thus in March 1985 the parliament elected Stefanopoulos as President of the Republic.

The Greek Parliament

In the mid nineties Greek politics appeared to be in the process of drastic change. Pasok, after the turbulent years of the 1989-1991 period, returned to power in 1993 with a comfortable majority. The new government under Andreas Papandreou embarked on a policy to stabilize the economy and to lead the country towards the targets defined by the Maastricht treaty. It is important to note that the government's performance signalled the beginning of a drastic change in PASOK's strategy. The party seemed to adopt a more realistic and modernizing attitude. The point is, however, that the economic exigencies, and the country's obligations within the context of the European Union dictated a moderate course leading to the stabilization and modernization of Greek economy and society. Significant grants form the European Union contributed to this end, but the whole process was neither easy nor always successful. Even more important is the fact that it caused the reaction of various segments of Greek society.

At the end of 1995, Papandreou was to be found in hospital in a very critical condition. The much-discussed subject of his succession became once again a central issue. Papandreou resigned in January 1996 and PASOK's parliamentary group elected Kostas Simitis as the new Prime Minister. The party proved that it could function without the presence of Papandreou and that its unity was not in serious danger. Thus all arguments about the disintegration of PASOK after Papandreou's departure were disproved and the party began to function as an open political force with its internal divisions and factional conflicts even more evident than in the past.

Simitis' leadership was reaffirmed in June 1996 when the national congress of the party elected him as party president. At the end of the summer, Simitis called for early elections. PASOK won the September 1996 elections and Simitis emerged as the indisputable political leader who put his mark on political developments in 1996. By contrast, the new defeat caused severe problems within the N.D. party which decided to re-orient its programme and to renew its political image. The end result of the debates and deliberations within the party was the election of Constantine Karamanlis, - the young nephew of the ex president of the republic - as new party leader.

The 1996 elections marked the beginning of considerable change in Greek politics. PASOK and ND continue to dominate the political scene but their appeal has been seriously undermined. The left of the political spectrum is represented by the Synaspismos which managed to exceed the 3% barrier and to win 10 seats and by the KKE which maintained its power (5.6% of the vote and 11 seats). A new party emerged in 1996 the "Dimokratiko Koinoniko Kinima - DEKKI" (Democratic Social Movement) founded by the ex PASOK minister Dimitris Tsovolas. DEKKI received 4.4% of the vote and 9 seats in parliament, appeared as a left wing party and capitalized on the anti-Maastricht climate. POL. AN. received less that 3% and thus no parliamentary represen-

tation. Thus, we have two major political forces and three, possibly four, minor parties. What is more important is that the 1996 elections registered, perhaps for the first time in Greek politics a growing frustration of the electorate as the percentage of abstentions increased as well as the number of blank and spoilt ballots. Public opinion surveys conducted before and after the 1996 election confirmed that a major change in Greek political culture is taking place characterized by rapidly growing signs of cynicism, apathy and political alienation. This is indeed a very interesting trend as Greece was in the eighties the country with the highest levels of participation and politicization in Southern Europe.

The policy of economic and fiscal stability through restrictions on public spending and incomes did stabilize the economy and led to an impressive improvement of several macroeconomic indicators. The country seemed to move according to the spirit of the Maastricht treaty along the tortuous road of convergence with the other European countries. This convergence, however, meant the continuation of an austerity policy which began in 1985, was briefly interrupted during the 1987-89 period, and was re-implemented in the nineties and was followed, notwithstanding some differences, by both the New Democracy party and PASOK throughout the decade. This apparently endless struggle to overcome the country's economic problems and to meet the standards of

Greece's partners in the European Union can be seen as the main causes of frustration and political alienation. What is more important is that this situation caused a long term disenchantment with party politics and with party ideologies and programmes.

It must be noted that after a decade of consistent efforts, Greece managed to achive the major objective of economic desciple and monetary stabilisation thus fulfilling, even at the very last moment the criteria of the Maastricht treaty. This success resulted in the country's entry into the Euro zone while at the same time changed to a considerable extent Greece's position and status within the European Union. It was perceived as a major success of the 1996-2000 Simitis government to win, although with a thin majority the 2000, parliamentary election.

The 2000 election proved one of the most closely contested in post war Greek electoral history. It was a clear choice between the two major political parties, and this fact enhanced the polarisation of the party system and, compared to the 1996 electoral results, led to the reinforcement of its' two main poles with PASOK receiving 43.8 per cent of the vote (and 158 seats) and New Democracy 42.7 per cent (and 125 seats). Thus the electoral results can be seen as a reversal of the tendency that appeared during the mid 90's indicating the emergence and crystallisation of new political parties. This tendency

proved stillborn, as only the KKE party maintained its electoral influence (5.5 per cent and 11 seats), while the Synaspismos party managed at a very marginal level to secure parliamentary representation with 3.2 pr cent of the vote and 6 seats in parliament. By contrast, the POL.AN did not participate in the election having suspended its political operation, while the DIKKI party received only 2.7 per cent of the vote and no parliamentary representation. Consequently, the attempts to create new parties proved unsuccessful, a fact well illustrated by the fate of the attempt made during the spring of 2001 by the popular ex mayor of Athens, Dimitris Avramopoulos, to create a new party, the Movement of Free Citizens, which a year later had to suspend its functioning; Avramopoulos, after a short period of independent political career, returned to the N.D. party a few months before the 2004 elections.

The polarization of the party system was reconfirmed during the last parliamentary election held in March 2004. It was a clear reversal of the balance of power between the two major parties registered in the previous elections: After eleven years in opposition N.D. returned to power under the leadership of Costas Karamanlis who became prime minister at the age of 47.

The return of the N.D. party to power can be seen as a significant political change marking Greece's entry in the 21st century. The N.D. victory confirmed a large-scale change regarding the political personnel, a development already visible since the mid-nineties. Indeed, by the end of the twentieth century both major Greek political parties had drastically renewed their political personnel including their leadership. As some of the dominant personalities of the seventies and eighties are gone (namely Andreas Papandreou and Constantine Karamanlis) both PASOK and ND have elected a new leader and the leading party and parliamentary personnel has been extensively renewed. Greek political parties can no longer be described as personalistic and poorly organised nor as exclusively relying on clientelistic networks.

The fact that the new Prime Minister Costas Karamanlis bears the name of his uncle (ex Prime Mimister and twice President of the Republic) should be seen as having a symbolic rather than real importance. Similarly, PASOK after the eight years period of the Simitis leadership, chose George Papandreou (son of Andreas Papandreou) as the new party leader. It was a political initiative inspired and backed by Costas Simitis and implemented a few weeks before the March 2004 election. The change of leadership did not prevent PASOK's electoral defeat. However, it indicates that both major parties have elected relatively young and at the same time well known political leaders following a new communication strategy and adopting a new style and a new approach in Greek party politics.

Last but not least, at a structural level, the Greek political system has proved that is able to withstand and overcome political crises with remarkable resilience. The capacity to overcome crises, as that of the 1989/90 period, shows that democratic institutions are well consolidated and that it is very likely that they will continue to function in the same smooth manner as in the past.

TABLE 1
PRESIDENTS SINCE 1973

A/A	PERIOD	PRESIDENTS
1	November 1973 - December 1974	Phaidon Gizikis
2	December 1974 - June 1975	Michael Stassinopoulos
3	June 1975 - May 1980	Constantine Tsatsos
4	May 1980 - March 1985	Constantine Karamanlis
5	March 1985 - March 1995	Christos Sartzetakis
6	March 1990 - March 1995	Constantine Karamanlis
7	March 1995 - present day	Kostis Stefanopoulos

TABLE 2
GOVERNMENTS SINCE 1974

A/A	PERIOD	PARTY	PRIME MINISTER
1	July 1974 - November 1974	"National Unity Government"	Constantine Karamanlis
2	November 1974 - May 1980	N.D.	Constantine Karamanlis
3	May 1980 - October 1981	N.D.	George Rallis
4	October 1981 - June 1989	PASOK	Andreas Papandreou
5	June 1989 - October 1989	"Coalition Government", (N.D. and SYNASPISMOS)	Tzanis Tzannetakis
6	October 1989 - November 1989	———————	John Grivas
7	November 1989 - April 1990	"Ecumenical Government", (N.D., PASOK, SYNASPISMOS)	Xenophon Zolotas
8	April 1990 - September 1993	N.D.	Constantine Mitsotakis
9	October 1993 - January 1996	PASOK	Andreas Papandreou
10	January 1996 - March 2004	PASOK	Kostas Simitis
11	March 2004 -	N.D.	Kostas Karamanlis

TABLE 3
Elections 1974-1981

Party	17/11/1974		20/11/1977		18/10/1981	
	%	Seats	%	Seats	%	Seats
Extreme Right	1,1	-	6,3	5	1,7	-
ND	54,4	216	41,8	171	35,9	115
EK-ND/EDIK	20,4	61	12,0	16	-	-
PASOK	13,6	15	25,3	93	48,1	172
KKE	9,5	8	9,4	11	10,9	13
KKE interior	-	-	2,7	2	1,3	
Others	1,0	-	2,5	2	2,1	-
TOTAL	100,0	300	100	300	100	300

TABLE 4
Elections 1985-1989

Party	2/6/1985		18/6/1989		5/11/1989	
	%	Seats	%	Seats	%	Seats
Extreme Right	0,6	-	-	-	-	-
ND	40,8	126	44,3	145	46,2	148
PASOK	45,8	161	39,1	125	40,7	128
KKE	9,9	12	-	-	-	-
KKE interior	1,8	1	-	-	-	-
SYNASPISMOS	-	-	13,1	28	11,0	21
Ecology Party	-	-	-	-	0,6	1
DIANA	-	-	1,0	1	-	-
Indep. Muslims	-	-	0,5	1	0,5	1
Others	1,1	-	2,0	-	1,0	1
TOTAL	100,0	300	100,0	300	100,0	300

TABLE 5
Elections 1990 -1996

Party	8/4/1990		10/10/1993		22/9/1996	
	%	Seats	%	Seats	%	Seats
ND	46,9	150	39,3	111	38,1	108
PASOK	39,3	125*	46,8	170	41,5	162
SYNASPISMOS	10,6	21*	2,9	-	5,1	10
KKE	-	-	4,5	9	5,6	11
POLAN	-	-	4,8	10	2,9	-
DIKKI	-	-	-	-	4,4	9
Ecology Party	0,8	1	-	-	-	-
DIANA	0,7	1	-	-	-	-
Indep. Muslims	0,7	2	-	-	-	-
Others	1,0	-	1,4	-	2,2	-
TOTAL	100,0	300	100,0	300	100,0	300

* The number of seats includes the MP's who have been supported jointly by Synaspismos and PASOK in five single member constituencies.

TABLE 6
Elections 2000

Party	Votes	%	Seats
PASOK	3.008.081	43,8	158
ND	2.934.948	42,7	125
KKE	379.280	5,5	11
SYNASPISMOS	219.988	3,2	6
DEKKI	184.648	2,7	-
Others	141.188	2,1	-
TOTAL	**6.868.133**	**100**	**300**

TABLE 7
Elections 2004

Party	Votes	%	Seats
ND	3.360.424	45,4	165
PASOK	3.003.988	40,5	117
KKE	436.818	5,9	12
SYNASPISMOS	241.714	3,3	6
DEKKI	132.933	1,8	-
Others	232.497	3,1	-
TOTAL	**7.408.374**	**100**	**300**

RECENT TRENDS OF THE PARTIES "BY PLAY"

By A. - J. D. Metaxas

1. Converging and non-converging parties

The potential of contemporary Greek political parties to differentiate themselves ideologically from each other - in order to represent, by definition, traditionally opposing social forces - seems very limited, due to political restraints.

Problems, especially the most important and urgent ones, appear to have specifically given solutions. Political parties do not seem to hold views or articulate ideas vastly different from each other. This holds true particularly on such issues as political and administrative modernisation, integration towards a European perspective, fiscal discipline, and telecommunication applications of an "open evolution". Even the terms governing the international presence of the country at multiple and adversarial levels are not a terrain for partisan politics. In other words, the solution of various problems is predestined, largely, by *unifying instructions* that emanate from international centres, European or global, which do not allow enough margin for national differentiation. A type of *local political globalisation* restricts political parties to roles of *prearranged action* and of a *controlled adversary*.

Parties, especially the governing ones, appear to be drawing nearer each

Costas Karamanlis, Prime Minister 2004-

other, so much so that the proximity is reflected not only on matters of essential choice and public speech but also on the "faces" and the body language of the persons who comprise them. It is not rare to ascertain that a high-ranking member of a political party could well belong to the opposing "other" one. Moreover, this refers to Ministers, party leaders or even Prime Ministers. Time and again the essential and stylistic behaviour of people who belong to different political parties is so alike that they remind us of portraits of a certain age. Even if they depict different persons, all portraits have something in common. This is certainly useful information for what constitutes a "legitimate style".

These similarities transform the parties from distinctly competitive to distinctly converging, particularly the "governmental" ones, i.e., PASOK and New Democracy that alternately seek power.

Converging parties are the parties for which antagonism ceases to be absolute and is restricted, by rule and despite the various attempts of rhetorical concealment, to a tonal confrontation.

On the other hand, *non-converging parties* are the ones that remain steadfast in their positions regarding the majority of aforementioned issues. Any retreat in public from the *clearly* supported ideological positions will not be without consequences.

The chances of the smaller political parties, i.e., Synaspismos and mainly KKE, to form a single-party-government are limited. Some of them though, keep the converging system at a state of critical contestation. It is for this reason that the converging parties try to approach the non-converging ones. The converging parties feel the need to appear respectful towards them. They also cultivate the impression that they can even co-operate, now or in the future, with some of the non-converging parties. This happens because they do not want to show that they are ignoring the ethos of the latter. By doing so, they minimise the impression that the prime target of the converging parties is blind pragmatism rather than social sensitivity.

George Papandreou, Leader of PASOK

Nevertheless, the general trend of the two large parties towards convergence does have some exceptions.

Some high-ranking members of PASOK - the officially "left progressive" party, to use a relatively conventional term - believe that important social, financial, and cultural imbalances continue to exist and that other, fairer solutions must be sought, which are different from the seemingly «necessary» ones. The country's essential convergence with the other member states of the European Union and admission into the Economic and Monetary Union cannot be an impersonal, bureaucratic goal. In other words, there are politicians who hold the view that certain misfortunes, individual or generic, continue to constitute a fundamental risk. At the same time, devotion to development, modernisation, and global co-operation (which is nearly tantamount to this) should not subjugate, justify or cover up every single issue.

Respectively, some high-ranking New Democrats - the party that is officially established as a "liberal" one - consider, on the contrary, that any adoption of a more generous social policy would bring the conservative party closer to the opposing progressive one. Some strong traditionalists would view such a scenario as an unjustified retreat from the "biblical" liberal faith.

We should not exclude, of course, the possibility that some of the non-converging positions of either party are not based on *strategic motives* but are *personality-centred*. In this case, the non-converging behaviour aims to achieve high-ranking status or leadership positions despite the fact that it happens in the name of (true or false) essential differences. It is not rare, for example, that if some people do not participate in the Government or in the Opposition leadership, this fact becomes the cause for *personal dispute*. However, we should not omit the case in which some high-ranking members, even though they lead the non-converging tendencies, act simultaneously within the boundaries of *visible legitimacy*. The latter is positively perceived on a socio-political level, while, on the other hand, these members are placed in an area of *open expectation*.

In conclusion, I would argue that the dominant *converging forces* encounter resistance, for a variety of reasons, from other converging forces. These are the ones that are substituted, as *counter-balancing reactions* vis-a-vis other outlooks within the actually and *symbolically* weakened classical partisan clash. The outcome of all these reactions is the creation of *non-converging groups* in every converging party, as well as temporal, usually loose, groupings. Their common feature is that they strongly question some choices, or persons who endorse those choices, despite the fact that they remain in the party and that they co-habit within the convergence. In the end, the party's *image of unity* breaks up.

A number of these non-converging threats, movements or groupings are treated by the dominant converging forces of every party, either in a *seemingly indifferent way* - a typical case of a *communicative surpassing*, or with a *calculated tolerance*. Special congresses, conventions, special meetings of committees or other organisations, reshuffles, et cetera, often operate beyond the provisions of their statutes. They are transformed-through tactical, mechanical acceptance of the other view-into mechanisms where differences are *publicly released*.

The confrontation of the inner party *non-converging pressure* aims to restrain, postpone and sometimes limit the negative consequences of a conflict.

In some other cases, a non-converging dispute might be considered even as a cause for support by converging forces. The justification is based on the theory that trends or even social groups should feel part of the system. The inner party opposition is shaped into forms of *controlled protest* that reinforce the *communication flexibility* of the party and create the feeling or the illusion of polyphony.

Despite the efforts and the inventiveness of the converging parties in offering satisfactory answers to social demands, the non-converging opposition does not seem satisfied and reacts intensely against any approach that aims at the incorporation or any communication trick or bargaining. The confrontation among the converging and the non-converging parties may relate to issues that are considered important, not only by themselves but by segments of the society as well. If so, the antitheses become acrimonious and threaten not only the party unity as an image but the very *converging function* of the Greek governing parties. This means that the pressure exercised by the forces of protest is not entirely absorbed. Consequently, we face the question of whether a political party can be simultaneously converging towards the opposite one, while some of its non-converging forces are effectively incorporated. In other words, both politically and socially, corresponding in order to achieve the preservation or the interchange of power.

This depends on many parameters, of which some have a structural and some have a contextual character. Yet, they are affected even by the *historic identity* of every party. This is what we call *experienced eponymy* and it comprises those values internalised by its followers, which you cannot divert from.

For New Democracy, a party with an *historic, "conservative" identity* (even though some party members dispute such classification), a turn towards a more socially sensitive program could ensure gains from a centre-bound, or more precisely, middle class audience that shares the same concerns. Simultaneously, this turn could cause losses from its right wing.

The opposite could happen to PASOK, a party with a *"progressive"* historic identity. Here a turn towards the opposing conservative camp could ensure gains from the respective centre or middle class area of the latter.

2. Multi-tendency parties or the multi-partisan camp

From what has been said, it is obvious that for each of the two large converging parties there is a critical relation between convergence/non-convergence that cannot be ignored. This is because it has serious consequences at the level of the party leadership, because *antileadership fractions* are formed in both parties.

In both cases, despite respective tensions, the daily harassment of the official leadership in an obvious or under-ground, publicised or muffled manner, leads to a situation in which the leaders or the party-presidents feel, but mainly appear, to be threatened and sometimes undermined. A sense of *continuous dispute*, drives them sometimes, and to a certain degree, to an objective hege-monism. This situation does not have precisely the same consequences for every party.

For a party that runs the Govern-ment, as PASOK did till 2004, the in-corporation of the inner party opposi-tion, even with chariot-like manoeuvres ("an heniochic attitude"), shows that, for the time being, it is easier. This is ac-commodated by the fact that this con-verging party is in power, which does not permit the non-converging forces to reach a certain point beyond which the exercise of power is endangered. The crises continue to "be welcomed and to be annoying", even though they are transformed to a certain degree into a *functional disagreement*.

In the other converging party, New Democracy, the rebuff of the dispute is harder. It cannot be achieved unless more decisive measures are taken. And to the extent that the overcoming of the protestation limits is without immediate cost, there are no consequences regard-ing the exercise of power for a party not running the Government. In this case, disputes originating from the inner party opposition are perceived by the leader-ship as an *objective disturbance* that

Aleka Papariga, General Secretary
of Communist Party (KKE)

does not permit the exercising of an ef-fective opposition, while protesters claim that this is exactly what they seek to achieve.

In a situation like this, where the var-ious attempts of *functional incorpo-ration* of the non-converging opposi-tions do not seem to succeed, how are the non-converging oppositions con-fronted? What tendencies do we ob-serve today? Is there any possibility of splits? Is a *preventive strategy* on how to preserve the big parties' indispens-able inner unity under debate?

Such a theme involves the transfor-mation of the two big parties into multi-tendency parties.

Multi-tendency parties are the con-verging parties that, typically or not, recognise the potential of their mem-bers to articulate different positions, as

*Nikos Konstantopoulos, President
of Coalition of the Left (Synaspismos)*

well as to form visible mechanisms in support of these positions, yet, they do not deny a *united partisan existence*.

Single-tendency parties are the ones that cannot adopt the principle of polyphonic choice, or even some of its versions, and choose as a *unifying substitute* the logic of the *super-leader's co-ordination*, where all positions can be expressed according to what the statute provides. Yet, they are covered up by a decision, while valid, the repre*sentational adequacy* of which is occasionally disputed.

Obviously every converging party that is transformed into a multi-tendency party basically accepts that *critical disputes* and objections expressed by non-converging forces - and we are interested in the ones that have an obvious social *response* - can, through the recognition of tendencies, not only be expressed but also organised. In a way, a multi-tendency party is driven to a system of *collective process* through which the various differences are mitigated.

The fact that tendencies are recognised is something that restricts, to a certain degree, the production of *periodical suspicion* that informs certain initiatives and machinations against the leadership. The possible evolution of the two large Greek converging parties into multi-tendency ones or into some type of multi-tendency version, that is to say an adoption of an informally organised pluralism-within-the-party, could mean:

1. that through the tendencies, proposal multiplicity, and indirectly, the best possible social representativeness of decisions can be reinforced

2. that through the tendencies, human aspirations, even those that are somehow unjustified are satisfied, or even considered, as long as they co-exist with an *effective* partisan policy, so that the necessity of a *perceptible leadership* is not disputed

3. and, that through the tendencies, a party, whether in power or not, becomes the main forum of *widely* debated proposals and perspectives, along with other financial, social and, mainly, cultural forces.

The possible choice even by Greek converging parties of adopting a multi-tendency version does not preclude them from being armoured with a greater inner flexibility. At the same time, it can reinforce them vis-a-vis certain non-converging parties, mainly Synaspismos (that appears as the cultivated Left). This can literally steal ideas, members and votes. The multi-tendency option should, reasonably at least, offer to the converging parties wider "catch-all" abilities ("multi-collective parties").

If the situation does not evolve, for whatever reason, towards inner party reformation, it is possible that certain leaderships or some non-converging groups or some persons could, in fact, contribute to the transformation of a *leader's party* into a *sovereign's* one. And this could happen both to PASOK and New Democracy. In other words a party type could be formed in which the reinforcement of the leader will be followed by the threat of a split which, regardless of its realisation, will sway constantly. Such a split will have differ-

ent consequences if it occurs or is retained as a threat during a pre-election period (or not) or if the split party is in power or in opposition. In any case, a party rarely welcomes a situation like this, unless it appears that it has a wide social and political *legitimisation*. I stress the word "appear" because even someone's simple departure, based on a different political platform, is condemned in the elections if it does not ensure this double legitimisation.

What is will happen if a break up or a state of break up occurs, without "seeming" justification? Is it possible that the party system will evolve from a two-party into a *two-camp* one, in other words, a system in which either the Government or the Opposition, or both of them, will be based on *plural majorities?*

The development of such a *multi-partisan* camp does not seem easy by Greek standards. Perhaps it is the first time that it cannot be entirely excluded.

PUBLIC ADMINISTRATION

By Calliope Spanou

President of the Republic

The President of the Hellenic Republic is the head of state. According to the Constitution, he is the "regulator" of the regime. His indirect mode of election and his limited powers, particularly after the 1986 Constitutional revision, exclude direct and active involvement in policy-making. Outside his political competencies (supra), he signs the necessary Decrees for the implementation of laws, appoints public officials and judges and is the (symbolic) leader of the military forces. Competent Ministers countersign the decrees. The President is the head of an autonomous public service that assists him in carrying out his responsibilities. The Presidency is a relatively recent institution, comprising the following Offices: Private, Legal, Diplomatic, Military, Economic Affairs and General Affairs.

The Presidential Residence

Presidents of the Hellenic Republic since 1974:	
Michael Stasinopoulos	1974 - 75 (transition to democracy)
Konstantinos Tsatsos	1975 - 80
Konstantinos Karamanlis	1980 - 85
Christos Sartzetakis	1985 - 90
Konstantinos Karamanlis	1990 - 95
Current President: Kostis Stefanopoulos 1995 -	

Central Government

As in other parliamentary regimes, the Prime Minister presides over the Cabinet. The *Prime Minister* concentrates the reality of governmental power and constitutes the strong pole of the executive. His /Her Constitutional role is to ensure the unity of government and the steering and overseeing of governmental action. The implementation of governmental policies is carried out by the public administration under his authority.

The *Prime Minister's Office* assists him/her in fulfilling the general overseeing of government and public administration. It is made up of the Strategic Planning Office, the Economic and Diplomatic Office and the Offices for the Quality of Life and for Social Dialogue and Communication. These monitor in a horizontal way the corresponding government activities. The heads of these offices together with a legal advisor are close collaborators of the Prime Minister.

In the Greek system of government, the Prime Minister is the primary figure of the Cabinet and the centre of most political decisions. Although this has deep historical roots, the 1986 constitutional revision placed even more emphasis on the Prime Minister at the expense of the President of the Republic. The extent to which the Prime Minister's primacy leads to centralisation in decision-making varies. In this respect, personalities matter as well as strong parliamentary majorities.

Prime Ministers Since 1974

K. Karamanlis (1974-80)
G. Rallis (1980-81)
A. Papandreou (1981-89)

The "Maximou megaron", the Prime Minister's Office

T. Tzannetakis
(June - November 1989)
X. Zolotas
(November 1989- April 1990)
K. Mitsotakis (1990-93)
A. Papandreou (1993-1996)
K. Simitis (1996-2004).
K. Karamanlis (2004 -)

The *Secretariat General of the government* is an autonomous public service, which assists the Prime Minister and the government in the exercising of their responsibilities. It is comprised of the following services: Office of the Secretary General, Office of Administrative and Financial Affairs, Office of Legislative Affairs, Office for the Co-ordination of Government Policies and Central Commission for the Drafting of Legislation and Telecommunications Office.

The Secretariat General of the goverment is directly accountable to the Prime Minister. It ensures the preparation of the agenda and the proceedings of the Cabinet and other collegiate governmental bodies as well as the monitoring of cabinet decisions. This service does not dispose of permanent personnel which changes following every governmental change. The Prime Minister makes all appointments. It is headed by the Secretariat General of the goverment who is the direct assistant to the Prime Minister.

The *Cabinet* (Council of Ministers) is comprised of the Prime Minister, the Ministers, alternate Ministers and Ministers without portfolio. It is currently composed of 18 Ministers and 1 Alternate Minister (Foreign Affairs). There are 22 Secretaries of State (junior Ministers) who are not part of the cabinet e.g. they neither participate nor vote in the deliberations. They can be invited to attend when matters falling within their scope of competence are discussed.

The cabinet meets in restricted composition following a labour division between the following collegiate governmental bodies. Most important among them are the Governmental Committee which co-ordinates governmental activities and decides on any issue referred to it by the Prime Minister and the Governmental Council for National Defence and Foreign Affairs. Other governmental bodies include the following: the Economic and Social Policy Committee, the Institutions Committee and the Public Works Committee, etc. The composition of these Committees varies according to their scope of competence and they are comprised of the relevant ministers.

Cabinet decisions are made by open voting and require the absolute majority of those present. In case of equally divided opinions, the Prime Minister's vote makes the difference in determining the outcome.

Ministerial Departments

The number of government departments is currently nineteen. Some of them correspond to previously separate ministries but they are currently placed under the authority of the same Minister.

Interior, Public Administration and
Decentralisation
Defence
Foreign Affairs
Economy
Development (Industry, Research
and Energy, Commerce, Tourism)
Environment, Physical Planning and
Public Works
Education and Religious Affairs
Agriculture
Labour and Social Security
Health and Welfare
Justice
Culture
Merchant Marine
Public Order
Macedonia and Thrace
Aegean
Transports and Communications
Press and Mass Media

The typical structure of a Ministry includes General Directorates, Directorates, Divisions, Bureaus. The political leadership of a Ministry, apart from the Minister, often includes junior Minister(s) and Secretary (-ies) General.

Central departments of a horizontal nature are the Ministry of the Interior, Public Administration and Decentralisation and the Ministry of the Economy. The latter is a result of a regrouping of the former ministries of National Economy and of Finance.

More specifically, the Ministry of Interior, Public Administration and Decentralisation is responsible, among other things, for deconcentrated and local government, human resource management in the public sector (recruitment, careers, etc.), relations between the administration and the citizens as well as elections and citizenship. The ministry of the Economy ensures a) financial management (budget, fiscal policy etc.) and b) a broader role in co-ordinating the various economic sectors and running the economy. This encompasses planning and regional development policies, macro-economic policies and public investment. Under the authority of the Ministry of the Economy, the Centre for Planning and Economic Research provides scientific expertise to assist the formulation of the above policies.

Advisory Bodies

Major advisory bodies assisting central government include the *Council of State, the Court of Accounts*, the *Legal Council of State and the National Council of Administrative Reform.*

More particularly, the Council of State, in operation since 1835-1844 and then since 1929, is the supreme administrative court of the country. At the same time, however, it is an administrative body whose competencies are provided for by the Constitution. The draft presidential decrees are submitted on an obligatory basis to the Council of State for its opinion regarding their conformity to the laws and the Constitution. Although the government is not obliged to follow the suggestions made, this is normal practice.

The *Court of Accounts*, created in 1833, has a double mission, as a supreme financial court and an administrative body with an advisory role concerning financial matters (e.g. pensions). It also verifies public accounts for legality and submits to the Parliament an annual report on the use of public funds, followed by suggestions. Both institutions were created according to the French model but the status of the members is that of a judge and not of a civil servant.

The *Legal Council of State*, established in 1882, is still in operation today, with a short interruption of almost 10 years. It is placed near the Minister of Finance; it advises government on legal matters and defends the legal interests of the state in court. It also assists administrative services in their everyday activities by rendering opinions on the handling of various administrative cases.

The importance of administrative reform is acknowledged by the creation of the *National Council of Administrative Reform* in 2000. This is an advisory body, formulating policy proposals and seeking to establish a consensus on administrative policies. Its composition includes representatives of various professional and interest organisations, experts, public institutions (Ombudsman, National Centre of Public Administration etc.) as well as party representatives. It is chaired by the Minister of the Interior, Public Administration and Decentralisation.

Administrative Structure of the country

Since 1986, the country has been divided into administrative regions, which form deconcentrated government services. There are 13 regions: 1) East Macedonia and Thrace, 2) Central Macedonia, 3) West Macedonia, 4) Epiros, 5) Thessaly, 6) Ionian Islands, 7) West Greece, 8) Central Greece, 9) Attica, 10) Peloponnese, 11) North Aegiean, 12) South Aegean, and 13) Crete.

A reform introduced in 1997 has upgraded the role of the regions and strengthened their administrative structure in order to assist them to perform their tasks. Regions implement domestic and European policies for the economic and social development of their geographic scope of competence. They play an important role in regional planning. In the same spirit, central government departments will gradually transfer executive powers to the regions and concentrate more on policy formation.

Each region is headed by a Secretary General, appointed by the Council of Ministers, who is the representative of central government at the regional level, responsible for ensuring the implementation of governmental policies. He/she can also be recalled or transferred to a different region in the same way.

Regional administration is organised within one General Directorate. Deconcentrated services at the regional level form thus a unified organisational unit.

They also have their own personnel, breaking with the tradition of vertical/sectoral dependence upon the corresponding central departments. Planning and regional development, public works, health, physical and urban planning, environment, forest management and agriculture are the main competencies of the new regions, supported by corresponding administrative units. The Secretary General of the region, assisted by the regional services ensures the overseeing of, and provides assistance to, both tiers of local government. Overseeing mainly concerns the legality of local government acts.

There is no self-government at the regional level. A *Regional Council* ensures representation of local interests through an advisory role. It is composed of the Secretary General of the Region, the elected Prefects *(infra)*, representatives of first tier local government associations and representatives of socio-professional groups. These groups include Chambers of Commerce, Industry, Technical Chamber, Geotechnical Chamber, Economic Chamber, Confederation of Civil Servants Unions, Panhellenic Confederation of Farmers Co-operatives and of the General Confederation of Labour.

The two tiers of local government at the departmental and municipality level are entrusted with the competencies concerning their respective geographical scope? he central government has no autonomous presence and competencies at this level and is limited to monitoring and control functions *(infra)*.

The Civil Service

The Greek civil service is basically organised along the lines of a career system. Civil servants have tenure, which is constitutionally guaranteed. They have the obligation of political neutrality, which involves refraining from expressing themselves in favour of a specific political party. The right of strike is subject to certain restrictions.

Civil service organisation is based on statutes dating from 1951. Despite occasional changes, the Civil Service Code has remained basically the same since then. Civil servants are recruited at the lower echelons and advance through promotions to the higher levels of bureaucracy. Apart from seniority, education level and performance appraisals are important criteria for career advancement. There are four categories of civil servants, according to their education level: University, Higher Technical School, High school and Compulsory education level.

Selection takes place through competitive examinations or through a form of the point system, depending on the specialities and qualifications required. A *High Council for the Selection of Personnel,* established in 1994, is an independent authority overseeing the selection process and ensuring the respect of the principles of merit, impartiality and transparency. Contract appointments complete the career system. This possibility is used mainly for scientific personnel as well as for responding to exceptional or occasional and seasonal needs. Subsequent laws have tightened up recruitment procedures in order to prevent over-staffing and guarantee impartiality and the use of the merit principal. The above mentioned High Council for the Selection of Personnel closely monitors recruitment and selection.

A civil servant's career is most likely to start and finish within the same ministry. Specialities are also linked to the specific ministry employing them. In other words, there are no inter-ministerial corps, though this possibility has often been envisaged and the relevant legal provisions are already in place. There is a widely shared belief among specialists that an inter-ministerial corps would en-

The National Centre of Public Administration

hance flexibility and work against compartmentalisation.

For a number of years, human resources policy has been seeking to increase public sector productivity. On the one hand, reforms attempt to provide a framework allowing for the best use of the existing personnel and encouraging civil servants to offer their talents and skills to serve Greek society. At the same time, the rights and obligations of civil servants have been reviewed in order to simplify disciplinary procedures and ensure conduct standards.

On the other hand there is a widely acknowledged need to reshape a rather heavy administrative machine. At the end of the year 2000, the public sector employed 404,920 employees (not included: army, police, education, justice, port-police, diplomatic corps, doctors, church) of whom 260,665 were tenured civil servants. First and 2nd tier local government (including dependent organisations) employs 61,226 employees.

In 1983, the *National Centre of Public Administration* was founded for the training of civil servants. The Centre has been in operation since 1985. Pre-entry training is more particularly the mission of the *National School of Public Administration*, meant to produce high level cadres for the civil service. Graduates of the 2-year programme of the School are then incorporated into the normal career pattern, benefiting from some initial acceleration of their career. The *Institute* for *In-service Training* is a second unit of the Centre, ensuring initial and continuous professional training.

Ensuring Sound Administration, Responsiveness and Citizen Rights Protection

In 1986, an important piece of legislation was passed which aimed at bringing the state - citizen relationship into equilibrium. Among other important rights, it has explicitly provided a right of access to government documents and has introduced simplifications in bureaucratic procedures. Later provisions have established further rights, such as, for instance, the obligation of the administration to respond to citizens' demands within a specific period of time accompanied by sanctions in cases of unjustified delay.

Building on these important reforms of the past decade, a consistent effort has been made during the recent years, to further promote transparency and accountability within the Greek political-administrative system. This important area of reform involves the introduction of new institutions and tools. Special bodies of inspectors (either horizontal such as the Administrative Inspectors, the Financial Inspectors and the Financial Crime Confrontation Body, or sectoral, such as transport, environment, health etc.) have been set up. Their target is to increase public control over bureaucracy, to combat corruption and to improve the effectiveness of specific policies. A General Inspector's Service was recently entrusted with the co-ordination of these control bodies. More particularly, the *Administrative Inspectors* placed under the authority of the Minister of Interior, Public Administration and Centralisation, undertake regular and ad hoc controls to ensure sound and efficient administration, quality of service and transparency. Their scope of competence encompasses all public services, including local government

To ensure sound financial management, the *Financial Inspectors*, placed under the authority of the Minister of the Economy, audit government financial services (e.g. tax offices, customs etc.), local governments, public agencies and public corporations as well as the allocation of subsidies and other forms of state grants.

With the intention of protecting citizens from bureaucratic arbitrariness, the recent establishment of an *Ombudsman* deserves special emphasis. This institution, which has been adopted by a great number of countries, aims at improving responsiveness to citizens' needs, ensuring transparency, combating poor administration and controlling the bureaucracy. It is equally expected to be a further source of ideas for new improvements in citizen/administration relationships.

According to the constitutional provisions of 2001, the Body of Parliamentary Chairpersons chooses the *Ombuds-*

Hellenic Post office

man unanimously or with a qualified majority of 4/5, for a 5-year (renewable) mandate. This is an Independent Administrative authority conceived as a mediator between citizens on one hand and public services, local government, public utilities (water electricity, transports, telecommunications, mail) on the other. This institution has proven quite successful during the first 5 years of its life.

Public Sector

Greece is traditionally characterised by a large public sector. It is made up of public corporations (such as the Public Electrical Power Corporation [DEH], the Hellenic Post [ELTA], Olympic Airways, the Public Petroleum Corporation [DEP] Hellenic Railways [OSE] etc.), banks

(ATE, ETE, ETVA...) and other agencies under state control. The criterion used to determine public sector agencies is the direct or indirect dependency on the state (capital share, decision-making, and appointment of leadership).

Over the past years a number of policy initiatives have aimed at reducing the size as well as increasing the productivity of public sector. Public sector modernisation currently encompasses two main sets of actions. The first is to enable public corporations to develop their policies and be accountable for their achievements and deficits. The new operational framework for public corporations revises their structure and operation. Public enterprises have taken the form of limited liability companies.

Thus, they can function according to private sector standards without losing their public utilities character.

Three main points deserve special mention. (i) Their relationship to the state is redefined to ensure the independence of their management from governmental interference. (ii) They have to function on the basis of strategic and operating plans. A contract between the government and management specifies the medium-term objectives to achieve. It is upon these that effectiveness is later assessed. The Ministry of the National Economy and the relevant Parliamentary Committee ensure the monitoring. (iii) To improve the service to the citizen, public enterprises are required to establish a Charter of obligations towards consumers. These provisions are expected to facilitate supervision and performance evaluation as well as to improve the quality of service provided.

Enhancing the competitiveness of the broader public sector requires further readjustments. Privatisation of several industrial firms under public control, as well as the listings on the Stock Exchange are meant to enable them to undertake their activities under more favourable conditions. The government's privatisation programme and more generally the economic liberalisation policy primarily affect companies such as the Hellenic Telecommunications Agency and the Public Petroleum Corporation.

LOCAL SELF GOVERNMENT

By N.-K. Hlepas

Local self-government has a long tradition in Greece that can be traced back to the late Middle Ages. During the long period of foreign domination, the "Greek communitarian spirit" contributed strongly to the survival of the nation. By the beginning of the nineteenth century, the Greek communes, which had been tolerated -if not supported- by the Ottoman occupants in their own interest, had reached a high level of autonomy. In most cases, quasi-democratic structures were familiar to them and every year general elections for the head of the community took place.

However, these "precursors of Greek statehood" that instructed the occupied people in politics and the secular elite in administration, presented a major handicap for the consolidation of a unitary national state during the French-influenced struggle for independence, as the so-called first Greek Republic (1821-1832) was established. Governor *Ioannis Kapodistrias* tried to unite the country under revolt but failed. In a country used to numerous centres of power, none of them could accept the rule of a national government. The iron hand of the Bavarian regents was the one that managed to abolish these thousands of historical communes (1833) and unify them in 750 Demoi (municipalities). These new

Demoi had many fewer responsibilities than the old communes and were obliged to engage in a process of state affairs in their district. Furthermore, the territory of the new-born state had been divided, according to the French model, into 10 prefectures ("nomoi"). The prefects were appointed by the King and were responsible for the supervision of municipalities.

MP's vs Mayors. Although the Demoi never managed to obtain significant administrative power, their political importance has been constantly growing. As they were already during the period of absolute monarchy (1833-1843) an institution based on the vote of the people, they gradually won a key role in the political system of the country, especially after the introduction - for the first time in the world - of universal suffrage (1864). Using the techniques of clientelism, the mayors became so powerful that members of Parliament (MP's) would hardly dare to ignore mayors of their constituencies. In 1912 the innovative statesman Eleftherios Venizelos, ordered the revival of the communes in an attempt to oppose clientelism and corruption but also to adhere to an ideology of the time that demanded the return "back to the roots of Hellenism". The MPs were, in this manner, liberated from the mayors but local government was fragmented into 6,000 units of Demoi (i.e., cities and towns of more than 10,000 inhabitants) and communes (in smaller towns and villages) - the latter dependent on state grants. Venizelos originally planned to "municipalise" the prefectures and remove the core of local government to this higher level. Due to political circumstances, but also the lack of resources, these plans fell through although the republican constitutions of the twenties (1925, 1927) foresaw "at least two tiers of local government". For the next decades, the municipalities constantly lost competencies. Most of them were much too small and depended on central government grants to survive. On the other hand, the prefectures and several state quangos took over the main functions of local administration.

Decentralisation: Starting in the fifties, a so-called "decentralisation-system" has been substantially strengthened. As it is understood in Greece, such a system is established when the central state creates non-central administrative units and gives them the power to decide on a considerable portion of public affairs within their district. These decentralised units are to be distinguished from municipalities since their heads - unlike the mayors- were appointed by the government. The latter were usually much more willing to hand over competence to the politically faithful "decentralised" prefects than to the mayors. Local government became little more than into a

The City Hall of Athens

The City Hall of Syros island

useful protest platform for political parties in opposition and a provider of elementary services. Furthermore, municipalities were subjugated to numerous and intensive controls from central and prefectural bureaucracies.

Third Republic: The fall of the military junta (1974) marked the beginning of an overall effort to democratise and reform the authoritarian, highly centralised state. The new constitution (1975) consolidated the "decentralisation system" (art. 101), while the local governmental bodies became solely responsible for local affairs (art. 102). The central government was supposed to maintain only the competence for national affairs, such as defence, monetary policy and industrial development. In spite of this, the state of local

government during the seventies was little different from that of the pre-dictatorship era. Limited functions, poor financial resources but strong political influence continued to characterise Greek local government.

The reform era: 1980 was the starting point for several reform efforts. The municipalities were proclaimed to be an institution to promote local economic and social development and were allowed to create profit-making enterprises. The management of water and sewage was handed over to flexibly organised, specially created enterprises called Municipal Enterprises of Water and Sewage. Several functions (urban transportation, nurseries, and maintenance of schools) were transferred from the central state to the local government.

New institutions for inter-municipal cooperation were introduced and the discretionary power of municipalities was enlarged through the abolition of a priori prefectural and other state controls. Nonetheless, the revenues of the municipalities remained inadequate for their tasks, so that they still depended on grants from the state. In 1989, the system of municipal revenue was reformed. Most of the state grants have been abolished and replaced by a new system based on the so-called "central autonomous funds". The latter comprised a proportion of certain government revenues (such as 20% of income tax, 50% of traffic duties etc.), which would be distributed among the municipalities according to objective criteria (such as the population), thus nearly eliminating government capabilities to utilise state grants. Furthermore, a growing number of municipalities were becoming familiar with the chances offered by European initiatives and programs, international networking and public-private partnership, so that traditional dependence on government funds could further be reduced.

New forms of participation. During the eighties, traditional attitudes were supposed to change through new institutions that would promote the - sometimes even direct - participation of citizens in municipal affairs. In the large cities, neighbourhood or "departmental", i.e., directly elected, councils have been established. In municipali-

ties with less than 10.000 inhabitants, the mayor is now able to convene the local citizen's assembly in order to discuss serious local problems. In many smaller municipalities this local assembly is also convened every year in May and the mayor reports to the citizens' assembly about his work during the previous months. Other, special laws foresee the local citizens' right to be informed about new building projects, urban development and planning, environmental impact assessments and environmental projects concerning their district. Furthermore, every citizen can refer to the council and present his opinion or ask for information about local affairs. Access to environmental information of all sorts is even easier and encouraged by a special ministerial decision implementing a European directive (90/313/EEC).

New responsibilities, new structures; The overwhelming majority of local authorities, however, were not substantially affected by this wave of reforms. A constantly expanding, wide spectrum of competence could only be

The City Hall of Thessaloniki

assumed by a small minority of the country's 5.775 municipalities. Out of the 5.318 communes (smaller towns and villages) some 85% had less than 1.001 inhabitants. They could only survive through state grants and were not able to offer modern services.

Venizelos, the regenerator of these communes, had already anticipated these problems in 1912. As compensation, municipal syndicates, according to the French model, were foreseen at that time. By the beginning of the eighties, about 200 such syndicates, mostly for irrigation and litter disposal, were in operation, but the institution as a whole was poles apart from resolving the problems caused by this extreme fragmentation of local government. By 1984, it was decided to deal with this problem in two ways. First there was an attempt to encourage, through grants and other incentives, the voluntary unification of smaller communes into Demoi. Second, new, "stronger" types of municipal syndicates ("development syndicates" replaced by "district councils" in 1994) were created.

The results of these efforts were not considered satisfactory. Thirteen years later, only 367 small communes (less than 10% of the target group) corresponded to the state incentives and transformed themselves into 108 Demoi, while the new types of syndicates did not live up to expectations. Furthermore, the absence of a higher (second) tier of local government deprived the municipalities of an important supporting in-

stitution, since the 54 state prefectures had proven incapable of filling this gap. In the cities, no important changes in internal administration and staffing were introduced, the new system of state grants ("autonomous funds") did not encourage local political accountability, while many mayors neglected strategic policy-making in favour of day-to-day action and clientelistic networking. By the early nineties, disappointment about such practices sometimes led to disillusionment about local government, but this turned out to be the point of a second reform era.

The "municipalisation" of prefectures: Efforts to establish a directly-elected representative body next to the prefect have been going on for more than a hundred years. In 1887, the enlightened statesman Charilaos Trikoupis established "prefectural councils", considering them a vehicle for liberty in the provinces and a "first step towards the democratisation of the whole administration system". Just three years later, the opposition party that came into power abolished these councils. Several laws targeting the transformation of the prefectures into local government units were passed later (1887, 1899, 1923) but none of them have in fact been enforced. In 1982, an indirectly elected "prefectural council" was established but the prefectures remained "decentralised" state institutions. New attempts at "municipalisation" failed twice (1986 and 1990), until finally in 1994 the 164-years-old state institution was transformed into a second tier of local government. The country's "decentralisation system" should, from now on, become gradually orientated towards the 13 state regions, which have been established since 1987.

In October 1994 prefectural councils and prefects were elected directly by the people. In most cases, each former "decentralised" prefecture has simply been transformed into a local government unit. In the metropolitan area of Athens, however, the "major prefecture Athens-Piraeus" was created and then subdivid-

tures have been subdivided into "provinces" ("eparchies") for geographical reasons. These provinces should ensure equal standard services also for the population of islands (where most of them exist) or highlands. In every province, a member of the prefectural council (called "eparchos") becomes the head of the local administration unit while a committee of members of the prefectural council constitutes the local, "provincial council".

Unique in southern Europe: The *"Capodistrias Program" of amalga-*

Table 1 : Distribution of the 50 "Prefectural Self-Governments" by orders of magnitude

Population	Pref. Self Government	%	Total Population	%
Up to 30,000	2	4.0	45,418	0.44
Up to 50,000	5	10.0	190,199	1.85
Up to 75,000	6	12.0	358,018	3.49
Up to 100,000	6	2.0	539,833	5.27
Up to 150,000	13	6.0	1.617,313	15.27
Up to 200,000	9	18.0	1.566,701	15.27
Up to 300,000	5	10.0	1.268,369	12.36
Up to 500,000	2	4.0	623,622	6.08
Bigger	2	4.0	4.048,831	39.47
Grand Totals	50	100	**10.258,364**	100

Source: National Statistical Service (1996)

ed into two "prefectural departments". Major prefectures have also been established in east Macedonia and Thrace - one of the country's poorest regions - embodying five former prefectures as "prefectural departments". On the other hand, some other communalised prefec-

mations Based on the experience of previous ineffectual attempts, the government decided to proceed with obligatory unifications of communes and reduce the number of communes from 5.318 down to 1.000 units. In February 1997, the Ministry of the Interior presented its plans for a final solution to the problems caused by the extreme fragmentation of local government in Greece. These plans constituted the subject of an animated public debate. Those against this particular program insisted on putting forward the idea of co-operation contracts among small communes as an alternative to obligatory unifications, while expressing their worries about the future of Greek rural culture.

The mandatory unification of municipalities in 1998 provides a unique, organisation of the first tier of local government, in its general principles. The so-called "Capodistrias Program" was not just a plan to merge municipalities, but also a national and regional development and works program, with a time scope of five years (1997-2001). The new local authorities would obtain the financial resources and the qualified staff they needed in order to set up a "modern and effective" unit of local administration that would act as an "instrument and a pole of development" for its district. At the same time, continued rep-

Table 2: Distribution of Municipalities by orders of magnitude and as a percentage of total population before (1996) and after (1999) the implementation of the 'Capodistrias' Program

Magnitude	Municipalities 1996	%	Municipalities 1999	%
Up to 300	2,043	35.1	33	3.2
Up to 500	1,180	20.2	14	1.3
Up to 1.000	1,357	23.3	46	4.5
Up to 2.000	672	11.5	93	9.0
Up to 5.000	337	5.8	380	36.8
Up to 10.000	102	1.8	281	27.2
Up to 20.000	48	0.9	95	9.2
Up to 50.000	54	0.9	56	5.4
Up to 100000	24	0.4	27	2.6
Up to 200000	6	0.1	6	0.6
Bigger	2	0.03	2	0.02
Totals	5,825	100	1.033	100

Source: Ministry of Interior, Public Administration and Decentralization

example of a radical reform through amalgamations in southern Europe to date. In 1997, a special Congress of the National Union of Municipalities approved the government plan for the re- resentation of the old rural municipalities was provided through local, directly elected community councils.

The total number of municipalities has been cut by 80%. This percentage would be even higher if the metropolitan areas of Athens and Thessaloniki, which were exempted from the amalgamations program and include more than 150 municipalities, were not taken into account. The average population of municipalities climbed up from about 1.600 to more than 11.000, while the average number of municipalities in each prefecture was reduced from about 120 (116.5) to a little over 20 (20.66) units. From this perspective, "prefectural local governments", especially outside the metropolitan regions, now seem to be too small to handle as a higher tier of local governance for the larger municipalities. On the other hand, quite a few of the new municipalities now seem to be too small to exercise several additional responsibilities (local police, minor harbours etc.) which have been transferred to the first tier of local government. Recent laws provided for the establishment of single or multi-purpose local associations ("syndicates") of municipalities that could carry out "demanding" tasks, such as local police, logistics and public works, while new types of contracting were introduced.

Despite these difficulties and several protests that the "Capodistrias Program" would not run as initially announced, there is no doubt that this major reform has already changed the landscape of local government in Greece. There is a new generation of politicians in the "Capodistrias municipalities". Most of them do not simply (as their predecessors used to do) stand for the interests of their local community at higher levels of politics and administration, but they also try to manage their own resources and cope with local problems. This type of mayor and councillor reflects the deep demographic, economic, communicative and cultural changes of the last decades that have tended to "urbanise" styles and views of life in the Greek countryside. Nowadays, local communities in "rural" areas would expect much more from public administration than they used to in the past. Consequently, the amalgamations of the nineties have responded to the changing social environment.

Municipal enterprises: This new, demanding social environment stimulated several local politicians to use the possibilities offered by law for the creation of municipal enterprises: Twenty years ago, less than a dozen such enterprises existed. Today, more than 1.200 units are to be found all over the country. They even include high-tech producers. The early eighties marked the starting point of this impressive process. Since then, different categories of municipal enterprises have been introduced. "Pure" (amigeis) municipal or inter-municipal enterprises are those owned entirely by municipalities. The municipal co-operative enterprises are those jointly owned by municipalities and co-operatives, while the "people-based" companies are those in which a considerable part of the shares is spread among private citizens (while no one of them is allowed to own more than 2%). The municipalities are also able to jointly create companies with private individuals and, in general, use any type of company foreseen by law. However, such initiatives can only be taken, if they are based on a so-called "viability-study", which should demonstrate whether an enterprise will be able to stand on its own feet. This -sometimes difficult- jump into entrepreneurial activities has been made easier through state investment incentives with a higher percentage than that of private enterprises and through several tax exemptions. Furthermore, municipal enterprises can hire personnel without taking into account the strict limitations affecting the rest of the widespread public sector.

cialised staff and flexible administrations, such as cultural and social services have been moved from the local government organisations themselves to the more efficient municipal enterprises. Several municipalities founded so-called "Development Companies" which do not simply provide consultant services and promote entrepreneurial activities of local government but are used as a flexible alternative for organising and offering any kind of municipal services.

Today, the great majority (75%) of municipal enterprises involves the provision of municipal services, while the rest develop entrepreneurial activities in areas such as tourism, manufacturing or

Table 3: The Development of the Number of Municipal Enterprises (1984-2000)

Year	1984	1985	1986	1987	1988	1989	1990	1991	1992
Number	73	104	135	158	212	278	326	360	397
Year	1993	1994	1995	1996	1997	1998	1999	2000	
Number	446	606	707	862	892	1101	1169	1221	

Source: Research/ Survey by the University of Athens (Department of Political Science and Public Administration) - including the municipal enterprises for water supply and sewage

In addition to the above, some new regulations allowing municipalities to assign public works directly to their own enterprises, led to the increasing use of municipal enterprises in order to by-pass local bureaucracies and several kinds of restrictions affecting public services. Municipal functions that required spe-

agriculture. It is no secret that many local policies, which are decided in the town halls of the cities, are enforced through these municipal enterprises. In a growing number of cases, contracting out and co-operation with private firms (especially in traffic and parking management) have been combined with such practices. Local government and local politics are increasingly expanding and becoming more and more complex. Multifarious municipal actions and administrative flexibility on one side, organisational fragmentation and diffusion of political responsibility on the other side, are the results of this process.

The citizen and local government. Demoi and communes have traditionally been the smallest cells in the Greek political system and are seen as the keystone of democracy. Since 1994, the municipalisation of prefectures added one more level of participation, where the local community can conduct its own affairs independently. The councils of the Demoi, communes and prefectures, but also the mayors and the prefects are elected directly by the citizens of their district. Their term in office is precisely four years, beginning on the first of January after the elections (which always take place during the first Sunday after the tenth of October). Political parties per se are not candidates, but in many cases (mostly in urban areas) they announce in public their support for certain candidates, while in the biggest cities (Athens, Piraeus, Thessaloniki) top cadres of the parties often use the position of mayor in order to pursue larger ambitions.

Mayors and prefects are both political masters and administrative directors of municipal bureaucracies. In the communes and the smaller Demoi, this dual role makes it possible for the citizens - who usually have quite easy access to their mayor - to resolve several bureaucratic problems with the assistance of his office. Furthermore, a special, rapid system of legal protection enables the local citizen to challenge any municipal measure that has affected him and violated his rights before an independent body - prior to appealing to the courts.

Since the early nineties, co-operation with NGOs and other private initiatives in order to cope with various social problems and to help the less privileged groups of people emerged as an important challenge. The formerly traditional, extremely homogeneous Greek society has been dramatically changing. Self-help groups of persons addicted to drugs and organisations that assist alien refugees and migrants are typical examples of partners that work with municipalities (especially in the big cities). They are gradually turning their attention to social minorities and trying to assist them.

A strong constitutional position: The amended (in April 2001) version of Art. 102 of the Greek Constitution provides for two tiers of local government (without identifying them). Furthermore, for the first time in modern Greek history, it is foreseen (Art. 102 par. 5) that local authorities should be able to impose local taxes, while the state will have to transfer the necessary funds whenever local authorities are obliged by law to undertake a new responsibility.

The Constitution ensures the twofold incorporation of local government agencies (LGA) into the democratic system of government. On the one hand, democratic procedures and rules for implementing the sovereignty of the people at the local level are introduced (Article 102, par. 2.). On the other, the Constitution itself defines, directly, a significant part of the executive function, that is, as the "administration" of local affairs as the field of responsibility of the LGAs (Article 102, par. 1). Thus, local government could be described as a junction of local policy and local administration. The Constitution clearly presupposes a balanced relationship between these two fundamental constituents of the institution. The decision-making competencies and the actual conditions for action on the part of the LGAs with regard to "local affairs" should, consequently, make possible the formation of an individual "local political will" and its transformation into acts of management of common (public) local interests.

The notion of "local affairs", in conjunction with a two-tier system of local government is supposed to restrict the competence of state administration, stricto sensu, and therefore the share of the executive power it possesses. Today there is an identification of the parliamentary majority with the central government and a great magnitude of the resources and activities are controlled by it. Given that this is so, such restrictions on the power of the national state and, by extension, on the governing party are obviously useful for a

smooth and balanced running of the democratic political system. Local Government can distribute important shares of executive power to a wide spectrum of political forces, thus creating new mechanisms of "checks and balances" within the overall state apparatus and ensuring local implementation of alternative proposals for the management of political power.

Pending reforms in the metropolitan areas. Although the time and scope of metropolitan reform were far from being clear, a paragraph in the Constitution concerning municipal associations was amended in 2001. This was done in order to facilitate the establishment of multi-purpose metropolitan associations of municipalities, which would be, in the future, one of the options coming into question.

For the time being, ministries or state-controlled quangos exercise quite a few functions of metropolitan administration, while local government structures remain fragmented. But in the face of the challenges due to the city's nomination for the Olympic Games of 2004, some necessary reforms of metropolitan governance could not be avoided. A new entity, named "Athens 2004", assumed the main responsibility for the co-ordination and promotion of several projects. Due to "Olympic pressures", several issue and project based mechanisms of co-ordination have been established and in most cases include social and private organisations as partners.

Public awareness about metropolitan problems in Athens has grown a lot, compared to the past. This is not only due to the Olympics as a mobilising mega-project. It also stems from the fact that the implemented modes of metropolitan governance, although structured by single issues and projects associated with the Olympics, did promote ties among sectors and agencies as well as between them and citizens. The public debate about the Olympics revitalised public debate about reforms and long-term strategies for the metropolitan area of Athens/Attica, while it initiated a kind of "reflex-debate" on reforms for the metropolitan area of Thessaloniki.

A new scheme of metropolitan governance is to be set up, that would promote effectiveness and efficiency and at the same time foster citizen participation as well as the accountability of decision-makers. The role of local government within this new system of metropolitan governance is expected to be very important.

In conclusion, it should be borne in mind that, in connection with any option for reforms, the main challenge for the future of local government remains the same. How will it be possible to preserve the democratic core of the institution inside an environment always asking for more and better services.

THE LEGAL SYSTEM

By J. Tassopoulos

Greek law belongs to the civil law tradition. The era of modern Greek law began with the National Revolution of 1821 against the Turks, which led to the creation of the Greek State in 1832.

In the Greek legal order, the division between civil (private) and public law is important. Public law is made up of constitutional, administrative, international and criminal law, and criminal and civil procedure. It is mainly civil law (general principles of civil law, law of obligations, property, family, and law of succession) and the various branches of commercial law that fall within the scope of private law. The importance of civil law as the heart of the legal system has diminished to a certain extent, while governmental intervention continues to expand and the state, with its administrative regulation, covers more aspects of life.

The most important codifications in Greek law are the following: the Civil Code, the Commercial Code, the Penal Code, the Code of Civil Procedure, the Code of Criminal Procedure, the Code of Private Maritime Law, the Code of Administrative Process, the Code of Administrative Procedure, and the Military Penal Code.

The Greek Civil Code of 1946 was greatly influenced by Byzantine law, which was applied in Greece before the promulgation of the Civil Code. The Civil Code is grounded on the principles of individual autonomy, private property and freedom of contract. It also protects the institution of family, grounded on equality of the sexes, which is constitutionally proclaimed. It contains, however, general clauses, leaving space for judicial adaptation to changing circumstances as well as for the introduction of elements of fairness.

The Constitutional Tradition

Greece is a country with a long constitutional tradition, which is marked by the existence of a written constitution. The present constitution was enacted in June 1975, after the fall of the dictatorship of 1967 and the re-establishment of democratic government in the country. The origins of the current constitution can be traced back to 1864.

Greece is a representative democracy, based on the principle of popular sovereignty. Greece has a parliamentary government and its president is elected by the parliament. The Government (the Prime Minister and the cabinet) is responsible to the democratically elected parliament. It is a multi-party system and the freedom of establishing political parties is guaranteed by the constitution. Direct, secret and universal ballot elect parliament. The amendments of 1986 abolished the presidential powers granted in the constitution of 1975. The role of the president of the republic has now become more or less ceremonial. As a result, the Prime Minister is the main locus of power. In 2001, the revision of the constitution improved the protection of individual rights, increased the role of the parliamentary committees in the legislative process and provided Independent Authorities, such as the Greek Ombudsman, with constitutional status.

Main Sources of Law

Despite the codification of Greek laws, custom is still recognised as a source of law, although, today, it is of minimal importance. Judicial decisions do not constitute binding precedent on subsequent similar cases, however they exert their influence through the need for a uniform application of the law.

Generally, recognised rules of international law, as well as international conventions form an integral part of Greek law and prevail over any contrary provision of law. International conventions are placed below the Constitution and above statutes.

The parliament and the president of the republic exercise legislative power. The role of the latter is limited to the promulgation and publishing of the laws. The constitution allows delegation of legislative power, except where a statute is required, e.g. for the imposition of taxes or for acts concerning the exercise and protection of individual rights. Delegation is mainly confined to the president of the republic and is exercised by presidential decrees, and countersigned by the proposing and politically responsible Minister under the following conditions. The statutes on which delegation is based must state the subject, the aim and the limits of the legal provisions for which delegation is granted. While they are in draft form, the Council of State, acting as an administrative organ examines Presidential Decrees for their legality, before the President of the Republic signs them. Parliament may also delegate legislative power to other organs of the executive, but only for the regulation of specialised, technical, or local matters. On proposal of the Cabinet, the president of the republic has the power to issue legislative acts, without statutory delegation, in extraordinary cases for the regulation of urgent and unforeseen needs. Within forty days after their adoption, these acts must be submitted for parliamentary approval. Failure to seek approval or in the case the Parliamentary disapproval, the legislative acts are rendered null and void.

European Community Law and the Greek Legal Order

Greece actively participates in the process of European unification. The

The ordinary criminal courts' building, at Evelpidon street, Athens

accession of Greece to the European Community was signed and ratified by the Greek Parliament in 1979 with a majority of 193 votes out of 300. Article 28 of the Constitution of 1975 provided the legal basis of the incorporation of Community law into the Greek legal order. According to art. 28 par. 2, competencies provided by the constitution, either treaties or agreements must be vested in agencies of international organisations, when this serves an important national interest and promotes co-operation with other states. Art. 28 par. 3 provides that Greece may freely proceed to limit the exercise of national sovereignty, insofar as this is dictated by an important principle of democratic government, and is effected on the basis of the principle of equality and under the coalition of reciprocity. European Community law has pervasive effects upon the Greek legal order and the reg-ulations have direct applicability and effect in Greece. When required, domestic law is adapted to the provisions of Community law.

A state under the rule of law.

Greece is a state under the rule of law. The Greek Constitution guarantees the principle of separation of powers, combined, however, with the notion of legislative supremacy. In fact only the judiciary is genuinely separated from the other state powers. However, the independence of the judiciary is relatively mitigated by the power of the Government to assign the heads of the three supreme courts (Council of State, Areios Pagos and Auditor's Court). Judicial review of the constitutionality of laws is actively exercised by Greek ordinary judges.

A judgement of unconstitutionality of a legislative act is binding solely between the parties. Only the Supreme Special Court has a quite circumscribed power to declare the provisions of a statute void, having effect erga omnes in case of conflicting judgements pronounced by the Council of State, the Areios Pagos or the Auditor's Court.

The Greek Constitution guarantees enumerated individual, political and social rights. Greece has also ratified the European Convention for the protection of Human Rights and Fundamental Freedoms of 1950 as well as the majority of its Protocols.

The Constitution proclaims that respect and protection of the value of the human being constitutes the primary obligation of the state. Personal liberty is inviolable. According to art. 5 par. 3, no one shall be prosecuted, arrested, imprisoned or otherwise confined except when and as the law provides. The Constitution guarantees for all persons living within Greece full protection of their life, honour and freedom. The extradition of aliens prosecuted for their action as freedom fighters is prohibited. Arrest or imprisonment is prohibited without a reasoned judicial warrant, which must be served at the moment of the arrest or detention pending trial. Such a warrant is not required in the case of arrest while committing a criminal act. Within twenty-four hours after the arrest, the arrested person must be brought before the examining magistrate who has to decide within three days whether the ar-

rested person will be released or imprisoned pending trial. Detention however is ordered in exceptional cases for grave offences. Pre-trial detention cannot exceed one year for felonies and six months for misdemeanours. Under exceptional circumstances this time limit may be extended for six and three months respectively.

Art. 7 par. 1 of the Constitution recognises the principal "Nullum Crimen, nulla poena sine lege". According to this principle, penal law must be written and precise. Finally, penal laws do not accept application by analogy and cannot be given retroactive effect. The defendant has the right to be heard, to be represented by counsel both at the pre-trial phase (interrogation) and during the trial, to review the file and obtain copies of the documents and to remain silent.

Intellectual freedoms are secured by the Greek legal order. Freedom of expression is interpreted as including the protection of freedom of information. Censorship and all other preventive measures are expressly prohibited. Seizure of the press is permitted after circulation by order of the public prosecutor, on limited occasions provided by the Constitution. The protective provisions for the press are not applicable to films, sound recordings, radio, television etc. Radio and television, are by constitutional mandate under direct state control, which aims at the objective transmission on equal terms of news reports and information, as well as works of literature and arts. According to presently valid law, this control is entrusted to and exercised by an independent administrative authority, the Radio and Television Council. Freedom of assembly, of association and of correspondence is also guaranteed.

Freedom of conscience and religion are constitutionally secured. In Greece there is neither complete separation between state and church nor an established religion. The Constitution recognises the Eastern Orthodox Church as the prevailing religion.

The Greek Constitution guarantees the principle of equality of all Greeks before the law. The principle is justiciable and concerns both the application of the law as well as the substantive provisions of legislation.

The Greek Constitution guarantees the right to privacy. Recently, an independent administrative authority for the protection of personal data has been established for the first time in the Greek legal order.

The Constitution guarantees private property, which is interpreted by the courts to include real property, excluding rights in personam. A special clause secures the protection of foreign investments in Greece. Taking (expropriation) of private property is constitutionally permitted for the public benefit, when and as specified by law and always following full compensation determined by the civil courts. A distinction must be made between expropriation and the imposition of regulations on the use of private property, which sometimes may be severe. Nevertheless such regulations must not amount to essential expropriation and must be consistent with the principle of proportionality.

Economic liberty (liberty of trade, free competition, free choice of profession) is constitutionally protected. All persons have the right to freely develop their personality and to participate in the social, economic and political life of the country insofar as they do not infringe upon the rights of others, or violate the Constitution and moral values. However, the Constitution allows state intervention in the free market economy mainly by declaring that private economic activity shall not be permitted to develop at the expense of freedom and human dignity or to the detriment of the national economy.

Protection of the environment.

The Constitution contains important provisions securing broad protection of the environment, both the natural and the cultural one. The protection of the environment is expressly indicated as a duty of the state, which is bound to adopt special preventive or repressive measures for environmental preservation. Art. 24 of the Constitution provides for urban planning as well as for the protection of forests. The environmental provisions of the Constitution have been broadly interpreted by the Council of State, whose jurisprudence has greatly contributed to the development of environmental law in Greece.

Social Justice

The Constitution guarantees social rights. The development and promotion of arts and sciences, research and teaching are obligations of the state. The Constitution protects family, motherhood, childhood, youth and the needy and poor members of society. According to the Constitution, education is a basic mission of the state and all Greeks are entitled to free education, at all levels, in state educational institutions. Exclusively fully self-governed public legal persons provide education at the university level. The establishment of private universities is constitutionally prohibited in Greece.

The Constitution proclaims the right to work. All working people are entitled equal pay for work of equal value, irrespective of sex or other distinctions. Trade union freedom enjoys constitutional protection. The right to strike is constitutionally protected if exercised by lawfully established trade unions, for the promotion of the financial and general labour interests of the working people. Collective bargaining and collective agreements have become the regular instrument for fixing the minimum wages. If collective bargaining proves to be ineffective, the law provides a procedure of arbitration.

Greece has also ratified many international conventions on labour law (e.g. European Social Charter of 1961, the UNO Convention etc.). The Constitution also provides for social security, which is recognised as a social right for working people. Care for the health of the citizens is a goal of the state. Greece has a national health system, established during the 1980's.

The Citizen and Public Administration

Greece is a unitary state. The administration of the state is organised on the basis of the principle of decentralisation. According to art. 101 par. 3 of the Constitution, regional state agencies have general decisive authority on matters of their region. As a consequence, competencies once transferred by law to regional agencies may not be given back to central agencies. Local self-government is constitutionally guaranteed. Municipalities and communities form the first level of local government agencies. The administration of local affairs belongs to the decisive competence of local governmental authorities. A second level of local self-government has recently has been established, i.e. prefectural local self-government. Local government agents of both levels are elected by universal and secret ballot every four years.

According to the fundamental principle of legality, administrative action must comply with the rules of law. The Greek legal system traditionally recognises the parliamentary control of administrative action, administrative self-control (hierarchical control of superior authorities to subordinate ones) and judicial control. Recently and for the first time in Greek legal order, the institution of Ombudsman (Commissioner) was introduced. It constitutes an independent administrative authority, mediating between the citizen and administrative authorities in cases of administrative malfunction. The Constitution guarantees the right to petition in writing to public authorities and the right to a prior hearing before any administrative action or measure is adopted at the expense of one's rights or interests. According to law, every citizen has the right of access to administrative documents, as long as they do not refer to the private or family life of third persons. However, the administrative authorities may bar access to secret documents.

Court Structure and the Legal Profession

The right of access to the courts is constitutionally guaranteed. According to art. 20 par. 1 of the Constitution, every person is entitled to legal protection by the courts and may plead before them his/her views concerning his/her rights and interests as specified by law.

Greece has three hierarchies of courts: Civil and criminal courts have jurisdiction on civil and criminal matters, where the same judges sit and judge either category of cases; and administrative courts with jurisdiction on administrative controversies, which are judged by administrative judges. There are also special courts.

There are three types of ordinary civil courts: District courts (justice of the peace, one-member district court and three-member district court), twelve courts of appeal and the Areios Pagos (Supreme Court). The subject-matter jurisdiction of the civil courts as a rule depends on the amount under question. An appeal usually leads to a trial de novo, extending to factual and legal matters.

Ordinary administrative courts have jurisdiction over all substantive administrative disputes. There are one-member and three-member administrative district courts as well as administrative courts of appeal. The supreme administrative court is the Council of State, formed along the model of the French Conseil d' Etat. The Council of State reviews the legality of administrative acts and has the power to annul them. It has general jurisdiction on annulment disputes. As a rule, the Council of State reviews the decisions of the administrative courts of appeal.

The Auditor's Court has jurisdiction over cases arising from pension grants and from the audit of accounts in genera. It also has jurisdiction over cases related to the liability of civil servants, military officers and local government agency employees, or disputes for any loss

through fraud or negligence, incurred upon the state or the above agencies and corporate bodies.

Finally, the punishment of crimes belongs to the jurisdiction of ordinary criminal courts, which are classified with respect to the category of the offence. As a rule, felonies are tried by a mixed court composed both of judges and jurors, as well as by the court of appeal (mixed, three-member and in the second instance five-member). Misdemeanours are tried by the two misdemeanour courts (one- and three-members, depending on the seriousness of the offence) while petty-violations are judged by the petty-violation court. Normally, the *Areios Pagos* stands also as supreme court reviewing the decisions of most of the lower criminal courts.

The Supreme Special Court, in addition to the aforementioned review of the constitutionality of laws, has jurisdiction over disputes arising from parliamentary elections, or referenda. It also has jurisdiction over disputes from conflicts of competence; controversies related to the designation of rules of international law as generally acknowledged and cases regarding the incompatibility or the forfeiture of office by a Member of Parliament.

The three law schools in the country at the undergraduate level offer basic legal education. It covers four years. There are however graduate programs as well. After graduation, a period of practical training follows. Judicial officers are career lawyers enjoying personal and functional independence. According to the former, judges after a probation period acquire life tenure. Their promotions, assignments, transfers and detachments are effected after prior decision by the Supreme Judicial Council. Functional independence concerns the independence of the judiciary as a separate branch of government. Lawyers who want to become judges must attend the National School of the Judiciary. Public prosecutors are parties in the criminal proceedings. They represent the state throughout all stages of the proceedings. However they are supposed to be objective authorities and their goal is to find the truth and apply the law correctly. As a consequence, they may plead in favour of the defendant.

Most lawyers pursue a career as private practitioners (attorneys at law). Their promotion to the higher ranks of courts (court of appeal and Supreme Court) takes place after specified periods of time. They have to be members of one of the Bar Associations of Greece.

GREECE AND THE WORLD

THE FOREIGN POLICY OF GREECE
By Constantine A. Stephanou

The background conditions
Cultural setting

Greece's 3000 year long history is one of a struggle to preserve its national identity or what is usually referred to as "Hellenism". This being said, many facets of this identity have been diffused throughout the world and have become part of other civilisations. Hellenism runs over and above the religious divide and what came to be known as the clash of civilisations. Greeks are famous for their openness and hospitality *(philoxenia)*. It is therefore not surprising that Christians, Muslims and Jews living around the Mediterranean, the Black Sea and elsewhere are attracted to Greece, the meeting point of civilisations.

Geopolitical setting

Greece's unique position at the crossroads of civilisations is coupled to its exceptional strategic location. It is the hub of transport and communications from Europe to the Middle East and is essential to the logistic support of neighbouring countries. The strategic importance of Greece has been a crucial factor in the shaping of the foreign policies of external powers. Greece, however, has been cautious in exploiting its strategic position, aligning itself with the western democracies in the two World Wars and contributing with its large merchant marine to the victories.

General foreign policy objectives
Promoting peace and security

Greece has been a staunch supporter of the United Nations and the specialised agencies since their inception and has been actively involved in their activities. Greece always deplored the blocking of Security Council resolutions by permanent members and the politicisation of some specialised agencies, which impaired their effectiveness.

Regional defence pacts such as NATO are, in Greece's view, an essential element of collective security. From 1952, when Greece became a member of NATO, until 1974, the main threats to Greece's security were deemed to originate from the Warsaw Pact. The invasion and occupation of Northern Cyprus and the claims in the Aegean by

A general view of Prague's Congress Centre during opening session of the NATO summit on Thursday, 21-11-2002

The President of the Hellenic Republic, Konstantinos Stephanopoulos, with the United Nations Secretary General, Kofi Annan, in Athens, 26-02-2003

another NATO member, Turkey, have affected Greek defence planning and expenditure. Nevertheless, Greece has fulfilled its obligations as a NATO member and, following the historical changes of 1989 and the emergence of NATO's new role, Greece has provided facilities for NATO operations in the Balkans, as well as substantial military contingents for peace-keeping purposes.

Promoting the European Political Union

Greek public opinion has consistently been pro-European. In the Eurobarometer polls, the deepening and widening of the European Union receives overwhelming support. Moreover, the leaders of the two major political parties, PASOK and New Democracy, frequently refer to the federal future of the European Union. Until, however, such a state is reached, Greece is strongly attached to the principle of equal footing in EU institutions and supports a strong role for the so-called supranational institutions, namely the European Commission and the European Parliament.

In addition, Greece is likely to support any measure enhancing the diplomatic capability of the Union, as long as this does not lead to the formation of a directoire of the larger member states. Europe should speak with one voice not only on trade and economic affairs but on security as well. The Treaty amendments at Maastricht and Amsterdam extended the scope of the European Union to the so-called Petersberg military tasks. In line with these treaties, Greece has actively contributed to efforts aimed at building a European Security and Defence Identity (ESDI) and

Prime Minister Costas Karamanlis with EU Commission President Romano Prodi

establishing a 60.000 man European Rapid Reaction Force by 1 July 2003. Greece pledged to contribute a 3.500 men contingent, to be composed of professional military personnel.

Preserving the US-Greek Strategic Partnership

US-Greek relations have been based on the common commitment of the two countries to freedom and democracy. US assistance was of critical importance for the economic recovery of Greece in the 1950s. Nevertheless, Greek public opinion has held the United States responsible for interference in Greek politics during the same period and for supporting the military dictatorship that ruled Greece from 1967 to 1974. More recently, however, it was the United States rather than Greece that complained about the conduct of its partner. The United States have been critical of Greek disarmament initiatives during the last period of the Cold War and of Greek attitudes towards liberation movements, deemed by the United States to be terrorist movements. Nevertheless, Greek governments have invariably supported US involvement in the security of south-eastern Europe and the eastern Mediterranean, because of the permanent threat of instability in the region. In Greece's view, the United States are capable of containing crises through the use of military power in the area, although in Greece's opinion, intervention should always be compatible with the provisions of the UN Charter. Moreover, co-operation with Russia and China is essential for the smooth functioning of the United Nations.

Promoting Stability, Democracy and Economic Recovery in South-Eastern Europe

Stability and Democracy

Greece has a long record of promoting the cause of stability in the Balkans. In the 1930s Greece negotiated a Balkan Pact with its neighbours and a conciliation and arbitration agreement with Turkey. In the post World War II Balkans, the Iron Curtain was an impediment to co-operation, with the exception however, of relations with non-aligned Yugoslavia. In the 1980s,

Greece provided unambiguous support to international initiatives such as arms reductions and confidence building measures under the Conventional Forces in Europe (CFE) Treaty, without asking for or enjoying exemptions.

Since the end of the cold war and the democratic transition in Bulgaria and Romania, Greece has actively supported the inclusion of these countries into the Euro-Atlantic structures. Greece believes that the gradual extension of the European Union and NATO to the Balkans is the most effective way to ensure stability and prosperity in the region. Greece has played an active role in shaping EU policies and related initiatives for political and economic reforms and institution building in the Balkans. These include the South East Europe Co-operation Initiative (SECI), the Royaumont Initiative. Since the end of the Kosovo war, Greece has participated in the Stability Pact for the Balkans under the auspices of the OSCE and the EU initiatives for the Western Balkans, including the conclusion of stabilisation and association agreements with these countries.

As reiterated at the EU-Balkan summit held in Zagreb, in November 2000, intra-Balkan co-operation is a prerequisite for the accession of the Balkan countries to the EU. In contrast to bilateral co-operation, multilateral co-operation among Balkan countries is minimal, particularly when compared to co-operation among Nordic, Baltic or Central European countries. Intra-Balkan co-operation was given a boost following Greece's 1997 initiative to host the first meeting of the South East Europe Co-operation Process at the level of Heads of Government in Heraklion, Crete. The second meeting took place in 1998 in Antalya, Turkey and the stage has been set for annual high-level

European leaders pose for a family photo after the EU-Western Balkans summit at Porto Carras resort, Greece, 21-06-2003

meetings enhancing confidence among the leaders of the Balkan nations. However, in addition to the Charter on good-neighbourly relations and co-operation, major co-operation initiatives have to be launched and a degree of institutionalisation has to be achieved.

Economic recovery

The Balkan and Black Sea countries have traditionally belonged to the economic periphery of Europe. For those countries that were behind the Iron Curtain, transition from the command economy to the market economy entailed substantial hardship to local societies. Greece has provided significant resources, including a military contingent, to the "Alba" operation, aimed at restoring Albania's infrastructure after the economic collapse of this country. Greece is still contributing to the reconstruction efforts and considers the Greek minority living in Southern Albania as a bridge between the two countries.

Economic deprivation has led to a large influx of immigrants from the former communist countries. Political refugees from Turkey, Irak and other countries also arrived in large numbers. Greek NGOs have provided critical support to asylum seekers and refugees, 7.000 of whom are living in Greece. The Greek government has also taken steps aimed at the legalisation of economic immigrants. Half a million illegal immigrants (mainly Albanians) living in Greece have availed themselves of the opportunity to be legalised since 1996. Once legalised they are subject to Greek labour and social security law. In addition, they are eligible for Greek citizenship after eight years of residence in Greece. Moreover, even illegal immigrants may benefit from the National Health System - and their children may enrol in the State Education System.

Greece has actively promoted assistance to the Balkan and Black Sea countries. Greek technical assistance to these countries has been provided under the "Phare", "Tempus" and "Tacis" programmes. Greece availed itself of the Interreg programme in order to finance projects of interest to neighbouring Balkan countries. Both Greek public and private sector enterprises have invested heavily in the area. Greece is now the largest foreign investor in the Former Yugoslav Republic of Macedonia and one of the main investors in Bulgaria and Romania. Greek enterprises have been assisted by Greek banks, most of which are present in the Balkan capitals and provide significant amounts of venture capital. Greek contractors are already participating in large infrastructure projects in the Balkan and Black Sea areas. Finally, Thessaloniki hosts among other international institutions, the Black Sea Development Bank and the Agency for Balkan Reconstruction.

Greece and the Yugoslav tinderbox

The end of communist rule has revived ethnic feelings in the Balkans and has led to the break-up of Yugoslavia. This process took place in a disorderly manner. Minorities did not receive international guarantees, and ethnic cleansing was practised or tolerated by most successor States. Moreover, national sensitivities of neighbouring countries were not taken care of. Greece objected to the Former Yugoslav Republic of Macedonia (FYROM) taking on the name Macedonia. At best it could lead to confusion with the Northern Greek Province of Macedonia or, even worse, imply expansionist designs by the newly born State. In October 1995, the two countries signed an interim agreement providing, among other things, for UN mediation on the name issue. The two countries have developed significant bilateral ties, as well as common security perceptions, thereby creating favourable conditions for a compromise on the name issue.

Greece has supported international initiatives aimed at the peaceful settlement of disputes in former Yugoslavia and has provided substantial humanitarian aid on a non-discriminatory basis. Greece understands Albanian and Serb sensitivities in the Kosovo conflict. Greece supports a peaceful settlement of the issue, ensuring the safe return of all refugees and the demilitarisation of Kosovo under effective international supervision. Greece favours a substantial degree of self-government for the territory, without, however, impinging on the territorial integrity of Yugoslavia -

except if the two sides agree to some kind of territorial division. Greece provided substantial humanitarian assistance to the conflicting sides during the Kosovo war and, more recently, deployed a military contingent of approximately 2.000 peacekeepers.

In conclusion, Greece has a unique knowledge and understanding of the intricacies of South-eastern Europe, is willing to contribute to the political and economic development of its neighbourhood and to assume the related risks. These factors makes it a key player in the area, the country through which most public aid and private investment is channelled and/or co-ordinated.

Greece and Turkey: From a strained to a normal relationship
The Aegean disputes

Although both Greece and Turkey joined NATO in 1952, they have different perceptions of their security interests. In Greece, there have been varied assessments of the security threat posed by Turkey. However, the general perception has been that since 1974 Turkey wanted to change the Aegean status quo in a manner which would annex Greece's Eastern Aegean islands into a Turkish zone of functional responsibility (continental shelf, Flight Information Region, sea and rescue responsibilities, NATO command responsibilities etc.). These goals, coupled with Turkish de-

Greek Prime Minister Costas Karamanlis with R.T. Erdogan, the Turkish Prime Minister

mands for the demilitarisation of the islands facing Turkey - which have been militarised after the Turkish invasion of Cyprus - were deemed by Greece as evidence of a policy aimed at undermining Greek sovereignty over the aforementioned islands.

Moreover, Turkey does not recognise the 10-mile limit of Greek air space and the Turkish position is that the expansion of the Greek territorial sea to 12 miles (in accordance with the UN Law of the Sea Convention) would constitute a casus belli. This was perceived in Greece as evidence of Turkish aggressiveness. It may also be recalled that in 1976 and 1987 Greek-Turkish disputes over the continental shelf and, in January 1996, the short-lived Turkish occupation of an uninhabited islet of the Imia group, came close to triggering a war between the two countries.

Furthermore, air warfare over the Aegean (frequent dogfights with sophisticated aircraft) carried serious risks of escalation.

Relations with Turkey have improved dramatically since the summer of 1999. A few weeks after the launching of negotiations aimed at promoting good neighbourliness and functional co-operation, catastrophic earthquakes hit Turkey and Greece. The unprecedented solidarity demonstrated by the peoples of the two countries paved the way for a fundamental reassessment of the relationship in the two capitals. Important bilateral agreements were signed in February 2000 and committees were established to promote co-operation in various fields. Confidence-building measures agreed in the past were finally being implemented and new measures were discussed in the NATO framework.

Moreover, the Greek position on EU-Turkish relations changed dramatically, as explained below.

The Cyprus conflict

A main cause of friction between Greece and Turkey is the Cyprus conflict. In 1974, Turkey invaded and occupied 36% of the territory of the Republic of Cyprus (where the Turkish Cypriots represented only 18% of the population, the remainder being almost exclusively Greek-Cypriots). This led to the displacement of 200.000 Greek Cypriots from the North to the South (subsequently replaced by 100.000 settlers from Turkey). A just settlement of the Cyprus issue, based on a bi-zonal and bi-communal federation, was agreed in the 1977 and 1979 summits between the Greek Cypriot and Turkish Cypriot leaders. More recently, the UN Secretary General Koffee Annan recommended this in the plans he submitted to the two communities in November 2002 and February 2003. These could pave the way for expanded co-operation between Greece and Turkey. The Turkish-Cypriot side, however, has demonstrated unwillingness to reach a final settlement and, instead, allowed the free movement of persons, a move that was followed up by the Cypriot government which took supplementary measures to encourage the employment of Turkish Cypriots by Greek Cypriot companies.

EU involvement in Greek-Turkish disputes

Belonging to the European Community was perceived as a valuable security asset when Greece submitted its application for membership in 1975. Greece has since benefited from its participation in EC / EU policy-making but has had trouble convincing its partners to contribute to the settlement of Greek-Turkish disputes.

The aforementioned involvement actually started with a dispute that is not Greek-Turkish as such, the Cyprus conflict. EU partners displayed solidarity on this issue, insofar as it was related to International Law. They refused to recognise the secession and independence of the self-proclaimed Turkish Republic of Northern Cyprus in 1983. They developed the relationship with the internationally recognised Republic and prepared the ground for its accession to the EU in May 2004, together with the nine other European countries which signed their accession agreements in Athens, on 16 April 2003.

Greek foreign policy was, however, frequently at odds with EU policy on Turkey. Greece's opposition to the Customs Union Agreement and related financial assistance to Turkey was lifted on 6 March 1995. This was only after Greece secured a promise from the Council that accession negotiations with Cyprus would start six months after the end of the Intergovernmental Conference scheduled to prepare the EU for enlargement.

The European partners of Greece, most of whom are members of NATO, have been reluctant to support Greece in cases of direct confrontation between this country and Turkey. Nevertheless, in the dispute over the Imia islets, the Council of Ministers called on Turkey to refer its claim to the International Court of Justice. Thereafter, the Luxemburg summit of the European Council in December 1997 refused to include Turkey among the countries eligible for EU membership on the grounds that this country did not meet the political requirements, including acceptance of the compulsory jurisdiction of the International Court of Justice. Interestingly, Greece made it known to Turkey that, notwithstanding the fact that this country had not accepted the compulsory jurisdiction of the Court, it would itself accept its jurisdiction in any proceedings instituted by Turkey.

Turkish accession to the EU

Greece was long perceived by Turkey as a country conspiring to achieve its permanent exclusion from Europe. Nevertheless, after the rebuff of Turkey by the European Popular Party (Christian Democrats) in 1997, the then Greek Foreign Minister Theodore Pangalos acknowledged publicly that Turkey is part of Europe from a historical viewpoint. A few months later, Prime Minister Constantine Simitis declared in the Greek Parliament that "we support the European perspective of Turkey, on the condition that this country complies with the European "acquis"". In Greece's view, Turkey is entitled to fair treatment, i.e. equivalent to that of the other candidate countries. Respect of international law and human rights by candidate countries remains, nevertheless, a high priority for Greece.

As a result of the fundamental reassessment of Greek-Turkish relations following the earthquakes that hit the two countries in 1999, Greece lifted its objections to EU financial assistance to Turkey. Part of this assistance was redirected to serve the reconstruction efforts in the area affected by the earthquakes. Moreover, at the Helsinki Summit of the EU in December 1999, Greece agreed to the inclusion of Turkey among the candidates for EU membership and, a year later, to the pre-accession partnership of the same country with the EU. Accession negotiations will begin when Turkey fulfils the criteria for EU membership laid down at the Copenhagen Summit in June 1993. With respect to Turkey, some criteria were further specified at the Helsinki Summit and include a provision calling upon Turkey to submit its claims against neighbours to the International Court of Justice. At the Copenhagen Summit in December 2003 the EU undertook the commitment to open accession negotiations with Turkey, if the European Commission made a positive assessment in its annual report scheduled for submission in October 2004.

Current Greek Foreign Minister George Papandreou has repeatedly described his vision of a "European Turkey", closely co-operating with Greece. Turkish accession to the EU, a not too distant prospect if Turkey decides to make the necessary adjustments, will entail among other things a common citizenship and a common currency between the two neighbours. This could open a new era of partnerships in business, civil society etc., over and above the substantial trade now taking place between the two countries as a result of the Customs Union.

Conclusion

In Greece's view, security and stability in the Mediterranean, Balkan and Black Sea areas are interrelated. The self-restraint of governments in the pursuit of national interests, although an important factor, cannot by itself achieve the said goals. Long-term security and stability depend on the economic development of the aforementioned areas, as well as cultural interchange between the peoples involved. Moreover, the anchoring of the European periphery to the Euro-Atlantic institutions remains a top priority of Greek foreign policy.

Costas Karamanlis, the Greek Prime Minister with the Greek Minister of foreign affairs Petros Molyviatis

GREECE IN THE EUROPEAN UNION
A POLITICAL / INSTITUTIONAL BALANCE SHEET

By Michael J. Tsinisizelis

Introduction

In attempting to present a balance sheet on the relations between a member state and the EEC, we usually have to come to terms with an immense amount of relevant information. Books, monographs and research theses have been and are being produced at an impressive rate throughout and outside the European Union. This holds equally true for the relations between Greece and the EEC.

Here we are concerned with the political / institutional affects of membership and in European policy terms with aspects of the domestic foundations of the Greek policies vis-a-vis Europe. In fact, we are concerned with an outline of the main effects of EU membership upon the operation of Greek political institutions.

1. An historical outline

Greece signed the first Association Agreement with the EEC in 1961 (applied for in 1958, in force since 1962). The "Athens Agreement" aimed at the accession of Greece into the EEC within 22 years. The Agreement was partly frozen for seven years (1967-1974), at the initiative of the Commission of the EEC. This was a reaction to the military regime that assumed power in Athens in 1967 (April 21), for the third time in this

Konstantinos Karamanlis, centre, poses in Athens with representatives of the six EEC member-states and his Cabinet ministers following the signing of the seminal EEC-Greece Association Agreement, 09-07-1961

century, and came into force again upon the restoration of a liberal parliamentary regime in 1974. Almost immediately after the collapse of the military regime (as a result of the Cyprus imbroglio and of a deepening economic crisis that was beginning to show its teeth) the Government then in power under K. Karamanlis, crowning its novel political project of liberal bourgeois modernisation (Mavrogordatos 1984), applied for full membership to the EEC, early in 1975. Greece joined the EEC, as its tenth member, in 1981.

The collapse of the military regime in 1974, the "Metapolitefsis", has had important consequences for the political system of the country. It is probably fair to suggest that this was not far short of a political revolution on a number of counts. First, the dire experiences from the seven years of military rule led to the legalisation in the collective consciousness of the population of the virtues of Representative Parliamentary Government, a fact that could not be easily assumed during the turbulent pre-coup years. Second, the Greek Communist Party became legal after almost 30 years (since 1947) and was allowed to contest the first democratically held elections after the collapse of the military regime, in 1974. Indeed the KKE and the KKE (interior), the two communist parties (as a result of a 1968 split of a united KKE) managed to capture almost 9% of the electorate. Third, the anticommunist ideology, a

pillar of the pre-coup state was driven *ad absurdum*. Fourth, to complete the "liquidation of the past image" policy pursued by the conservative Government of the day, the monarchy was brought to an end through the December 1974 free and fair referendum. Fifth, the composition and structure of the political personnel changed radically. This change was more obvious with regard to the middle and lower party political personnel than at the level of the leadership of the parties.

The "Right" vs. "Left" cleavage that frustrated the country for almost 30 years, spilled over in 1974 to the level of international relations due to the British and American intervention (Truman Doctrine) in the 1946-1949 civil war against the communist led ELAS (National Liberation Army). The ensuing anti-western attitude of the populace was revitalised in 1974 with the British and NATO unwillingness to prevent or reverse the Turkish invasion of Cyprus. Fuel was added to this fire by their alleged action to prevent the Greek army from landing on the island and the alleged role and support of the USA with regard to the military regime. For the latter, the US officially apologised through its Ambassador Burns and President Clinton himself on a visit to Athens in early 2000). It was also against this background of xenophobia, that owes its existence to the history of the modern Greek state since 1831, an element of the political culture that draws much of the responsibility, that the political parties representing the broad "Left" flourished in the period from 1974 onwards. A population accustomed to real or perceived threats to its national integrity throughout the years of its existence as an independent state under International Law, would be easily drawn by arguments of the kind. Andreas Papandreou's PASOK skilfully managed to utilise this element as well. Seven years after its appearance, this party in the 1981 elections received 48% of the vote and a handsome majority in Parliament (actually, in three consecutive elections in 1974, 1977 and in 1981 PASOK almost doubled its share of the vote each time!). The irony of history had brought to power a political party that was elected on a ticket to withdraw from the EEC, at the time that Greece was becoming a full member! Ironically enough, the government of the day which managed the accession of the country in the EEC, a fact which by now is regarded as the most significant post World War II improvement in the status of the country in the international system, lost the elections held immediately after accession. Contemporary European history abounds with such ironies, starting from the 1946 British General elections.

The major parties of the broad Left were against the country accession to the EEC (PASOK-KKE, mainly since the smaller KKE interior was more concerned with the terms of the accession to the EEC). This exemplified by the fact that both parties walked out of Parliament during the discussion on the ratification of the Treaty of Accession to the EEC in 1979. As a result the majority party in Parliament ratified the Treaty. To be fair to the anti EEC forces, however, at the time the EEC represented no more than a mere customs union with a few common policies, hit by the consecutive energy crises of the 70's and betrothed with fierce debates internally over budgetary contributions. The European Monetary System (EMS) in 1979 was the most important institutional development of the period but this, to reinforce the point, was arranged outside the Treaty framework at the time. To be fair, there was no way for PASOK or any of the parties of the "Left" to have foreseen the dramatic systemic changes of the 1989 European *annus mirabilis* or those that began in the EEC a few years earlier with the introduction of the Single European Act (SEA) and the consecutive Treaty changes in the 90's. Furthermore, PASOK came to power with a clear social agenda, which was long overdue in Greece but not easily reconciled with the conditions of the European System of Co-operation. This was in spite of the existence of all sorts of non-tariff barriers to trade not only between Greece and the rest of the EEC but also intra-EEC, and which nevertheless, became a top priority for the newly elected government. As a result, divergence not convergence with the rest of the EEC member states, was the inevitable result. For the best part of its EEC/EU membership Greece has been the poorest Member State in terms of GNP per capita. Divergence, especially during the 80s, also occurred at the level of foreign policy, at the level of European Political Co-operation (EPC) level. This was when A. Papandreou tried to balance between the two blocks of the cold war period, in spite of the fact that Greece has been a member of NATO since the mid fifties!

In general the debate in Greece on the European System of Co-operation either before or after the accession of the country into the EEC has been conducted within a small circle of bureaucratic and party political elites without wider participation. This is however slowly changing. Fatouros (1992) pointed out that the issue of the entry of the country into the EEC was entangled in the old cleavage be-

tween "westernisers" and "traditionalists". This cleavage draws its existence in the years before the independence of the Modern Greek State in 1831. This cleavage refers to the age-old question as to whether Greece belongs to the "East" or to the "West". The "Westernisers" (modernisers) were historically identified, *grosso modo*, with the rational inquiry and the political liberalism of the Continent, a sometimes cosmopolitan view of the world. The "Easterners" (traditionalists) on the other hand, were represented chiefly by the Orthodox Church, advocating the defence of the status quo e.g. religion, tradition and social hierarchy. A clear indication that this cleavage is still active, reminiscent and echoing perhaps of the early, but still active, religious cleavages in Europe, was provided by the recent controversy over the recording of religion on the Identity Cards. This issue between the state and the church tor-

The accession ceremony at the Zappeion Hall in Athens-Greece formally accedes to the EC, 28-05-1979

mented the country for almost fourteen months after the 2000 elections. On these grounds the challenge facing the country upon entry into the EEC in 1981 was, as Valinakis (1994) pointed out, how to bridge the gap between its political, economic and cultural identity as a western European nation, with its East European location and traditions. This rather schizophrenic situation is probably a good explanatory variable of many of the problems that the country faced in the EEC/EU.

Overall, the Greek case in the EEC, therefore, was not or could not have been a success story. This, *inter alia*, may be due to the fact that the country joined the Community on political rather than economic grounds. Certainly, it appears that the charismatic authority and consummate statesmanship of the Prime Minister at the time has been instrumental in the success of the Greek application, as much as it was a result of the influence of the Franco (D'Estaing) - German (Schmidt) entente in the EEC.

In Greek eyes, the new (as of 1974) situation in the neighbourhood of the country necessitated additional structures of support in its international relations. In internal political terms, the EEC was seen as: (a) the additional support required for the protection of the new and fragile liberal parliamentary regime; and (b) the political and economic context that would facilitate the economic development of the country. The strategy of the Government of the

day was based on a theory of induced modernisation e.g. that the country as a whole would have to adjust to this new and much more competitive environment or perish. In short, "Right" vs. "Left", "East" vs. "West" (and possibly "Third World" vs. "East" and "West"), these cleavages (and their by-products) initially marked the development of Greco-EEC relations.

The first PASOK EEC years (1981-1989) went through a number of phases. Initially, during its opposition years, the leadership of the party was caught in a North-South analysis, which almost naturally resulted in the rejection of the EEC as a solution for the economic development of the country. The impassioned anti-EEC stance of the Party during its opposition years was to a large extent responsible for many of the problems, which the country faced inside the EEC. For, if anything this attitude affected the grassroots and more importantly the cadre of the party, that is to say the very people that were responsible for the creation and implementation of Government policies both in Greece as well as in the EEC institutions. The "memorandum to the EEC" of March 1982 marked the second phase of the PASOK attitude, and the change was completed with the support offered for the Single European Act (SEA.). In essence, it took more than half of PASOK's first period in Government for the party to decide whether the country should stay in the EEC and on what terms. In the early eighties the European Commission presented the chance to PASOK in the form of the Integrated Mediterranean Programmes (IMPs) under consideration. Tsoukalis (1988) has concluded that the policies of PASOK in the EEC were directed towards two ends: (a) the maximisation of currency flows from the various Community funds, and (b) the widening of the Greek degree of freedom in economic policy making.

The 1989 *annus mirabilis* in Europe and internal developments in Greece led to a significant change in PASOK's attitude vis-a-vis the EEC. The collapse of the former Soviet block and the *"Europa offenheit"* policies of the former Warsaw Pact countries seeking rapprochement with all western dominated international institutions -from NATO to the OECD- made the EEC a desirable reality. The anti-imperialist / anti-western attitude in PASOK crumbled, although it does resurface in times of crises such as the recent Yugoslav and Gulf crises, in a large chunk of the party and the society, a fact that the leadership of the party and the Government must take into account. This may be an explanatory factor in the reasons for the Greek feelings of insecurity during the recent Balkan bewilderment and its still pending issues. This dormant legacy of the past is still part of the "zero point energy" political culture of the country.

The 1989-1990 political crises, with the formation of three consecutive ecu-

menical governments, ended with PASOK loosing the 1990 elections after a decade in power and returning to opposition until the premature downfall of the neo-liberal orientated Government of the day. At the 1994 elections PASOK returned to power. In 1996, A. Papandreou the founder of PASOK and Prime Minister of the country died and K. Simitis was elected as party leader and consequently as the new P.M. The election of Simitis to the leadership of the party signified a radical change to the profile of PASOK. The *"Allagi"* (Change) slogan used during the Papandreou years acquired a strong modernising dimension, which was exemplified by a number of institutional changes regarding Ed-

Ex-Prime Minister Costas Simitis receives the first euro banknotes circulated in Greece during a New Year's Eve reception celebrating the country's introduction in 12 "euro zone" members, 01-01-2002

ucation (Metarithmisi) and the Local Authorities (Kapodistrias Programme) as well as changes at the level of economic policy making. The Simitis Government helped to change the attitude of the country vis-a-vis Europe. The primary objective of the Government evolved around the entry of the country in the Economic and Monetary Union and the satisfaction of the Maastricht criteria and the change of the "black sheep" image of the country in the EU.

2. The role of the parliament

The literature on the democratic deficit in the EU has been blown out of proportion in recent years. This is a structural problem of the EEC. It is due to the logic of the neo-functionalist Community Method and its legal guarantees that have helped to shape the integration process by affording roles, powers and capabilities to the European Institutions and especially the European Commission, within the policy making process. This ongoing debate however, has helped to bring to light issues central to parliamentary democracies such as those related to the legitimisation of the policy processes, or those related to the very physiognomy of the European System of Co-operation and its future directions. Nowadays it seems to be a rather topical issue, in view of the 2004 IGC (Intra-governmental Conference), which will be convened in order to try and settle issues of a constitutional nature.

Greece, for that matter, has been among the staunchest supporters of improving the democratic physiognomy of the EU during the 90s a fact that the Government did not fail to point out during the recent IGCs of 1996-7 and 2000.

In Greece, liberal parliamentary institutions were introduced comparatively early in the Greek political system but these were never fully "embraced by the Greek soul" (Kioukias 1993); as is the case with western liberal ideas in general. Diamandouros (1983) pointed out that this is due to a number of factors. These include the impact of the patriarchal Ottoman rule, the dire experiences inflicted by the behaviour of western powers towards Greece, the weaknesses of the Greek bourgeoisie. Other factors include the powers of traditionalist elites, the dominance of nationalist and irredentist ideologies as well as the absence of long and stable links with European Enlightenment. These inadequacies, although possibly not to the same extent, are still with us today, perhaps in a more clandestine form, shaping the quality of the Greco-EEC relations

It is probably fair to suggest that the overall influence of the Parliament in foreign policy formulation is marginal. This is true in the case of the European Policy of Greece, which is regarded, technically at least, as part of the international relations of the country in spite of the occasional declarations to the contrary by various influential individuals inside or outside the main political parties. This attitude is gradually changing, given the evolution of the EU system, but it is fairly early to come to conclusions on the implications or the extent of such a change. The most important function that the 1975 and the 2000 constitutions recognise in the field of foreign policy for the Parliament is the ratification of international treaties, provided for by new art. 36, para. 2. Papadimitriou concluded that during the decade 1975-1985 (1974-1977,1977-1981,1981-1985) the Parliament exercised its ratification powers without a substantial debate, either on the whole or on parts of these agreements, a remarkably consistent practice throughout the decade under examination. Additionally, a large number of international agreements were excluded from the ratification procedures of the Parliament in spite of specific constitutional provisions to the contrary. Both the 1975 and the 2000 constitutions do not recognise any specific role for the Parliament in the formulation of the foreign policy of the country, including its European policy.

The position of the country in the European System of Co-operation is usually discussed in Parliament on the occasion of more general debates on "the state of the country" between party political leaders, or on the eve of major European Councils. This is a practice that has largely been used during more recent years, due to the rapid developments in the EEC since the mid 80s. In any case, debates of this sort are always conducted within the context of the foreign policy of the country and the information provided during these meetings is at best trivial. The only exceptions to this rule so far were the debates on the occasion of the ratification of the Treaties of Accession of Spain and Portugal, and of the Single European Act.

The role of the Greek Parliament in the case of the incorporation of EEC legislation is minimal. Indeed Law 945/1979, by which the Accession Treaty was ratified, stipulates that the final responsibility for the incorporation of the EEC legislation in the Greek Legal order rests with the Executive of the country. This is on the basis of the general authorisation of art. 43, Para 4 of the 1975 constitution, e.g. through Presidential Decrees. Earlier, in the period between 1975-1979, during this second phase of the Association years, the Parliament was involved four times in legislation of relevance to the EEC. For example, once Greece was part of the Community and in the space of nine years (1983-1993) only 31(!) were laws ratified by Parliament. This number also includes all the major pieces of EEC legislation such as the Accession Treaty, the SEA, and the Treaty on European Union.

Parliamentary committees for the scrutiny of Community Legislation (e.g.

the House of Lords Select Committee on European Integration) or for the closest possible involvement in EEC policy making of the Parliamentary institutions *(Folketing)* have been well known for quite some time in the EEC and their cases are well documented. The Greek Parliamentary committee on European Integration is a mixed committee consisting of 24 MPs (12) and MEPs (12) and one of the vice chairmen of the House as the chairman of the committee (Total 25). It was set up by a decision of the Chair of the House on the 13th of June 1990. Both MPs and MEPs are voting members and are chosen on the basis of the electoral strength of their parties in both the National and the European Parliaments, although the electoral system is not the same in both instances. The tasks of this committee are defined in the same decision. Thus, the committee deliberates on: (a) institutional issues of the EEC (b) co-operation between the national and the European Parliaments (c) the EEC Legislation due for incorporation into the national legal order (d) the decisions of the ad hoc or permanent parliamentary committees of relevance to the EEC. It was for the relative elevation of the European Parliament after the Single European Act and the introduction of the co-operation procedure between the EP and the Council that the necessary impetus for the creation of this committee was established.

In more general terms, political parties are central to the operation of western parliamentary democracies. As Gaffney (1996) or Mair (2001) put it, they are the organised expression of cleavages within societies. The relevant literature suggests that, on the whole, the significance of political parties tends to be diminishing, although account must be taken of the changing circumstances in which they operate. This seems to be truer nowadays with the current state of affairs in the EU and the need to operate in an environment of multilevel governance. Greek political parties are present at the European level, participating actively in the European political parties and other forums. They have not however, refocused their attention from the national level where their primary interest lies, as is the case in the EU countries in general. This seems to be more the case for the opposition parties, in spite of the relative increase in the powers of the EP in recent years. The European System of Co-operation is still dominated by the preferences of the executives and Governments run these.

3. State and public administration

Anastopoulos (1993), Makridimitris-Passas (1992) and Spanou (2001) discussed the problems that the Greek Public Administration faces within the EEC. Hellinocentrism, a defensive attitude, a narrow financial approach as well as inflexibility are some of its major shortcomings. As a result, the credibility of the Administration in the EEC is seriously impeded. Passas (1993) points out that in organisational terms, the main problem seems to lie in the poor co-ordination between the vertically organised units, the understaffing of those units and the wide mobility of personnel mainly through party political activity.

As a result of EEC membership, the style of policymaking has become more open Experts from other Departments/ Ministries as well as independent experts are brought in. Ioakimides (2001) talks about the "de-externalisation of foreign policy ...in the sense that many "outsiders" seek to influence foreign policy outcomes".

Internally, the responsibility for European issues was given to the Ministry of the National Economy, largely to the CEA -The Council of Economic Advisers. This is a unit of strategic importance within the Ministry of the National Economy. Under the Minister of the National Economy Arsenis (as under Minister Manos, the late Minister Genimatas and the current Minister Papantoniou) both of these had almost absolute authority on issues of economic policy broadly conceived, following a politics/ economics dichotomy. Gradually however, under the influence of a certain "economism" of the Single European Act and of the Treaty on European Union, but also due to the poor comparative economic performance of the country, the Ministry of National Economy has acquired the greater part of the

responsibility for European Affairs. This process of power reallocation between the various Ministries has become all the more obvious. This took place during the term of the previous Government (1996-2000) given the very difficult yet unprecedented and successful effort to join the third stage of the EMU and satisfy the Maastricht criteria - a task considered at the time as a mission impossible. Reduction of Public debt, reduction of the Public deficit, lowering of the interest rates and monetary and fiscal stability - macroeconomic stabilisation - on the basis of the 1993 and 1994 convergence programmes - all these pushed the Ministry of National Economy to the centre of the game. Of course this has been a source of tension between the various Ministries, which is compounded by the fact that to all intents and purposes the EEC Council of Ministers is a "legal fiction". More difficult problems arise out of the allocation of funds from the Structural Funds to the various Ministries. This is a sine qua non for the convergence and rationalisation of the Greek economy. It has interesting implications for the decentralisation of the political system as a whole and the various financial instruments arising out of the 1988 restructuring of the Funds and the various reforms such as those included in the Commission's Agenda 2000. Conflicts between the various Ministries are resolved at a higher level, at the cabinet level *(KISIM)* or even

personally by the Prime Minister. It must be said, however, that in general the effectiveness of such bodies of collective responsibility as the cabinet *(KISIM)*, is at best dubious.

Considerable efforts have been made in recent years to change the prevailing culture in the bureaucracy and to check those of its aspects not considered friendly to the citizen. The office of the Ombudsman was created in 1995 and a number of Independent Authorities were set up based upon the EU or European models dealing *inter alia* with the protection of civil rights. These helped to re-emphasise the obvious point that the citizen is at the centre of any political system and also helped the corroboration of political democracy in Greece. Community funds are also used to modernise the public bureaucracy through the application of a vast number of programmes introducing and extending the application of information technologies - e administration- or to improve the skills of civil servants such as the "Politeia" programme. Transparency is slowly but steadily being introduced within the system but on the whole as Ioakimides (2001) argued, these changes (and others as well) helped to rebalance state - society relations in favour of the latter. It should be mentioned, however, that in spite of the various EU initiatives on issues traditionally outside the political agenda, mobilisation and quantifiable public awareness have been rather low. Environmental movements, feminist movements etc. or any of those included in Ingelhart's typologies, do not seem capable of mobilising citizens at any impressive rate. In addition, political parties were quick to include such post - materialist issues in their manifestos, precluding in way, the development of such movements. Civil society is still in a state of development. Migration on the other hand is a totally new issue to be dealt with in the political system. It is a direct result of the post- 1989 developments and also touches upon the foreign policy of the country. Greece has traditionally been a labour exporting country, where throughout the 20th century, migration flows were recorded towards the more developed economies of the countries of western Europe, the USA and Australia, while repatriation flows occurred from the prosperous Greek communities in Africa and the Asia minor. Data show that the vast number of migrant workers originates from neighbouring Balkan countries although there also seem to be migration flows similar to the rest of the EU. The response, however, of the Greek state has at best been dubious, avoiding on the whole the confrontation of such issues of paramount importance as the ways to integrate migrant populations into Greek society or the rights of migrants. As a result, xenophobic reactions capturing the attention of the media are not a rare phenomenon.

The Modern Greek State matured in a hostile neighbourhood whose continuous turbulence triggered a series of political crises internally. Thus the centralisation of the political system was the inevitable result, with the Greek state in the role of modern Leviathan or a Colossus but with "feet of clay" as Mouzelis (1990) colourfully suggests. Traditional political parties with extensive networks of clientelistic relations, offering, *inter alia*, public sector enrolment, became the chief stabilisation mechanism in support of the system

On the EEC/EU issues, the Panhellenic Confederation of the Unions of Agricultural Co-operatives (PASEGES) and the Government of the country, through a process of consultation, manage to adopt a unanimous stance on the Community issues in most cases. This may also be explained with reference to the importance of the agricultural economy of the country. Indeed, agriculture contributes 17.4% of the gross value added in Greece and accounts for 31.3% of the value of total exports. Approximately 20% approximately of the total labour force is still employed in the agricultural sector but the number is steadily declining. The existence of the CAP has been the chief parameter of successive Governments in their decision to associate, join and finally stay in the EEC, in spite of the comparatively poor support for Mediterranean production under the CAP regulations. The defence of the national interest, therefore, requires unanimity at the EEC level. On the other hand GSEE is one of the two top unions (the other one is ADEDY representing public sector employees *stricto sensu*) and is member of the ETUC, the workers confederations umbrella organisation at the EEC level.

GSEE appears at the top of an organisational pyramid in which the unions of the private as well as the wider public sector (banks, common utilities organisations etc.) are represented. Today the picture is one of extreme apportionment as there are over 5000 first level unions and 84 federations. A measure of the lack of political autonomy of the organisation may be provided by the fact that in every instance until 1989 the leadership of the *GSEE* was of the same party political affiliation as the Government of the country. Nevertheless, at the national level, the organisation has developed a network of linkages with the Ministry of Employment, especially after the Amsterdam Treaty and the Lisbon European Council. Currently however, the country lacks a clear forum for the dialogue between the social partners. Through party political connections the *GSEE* remained calm for the time required for the country to join the Euro zone. Tension has grown once again due to the failed attempt by the Government to reform the social security system, an item which triggered a serious party and Governmental crisis and which resulted in the reformulation of the Government in October 2001.

The *SEV* (Federation of Greek Industries) is an active participant in UNICE and has developed close links with the EU institutions through its Bureau in Brussels. The SEV consists mainly of large industries (two out of three of the more profitable industries of the country) including those representing multinational capital. In contrast with the other two organisations referred to above, the *SEV* exhibits a higher degree of political autonomy. This is likely better explained with reference to the importance of its political resources, e.g. its significance in economic terms. More recently the SEV, with the occasional hitches, acted as a powerful ally in Government efforts to rationalise the public sector and the economy and to attain the Maastricht criteria, although tension between the two sides grew as a result of Government hesitation to further deregulate the economy.

Throughout the term of the previous and the present Government under Simitis, the efforts to adapt the society to the new European environment took a more concrete form. There were also a number of efforts internally to streamline the various sectors of the economy and the society in order to adapt more successfully to the new and more difficult environment. Internally, the initiative depended on the premise that at the present stage of development of the European System of Co-operation competition is not only about firms but extends to the competition of systems, modes of organisation, and finally to roles and identities. Education and the system of local authorities were chosen as the first sectors to adapt. Both of these initiatives were not without problems and revealed the limits of the adaptive capacity of the sectors concerned and perhaps of the society as a whole. Wider European initiatives such as the Sorbonne, the Bologna and recently the Prague Declarations coincided with internal reforms and triggered a wider debate internally. The "Ekpedeftiki Metarrithmisi" of 1997-2000 was a vigorous effort, at considerable political cost, to modernise the educational system at all levels, focussing on the secondary level (Lyceum). Party political considerations, traditional attitudes, financial considerations and opposition from interest groups (the Federation of High School Teachers *[OLME]* - the Federation of Greek Primary School Teachers *[DOE]*) in defence of the status quo stood well in the way. In spite of the above-mentioned difficulties, the programme was carried through.

On the other hand the name "Kapodistrias", the founder of the Modern Greek state, was given to the programme to rationalise the system of local authorities. The picture of the system before the Kapodistrias plan was one of extreme fragmentation, in that there existed 5999 *Koinotites* - with less than 10,000 inhabitants *(communes)*- and 304 *Demoi* - with more than 10,000 in-

habitants. The plan aimed at a reduction of the overall numbers to rationalise the system and streamline expenditure, given that these bodies depend heavily on state funding for their survival. Although the programme was carried through, it still in need of further action for its stabilisation. In essence, the plan helped to accommodate the EEC inspired decentralisation process of the political system which began as early as 1984 when the country was divided into 13 regions for the purposes of the EEC's regional policy. Although this has been for some time a mere administrative division, a nominal devolution, it was in 1994 that the first sub-government elections were held (prefecture councils) which added an interesting new dimension to the political system as a whole (Tsinisizelis 1996, Ioakimides 2001).

4. Public Opinion and European Integration

Public opinion data cover the period from 1974 to 2000. In some cases, which are mentioned in the table, the data used relate to shorter periods, as from 1981 (Greek entry in the EEC).

Generally speaking Greek public opinion is responding within the trend recorded for the rest of the EU members, although it seems to be more responsive to developments not immediately associated with the EU per se which are related to the "zero point energy" culture referred to above. In this regard I am inclined to treat these data with caution,

How Europeans see themselves

Looking through the mirror with public opinion surveys

favour to some extent (these two categories together amounted to approximately 70%) while approximately only 15% were found to be against to some extent or very much against the unification attempts.

In every instance, during the 20 year period, more respondents considered the EEC a "good thing" than those that who considered it a "bad thing" by a factor of 2.5 up to 1983 and by a factor of 5-10 from then onwards. The factor reached a peak of approximately 13% with 75% positive and 6% negative in 1990. Data concerning the feeling of the respondents whether their country had benefited from the EEC

especially those related to the CFSP or the CFSDP. That is to say High politics, even in cases not related with the EU affect the attitude towards the EU itself.

A large majority was recorded in favour of the unification attempts in Western Europe in every instance during the period 1983-2000. In response to the question of whether they were in favour of the efforts to unify Western Europe, 40% on average replied that they were strongly in favour. 30% were in

show that since 1989 onwards the percentages in favour of European Unification match with those that feel that their country has benefited from the EEC. In every other instance up to 1989 (1980 - 1993) those respondents who thought that their country had benefited from the EEC are more by a factor of 2 than those who thought the opposite. If we observe the trend in both questions, we may conclude that the anti - EEC attitude is declining sharply from 1990 onwards. It was becoming apparent that the EU is the only block of stability in Europe as well as what the real situation in the former Soviet block countries was.

A similar point can be made with respect to the feelings of the respondents had the EEC been scrapped. It is only since 1988 that those who replied that they would lave been indifferent had the EEC been scrapped were less than those who replied that they would have been sorry! Still 10% of the respondents (average 1981 - 1998) declared that they would have been relieved had the EEC been scrapped. This percentage declines however from 1986 onwards to a mere 4% in 1990 from the 50% where it stood during the second six months of 1982 and it becomes irrelevant from then onwards.

The Macedonia question at its peak in the early 90s and the war in Yugoslavia at the end of that decade are the only instances during which support for the European integration actually declines. By the same token, it increases during instances in which the EU is seen as protective of the national interests of the country as during the immediate aftermath of the Helsinki European Council with reference to Greco-Turkish relations. On the whole, data available Euro barometer show that there broad support for European Integration, amongst the highest in the EU, which slightly declines in times of international crises seen as affecting vital national interests.

Concluding Remarks

Greece has been a member of the EEC / EU almost twenty years. The Pendulum theory (Kazakos 1993) that was used to describe the Greco - EEC relations has some explanatory value. Nowadays, the pendulum seems to have been stabilised, at long last. The three major parties in Parliament, e.g. New Democracy, PASOK and the smaller Alliance of the Left (Synaspismos) and other parties outside Parliament are unanimous that the country must adapt positively to the new European environment and this attitude is unequivocally supported by a huge majority of the population. With the possible exception of the small Greek Communist Party, no other party rejects European Integration.

The European policy of Greece is primarily the responsibility of the Government of the country. Internally the Government enjoys a near monopoly position since there are no any other power centres capable of challenging its authority. At the societal level the pattern seems the same: party political intervention ensures that no other form of political representation is capable of challenging that authority. At the European level the relations between the Government and organised interests still project "a billiard ball image" as different actors promote the same positions in different forums. To a certain extent this is a structural problem in the sense that the differing levels of economic development between Greece and the other EEC member states facilitate a compromise internally on the need for more resources from the various Community funds. This has been the main concern of the Greek European policy since 1981. Internally, although improvements are required on a number of issues, the political system has become more open, more transparent and less centralised throughout its EU membership.

European and International realities have changed considerably since the entry of the country into the EEC/EU. In the space of just fifteen years, the original EEC treaties have been extensively modified, creating a system of multi-level governance in search of its physiognomy.

Quite recently, the Prime Minister of the country called for the creation of a European federation, thus joining in the debate on the future of Europe in view of the 2004 IGC. This denotes the tremendous changes that the country has undergone from a state of denial to become one of the more pro-integrationist member states. Nowadays the Government has set the target of attaining real convergence by the year 2010. It is an awesome task requiring multilevel and daring changes in the ideology, the customs and the norms of the system as a whole.

THE FOURTH GREEK PRESIDENCY OF THE EUROPEAN UNION

By Michael J. Tsinisizelis

In January 2003, Greece took on once again the Presidency of the European Union for the standard six-month term, until the end of June 2003. This is the fourth time since 1981, when Greece became a full member that holds the Presidency of the EU. This took place at a very important moment in the history of the EU. A number of important EU initiatives were planned to be completed during the Hellenic Presidency and are the priorities of the Presidency's action program. In the following pages an attempt is made to briefly present the priorities of the Hellenic Presidency as these are presented in a number of official documents.

The first priority action was the completion of the enlargement process with ten new members from Central and Eastern Europe, Malta and Cyprus so as to finally bring to an end the "false divi-

A 4,500-year-old mural from the island of Santorini inspired the emblem to mark Greece's EU Presidency. A swallow, the harbinger of spring, symbolizes a new beginning and hope as Europe embarks on its enlargement process, and also promotes freedom of expression and peace

sions that kept for a long period the European continent apart". This is correctly considered a major challenge for the EU and due attention was granted to the smooth completion of this process by the Hellenic Presidency. The ten countries about to join the EU after the Copenhagen Summit decision of December 2002 are Cyprus, Malta, the Czech Republic, Estonia, Lithuania, Latvia, Hungary, Poland, Slovakia and Slovenia. These countries are scheduled to become full members by May 1, 2004. The EU prepared itself institutionally to accept the new members with the Nice Treaty, which will come in force by the end of 2003. In this context Greece was very concerned about the Cyprus application to become a full member of the EU given the political problems on the island and the relations between Greece, Turkey and the EU. A political solution put forward by K. Anan, the UN Secretary General, for a lasting solution via the creation of a Federal structure on the Swiss and Belgian models, was supported by Greece but not by Turkey. Had it been successful, this proposal would have had the merit of enabling the accession into the EU of the whole of the island. Negotiations between the two sides came to an end during the Hague meeting of

The signing ceremony of the Accession Treaty of 10 new EU member-states, at the Stoa of Attalos, in Athens, during the Informal European Council and European Conference, 16-04-2003

March 2003. The Cyprus Republic will join the EU and will sign the Accession Treaty on the 16th of April in Athens along with the nine other countries but with the proviso that the acquis communautaire will be temporarily applicable only for the Greek part of the divided island.

The future accession of Romania, Bulgaria and Turkey into the EU and their preparation for that goal were also corollary priorities of the Presidency following the enlargement discussions according to the Copenhagen and the Brussels Summit decisions.

Further progress in the "Lisbon process" is the second priority area of the Hellenic Presidency. The extraordinary European Council, in Lisbon of June 1999, put forward an action program until 2010. It is targeted at the gradual adaptation of the European economy within the contemporary Society of Knowledge, with due respect to improving employment opportunities,

necessary economic transformations and adaptations and the attainment of Social cohesion.

The Presidency has pledged to undertake specific initiatives in order to advance the Lisbon process. These are aimed at the following broad issue areas to be discussed at the Autumn Summit in Brussels:

1. Entrepreneurship and Small and Medium enterprises,
2. The European Economy of Knowledge,
3. Trans-European networks along with initiatives included in the Sixth Action Program on the Environment,
4. Increases of the employment opportunities along with improvements in the quality of employment,
5. The strengthening of Social Cohesion,
6. Sustainable development and environmental protection.

Migration and asylum constitute the third priority action area of the Hellenic Presidency. This is a hot issue for the European Union as well as Greece, particularly with regard to illegal migration. The objective of the Presidency was to set the framework for a comprehensive Asylum and Migration policy for the EU. At the Seville European Council it was decided to pursue policies designed to combat migration flows into the EU. This was to be accomplished by assisting migrant exporting countries to create better economic and social conditions at home and thus lower out-migration flows, along on the line of the Barcelona process on Euro-Mediterranean partnership. Although the Hellenic Presidency emphasised this policy area, it was acknowledged that controlled migration flows may be useful for the European economies, especially in view of demographic trends in the EU.

The Future of Europe debate within the Convention preparing the new Constitutional Treaty also constituted a priority of the Hellenic Presidency. According to the existing timetable, the Convention was to present its results and its proposals for a new constitutional treaty at the Thessaloniki European Council in June 2003 and a new Intra-governmental Conference (IGC) would begin shortly afterwards. The Hellenic Presidency noted that the further advancement of the integration process and the clarification of the physiognomy of the EU should be based on the following premises:

1. the enlarged Union should be a democratically organised entity, concerned about the needs of its citizens. It should be characterised by the principles of the Rule of Law common to all member states, the protection of Fundamental Rights and Freedoms. Furthermore, the Charter of Fundamental Rights should be included in the new Treaty, egalitarian relations between the component states of the EU institutionally guaranteed, and the principles of solidarity and subsidiarity applied.

2. The EU should become a more effective a system, able to make decisions. The EU should be in possession of all the necessary means to seek, approach and eventually tackle societal needs and problems, strengthen social cohesion, attain real convergence and reduce economic disparities between its regions. It should also be able to pursue sustainable development along with the necessary transformations and adaptations of the European Economy to increase its competitiveness in global terms.

3. The EU should strengthen its position in global international relations as an agent of peace and security basing its actions firmly upon the principles of international law.

The final priority of the Hellenic Presidency concerned the domain of the international relations of EU Defence cooperation. This is a relatively new item on the EU agenda that, since the Helsinki Summit of December 1999, is crucial to the clarification of its physiognomy especially after enlargement. Improving relations with the Balkan countries especially Romania and Bulgaria, Russia, Ukraine, Byelorussia and Moldavia, the wider Caucasian region and the countries of the Mediterranean sea is a major concern of the Hellenic Presidency.

Fighting international terrorism is a major problem world-wide, especially since the tragic events of September 11th. This was a major priority area of the Hellenic Presidency together with fighting its component parts: the proliferation of nuclear and chemical weapons or weapons of mass destruction in general; drug trafficking etc. In this context the Hellenic Presidency advocated close co-operation with the USA in view of a joint stance on these major security issues.

The further development of the Community Funds Support Programme (CFSP) mechanisms, especially of joint positions and strategies was considered a major and indispensable priority area of the Hellenic Presidency. This was considered crucial for the further advancement of the integration process, so that the EU could at long last acquire a single voice in the international forums and on major international issues. However, the history of the European Political Co-operation and later of the CFSP suggests that this has never been the strongest feature of the EU.

GREECE AND SOUTH-EASTERN EUROPE

By Kostas Ifantis

At the dawn of a new century, Greek foreign policy has also entered a new era. Recent years have seen enormous changes within Greek society and domestic politics. In nearly every respect, the country is more deeply integrated in Europe and closer to the European mainstream than never before. Athens has become a member of the European Monetary Union (EMU), confounding sceptics both inside and outside Greece. The country's relations with its northern neighbours have improved dramatically, and Athens has remained insulated from a serious of devastating regional upheavals. Overall, Greek foreign policy horizons have expanded, and the country has developed a more active, confident approach aware of potential at a regional level. Indeed, Greece itself has the potential to emerge as the leading stabiliser in the region of South-eastern Europe and is, to a certain extent, already playing this role in some fields.

The Strategic Environment

Powerful processes of change and transition in the global environment, on its borders and within the country itself have profoundly affected Greece. Since the mid-1990s, the country has undergone rapid modernisation, a continual process of development. It has become progressively more European, and its foreign policy has become more sophisticated. At the same time, the geopolitical scene has evolved in ways that present new challenges and opportunities for Greece in its relations with other regional actors and beyond. The geopolitical physiognomy of Greece is well defined. The country is located at the crossroads of three continents. It is in close proximity to the Black Sea and the oil-rich regions of the Middle East and the Caucasus. It is the only Southeast European country that is a member of the EU and NATO. The Aegean Archipelago is a vital naval route, connecting the Black Sea with the Mediterranean, and an extremely important transit route for the transport of energy products, especially after the construction and operation of pipelines from Central Asia and the Transcaucasus.

The world at the country's borders has changed radically in the last decade. To the north, old and new states are trying to survive and make the transition to western democratic standards and market economies. To the south, the Middle East is no longer the stage on which Cold War rivalries are played out, but sadly it remains a source of global instability, a melange of religious fundamentalism, authoritarianism, and militarism. Most of these old and new challenges cross traditional boundaries and underscore Greece's

President of Bosnia-Herzegovina,Borislav Paravac, ex Greek Foreign minister George Papandreou, FYROM President Boris Trajkovski, Albanian Alfred Moisiu, Croatian Stjepan Mesic and Serbian Svetozar Marovic pose for a family photo after the meeting of the presidents of the Stabilization Association Process (SAP)countries in the southern FYROM town of Ohrid,01-06-2003

potential to play a trans-regional role, looking outward from Europe to the Mediterranean, Eurasia, and the Middle East. This is the area of strategic consequence for Greece, and it is obviously far wider than what immediate geography indicates.

Changes across this vast region easily affect Greek interests. Stability around the Black Sea will be shaped by the prospects for political and economic development in Russia, Ukraine, and the southern Caucasus. Black Sea developments can in turn influence the evolution of the Balkans and the eastern Mediterranean, where Greek interests are directly engaged. The evolution of the Middle East, including the Arab-Israeli conflict and the strategic equation in the Persian Gulf, can also have a direct impact on Greek security interests. The breakdown of the peace

process can lead to regional spillovers of terrorism and political violence affecting a range of interests, from tourism to maritime industry. In the wake of 11 September 2001 terrorist attack in New York and Washington and the subsequent US-led campaign against mass terrorism, the security stakes have become extremely high.

It is profoundly true that the developments spanning Greece's abroad are indeed trans-regional. Trans-regional and trans-sovereign are the political, economic and security issues and risks for that matter. In this context, the country is exposed to the less positive aspects of an increasingly trans-regional environment. Non-traditional security concerns are characteristic of it. They include heightened environmental risks, refugee flows, contagious diseases, cross-border organised crime and drug trafficking. They also include nuclear smuggling and proliferation of weapons of mass destruction (WMD) - nuclear, chemical, biological, and radiological - and the means for their delivery at long ranges in the Middle East and around the Mediterranean, terrorism, and spillovers of political violence.

The costs of addressing these challenges on a national basis are high and perhaps unsupportable in the Greek case. In other areas, from terrorism to drug trafficking, to international criminal activities, the continued Europeanisation of Greek policy is essential, driven on the one hand by the need to face policy problems multilaterally and, on the other, by requirements emanating from Brussels in an era of increasing European integration.

Leadership in Co-operation

After a short period of adjustment to the new realities, Greece seems to be discovering its role and unfolding its capabilities to respond successfully to the regional challenges. By formulating a comprehensive and co-operative approach to the region's problems, Greece opted for a multilateral foreign policy (together with its EU, WEU, OSCE and NATO partners) designed to contribute to successful transition policies towards democracy and market economy in each of the states north of its borders. After smoothing its troubled relations with Albania and FYROM and

while continuing to cultivate excellent relations with Bulgaria and Romania, Greece has also proceeded to adopt a purely equi-distant stance (vis-a-vis Serbia, Croatia, and Albania) on the questions of Bosnia and Kosovo, respectively. The Greek Balkan policy could be summarised as joining the coalitions of the willing that act collectively in the drive for the stabilisation of the region. In this respect, Greece has joined Western peacekeeping and peace enforcement missions in the conflict zones of the region. This includes its mid-May 1997 participation in PfP military exercises in the territory of FYROM and mid-summer 1998 NATO exercises in Albania, together with troops from the United States, Italy, and Turkey, among others.

The endeavour to define and pursue an appropriate strategy continued, with considerable success, in the Kosovo and FYROM crises as well as in the Yugoslav domestic developments. The latter led to the dramatic "change of guard" in Belgrade, a change that paved the way for the democratisation of that country and its return to international legitimacy. Milosevic's departure has changed the dynamics of Balkan politics and has opened up new opportunities to integrate the region into a broader European economic and political space. In the cases of Kosovo and FYROM, Athens undertook a series of diplomatic and humanitarian initiatives to restore regional peace and stability.

Departure of greek soldiers participating at the international military forces in Albania, Thessaloniki, 16-04-1997

These initiatives demonstrated a combination of political responsibility, determination and level-headedness. They also established Greece as a trustworthy mediator during challenging and critical times.

Fighting Organised Crime for Regional Security and Stability

In the field of domestic security, one of the most serious threats in the Balkan Peninsula is the instability that can be triggered by organised crime. In this sense, being part of the region has not worked to the country's advantage in that it has placed it in danger of spillover. Indeed, crime had increased dramatically. Greece still boasted the lowest levels of crime within Europe and had been quite successful in resolving crimes, reforms and modernisation within Greece's law enforcement infrastructure. These were necessary and prudent and have led to a significant reduction in overall crime, including large seizures of narcotics and weapons. Additionally, co-operation has been intensified with each of Greece's neighbours, as well as the larger international community. Greece is involved in a series of bilateral and trilateral meetings with states such as Albania, FYROM, and Italy, displaying collective political will and commitment to co-operate on issues of law and order. Efforts include education and training, and sharing know-how and technology.

Greece has been working closely with the Albanian government on various types of assistance. It has provided logistical support and equipment ranging from armoured transport vehicles and patrol cars to computers and bullet-proof vests. It has also offered successful forms of training and shared know-how on matters such as investigating economic crimes, detonating explosives safely, and cracking down on police corruption. All these endeavours, in their diversity, proved to be valuable, constructive, and beneficial. As a result, Greece has brought a more comprehensive proposal to the Stability Pact, involving the training of a combined Balkan police force. The proposal has enthusiastically been adopted. Moreover, Greece has been discussing proposals with its regional neighbours and has also been discussing initiatives with its European partners. For Athens, there is nothing more imperative for regional security in the Balkans.

Geo-economics

Greece's upgraded role in Southeastern Europe is based on its strong economic performance. Solid progress over the second half of the 1990s has guaranteed Greece's participation in the European Monetary Union - the 'hard core' of the European integration process - as well as a constructive and continuing presence on the regional scene. Extensive modernisation programmes and intensive institutional reforms have generated a new self-confidence and have been helped Greece. A stable and dynamic economy is broadening its foreign policy perspectives and enhancing its capabilities as a partner in stabilisation. Greece's role has been enhanced in the Balkans. Its potential to promote stability in the region, as well as to help Balkan states integrate into an international system of political democratisation, economic liberalism and the corresponding comprising institutions which support it, is recognised by the international community. Cultural and economic ties to the peoples of this region, in conjunction with Greece's privileged location at the crossroads of three continents, has created the potential for Greece to become an efficient gateway to the emerging regional markets. Greece has started to realise this potential by promoting free-market principles and securing democratic institutions. Since the mid-1990s, Greek policy can be summarised as involving three major strategic objectives. The first is the rapid development of close economic ties with all the Balkan states and economic reconstruction of the region through trade transactions, investments and through the implementation of a development assistance programme. The second is the promotion of regional co-operation as a means of fostering stability and prosperity in the wider region. The third is the integration of the countries of the region into the European Union.

On the business front, the number of Greek enterprises in the Balkan countries has increased considerably. The number of sectors within which they are active is already quite large and extends from the more traditional sectors, such as foods and drinks, clothing and construction to the more specialised technological sectors, (such as telecommunications), where Greek enterprises hold a strong position among other foreign investments. Banks and companies are active, especially in the financial sector, which facilitates and encourages new Greek companies to establish themselves there They also act as a guarantee as to their smooth functioning in the country of establishment. By way of illustration, the presence of Greek private and state banks in FYROM, Romania, Bulgaria and Albania and of insurance companies in Romania and Yugoslavia should be noted. The initiative of the Greek banking sector motivated the large Greek corporations to follow, since the latter could afford the necessary financial backing. Large Greek companies swiftly elaborated extensive market research and business plans and developed numerous joint ventures with local companies in the process of undergoing privatisation.

By the end of the 1990s, there were more than 1,200 Foreign Direct Investments of Greek interest in Central and Eastern Europe. Eighty-two per cent of these are in three countries: Bulgaria (41%), Albania (20.5%) and Romania (20.5%). In Albania, the Greek invested capital exceeds 200 million Euro with more than 10,000 new jobs created, while in FYROM the amount of Greek foreign direct investment (FDI) exceeds the 300 million Euro, with more than 5000 new jobs. These investments principally focus on trade (47%), and

to a lesser extent on industry (36%), while the clothing sector accounts for 48% and food and drink for 26%. Greek foreign investments show the importance of geography in the sense that they are centred on neighbouring countries (Albania, FYROM, Bulgaria and Romania) and especially in terms of their distribution within each country (i.e. in the south, close to Greece). On a bilateral basis, Greece is the second largest foreign investor in Albania, and the third largest foreign investor in Bulgaria. Greece is the most important trading partner of the Former Yugoslav Republic of Macedonia. It ranks first among foreign investors in terms of invested capital and in the number of investing groups. In Romania, Greece ranked eighth in terms of invested capital and fourth in terms of established enterprises.

At the same time, the Balkans is an area where Greek trade has shown a remarkable increase. The following examples testify to the exceptionally high Greek export penetration. In 2000, Greek exports to Albania amounted to more than $230 million, more than a third of the country's overall import value. Greece is also FYROM's second largest trading partner, with Greek exports exceeding $430 million in 2000. Although suffering severely from political and economic crises, Greek exports to Yugoslavia have gradually been increasing. Bilateral economic relations between

The European Agency for "Reconstruction of the Balkans" headquarters in Thessaloniki, Hotel "Vienna"

Greece and Romania have also followed an upward trend since the early 1990s, especially in terms of trade. Greece accounts for more than 5% of the country's overall external trade in terms of value. Trade with Bosnia Herzegovina has also enjoyed significant growth in the post-Dayton era, leading to a further boosting of bilateral joint business activity.

On another equally important front, the Greek Ministry of Foreign Affairs spends millions of Euros every year on developmental aid to other countries. The turbulent conditions in the region in recent years have on numerous occasions created the need for urgent action in order to save human lives and minimise suffering. Greece funds NGO programmes covering a wide range of activities, such as dealing with humanitarian crises (distributing medicine and food), reconstruction efforts (repairing schools or building hospitals) and building democratic institutions (civil society). In 1999, 50% of the more than 2 million Euro given to South-eastern European countries was used to help refugees from Kosovo. In 1999, in association with the Ministry of Finance, the Ministry of Foreign Affairs established the first Greek International Developmental Co-operation Agency to support the work of Greek NGOs. Strengthening civil society allows citizens to participate equally in shaping foreign policy. The importance of the role of developmental and humanitarian co-operation was evident during the recent crisis in Kosovo. Whether setting up refugee camps in Albania and FYROM, or distributing humanitarian aid, Greek NGOs made a vital contribution to the stability, security and protection of Balkan populations. The Greek Ministry of the National Economy has also been implementing another separate programme devoted primarily to development aid. In 1997 this aid amounted to $30.5 million and in

A Grand Strategic Choice

In recent years, few countries have seen as much change, and as much turbulence along their borders as Greece. Despite being a member of the EU and NATO, Greece is geographically situated in and near conflict-prone regions where the use of force in inter-state relations has been an option in the not too distant past. Greece's role has evolved into that of a stabiliser, promoting peace, security and development. Athens credibly remains steadfast to its position concerning internationally agreed upon and legally defined borders and the exercise of sovereign rights. It relies both on internal and external balancing for national security and defence, and actively promotes the peaceful settlement of disputes.

In the Balkans, the current period is crucial. The process of transition to stable social, economic and political conditions, the construction of a modern political system and a new social-economic organisation, has been a very difficult project, with setbacks and uncertainties. Greece's main policy towards the countries of the Balkan region is to provide them with help for the reconstruction and stabilisation of their democratic institutions. It aims at assisting these countries' efforts to achieve convergence with the EU and at promoting a policy for South-eastern Europe within the framework of the Union. The political contribution to such processes is made in a flexible manner. The experience of tripartite relations with Bulgaria and Romania has shown that there is much to gain from such initiatives. Greece's financial contribution to reconstruction is not limited only to the governmental level although it does seek to improve co-operation at non-governmental levels. The stabilisation and improvement of the situation in the Balkans enriches the European spirit. Based on this idea, Greece supports all efforts in the Balkans that strengthen democracy and all initiatives that boost civic society.

As we enter the 21st century, Greek foreign policy debate has become broader in terms of interests, actors, and preferences. The strategic choice to integrate political, economic, and security objectives has meant a sharper view of Greek national interests, based on the tremendous advantage that membership in all European and Euro-Atlantic institutions confers. Overall, as the only South-eastern European and eastern Mediterranean country (fully) integrated with Europe, Greece has been able to bring to the fore considerable capabilities to address demanding political, economic, and security challenges.

1998 to $44.7 million. Greece has committed resources amounting to more than $160 million between 1997 and 2001 for development assistance in the Balkans.

But in its most important endeavour, Greece was the first country to draw up a comprehensive Reconstruction Plan for the Balkans. For the 2000 - 2004 period, it has pledged a total of more than 500 million Euro for the reconstruction of Kosovo, Albania, Bulgaria, Romania and FYROM. Financing of the plan comes directly from the Greek State Budget, thus underlining the sincere Greek intentions to promote regional development and prosperity.

The underlying rationale of the plan is the linkage between infrastructures, economic development and democratic institution building. That is why it has been incorporated to the Stability Pact. Support is to be provided to projects dealing with social and economic infrastructure (more than $188 and $240 million respectively), and the production capacity (more than $150 million) of the recipient countries. Social infrastructure involves financing of projects in the fields of education, health and housing. Promotion of regional co-operation and understanding is imperative. In that context, the priorities include mainly the preparation and completion of trans-regional infrastructure projects such as transportation, energy, telecommunications and financing. These infrastructures will reinforce the bonds between Balkan states. Moreover, these measures will promote market economy structures, which will undoubtedly lead to stable economic growth.

GREECE AND MEDITERRANEAN SECURITY-BUILDING

By Dimitris N. Chryssochoou

Greece, a country located at the eastern hub of a strategic theatre lying at the crossroads of three continents - Europe, Asia, and Africa - is well anchored to the European zone of peace and stability. At the centre of a volatile regional triangle made up of South-eastern Europe, the Middle East and the Caucasus, the Mediterranean plays a pivotal role in the country's history, politics and society. Greece is also an integral part of the Balkan state system, whilst the Aegean passage constitutes an important shipping route for the transportation of energy supplies to continental Europe.

After the Mediterranean enlargements of the European Union (EU) in the early (Greece) and mid-1980s (Spain and Portugal), Greece's position has enhanced further the strategic significance of the Mediterranean for the EU. It is not least because this "unique body of water," to borrow a phrase, constitutes a crucial fault-line between the rich Christian North and the poor Islamic South.

Today, the challenges confronting the Greek polity are numerous. These include the safeguarding of its territorial integrity (especially from the East), furthering the process (but also the quality) of Europeanisation within its domestic governance structures, and projecting its civilian values in its oft-troubled peripheries (in its northern borders, after the successive Balkan crisis).

With Greek politics being formulated in relation to an ever globalising, if not already globalised, world, the time is ripe for the country to redefine its strategic orientation in the new multi-cultural settings, including the Mediterranean.

Today, Greece exhibits a firm European orientation, being one of the firmest supporters of European integration in general and the federalisation of the EU political system in particular. The once problematic relationship with the then European Economic Community, conceptualised along the lines of an "uneasy interdependence," is long gone. Greece is an integral part of the "Eurozone," and has a generally increasing propensity to internalise European norms.

Consequently, Greece is a polity that strives towards a more profound "deepening" of the integration process, especially in the field of European Security and Defence Policy (ESDP), perceiving it as a prelude to a common European defence.

At the same time, Greece maintains particular Mediterranean concerns that relate to both internal and external security. Respect of internationally recognised borders, stability, peace, security, and full respect for human and minority rights guide its "principled" policy. Despite the many complex problems faced by the littoral countries, Greek foreign policy aims to develop multilevel and multilateral links with them based on historical and cultural ties and affinities, as well as on common economic and commercial experience. Greece has intensified its efforts to foster links with its southern partners, acting as a factor of stability throughout their transitional phase. Building on an ESDP Mediterranean dimension, the new regional space becomes a rediscovered land of opportunity and belonging for Greek policy-makers.

The EU agenda has been reshaped to accommodate regional transformations at its periphery.

Since the launching of the Euro-Mediterranean Partnership (EMP) in November 1995 - following the adoption of the Barcelona Declaration between the EU and its twelve Mediterranean partners - EU Mediterranean policy has gained both in strategic importance and, compared with previous policy regimes, internal cohesion.

By putting an institutional face on a more balanced as well as comprehensive approach, the EMP became crucial to Mediterranean order-building through a principled policy orientation, based on the norms and principles of good governance.

In promoting the Mediterranean dimension of the recently instituted ESDP, the Spanish Presidency (January-June 2002) held a seminar in Barcelona on 20-21 May 2002. Representatives from EU and EMP partner-nations (as well as Libya and Mauritania, although they are not members of the EMP) as well as academic and policy experts from relevant institutions were invited. The seminar focused largely on the structure and process of the Helsinki Headline Goal (according to which, the EU should be ready to employ a force up to 60,000 men by 2003), the nature of the "Petersberg tasks" (including peacekeeping and humanitarian missions) and, crucially, conflict prevention.

What follows reflects some of the main issues and challenges facing, on the one hand, the relationship between the ESDP and the EMP and, on the other, the prospects for developing a "capacity for dialogue" on how best to advance Mediterranean security-building. An analysis of this kind should be conducted in line with two criteria. First, it should reflect current priorities; and second, it should strive to reach new insights into a "heterarchical regional space' which, after centuries of co-operation and discord, is groping for the emergence, if not indeed institutionalisation, of a regional regime 'proper". At this stage, however, some general views on the Mediterranean are in order.

To begin with, much like Europe itself, the Mediterranean - for some, Europe's birthplace - constitutes a composite of different cultures, each having a distinctive sense of being and belonging. To borrow a phrase, it is "a patchwork of images, composed partly of myths, partly of realities". But the extent to which old images are replaced by new in the region's cultural tapestry remains open.

Mythical constructs aside, in the light of current constellations, the Mediterranean region reveals a pluricausal and multilogical dynamism towards a new socio-cultural and political mapping of its component collectivities.

Elements of convergence and divergence are reformulated through a dialectical union of old stereotypes, novel ways of thinking and acting, modified security perceptions, and an ascending pluralism in its emerging human governance structures.

In large measure, the extent to which the old images are replaced by new in this unique cultural tapestry ultimately depends upon different understandings of its sense of unity and diversity.

At a time however, when both Mediterranean shores are groping for change, the strategic orientation and rationale of the ESDP in the Mediterranean becomes a focal point of attention. It is important to clarify what the ESDP is not. It is not a threat or for that matter an extension of EU military or for that matter strategic influence in the Mediterranean region. Nor is such policy, meant to act as a reinforcement of western military power to the South and, by extension, as a force unchecked, even unre-stricted, by the principles of international legality. Nor, finally, is the ESDP, under its present design, building a capacity to intervene in the domestic affairs of other states or groups of states.

On the contrary, crisis-management operations within the ESDP context are linked only to Petersberg-type missions, including humanitarian tasks, peace-making, and peace building. ESDP functions should thus be seen as a reliable confidence-building measure, aimed at a complementary framework for co-ordinated collective action in the region.

But to achieve intended outcomes, the EU has to identify, first and foremost, a commonality of interests, aspirations and, above all, a shared Mediterranean vision with its Mediterranean partners. As for the latter, they would also have to employ reliable strategies towards a more balanced network of relations in their dealings with Europe.

The aim is to develop a "capacity for dialogue" so as to alleviate historically rooted prejudices, including long-standing security misperceptions. In international politics, however, experience teaches us that it is the threat itself, as much as its perception, which guide policy-makers. Discourses on Mediterranean security are full of misunderstandings about distorted perceptions, images of political Islam, and the threat of terrorism by extremist nationalist movements.

These often emanate from mutual ignorance and, many times, intentional confusion. Hence the need to redefine terms that reduce intelligent dialogue to a series of "parallel monologues," with a view to dispelling the clouds of deliberate myth-making and revengeful rhetoric.

Since the collapse of the entire deterrence regime, Mediterranean security became increasingly indivisible, often regardless of diverse sub-regional features. Such questions are largely products of changing power politics constellations. Some have tried to project, both before and after the horrific terrorist attacks on the US, a historical Mediterranean fragmentation, by perceiving the dominant conflict as one between "Occidental" and "Oriental" value systems.

This approach favours the cultural dimension security, prophesying, by and large, an almost inevitable "clash" among different civilisations. Yet, others focus on "new" security threats and

risks, including terrorism, transnational criminal activities, nuclear smuggling, drug trafficking, refugee movements, illegal immigration, structural economic asymmetries, and environmental risks.

The post-bipolar global scene has lent great fluidity and instability to the region, which is still not well equipped in terms of competencies and institutions to deal with the new security threats and challenges. What is needed most therefore, is a structured security dialogue on the root-causes of conflict, combined with the prevention of immediate crises through a long-term strategy within integrated multilateral institutions.

To put it differently, there is urgent need for a renewed focus on institutional response adaptation to structural changes on the global scene, and the development of a "common strategic language" to redefine older and emergent security concerns.

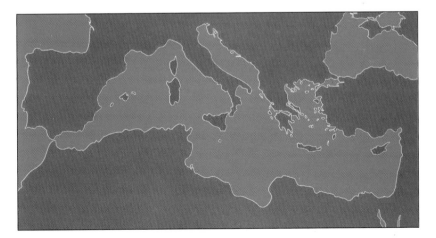

Doubtless, the further integration of foreign, security and defence policies in the European context is bound to have an impact on the EMP.

The reasons for this are obvious, for the rationale of the latter is, by and large, that Europe should attempt to extend its integrative potential to the Mediterranean South.

At the same time, demands for greater transparency cut across EU common policies and assorted decision-making processes. Transparency emanates as an institutional property central to the political and economic governance of the Mediterranean, especially in relation to the multi-dimensional structures of the Barcelona Process. For, if anything else, mutual trust-building among the partners, should be at the top of the emerging Euro-Mediterranean agenda.

Although the development of the ES-DP arguably represents a new element in Euro-Mediterranean relations, past experiences, like the creation of Eurofor and Euromarfor, generated negative public response.

This has led some to believe that a similar reaction could be expected to the creation of a European defence capability. In its effort to construct a common defence and security policy, the EU has created, and in some cases is in the process of setting up, the relevant institutional mechanisms to confront the new security risks and challenges.

However, external perceptions and misperceptions are equally important. It is particularly the case that as long as misperceptions persist, then the relationship between North and South will remain particularly tense, offering an apology for keeping sustainable co-operation out of reach.

What is needed, therefore, as many have argued, is a reciprocal exchange that does away with any subjectivist view that wants the "West" to act as a universal civilising force based on an almost metaphysical obligation to humanity.

Hence there is also a need for the EU, both as a collective polity and an ascending global actor, to re-invest in Mediterranean security building. This is even more the case since the September 11th events and assorted security threats of an asymmetrical kind.

But while the Barcelona Process remains the best option for North-South economic co-operation, there are those who see no reason as to why it should be the preferred framework for Mediterranean security, given the wealth of bilateral ties that already exist across the region. There is however still evidence to suggest that multilateralism is important, and so is the prospect for a substantive dialogue on Mediterranean security.

This is seen not only as a means of rectifying existing asymmetries and redressing current imbalances, but also as an expression of a higher purpose, if not indeed of a higher normative order. It is seen as an effort to assist in the elaboration of mutually rewarding guidelines for a "common Mediterranean security space" to emerge and consolidate itself.

Such a dialogue was recently proposed by The Hellenic Presidency of the ESDP (July-December 2002, due to the Danish optout), through a follow-up seminar to that organised by Spain, held on the all-Mediterranean island of Rhodes on 1-2 November 2002.

The Hellenic Ministry of National Defence was responsible for organising the Seminar.

The Ministry made the case for the necessity of endowing the regional process with a new sense of purpose, and process too, through the active engagement of EU and EMP partners in an open and constructive security dialogue in the Mediterranean. Such a political dialogue, the argument goes, is an additional window of opportunity for increasing the levels of systemic openness, transparency and internal cohesion in the relationship between European and Mediterranean countries.

The proposed dialogue also gives priority to the human dimension of security, which enhances civilian engagement in crisis management, always within the norms of good governance and the rules of international legality. The idea of a Mediterranean security dialogue opens up a wide range of possibilities for crucial issues to be brought into fore.

These include questions of operational readiness, doctrinal convergence over both conflict prevention and conflict resolution, information exchange practices, export control regimes, civilian emergency planning, disaster-management techniques, emergency rescue missions, and a reconceptualisation of the defence mechanisms themselves.

Of importance here is also the extent to which the strategic ramifications of new geopolitical realities and security risks in the Mediterranean can adequately "provide" principles, norms and decisionmaking rules for a cooperative security regime to be set in motion. In that sense, discussion can be directed towards institutional response adaptation to global change, assessment of diverse strategies, and of the different perceptions of security risks.

Moreover, an inclusive, elaborate and comprehensive security dialogue in the Mediterranean can offer a discursive platform from which international norms can facilitate agreement on the basis of mutuality and reciprocity.

Turning to the EU itself, the Common Strategy for the Mediterranean represents a comprehensive guide, whose primary objective is "to establish a common area of peace and stability through political and security partnership".

It also reaffirms that the EU intends to make use of the ESDP so as to strengthen co-operative security in the region. Indeed, the ESDP is better equipped to deal with crisis-management operations than the existing EMP structures, which were not intended to act either as a peacekeeper or as a peacemaker. At the same time, it is important for the two multilateral settings to arrive at common definitions and responses to problems.

These definitions are related to the new asymmetrical threats, as well as to issues of justice, tolerance, the improvement of information flows between the two shores, together with the fact that complementarity of functions and trust-building must be accorded priority.

At the policy level, many co-operative actions need to be explored, in the form of confidence and partnership-building measures. Such actions may range from the development of human security networks, the intensification of co-ordination mechanisms for information exchange to the setting up of emergency rescue and common training exercises.

Others may include exchanges among military personnel, civil society involvement through specialised consultative bodies, and positive public awareness formation through the conducting of regular seminars. In brief, central to a viable Mediterranean order is the emergence of a co-operative security culture, through the organisation of regional governance out of the systemic complexity of a fledging heterarchical space.

However, in order to break down such complexity, one first to realise the importance of diversity. The Mediterranean is located within the clash of different subsystems, which minimises homogeneity as the principal referent for regional stability.

This reflexive approximation to Mediterranean reality resonates with a broader aspiration of "partnership" that stresses the complex character of a common vocation.

Whatever the legitimising ethos of the prevailing worldviews, a security dialogue based on transparency, cultural pluriformity and symbiotic association is central to any attempt at revitalising a cross-fertilisation among highly diverse units.

The ESDP can thus be seen as an opportunity for Mediterranean co-operation, not as an alternative to it. After all, developing a "capacity for dialogue" is not a solution, but a way of seeking solutions, assigning meaning to a new politics of mutualism, civility, and hope.

GREEKS ABROAD

By Demetri Dollis

Institutional Framework - Policies

The Greek Diaspora has always been one of the major components of Hellenism, because migration has been, since antiquity, a way of life for Greeks.

The history of the contemporary migrations of Greeks is divided into three major periods: from the mid 15th century to the early 19th century, from the establishment of the Greek State (1828) to the World War II and from the early 1950s to the end of the 1970s.

Today, approximately 6-7 million Greeks are scattered in 140 countries around the world. The largest centres of Greeks living abroad can be found in the USA, Australia, Canada, Germany, Great Britain, in Black Sea countries and in South Africa.

The way that metropolitan Greece developed policy for Greeks living abroad has altered throughout the years. Three main periods can be determined so far as state policy is concerned. The first is from 1828, when the modern Greek State was established. The second is from the end of World War

I, i.e. from the 1920s to 1974. The third is from 1974 until today.

In the first period, the contribution of the Greek Diaspora was decisive and greatly assisted the struggle for Independence (1821), and the creation of Modern Greek State. At that time, Greeks living abroad had considerable financial and political resources that helped Greece consolidate its presence as a state, nationally, as well as internationally.

From the era of Prime Minister Eleftherios Venizelos, who set the foundations of a realistic national policy for the Greeks Abroad, and up to 1974, relations between the Greeks within the

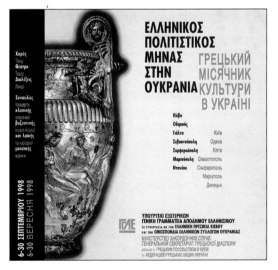

Cultural manifestation of the Ukraine's Greek Community

national territory and those who lived abroad remained at the level of family and place of origin.

The main scope of Greek policy during this period was to secure the interests for Greeks Abroad through diplomatic channels alone. Relations between Greece and Greeks living in countries of the former Warsaw Pact were non existent at the official level.

Since the mid 70s, Greek policy on Greek Expatriates started to change. The growing importance of the Greek presence in the US, as well as in other countries, led to the awareness that the Greek Diaspora constitutes a national asset and that preservation of its national identity is an obligation for the Greek State. As a result of that awareness, Greece started shaping an overall and flexible national policy for Greeks Abroad, aiming at safeguarding Greek identity.

A key date that cemented this change, was the establishment of the General Secretariat for Greeks Abroad, through Law 1228/1982, an autonomous body within the Ministry of Culture, which constitutes, ever since the "Headquarters" for Greeks abroad.

Presidential Decree No 104/1983 specified the responsibilities of the Secretariat reflecting the strategic goals of the governmental policy of that period which safeguarded:

• rights and interests of Greeks abroad,

• application of measures for their social, cultural, economic development,

the monitoring educational and religion issues,

• provision and implementation of national migration policy and relevant international and bilateral conventions

• formation of policies for repatriation.

In 1993, the General Secretariat for Greeks Abroad was transferred from the Ministry of Culture to the Ministry of Foreign Affairs; a change that signals a transition from an introverted national policy to an extroverted one, as well as interactive and internationally oriented policy. This change provided an impetus to the new, diversified activities of the Greek State, while it fully respected the status of Greeks living abroad, as national citizens of another country.

In 1995, Presidential Decree No 196/1995 set up the Council for Greeks Abroad (SAE), which constitutes the highest collective and autonomous institution, composed of organisations of the Greek Diaspora and has a consulting and introductory role to the Greek State on issues pertaining to Greeks abroad. SAE headquarters is located in Thessaloniki, "the Capital of Greeks Abroad". In 1999, Presidential Decree No 191/1999 broadened the representation of Greeks abroad in SAE, thus strengthening regional structures.

In the spring of 1996, the institutional framework relating to Greeks Abroad was further strengthened by the decision to modify the status of the Committee of the Parliament for Greeks Abroad from an ad hoc to a standing and permanent one.

This Special Permanent Committee of the Greek Parliament (consisting of all parties) secures the substantial dialogue of the political forces of the country on this issue and has, ever since its establishment, elaborated several proposals, covering the whole spectrum of national strategies for Greeks Abroad.

Again in 1996, at the initiative of Greeks - members of national Parliaments in their countries of residence, the "World Inter-parliamentary Union of Hellenism" was founded, aimed at promoting the interests of Greeks abroad and tightening Greek ties with other countries where Greeks reside.

During the same period, the "Greek Institution of Culture", the "Co-ordinating Committee of Research Institutes of Hellenism" and the "Centre of Studies and Development of the Greek Culture of the Black Sea" were being established.

The "Greek Institution of Culture" has annexes in Berlin, London, Paris, Odessa, and is primarily dealing with teaching the Greek language and promoting Greek culture abroad.

The "Black Sea Centre" has set as primary goal the support of cultural, social and economic development of Greeks in Black Sea Countries. At the same time, it promotes relations between Greek Local Government Authorities and those of Black Sea countries, using Greeks living in those countries as a direct channel.

In a search to find ways to broaden and develop different policies on Greeks Abroad, the Greek State has set the following main axes of a national strategy:

Organisation of Greeks Abroad: providing material and moral support to Greek organisations throughout the world, including SAE and other institutional networks (such as youth, women, businessmen, scientists, and culture).

Communication: the use of modern technology offers possibilities to achieve constant communication through the immediate exchange of information and interaction among Greeks all over the World.

Education: offering the possibility to young people, second or even third generation Greeks, to have Greek education in their resident countries. This promotes national cultural identity by acquainting them with the Greek language, history and wider culture.

Cultural policy: includes both support and promotion of cultural events organised by Greeks Abroad, as well as cultural exchange between metropolitan Greece and Greeks living abroad.

Policy on Repatriation: focuses on supporting Greeks who have returned to their homeland, as well as on fighting the social seclusion they face.

Promotion of financial issues which concern Greeks Abroad with emphasis on granting support to Greeks living in former socialist countries and facing harsh socio-economic conditions.

New York,
15-04-2002: the
Greek Community
celebrates the
National Day of
25th Mars

Moreover, a priority target of economic policy for Greeks Abroad is to help them develop business activities.

Another initiative undertaken by the Greek State is to assign Universities and Research Centres with the elaboration of studies and researches on issues related to the lives and interests of Greeks Abroad.

The Athens Olympic Games of 2004 offered a new opportunity to Greece to expand its policies on the Greek Diaspora. A Memorandum of Understanding signed between Organising Committee "Athens 2004" and the Greek Ministry of Foreign Affairs, undertakes the initiative to promote Greek culture and the Olympic spirit throughout the world with the assistance of the Greeks Abroad. Moreover, a ceiling of 5000 individuals has been set for Greek youngsters living abroad, who would like to serve as volunteers at the Athens Olympic Games of 2004.

The Olympic Games became a starting point for the biennial organisation of Athletic Games among Greek athletes living abroad in the city of Thessaloniki, combined also with cultural festivities. This event is named "Hellenias". Thus a detailed list of all Greek athletes throughout the world will be kept and unfamiliar Olympic sports will gain wider public awareness in Greece.

Another initiative of great importance is the program of hosting each year, children, students and elderly people in summer camps in Greece. This program has made a decisive contribution to the tightening of ties among metropolitan Greece and its Diaspora. Especially during the last 10 years, the number of people who visited Greece has considerably increased.

These programs have now been expanded to cover all geographic parts of

Greece with the assistance of the Ministry of Interior and the Local Government Associations. The aim of these programs is to give the opportunity to Greeks overseas born to visit the country.

The current global strategy on Greeks Abroad, adopted by Greek governments, especially during the last 20 years, aims at the shaping of a strong and interactive relationship between Greece and its Diaspora, a challenge that meets the needs of globalisation and promotes Greek culture and spirit ecumenically.

Greece, one of the leading countries in this area in terms of organisational structure of its Diaspora, and existing internal legislation, soon realised the importance of safeguarding "national memory". It also understood the importance of providing individuals with the opportunity to value their Greek origin, while at the same time totally and successfully integrating themselves in their host countries.

Greeks abroad, preserving their special ethnic characteristics, adapt, create and advance in their countries of residence. Greece, as a country of origin, maintains close relations with the Greek Diaspora, capitalising on this interactive relation, both domestically and internationally.

The new structural framework of the General Secretariat for Greeks Abroad, which is currently under approval, is responding to the new orientation of Greek governmental policy. It also takes into consideration Greece's role within the European Union.

Greece has a rich historical experience as a country of origin for Expatriates - Immigrants and as a transit and host country as well, therefore, rightfully claiming a primary role in the shaping of a policy for migration.

Holding EU Presidency during the first semester 2003 provided a better opportunity for Greece to accelerate modifications of these policies. This was done not only domestically but also within EU territory, by bringing together expatriates from all over Europe and setting the principles of closer co-operation, so that common problems can have common solutions. Such a process of co-ordinating legislative frameworks and actions of the EU member States, although daring, would meet the needs of modern Europe in the new Millennium.

ECONOMY

THE ECONOMY OF GREECE

By Panos Kazakos and Panagiotis Liargovas

During the last decade, Greece has enjoyed economic and political stability. It has undergone significant infrastructure improvements and major reforms in the public sector as well as a programme of market liberalisation, all of which have improved its economic profile.

Since January 1st 2001, Greece entered the Economic and Monetary Union (EMU). A year later Greece, together with 10 more EMU countries replaced its local currency (Drachma) with the Euro. This has been a result of impressive economic policy changes and growth over the last years, during which convergence towards European Union economic performance standards, in both nominal and real terms, has evolved at a rapid pace.

Moreover, the upcoming Olympic Games to be hosted in Athens in 2004, the Greek Reconstruction Plan for the Balkan Region and the continuous expansion of Greek activities covering the entire Balkan and Black Sea regions, have indeed created significant business opportunities.

Macro-economic stability and growth

Although the international economic environment remains highly uncertain, the medium-term perspectives of the Greek economy are positive. Buoyant domestic demand, the large inflows of funds from the 3rd EU Community Support Framework and the preparations for the 2004 Olympic Games to be hosted in Athens are contributing to a sustained high level of economic activity. For the period 2003-2006, a robust sustainable growth rate is projected, with continuing fiscal consolidation, and declining public debt as a percent of GDP. Moreover, continued structural reforms and the adopted social insurance and pension system reform are expected to contribute to the long-term sustainability of public finances and growth.

For the period 2003-2004 GDP is projected to increase on average by 3.9 per cent, while for the period 2005-2006, GDP growth is projected to be approximately 3.7 per cent annually. Fixed capital formation is expected to increase by an average growth rate of 6.9 per cent for the period 2003-2006, while business investment growth is projected at 8.5 per cent annually. The share of investments in GDP will be at about 26 per cent in 2006, from 23 per cent in 2002. As far as the other components of GDP are concerned, private consumption in the 2003-2006 period

Selected Economic Indicators 2003-2006

	2003		2004		2005	2006
	SGP2001	SGP2002	SGP2001	SGP2002	SGP2002	SGP2002
1. GDP GROWTH	4.0%	3.8%	4.0%	4.0%	3.7%	3.6%
2. GROSS FIXED CAPITAL FORMATION	9.9%	9.5%	7.4%	7.0%	6.1%	5.1%
3. REAL UNIT LABOUR COST	-0.4%	-1.2%	0.0%	-0.7%	-0.7%	-0.7%
4. PRIVATE CONSUMPTION DEFLATOR	2.7%	2.7%	2.8%	2.8%	2.6%	2.6%
5. GENERAL GOVERNMENT BALANCE (% GDP)	1.0%	-0.9%	1.2%	-0.4%	0.2%	0.6%
6. GENERAL GOVERNMENT DEBT (% GDP)	94.4%	100.2%	90.0%	96.1%	92.1%	87.9%
7. UNEMPLOYMENT RATE	9.8%	9.1%	9.0%	8.4%	7.7%	7.1%

Notes: SGP = Stability and Growth Programme
Source: Ministry of the Economy

is projected to remain strong, above 3 per cent for each year, while trade balance will be kept constantly above 14 percentage points of GDP.

Employment for the years 2003-2006 is projected to increase as a consequence of high growth rates. The average annual rate of increase in total employment is estimated to be 1.1 per cent. The rise in the employment rate is justified by the fact that migration from the agricultural sector into the urban sector will be much smaller in the coming years. Continuing structural reforms and the implementation of the National Action Plans on employment are also expected to contribute to higher employment. As a result, the unemployment rate is expected to decrease from 10 per cent in 2002 to 7.1 per cent in 2006.

The medium-term outlook for *public finances* is compatible with the Stability and Growth Pact. In the period 2003-2004, the general government balance is projected to be negative but improving over the period, from -1.1 per cent of GDP in 2002, to -0.9 per cent in 2003 and -0.4 per cent in 2004. In 2005, a small surplus of 0.2 per cent of GDP is predicted, which will increase in 2006, to 0.6 per cent of GDP. For the whole period, the primary surplus is estimated to range between 4.4 per cent and 5.2 per cent of GDP and it will be increase progressively. These primary surpluses will secure a decline in the general government debt ratio, from 105.3 percent of GDP in 2002, to 87.9 percent in 2006.

For the period 2003-2006, *inflation* is projected to decline although it will remain above the European average. The average annual rate of increase of the private consumption deflator is projected to be 2.7 per cent, influenced by the high growth rates and the ending of the previously large under-utilisation of economic resources. The annual average nominal unit labour cost is projected to be 2.3 per cent, which is compatible with an estimated increase of labour productivity by 2.6 per cent annually and an increase in the nominal compensation of employees per head by 5.0 per cent.

The continuous *upgrading of the ratings* by the various international evaluation agencies constitutes the seal of approval by the international business community of Greece's solid economic performance. Greece is rated A2 by Moody's, A- by Standard and Poor's, BBB+ by Fitch IBCA, and B by the Japan Centre for International Finance.

Economic policy in the medium term

Economic policy, in the medium term is oriented towards sustaining the significant improvement of macroeconomic fundamentals, which was accomplished over the previous years, and by pursuing real convergence. Furthermore, the need to reduce the public debt, which is still very high, calls for a prudent fiscal policy and higher primary surpluses in the budget. The task might prove to be equally tedious as in the last few years, given that the external

prospects are not particularly favourable. Further fiscal consolidation is also expected to contribute to the containing of inflationary pressures, which still persist in the Greek economy. Since monetary policy is the competence of the European Central Bank, budgetary policy has become the main instrument for demand management.

It is true, however, that Greece still needs large investments in the area of infrastructure and public services. Hence, the above task becomes quite demanding, and will be achieved not only through fiscal policy but also the extending and deepening of structural reforms and the adopted social insurance and pension system.

Budgetary implications of the structural reforms

In the spirit of Lisbon, the Greek economic policy agenda involves the deepening of structural reforms in product, capital and labour markets, so as to sustain a strong economic performance and accelerate the process of convergence with the other EU countries. Struc-

tural policy is directed towards the enhancement of productivity, competitiveness and the potential of the Greek economy for growth and job creation. Meanwhile, the privatisation programme brings market incentives and discipline to an increasing part of the economy.

Reducing administrative barriers and simplifying the business environment for enterprises, in general, and SMEs, in particular, opening up network utilities, as well as reforming the tax and pension systems are some of the areas where significant initiatives have been taken. A large number of items in tax reform concerned the simplification of tax administration for SMEs, so as to enhance their role in generating growth and employment.

The privatisation programme is being pursued with renewed vigour. The government decided to follow a more proactive approach by introducing new methods of privatisation and by lifting the upper level privatisation limit for some companies. In 2001, the total amount raised, either by the State or by public entities came up to 4.4 billion

Main Structural Reforms Realised in 2002	
Reform of pension system (L3029/2002)	June 2002
Law on corporate governance and internal auditing	September 2002
Parliamentary lodgement of law concerning the application of International Accounting Standards	September 2002
Effective liberalisation of coastal shipping and sea transport	November 2002
Draft law concerning the first wave of tax reform	November 2002

Euros[1], bringing the whole amount raised during the period 1998-2001 up to 11.8 billion Euros. The privatisations completed within 2002 concerned the sale of an additional 67% of the Hellenic Industrial Bank, the acquisition of 49% of the Hellenic Casino of "Mont Parnes" by a strategic partner (the

Recent Privatisation of State-owned Enterprises, 2001-2002

Company	Method of Privatisation & % sold	Total amount raised (in bn €)	Stat Control (%)
Licensing for second and third generation mobile telephony (2001)		0.5	
Football Prognostics Organisation (OPAP) (2001)	Initial Public Offering (5.4%)	0.09	94.6
Corinth Canal (2001)	Concession Agreement (100%)	0.03	0
Hellenic Telecommunications Organisation (OTE) IV (2001)	Exchangeable bonds (9%)	1.0	41.7
Salonica Port Authority (2001)	Initial Public Offering (25%)	0.02	74.3
Salonica Water and Sewage (2001)	Initial Public Offering (26%)	0.01	74.5
Skaramaga Shipyards (2001)	Trade Sale (100%)	0.05	0
Public Power Corporation (2001)	Initial Public Offering (16%)	0.46	84
Issuance of Privatisation Certificates ("prometoxa") (2001)		1.94	
Hellenic Industrial Bank (2002)	Trade sale (67%)	0.51	7.8
Hellenic Casino of 'Mont Parnes' SA (2002)	Strategic Investor (49%)	0.12	51
Football Prognostics Organisation (OPAP) (2002)	Additional Offering (19%)	0.51	75.6
Hellenic Telecommunications Organisation (OTE) (2002)	Additional Offering (8%)	0.65	33.7

Source: Ministry of Economy and Finance.

---

[1] Including revenues from privatisation certificates and exchangeable bonds

Envisioned Privatisations for the forthcoming period

Public Enterprise	Currently under State Control (%)	Method of privatisation & % to be sold	
Hellenic Petroleum	58.2 [1]	Strategic investor	23%
Piraeus Port Authority	100	IPO	25%
Olympic Airways (OA)	100	Divestment	
Hellenic Postal Services (ELTA)	100	- Strategic partner through a rights issue and formation of a 50-50% joint venture in express delivery mail service - IPO	up to 10%
Athens Water & Sewage Company (EYDAP)	61	To be determined	10%
Hellenic Stock Exchanges	33	To be determined	33%
Postal Savings Bank	100	To be determined	To be determined
Public Gas Corporation (DEPA)	65 (2)	Strategic investor	35%
Hellenic Tourist Properties (ETA)	100	IPO	25%
Agricultural Bank	82.3	To be determined	To be determined
Public Power Corporation	84	Additional Offering	15%

Source: Ministry of Economy and Finance

Notes:
(1) Currently outstanding an exchangeable bond, representing 9.6% of the company's share capital
(2) The Public Power Corporation has an option to acquire a 30% stake in DEPA.

remaining 51% belongs to Hellenic Tourist Properties). Also included were the additional offerings of the Football Prognostics Organisation (OPAP) and Telecommunications. Revenues raised in 2002 were about 2.25 billion Euros.

Admittedly, the continuing deterioration of the Stock exchange has affected the privatisation momentum.

Since the 1st of January 2001, the *telecommunications* sector has been fully liberalised and licences for the local loop wireless networks have been awarded. Over 250 enterprises are already active in the sector. The mobile telephony market has been open to competition since 1992 and value-added services (private networks, etc.) since 1996.

The process for the auctioning of 3rd generation mobile networks has begun.

The *electricity* sector has been partially liberalised. 993 statements of interest have already been filed. The envisaged investments could lead to an increase in installed capacity of about 40 percent.

Regarding *oil refineries,* the biggest player in the market is Hellenic Petroleum. Two trances of stock have been sold and the state holding has been reduced to 51%.

Preparations are under way for an additional offering of stocks (15%) of the Public Power Corporation within 2002. The process of selecting a strategic partner for the Hellenic Telecommunications Organisation is continuing. The state is holding less than 42% of the shares. A strategic investor is being sought for a majority stake in Hellenic Petroleum.

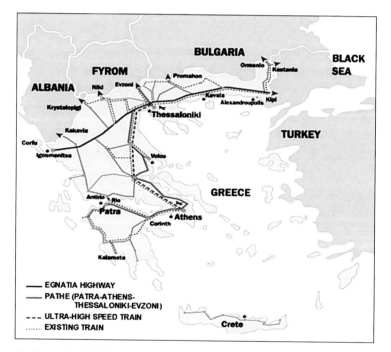

Egnatia Higway, the PATHE motorway and the modemisation of the rail network are the three basic axes that form part of the Trans European Network

Following the financial markets' liberalisation, the banking system has undergone deep changes. Five banks have already been sold to the private sector. The sale of the Ionian Bank in 1999 was the largest ever privatisation in Greece and has initiated a major restructuring of the banking sector. Even in the National Bank of Greece, private investors hold more than 50% of share capital.

The Structural Funds in Greece in 2000-2006

Having already received about 32 billion Euros in aid during 1994-1999 from the 2nd Community Support Framework, Greece will gain a further 48 billion Euros over the years 2000-2006 from the 3rd Community Support Framework. This amounts to about 4% of GDP yearly and will be partially allocated, along with private sector funds, towards the completion of large infrastructure projects - the basis for long-term growth.

The total budget available to projects under the four Structural Funds, namely the European Regional Development Fund (ERDF), the European Social Fund (ESF), the European Agricultural Guidance and Guarantee Fund - Guidance Section (EAGGF Guidance Section), and the Financial Instrument for Fisheries Guidance (FIFG), is divided into three priority Objectives:

• Objective 1: Regions whose development is lagging behind

Objective 1 is designed to promote the development and structural adjustment of less developed regions. Only those regions whose per capita GDP is less than 75% of the Community average are eligible for Objective 1.

From 2000-06, all the Greek regions will continue to qualify for Objective 1 assistance (East Macedonia, Central Macedonia, Western Macedonia, Thessaly, Epirus, the Ionian Islands, Western Greece, Continental Greece, Peloponnese, Attica, North Aegean, South Aegean and Crete). The Objective 1 budget for Greece in 2000-06 stands at 21 billion Euros compared with 15.236 billion Euros in 1995-99.

• Objective 2: Regions undergoing structural conversion

Objective 2 (which replaces Objectives 2 and 5(b) from the 1994-99 period) is intended to support the economic and social conversion of areas facing structural problems. In 2000-06, four types of areas are recognised as having structural problems: industrial, rural and urban areas and areas dependent on fisheries.

Since the whole of Greece qualifies for Objective 1, Objective 2 does not apply.

• Objective 3: Education, training and employment

Objective 3 is designed to support the adaptation and modernisation of education, training and employment policies and systems. It combines the old Objectives 3 and 4 and is closely connected to the new Title on employment in the EC Treaty as amended by the Treaty of Amsterdam.

Since Objective 3 is only operative outside Objective 1 areas, Greece is not affected by it.

Besides the three priority Objectives, the Structural Funds are also providing finance in the new period through four Community Initiatives:

• Interreg: promoting cross-border, transnational and interregional co-operation, with a view to stimulating balanced development and spatial planning within Europe;

• Urban: financing economic and social regeneration of cities with serious structural problems, to promote sustainable urban development;

• Leader: supporting rural development;

• Equal: funding for transnational co-operation to promote new practices that guarantee full equality of opportunity in access to the labour market.

The 2000-06 budget for these Initiatives in Greece is 862 billion Euros, broken down as follows:

• INTERREG   EUR 568 million
• EQUAL   EUR 98 million
• LEADER   EUR 172 million
• URBAN   EUR 24 million

The Treaty of Maastricht set up the Cohesion Fund. Its purpose is to help those Member States whose per capita GNP is less than 90% of the Community average (namely Greece, Ireland, Portugal and Spain) adjust to the challenges of economic and monetary union. This is to be done through the partial financing of projects in the fields of the environment and trans-European transport infrastructure.

In 2000-06 Greece should receive some 3.060 billion Euros, compared to 2.836 billion Euros in 1994-99.

Lastly, although this is not, strictly speaking, structural assistance, it is worth noting that Greece also receives rural development assistance from the EAGGF Guarantee Section. Since the Berlin summit agreement of March 1999, rural development policy has become a key element of the common agricultural policy (CAP). The EAGGF Guarantee Section will in future provide support for four measures to be applied throughout the Community (early retirement, compensatory allowances for farmers in less-favoured areas, woodland management on farms, and agri-environmental measures). In addition six other measures will be undertaken by the Guarantee Section which are restricted to regions not covered by Objective 1 (investment in agricultural holdings, start-up assistance for new entrants to farming, training, forestry, processing and marketing of agricultural products, and adaptation and diversification of rural areas). Thus, rural development assistance is not linked to specific regions.

The annual rural development budget for Greece is 131 million Euros or 3% of the total Community budget in this domain.

In general, Structural Funds are expected to have demand effects generated by the rise in the income of persons and firms involved in the implementation of CSF programs. On the other hand, supply-side effects stem from the improvement of factor productivity generated either as an externality through the improved infrastructure or directly by augmenting labour productivity through training. The effects of CSF intervention follow two parallel paths: first, the CSF flows cause a rise in total demand, through domestic expenditure and personal income; second, in domestic supply through the rise in sectoral productivity due to improved infrastructure, reduction of unit labour costs and increase in capital formation.

The contribution of Structural Funds to the acceleration of growth depends to a large extend upon the magnitude of supply-side externalities. When supply-side externalities are fully in operation, the rise in the output growth rate is significantly higher compared to the demand-push effects, while employment rises sharply and around 200 thousand jobs will have been created by the end of the decade.

The 2004 Olympics

Athens, the city where the first modern Olympic Games were revived in 1896, will host the 2004 Olympic Games. Greece's vision is to glorify the Games in the land that gave birth to the Olympic ideals.

Besides the Sports and Cultural aspects of the Games, excellent opportunities also arise for investment in the development of sports facilities and Olympics related projects. For the preparation of the Games, the total budget reaches to 5.6 billion Euros. The Greek state will contribute 3.5 billion Euros and the EU will contribute 0.9 billion Euros - for the balance 1.2 billion Euros Greece is requesting the participation of the private investors, to invest in partnership with the Greek Government.

The 2004 Olympic Games are also expected to have strong positive effects on the basic business sectors of the Greek economy, opening up new investment opportunities. According to a research by the Foundation of Economic and Industrial Research (Oct. 2000):

• The minimum increase in the turnover of the tourism industry will be 160 million Euros for year 2004. During the period of the Games only, 2 million tourist-days are forecast for foreign tourists.

• Local industrial enterprises will increase their turnover during 2001-2004 by 755 million Euros, mainly by acting as sponsors of the Game, thereby promoting their image in international markets.

• Construction companies will be called to undertake projects directly related to the Games with a total budget of 580-700 million Euros.

The demand for telecom services, as well as transport, financial, trade, consulting and other services is expected to boom.

Greece's geopolitical situation in the Balkans

Economic growth is also supported by the new geopolitical situation in the Balkans. In the past, Greece was confronted with an unfavourable situation not to be found anywhere else in Europe. The northern borders of the country were real barriers to communication, trade and investment with neighbouring countries. This situation generated two serious problems. First it effectively increased the economic distance between Greece and the EU and second it did not allow the forces of comparative advantages to develop. As a result, there was limited market accessibility for exporting industries and very limited prospects for export-led growth.

Political tensions aside, severe economic distortions had been produced for Greece and the other countries in the area. The rehabilitation of these distortions is an obvious political and economic benefit for all the European nations and markets, and Greece can play a pivotal role in this process.

The geopolitical isolation of Greece, combined with the small size of the domestic market perpetuated structural deficiencies in the economy and resulted in a situation that was unique in Europe:

- Greek industry is one of the smallest and most fragmented in the EU.
- Trade with other EU countries takes place between sectors, based on the traditional pattern of comparative advantage.
- Business alliances and partnerships with foreign counterparts are rare, especially in the industrial sector.
- In several sectors, where economies of scale were present, there was either no domestic activity, or the state had to provide protection. This led to an economy with a high degree of state activity and ownership.

This unfavourable situation no longer exists. From the moment the economic border of Eastern Europe and the Balkans opened to international competition, the Greeks once again took the traditional trade routes to the Balkans and to the rest of the countries in the area.

The results are encouraging. In less than five years, Greek companies have thrived in Albania, Bulgaria, Romania, Ukraine, Russia, the Black Sea region and other Balkan countries, thus contributing to the progress and prosperity of these nations. Greek companies have taken full advantage of their historical knowledge of how to do business in these areas.

Greece is ranked
- 1st direct foreign investor in Yugoslavia and FYROM
- 2nd in Albania
- 3rd in Bulgaria
- 6th in Romania

There are already several positive developments in trade between Greece and the Balkan countries. It is not only the fact that exports have risen since 1990 and that this has led to an amelioration of the current account, measured on a customs basis. Even more important is the fact that two thirds of Greek-Balkan trade has an intra-industry character, that is, trade within broadly similar sectors. This will create the conditions for economies of scale, enabling an increase in the average size of industry, compared to the currently small size of firms and the establishment of firms in sectors so far deemed

The National Bank of Greece branch at Tirana, Albania

unsuitable due to insufficient market size.

It needs to be stressed that this is no substitute for the need of Greek firms to play competitive role in the European single market, but it will help to achieve better size and capacity. Additionally, a more efficient structure in the economies of neighbouring countries will have major benefits for the European Union, such as:

• the creation of modern dynamic markets in the vicinity of EU, thus enhancing trade potential, welfare prospects and stabilising the workforce movements from the periphery to the core countries.

• the economic, political and institutional upgrading in the Balkan countries, which is the best means towards their eventual accession to European Union.

• the creation of better conditions for an efficient utilisation of Structural Programmes for the Balkan Countries and Eastern Europe.

The Greek government is assisting the penetration of Greek companies into the neighbouring markets either directly or through cash grants and tax incentives (e.g. in Albania) or indirectly through regional institutions and initiatives. The Greek export Guarantee Board along with MIGA (Multilateral Investment Guarantee Agency) also provides insurance coverage for investment projects in the region.

In September 1999, the Greek

government unveiled a plan for the reconstruction of the Balkans, after the war in Yugoslavia earlier in that year. Accordingly, the authorities propose to spend, in the period from 2000-2004, the sum of 180 billion drachmas (528 mil. ☐). The Plan demonstrates the special interest of Greece and the strategic importance it attaches to the development of the region. The annual distribution of the funds is compatible with the needs arising in the affected areas/countries and with the necessity to incorporate the region of SE Europe into the European Union. Actions and initiatives to be taken within the context of this National Plan will correspond to the needs and targets of the recipient countries and to be in synergy with the international plans. The programme will be administered with flexibility, mainly as far as the allocation of funds between sectors and countries is concerned and will take into account the specific conditions, which prevail in the recipient countries. Greece is a major shareholder in the Black Sea Trade & Development Bank. It is also a member of the Southeast Europe Co-operative Initiative (SECI).

Greece: An attractive region for Investment

Growth and investment supported by financial flows from the European Union are the key components of the government's blueprint for change. Radical economic policy changes,

massive infrastructure developments, deregulation and privatisation have fostered international confidence in Greece as a corporate location. A competitive investment climate is supported by a rapidly advancing telecommunications network, low labour costs coupled with increasing productivity, which are reinforced by an improved energy supply and lowered costs. Plentiful opportunities for expansion make Greece an investment location with long-term prospects. Opportunities for joint ventures can help reach the virtually untapped and sizeable markets of the Balkan, Black Sea, Eastern Europe and eastern Mediterranean regions, all of which can be accessed directly from Greece. Competitive incentives are currently available and further reinforced for specific regions and sectors, providing additional impetus to the investment.

Human Resources

Greeks with university degrees who have studied abroad - either in North America or Europe - represent approximately 11% of the Greek population.

A 1996 study conducted by the Greek Association of CEOs (EASE) in association with INSEAD (the French Institute for Economic Research and Development) demonstrates that 94% of Greek managers are university graduates, of whom 54% are postgraduates. Some 45% of Greek managers speak a foreign language - mainly English - and half of these speak a second foreign

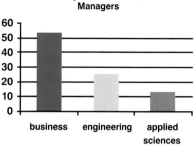

University Education of Greek Managers

Source: EASE and INSEAD
study on "Greek Management"

language (largely French, German or Italian).

The study also indicates that university education of management executives is approximately 55% in business, 25% in engineering and 15% in applied sciences.

Greece combines a reasonable pool of skilled workers and a good supply of unskilled labour. It also has the second lowest industrial labour costs in the EU.

In terms of labour costs, Greece is one of the most advantageous EU countries. Any potential investor who makes investments equivalent to in Germany or France will achieve the same productivity results in Greece.

Investment Incentives

The Greek government currently provides a generous incentives package for productive investments in the primary, secondary and services sectors of the economy, including tourism. The incentives take the form of either cash grants and interest rate subsidies or tax-free reserves. The location, the sector and the employment potential of the investment determine the precise incentives on offer in each case.

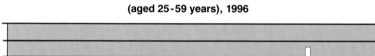

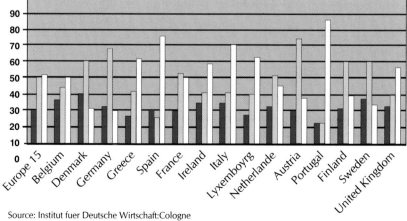

Educational Attairment Level of Labour Force as % of Total Labour Force (aged 25-59 years), 1996

Source: Institut fuer Deutsche Wirtschaft:Cologne

Hourly Labour Cost in 1997 ($)

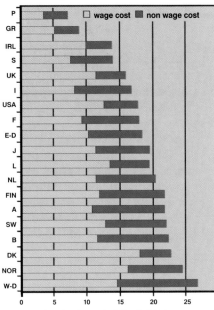

Source: Institut fuer Deutsche Wirtschaft:Cologne

The government formulated its policy in support of the following objectives:

• The development of new technologies, products and informatics.

• The modernisation of industry in terms of technology, management and operations through comprehensive business plans.

• The upgrading of tourism investments and the promotion of new forms of tourism.

• The quality control of standardised products and the improvement of company competitiveness.

• Environmental protection and energy conservation.

• The advancement of industrial research.

For the application of the above incentives, Greece is divided into 4 zones, as follows:

Zone D: Perfectures of Xanthi, Rodopi and Evros, the Northern Aegean islands, Thasos island, the perfecture of Dodecanese except for the city of Rhodes, all areas within 20 km of the border and ETVA Industrial Zones of the Epiros region.

Zone C: Areas of Greece with acute problems of unemployment and/or population loss. The Ministry of National Economy shall define these areas in a future decree.

Zone B: Some areas of Attica and Thessaloniki, and all other areas that are not included in zones C, D or A.

Zone A: Perfectures of Attica and Thessaloniki, except for the parts that may be included in zone B or C.

In the case of investments in industry, mining and tourism of at least 25 billion drachmas with the creation of at least 300 permanent jobs, all types of incentives are alternatively applicable. Also, divergences are allowed from the limitations in self-participation, the submission deadlines, and the procedure for the awarding of the grants, the size of the grants, the interest subsidy (duration and percentage). Divergences are also allowed with regard to the maximum amount of the bank loan, the percent-

Investment Incentives by Zone						
	New Corporations (less than 5 years)				Existing Corporations (more than 5 years)	
	Cash Grant	Loan Interest Subsidy	Leasing Subsidy	Tax Allowance	Loan Interest Subsidy	Tax Allowance
D	40%	40%	40%	100%	40%	100%
C	30%	30%	30%	70%	30%	70%
B	15%	15%	15%	40%	15%	40%
A	(1)	(1)	(1)	(1)	(1)	(1)

This chart covers all investment categories up to GRD 25bn.

1. In Zone A, cash grants up to 40% and tax allowances up to 100% are applicable for the following kind of projects: tourist, state-of-the-art technological products and services, utilisation of renewable sources of energy, software development, establishment of R&D centres, protection of the environment, and production of innovative products.
2. Zone B also includes the industrial estate of Thessaloniki.
3. Zone D also includes the industrial estates of Ioannina and Preveza.

ages of tax allowances and allowances in the leasing of equipment, the conditions of company shares' transfer, as well as the possibility of public corporations participating in the investment

Areas of potential Investment

Telecommunications

OTE holds 12th position among the OECD countries and 1st among the Objective 1 countries (Spain, Portugal, Ireland) with regard to the infrastructure of the telephone line network. Telephone services are provided by Hellenic Telecommunications Organisation (OTE) the state-owned company, which has been partially privatised through public offering on the Athens Stock Exchange

and the NYSE (30% of the share capital).

In the mobile telephone sector there is high competition among TELESTET, PANAFON and COSMOTE. The sector enjoys high growth rates. The heavy investment programme of OTE has resulted in the continuous development of the infrastructure (ISDN lines) and in the improvement of the quality of the services provided. Currently the network is fully digitalised. At the same time, it offers very competitive pricing - among the lowest in the EU. For international calls, Greek tariffs are as much as 40% lower than the OECD average.

The provision of the following services has been liberalised:

• Data transmission and conveyance

services, such as data networks, internet access services, etc.

• Voice services to corporate networks and closed user groups

• Value added services such as electronic mail (E-mail), audio-text, access to databases, etc.

• Mobile and personal communications such as paging, mobile telephony, etc.

• Satellite communications

• Operation and exploitation of the Public Switched Telecommunications Network, (PSTN)

• voice telephone services

Railways

The Hellenic Railways Organisation's (OSE) investment plan of 3.245 billion Euros involves a large expansion programme to modernise Greece's main rail access, opening a rail gateway to Europe via the Port of Patras.

The project entails the construction of a double-track railway line in accordance with international specifications (to link Patras - Athens - Thessaloniki - borders, i.e. border with FYROM (Evzones), Bulgaria (Promachonas to Sofia, border with Turkey (Kipi Bridge to Instabul, and also the border with Turkey at Kastania to Adrianoupolis. It also includes a second branch line to the border with Bulgaria (Ormenio to Sofia). The project has been designed for trains with high specifications and standards of manufacture/luxury/comfort etc. as well as average, high and top speeds.

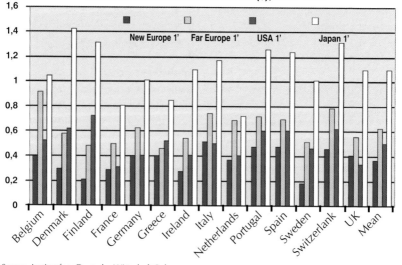

TELECOMMUNICATIONS TARIFFS ($), JULY 1998

New Europe 1' Far Europe 1' USA 1' Japan 1'

Source: Institut fuer Deutsche Wirtschaft:Cologne

Energy
Electricity

At the moment, the production and distribution of electricity is dominated by the Public Power Corporation (PPC). Production of electricity with the use of Renewable Energy Sources by private individuals is allowed, according to Law 2244/90. The distri-

bution network is owned and operated only by PPC.

However, the PPC monopoly will cease to exist by the year 2004 when the deregulation of the energy market will take place in Greece.

The installed capacity in Greece in 1997 was 9,859 MW. This will be increased by 1,788 - 1,858 MW (Thermoelectric) and by 316 MW (Hydroelectric) until the year 2003 (total cost estimated at 630 billion drachmas).

Natural gas

The Public Gas Corporation project to introduce Russian and Algerian natural gas into Greek energy mix is proceeding. The project includes the conveyance of natural gas (mainly by pipeline) from Russia, via Bulgaria, to Athens. It also involves the creation of cryogenic installations for storing liquefied gas from Algeria in Attica, on the isle of Revythousa (near Elefsina). It further includes the construction of the necessary local and urban distribution centres along the length of the pipeline

throughout the country. It is estimated that Greece will import 4 billion m3 of natural gas annually, intended for industrial and residential use. Budget of the project 1989-2002: 1.839 million US $ (Constant Prices 1997).

Shipping

The abolition in 2004 of "cabotage", the EU policy allowing coastal transportation within EU countries to be undertaken exclusively by ships carrying the flag of the particular country, has already brought opportunities to the shipping industry. Further changes are expected, subsequent to recent EU legislation, to increase the competitiveness of the EU shipping fleet.

Banking and insurance

The Greek Banking system has been liberalised since 1987, enabling some foreign banks to earn their highest world-wide returns in Greece. Significant restructuring is taking place through consolidation, mergers, acquisitions and privatisation. Banks in Greece are well positioned to become regional financial centres of trade in the Balkans, the eastern Mediterranean. They will also be well placed to trade in eastern European currencies, as well as in the transfer of technical and financial skills.

Significant restructuring or consolidation will occur in the insurance sector as well. Finally, the prospect of more active management of the huge state-controlled pension funds will lead to added opportunity.

Sectors of the economy
Money and banking

Until 2000, the unit of currency in Greece was the Drachma. On 19 June 2000 in the EU Council of Santa Maria de Feira, Greece was approved to access the Euro area as its twelfth member. The other eleven members

Tourism

Greece's tourist industry is a strong force in its economy. Annual arrivals approximate the country's population. A concerted effort is being made to reposition the tourist industry as more up-market with the establishment of integrated and specialised resort areas. Luxury hotels, golf courses and theme parks are only examples of investment opportunities while more specific ones are available from the Greek National Tourist Organisation.

(Austria, Belgium, Finland, France, Germany, Ireland, Italy Luxembourg the Netherlands, Portugal and Spain) had already adopted the Euro as their national currency, in scriptural form, of course, from 1st January 1999. The irrevocable conversion rate of the Drachma vis-a-vis the Euro was set at 340,750 drachmas. The Euro began to circulate in Greece and in the other eleven countries from 1st January 2001.

The Bank of Greece.

It was established in accordance with the Geneva Protocol of 15 September 1927 and began operations on 14 May 1928. The proposal to establish a central bank was put forward by the League of Nations in order to support the Greek government's efforts at overcoming serious economic and budgetary problems. To a considerable extent the economic hardships could be traced back to the displacement of Greek populations from Asia Minor in 1922, which led them to seek refuge and to resettle on a massive scale on the Greek mainland. Indeed, in the period from 1922 to the establishment of the Bank of Greece (1927), public expenditures rose more than twofold, inflation was escalating on average, at round 20% annually, the trade deficit had increased more than tenfold while the drachma has depreciated by over 100% vis-a-vis the pound sterling.

Until the establishment of the Bank of Greece, central banking functions had been exercised largely by the major commercial bank, the National Bank of Greece, which had been founded in 1841 and had gradually acquired a monopoly over note issue. The Bank of Greece began operations in May 1928 with a staff of 500 (compared with the staff of about 3,086 in January 2002). Subsequently the Bank opened a number of branches and agencies serving mainly to supply currency locally as well as to disburse and/or to collect funds for the government accounts. On 4 April 1938 the headquarters of the Bank was moved to its present location.

The Bank of Greece is a member of the European System of Central Banks (ESCB), which comprises the European Central Bank (ECB) and the National Central Banks (NCBs) of all EU member states. From 1st January 2001 forms part of the Euro system, which consists of the ECB and NCBs of Euro area member states.

The governing body of the Bank is the General Council. The General Council is entrusted with the general operational, administrative and financial affairs of the Bank. On issues relating to monetary and exchange rate policies, authority rests with the Governor, who consults an internal committee on monetary and credit affairs. The General Council is accountable to the General Meeting of shareholders. The General Meeting has certain specific powers reserved to it. In particular, the General Meeting has the power, inter alia, to approve the Annual Report and the accounts of the Bank, to appoint members of the General Council and to propose amendments to the Statute, which, subsequently, must be ratified by Parliament as a Law. Every person registered as holding twenty-five or more shares in the share capital of the Bank is entitled to attend and to vote at the General Meeting.

The General Council consists of the Governor, the Deputy Governors and nine-executive Councillors. The Governor and the Deputy Governors are appointed by the President of the Republic of Greece, following a proposal by the General Council, which is endorsed by the Government, for renewable three-year terms. The General Meeting elects the nine Councillors for renewable three-year terms.

The Minister of Finance may nominate a non-voting Government Commissioner. He/she attends the General meeting and the Meetings of the General Council and can veto decisions if he/she considers them to be contrary to the Statute or any other laws of the State. However, the final arbiter of any such veto challenge initiated by the Government Commissioner is a Commission of three persons appointed to rule on such matters. The Government chooses one member of the Commission; the President of the Supreme Court rules on one suggested by the Bank and the third is agreed upon between the Government and the Bank or, fail in such agreement.

The Banc of Greece

In addition to its tasks in the field of monetary and exchange rate policy, the Bank:

- Holds and manages the country's official foreign reserves
- Issues banknotes, which have the status of legal tender
- Exercises the prudent supervision of credit institutions and other financial institutions
- Promotes and oversees the smooth operation of payment and securities settlement systems
- Acts as a treasurer and fiscal agent for the government.

The Statute of the Bank of Greece was amended by the decisions of the General Meeting of Shareholders of the Bank of Greece held on 22.12.1997 and 25.4.2000, (ratified by laws 2609/98 and 2832/00 respectively) to meet the requirements of the Treaty on EU. The new statute:

- Explicitly states that the Bank's primacy objective is to ensure price stability.
- Safeguards the Bank's independence and establishes its accountability to Parliament.
- Establishes a new body in the Bank of Greece, the Monetary Policy Council.
- Recognises the Bank's legal integration into the Euro system from the adoption of the single currency in Greece (1.1.2002). Within this context, the Bank of Greece contributes to the implementation of monetary policy in the Euro area, as formulated by the exchange rate policy.

Financial Reform and the Banking System

Until the mid-1980s, the banking system operated in an environment characterised by selective controls and regulations, which gradually led to allocative inefficiencies and to serious distortions in the functioning of the financial system. As a result, the Bank of Greece was not in the position to pursue an effective monetary policy, which was further constrained by the increasing public debt. A large part of the PSBR was financed either directly by the Bank of Greece or by commercial banks, which were required to invest a proportion of their funds in Government securities. In addition, the refinancing of specialised credit institutions by the Bank of Greece inflated the monetary base, thus undermining the effectiveness of monetary policy. Clearly, there was an imperative need for a modern, flexible and market-oriented financial system.

The first step towards the deregulation of the financial system was the abolition of the Currency Committee (Law 1266/1982), a government body responsible for the formulation and implementation of monetary policy, and the assignment of its tasks to the Bank of Greece. More specifically, this law enhanced the role of the Bank of Greece in the conduct of monetary policy and set a ceiling on central bank financing of the central government (10% of the annual budgeted expenditure). Since 1982, monetary authorities have taken a series of measures to simplify the interest rate structure, which was considered necessary for their gradual liberalisation. These measures enabled the Bank of Greece to proceed, in the period 1985-90, with an extensive liberalisation of interest rates and the abolition of the reserve/rebate system along with a large number of specific credit controls and regulations. Since Greece entered the Euro Zone, the Central Bank of Greece has become independent, joining the European System of Central Banks. The government can no longer use the Central Bank and monetary policy in order to stabilise the economy.

Credit institutions and specialised financial companies were also allowed to offer new products, including leasing, factoring, forfeiting and venture capital. Furthermore, firms were permitted to borrow in foreign exchange, at home and abroad, without the prior approval of the Bank of Greece. In the same period, direct investments from and to the EU member-states were liberalised, the operation of the Athens Stock Exchange was set on a new basis and new types of activities were introduced.

Foreign exchange controls concerning current transactions were lifted in 1992, while capital movements were completely liberalised in May 1994, following the removal of all remaining restrictions applying to short-term capital movements. Banks have been allowed to use new financial products, such as futures, options and swaps, for hedging against potential risks arising from foreign borrowing and foreign exchange liberalisation. Various measures were also taken to promote the modernisation of the capital market.

By removing restrictions on the operation of the financial system and the supply of financial products and services, liberalisation has resulted in important structural benefits. Above all, financial liberalisation has been linked with major improvements in the efficiency of financial institutions, although other factors, such as technological advances, may also have been important.

The number of financial institutions (excluding insurance firms) has increased rapidly over the last ten years, though more significantly so during recent years, when the process of liberalisation was accelerated and completed. More spectacular however, is the proliferation of collective investment institutions (mutual funds and investment firms) and brokerage firms. As a result, both investment and employment in the financial sector has increased at a fast pace. In two years time (2000-2001), seven new credit institutions were founded. From 1998 until 2001, many repurchases and incorporations have taken place (see table below). The recent rapid improvement in information and telecommunication systems, combined with the liberalisation of financial markets and capital movements, have allowed the introduction of new and often highly complicated financial products. They have also eliminated geographical boundaries between sectors and markets and led to market integration both domestically and internationally. At the same time, due to liberalisation of capital movements, cross-border capital mobility has also been increased. It cannot be argued that satisfactory competitive conditions have already been established in the Greek banking system. However, the financial changes of the last decade and the liberalisation of the banking sector have dramatically altered the conditions of the supervision of credit institutions in Greece and the conduct of monetary policy since the entry in the Euro zone.

Greek Credit System
(End of 2001)

	Institutions	Branches	Asset%	Grants%	Deposits%
Greek Commercial Banks	21	2.734	79,4	82,1	82,8
Foreign Banks	21	188	9,6	9,4	7,8
Associate Banks	15	56	0,4	0,7	0,4
Specialised Credit Organisations	4	156	10,6	7,8	8,9
Total	61	3.134	100,0	100,0	100,0

Source: Bank of Greece

**Repurchases and Incorporations of Banks in Greece
(1998-2001)**

Year	Buyer	Acquisition
1998	Peiraios Bank	Macedonias-Thraces Bank, Credit Lyonnnais Grece,Chios Bank
	Eurobank	Athinon Bank, Crete Bank
	Egnatia Bank	Kentrikis Ellados Bank
	National Bank	EKTE
1999	Peiraios Bank	Nat. Westminister (Greek network)
	Alpha Pisteos	Ionian Bank
	Telesis Stockholders	Doriki Bank
	Eurobank	Ergasias Bank
2001	Eurobank-Ergasias	Telesis Investment Bank
	Marfin AEPEY	Peiraios Prime
	Peiraios Bank	ETBA

Source: Bank of Greece

With regard to public and private banks in Greece, it appears that the latter seem to be increasing their profits at a faster rate than the former. Preliminary results of the annual industry survey of the economic and business research company ICAP, indicated that 1995 was a poor year for public-sector banks. Deposits in all 19 commercial banks grew by 14.1% and loans by 28.3%, but net profits rose by just 1.7% to 183.6 billion drachmas, compared with 180.5 billion in 1994. The large state-controlled banks National and Commercial each displayed a steep downturn in profitability. In contrast, Alpha Credit and Eurobank-Ergasias, both private-sector banks, displayed strong gains and moved into first and third place respectively in the profitability league table. In 2000, the National and the Commercial moved into the first and second place, respectively (see table below).

The state banks are heavily overstaffed and unproductive, as demonstrated by the figures on profitability per employee. A large share of non-performing debts also adversely affects state bank profitability. The National took a step towards rehabilitation by writing off 118 billion drachmas of such debts at the beginning of 1997.

Agriculture

Primary sector activities and their share in the GDP have always been important for the Greek economy. In 1993, 11.2% of Greek GDP consisted of primary-sector activities: agriculture, fisheries and forestry. This compares with only 2.4% for the EU as a whole! Greek agriculture is heavily constrained by topography. The mountainous terrain means that only 26.5% of the land is cultivated. Of this, 65.7% is devoted to arable farming and 26.8% to orchards (citrus fruits, peaches, apricots, apples, pears, cherries and figs), nuts (walnuts, almonds and pistachios) and olives. Despite the country's reputation for its raisins and currants, and increasingly, for its wines, only 4% of the land is given to vineyards. Vegetable production uses 3.4% of the land. Of the cultivated land in Greece, 38% is irrigated. Greece's main industrial crops are tobacco and cotton.

For many years, the state used to provide cheap fertilisers to the farm community but in 1992 the EU finally forced it to stop. The extra cost of this, plus the soaring cost of credit and the disruption of exports caused by the civil war in Yugoslavia, meant that in the early 1990s many farm co-operatives fell into arrears on loans and started to accumulate penalty charges. However the Agricultural Bank in 1994 was permitted to reschedule 220 billion drachmas in loans over a period of 10-15 years.

Seven Most Profitable Greek Commercial banks in 2000 (In thousand Drachmas)		
	Gross Profit	**Net Income**
National	622,518,119	298,014,472
Alpha Credit	360,505,809	115,018,752
Commercial	291,671,306	115,049,909
Eurobank-Ergasias	280,640,000	107,140,000
Agricultural	249,660,503	83,948,175
Piraeus	104,698,716	63,692,521
General	42,074,181	1,882,642

Notes: Investment and mortgage banks are not included. The Agricultural bank is included because its charter has been amended to define it as a universal bank, even though it is wholly owned by the Greek state and continues to have an administrative role as the conduit for Common Agricultural Policy subsidies and the monitoring of the co-operative movement.

Source: Bank of Greece

**Repurchases and Incorporations of Banks in Greece
(1998-2001)**

	1999	2000	2001*	% Change 2000/01
Wheat durum	1,400	1,450	1,390	-4.1
Wheat soft	622	408	380	-6.8
Maize	2,070	1,850	1,657	-10.4
Barley	320	258	195	-24.4
Tobacco	126	122	124	+1.4
Cotton	1,320	1,250	1,140	-8.8
Rice	167	169	147	-13.0
Sugar beets	2,160	3,116	2,625	-15.7
Oats	114	72	78	+7.7
Edible pulses	30	35	33	-5.7
Sunflower	33	20	19	-6.0
Fodder plants	1,260	1,500	1,400	-6.6
Fruit & Vegetables (basic crops)	3,604	3,100	3,200	+3.3
MEAT PRODUCTION				
	490,200	491,490	484,311	-1.5
Beef	66,605	60,930	61,634	+1.1
Sheep	80,977	79,569	78,699	-1.1
Goat	44,814	43,700	42,361	-3.2
Pork	139,844	138,963	135,164	-2.8
Poultry	153,807	163,787	161,953	-1.1
Rabbit	4,453	4,541	4,500	-0.9
Cow's	776,800	789,000	776,900	-1.6
Ewe's	653,800	667,300	678,300	+1.7
Goat's	434,800	490,300	460,200	-6.5
Eggs	117,840	121,800	130,718	+7.3
MILK PRODUCTION				
	1,865,400	1,946,100	1,915,400	-1.6

* Estimates, Source: Ministry of Agriculture

According to the provisional estimates of the National Statistical Service of Greece, agricultural output per unit of labour increased by 1.2% at nominal prices in 2001, relative to the previous year. In 2001, it is estimated that total financial aid to Greek agriculture, from national and Community resources, totalled 5,565.12 million Euros, which marks an increase of 10.2% over 2000.

A sum of 2,569.15 million Euros or 46.15% of the total aid comes from the Community resources and specifically the Guarantee Section of the European Agricultural Guidance and Guarantee Fund, while the amount of 2,995.97 Euros or 53.85% of total aid comes from national resources. During 2001 and within the framework of the 3rd Community Support Framework, the implementation of the Operational Programmes began for the new programming period 2000-2006 relating to agriculture. Implementation commenced of the operational programme "Agricultural Development and Rural Restructuring" with a total budget of 3 billion Euros. This programme is expected to provide strong impetus to investments in agricultural holdings as well as the processing and trading of farm products, while helping to improve the age composition of the agricultural population. Implementation of "The Programming Document for Agricultural Development and Rural Restructuring 2000-2006", has also begun, with a total cost of 2.7 billion Euros. It is being used to finance early retirement, compensation, allowances, agro-environmental measures and the afforestation of farmland.

On 1 July 1995, the implementation of the GATT accord called for a six-year period of gradual reductions in import duties and subsidies. It also called for reductions in the regulations which, in the context of the reformed Common Agricultural Policy (CAP) then in force,

governed the markets for products such as cotton, fruit, vegetables and rice. These products are very important to Greece and such measures led to an intensification of international competitive pressures on Greek agricultural production. It is thus imperative to exploit Greece's potential (especially by promoting dynamic Mediterranean products) and establish flexible forms of collaboration among producers, manufacturers and exporters, in order to penetrate international markets with products of higher value added and, therefore, increase agricultural income.

Fishing. Although it contributes only a small amount to GDP - 0.36% for 1997, fishing is important to the Greek economy because promotes the social and economical coherence of large Greek regions such as the islands of the Aegean and the Ionian Sea. 40.000 people are employed in the fishing sector.

The Greek fishing fleet is becoming smaller. Nevertheless, in 1997 Greece still remained the first country in the EU with regard to the size of its fishing fleet. Greeks owned 20,243 fishing-boats at that time. The catch is also decreasing: 191,000 tons in 1994 compared with 152,9 tons three years later and 116 tons in 1999.

Greek producers are European leaders in marine fish farming, with 54% of total production in 1994 (22,300 tons) and sales in 1994 with a value of 25 billion Dr. The principal species farmed are sea bass and sea bream. From 1994

and on, marine fish farming has increased its productivity. In 1999, production reached 72,650 tons. There are about a dozen producers based in the islands, in the northern Aegean and in the lagoon at Messolonghi near the western mouth of the Gulf of Corinth. A series of mergers and acquisitions has resulted in the formation of Europe's two largest marine fish-farming groups, Nereus and Selonda.

Industry

Industry constitutes significantly to the country's economic base, and is made up of a large number of small and medium-size enterprises, characterised by a high degree of flexibility and initiative. Major branches include food and beverages, clothing and textiles, shoes, chemicals and plastics, oil and coal products, glass products and cement. The last few years have witnessed the appearance of dynamic businesses, establishing a new environment for the development of Greek industry. Through a systematic process of adaptation, a major proportion of Greek industry has been modernised, strengthening its competitive base, improving its profits and making it better able to compete.

In 1998, Greek industry demonstrated the highest growth rate among

Fish catch
('000 tons unless otherwise indicated)

	1993	1997	1998	1999
Overseas	14.7	5.1	5.9	6.0
Greek waters:				
Open seas	68.1	76.3	59.1	60.0
Inshore	87.1	71.5	47.9	50.0
Total	169.9	152.9	112.9	116.0

Source: NSSG, Sea Fishery Survey

the EU countries. Production rose for the 5th year in a row by 3.2% reaching the highest level since 1988. This was achieved mainly due to the revaluation of the Drachma and its entry in the European Exchange Rate Mechanism. The Greek industrial sector includes 1,440 industries. In 1998 sales increased by 7.9% exceeding 1 billion drachmas and gross profits that increased on an annual basis by more than 16.5%.

The manufacturing sector accounts for 60% of total Greek exports. This ratio represents the great importance of the sector's development for achieving higher economic growth rates in the near future. Of course, the Greek manufacturing sector is small by European standards, accounting for less than 15% of GDP in 1994 compared with 21.2% for the EU as a whole. Although it has been declining for the last number of years, it still makes a vital contribution to Greek exports. Small family businesses make up majority of manufacturing firms. Most of them employ fewer than

ten people. It is estimated that income from secondary production increased considerably in 1995, while it had remained virtually unchanged in 1994. This development was due to a substantial rise in public construction activity; an increase in manufacturing output at a faster pace than in 1994; and the acceleration of the already high growth rate of electricity and gas production. On the other hand, mining and quarrying output and private construction activity have been declining. The expansion of manufacturing production was due to a rise in domestic investment demand and increased foreign demand, owing to favourable international conditions, which enabled industrial firms to step up their exports.

The largest and generally most profitable sectors produce consumer goods: textiles, shoes, foodstuffs, beverages and tobacco. They have the advantage of local raw materials and, until the 1980s, cheap labour. In the textiles sector, however, it is now cheaper to import some basic goods, such as underwear, from the Far East than it is to manufacture them in Greece. Furthermore, increased economic integration with Europe during the 1980s has led to the decline of many of the low-technology import-substitution industries founded in the 1950s and 1960s. Manufacturers are being forced to diversify into products with higher added value, such as fashion garments, to compensate for higher wage costs. Some Greek firms, particularly in the garment sector, now subcontract their labour intensive processes to the Balkan countries. However many industries have shut down because they could not cope with the international competition. This has resulted in higher unemployment.

After a disastrous period in the early 1980s, when corporate margins were destroyed by high inflation and administratively fixed prices, industry gradually turned to profitability after the first stabilisation programme of 1986-1987. Legislation was passed in 1996 for the creation of the Hellenic Centre of Investments (ELKE), a "one-stop shop" to help foreign investors through the bureaucratic maze. It is actually a private company reporting to the Ministry of the National Economy and allocates individual account executives to potential investors to facilitate the latter's efforts to obtain licences and approvals.

Recent developments point to the conclusion that Greek industry is going

Industrial Production Indices
(1993=100)

	1998	1999	2000	2001
GENERAL INDEX	112.2	115.4	124.3	125.4
INDICES BY SECTOR				
Food and Drinks	114.4	115.3	119.4	122.8
Tobacco	101.5	109.3	107.7	111.3
Textiles	78.6	77.6	84.5	80.8
Clothing	71.2	68.2	67.0	63.7
Wood and Cork	61.9	61.5	100.4	101.8
Paper and products from paper	135.6	137.1	116.4	110.9
Printing-Publishing	91.0	100.6	112.7	114.5
Leather and Footwear	63.2	66.6	67.2	65.8
Rubber articles and plastics	137.0	147.9	148.7	154.3
Chemicals	122.2	126.8	129.0	138.0
Petroleum and coal products	161.9	137.2	162.3	160.7
Non metallic minerals	112.9	113.2	115.5	118.1
Basic metallurgy	113.6	122.4	137.7	147.8
Metal products	102.6	119.8	121.3	123.2
Machines and apparatus	137.0	128.6	152.1	147.4
Electrical machinery and appliances	104.3	108.4	122.2	123.0
Transport equipment	77.5	73.2	69.2	69.5
Furniture-Other industries	108.2	115.9	125.1	121.4

Source: National Statistical Service of Greece

through a painful reorganisation phase, which will result in improved performance. The reorganisation process has been accompanied by the materialisation of ambitious investment plans, which has transformed many industrial groups to modernised and highly comparative enterprises.

The craft sector

The Greek - non-legally defined - craft and small-medium enterprise sector includes handicraft, artistic small industry, and all micro business in trade and services.

Greek small to medium enterprises (SMEs) in 1995 accounted for 746,860 enterprises, employing 1.7 million, with a turnover of 357 billion Euro. The share of SMEs in total employment was 86.5%. The Micro enterprise share in total employment was 58%. Trade and Crafts are the sectors of activity employing most Greeks (48.7% in 1995 of the total labour force) followed by industry and energy (19.4%) and construction (18.9%).

Craft and micro enterprises are commonly accepted as being low technology, using firms dependent on traditional work methods with a labour force of up to 10 employees. The majority of these firms are owned and operated by sole proprietors who depend on the assistance of family members, usually their spouse in order to deal with their daily responsibility.

The organisation and infrastructure of the Crafts Trade.

Recently all enterprises except for some services had to register with the Chamber of Commerce and Industry. A substantial number of enterprises in the so-called cottage sector are in fact not registered: this sector consists mostly of small subcontractor craft and handicraft enterprises.

Most craft enterprises are not organised in a special craft, but in sector specific SME organisations. In the handicraft sector, organisation by type of activity is more common, but only regionally. Most of them are organised in co-operatives on both sectoral and regional basis. The majority of all professional associations are member of the GSEBEE: the General Confederation of SMEs, Traders and Craftsmen of Greece. GSEBEE is one of the three social partners of Greek government, representing the interests of SME and craft in economic and social policy issues.

In 1987, handicraft co-operatives established PESKAHIVO, the Panhellenic Federation of Artistic Handicraft and Craft Co-operatives and Home-craft. PESKAHIVO objectives are: promotion of handicraft products and the provision of services to members such as technical assistance, training and consultancy.

Enterprises and Employment in the Craft Sector in Greece 1988			
	Enterprises	**Employment**	**Average enterprise size**
Manufacturing craft	133,000	287,000	2.2
Trade	167,000	275,000	1.6
Service	20,000	28,000	1.4
Total	320,000	590,000	1.8

Other facilities dedicated to the support of handicrafts are Handicraft Centres and Sectoral Institutes, established by EOMMEX, the Greek Organization for SMEs and Handicraft. The Handicraft Centres will offer technical assistance, training and consultancy, marketing and promotion services, and quality testing. There are sectoral institutes for leather, clothing fur, gold and silver, marble, furniture and wooden products. EOMMEX is a state organisation for the implementation of SME policy measures, including handicraft.

Balance of payments and foreign trade

Greece has historically been an active trading nation. However, it has a large trade and balance of payments deficit. The trade deficit in 2001 was 608 million Euros less than in 2000, amounting to 16.3% of the GDP. The balance of payments on current account, was also 303 million Euros less in 2001 than in 2000. As percentage of the GDP, it declined 6.2% in 2001. Its main exports are food (fresh and processed), textiles (yarns, fabrics and ready-made clothing), chemicals, semi-processed mineral products, cement and refined oil products. It imports a large proportion of energy, some food (largely protein products), virtually all its transport equipment and much of its machinery and electrical goods.

Some three-fifths of Greek trade is with other EU members. Markets were developed in a period when Greece was a low-wage economy. Today its products face stiff competition from countries where the labour is cheap enough to keep prices low even after payment of the common external tariff. Greek firms therefore have to reorient production towards goods of higher quality and higher added value. Furthermore, in the 30 years up to 1994, Greek textiles benefited from the bilateral quota and tariff arrangements of the Multi-Fibre Arrangement under the General Agreement on Tariffs and Trades (GATT). However, the inauguration of the World Trade Organisation (WTO) has meant that this will be gradually phased out over the decade 1995 - 2005.

The trade deficit began to grow sharply after Greece's entry into the common market in 1981. It has been calculated that, before then, Greek industrial products were subject to 45% effective protection - including tariffs, quotas and other restrictive measures. It is only in the 1990s that Greek traders began to operate in a fully free market without subsidies, foreign exchange controls or restrictions on capital movements. Nowadays the trade deficit decreases steadily every year. In 2000, the trade deficit accounted for 17.8% of the GDP and in 2001 16.3% of the GDP.

Greek traders have been quick to capitalise on the opening up of new markets in former communist countries and have made inroads into the countries of the Balkans and the Black Sea region. The government has supported the effort by providing, through state-controlled banks, rolling commercial credit to countries such as Ukraine, Romania, Armenia, Georgia, Albania, Bulgaria, Moldova, Azerbaijan and Russia. Greek exports to the Balkan countries are increasing dramatically. Exports to former Soviet countries are increasing also but at slower rates. As a result Greek exports to the OECD countries and the EU have declined from 51.5% in 2000 to 49.1% in 2001 and from 86.1% to 82.4% respectively.

In the mid-1980s the government created the Export Credit Insurance Organisation (OAEP). OAEP policies cover risks for business done with foreign governments or public-sector agencies only. Coverage for commercial risk must be obtained through banks or insurance companies. Since 1995 a number of banks have begun to provide such services. Legislation to permit factoring was first introduced in 1988. However, it was not until 1995 that four independent factoring companies were actually established.

Energy

Nowadays, energy has become an economic policy domain, assuming an increasing role in development. Growth rates in the Asian and Southeast European countries demand larger and larger quantities of electricity and raw materials. On the other hand, the exploitation of the new petroleum and natural gas deposits in the countries of the former Soviet Union has created a new scenario on the world energy map, over which many countries "are battling" to obtain a strategic position.

Greece, due to its geographical position and its proximity to countries that do not possess the necessary infrastructure on the energy sector, has recently started to systematise its efforts to become the energy crossroad of the entire region. The normal functioning of its internal market and its existing infrastructure in the elaboration of electricity and petroleum, make Greece the only player in the region capable of organising the potential regional energy networks and co-operation among the countries of the Balkans, Black Sea and Central Asia.

A partial liberalisation of the electricity market took place in Greece (and in all the other EU member-states) in 2001 and the liberalisation of the natural gas market is anticipated. Thus conditions were laid down for co-operation among the Greek public and private sectors, which would allow the expansion of Greek entrepreneurial activities outside Greek borders. At present, Greece is the only EU country in the Balkans. It is thus in a good position to develop modern technologies and modernise current infrastructure in order to play a leading role in the works and the EU energy development projects (Trans-European

Networks) aimed at linking the East to the West and the European North to the South.

Transport

Greece is the only member of the EU that does not share a border with any other member state; yet two-thirds of all its trade is with the EU. The poor quality of its transport and communications network is a contributing factor in its persistent trade deficit. To improve the situation, more than one-quarter of all the expenditure under the Second Community Support Framework was to be spent on transport infrastructure. The Third Community Support Framework also provides substantial funds for the very same reason (see in the related chapter).

Rail. The state-owned railway, Hellenic Railways Organisation (OSE), operates 2,500 km of track. The rolling stock is old, its passenger facilities are poor and freight carriage is slow. However, investment in the system has been earmarked by the EU programme of the Trans European Networks (TENs), and a 642 billion drachmas (2.7 billion Euros) programme of investments had been drawn up for implementation by the end of the century, funded partly from domestic resources. The effort to modernise the Hellenic Railways will continue during the 2000-2006 period. The programmes under the 3rd CSF have a budget of 90,000,361 Euros.

Furthermore, work has been completed on the two new metro lines in Athens, which connect with the 130-

year-old line and are estimated to expand capacity by a further 140 million passengers a year (the old line carried an estimated 110 million passengers a year). The 705 billion-drachma extension opened to the public in January 2000. Launched in 1999, the 18-km extension consists of two new lines cutting through the city centre which meet beneath the Syntagma Square. The metro will

The Athens Metro

expand further over the next seven years to serve more residential districts. Funding from the EU 3rd CSF has been requested to extend the two new lines to low income districts in western Athens. The northern line will also be extended as far as the Stavros crossing, where it will connect with a light railway to the new international airport.

Roads. There are approximately 9,255 km of highways in Greece and some 29,350-km of provincial roads. Construction of two new international-standard, six-lane motorways with bypasses around major conurbations is under way. Funding for these projects was provided in part by the EU CSF II

The Egnatia motorway

and the TENs programme. The 3ʳᵈ CSF continues the partial funding for the completion of the construction (for details about the Patra-Athens-Thessaloniki motorway, the Egnatia road, the Elefsina-Spata highway etc. see in the relative chapter).

Ports and ferries. Greece has 444 ports, of which 123 have some passenger or freight traffic. In 1993, there were 36.6 million passenger movements, 2.5 million international and 34.1 million domestic. Although the Single Market Act technically opened up Greek passenger-ferry services to foreign competition, Greece managed to negotiate derogations, which prevent the entry of foreign competitors until the end of 2003. However many routes, especially in the Adriatic, are already fiercely competitive. In any case, most Greek ports are purely commercial.

The New Athens (Eleftherios Venizelos) Airport

Olympic Airways, the state-owned airline, has a fleet of 60 aircraft. Half of these are short-haul craft used by its domestic subsidiary Olympic Aviation. By 1993, the loss-incurring airline had accumulated debts totalling 521 billion Dr. The Greek government and the European Commission agreed on a restructuring plan whereby the state would write off 427 billion drachmas in accumulated debt and inject 54 billion drachmas in capital into the airline in three doses. In exchange, the airline would freeze aircraft purchases for three years, cut operating expenses by 30% within two years and freeze staff pay and benefits until the airline once again became profitable. As a result, the airline returned to profitability in 1995.

However, the liberalisation of the European passenger air transport market has meant greater competition from foreign, especially German, carriers. This

increased further after 1997 when certain Greek derogations from European competition policy began to expire. Olympic Airways has had to compete not only with foreign carriers but also with private national carriers that entered the scene dynamically. Thus further measures have to be taken in order for the airline to survive on the one hand and on the other for it to begin acting as an important player in the international competition map.

Pireus Port, the passenger terminal

Air. Greece has 39 airports capable of receiving international flights, the largest number of any country in Europe. In 1995, there were a total of 13.02 million passenger arrivals and 13.06 million departures. A total of 149,803 tons of freight was handled. Two-thirds of these airports are on the islands and in most instances also serve as military bases. Athens' Hellinikon airport handled until recently the largest volume of traffic. In 2001, a state-of-the-art airport has been delivered in terms of technology and equipment, focused on safety, user-friendliness and service excellence. Europe's new southern gateway to the world, the new Athens International Airport in Spata is the biggest infrastructure project in Greece. The capacity of the new airport is up to 16 million passengers annually during the first phase. It is designed for 220,000 tonnes cargo traffic a year. This airport can handle 65 landings and take-offs per hour or 600 per day.

Tourism

Tourism may have a long historical background as a social phenomenon in Greece, but only after the Second World War did it start to become significant as an organised economic activity. Greece is famous world-wide for its sun, clean beaches, beautiful islands in the Aegean sea, picturesque villages on the mainland and the hospitality *("philoxenia")* of its people. Among tertiary sector activities, tourism is one of the most important sectors of the Greek economy,

Tourism

	1991	1992	1993	1994	1995
Gross receipts* ($m)	2,567	3,255	3,345	3,905	4,106
Foreign exchange indent receipts per tourist ($)	320	349	345	346	383
Tourist arrivals					
Cruise passengers ('000)	235	425	500	589	582
Other tourists ('000)	8,036	9,331	9,413	11,302	10,712

*Excluding cruise passengers
Source: Greek National Tourism Organisation

accounting for about 20% of total invisible earnings.

Greek tourism, after displaying an increasing trend for many years, began in the middle of the last decade to signs of fatigue. Over 11 million people visited Greece during 1994, with slightly fewer in 1995. 2001 found Greece in 15th place in the world classification of tourist entries, receiving over 14 million tourists. The majority (92.25%) come from Europe. The accommodation capacity of the 8,209 hotels is 601,034 beds (1/2002). Some 28,000 secondary accommodation establishments provide another 450,000 beds. There are also 351 camping sites with 30,643 pitches and 949 bungalows.

The tourist industry provides jobs for more than 350,000 people (about 10% of the employed labour force, 6.1% direct employment and 3.9% indirect) and in 2001, the tourism contribution to the GDP is estimated at up to 8%. The tourism receipts in 2001 were

9.121 million USD. Even these figures fail to capture other earnings such as credit-card sales, cruise-ticket expenditures and purchases of drachmas by tourists from banks in their own coun-

Arrivals of Tourists Nationality %

Year	Europe	Asia	Africa	America	Oceania	Others
1960	53.0	5.7	1.9	22.4	1.0	1.0
1965	57.9	4.3	1.7	20.7	1.5	0.2
1970	52.4	4.5	2.5	24.5	2.1	0.1
1975	64.0	3.7	1.7	17.5	1.8	0.1
1980	72.8	5.7	2.0	7.8	2.5	0.2
1985	76.7	4.2	1.6	8.8	2.0	0.1
1990	85.8	3.0	0.7	4.1	1.2	0.4
1995	87.8	2.7	0.5	3.0	0.6	0.0

Source: National Statistical Service of Greece

tries, which are estimated to increase present earnings to over $7 billion.

Tourist earnings per head nearly trebled during the 1970s, but a rush to provide more beds led to over-capacity in the 1980s. Greece gained a reputation as a last minute, cut-price destination and receipts fell from $361 per head in 1980 to $217 per head in 1985. Since then, successive governments have pursued a policy of attracting fewer, higher-spending tourists and, to this end, limited investments have provided facilities such as conference centres, casinos and winter sports facilities in an effort to spread arrivals more evenly throughout the year. However, the figures up to 1995 demonstrate that spending per head has not kept pace with inflation.

These disappointing figures could be a result of the fact that in past years the state has spent less than 2% of its investment budget on tourism, museums and monuments and the spending of the Ministry of Tourism amounted to less than 0.1 % of total budget spending. Furthermore, tourism development had been allocated just 517.7 m Ecu or 1.7 % of the funds to be invested under the Second Community Support Framework scheme. Nevertheless, under the 3rd Community Support Framework 139,759,784 Euros will be invested in tourism. The present government has introduced investment incentives designed to create an Integrated Tourism Development Area, which will group together luxury hotels with other amenities such as golf courses, marinas, winter-sports centres, health spas and convention centres.

Other objectives include the development of alternative forms of tourism (marine tourism, mountain tourism, eco-tourism, cultural and health tourism), the creation of tourist supply in less developed areas, a decrease of seasonality in tourist demand and the protection and

Arrivals of Foreign Tourists at Frontiers.

Region	1998	1999	2000	2001	Variation% 2001/2002
EU	7,663,483	8,789,371	9,219,271	9,484,582	2.88
Total Europe	10,174,303	11,320,013	12,080,211	13,032,334	7.88
Total Asia	358,574	434,276	586,569	606,640	3.42
Total Africa	38,738	48,040	60,955	57,891	-5.03
Total America	291,507	305,261	300,213	266,723	-11.16
Total Oceania	52,924	56,498	67,597	69,790	3.24
Total of Foreign Tourists	18,579,529	20,953,459	13,095,545	14,033,378	7.16
Cruises			471,908	621,357	31.67
Grand total			13,567,453	14,654,735	8.01

Source: Greek National Tourism Organization

promotion of important elements of the natural and cultural environment.

Shipping

Hellenic shipping is a dynamic development factor in the National economy and an effective world representative of Greece. Simple reference to the fact that today Greece owns the largest international merchant fleet may not suffice to make one realise the important role that Hellenic Merchant Shipping plays today. Hellenic Shipping today (including all Hellenic owned ships under foreign flags) is the world leader with a fleet of 3,800 ships of all types (over 1000 gross tons) totalling 7,156,763 gross tons, which constitutes 16% of world capacity. On the other hand, Hellenic flagged ships make up only 8% of world tonnage, which places Greece in the third among the leading shipping countries world-wide.

The Hellenic merchant fleet, which includes all types of freighters (for special cargoes, tankers etc.), together with vessels for other purposes (cruise ships, coastal craft, ferry boats etc.) currently numbers 2,100 vessels with a total capacity of 24.5 million gross tons.

Thus, Greece, with its merchant fleet, ranks first among European Union states, owning about 50% of total Union fleet. Furthermore, over 50,000 seamen are employed in the field of merchant shipping, which represent about 3% of the total manpower and income to 5% of Greek families.

Merchant shipping has steadily supported the Greek economy over the years. In 1995 alone, shipping operations made it possible for Greece to import 2.191 billion US dollars, offering a significant contribution to the National Balance of Payments. At this point, it should be noted that maritime foreign exchange is a "net" exchange created at no cost to the economy (as in the case of the tourist foreign exchange flow). This is due to the fact that the vast majority of Greek ships is engaged in cross-trade activities between third countries and thus affected by world economy and Shipping Market conditions.

Greece as a traditional maritime country, surrounded by the sea, with thousands of islands, requires a sufficient and appropriate cabotage service. The development of domestic and foreign

trade as well as tourism, among other things, depends upon this. It is therefore easy to realise the critical contribution of Hellenic Merchant Shipping to these important fields of the economy. Coastal Passenger ships and car ferries link the mainland with the islands and provide services necessary to the life and development of the islands.

Greece as a European Union Member-State submits to competent international organisations proposals aimed at increasing competitiveness of Community shipping relative that of third countries, as well as stamping out protectionist measures whenever and in whatever form they are applied. The decisive role of shipping in the world economy and trade is well known for three particular reasons:

• it offers lower transport cost relative to other means

• it is an indispensable means of

World Ranking of Merchant fleets

Shipping	Total in million tons DW	National flag	Foreign flags
Greece	120	50	70
Japan	86	23	63
USA	50	13	35
Norway	48	28	19
China	35	23	12
Hong-Kong	31	7	24
UK	22	5	17
S. Korea	21	10	11
Russia	18	14	4
Germany	17	6	11
Taiwan	14	6.5	7.5
Sweden	13	2	11

Source: UNCTAD

transport for raw materials necessary to world industry
 • it is a contributing factor in the

establishment of smooth and stable international relations between countries involved in shipping, which are necessary for the growth of the economy.

The fact that sea transport presents each year constant and significant growth is not accidental. In particular: 90% of European trade with the rest of the world is carried out by sea, 35% of internal European trade is likewise carried out and 60% of crude oil transported world-wide uses tankers.

Fairs and exhibitions

The official Hellenic Organisation of International Trade Fairs, Exhibitions, Festivals and Congresses is *HELEXPO,* an organisation with a successful background of more than 60 years in the organising of fairs and exhibitions. Every year, HELEXPO opens its gates to Greek and foreign companies in September at Thessaloniki for the Thessaloniki International Trade Fair.

The HELEXPO, in Thessaloniki

HELLENIC MERCHANT SHIPPING : A LEADING SECTOR AT INTERNATIONAL AND EUROPEAN LEVEL

By G. Samiotis, G.P. Vlachos and B.S. Tselentis

Introduction

The fact that Greece today is a worldwide leading power in merchant shipping, is neither by chance nor coincidental. The very existence and evolution of Greece as a nation, has been throughout its history, strongly associated and dependent upon activities in the marine environment. It is well known that in ancient times, the creation and maintenance of naval and merchant fleets, in addition to developments in naval architecture and institutions (e.g. the sea law of Rhodes in the 9th century BC),

rendered Greece a dominant maritime power in the Mediterranean. The significant role that shipping played during the 1821 uprising of the Greek nation against the Ottoman Empire and the creation of the contemporary Greek state, have been pointed out by many historians and scholars.

1. The status and role of Greece in the international maritime market

The 21st century still finds the Greek owned merchant fleet in the top posi-

Piraeus Port, the container terminal

tion, as well as the national flag maintaining one of the highest places globally, as far as tonnage is concerned. The Hellenic owned fleet today, amounts to over 3,400 ships and its transporting capability reaches 139,000,000 DWT. In terms of investment it corresponds to about 40 billion US $ and meets 16.3% of world transportation needs.

The Greek owned commercial fleet has some particular characteristics that differentiate it from fleets of other traditional maritime countries.

These characteristics include its specialisation and spatial activities, its financial sources, etc. In particular, Hellenic shipping consists of ships that are mainly specialised in bulk transportation of dry and liquid cargo (crude oil and its products, coal, grain, minerals, etc.), as well as in the transportation of traditional general cargoes. These ships account for approximately 95% of the Hellenic owned fleet, while the remaining 5% include cruisers, commercial and coastal ships.

As a leading world power in maritime transportation, Greek-owned shipping operates on a world scale covering the transportation needs of countries well beyond the Greek state.

Indeed, this fleet serves the trade needs of many countries throughout the world. In addition, a series of activities associated with Greek owned shipping take place abroad (e.g. shipbuilding credits, financing, chartering, marine insurance, shipbuilding, repairs, mainte-nance, conversions, ship scrapping etc.).

Furthermore, even nowadays, the management of Hellenic owned shipping is undertaken within the administrative framework of foreign countries such as the City of London in Great Britain, contributing to the development of these important business centres.

It is thus obvious that Greek shipping associates its leading role and its development globally, to the very basics of world trade, such as: the international charter market, the international stock market, and other relevant economic activities. Greek-owned shipping has survived and developed thanks to the flexibility, knowledge and adaptability of Greek ship operators and ship owners, in relation to a series of international variables that affect the industry and influence business decisions with regard to a number of choices (flag, specialisation, markets, etc.).

2. Hellenic shipping and the European Union

The Hellenic maritime industry is influenced both positively and negatively by developments in the European Union (EU), since Greece has been a full member of the Union from the early 1980s.

The EU, only recently (in mid 1980s) formed and modulated a discreet European policy on shipping. Within this framework of discussions (the Council of Merchant Marine Ministers), Greece has played a decisive role, since, in addition to its leading influence on global

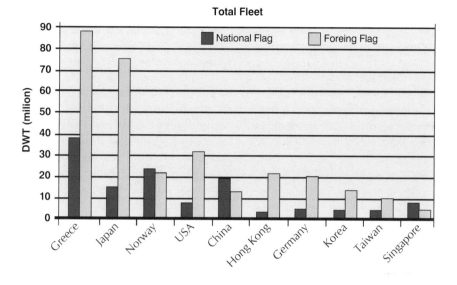

sea transport, it is also the dominant maritime power in the EU, owning 50% of the total EU commercial fleet.

This leading role, in combination with the fact that 90% of all foreign trade and 30% of intra European trade is undertaken at sea, is further strengthened, allowing Greece to play an active role in shipping centres and forums where policy and other issues relevant to the industry are discussed. Greece, as an active member of the EU, especially in matters of commercial shipping, has often joined forces with other countries supporting a Community shipping industry based on fair and free competition without governmental interventions, that will ensure the safety and protection of the marine environment. It is unfortunate that often these endeavours

are hindered by mishaps that threaten the competitiveness of EU shipping.

This last point appears to be the main reason why the EU has been so unsuccessful in developing and applying effective and efficient policy decisions, concerning important shipping matters, even though Greece responded positively to all these efforts. A prominent case is the stalemate reached during the negotiations for establishing the European Registry called EUROS.

These developments seem to have increased the trend towards establishing international and parallel registries by countries of the EU, as a separatist way of maintaining their country's competitiveness in the maritime sector. It must be pointed out that Greece has not moved along a similar legal and procedural line, despite the serious problems, of competitiveness and losses from its national registry, it is facing.

Despite the fact that the EU has not as yet adopted a discernible and strong maritime policy, many positive steps have, in general, been taken, especially concerning the impact of shipping on the marine environment and the safety of navigation.

Navigation safety and the European marine environment have been subject to serious incidents, due to the lack and/or the deficiency of protection and safety institutions (e.g. Torrey Canyon 1967, Amoco Cadiz 1978, Haven 1991, Aegean Sea 1992, Braer 1993, Estonia 1994, Sea Empress 1996, Erika 1999, and Prestige 2002).

Greece, as a member-state of international institutions, has supported all attempts aimed at the protection of the marine environment (IMO, UNEP, etc.), as well as at the development of a modern national institutional framework.

Greece and Greek shipping have contributed to international attempts concerned with the development and adoption of relevant measures and have always been prompt in harmonising and applying this legislation within its national boundaries.

Another important issue at the top of the agenda for Greece and the EU over the last years, has been the issue of lifting the protectionism of sea transportation within territorial waters of member states, known as cabotage. This

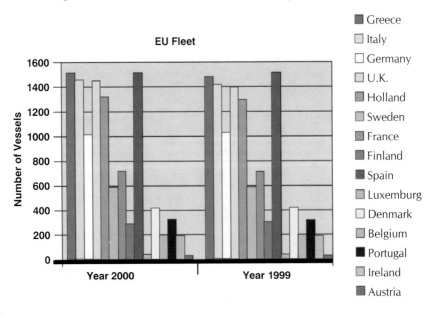

has been an extremely important as well as a sensitive issue for a county like Greece, where coastal shipping has developed to serve over 3,500 small and larger islands (about 19% of mainland Greece), on which about 14% of the total population resides. Greece also possesses one of the largest shorelines in the world, over 15,000-km in length. It is clear that within this context, Hellenic coastal shipping functions as a critical communication and trade link, between the mainland and insular areas. Furthermore, it provides a basic tool for the development and implementation of legal, social and regional strategies and policies of the state, for this particular island environment.

One of the most important problems still facing the Greek State is the lack of business interest within a totally liberalised internal transport market, after the lifting of cabotage, in providing services to a number of small islands with few inhabitants, especially during the winter period. Problems concerning this liberalisation, however were confronted in a positive manner by Greece (by both the public and the private sector) as well as the EU, within the newly negotiated adaptation period (until 2004) that was agreed upon after lengthy but constructive discussions.

3. Contribution to national economic and social development

The leading position of the Hellenic-owned commercial fleet obviously plays an important role in the development of a country with a small population and territory, such as Greece.

The positive impact of the Greek shipping industry on the Hellenic economy and on state development is based mainly on the foreign currency entering the country. This is attributable to the fact that this transport sector has an autonomous development based on its globalised activities. It is interesting to note that Greek ship operators and owners were active in 43 different national registries, in the year 2001.

It is true that transport services, shipbuilding and repair, vessel purchase transactions, scraping, etc., associated with Hellenic owned shipping, take place in countries other than Greece. In these countries large amounts of capital are deposited, while the Greek State is not affected negatively by economic, social and environmental costs that are associated with these activities.

Part of the positive impact arising from shipping, is the important contribution of imported foreign currency. It contribute to the National Balance of Payments, as well as the vivification of the national economy and local communities (recipients of this foreign currency), the creation of employment at sea and on land, the development of activities associated with the industry and associated sectors, the national economy etc.

The amounts of foreign currency from shipping, comprised of amounts transferred by ship owners and seamen, demonstrate a high degree of consistency over the years, contributing greatly to the improvement of the National Balance of Payments, which has been in deficit ever since the end of the 2nd World War.

Foreign currency from shipping over the past years, has risen to 2 billion US dollars per annum, and represents about 6% of the Gross National Product (GNP). Taking into account the relevant economic indicators, almost the entire net national product created abroad comes from the maritime sector. Apart from the positive impacts to the national economy the above-mentioned inputs (the diverse positive effects), are also a vital part of the prosperity of local communities, which actually receive this foreign currency.

Furthermore the maritime sector contributes decisively to the economic and social development of the country, by employing, in recent years, a total of 55,000 people. In particular about 30,000 are employed aboard ships and 15,000 on land, serving the maritime enterprises as well as the associated industries. It must be noted, however, that employment numbers and opportunities in Hellenic owned shipping, during the last decade, have been decreasing. This seems to be a wider problem facing most traditionally important shipping nations and is associated directly with the strong international competition, inevitably leading to the employment of cheaper foreign labour, in order to minimise operational costs. The decrease in employment figures is also attributed to the fact

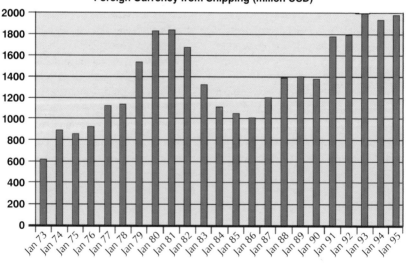

Foreign Currency from Shipping (milion USD)

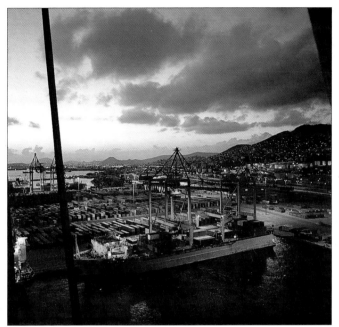

*Piraeus Port,
the container
terminal*

that the shipping sector is evolving into a highly capital intensive industry.

Even though Hellenic shipping still maintains its leading role internationally, there has been no equivalent development in other shipping related sectors within Greece. This can be accounted for by the fact that the necessary co-operation between the Hellenic owned shipping (ship operators and owners) and the Greek State (appropriate maritime policy and relevant economic planning) has not developed well. Up to the 1960s, the development of shipping related services such as banking insurance and brokerage services, shipbuilding and technological infrastructure,

shipping business management etc., was extremely slow. During the 1970s, the situation improved, due to the efforts of all parties involved, leading to a steady improvement in all sectors. In more recent decades, the competitiveness of maritime business, ship-repair/ building/refurbishing industry, banking and insurance, brokering and supply services, as well as vessel purchase transactions has evolved, and is striving for better standards. There are obviously differences in how each sector attains higher standards, but as a whole, these advances are unquestionably insufficient relative to the vitality of the Greek shipping industry.

4. Striving for quality in shipping and marine environmental protection

As pointed out above, Hellenic owned shipping is by far a globalised activity, which develops and operates within a defined business and institutional framework.

This framework influences the industry directly, but can also be influenced, in some ways, by the Hellenic maritime community, due to its leading international status. It is true that recent trends in international shipping, especially within the EU and Organisation for Economic Co-operation and Development (OECD) countries, focus on the development of a free and competitive maritime market, where transport services strive for quality at the lowest possible price. At the same time, efforts to ensure vessel and navigational safety, as well as the protection of the marine environment, are also high among their priorities.

The above mentioned goals have been adopted by the Hellenic State and shipping community, both within the domestic legal and institutional framework, as well as in international forums (EU, UN, UNEP, IMO etc.), in which Greece's leading position allows for further improvement and influence. Greece has inevitably proved that, as a member of the OECD and the EU, it has worked positively and constructively

towards attaining a high quality level in world-wide shipping. It is important to note that Greek ship owners set up, as early as 1982, a non governmental organisation for promoting quality in shipping mainly through the protection of the marine environment. This organisation known as the Hellenic Marine Environment Protection Association (HELMEPA) has been very active both within Greece as well as in international institutions (IMO etc.).

It must be stressed, however, that attaining a high quality level in the shipping industry, is an extremely difficult and painstaking process, since it involves international co-operation and is affected by many factors. Major maritime nations in particular, face these difficulties within the globalisation process that the industry is going through. Intense and often vicious competition in freight trends to compete with quality in shipping services.

The numerous legal opportunities open to shipping firms allowing them to spread their activities throughout different parts of the world (different registries, headquarters, company holdings etc.), leads to anonymity and increased difficulties when investigating pollution incidents, breaches of contractual duties etc.

The ease with which a shipping firm can change registries nowadays, selecting those that allow increased profits while minimising running and maintenance costs, appears to be one of the most serious problems facing the industry.

As pointed out previously, Greece is extremely active within many open registries, as are many other OECD countries.

In addition, many EU countries resort to international as well as parallel registries, to minimise losses to their national registries.

This situation affects not only the stability and improvement of the maritime sector, but also poses a serious threat to maritime safety as well as to the marine environment.

Quality shipping, today, appears to be a difficult objective achievable only through international co-operation within which the OECD and EU countries play an important role.

So, it seems reasonable to suggest that the only way forward is to strive for quality shipping throughout the world. Efforts should be made to confront the split that exists in the maritime sector between first class shipping, serving OECD and EU countries, and second class, comprised of substandard ships under flags of convenience mainly owned by firms originating from EU and OECD states, serving the rest of the world.

THE 3rd COMMUNITY SUPPORT FRAMEWORK FOR GREECE

By Nikos Komnenides & Maria Kostopoulou

A preferential area in which the target for social and economic cohesion in the European Union is to be achived

Greece is one of the more interesting cases in which structural interventions are applied propitiously can be seen to achieve the target for social and economic cohesion in the European Union.

Greece, since its accession to the European Union, has successively executed developmental programmes lasting for many years. This began with the Mediterranean Integrated Programmes in 1984 and continues to the present, with the 3rd Community Support Framework to be completed by the year 2008.

These programmes have contributed to the gradual change in the developmental model of the nation. The country has evolved from a mainly rural economy without any particular specialisation and a mediocre developmental performance, to a gradually and increasingly more integrated economy able to depend on its own strengths in the international and European competitive arena.

The prerequisites were already met through the long-term programmes of the past for the 3rd Community Support Framework focusing on interventions and investments of high added value to the economy and the prosperity of the population of the country.

The European Union approved the 3rd Community Support Framework on September 3rd 1999. This constitutes a gigantic developmental programme valued at 44.6 billion Euros for the period 2000-2006. It covers the whole spectrum of an integrated structural effort aimed at a developmental upgrading within the framework of the European whole.

The European Union is contributing about 51% of the project funding. The remaining resources are to be met through national funding - 25% from state resources and 24% from the private sector either through private investments or through the joint funding of large-scale works in mainly infrastructure and transport.

An integrated strategy for the development of the Greek State

A developmental programme of such dimensions is particularly complex and includes demands to meet the needs of the existing conditions but also to adapt the whole country to the rapid developments of the international economy. It must contribute to the shaping of a functional and contemporary network of economic infrastructure (transport, energy, etc.) It must also formulate an institutional and operational framework for the uninterrupted exercise of private initiatives in the investment sector. It must support modern forms of investments and research throughout all of the geographical regions of the country without excluding areas where private initiatives are not particularly strong.

This developmental endeavour also depends on the extent to which the characteristics of occupational training and education in Greece are restructured as well as on other actions relating to the adaptation of human resources to the job requirements of a contemporary economy.

Besides these immediate developmental choices, however, a balance must be kept in investing both in issues

FINANCING TABLE FOR CSF 2000-2006 (in €)					
Title of Operational Programme	Total Cost	Total State Cost	Community Participation	National State Participation	Participation Participation
O.P. EDUCATION AND INITIAL OCCUP. TRAINING	2,484,599,225	2,484,599 ,225	1,863,449,418	621,149,807	
O.P. EMPLOYMENT AND OCCUPATIONAL TRAINING	1,998,895,185	1,888,895,185	1,416,671,389	472,223,796	110,000,000
O.P. ROAD SYSTEMS, PORTS, URBAN DEVELOPMENT	9,317,357,643	5,883,977,981	3,033,003,071	2,850,974,910	3,433,379,662
O.P. RAILWAYS, AIRPORTS, URBAN TRANSPORT	2,937,600,380	2,859,150,380	1,468,752,690	1,390,397,690	78,450,000
O.P. COMPETITIVENESS	6,392,333,212	3,217,420,737	1,976,705,391	1,240,715,346	3,174,912,475
O.P. AGRICULTURAL DEVEL. RESHAPING OF RURAL AREAS	3,010,155,273	1,776,211,026	1,233,418,499	542,792,527	1,233,944,247
O.P. FISHERY	499,292,920	320,072,310	236,595,752	83,476,558	179,220,610
O.P. ENVIRONMENT	677,855,545	677,855,545	485,073,656	192,781,889	0
O.P. CULTURE	604,900,000	590,400,000	414,300,002	176,099,998	14,500,000
O.P. HEALTH - WELFARE	513,306,663	513,306,663	384,979,997	128,326,666	
O.P. INFORMATION SOCIETY	2,839,078,394	2,269,578,394	1,702,183,796	567,394,598	569,500,000
O.P. TECHNICAL ASSISTANCE	84,971,613	84,971,613	63,728,709	21,242,904	
TOTAL OF SECTORS	**31,360,346,053**	**22,566,439,059**	**14,278,862,370**	**8,287,576,689**	**8,793,906,994**
TOTAL REGIONAL	**10,909,204,445**	**9,363,575,924**	**7,041,737,593**	**2,321,838,331**	**1,545,628,521**
TOTAL CSF	**42,269,550,498**	**31,930,014,983**	**21,320,599,963**	**10,609,415,020**	**10,339,535,315**
RESERVES	2,288,810,262	2,074,610,262	1,386,400,000	688,210,262	214,200,000
GENERAL TOTAL CSF	**44,558,360,760**	**34,004,625,245**	**22,706,999,963**	**11,297,625,282**	**10,553,735,515**

COHESION FUND					
TRANSPORT	1,660,000,000				
IMPROVEMENT OF QUALITY OF LIVING	1,660,000,000				
TOTAL	**3,320,000,000**				

of social and cultural infrastructure as well as in the environmental upgrading of the sensitive area that has to do with the every day matters of Greeks citizens.

This endeavour takes into account the multi-faceted developmental procedure within the entire Greek reality. It covers large urban centres with their own requirements but also rural Greece that has to deal with the difficult demands of modernisation, especially those concerning agricultural activities, within the context of the target of maintaining a balance in the development of all the regions in the country.

This strategy will be realised through a series of twenty-five developmental operational programmes, which cover the major national sectors (12 programmes)

and the Greek regions (13 programmes), one for each of them.

In the table and diagram that follow, the principal priorities of the developmental programme can be seen as well as the operational programmes through which the achievement of specific targets is planned for the years 2000-2006. The principal economic allocations for each of these programmes are also shown.

The 3rd Community Support Framework (CSF) is a significant financial lever for development and it contributes to long-term stability and prosperity. Through the execution of the programme, Gross Domestic Product is expected to increase by 3.6% annually. Indicative estimations are shown below:

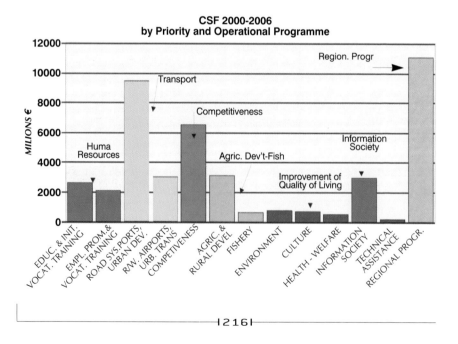

**CSF 2000-2006
by Priority and Operational Programme**

The Rio-Antirio Bridge

	2000-2006
CSF as % National Developmental Programme	65%
CSF as % of GDP	4%
Community participation in CSF	50,5%

The high rates of development, improvement in economic conditions and structural interventions have had positive results in dealing with unemployment, employment and in the creation of new jobs.

The CSF has contributed to the reduction in unemployment by about 6.2%, with the creation of 120,000 new jobs during the programme and approximately 60,000 to 80,000 permanent jobs after the completion of the programme.

Other characteristic features are the following:

Significant results with particularly positive social and economic implications (greater facility in citizen mobility, strengthening of competitiveness, reduction in costs of *transport* and increases in speed as well as improvement in the provision of tourist services) are expected through the transport programme. It includes the construction of 1,100 kilometres of motorways to be added to those constructed during the 2nd CSF, comprising the first integrated network covering the entire country. The network is supplemented by corresponding national, local and urban networks, as well as by the construction of mass transport systems in Athens and Thessalonica, basic infrastructures for

The Patras-Athens-Thessaloniki-Evzonoi (P.A.TH.E)motorway

port and airport networks, and improvements in transport safety, etc.

In the area of the railways, the Patras - Athens - Thessalonica - Eidomeni network is being completed and will reduce the time length of the journey from Thessalonica to Athens to 4 hours and 40 minutes (90 minutes shorter). The saving in travelling time is about 20-30% in road transport, by 10% in railway transport and by 50% in urban transport.

Concrete results have been seen in the development of *the natural gas network* both in links with neighbouring countries and in the distribution networks in urban centres, resulting in the less dependence of Greece on oil.

This spectrum of economic infrastructures at the end of the period will constitute a strong foundation for the modernisation of the developmental dynamics and enhancement of the quality of life of the residents.

In the *sector of production* emphasis is being placed on supporting research and the rationalisation of technological and research techniques through a special operational programme, directed at developing an information society. It meets a wide spectrum in social and economic life, has an innovative and horizontal thrust in the sectors of communications, (complementary to private initiatives), development and employment in the digital economy, education and culture as well as in catering to citizens' needs and improving the quality of life.

The incentives for private investments meet a wide range of economic activities. These actions deal with supporting business plans, strengthening small and medium sized enterprises for activities related to the quality of life, qualitative modernisation in the tourist sector, the development of entrepreneurship for women and the youth. At the same time, the adaptation of businesses to the new economy is to be promoted through a variety of programmes.

Almost the all of the funding for businesses is being directed to small and medium sized businesses that cover 73.5% of total employment.

Numbers indicative of the efforts being placed in the sector of *human resources*, which is being hit by high unemployment and a low percentage of employment, are the large percentage of the unemployed who have the opportunity for training or employment - about 70%. 70,000 threatened by social exclusion are currently being trained or placed in jobs. 20,000 working in mass media and 120,000 self- employed will also be trained. A significant number of new jobs are being created in social care structures.

In the sector of *education and initial occupational* training, the priorities concern improvement of the educational system and its services. This will allow the more effective confrontation of the real needs of society, opening channels of communication and linkage to the job market. Improvements will be made to infrastructure, means and educational programmes. The educational task will be upgraded and life long education will be promoted. Equality of opportunity will be encouraged, entrepreneurial action and occupational orientation will be facilitated.

In the area of *social infrastructure*, the main intervention has to do with the sector of health and mental health, completion of the structures and the organisational reformation of the National Health System, improvement in the services provided and the development of welfare services.

The Operational Programme for

Unification of the Archaeological Sites of Athens

culture places particular emphasis on the protection and promotion of our cultural heritage as well as the development of contemporary culture. The aim is to protect and display monuments and archaeological sites, the upgrading of the existing infrastructure as well as the creation of new infrastructure for museums and the improvement of the services provided. Moreover, it has targeted improvements in the infrastructure and large promotional events of contemporary culture as well as the construction of modern conference and cultural centres.

In the sector of the *environment,* Greece is finally complying with Community legislation concerning the environment wherever Greek law had not met requirements.

Indicative actions concern the aquatic environment (in addition to the actions of the Cohesion Fund), solid wastes, atmospheric environment and noise, protection of the landscape and marine environment, land registry, management of protected regions and individuals, remodelling, promotion of city and land planning and the development of environmental institutions.

These national policies are complemented through programmes that have a more direct relation to the geographical sector such as the programme for the development of the countryside, the restructuring of fisheries and the thirteen (13) Regional Operational Programmes.

In the *agricultural and fisheries* sector, the aim is to reinforce competitiveness in agriculture, improve the quality of agricultural products and improve the age-factor of farming population. Integrated interventions in mountainous and disadvantaged regions are being met with actions to promote mountain agriculture, supplementary activities in the sector of tourism and small and medium-sized enterprises, cultural actions and initiatives to promote agricultural tourism.

Thirteen (13) Regional Operational Programmes are being carried out under the responsibility of the regional and local authorities. They deal mainly with the needs at a regional and local scale. Concerned parties are more directly interested either because they are directly active in the economy or as users of social and cultural services.

In other words, in these programmes one encounters transport networks of regional and local significance, support of social, economic and environmental infrastructures, of urban and rural centres, actions related more directly to human resources as well as subsidies for the modernisation of economic activities in the agricultural, tourist, manufacturing and services sector.

Mobilisation of a powerful management mechanism in the public and private sector

The comprehensive implementation of the programme is mobilising powerful administrative and executive forces in the public and private sector. In order to implement the programme, the competent administrative services of the state have been reorganised. This has been accomplished according to the uniform standards of the European Union, with twenty-five (25) administrative authorities comprised of about 800 people for all the Ministries and the Regions and they are responsible for their respective operational programmes.

Of course, executive authority lies within a larger number of public services that are involved in the execution of works and actions of the multifarious programme, where great efforts are being made to overcome the innate problems of a Greek administration that badly needs to be modernised.

Similarly, the private sector, which will ultimately be the one to carry out the implementation of the programmes, is providing improved services relative to the past.

The demands for proper management are indeed greater than those observed during the execution of these programmes and so the improvement in institutions and mechanisms is constant. Areas that could do with further improvement include the efficiency of the competent services for the carrying out of the actions and the projects, more active participation from the private sector, simplification of procedures and the improvement of legislation pertaining to public works.

From an objective point of view, the administrative and economic organisa-

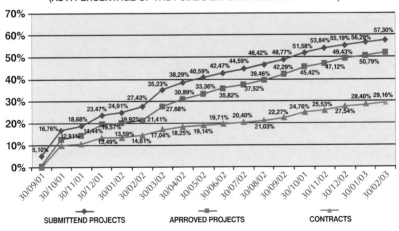

PROGRESS OF SUBMITTED AND APPROVED PROJECTS & CONTRACTS BUDGETS (AS A PERCENTAGE OF THE PUBLIC EXPENDITURE COMMITMENT)

Source: M.I.S. «Ergorama»

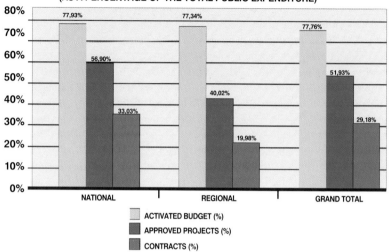

PROGRESS OF THE CSF 2000 - 2006
(AS A PERCENTAGE OF THE TOTAL PUBLIC EXPENDITURE)

Source: M.I.S. «Ergorama»

tion has improved significantly from the past.

Speeding up in the implementation of the programme

In early 2003 the course the implementation of the programme has been taking can be seen as follows:

The difficulties and the inevitable failures inherent in such a significant endeavour go without saying. The implementation of such a programme cannot always meet its goals completely nor can it be carried out exactly as budgeted to the exact penny. On the other hand, the demands of society and the econo-

my are developing so rapidly so that the end result can be evaluated not in absolute terms but rather in relation to the justifiable demands placed by society itself.

Doubtless, the shaping of a modernised economic and social infrastructure of Greece as a follow-up to previous programmes will allow the involvement of an active Greek population in the quest for progress and prosperity in a contemporary democratic and socially sensitive state within the framework of a European Union that is currently forming its new ambitions.

DEMOGRAPHIC TRENDS AND SOCIO-ECONOMIC INDICATORS IN THE EU AND GREECE

By Y. Yfantopoulos

Introduction

The main aim of this section is to provide general information concerning demographic trends, and socio-economic indicators in the EU Member States and Greece. It is generally accepted that there are many dimensions through which demography, health and quality of life could be measured. From a wide range of macro and micro indicators, we have selected some indicative indexes, which portray the current state of development in life expectancy, health status and quality of life in Greece and the EU.

This chapter is divided into three parts. The first part presents a compara-tive view of population trends, life expectancy, mortality, disability and quality of life in the EU-15. The second part focuses on Greece and discusses population growth and infant mortality trends over the period 1955-2000. Finally, in the third section, we make use of some demographic and socio-economic indicators to analyse social cohesion and income inequalities in the accession countries.

European Comparisons

This section considers some international comparisons of demographic trends in the EU-15. There are some

Central Metro station at Syntagma

problems concerning the comparability of the international statistics, and the value of the calculated indexes. In order to avoid any conceptual miss-interpretations we focus only on validated indicators which have been developed by the Eurostat, the World Health Organization and the European Commission.

Population trends in Europe

On January 1, 2002, the population of the European Union (EU-15) was 379 million. On the base of this estimate, Europe is the third largest geographic unity in the world, after China (1253 million), and India (1009 million). It is also ahead in comparison to the population of United States (274 million) and Japan (126 million). The population of the accession members, i.e., the twelve countries that are in the face of membership

negotiations, is around 106 millions.

In the forthcoming decades of the second millennium, one of the striking aspects of the European Community's Social and Demographic problems is the increasing rate of the ageing. The extent and form of ageing varies significantly from one Member State to another.

In 1960 there were only 34 million elderly (above 65 years of age). In 2000 this figure was almost double reaching the level of 60 million. The future prospects are gloomier since the proportion of elderly is expected to rise from 16% in 2000 to 27% in 2010.

In an effort to qualify the expected demographic trends over the period of the next 20 years (i.e., 2000-2020) we can clearly distinguish (see Diagram 1) between three broad age groups, which will undergo impressive changes.

Diagram 1

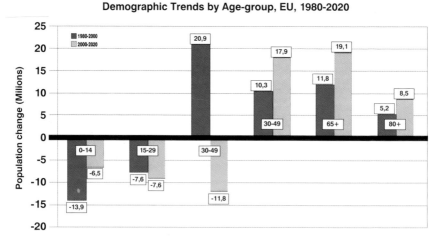

Demographic Trends by Age-group, EU, 1980-2020

Source: Eurostat-1995 based (baseline) household projections

1).The group of young people (0-29) is expected to fall by 15.4%. This reduction is expected to have an immediate impact on the educational infrastructure as well as on the social and health services relevant to the younger population. Despite this reduction, it has been proposed by the European Commission and the OECD that attention must be paid to ensuring a high equality of educational services. (diagramme 1)

2) The age group of working population (29-64) will present initially a decline by 11.8% in the age group 30-49, followed by a substantial increase by 17.9% in the age group 50-64 years. The net effect of the group (29-64) is expected to be an overall increase by 6.1%. This change will bring a profound impact in the labour force and the corresponding productivity.

3) The group of elderly (+ 65) will witness an impressive increase by 27.7% generating new demands for elder services and imposing an extra burden in the pensions and health care services.

There are there predominant factors that have an important impact on the ageing of the European Population.

• The first is the continuous fall in fertility rates
• The second is the extended longevity and
• The third is the impressive decline in mortality.

The rate of fertility has fallen from 2.59 in 1960, to 1,45 in 1999. The Southern European Countries with the

Diagram 2

Total Fertility Rates 2000

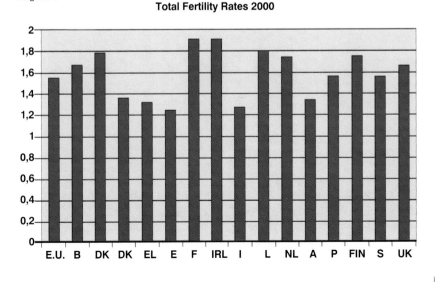

Diagram 3

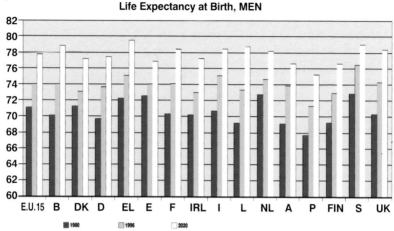

Diagram 4

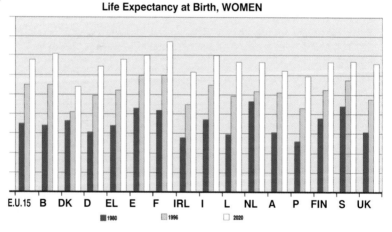

highest fertility trends in the 1970's and 1980's present currently (in 2000) the lowest rates. Spain (1.19) and Italy (1.21) record the lowest fertility, with Ireland (1.89) showing the highest (diagramme 2).

Life Expectancy at birth

A measure of the expectation of life at birth has the advantage of describing the overall mortality of a population in a more summary fashion than the mortality rates. Life expectancy indicators are calculated from life tables which present the record of survival and mortality within a hypothetical cohort (tables of life's generation), subject to the sequence of age specific mortality rates, estimated during a given calendar period among actual age cohorts.

Life expectancy has been constantly increasing across all Member States.

The total gain in years during the second half of the century is around ten years. In diagrammes 3 and 4 we present life expectancy gains for both males and females over the period 1980-2000 and the forecasted gains for the years 2000-2020.

The decrease in fertility and the increase in life expectancy are responsible for the ageing of the population; in the EU countries.

Mortality Trends

One of many purposes for measuring mortality is to enable us to draw inferences about the likelihood of death occurring within a specific period of time (age). A reason for doing this is that the risk of dying varies with a number of factors such as: age, sex, geographical locality of residence, occupation, income, life-style, as well as the availability of health services.

Examining the total causes of deaths which have been standardised (direct method) for age and sex, and are expressed in rates per 100,000 individuals, we found that Greece appears to be a country with the lowest death rates among the EU states. In the case of male mortality (see diagramme 5) Greece is the second best Country of Europe after Sweden. The same position is main-

Diagram 5

Mortality: Standardised Death Rates. per 100 000 population, All causes of death, Men, 1998, EU-15

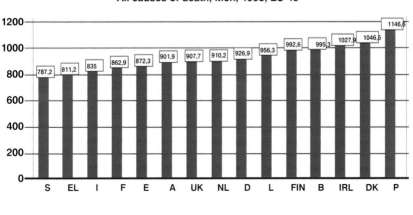

Diagram 6

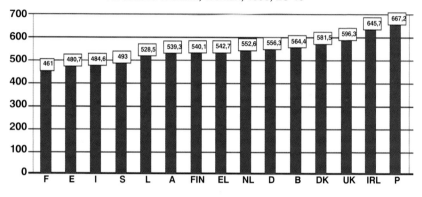

**Mortality: Standardised Death Rates. per 100 000 population,
All causes of death, Woman, 1998, EU-15**

tened for the case of female mortality (see diagramme 6).

As far as the rest of causes of death are concerned, we found that ischaemic heart diseases, cerebrovascular diseases and malignant neoplasm's exhibit the highest proportional rates of all diseases specified. Generally deaths caused by circulatory system diseases and diabetes mellitus are proportionately higher in the more developed areas of Europe This is attributed to epidemiological profile as wel as to the overall life style

Disability Adjusted Life Years

The World Health Organization (WHO) has developed a widely accepted methodology in measuring the health status of different nations across the globe.

The main idea was to device an indicator, which is not restricted to the description of death, but to reflect the impact of a wide range of risk factors upon health.

Christopher Murray, Executive Director of WHO's Global Programme on Evidence for Health Policy, undertook the responsibility to develop a comparable approach based on the combination of mortality and morbidity.

The new indicator was called DALY (Disability, Adjusted Life Years) and it is a. composite indicator taking into account the impact of several risk factors upon mortality and morbidity. The loss of one healthy year of life is equal to one DALY.

In diagramme 7 we present the relationship between per capita health expenditure and the estimated DALYS for different European and Accession Countries We witness a positive relationship between DALYS and health

Diagram 7   DALYS and Health Expenditure

Health Expenditure per Capita in DALE

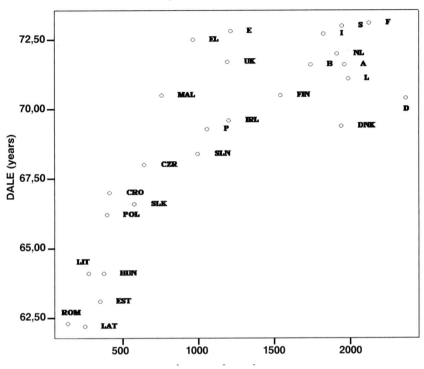

Health Expenditure per Capita in Dollars

expenditure supporting the hypothesis that more economic resources would improve markedly the health of the accession countries. However the effect on the wealthier nations of the European Union is only marginal.

Factors contributing to living standards and Quality of life.

During the last decade it has been a growing interest among politicians, ad-ministrators and social policy analysts to investigate the quality of life issues and to devise methodologies aiming at its measurement. Several International Organizations like the WHO, and the OECD have launched several studies on living conditions promoting quality of life issues as a key concept for assessing subjective valuation of several dimensions of well being in different cultural settings.

In early 1995 the Executive Board of WHO approved a programme on quality of life of the elderly aiming at the investigation of different perspectives related to:

1)Life Course of the elderly who are not compartmentalized, 2) Health promotion for the elderly 3) Cultural settings 4) Gender differences 5) Inter generational cohesion and 6) Ethical considerations. The programme aimed at the collaborative work between various academic and non-governmental organizations in order to create data bases for policy strengthening, advocacy, and implementing community based programmes.

Further to WHO, the OECD initiated several studies on social indicators promoting the measurement of quality of life as a key instrument for assessing subjective well being.

Taking this experience into account the European Commission launched in 1999 the Eurobarometre study EB 52.1 aiming at the measurement of quality of life and the factors influencing it, using a multidimensional set of indicators. The validity and reliability of the obtained results were compared with other studies and it was faound that the developed methodology was feasible for comparing quality of life across counries.

The term quality of life is defined here as the European Citizen's subjective perception of happiness or satisfaction with his/her living standards and the consumption of public goods and services. There are many factors influencing quality of life. Health, consumption patterns, income, family relations, housing and social environment and personal security are only a few indicative factors which are discussed at some length below. The term quality of life, despite its multidimensional aspects (i.e. physical, psychological, social participation, cognitive etc.) it is used here in a generic form, capturing the widest possible factors that describing personal satisfaction with all conditions of living. As such, the term encompasses all individual's perceptions and attitudes towards the general concepts of quality and living standards which are the core concepts for our here.

Examining the factors influencing the quality of life stahdards across the European memebr states it was found that: good health (25%), sufficient income (15%), a caring family, nice home and friendly neiborhood are among the core factors acording to Europeans' subjective evaluation that contribute to their quality of life.

Obviously there are several differences among the European countries in the hierarchical order of listing the factors. However good health and sufficient income are the most prominent issues which came on the top of the list across all member states. Analysing further the responses on the relationship between quality of life and health we found that among all the European Citizens the Greeks assign the greatest

Diagram 8   Quality of Life in EU.

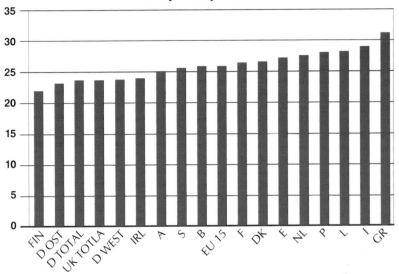

Being in Good Health is an Important Factor Contributing to my Quality of Life

value on their health. (Diagramme 8). Being in good health is the top priority among the greek citizens.

Geography and population growth in Greece
Geography

Greece is geographically characterised by mountains and a scattering of small islands. The total land area amounts to 131,944 km^2 , of which 29 per cent is arable, 39 per cent is permanent meadow and pasture and only 12 percent is urban.

Officially Greece is divided into fifty-one counties (nomos) and thirteen regions. There exist one hundred and sixty nine inhabited islands which constitute about 19 per cent of the total land area and they are populated by 17 per cent of the total population.

Communications between the islands and the mainland have improved considerably in recent years mainly as a result of tourism, but still certain difficulties remain in comparison with the rest of the European Countries.

Population Growth

The rate of natural increase in a population over time is defined as the difference between the crude birth rate and crude death rate, plus the rate of net migration. In studying the nature of population growth in Greece it suffices to say that natural, ethnical and historical reasons have combined to produce an uneven distribution of the population, so that more than one third of the population now lives in the Athens Area, which represents less than 5 per cent of Greece's territory.

Some 56 per cent of the industrial establishments in the country and 48 per cent of the wage earners in manufacturing industries are located in this area.

According to the 2001 population census, there were 10,939,605 inhabitants in Greece of which 49.58 per cent were men and the rest 50.42 per cent women. In the period 1971 - 1991 the proportion of males has remained fairly constant, ranged from 48.9 to 49.0 of the total population.

The population of Greece grew by 4.7% between 1981 and 1991, following an increase of 11.1% during the previous periods. In the decade 1991-2001 the rate of growth was 6.7%. (see table 1)

During the 1960's amd 1970's a substantial migration took place from the rural to the urban areas. The decline in most rural areas (especially the Ionian and Aegean Islands) occurred mainly due to an exodus of the younger generation (from 25 to 45 years of age) from their villages to Athens or Salonica, or alternatively to other developed countries. This movement is responsible for a profound demographic change which has resulted in a skewed distribution towards the aged combined with a negative growth in most of the rural areas.

Table 1

Population of Greece by Sex and Major Age Groups

YEAR	TOTAL	MALES	FEMALES	0-14 YEARS	15-64 YEARS	65 & OVER YEARS
1971	8.768.372	4.286.748	4.481.624	2.223.904	5.587.352	957.116
1981	9.739.589	4.779.571	4.960.018	2.307.297	6.192.751	1.239.541
1991	10.252.580	5.051.553	5.201.027	1.880.800	6.866.400	1.452.800
2001	10.939.605	5.424.089	5.515.516			

Source: National Statistic Service of Greece

By studying the reproduction rates of rural and urban populations in Greece, we get the impression that since 1950 live births increased in the urban population and decreased in the rural population. But the number of deaths increased in both segments. The excess of births over deaths increased in the urban areas and decreased precipitously in the rural areas. Evidently the problem of low-natality appeared strongly in the rural population. Depletion of the rural population through migration to large cities and the progressive ageing of the remaining population are the main causes for the low-natality observed in the rural population.

Infant mortality trends

Infant death rates refer to deaths which occur within the first year of life. Neonatal death rates refer to deaths which occur after the first day of birth until the 27th day, and the post-neonatal death rate refers to the period between the 28th day after birth until the 365th day. These death rates are often espe-

cially responsive to changing conditions of infectious diseases, nutrition and medical care, and they are widely considered to be more sensitive indicators of the environmental factors affecting the level of health than are death rates at later ages.

By analysing infant, neonatal, and post-neonatal mortality rates according to their cause of death, and by distinguishing between rural and urban populations, the most common causes of death, especially in rural areas, are seen to be due to infectious diseases, injuries incurred at birth, post-natal asphyxia, diseases peculiar to early infancy and immaturity.

Analysing the Greek data we can describe briefly the following facts:

(a) The rate of infant mortality is decreasing in the urban areas, but it is rather difficult to identify the rural rates due to statistical deficiencies. It should be noted that infant mortality in the 1950's and 1960's has been systematically under - reported (especially neonatal) in rural areas. The registration of infant deaths in rural areas has shown a little improvement since the early 1960's when the majority of these events occur in maternity clinics or hospitals, however still there exists a lack of completeness in the registration of infant deaths.

(b) The rate of neonatal mortality showed an upward trend in urban areas until the middle 1960s. After 1966 this rate has been declining constantly. The rural areas has been showing a decreasing rate of neonatal mortality but as it has been reported by the Greek Statistical Office, this is an error attributed to the lack of efficient statistical services in rural areas.

(c) The rate of post-neonatal mortality is generally decreasing. The rate of decrease appears to be much higher in urban rather than in rural areas, and there has been observed a continuously widening gap between rural and urban post-neonatal mortality rates.

Infant mortality in Greece is reported adequately, with some minor problems in rural regions, particularly with regard to neonatal mortality. Total infant mortality has declined significantly over time, (see diagramme 9) from 43.52 %0 in 1955 to 6,15 %0 in 1999.

Accession countries

In 2000, all the applicant countries had a lower GDP per capita than the EU-15 average of about 22,500 PPS. However the range among the 13 Accession countries is considerable, from 5,400 PPS in Bulgaria to 18,500 PPS in Cyprus. In other terms, GDP per capita in the applicant countries ranges from 24% to 82% of the EU-15 average.

Diagram 9

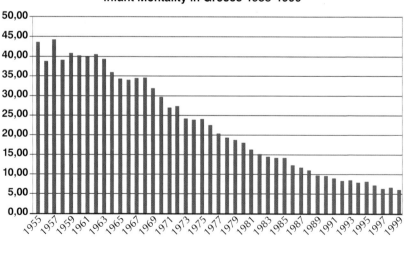

Infant Montality in Greece 1955-1999

Diagram 10 provides an overview of the income variation among the EU and the Accession Countries. Excluding Luxembourg, all the rest of EU countries present a variation of their GDP per capita around 15% of the average. The Enlargement countries, after marked declines in their GDP growth rates, during the transition period to a marked economy, they present convergent trends with the rest of EU States. However, still they confront considerable lags in the catch up process. In 1997, Slovenia and Czech Republic had an income per capita much closer to Portugal and Greece reaching the bottom limit of the EU Countries. Romania, Lithuania, Latvia and Bulgaria had a per capita income less than one third of the European average.

Examining the difference in per capita income between the EU and Accession countries we found that income levels among the Enlargement countries are much larger than those of EU member states.

In order to obtain an overall impression of the population size and the socio-economic situation in the Accession countries we present in table 2 some indicative indicators.

The largest population is registered in Turkey, (68,6 millions), Poland (38,6 millions) Romania (22,4 millions) and the lowest in Malta (0,4 millions) and Cyprus (0,8 millions). Cyprus (18.500 Euros) and the Czech Republic (13.300 Euros) are the wealthiest among the accession countries

Diagram 10

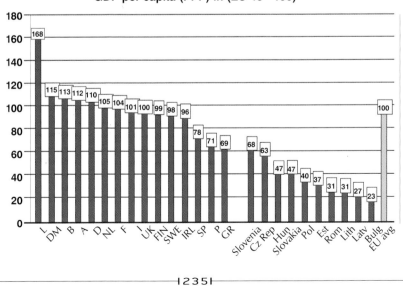

GDP per capita (PPP) in (EU-15=100)

Table 2   Socio-economic Indicators in the Accession countries

Candidate Countries	Population (million inhabitants)	(million Km²)	G.D.P. per inhabitant (euro)	Economic Growth %	Unemployment (% of active (population
Cyprus	0,8	9	18.500	4,0	4,0
Czech Republic	10,2	79	13.300	3,3	8,0
Estonia	1,4	45	9.800	5,0	12,4
Hungary	10,2	93	11.900	3,8	5,7
Latvia	2,4	65	7.700	7,7	13,1
Lithuania	3,5	65	8.700	5,9	16,5
Malta	0,4	0,3	11.700	-0,8	6,5
Poland	38,6	313	9.200	1,1	18,4
Slovak Republic	5,4	49	11.100	3,3	19,4
Slovenia	2,0	20	16.000	3,0	5,7
Bulgaria	7,9	111	6.500	4,0	19,9
Romania	22,4	238	5.900	5,3	6,6
Turkey	68,6	775	5.200	-7,4	8,5

One of the EU's principal objectives is to strength the economic and social cohesion by ensuring an overall harmonious development. As it is stated in the EC Treaty (Art.2) "the Community shall have at its task"...the continuos "raising of the standard of living and quality of life". Social cohesion often implies "greater equality in economic and social opportunities".

Examining social cohesion in the Accession Countries we shall adopt the common methodology which argues that one of the dimensions of social cohesion is the income inequality. We should underline here the difficulties in drawing comparisons between Eastern and Western European Countries, as well as within the Eastern countries since the publication of income data under the Communist regimes were extremely restricted.

There had been several supporters of the hypothesis that socialism had reduced income differentials and had abolished poverty. Despite the lack of income statistics, an effort is made here to provide evidence presented by several European researchers (Atkinson A., Micklewright J and others) supporting the hypothesis that income distribution was more egaliterian in the Eastern European Countries than in then Western European States. Estimates of Gini Coefficients during the mid 1980's reveal the following values: Czechoslovakia (1985) Gini = 19.9, Hungary (1982) Gini = 20.9, Poland (1985) Gini = 25.3, and United Kingdom (1985) Gini = 29.7. (Source Atkinson A. Income distribution in the Eastern European Countries) However, we should be very cautious in interpreting these results since the concept of income is dissimilar and the structure of the economy in the Eastern Countries incorporated a significant component of non reported *underground income.*

Examining income inequalities in 1997 among the Enlargement countries, one see levels of inequality not so dissimilar to those of the EU Member States.(see diagramme 11) The richer Countries present lower inequality levels. In the case of Slovakia, Hungary and the Czech Republic the Gini coefficients are lower than the E. U. average.

Looking at indicators on the distribution of income such as the Gini coefficient and the income share ratio (share of income of top 20% of population compared with the bottom 20%), one

Diagram 11

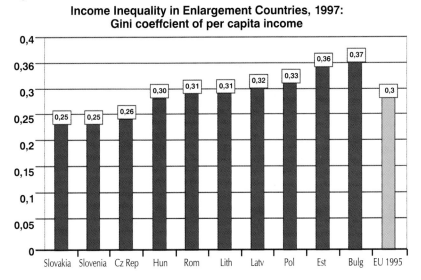

Income Inequality in Enlargement Countries, 1997:
Gini coeffcient of per capita income

Source: World Bank. No data for Cyprus and Malta. 1998 data - Estonia, Hungary, Latvia, Poland, Slovenia. 1997 data - Bulgaria. 1996 data - Czech Republic, Lithuania. 1994 data - Romania, Turkey. 1992 data - Slovakia

sees levels of inequality not so dissimilar to those of the EU Member States.

In fact, in many cases, the distribution of income is more even in the applicant countries, albeit that the average income may be considerably lower. Using data for selected years during the 1990s (owing to data availability), the Gini coefficient is highest (i.e. more inequality) in Turkey and Estonia (41.5 and 37.6) and lowest in Slovakia, Hungary and the Czech Republic (19.5, 24.4 and 25.4).

Conclusions

Concluding this chapter, we may argue that there has been a broad acceptance among the European Governments and policy makers to improve longevity, health status and the overall quality of life among the EU Citizens. Despite the noble intentions we found out that there are significant differences not only between the countries but also within the countries among the regions and the rural / urban populations.

Greece, a country of 10,9 millions, has achived the longest longevity and the lowest rates in mortality among the European Member States. In addition Greeks believe that the most important factor contributing to their quality of life is to be in good health.

This view is also shared with all the rest of EU countries.

The Accession countries present significant differences in GDP per capita and in living standards in comparison to Europe. Income inequalities are much higher in the accession countries and this is attributed to the economic crisis confronted during the liberalization of the prices and the transition from a planned to a market economy. However during the last few years some countries have shown impressive convergence trends.

SOCIETY

LABOUR AND INDUSTRIAL RELATIONS

By G.P. Koukoules

Industrial Relations

In the presentation of Greek industrial relations that follows, there are references to the agents of industrial relations (the state, labour unions, management organisations). Then the institution of collective bargaining is examined and then the parallel institutions of conciliation, mediation and arbitration. These are clearly marked by their legal structure. Then an examination of labour conflicts is made (strikes, lockouts) and the legal response to them. The presentation concludes with reference to the participatory institutions that are developing.

The Agents of Industrial Relations
The State

The primary characteristic of the national system of industrial relations is its legal foundation, a result of the interventionist role of the state.

The process of modernisation begins with the rise to power of the Liberal Party (1911-1915) and in the process, its compromises towards the working and bourgeois classes. During the Interwar period, the Interventionist State expands and becomes oriented toward the creation of developmental infrastructure (major public works, multitude of important institutional reforms).

The devastation resulting from the Second World War and the civil war, which ensued thereafter, strengthened the state interventionist role even further. This resulted in the creation of an oversized state sector and the state came to the fore as one of the largest employers. This development constituted one of the most important vehicles for social policies.

Having undertaken economic development in a responsible manner, and in order to control the various economic sectors, the state also intervened systematically in the shaping of industrial relations. This was done either through a controlled system of collective negotiations or through the various policies of wage controls in the cases in which the control of the collective negotiations was not possible.

After 1985, the systematic freeing of industrial relations began. This process was hastened with the rise to power of New Democracy (1990-1993) and continues to this day. The reorientation of the interventionist role of the state, justified by the economic situation and necessitated by Greece's obligations towards the European Union had two important impacts. It resulted on the one hand, in the dispensation of the government from the burden of the so-called "problematic enterprises" and on the other, the tendency towards privatisation of the profitable enterprises of the public sector.

The Labour Unions

According National Statistical Service data (*Manpower Research* 1999), of a total of 3,939,79 individuals employed, 2,296,06 were wage earners (1,392,97 men and 903,08 women) and 964,09 were self-employed.

Union freedom is protected under Article 23 of the 1975 Constitution, by a number of international agreements ratified by the parliament, and is regulated under Law 1264/1982.

The *structure* of the union hierarchy is the following. The basic core are the locals at the rank and file level (the first degree union organisations) which are united on a local and occupational level in labour centres (horizontal second de-gree organisations) and at a branch and craft level in federations (vertical second degree organisations). The union locals of the rank and file are united through the Labour Centres and Labour Federations, at the third degree organisational level, which is the Confederation. The General Confederation of Greek Labour (GSEE) is made up of 2,264 rank and file locals (2002), 82 Labour Centres and 69 Federations (2002).

This fragmentation can be explained by the small size of Greek enterprises, 94% of which employ 1-9 employees, 5% employ 10-49 employees and 1% employ more than 100 employees (2000). With regard to the choice of craft unions rather than industrial or sectoral unions, the level of economic development initially justified the latter but it remained for reasons of more general union tactics. The Law 1876/1990 on

collective bargaining (civil law) attempts to limit craft union structure to some extent.

With respect to *union coverage*, according to a recent study (2002), the proportion of unionised wage earners reaches 29.2% (civil servants included). However, with the exemption of civil servants, there is a noticeable discrepancy in unionisation between the public (49.4%) and private (24%) sectors as well as within the same sector, between the sexes and between age groups.

According to Greek law, both *positive* and *negative* trade union rights and freedoms are protected. Consequently, measures of union security such as closed shop or union shop are illegal and null.

Every Greek party, through its trade union front organisation, is represented in one way or the another within all levels of the trade union structure. The major *party trade union front organisations* are The Panhellenic Militant Labour Union Movement (PASKE) which is associated with PASOK and the Democratic Independent Labour Movement (DAKE) which is associated with New Democracy. The United Militant Labour Movement and Associates (ESAK-S) is affiliated with the Communist Party and the Autonomous Interposition is associated with the other left party Synaspismos (Alliance of Progressive and Left Forces). This relative fragmentation of the Trade Union structure along party lines contributes to the pluralistic orientation strategy and programs of Greek trade unionism. In 1999 a front organisation appeared, the All Workers Militant Front (PAME), with a pro-Communist leadership.

The *economic self-sufficiency* of the union organisations is complete. Membership dues are slow in coming and deficits are covered by significant contributions from the Labour Centre (Ergatike Hestia), which operates under Ministry of Labour control and manages funds generated from the dues of both employees and employers.

Research and *scientific support* for the trade unions comes primarily from the Institute of Labour, which is under the aegis of the Confederation of Labour (GSEE) and is run by university professors. The Institute provides a permanent staff at times supported by external researchers and its scientific activities are directed by an academic. The activities of the Institute are research oriented and concern not only industrial relations but also more general economic issues (e.g. sectoral studies). The results of these studies support the positions of the Confederation during negotiations, and are used more generally to support the programmatic demands of the organisation. There is a plethora of scientific and well-documented publications that support the positions of the Institute.

Educational and Other Activities

With the support of the Institute of Labour, GSEE organises seminars of various lengths providing union education at the central and regional level. The labour centres and the federations undertake similar activities. The National General Collective Labour Agreement foresees the provision of leave of absence for participation in the educational seminars of the union organisations.

A *Women's Secretariat* functions within GSEE, which brings to the fore and often deals with issues concerning working women (e.g. issues of equality, sexual harassment, etc.)

The Confederation organises or participates in cultural and other events (e.g. campaigns against drugs).

Participation in Collective Bodies of Social Policy

GSEE participates in all the public collective bodies or other institutions that are involved in social policy. These include for example the "Foundation of Social Security" (IKA), in the "Organisation for the Employment of Manpower" (OAED), in the "Workers' Welfare Foundation" (Ergatike Hestia), in the "Organisation for Labour Housing", in the "Committee of Economic and Social Policy", a body with consulting responsibilities etc.

Participation in the administration of the "Workers' Welfare Foundation" is of decisive importance because this organisation has the responsibility for a variety of after hour and leisure time programmes for workers but also for pensioners. In addition to the programmes of social tourism (7.5 billion drachmas

in 1997), the above institution administers programmes for the purchase of books and entertainment.

Social Dialogue

With the initiative and participation of the government and also the social partners, a process of social dialogue recently began which concerns labour, social insurance, economic and development issues.

After the social partners reach common assessments, the goal of the social dialogue is to attend to social contracts. This new practice which is thought to assist, if not in the overcoming then at least in the gradual setting aside of the traditionally confrontational relations between the social partners, does not imply that the government has forsaken its legislative responsibilities. In any case, to the extent to which the disagreement or even agreement between partners does not comply with governmental choices, the government can intervene with legislative changes.

The majority of members of the administration of GSEE have expressed support for the participation of their organisation in the process of social dialogue. This participation however does not imply agreement with the positions and the proposals of the government or of the employers.

International and Regional Participation

GSEE is the founding member of the

International Confederation of Free Labour Unions and its federations participate in the respective professional secretariats. GSEE is also a member of the European Union Confederation and its federations are part of the respective European Union Federations.

Representation of Public Employees

Public employees are represented by the Confederation of Public Servants (ADEDY). Until recently (see below) collective bargaining was not allowed on the terms and conditions of work of public employees. In order to deal with the dysfunctional aspects of unionism in the private sector, negotiations were carried on for the unification of the two most representative (third degree) union organisations (GSEE/ADEDY).

Employer Organisations

The employer organisations are structured according to the professional interests they represent.

Industry

The Federation of Greek Industries (SEV). This is the most representative organisation of the sector. It is organised on a regional and sectoral basis. SEV has responsibility for the signing of national general collective labour agreements (see below).

The Association of the Industries of Northern Greece (SVVE). This association represents the industrial interests in the region of northern Greece and co-

The G.S.E.E. building in Athens

operates with SEV. Both organisations participate in various bodies for social and other policies. At a scientific level they co-operate with the Institute for Economic and Industrial Research. SEV is a member of the respective European Employers' Organisation (UNICE) which represents SBBE indirectly. SEV represents the Greek Employers at the International Labour Organisation.

Commerce

The General Confederation of Small Businesses and Trades (GSEVE). This confederation represents a wide spectrum of small businesses of the productive sector of the economy.

National Confederation of Hellenic Commerce. This federation is also in the area of commercial activity and to some degree overlaps with GSEVE. Both these organisations co-sign the National General Collective Labour Agreement and are generally differentiated downwards, in relation to the members of SEV, with regard to wage scales. Both organisations participate in different bodies involved in social and other policies. Other important employer organisations are the Association of Greek Banks and the Federation of Greek Shipowners.

Collective Bargaining, Collective Agreements, Mechanisms of Solving Deadlock

Collective bargaining and collective agreements constitute the essential complement to union freedom and for this reason, are safeguarded in the Constitution (Article 22, paragraph 2).

For historical, political and economic reasons, the system of collective industrial relations which was established in Greece after the Second World War, displays significant differences from that of other European countries.

The system previously in force (Law 3239/1955)

Up to 1990, collective labour disputes were regulated by Law 3239/55. Its provisions reflect post-war conditions in Greece, and make the state the primary regulator of industrial relations, essentially eliminating any concept of consensus in settling collective disputes.

In the past, according to Law 3239, if negotiations broke down between management and labour and a collective labour agreement (CLA) was not signed, the parties were obliged to seek recourse in a system of compulsory arbitration. The compulsory factor ran through the initiation of the arbitration process, the composition of the arbitration board (tribunal) and the binding nature of the arbitration awards.

Regarding the initiation of the pro-

cess, it was not necessary to ensure agreement between the two sides (management and labour). The desire of just one side was sufficient and expressed by a simple application to the Ministry of Labour. The role of arbitrator was played by arbitration tribunals that were composed of one regular judge as President with a double vote, one Ministry of Labour employee (both were appointed by the Ministry of Labour), one representative of the employers and one of the workers.

Compulsory arbitration was in essence the only way of settling collective labour disputes, given that no provision was made for mediation, and the conciliation process was limited to a formal procedure whose purpose was to bring the collective dispute under compulsory arbitration.

In addition, one consequence of the referral of a collective dispute to arbitration was to prohibit continuation of the strike, or the proclamation of a new one. Failure to observe this prohibitive clause was seen as termination of the individual labour contact, with penal repercussions for the strike leaders.

And finally, in order for the arbitration award to take on normative force, the Ministry of Labour had to issue a decision. This presupposed administrative approval of the content of the arbitration awards, since the Administration had the power to amend or to refuse to approve their content if they were opposed to government policy.

These settlements caused intense social conflicts, successive and dynamic strikes, judicial interventions, denunciations and appeals to international organisations (ILO), etc. It is characteristic that during that period, more than 50% of collective settlements (both collective agreements and arbitration awards) were the result of arbitration, whereas today (from 1992 to 2001) arbitration awards represent only 14.8% of all collective settlements (see table 1).

The need to replace this authoritarian regime with modern democratic legislation began to be manifested more and more intensely after the 1980s. Nevertheless, ten (10) years were required for ideas concerning the reform of the collective bargaining system to "mature". The preliminary work and consultations required to draft the new law took more than a year and a half.

Finally in 1990, under a coalition government, Law 1876 was passed, which is still in force, with the unanimous consent of the three political parties, the representatives of GSEE and the three employers' organisations (SEV, GSEVEE, ESEE).

Main features of Law 1876/1990: free collective bargainning

The new law contains provisions referring to *the process of collective bargaining* and in that sense, the rights and obligations of those on both sides of the process (labour union organisations, employer associations and individual employers) of negotiations. Negotiations must be conducted in good faith and labour may draw complete and accurate information from the employers' side. During the course of negotiations, and of the process of mediation and arbitration, strikes are allowed unless otherwise stated in the previous collective agreement.

The content of the collective labour agreement has been opened. It may now regulate not only all issues of individual labour relations but also all issues concerning the relations between capital and labour in general (e.g. additional health and maternity coverage, the exercise of company policy to the degree to which it influences labour relations, additional facilities for the exercise of union rights at the enterprise level).

Pension issues and issues regulated by provisions of compulsory law binding to both parties (e.g. provisions of a penal nature, provisions concerning the jurisdiction of the courts, etc.) are excluded from negotiations.

The collective agreement may contain peace clauses related to the issues it regulates. As a result, and if such a clause has not been agreed upon, then a strike based on amendment of the provisions of the collective agreement, is legal during the time it is in effect.

The Levels of Collective Negotiations, Types of Collective Agreements, Pertinence of Entering.

A multilevel bargaining process is characteristic of the Greek practice.

The Law of 1990 created a decentralised bargaining system in the form of successive negotiations, instead of the decentralised and hierarchically structured system established by Law 3232/1955. This means that bargaining is free at every level.

The national general collective agreements, which regulate minimum wage issues, salaries, hourly wages and other basic working conditions, are concluded on the side of the workers by GSEE and on the employers' side by the respective organisations to which we have referred. These types of agreements cover all the workers in the country who are employed in the private sector.

Through these contracts, the establishment of minimum wages and salaries or hourly wages for all the workers covered makes up for the lack of related legal regulations.

Other categories of collective agreements are the sectoral, the enterprise, (when the employer employs at least 50 salaried employees), the national craft or the local craft agreements.

The above agreements are concluded, on the part of the workers, by the most representative union organisation.

Collective agreements at the middle level, may not contain terms of work more detrimental to the workers than those of the national general collective agreement. If the national general collective agreement and the other categories of collective agreement amend legal regulations (laws, presidential decrees, customs, etc.), then these amendments are valid, provided that they put forward regulation beneficial to the workers.

Obligations.

The sectoral collective agreements, the national craft and local craft agreements, bind the workers and the employers who are members of the union and employer organisations under agreement, unless the Minister of Labour extends the scope of who is bound under those agreements.

The Binding Power of Collective Agreements

The provisions and terms of the collective agreements have an immediate and compulsory effect and are of a higher order than individual agreements since they contain greater protection for the workers.

As we have already observed, the above regulations cover the employees in enterprises which are regulated by private corporate law, regardless of whether the employer, the enterprise, etc. is part in the private or public sectors of the economy.

Consequently civil servants are excepted and their wages and other terms of employment are determined by law and through the action of executive power. Within the context of the modernisation of public administration under way, Greece put forward (June 1996) International Conventions 154 and 151, which recognise the right of collective bargaining for the different categories of public employees. The Law 2738/1999 puts these international provisions into effect but among other things the negotiation of wages is excluded.

Mechanisms for Dealing with Negotiation Deadlocks.

The abolition of Law 3239/1955 also meant the abolition of compulsory arbitration. Today deadlocks that result from the process of collective bargaining are dealt with through the mechanisms of conciliation, mediation, and arbitration (Law 1876/1990).

During the process of conciliation, the conciliator, an employee of the Ministry of Labour, attempts to bring the positions of the two parties closer together. If the conciliation process ends in an agreement, a collective agreement is concluded.

Mediation

This is an independent process for resolution of collective differences. Either party may request mediation. The mediator may demand the information and data from the employers and from any responsible party. The mediator has the right - under certain circumstances - to submit his proposal. So long as his proposal is accepted and so long as both parties sign it, then it is equivalent to a collective agreement. The process of mediation takes approximately 30 days.

Arbitration

Arbitration is a final means for dealing with deadlocked negotiations and it is foreseen in the Constitution (Article 22 paragraph 2). According to the existing system, appeal to this process is possible in four cases. a) The first is at any stage of the negotiations, if the parties agree. b) The second is from only one side if the other party refuses mediation. c) The third is unilaterally from union organisations, if it is proven that the employer has rejected the proposal of the mediator, in this case, the right to strike is deferred for a period of 10 days from the day of the appeal. d) The fourth is in the case of collective agreements in enterprises and public utilities companies in which the right of appeal to this process is given to the party which accepts the arbitrator's proposal, while the other party has refused to do so.

The decision of the arbitrator is equated with a collective agreement. The arbitration decision is reached within 10 days from the time of the arbitrator's establishment in office if mediation has preceded and within 30 days if it did not.

The above processes are a kind of support, and thus the parties are free to determine the terms of the contract in order to avoid the entire process. If from existing information it can be concluded that the parties have not put that option to use, then the respective provisions of Law 1876/1990 will be applied. According to the statistical data (1992-1996) of the Organisation of Mediation and Arbitration (see below), collective bargaining in the private sector, where union organisations are weak, is largely arbitrated (76%-83%). On the contrary, in the wider public sector where there is a strong union presence, the percentages are much lower (5%), while relatively low percentages for the same procedure are noted (20%-23%) in the public sector and in the enterprises which operate under public law regulations.

Organisation of Mediation and Arbitration (OMED). This organisation has been functioning since January of 1992. It is an independent organisation which is funded by the "Workers' Welfare Foundation" (Ergatiki Hestia) and by the Budget of the Ministry of Labour.

The mediators/arbitrators serve a public function without being civil servants and are completely independent while carrying out their duties.

The mediators/arbitrators are individuals who offer theoretical and practical knowledge on the issues they deal with in industrial relations. The hiring of mediators/arbitrators is undertaken on a three-year contract term for the provision of independent services. OMED offers mediation and arbitration services for the solution of collective labour differences. The mediator or the arbitrator is chosen by the parties from a special list. In the case in which agreement cannot be reached, the choice is made by lot. OMED also provides advice on issues of industrial relations, assistance in the improvement of collective bargaining, undertakes research related to labour relations and writes "Codes for Practice".

Another important activity of the organisation is the undertaking of the continuous training of mediators and arbitrators and, with the participation of social partners, the organising of seminars and workshops during which discussions develop on issues related to the entire spectrum of industrial relations.

Strikes: The Right to Strike, Public Dialogue, Lock-out

Strike activity is a customary phenomenon in the realm of labour relations. But the frequency of strikes, the degree of participation by the working people and the number of lost hours of labour are a function of policy at the particular economic conjuncture.

Strike data are collected by the local Labour Inspectorates and the Ministry of Labour, and are usually incomplete. The overall Table (Table 1), which covers the period from 1990 to May of 1999, provides a picture of strike activity.

Table 1.1 shows the special weight of the public sector. Trade union density in this sector is very high (in some cases, it exceeds 70%), while the wave of privatisations taking place since the early 1990s fosters strike mobilisations.

The same Table shows that we have no data for the period after the first half of 1999. We should note the national general strike of April 2001, on the occasion of the government's effort to amend the existing social security system, which resulted in the loss of many hundreds of thousands of hours of labour. It is, however, indisputable that after the tension that culminated in the year 1990, a constant decline in strike activity has been noted, which is due among other things to unemployment (11.2% in 2000, 10.2% in 2001) as well as to the more general economic crisis.

The Right to Strike

It is recognised in the Constitution (Article 23) and its details are regulated under Law 1264/1982 and the related legislation. Declaration of a strike by the appropriate union organisation is of fundamental importance for the legality of strikes. Strikes of the first-degree union organisation (local) are declared upon the decision of the general assembly of union members. The second degree (Labour Centres, Federations) and the third degree (Confederations) union organisation declare strikes upon the decision of their administrative council, unless their constitution defines it otherwise.

The declaration of solidarity strikes in enterprises dependent upon multinational companies is made by the most representative third degree union organisation.

Other preconditions for the legality of a strike are that the employer and the employer organisations to which he belongs must be informed 24 hours prior to initiation of the strike. It is also the

STATISTICAL DATA on OMED operation from 1992 - 2001
1. GENERAL DATA

	1992	1993	1994	1995	1996	1997	1998	1999	2000	2001	Totals
MEDIATION											
Mediation Applications	86	109	109	101	115	119	132	123	127	96	**1117**
Collective Agreements	32	52	55	46	47	51	61	49	75	44	**512**
Mediation Proposals	47	58	68	57	68	81	97	86	69	53	**684**
Proprosals resulted into striking a Collective Agreement	7	20	17	13	16	27	33	26	29	9	**197**
ARBITRATION											
Arbitration Applications	36	41	42	48	56	72	70	65	59	46	**535**
Arbitration Awards	32	31	39	39	51	62	60	58	49	43	**464**
Collective Agreements	3	8	3	8	4	9	7	7	10	3	**62**
Arbitration Award and simultaneous Collective Agreement	0	0	0	1	1	1	2	0	0	0	**5**
Suspended procedure	1	2	0	0	0	0	0	0	0	0	**3**
SAFETY PERSONNEL											
Safety Personnel Applications			13	18	14	8	20	10	4	6	**93**
Successful conclusion			5	9	6	5	8	3	2	5	**43**
PUBLIC DIALOGUE											
Public Dialogue Applications			4	9	9	10	7	14	9	18	**80**
Successful conclusion			4	5	6	8	3	6	4	3	**39**
											1825

NOTE 1: The application numbers of Mediation, Arbitration, Public Dialogue and Safety Personnel are net, meaning the gross number of applications less those which for various legal or technical reasons were characterised as Invalid or classified as File.
NOTE 2: The data for 2001 pertain to the completed number of 96 cases, out of a total of 118 applications.
NOTE 3: In Arbitration case 073/98 regarding the Economists in Agricultural Organisations, an Arrangement was signed, which does not constitute a Collective Labour Agreement. This accounts for the discrepancy of one case short out of the total of 70 for the year at hand.

obligation of the organisation that declares the strike to make the necessary staff available for the safety of the enterprise's establishment and the prevention of damage or accidents.

There are also additional preconditions for the legality of a strike. These are imposed upon the union organisation in areas of the public sector, local government organisations that do not fall under public law regulations, and in the social services organisations (4 day warning and invitation to the employer for a public dialogue).

A legal strike postpones the contract obligations of the employer, as s/he is not required to pay salaries for the duration of the strike. Thus, given that the Greek trade union organisations have no strike funds, the strikers are deprived of any financial assistance whatsoever.

The period of the strike is considered time spent in service, that is, it counts towards the calculation of the various allowances, compensation, etc.

Social security is cut off throughout the period during which no wage is being paid. If the strike is short term, the continuation of the social security depends upon claims and the payment of wages during the strike.

Public Dialogue

Although Greek law does not foresee independent institutions of conciliation, mediation and arbitration, in the case of strikes, resort to the services of the Organisation of Mediation and Arbitration is possible. In addition, the legislation imposes another process of mediation upon the social parties. This process is public dialogue (Article 3, Law 2224/1994).

Public dialogue is obligatory when the strike concerns workers whose legal status is regulated under civil law and who are employed in the public sector, in organisations of local government, in organisations regulated by the public

From the celebration of the 1st May

TABLE 2
Strike Activity in Greece 1990 - 1999

Year	PRIVATE SECTOR			BANKS - PUBLIC UTILITIES			TOTAL		
	Strikes	Strikers	Hours Lost	Strikes	Strikers	Hours Lost	Strikes	Strikers	Hours Lost
1990	135	798,405	10,258,638	65	607,092	10,076,675	200	1,405,497	20,335,313
1991	98	345,294	3,769,877	63	131,288	2,069,786	161	476,582	5,839,663
1992	110	366,566	2,740,698	56	602,918	4,331,310	166	969,484	7,072,008
1993	42	326,664	2,286,648	41	174,610	1,222,396	83	501,274	3,509,044
1994	48	149,029	1,046,514	8	77,126	826,385	56	226,155	1,872,899
1995	30	101,697	570,177	12	20,353	95,853	42	122,050	666,030
1996	20	190,451	1,330,744	11	43,223	302,764	31	233,674	1,633,508
1997	21	159,700	1,122,884	15	57,099	405,720	36	216,799	1,528,604
1998	8	94,469	661,283	30	119,438	854,064	38	213,907	1,515,347
1999 *	5	439	29,180	10	3,972	16,462	15	4,411	45,642
Totals	517	2,532,714	23,816,643	311	1,837,119	20,201,415	828	4,369,833	44,018,058

* May 1999
Source: Ministry of Labour

law and in public enterprises of social services. In this case, prior to exercising their right to strike, the union organisations are obligated to call upon the employer to engage in a public dialogue on their demands. In other enterprises, the union organisation that declares the strike may ask for a public dialogue to be conducted before or during the period of the strike. The employer also has the right to request a public dialogue. A mediator chosen from the list of mediators/arbitrators of OMED directs the public dialogue.

If the mediator cannot bring the two parties together within 48 hours, then he has the right to submit to the parties, a report of the demands of the strike based on their viewpoints and the related supporting material. This report, under certain circumstances, may be published in the daily press by the mediator or by one of the two parties involved. The conducting of the public dialogue does not suspend the right to strike.

Lock-Out

Aggressive or defensive lockouts, under Law 1268/1982, article 22, paragraph 2, along with the hiring of strikebreakers is not allowed. The employers however, may respond with the use of other rights.

Participatory Institutions

The meaning of participation, either in the form of co-decision making or in the form of influencing decisions or ultimately in the form of profit sharing, was shaped within the different national systems of industrial relations during the First World War and was systematised following the Second World War.

The appearance of such institutions within the Greek system was connected either with certain professions (e.g. tobacco workers in the inter-war period) or it was conjectural (e.g. bank workers after the withdrawal of the occupying forces at the end of the World War Two). Of course initiatives by individual business are not prohibited.

Within the context of the structural changes stemming from the European and other obligations of Greece in the last twenty years, but also for ideological reasons, in the early 1980's, the introduction of participatory institutions has developed at a faster pace. The prime mover behind these institutions is the state. These institutions modernise the Greek system of industrial relations and although they have not yet been consolidated, they do not cease to be important for its further development. The introduction and the regulation of participatory institutions in the Greek legal system correspond to the multiformity of the notion of participation. However, with the exception of certain agreements, the institution of profit sharing does not exist.

Advisory Labour Councils

These are foreseen by Law 1767/1988 and concern businesses employing at least 50 people or those employing 20 persons, on the condition that union lo-cals have not been established within them.

The number of members on the advisory council depends upon the size of the enterprise: 3 members in enterprises employing up to 300 workers; 5 members in enterprises employing from 301 to 1000 workers, and 7 members in enterprises employing from 1001 or more workers. The members of the advisory council, directly elected every two years by secret ballot, enjoy legal immunity from firing. In contrast to other legislation, the union organisations do not have a "monopoly" on the list of candidates.

The president of the labour advisory council, or his deputy, is excused from the obligation to provide work for two hours a week, as long as this is necessary for the exercise of these duties.

The employer and the advisory labour council meet within the first 10 days of every second month.

The employer is obligated to provide appropriate office space for the advisory council in the work place and an appropriate location for the placing of its announcements.

Jurisdiction of the Advisory Councils

The functioning of the labour council is participatory and consultative and is aimed at the improvement of working conditions in combination with business development.

The labour councils co-operate with

the union organisation of the enterprise and they inform it concerning issues within their jurisdiction. Along with the employer, the Labour Councils decide on: a) the establishment of internal rules, b) the rules concerning health and safety of the enterprise, c) the establishment of information programmes on the new organisational methods of the company and the use of new technologies, d) the planning of training and continuing education, e) methods for control of the presence and behaviour of staff within the framework of the protection of the worker's individual identity, f) the planning of social leave g) the rehabilitation of those disabled as a result of work site accidents, j) the planning and the control of cultural, entertainment and social activities.

The Council carries out these functions, as we have seen, only to the extent that a union does not exist and that these issues are not regulated by collective agreement.

The Labour Council studies and proposes ways of improving the productivity of all the factors of production, proposes measures for the improvement of terms and conditions of work, and proposes people for the Health and Safety Committee from its membership.

Provision of Information

The employer is obligated to inform the Labour Council on some issues, prior to the implementation of the respective decisions (e.g. changes in the legal standing of the enterprise, the introduction of new technology, the planning of production, the introduction of the enterprise budget, etc.). The institution of the Labour Advisory Councils, due to the small size of Greek businesses and other historical reasons, has not been fully consolidated as an institution which complements the daily activity of the trade unions.

Participation in Public Corporations and Public Utilities

(Electrical power, telecommunications, post, radio or television, banks or insurance companies which belong to the public sector, etc.).

Here, participation exclusively concerns the so-called "socialised companies" and refers to participation in the administration, in the laying out of strategy, in the planning and controlling of these enterprises (Law 1365/1983).

Participation is implemented through the *Representative Council of Social Control* in which representatives of the workers, of the state, of the local government, as well as representatives from social agencies and organisations that are related to or are influenced by these companies participate.

So far, the participatory institution has not developed as much as anticipated by legislators in the 1980s. As was expected however, the extensive privatisations in recent years have not facilitated the further implementation and consolidation of this form of participation.

Law 2414/1996 concerning the modernisation of public enterprises and organisations provides the possibility for transforming the public corporations into market oriented companies.

Two worker representatives participate on the Board of Directors of these enterprises. These representatives are elected directly by secret ballot. (Article 6 in Law 2414/1996 and Article 17 in Law 2469/1997).

Worker representatives are also foreseen in the *Supervising Councils* of the enterprise in the mining and metals sector (Law 1385/1983). However, this law was never implemented and was finally abolished (Law 2000/1991).

Health and Safety Committee

The workers participate with represen-tatives on these councils, if the enterprise employs more than fifty persons. If the enterprise employs from 20-50 persons, an elected representative is appointed for the work health and safety in the company (Law 1568/1985). If a Labour Advisory Council is functioning within the enterprise, then the Council suggests members for the Health and Safety Committee from among its members.

In the case of direct and serious danger, the committee (or representative) calls upon the employer to take immediate measures without ruling out the shutting down of the factory and its production.

The final form of participation is the *union action at the enterprise* level which is recognised and strengthened legally (Law 1264/1982).

THE SOCIAL DIALOGUE IN GREECE

By Valia Aranitou and Matina Yannakourou

In the course of the last two decades the role of organised interests in the Greek political system has become differentiated to a great degree. Whereas an issue of legitimacy had been raised, there is presently a reversal of the terms and a strengthening of their role to the point, at the turn of the new century, the celebrated social partners possess a privileged position in the legitimation of social and political choices. It should be noted that the introduction of social dialogue institutions and their establishment in the minds of the parties involved (such as the government, the employers and the work force) has been delayed remarkably in Greece in comparison to the rest of the European Union (EU) member states. This delay is due to the lack of a social dialogue tradition, a lack of familiarisation with the philosophy and the processes of such a tradition, as well as a predominant atmosphere of suspicion and conflict in the relations of the parties involved.

For quite a period of time in Greece the term "social dialogue" was identified with collective bargaining leading eventually to the conclusion of a collective labour agreement (SSE). A broader use of the term increasingly started to become evident, which included:

a. autonomous social dialogue, that is, collective bargaining among the representative organisations of the employers and the working people.

b. institutionalised deliberation of the government with delegates of the social partners conducted within established national-level dialogue structures (the Economic and Social Council by virtue of Law No. 2232/1994, the National Land Planning Council by virtue of Law No. 2742/1999, etc), as well as through the participation of the social partners in the decision-making bodies (the Boards of Directors and the Public Policy Commissions), and

c. non-institutionalised deliberation, conducted either in on-going informal agencies (e.g., the National Council on Competitiveness) or provisional forums (for example, the National Co-ordination Committee on the Euro), or it may assume the form of more or less structured tri-partisan or bipartisan contacts among the government and the social partners.

It is generally understood that *social partners* participating and implementing the social dialogue are the following most representative summit-level trade union organisations of the employers and the working people who sign the General National Labour Collective Agreement (EGSSE). To be specific:

On the part of the workers: The General Workers Confederation of Greece (GSEE) is the only representative organisation by law on a federated level. Another leading trade union organisation participating in the said dialogue is the Supreme Public Employee Unions Directorate (ADEDY).

On the part of the employers: The Greek Industrialist Association (SEV) was founded in 1907. The General Small-Industry, Professionals and Merchants Confederation (GSEVEE) was founded in 1919. The federated organisation for trade, the National Confederation for Hellenic Trade (ESEE) was founded as late as 1994, long after the other respective trade organisations.

Other organisations may participate in this social dialogue process, depending on the circumstances. These include farmer representative organisations, consumer organisations, scientific associations and the various Chambers of Greece, the delegates from local and prefectural governments, etc.

Social dialogue in Greece nowadays yields substantial results on a national level mainly in milieus that foster positive preconditions for a culture of debate.

On the contrary, with regards to the provincial, local and co-operative levels, the establishment of institutions and instruments by legislation favouring such social dialogue has not managed so far to create the necessary potential.

Institutional social dialogue on a national level in Greece

The most important manifestations of this kind of dialogue process is the par-

ticipation of the representatives of the social partners in the decision-making centres (Ia), the collective bargaining for the signing of the General National Labour Collective Agreement *(EGSEE)* (Ib) and the operation of the Economic and Social Council (Ic).

Participation of social partners in commissions and public policy councils

In the 90s there was a significant increase in the participation of the social partners in policy proceedings.

Representatives of the General Workers Confederation of Greece participate in 140 Committees and Council under the authority of various ministries (with dominant presence on the boards of the Ministry of Labour, the Ministry of Health, Welfare and the Ministry of National Education). They also participate in three District Councils, nine Committees of the Prefecture of Attica and Piraeus and on all the Monitoring Committees of the progress of the Third Community Support Framework.

The representatives of three employers' organisations participate in more than sixty permanent national-level structures and in many more on a local level. They also take part in deliberation committees on specific issues, such as the social security and the taxation issues. The most indicative of these are the Board of Directors of the Social Security Foundation (IKA), the National Consumer Council, the National Export Council and the Organisations of Workforce Employment *(OAED)*, in which the administration is tripartite and equally distributed, the two social partners designating their own delegates as representatives. They also participate in the National Commission on Competitiveness and the Competition Committee, the Capital Market Commission, the Monitoring Committees of the Third Community Support Framework for Greece, the Boards of Directors of the Workers' Welfare Organisation, the Worker's Housing Organisations, etc.

Traditional forms of social dialogue: the collective bargaining for the general national labour collective agreement

The process applied for the negotiations and the conclusion of the General National Labour Collective Agreement is the expression of an embedded climate of social peace par excellence. It reflects the willingness of the parties involved (the GSEE, SEV, ESEE, GSEVEE) to commit themselves and work out mutually accepted solutions not only for worker's rights, but also for more encompassing issues. These issues pertain to employment, vocational training, competitiveness and productivity, free of any state intervention or any appeal to mediation from other persons or agencies. At the same time, the maturity in the relations of the parties involved is verified by the terms of the General National Labour Collective Agreement,

renewable every two years as a rule.

Furthermore, the contents of the General National Labour Collective Agreement has expanded to significant degree with innovative approaches on issues pointing to the connection of the collective negotiations with employment policies and in general with social policies. Very indicative of such an approach is the establishment of the Employment-Unemployment Fund (LAEK) in 1993, whose management and funding has been undertaken solely by the social partners in question.

The social dialogue in the economic and social council *(oke)*

The Economic and Social Council (OKE) was founded by virtue of Law No. 2232/1994 as a central platform for social dialogue with the most representative of the country's social agents on economic and social policy issues.

The makeup of the OKE was based on the respective composition of the OKE in the EU. For this reason, it is further broken down into three groups. The first reflects the business sector-employers, the second private sector and public administration workers, and the third the remaining productive classes (such as farmers, professionals, local municipal and community governments, the Chambers, etc). The law expressly stipulates which organisations are to participate in the OKE, which shall be federated and representative of the sector that they reflect.

The OKE exercises a mainly opinion-issuing and advisory authority over legislation bills on labour, social security, investment, internal revenue, competition, development issues among others. In the recent 2001 constitutional amendment, the OKE was granted constitutionally protected institutional status (Article 82, Section 3-1975/1986/2001 Const.).

By the end of 2002, the OKE had issued a total of 86 opinions (55 of them at the request of the Ministry and 31 on its own initiative). In the period between 1996 and 2001 the government requested the opinion of the OKE on about an average 42.3% of legislation bills pushed through to Parliament under the jurisdiction of the Commission. The actual speciality of the OKE by nature constitutes a multi-participatory and polyphonic institution (eighteen federated social and professional associations are represented on its board) aimed at the expression, the debate, the contest and hopefully the coalescence of the divergent interests manifested in Greek society.

By the end of 2003, two new national-level dialogue bodies will have been institutionalised: the National Employment Committee and the National Social Protection Committee. The first will pursue the formation of policies that promote an increase in employment figures and dealing with unemployment, while the latter will aim at confronting poverty and social exclusion.

Non-institutionalised social dialogue on a national level in Greece

Besides the aforementioned permanent structures of social dialogue, whether presently operating on an established basis, such as the OKE or in the process of preparation, such as the National Employment Committee and the National Social Protection Committee, there are also other permanent non-institutional agencies such as the National Council on Competitiveness (ESA). The ESA commenced operations following an initiative of the Ministry of Development and the request of the Greek Industrialist Association (SEV) as an agency to help promote competitiveness in the Greek economy with no provision as to its composition.

The first attempt to conduct a general tripartite dialogue with the social partners aimed at reaching consensus on reforms vis-a-vis the induction of Greece into the Economic Monetary Union took place in 1997.

Following discussions that lasted for six months, an agreement was signed that came to be more widely known as the "Government - Social Partners Confidence Agreement on the Course to the Year 2000".

Other significant experiences with expanded non-institutional dialogue on a national level were recorded during the preparation of social security and taxation reform.

The dialogue on social security was

conducted in many more stages. The first stage lasted from May 1997 until May 1998, processing the proposals on measures for the direct support *(the small package)* of the social security system aiming at the rationalisation and the efficient functioning of the system. The second phase of the dialogue for the promotion of the subsidy base of the social security system was inaugurated in April 2001 upon the initiative taken by the Ministry of Labour and Social Security. The course of the dialogue, however, was halted even before its formal opening due to pronounced opposition on the side of the workers. The third phase of the dialogue began in March 2002 from a blank slate under the pressure of the EU and finally assumed the form of a political arrangement of the whole issue. It was finally completed in July 2002 with the ratification of Law No. 3029/2002.

The taxation reform debate seems to have been more successful and effective in that it is more structured and wider in scope. This discussion began in April 2002 and lasted for two months. This dialogue was conducted within the framework of the Central Co-ordinating Social Dialogue Committee, comprised of representatives from the social agencies, political parties, the Ministry of Finance and special experts, meeting regularly under the co-ordination of the Secretary General of the Ministry of Finance. Both the principles and the positions processed by the Central Com-

mittee were reflected in the subsequent taxation legislation bills for the simplification of the Bookkeeping and Accounting Figures Code *(KVS)*, the manner of paying the value-added tax *(FPA)* and income and capital tax.

Conclusions

Social dialogue in Greece has developed in a piecemeal and painful manner, facing many difficulties due to the long tradition of state intervention in the charting and implementation of financial and social policies. This kind of interventionism expressed in the reduction of legislation to the dominant source of regulation has contributed to the lack of a dialogue culture on the part of all the parties involved. It should be stressed that the role of the social partners has been remarkably strengthened in recent years with regard to the making of financial and social decisions. An indication of this is the tendency towards the institutionalisation of permanent national-level structures of dialogue with the social partners and/or agencies or in the direction of mapping the overall national policy *(OKE)*, either in separate policy sectors (the National Land Planning Council, the National Council on Competitiveness, the National Employment, the National Social Protection Committee).

This favourable direction has been paved by a variety of factors. These include the positive climate fostered by the employer and trade union summit organisations, the institutionalisation of permanent organisations facilitating the convergence of these organisation in the same conference room and also by the participation of our country in the EU, where dialogue is part and parcel of the Community *acquis*. The government has been drawn into committing itself to discussions with all social partners (as for example in the preparation of the National Action Employment Plans) for economic and social policies. This process has been facilitated by the familiarisation of the leaderships of these social partner groups who have finally arrived at the philosophy of social dialogue, through extensive participation in institutions and committees encompassing European social dialogue.

THE WELFARE STATE IN GREECE

By Y. Yfantopoulos

Indroduction

Throughout the 1980s Greece was in the phase of regulating the welfare system by introducing important legislative acts. After the reestablishment of democracy in 1974, the social objectives were redefined and new policies were introduced, aimed at the expansion of social insurance coverage, improving access to social services, balancing regional inequalities and reallocating resources towards the needy and the lower income classes. The objective of equity was very well expressed in many legislative acts introduced during the 1980s. However, despite the good intentions of the reformists, neither the public administration machinery, nor the economic climate was supportive of launching large-scale social reforms. The civil services was not qualified enough to implement new public management techniques, and there was a low incentive for productive and efficient utilisation of public resources. The lack of qualified public managers in the civil service contributed to the limited absorption of the European Structural Funds. Furthermore, in the 1980s, the sluggish economic growth, the high rate of inflation combined with mismanagement, lead to increasing public deficits and economic imbalances. At the same time the government faced an accumulated social demand for health and social reforms. Major reforms were introduced including the establishment of a National Health Service System (Law Act 1397 in 1983) but these reforms were not accompanied by the necessary public management steps in order to ensure an efficient implementation of the stated objectives.

The 1990s brought a new era of scepticism and a rethinking of social objectives. Equity was reconsidered by taking into account efficiency, effectiveness, economic growth, and public satisfaction with the anticipated reforms. Party politics within the public sector were criticised and several privatisation schemes were introduced. At the same time the European Commission demanded better utilisation of European Funds and the Government was asked to submit proposals for funding supported by rigorous economic feasibility studies. Hence the period of 1990-1997 is characterised by the introduction of a new concept of public efficiency based on large scale monitoring and the evaluation of the implemented reforms.

Similar developments in the social and economic spheres have been identified in Spain, Portugal and Italy. In the social science literature these developments have often been discussed and analysed and because of many similari-

*The IKA Building at
Kerameikos, Athens*

ties among these Countries we often make reference to the so-called Southern European Welfare Model.

The purpose of this paper is to discuss the evolution of the Greek Welfare system in conjunction with social policy developments in the European Union.

Section 1 presents the evolution of social expenditures in the EU and Greece. Emphasis is given to the converging trends witnessed in Greece after 1994.

Section 2 focuses on poverty and social exclusion and analyses the relative position of Greece with respect to the rest of the European Member States. Section 3 discusses the organisational structure of the welfare state in Greece and provides a brief overview of the financing and distribution of social insur-

ance expenditures. Finally section 4 critically assesses the welfare policies and reforms launched during the period 1990-2002.

Social protection in the EU and Greece

The evolution of social expenditure in the European Union OVER the last decade displays an irregular path of development. Examining the evolutionary process, we may distinguish two different paths:

The *First Path* covers the period 1990-1993, and it is characterised by the expansionary role of the Welfare State. The expenditure in social protection as a percentage of GDP increased on the average, in the EU-15 Members by 3.3 percentage points i.e. from

25.5% in 1990 to 28.8% in 1993. (see diagram 1).

This increase is attributable to three major factors:

1) To a substantial rise in unemployment benefits.

2) To an overall rise in public expenditure

3) To a decline of economic growth.

In its economic report, the OECD argued that social policies should not have been implemented outside the reality of budget constraints and invited the Member States to:

1) Redefine social priorities and social objectives

2) Re-examine the evolutionary process of social expenditure

3) Introduce more cost effective thinking in order to increase efficiency

4) Reallocate responsibilities and actions from the public to the private sector.

On the basis of the above proposals the Governments of the European Union introduced several measures to control their social spending. The result of these policies was the downsizing of the social sector. (see diagram 1)

The *Second Path* covers the years 1994-1999, where after a short stabilisation during the period 1994 to 1996, a downward trend in social expenditure was observed. (see diagram 1). The fall in the share of social expenditure in GDP was 0.8 percentage points. The main reason for this reduction is attributable to:

Diagram 1

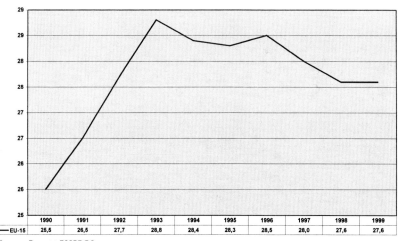

Expediture on Social Protection in EU-15 (as % of GDP)

	1990	1991	1992	1993	1994	1995	1996	1997	1998	1999
EU-15	25,5	26,5	27,7	28,8	28,4	28,3	28,5	28,0	27,6	27,6

Source: Eurostat-ESSPROS

1) a slow-down of unemployment benefits

2) a slight upturn of economic growth.

Although the downsizing of social protection expenditure was fairly general in all EU Countries, some States such as Greece and Portugal have managed to adopt different paths of development.

Examining the evolutionary process of social expenditure in Greece during the 1990s we can see:

1) *Diverging* trends in the first period 1990-1993 where a drop in social expenditure of 0.9 percentage points is observed (from 22.9% in 1990 to 22.0% in 1993) (Diagram 2).

2) *Converging* trends during the period 1994-1999 with a corresponding increase of social expenditure of 3.5 percentage points (i.e. from 22.0% to 25.5% in 1999) (Diagram 2).

A comparative view of the different paths of development is shown in diagram 2.

A plausible explanation for these differences in the path of social development may be attributed to historical delays in the evolution of the welfare system in Greece as well as to the lack of trained public administration personnel to implement the necessary social reforms.

In 1999 the per capita social protection expenditure in the EU-15 was 5.93 Euro (see diagram 3). In order to establish better comparisons among the Member States we express the expenditure in purchasing power standards. Greece, Portugal and Spain representing

Diagram 2

Expediture on social protection (as % of GDP)

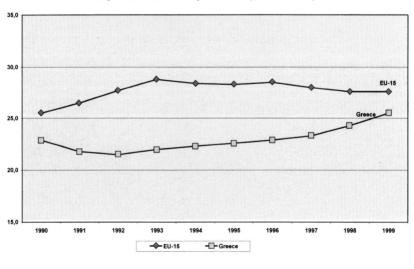

Diagram 3

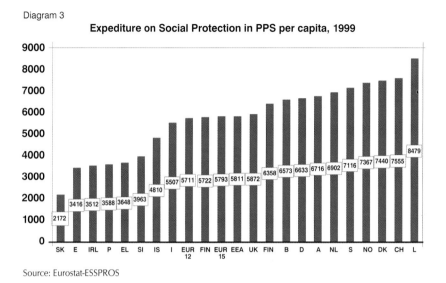

Expediture on Social Protection in PPS per capita, 1999

Source: Eurostat-ESSPROS

the Southern European block, spend relatively less than the EU average on social protection. Luxembourg, Denmark and the rest of the Northern European countries, in comparison to Southern Member States, devote twice as much for their social spending (see diagram 3). The disparities between countries are related to i) different levels of socio-economic development, ii) organisational structures between the welfare systems, iii) demographic profiles of the population iv) unemployment rates, v) effectiveness of the welfare system to accomplish social objectives.

Poverty and social exclusion

The Nice Summit in December 2000 confirmed social policy as an integral part of the overall economic policies of the Union. However, despite the good will of the European policy makers, as many as 17% of European Citizens live below the poverty line, defined as 60% of the national median income (Diagram 4). Poverty varies significantly among the Member States ranging from 24% in Portugal, and 21% in Greece and Ireland, to 10% in the Netherlands and Denmark (11%). These differences may be attributed to economic, political and cultural factors that have contributed to the evolution of the welfare states in Europe. In addition, almost all European Countries (except Greece), have developed minimum income schemes to protect EU citizens from poverty and social deprivation. Some governments like the northern European and the Scandinavian ones have developed effective targeted social policies to combat poverty and social exclusion. In Greece, despite the evolution of the welfare services and the implemented reforms in the National Health Service system and the Social Insurance sector, there are some institutional and bureaucratic obstacles that prevent the effective redistribution of resources towards the poor and socially excluded persons.

Following the proposal of the European Commission, each Member State undertook the responsibility to submit in September 2001, a National Action Plan to fight poverty and social exclusion. The Greek report presented some "stylised facts" indicating the social groups which are at a high risk of poverty and social exclusion:

1) The elderly and the very old confront a high risk of poverty. This risk is much higher in Greece relative to the EU average. In Greece, the poverty rate for the age group 65 and above is 33%. The corresponding figure for the EU is 20%.

2) The economic position of the pensioners appeared to deteriorate up to 1994. Some positive improvements have been realised since then.

3) Poverty is related to geographical areas and is more apparent in rural areas.

4) Unemployment and access to the labour market and social services appear to be the major factors contributing to poverty.

5) The informal social networks and the "family" as nucleus of Greek society still play and important role in preventing poverty and social exclusion.

The welfare state in Greece

The Welfare State in Greece is administered through a complex system of public and private institutions. According to the 2002 Social Budget, more than 170 insurance agencies and institutions are functioning, supervised by six different Ministries with a multiplicity of social objectives and overlapping services. The Ministry of Labour and Social Insurance is responsible for the organisation and administration of social insurance services. There are approximately 95 insurance agencies supervised by the Ministry of Labour and Social Insurance. The Ministry of Health and Welfare deals with the primary health centres, the hospitals, the social centres for the children and the elderly, as well as the regional distribution of health and welfare services. The Ministry of Defence supervises 10 insurance units that provide health services and pensions schemes for the army personnel and their dependants. The Ministry of Agriculture deals with the provision of health care to the rural population. The Ministry of the Merchant Navy supervises 7 insurance schemes that cover seamen and their dependants. Finally, the Ministry of Finance undertakes the role of financing the above services. In addition to above, there are approximately 56 sickness and pension funds specialised in

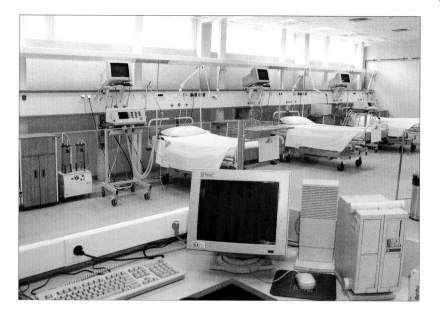

the provision of supplementary welfare services.

Approximately one hundred of the above institutions provide medical health care benefits and the remaining offer varying forms of pension schemes, unemployment benefits and other types of insurance.

Organisational and Administrative Structures

At present the largest insurance units which provide various forms of insurance benefits are the following:

- IKA (Institute of Social Insurance) Insurance coverage is provided to urban population - blue and white collar workers)
  - OGA (Organisation of Agricultural

Insurance) The rural population is covered under by a means test system

- TEVE TAE (Insurance Fund for Merchants Manufacturers, and small trade Businessmen)
  - Civil Servants
  - OTE (Telecommunications personnel)
    - DEH (Electricity personnel)
    - BANK INSURANCE UNITS (Banking personnel)

Table 1 presents the number of directly and indirectly insured individuals under each of the above organisations. The majority of the Greek population is covered under IKA (50.35%), OGA (19.6%) and TEVE-TAE (14.3%).

In an attempt to describe the spectrum of services provided by the insur-

Table 1 Insured Population by Insurance Scheme

Insurance Fund	Directly Insured	Indirectly Insured	Total	% of total Population
IKA	2,900,000	2,620,000	5,520,000	50.35%
OGA	1,543,000	607,000	2,150,000	19.6%
TEVE	500,390	758,085	1,258,475	11.5%
TAE	113,000	192,000	305,000	2.8%
OTE	87,315	114,395	201,710	1.8%
DEH	59,500	74,015	133,515	1.2%
Banks	8,010	9,445	17,455	0.2%
Total (Census2001)	5,595,244	4,768,615	10,363,859	10,964,020

Source: Social Budget

ance organisations we show in table 2 the insurance coverage for outpatient, hospital, pharmaceutical, dental, laboratory and other services.

In Diagram 5 we present the organisational structure of the Greek Health Insurance Services. We follow the OECD approach to present the interaction between:

- Population
- Central Government
- Social insurance funds
- Private agents

Diagram 5 describes the complexity of the Greek health services on the financing and delivery side.

Co-ordination is required among the insurance agencies in order to ensure a better organisation of the various insurance schemes, as well as, to protect peo-

Table 2 Spectrum of Services provided by the Insurance Funds

Insurance Fund	Out patient	Hospital	Pharma-ceutical	Dental	Laboratory	Other
IKA	+	+	+	+	+	+
OGA	+	+	+	-	+	+
TEVE	+	+	+	-	+	+
TAE	+	+	+	-	-	+
OTE	+	+	+	+	+	+
DEH	+	+	+	+	+	+
Banks	+	+	+	+	+	

Source: Social Budget

Diagramme 5 THE GREEK SOCIAL INSURANCE SYSTEM

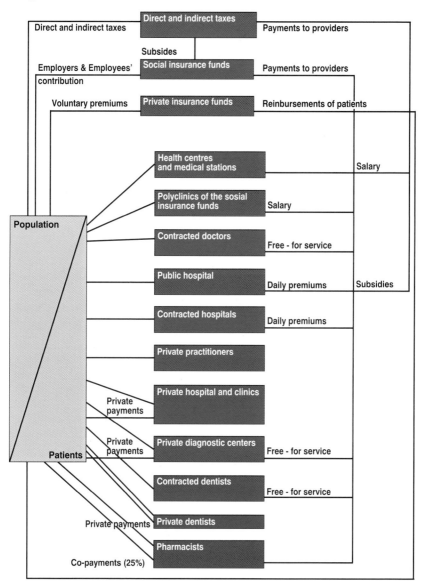

ple from heavy double or triple insurance coverage. As long as this co-ordination is not achieved, the injustice and the inequalities in the distribution should be faced gradually by specifying common objectives and developing synchronised policies. A short-term objective to be further discussed below is to develop harmonised policies, which will lead to the gradual integration of OGA, IKA, TEBE and other units under a unified insurance system. The cost of social insurance may be reduced due to economies of scale, as well as to possible reductions in the over-utilisation of services. New methods of management should be developed among the insurance agencies in order to control the increasing defect and develop rational cost-containment policies. The different insurance system schemes should be adequately administrated in order to obtain the best cost-benefit ratio.

Financing

The main source of financing for social insurance in Greece are the employers' and employees' contributions. (Diagram 6). Employers' contributions represent 31% of the total revenues whereas the corresponding figure for employees' contribution reaches a similar level of 33%. (Diagram 6).

The figures for employees' contributions include the self employed. There are great disparities among the social insurance organisations in their contribution rates. The financing of IKA,

TEVE, OTE, and the Banking insurance units is mainly from employers and employees contributions. In the case of OGA, the State covers the total Budget through earmarked and community taxation. During the last decade there were increasing pressures in the financing of social insurance services. The Government could not increase the contribution rates, and at the same time, the cost of social care had been escalating. The result has been increasing deficits in the major insurance units, which had a profound impact on the reduction of the quality of provided services.

Furthermore, the level of minimum pension benefits was below the poverty limit. However, at the same time a relatively large proportion of people enjoyed pension benefits without fulfilling the age criterion (65 years). It has often been argued that the distribution of social benefits and pensions in particular has been influenced by "political and clientelistic" relationships. Recently, there have several attempts to re-consider the eligibility criteria for providing pensions. Despite the implemented policies, the burden of financing social services is still severe and there is no sign at least in the short run of an ability to combat the deficit.

Social Insurance Expenditure

As presented above, there are several Ministries involved in the provision of Social Services in Greece. The Ministry of Labour and Social Insurance plays the

Diagram 6 Social insurance Revenues 2002

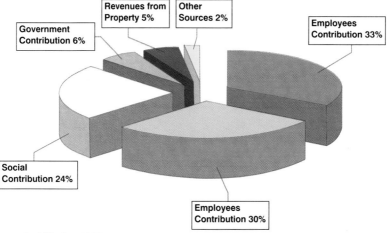

Source: Social Budget 2002

leading role in the provision of benefits (both in cash and in kind), and in budgetary terms, it absorbs the highest percentage, accounting more than 81% of the total funds devoted to the social sector. The rest of the Ministries play a relatively minor role and the funds devoted to them out of the Social Budget constitute only 13% for the Ministry of Finance, and 6% for the rest of the Ministries. Since the Ministry of Labour and Social Insurance is the responsible administrative and political entity for providing social services, it is crucial to further examine the allocation of funds among the major social functions.

Pensions represent one of the largest functions of the modern welfare world. In all Members of the European Union

the expenditure on pension are growing exponentially due to the ageing effect. Among all the EU Member States, Greece is the only Country with the highest share of social expenditure devoted to Pensions. As much as 69% of the Social budget goes for pensions (see Diagram 7). For this reason the Greek welfare system, it was often argued, serves largely one function, that of the elderly, leaving little space for the development of the rest of the Welfare Services.

Sickness is the second function absorbing 21% of the Social Budget. It should be noted here that several reforms have been undertaken in the health sector, which were explored at some length above. Despite the expansion in social coverage since the 1960s, after the establishment of OGA, public expenditure on health has not shown a growth similar to those of other European countries, which have undergone similar institutional changes. The fact that the expansion in social insurance has not been accompanied by a corresponding increase in public expenditure has resulted in a decline in the quality of services provided.

In Greece, social expenditure has been devoted to various functions and services without taking into account the efficiency and the effectiveness aspects of the system. Very little economic analysis has been undertaken in the social field and the provision of social benefits is distributed without taking into account the alternative cost benefit options. Any proposal for reform should be accompanied with a detailed feasibility study highlighting the social costs and benefits of the proposed actions.

Health reforms

All the Member States have faced increasing demands for more and better quality services. Given the commitment of the European Health models to principles of equity and universality of access to health services, several reforms have been introduced aimed at cost containment and efficiency in the utilisation of services. The European Commission invited the Member States to:

Contribute to improve the efficiency and effectiveness of health systems so that they achieve their objectives within available resources. To this end, ensure that medical knowledge and technology is used in the most effective way possi-

Diagram 7   Social insurance Expenditure by Function 2000

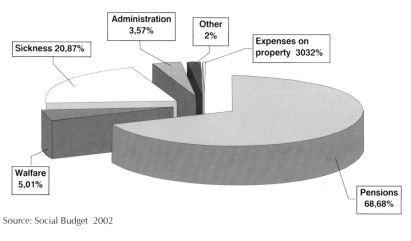

Source: Social Budget 2002

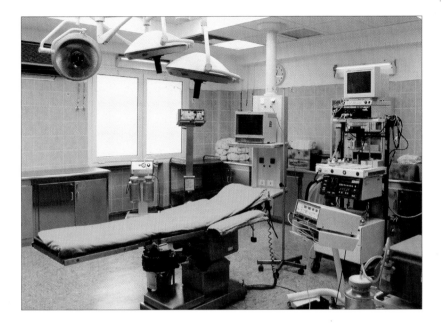

ble and strengthen co-operation between Member States on evaluation of policies and techniques.

In order to achieve greater efficiency health reforms have been introduced aiming at the regionalisation and decentralisation of services. Greater responsibilities have been given to regions to organise their hospitals and general practitioners. Greece has not been an exception to this rule. Legislative act 2889 passed on 2 March, 2001 established 17 Regional Health Authorities (PESYS). Under this law, hospitals and primary care centres have become decentralised units run by professional managers. Each PESY is responsible for developing an operational plan and for devising pri-

orities to allocate resources efficiently. At the same time an integrated geographical information system is being put together to record and monitor health care needs.

Furthermore a new administrative body has been proposed called ODIPY. It has undertaken the major role of pooling all the funds from the public and private insurance agencies and allocating resources to each PESY on the basis of demographic, epidemiological, social and economic criteria. ODIPY is based on the philosophy of quasi-market thinking according to which is would purchase services from hospital and primary health centres and other public or private providers of services.

The overall picture and policy implications

In this section we bring together the principal results of the preceding analysis and we identify and categorise the kinds of problems which face the Greek Social Service Sector today. After a review of these problems we propose a framework and discuss the principal areas upon which research activity should be focused. Reviewing the main issues of the Greek social insurance system, we can identify two major problem categories.

• Problems associated with the insurance system and the quality of services.

• Problems related to efficiency and allocation of social expenditure.

Problems associated with the Insurance System

In the Social Insurance sector, a major objective is the achievement of one comprehensive and universal system, which will enable people to have better access to social insurance benefits. The great disparities, which are observed in the provision of social benefits, are not only socially unjust, but also economically dangerous since they present obstacles to the efficient functioning of the labour market. The inequalities in the provision of social services and benefits have been estimated by several researchers through the use of the Gini coefficient. This is a measure of inequality taking a range of values between zero = absence of inequality, and one = extreme inequality. Any value between this range reveals the extent of inequality within a society or a social group. Gini coefficients are shown below for the per capita social insurance benefits provided for medical care and for pensions. Gini Coefficients for the per capita Medical Benefits provided by the insurance organisations are:

G = 0.4658 for outpatient care
G = 0.3507 for hospital care
G = 0.4111 for total health benefits

In the case of per-capita expenditure on pensions, it was found that there exist higher inequalities in the lower pension categories. This finding highlights the lack of a comprehensive "social net" for the provision of minimum pensions. The Gini coefficients for the pension categories are the following:

1) Very low pensions
(less than 300,000 annually) G = 0.256
2) Low Pensions
(up to 550,000 annually) G = 0.208
3) Average Pensions
(551,000 to 1,400,000) G = 0.127
4) High Pensions
(1,401,000 to 5,000,000) G = 0.036

The limited insurance benefits provided by certain organisations should be increased, and the whole system should be reorganised towards a more comprehensive one.

Although there have been many studies concerning the organisation of insurance coverage and the financing of different insurance schemes (both centralised and decentralised), very few have considered what seem to be the vital factors concerning the optimality aspect of a social insurance system. It has been argued in the literature that, whatever the harmonising intention of different insurance schemes, choice of the insurance coverage, co-insurance and deductible policies adopted by a system, a crucial factor for evaluating these policies should be related to the analysis of equity and efficiency aspects of the system. The optimal degree of insurance coverage for a group (or different groups) of people should not only be related to the level of income (as it has often been argued, but furthermore, it should also be related to the level of social needs of these people. Any analysis which is based on the consumption of social services provided by an insurance scheme, without considering social needs as a significant variable and the impact which social services have upon social risks, seems to omit one of the crucial factors for policy evaluation. The degree of insurance coverage may vary with the level of needs.

For example in the case of health services, if the health status of the rural population (OGA) is produced under conditions of decreasing cost, then a potential increase in the level of health status for these people would decrease the average cost of producing it. Hence OGA could achieve a net economic

benefit without decreasing the quality and quantity of services.

It has been proposed by the group of experts that in order to simplify the complexity of the Greek insurance system a possible solution may be the integration of OGA, IKA and TEBE under a unified insurance system, although they do not mention how this can be achieved. Such a proposal, as well as any other proposal of this kind, requires an empirical investigation to identify to what extent such an integration would prove more effective and more efficient, in terms of increases in output and reductions of unit costs.

Problems related to efficiency and the allocation of Social Expenditure

From the preceding analysis, we saw that Greece, after 1993, has increased substantially the share of GDP for social protection expenditure. However, despite relatively high spending, the effectiveness of the social sector in combating poverty and social exclusion has not very high.

The group of experts has proposed that an assessment of the efficiency and the allocation of social expenditure is urgently required in order to partially satisfy the unfulfilled needs of Greek people for social services. However, before asserting to what degree social insurance resources or public institutions (public hospitals, social centres etc.) should be increased, we should introduce some methods for evaluating and controlling the performance of the numerous insurance agencies. The significance of the methods lies in their generality. This implies that whatever the form of financing an insurance scheme and whatever the insurance system (centralised or noncentralised), the information provided by these methods are fundamental and significant to the policy decision requiring the assessment of an efficient allocation of resources.

The crucial instrument for policy valuation is to study the impact of public expenditure upon social needs. In the vast literature of white papers, preambles to parliament acts, and Public policy reports, there appear to have been two underlying concerns throughout the OECD region to justify public expenditure on social protection.

(i) reduction of inequality of access to and use of social services.

(ii) an increase of the Social welfare Status and well being of the population in general.

Greece, being a member of the European Union and the OECD, may accept there is a need within the Ministry of Labour and Social Insurance as well as in the Ministry of Health and welfare for evaluating the allocation of public expenditure among programmes. However this is not the only piece of information required for assessing the efficiency aspects of the Welfare State. In order to allocate budgets or public money among different regions, insurance

schemes or institutions, it is not only knowledge of output that may prove useful, but also knowledge regarding the productivity of different inputs, as well as the interrelationship between the different institutions providing welfare services. This would help us to identify what the optimal combination of services is and to what extent possible increases in these services (through increases in public expenditure) would increase the Welfare Status and well being of Greek Citizens.

Conclusion

In our analysis so far we have identified the major problem areas concerning the regional distribution of health resources, insurance coverage and financing of different health care systems in Greece and in Europe.

Although there have been many studies concerning the managerial, the organisational, the inter- and intra-institutional relationships of the different insurance schemes (both centralised and decentralised), very few have considered what seem to be one of the vital factors concerning the efficiency, equity and effectiveness aspects of the Social Insurance System.

The optimal degree of insurance coverage, co-insurance and deductible policies adopted by a system should not be related to the level of income, or the level of risk, but rather it should also be related to the level of social need. The degree of insurance coverage may vary with the level of need, of various professions. Any analysis which is based on the consumption of social services provided by an insurance scheme, without considering the effectiveness and the efficiency aspects of resources as well as the distributional issues of these benefits seems to omit some crucial factors for policy evaluation.

There is currently, to the best of our knowledge, no research being undertaken to measure the alternative cost-effective procedures for providing social services through different insurance programmes. Also there has been a lack of research into measuring the redistributive impact of social insurance benefits by establishing who bears the cost of different insurance schemes and who receives the benefits.

Whatever the research interests, whatever the social regimes, what really matters in Greece is not so much to expand the insurance schemes and finance inefficient organisations but rather to guarantee that in the immediate future a certain level of quality of services will be accessible to everyone, in an efficient and effective way.

THE GREEK OMBUDSMAN

By N. Diamantouros and Chr. Adam

A) Background

The creation of the institution of the Greek Ombudsman in 1997 reflected the steadily increasing strength of democracy in Greece. The starting point occurred in 1974 with the establishment of the first genuinely democratic regime in the country's modern history. Consolidation of the democratic system in the late 1970s and early 1980s was a major achievement, indicating a new maturity of Greek society and its political culture. Yet, the consolidation of democracy, while now considered an indisputable fact, had obviously left still considerable margins for improvement in its quality.

Self-evaluation and the ability to create mechanisms of accountability easily accessible to citizens is one such critical aspect. Mechanisms of this nature make it feasible to identify in practice existing deficiencies of the institutions and functions of the state (both central and local) suggesting the remedial actions to be taken wherever necessary. In this sense, grassroots accountability and control become additional complimentary safeguarding tools of contemporary high quality democracy.

The Ombudsman is such an institution of grassroots accountability and control since it is primarily the citizens that trigger its business i.e. investigating complaints regarding problems they face during their everyday dealings with the state. As no Ministry oversees or restricts its operations, it is an independent administrative authority reporting on a regular basis directly to the highest level of government. According to its founding law, its aim is to protect citizens, to combat misadministration and to ensure observance of the laws through extra-judicial and mediatory means. Therefore, by its very set-up, it identifies the existing deficiencies of government in practice and acts as an early warning monitoring system indicating the path to be followed in order to remove everyday malfunctions in the running of the state. Thus, in a way, the Ombudsman is to the gov-

The Greek Ombudsman headquarters in Athens

ernment what a market poll is to the economy: a politics-free listening tool, when properly utilised, can allow for the fine-tuning of the state machine leading to the removal of its friction points.

Furthermore, the creation of the Greek Ombudsman is an additional step towards the development of the common institutional infrastructure necessary for streamlining the tools and political culture of the European Union member states[1], thus facilitating the creation of the new geopolitical entity currently under formation. This role dimension has instigated a series of contacts and activities of the Greek Ombudsman with fellow institutions abroad (including the European Ombudsman and thematically responsible EU services) and has already resulted in officially established lines of co-operation, presented further below.

B) Setting up a new model:

The headquarters of the Ombudsman are located at a central, easily accessible modern office building in Athens (5, Hadjiyanni Mexi St.). Nearby mass transportation networks (bus line and metro stops) and special street measures (restricted car parking, ramps, street signs) provide unimpeded access for people, including those with special needs. In a further effort to create a new model of public service and to increase effectiveness and transparency, up-to-date advanced modern electronic technology has been used throughout, while all levels of work are executed through electronic means and custom-tailored software programs. This not only facilitates day-to-day work, case monitoring and archiving, but also further allows for the automatic extraction of the all-important statistical data, which substantiate the findings. Independent researchers and students are welcome to use this information in specially reserved work-posts supplied with PCs connected to the office network, while a staffed library has been created in order to provide the necessary bibliographical support. The contents of the library are periodically increased by new volume additions while the staff is encouraged to request whatever editions it deems necessary for its work.

The Office of the Ombudsman was set up in three stages:

The first was the selection of the first Ombudsman, *Nikiforos Diamandouros*, Professor of Political Science in the Department of Political Science and Public Administration at the University of Athens. He assumed office on 1 May 1998.

---

[1] The institution of the Ombudsman was first set up by Sweden just over 200 years ago and was progressively followed by other States since. Though each State has developed different legal frameworks governing the duties and activities of their Ombudsmen, the basic model has remained similar in nature, i.e. safeguarding the legality of state actions.

The second involved the selection of the four Deputy Ombudsmen in July 1998:

- *George Kaminis,* Assistant Professor of Constitutional Law at the University of Athens,
- *Maria Mitrossili-Asimakopoulou,* PhD, lawyer, specialist in health and welfare issues,
- *Yannis Michail,* architect-urban planner, member of the German Academy of Urban Planning and Urban Design and
- *Aliki Koutsoumari,* lawyer, former Director of the Ministry of the Interior, Public Administration and Decentralisation.

Immediately afterwards, the process began of appointing the professional staff, an eventual total of 112 persons (47 senior investigators, 28 junior investigators, administrative staff, PC support etc.). All Senior and Junior Investigators hold university degrees while over 70% of these hold graduate and PhD degrees. Unlike the Ombudsman Bureaus of other nations staffed almost exclusively by lawyers, the professional personnel of the Greek Ombudsman covers a wide range of specialisation in order to be able to provide a comprehensive investigation of the complaints received through a multi-disciplinary approach. The selection of staff was completed in sub-stages in order to provide the time necessary to evaluate and validate the disciplinary needs of the different departments, based on the nature of the cases submitted by the citizens. Strict meritocracy was consistently observed in the process of the selection procedures attracting professional staff of the highest standing, an accomplishment which is one of the Authority's most significant assets.

Finally, on 24 September 1998, the institution of the Greek Ombudsman was formally inaugurated and began accepting citizens' complaints on 1 October 1998. By year's end and after just three months of operation, a total of 1,430 complaints had been submitted. This number increased dramatically over the next 4 years reaching a total of approximately 42,000 complaints between Oct. 1998 - Dec. 2002, thus offering a clear indication that the new institution has been widely accepted by the public.

C) Jurisdiction,

The Ombudsman is an Independent Administrative Authority empowered by its founding law (2477/1997) to combat misadministration (i.e. acts in violation of the principles of good administration, transparency or abuse of power), to defend citizens' rights and to ensure respect for legality (including acts of omission). The Ombudsman acts as an independent extra-judicial control body and mediator and his powers range from simple intervention aimed at resolving conflicts between citizens and public services to the publication of the results of investigations conducted by the Authority. He has jurisdiction over issues pertaining to the public sector, first and second tiers of local government, public corporate bodies, public utility companies and cases related to the protection of the environment. He can also proceed ex officio to the investigation of cases, which have aroused particular public interest. The Ombudsman cannot investigate cases pending before a judicial authority and has no jurisdiction over government ministers or deputy ministers for acts pertaining to their political function. Furthermore, he has no jurisdiction over religious public corporate agencies, the military services with regard to issues of national defence and security, the National Intelligence Service, the Ministry of Foreign Affairs for matters related to the country's foreign policy, the Legal Council of the State and the Independent Administrative Authorities with regard to their main function. As of the year 2000, the Ombudsman is also a member of two more bodies, which benefit from his experience on issues related to the protection of human rights and the fight against misadministration. These are the National Committee for Human Rights (full member) and the National Council for Administrative Reform (established by virtue of article 2 of law 2889/2000).

D) Institutional means available

The institutional possibilities given to the Ombudsman to allow him to fulfil his mission are laid down in the Authority's founding law (2477/97) and oper-

ating regulations (Pres. Decree 273/1999) and include:

● The drawing up of an annual report on the work of the Authority, presenting the most important cases dealt with during the year, indicating deficiencies of the administration and formulating recommendations for the improvement of the public services and the adoption of the necessary legislative measures. This report is submitted each March to the Prime Minister and the President of Parliament and it is also communicated to the Minister of Interior, Public Administration and Decentralisation. The annual report is debated in a special plenary session of Parliament, in accordance with the provisions of the Parliamentary Rules of Procedure and is published in a special edition by the Government Printing Office. An abridged English version of this report is also prepared and made available to interested parties.

● During the course of the year, the Ombudsman may submit additional thematic reports on important issues in need of correction. These reports are presented to the Prime Minister and to the Speaker of the House of Parliament and the relevant ministries are notified.

● Specific findings are presented to the relevant minister and departments involved. Should there be no amending response on their part, the Ombudsman may proceed to publish his findings in the Mass Media.

● Should investigated cases come across sufficient indication of a criminal act, the Ombudsman hands over the case to the prosecuting authorities.

E) Structure

The work of the Greek Ombudsman is divided into the following four areas/departments:

1. The "Human Rights" Department supervised by Deputy Ombudsman George Kaminis. This undertakes cases involving individual, political or social rights. Cases of misadministration and other infringements of legal principles by public services are handled as violations of citizens' rights, which are protected by the Constitution, by international agreements, or by law. Investigations cover the full spectrum of public administration, including:

• violations of personal freedom by the police;

• unjustified discrimination on the basis of nationality or ethnic origin in the provision of administrative services;

• violations of the principle of meritocracy in selection procedures for public sector positions;

• denial of the right of petition or the right to effective legal protection;

• refusal to implement irrevocable judicial decisions.

1998-2002 overall statistics show that of all complaints submitted to the Ombudsman, this department handled approximately 11%[2]. Of this, one third were filed by foreigners and economic immigrants. Their complaints deal with issues of discrimination based on nationality and point to the malfunctioning of the legal system governing entry, residence and employment of aliens as well as the existing naturalisation procedure. Misadministration, in the wider sense of the term, is perhaps the most serious cause of human rights violations in this country.

The remainder of the cases handled by the Department concerned the investigation and substantiation of human rights violations committed by public bodies. They pertained to freedom of religion and religious belief, education, employment and professional freedom, equality of citizens, freedom of access to information, freedom of the mass media, protection of personality and effective judicial protection.

2. The "Health and Social Welfare" Department, is supervised by Deputy Ombudsman Maria Mitrossili-Asimakopoulou. It is responsible for complaints concerning:

• social insurance, including pension rights, payment of and receipts for contributions, register of insured persons, etc.;

• health, including issues of public hospital and outpatient care, sickness

---

[2] Since percentages vary slightly from year to year, average figures are presented in this report. Exact annual figures with extensive analysis of findings are presented in the Ombudsman's annual reports as well as their abridged English language versions.

benefits, health professionals and in general the National Health System;

- public health;
- welfare, including different benefits (for permanent disabilities, maternity, large families, social tourism, workers' housing, etc.);
- care of the elderly, children, people with special needs and the unemployed;

The cases handled cover a wide spectrum of public services, including insurance funds, welfare services, prefecture health committees, the Treasury, hospitals, etc. Complaints addressed to the Social Welfare Department come from Greek citizens, foreign economic immigrants and refugees as well as other socially excluded groups or categories in need of special care, such as children, the elderly, the physically and mentally ill, people with special needs, the Roma, the unemployed, etc.

1998-2002 overall statistics show that this department handled approximately 30% of all complaints submitted to the Ombudsman. The main problems with regard to administrative action were linked to instances of misadministration, particularly within social security institutions and Supplementary Insurance & Pension Funds. The fundamental conclusion to be drawn is that social administration, in as much as it is directly linked to major problem areas in this country, such as social security and health care, is riddled by excessive red tape, deficient organisation and op-

erational insufficiencies.

3. The "Quality of Life" Department supervised by Deputy Ombudsman Yannis Michail. The Department investigates complaints regarding misadministration actions involving issues primarily related to:

- the built-up environment, (urban plans, building permits, violations of the Building Code),
- land uses (such as industrial parks, waste disposal or sewage treatment plants),
- the natural environment (i.e. violations of protection measures and restrictions pertaining to forests, lakes, rivers and coastline zones),
- public works misconstructions posing dangers to users or neighbouring properties,
- violations of legislated protection measures for monuments, historical settlements or traditional buildings,
- misconstructions or malfunctions of Public Utility Company networks,
- certain aspects related to the Port and Airport Authorities, (such as fair allocations of rented port zone open areas to restaurants and cafeterias) as well as the Armed Forces, and, finally,
- air, water noise and visual negative side effects of the above (pollution issues).

These investigations cover the activities of all levels (central, district and local) of public administration agencies such as the Ministry of the Environment, Urban Planning and Public Works, town planning bureaux, Prefectures, forestry, local authority technical agencies, etc.

1998-2002 overall statistics show that this department handled approximately 26% of all complaints submitted to the Ombudsman. Two thirds of its complaints are related to issues falling within the responsibility of Local and Regional Authorities. The remaining findings clearly indicated extensive and serious violations of environmental legislation and particularly in ecologically vulnerable areas, such as those included in the NATURA 2000 network. Through its mediation work, as recorded in its reports and proposals for the improved operation of public services, the Department seeks to contribute to the administration's work in order to:

a) Achieve the delicate, but crucial balance between the right to the environment and the right to property (in particular in connection with land use) as required by law, the Constitution and EC directives pertinent to the subject.

b) Clearly specify essential concepts and rules contained in national and community legislation on the environment. The recent revision of article 24 of the Constitution, which establishes the individual right to the environment and the principle of sustainability and expressly recognises the obligation of the state to draw up a forest and land registry, significantly extends the Ombudsman's capacity to investigate and mediate in environmental matters.

4. The "State-Citizen Relations" Department, supervised by Deputy Ombudsman Aliki Koutsoumari. The Department is responsible for issues concerning information and communication with public services, the quality of services provided, misadministration by local government authorities, public utility companies, transport and communications, labour, industry, energy, taxation, customs, fiscal matters, commerce and state procurement, agriculture and agricultural policy, and education. The complaints submitted concern:

• Misadministration in general (including the civil service in the narrow sense, i.e. ministries, general secretariats, etc.);

• Tax Offices - taxation issues;

• Public Institutions of Education - Centre for the Recognition of foreign academic titles

• Local government

• Billings of public utility corporations (water, electricity, etc.)

• Greek Post Office;

• Other public services (Customs, Deposit and Loan Fund, Treasury etc.)

1998-2002 overall statistics show that this department handled approximately 33% of all complaints submitted to the Ombudsman. The most important instances of misadministration concern: general problems of organisation in public enterprises; delays or refusal on the part of the services involved to respond to requests from citizens and supply them with requested information; incidents of direct violation of substantive law; anti-contractual behaviour or failure to act as required by law. Moreover, the identification of cases of sudden and unjustified modification of the terms and conditions for receiving benefits and allowances, or the issuing of individual administrative acts, was of particular concern to the Department, since these cases constitute typical examples of the flagrant violation of the principle of justified trust, which should govern the actions of the administration. The non-enforcement of court decisions was the main cause of violation of the legality principle, a fact which led to the introduction of constitutional provisions allowing for sanctions, should the administration fail to comply with the decision of the court (article 95, paragraph 5 of the Constitution).

F) Modus operandi

The Ombudsman undertakes the investigation of any issue within his jurisdiction, following a signed written complaint lodged by any directly concerned person or legal entity or union of persons that has dealings with the Greek public sector, whether inside or outside the borders of the state. A complaint must be lodged within six months from the date on which the applicant is informed of the acts or omissions for which he/she has the right of recourse to the Ombudsman. Complaints can be sent by mail, e-mail, or fax, or can be delivered in person at the Citizens' Reception and Information Bureau located on the third floor of the building. This Bureau is staffed by Senior and Junior Investigators on a daily rotation basis (the Ombudsman and the four Deputy Ombudsmen also periodically man the desks). It assists citizens in need of help to prepare their documents or advise them on the line of action they should follow to solve their problem. Likewise, two additional Investigators answer incoming phone calls of citizens. Through these means, the Ombudsman ensures direct, personal and friendly communication with citizens.

Furthermore, on a biannual basis, the Ombudsman and/or Deputy Ombudsmen and a skeleton interdepartmental staff, set up temporary premises each time at a different city. Representatives of the Administration are also invited to attend. During these publicly pre-announced sessions (through local radio and press inserts), citizens are encouraged to visit the staff, receive information, discuss their problems and submit their complaints. Direct communication enables the Ombudsman to better understand the problems faced by people living outside Attica, to inform them about the office, and to help them

understand and take action concerning their rights. It also allows the establishment of first hand contact with the local public services/administrators, thus building a more personal line of communication and trust.

As mentioned earlier, the Ombudsman on his own authority (i.e. without receiving a written complaint) may also proceed in the investigation of cases, which have aroused particular public interest.

Complaints received are entered in the electronic register. This allows the progress of each case to be monitored easily and also ensures the essential follow-up, control and transparency in the operation of the institution. Once a complaint has been registered, it is given a preliminary examination ascertaining whether there are any reasons for which the complaint falls outside the Ombudsman's jurisdiction, as defined in the law, after which it is assigned to the relevant department. A letter is mailed out to the complainant, informing him/her of the department and name/phone number of the Senior Investigator who has undertaken the case.

The investigation of a case follows a series of steps safeguarding the fairness of the results:

• Determine competency and jurisdiction parameters of the Ombudsman.

• Identifying all relevant to case legislation, EC directives, international agreements, etc.

• Contacting, by phone or in writing, the public service(s)/administrator(s) involved, communicating the nature of the complaint, in order to receive the input and point of view of the other side. All public sector services are obliged by law to facilitate the investigation in every possible way. Refusal of a person or service to co-operate becomes the object of a special report by the Ombudsman to the competent Minister.

In many instances, this first contact proves sufficient for the solution of the problem. If not, the actual investigation works starts through:

• Verification of actual case events. This often involves on-site visits of specialists (members of the Ombudsman's staff and/or outside experts) to establish the facts and parameters of the case. Furthermore, other aspects (such as possible negative environmental side affects, violations of constitutional rights, etc.), of which the complainant may not be aware, may be introduced to the case by the Investigator. In this way, the Ombudsman utilises its inter-disciplinary staffing to carry out a more in-depth comprehensive approach[3], not limiting the investigation to legal matters alone (i.e. the respect of legality). Once all the

---

[3] This has been particularly appreciated by subsequent court proceedings, as judges have often found the comprehensive case presentation very informative as to the parameters of the problem examined

pieces are in, the Senior Investigator - often assisted by the input opinions of other scientific disciplines - proceeds to:

• Drawing up conclusions and submitting solution/suggestions for the public service/person(s) involved. The service is obliged by law to respond informing the Ombudsman on actions intended to be taken to remedy the problem, or to submit its legally documented and substantiated positions in case of non-agreement. Should there be no response, once again this becomes the object of a special report by the Ombudsman to the competent Minister or it can be presented through the Mass Media (Press, TV). As stated earlier, should the investigation findings produce:

a) sufficient evidence that a public functionary, civil servant or member of the administration has committed a criminal act, the Ombudsman refers this to the relevant Public Prosecutor. Once a case has been turned over to the judicial system, the Ombudsman has no authority to intervene or even follow up;

b) establish that there has been unlawful behaviour on the part of the public functionary, civil servant or member of the administration, the Ombudsman must submit a report to the competent supervising authority calling for disciplinary action.

• The Ombudsman may further define a reasonable time limit, in view of the circumstances, at the expiry of which, if no action has been taken, he may himself order the procedure.

A standardised electronic record is kept for each case, including its specific data/characteristics, a log of the investigation actions, inputs received, results, etc. This information is automatically passed on to a central data basis where it is statistically processed, providing the service with fingertip updated overall progress figures and facts (such as geographic distribution of complaints and administrative services involved, thematic of complaints, etc.). It thus also acts as a special problem identification warning system by marking-out:

• specific administrative deficiencies with high occurrence rates. This often leads to the preparation of special thematic reports focussing on the systematic weaknesses of the administration, which are then submitted to the Government. In the years 2000-1, three such reports were submitted ("Local & Regional Authorities", "Operation of the Supplementary Insurance Fund for Metal Workers", "Military Service Conscientious Objectors");

• specific services or administrators with unusually bad records are often the result of corrupt practices. In such instances, the Ombudsman contacts the responsible overseeing administrative authority (or the Public Prosecutor) so that an in-depth investigation is carried out and measures are taken to establish legality.

At the end of the year, each Department prepares input sections for the annual report. This includes a selection of important/characteristic cases corresponding to the findings of the statistical data, both of which identify specific deficiencies of the administration. Conclusions are drawn and specific measures addressing the deficiencies are proposed. The final document is submitted to the Government by end of March.

G) Other activities of the ombudsman
International activities:

a) Stability Pact for South-eastern Europe. The Ombudsman responded to the invitation from the Minister of Foreign Affairs to promote the institution of the Ombudsman in the member states of the Stability Pact for South-eastern Europe within the framework of the First Table, concerning democratisation and human rights. In close co-operation with the Council of Europe, this initiative provides technical know-how and advice to newly established ombudsman institutions in the Balkan countries, through systematic interaction with the Greek Ombudsman's professional staff through a series of visits and seminars. This activity constitutes a major undertaking for the Office of the Ombudsman, whose scope is meant to broaden through further networking in other in European countries. During the year 2000, the Ombudsman drew up a project under the title "Contribution to the creation of mediator institutions focusing on Southeast European countries and

their respective networking" which has been included in the relevant cycle of activities by the Directorate of Human Rights of the Council of Europe. The Ombudsman, the Deputy Ombudsmen and staff members visited Albania, Bulgaria, Yugoslavia (Serbia and Kosovo), Slovakia and Slovenia in order to provide support to existing institutions or efforts being undertaken to create such institutions, through the transfer of know-how.

b) The Athens Network. Frequently, environmental problems do not limit themselves within national boarders. As a result, dealing with these requires international co-operation aimed at streamlining legislation. The member state ombudsmen - as control mechanisms - need also to harmonise and co-ordinate their interventions. The Athens Network is an EU supported programme, which is in the process of creating an establishing official co-operation between the national Ombudsmen of the EU member states and EU services on issues pertinent to the protection of the environment. Over a period of two years, a series of meetings have been held in Athens in which a good number of European Ombudsmen and EU representatives have participated. A database to include legislation and best practices in member states pertinent to protection of the environment has been agreed upon and will soon be set up in Athens while venues of official co-operation are in the process of being identified.

c) In addition, the Ombudsman has continued and extended his contacts with his international counterparts. He gave lectures at international conferences, universities, and public policy research centres and also participated in international meetings on issues related to the institution of the Ombudsman. The Deputy Ombudsmen and the Senior Investigators have also participated in similar activities. Special reference is made to the participation of the Greek Ombudsman's delegation in the:

- 7th Conference of the International Ombudsman Institute, (held in Durban, South Africa in the year 2000);

- Seminar organised by the European Board for Democracy through Law, of the Council of Europe (Venice Commission) and the Marangopoulos Foundation for Human Rights held in Athens.

- Workshop "The model of an Ombudsman Institution for the Fed. Republic of Yugoslavia" (Belgrade, July 2001).

All of the above mentioned contacts contributed substantially to the adhesion of the Greek Ombudsman to international networks related to ombudsman activities. These contacts also facilitated the transfer of experience and know-how, and enhanced its outward orientation, creating possibilities for initiatives and co-operation within the framework of both the European and the wider international community of ombudsmen.

National level activities:

-"Turn toward public admin-

istration". There has been a considerable increase in the flow of complaints submitted. Irritation often emerges in the investigated administration services resulting in resentment and non-co-operation. As a result, the Ombudsman decided to introduce the "turn toward the public administration" approach. Through a series of contacts, it aims at ironing-out the wrinkles of communication, promoting the logic of resolution and "positive sum" for both sides. This has assumed two main forms:

• Regular and closer communications between the Ombudsman's staff and all levels of the public administration, including the political leadership.

• Organising full-day meetings with ministerial departments to systematically inform officials about the nature of the Office of the Ombudsman as a mediating institution able to operate as an alternative, extra-judicial mechanism providing fast and flexible resolutions for disputes arising between individuals and the administration.

The common denominator of both, is the search for ways to simplify the administration's operating procedures and contribute to their enhanced rationality. At the same time, administrators are encouraged to use the Ombudsman's reports as an additional venue to communicate proposals for reforms to the central government or the prefecture administration.

- Professional staff members of the Ombudsman have appeared at an extensive number of seminars, university events and Local Authority meetings with the public, presenting the new institution.

- Following the 7 Sept. 1999 earthquake, all the Ombudsman's staff visited, on a 15-member-team rotation basis, the areas of Attica that were hit. The teams worked with the relevant administrative local authorities and effectively contributed to the solution of many pressing problems faced by the victims.

- The Ombudsman has carried out two self-initiated investigations on cases that have attracted public interest. The first was at the detention centre of the Attica Police Headquarters (Aliens Sub-Directorate, GADA) in order to check the conditions under which foreigners are detained in this facility. The second investigation involved the Therapy Centre for Dependent Persons (KETHEA).

-The staff has also participated in several environmental awareness events such as bicycle-days, rafting and marathon running, etc.

H) Constitutional recognition of the ombudsman as an independent authority

After its revision in 2001, the Constitution recognised the Office of the Ombudsman as an independent Authority (article 103, par. 9). In conformity with this same provision, the ordinary legislation regulates the Authority's constitution and mandate. Of course, the provisions of law 2477/1997, still apply to the extent that they comply with new constitutional provisions on independent authorities (article 101 A). They must also comply with the relevant provisions of the Parliamentary Rules and the uniform arrangements governing the organisation and operation of independent authorities, after the passing of the Constitution's implementing law, as provided in article 101 A of the Constitution.

The Parliamentary procedures implementing law of article 101 A of the Constitution and the above mentioned provisions of Parliamentary Rules were passed by Parliament in Feb 2003. It should be noted here that a fifth area - that of the protection of children's rights - has been added to the duties of the Office.

I) Assessments

The completion of approximately four and a half years since the start of the Ombudsman's activities is an appropriate milestone at which to draw some general conclusions concerning the progress of the Greek Ombudsman to date.

The Ombudsman emphasises in particular the conditions that ensure the success of the institution and safeguard its independence. These include recognition by the citizen/user, the creation of a relationship of trust with the mass media and the support of the political leadership. The progress made has been satisfactory in all these areas.

The Ombudsman's work with regard to the main object of his mission, i.e. the handling of citizens' complaints, has also developed satisfactorily. The flow of complaints has increased considerably. The total number of complaints examined in the first four and a half years exceeded 42,000 and the resolution rate was high (47% of all admissible complaints and 91% of all justified complaints). The large number of letters received from citizens expressing thanks clearly demonstrate that this institution has been accepted by the public and is acquiring a steadily increasing legitimisation in their eyes.

Relations with the mass media have been established in an equally satisfactory manner. The ultimate aim of the Ombudsman is to promote the work of the Authority by making its activities known to the public and informing citizens about its efforts. In the period of time that has elapsed since the establishment of the Greek Ombudsman's Office, the latter seems to have successfully created information and communication mechanisms for the mass media based on mutual trust and openness. The launching of the Authority's web site in 2001, as well as its expanding communications policy, further enhances these relations.

Furthermore, the confidence shown in this institution by the political leadership of our country has also had a catalytic effect on its legitimisation and guaranteed independence. The recent constitutional recognition of the institution has confirmed the broad political support it enjoys, as do the positive statements about the Ombudsman's work at the yearly meetings of the Authority's leadership with the Greek Parliament's Standing Committee for Institutions and Transparency. The same effect was achieved by the Ombudsman's participation in recently founded advisory bodies of national scope, such as the National Committee for Human Rights and the National Council for Administrative Reform, operating under the Prime Minister and the Minister of the Interior, Public Administration and Decentralisation respectively. At the same time, the Prime Minister himself has shown considerable interest in the Ombudsman's work, which receives support from all the ministries. These, as well as the progressive establishment of good relations with the administration, have given the necessary momentum to the Authority's development over the past three years and have allowed it to look to the future with increased self-confidence and measured optimism.

These generally positive statements should in no way be misinterpreted as complacency or lack of vigilance. On the contrary, any success achieved in the past, serves as an incentive for the Authority to intensify its efforts towards its main objective as laid down by the state in its founding law: to defend the rights of the citizen, combat misadministration and safeguard legality. In other words, to contribute in every possible way towards the deepening and enlargement of the principle of the rule of law in our country, this being the foremost criterion for evaluating the quality of democracy in Greece.

In order to achieve this objective, based on the conditions for success referred to previously, the Ombudsman has set the improvement of relations with public administration as a top priority. This improvement extends to all echelons of administration, from the lowest to the very highest, and, over time, has acquired many different forms and operates at various levels. To this end, the Authority has adopted the "logic of resolution" - as opposed to the "logic of confrontation and denunciation" - as a basic rule for approaching public administration and seeking ways of resolving systemic and individual problems, as they are reflected in the complaints from citizens received by the Ombudsman. To be applied it must be linked to the logic of the "positive sum", the basic principle of which is that in the overwhelming majority of cases, conflicts should be resolved in a way that will provide sufficient satisfaction to both parties and avoid favouring one over the other. This type of approach differs from the other predominant model, that of the logic of the "negative sum" according to which the satisfaction of a demand calls for the "victory" of one party and the "defeat" of the other, with evident adverse effects for their mutual relations.

In conclusion, the initiatives taken by the Ombudsman are totally in line with his overall efforts at promoting his role as a mechanism of control, mediation and consultation. Performance statistics show that the Office has proven capable of:

• efficiently contributing to the defence of citizens' rights,

• promoting the improvement of the level of service provided by public administration to those dealing with it, irrespective of nationality, within and beyond the boundaries of the Greek State, thus...

• developing the image of a new model of modern democratic and committed public administration.

CITIZEN SERVICE CENTERS: THE GREEK PUBLIC ADMINISTRATION OF THE 21RST CENTURY

The citizen service centers (KEP)

The Citizen Service Centers (KEP) can be viewed as the answer to modern requirements for quality service provision to citizens. They are branches, like bank branches, of the central public administration, instituted solely for the improvement of services provided to citizens and businesses.

Citizen Service Centers (KEP) are One Stop Shops, where citizens may:

- Ask for information regarding any public sector organization, procedure or requirement
- Request for a certificate, license etc to be issued
- File an application
- File a complaint

Most of KEPs services are provided through outsourced IT systems.

The Citizen Service Centers (KEP) have two strategic goals:

- To offer improved service provision to citizens and businesses all over the country, implementing the model of "one-stop shops".
- To utilize the potential of Information Technology and Communications, in order to implement electronic transactions.

The programme's objectives

The Citizen Service Centers were created in order to:

- To ameliorate the relations between the citizens and the Public Administration
- To enhance the public administration's reform programme
- To introduce e-government appli-

cations to the public cervices
- To strengthen administrative Democracy

The benefits of the programme:

The concrete benefits of the programme, in the long term, are :
- Better service to the citizen (less time wasted in queues, fewer trips to and from public sector units, simpler documents & procedures, staff responsive to citizen needs)
- Lower transaction costs (benefit the entire economy)
- Reduced application processing costs for citizen-facing public sector units In the medium term, KEPs also

guide the transformation of the public sector by:
- Increasing citizen expectations
- Forcing Quality of Service standardization to all public sector units
- Introducing e-Gov the right way round: from citizen requirements to systems

Deployment well under way
Citizen Service Centers (KEP):
- Will operate in 1.132 units throughout the country (700 already in place)
- All local governments
- All prefectures
- All Regions

KEP Certified Procedures

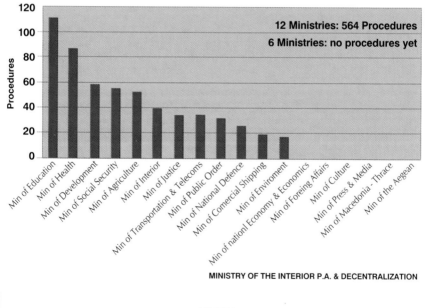

12 Ministries: 564 Procedures
6 Ministries: no procedures yet

MINISTRY OF THE INTERIOR P.A. & DECENTRALIZATION

Volume of Transactions

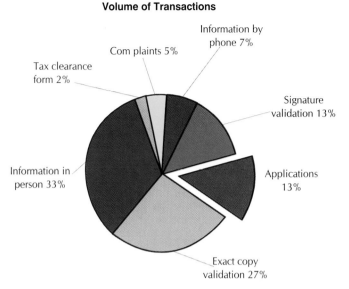

MINISTRY OF THE INTERIOR P.A. & DECENTRALIZATION

• Will include all (1200 certified) Public Administration procedures (750 already certified)

• Will be recruited by highly specialized Employees (2.500 already working, the majority of them being University graduates)

KEP sources of funding:

The main sources of funding are:
• Central Government Budget
• OP Information Society
• Independent Local Authority Revenues
• Regional Development Funds
• Hellenic Manpower & Employment Organization (OAED)
• OP Politeia

KEP and e- government applications:

KEPs have the following characteristics:

• Banking approach (they operate

like bank branches)
- Every desk is the right desk (equal quality service in every desk)
- One contact person
- Intergovernmental processes

KEP serve as a bridge to e-government applications:

- 1100 CSC connected to the Internet by the end of 2003.
- PKI certificates for every Kep
- On line transactions:

STAGE 1: Information. On line information

All administrative information in Internet (available now)

STAGE 2: Interaction. Downloading of forms.

780 Forms are available now.

1200 forms will be available by December

STAGE 3 Two - way interaction.Processing of forms will be available by December

STAGE 4: Transaction. Case handling and delivery will be available by December (for a large number of high priority administrative procedures and services)

KEP and administrative democracy:

Every citizen has got the undisputable right to enjoy the merits of Administrative Democracy:

- Equal Administrative products and services
- Quality Administrative Products and services
- Homogeneous Administrative Products and services
- Free of charge Administrative Products and services from all the public Services

KEP as a tool to public administration reform

The end of the 20th century was marked by continuous and complicated changes, in geopolitical, economic and political terms. Such changes constitute the starting point of a new era in governance with different problems than the past ones and with new demands put forward by the citizens. One of the major tasks of the modern Public Administration is to ensure the quality of service provision to all citizens.

Within this framework, the Citizen Service Centers can be viewed as a tool to Public Administration reform by:

• Changing the structure of the Public Services

• Changing the functioning of the Public Services

• Changing the Personnel of the Public Services

Succeeding to fulfill the afore mentioned objectives:

• To ameliorate the relations between the citizens and the Public Administration

• To enhance the public administration's reform programme

• To introduce e-government applications to the public cervices, and

• To strengthen administrative Democracy

Greece with the Citizen Service Centers (KEPs) sets a concrete paradigm of 21rst century modern Public Administration in the emerging "new" Europe.

EDUCATION IN GREECE

By M. Defigou

1. Greece - General Information

Greece is a Southern European country, bordering the Aegean Sea, Ionian Sea, and the Mediterranean Sea, between Albania and Turkey.

The total area is 131,940 square km (land area: 130,800 square km). Greece has a total of 1,210 km. of land boundaries (with Albania 282 km, Bulgaria 494 km, Turkey 206 km, the Former Yugoslav Republic of Macedonia 228 km). It has a coastline of 13,676 km. Greece is a peninsular country with an archipelago of about 2,000 islands.

1.1 Population

The population of the country is 10,964,020 (2001 estimate). The population growth rate is 0.21% (2001 est.) and the birth rate: 9.6 births/1,000 population (1999 est.). Greece has one of the highest levels of life expectancy at birth for the total population (78.59 years, males: 76.03 years, females: 81.32 years (2001 est.) but is among the countries with the lowest level of fertility rate in the EU (1.3 children born per woman (2001 World Bank est.). The most common religion is Orthodox (98%), but there are also Muslims (1.3%), Roman Catholics and others.

A percentage of 97.4% of the population aged 15 and over can read and write (UNESCO 2002 est.), but the percentage of males is higher than females (male: 98.6% female 96.2%.)

According to UNESCO, the percentage of the population aged 15 and older in Greece which is illiterate, has been steadily dropping over the years and it has been estimated that it will fall to 2.3% in the year 2005 and 1.1% in 2015.

The labour force of the country is about 4.369 million (services 59%, agriculture 20%, industry 21% -2000 est.). A peculiar characteristic of Greek economy is the large number of employers and self-employed (about 40% of the total labour force)

There is a high degree of urbanisation, with about 65.7% of the population living in urban areas (about 40% in Athens the capital), and the population density is 80 inhabitants per sq. km.

Over the last decades, there has been an increasing number of newcomers to the country. Thus, it is estimated that more 500,000 newcomers live in the country.

1.2 Economy

The Greek economy is dominated by a large public sector (about 60% of GDP). Tourism is a major source of foreign exchange. Agriculture is self-sufficient except for meat, dairy products, and animal foodstuffs.

Over the last decade, real GDP growth has averaged 1.6% a year (compared with the EU average of 2.2%) but in recent years it has shown a significant increase. During the year 2002, the growth rate of the Greek Economy was the highest in the European Union. The country's GDP growth is estimated to have reached 3.5% compared to 4.1% in 2001, exceeding that of Ireland which demonstrated a growth rate of 3.3% compared to 5.7%. It was much more dynamic than the 0.9% which is estimated to be the EU average. At the same time however, the country's GDP per capita is still the lowest in the European Union. During 2002, the latter is estimated to have reached 69.9% of the EU average compared to the 68.1% during the last year.

Inflation is above the EU average, as in 2001 it reached 3.7% compared to 2.3% which was the EU average among the 15 member countries, thus making it the fourth highest.

The national debt for the year 2001 reached 107% of GDP, which is the third highest in the EU and much higher than the EU average which is 63.1%.

Eurostat estimates that for the year 1999, public expenditure on education in Greece reached 3.6% of GDP, while in 2000 it was estimated to have increased to 3.8% and consequently fell to 3.5% during 2001. These percentages are the lowest in the EU, while especially in 1999, the last year for which there are complete figures, the EU average reached 5%.

The GDP is about $189.7 billion (2001 est.) and the GDP per capita is $17,900 (2001 est.).

2. Education in Greece

The level of education in Greece is in generally low and varies considerably between the different age groups. A large number of people (mainly older people) had completed only primary education, while post secondary degree holders represent about 11% of the work force.

The average number of years of schooling for a child is about 14.29, which situates Greece in a mid-level position in comparison with other countries.

Country	Total	Male	Female
Greece	14.29	14.15	14.44
USA	15.22	14.78	15.65
Spain	15.30	15.01	15.60
United Kingdom	16.38	15.96	16.82
Ireland	14.87	14.45	15.30

Table 1. School Life expectancy by Country and by Gender for the School Years 1999/2000.
[Source UNESCO, Institute for Statistics, Education Sector, September 2002]

The age of at which compulsory education in Greece comes to an end is 14.5, which is slightly lower than in other developed countries. A comparatively high percentage though, stays in education until the age of 19.

Country	Ending age of compulsory education	Students Aged:		
		5-14 as a percentage of the population of 5 to 14-year-olds	15-19 as a percentage of the population of 15 to 19-year-olds	20-29 as a percentage of the population of 20 to 29-year-olds
Greece	**14.5**	**99.8**	**87.4**	**16.9**
USA	17	99.3	73.9	21.2
Spain	16	104.4	79.5	24.3
United Kingdom	16	98.9	73.3	23.8
Turkey	14	80.2	28.4	5.2
Ireland	15	10.5	79.8	15.6

*Not available

Table 2. *Enrolment rates (2000) Full-time and Part-time students in public and private institutions, by age. (Source OECD, Centre for educational Research and Innovation)*

The provision of lifelong learning is especially low in Greece, placing the country in the last position among the EU 15. In the year 2001, about 1.4% of the population aged between 25 to 64 attended vocational education and training programs. This percentage is by far the lowest in the EU, which has an average of 8.4%.

3. The Education System

According to the Greek Constitution the entire educational system is under the supervision of the state.

The Ministry of National Education and the Pedagogical Institute formulates educational policy and the goals of the educational system. The latter is responsible for the study of educational policies and curriculum development. Local educational districts, which are located in every *Nomos* (Prefecture), under the authority of the Ministry, ensure that schools follow a centrally prescribed curriculum.

School attendance is compulsory from ages 6 to 15, that is, for 9 years. Pupils must attend a full-time primary school *(Dimotico)* for 6 years and after that a three year *Gymnasio* (Lower secondary education school). Between the ages 3½ to 6 they may follow a 1- 2 years *Nipiagogio* (Kindergarten)

After a pupil finishes Gymnasium she/he may attend either a Unified Lyceum (UL), or Technical Vocational School (TVS). At this stage of the secondary education system there are also vocational and professional schools.

Post-secondary education is made up of Universities and Technological Educational Institutes - TEI (3 - year colleges of higher education without university status). Every year the Ministry of Education decides upon the number for entrants to be allowed in each University department. Within the framework of the policy applied since 1996, the number of positions offered in the last years has doubled, in view of the goal of unhindered access to higher education. In cases where the number of positions offered fails to cover the demand, there are some criteria that determine the final number of eligibility points for each candidate.

Attendance in all public schools and Universities is free of charge. The ed-

ucational materials, especially textbooks are also provided free of charge.

The school period extends from September 1 to August 31, no teaching takes place between the end of June and the end of August in primary and secondary education.

Within primary and secondary education there is the possibility of the creation of private schools. They are obligated to follow the same curricula as the public ones, but there are no state recognised private institutes of higher education.

Those who do not have the opportunity to enter University may attend 2 years vocational courses in the Institutes of Vocational Training (VTI). These are public or private and are incorporated into the formal educational system or as special vocational courses and seminars organised by private or other public authorities. They fall under the umbrella of the informal vocational educational system (Centres of Vocational Training, Free Studies Institutes, and so on).

During the school period 2000/2001 there were 332,407 students in primary education. There were in total 1,768 public primary schools and the total number of teachers was 34,689 - for a teacher/student ratio of 1/9.6. During the same period there were 224,573 students in Unified Lyceum (UL) and 117,603 in Technical Vocational Schools (TVS) of secondary education. The total number of public schools were

1,185 units in UL and 412 units in TVS and the total number of teachers 21,092 in UL and 15,173 in TVS- with a teacher/student ratio of 1/10.6 in Unified Lyceum and 1/7.8 in Technical Vocational Schools.

In 2002, 83,050 students entered the country's 20 Universities and 14 Tech- nological Educational Institutes.

Teachers at public schools are professional civil servants in the services of the state. Students and pupils who have graduated from one level of education may freely enrol in the next, with the exception of Universities and TEI, where enrolment is based on examinations.

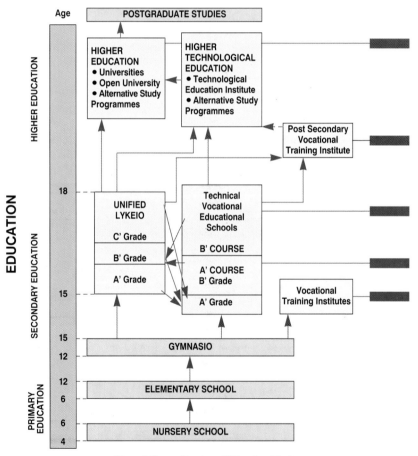

Figure 1. Greece: Structure of Educational System

3.1 Pre-school Education

Before entering primary school children aged 3½ - 5½ may attend kindergarten, of which there are both public and private. Attendance at kindergarten is for two years and is gradually being made compulsory throughout the country. The kindergarten is intended to support and supplement the education provided by the family and to compensate for development deficiencies in order to provide children with a broad range of opportunities for education and development. Children learn through play. As a rule, children attend kindergarten only in the morning. In total, the hours of creative engagement of children in public kindergartens, according to Presidential Decree, are three and one-half hours, beginning at 9:00 a.m. and finishing at 12:30 p.m.

At the beginning of the 1997-98 school year, 160 all-day kindergartens were opened on a trial basis with an extended timetable, engaging the children in creative activities (at least eight hours per day, beginning at 7:45 a.m. and finishing at 16:00 p.m.)

In the school year 1998-1999, this pilot program, that is, all-day public kindergartens, was expanded to include 350 kindergartens. This number has been doubled for the school year 1999-2000 within the context of the goal for all kindergartens to operate all day.

The number of children attending kindergarten centres under the Ministry of Education in 2001/02 was 144,055, slightly higher than about ten years ago (136,536 in 1990/91). In the same period, there were 5,694 kindergartens (5,518 in 1990/91) and 10,211 teachers (8,400 in 1990/91). - Source: National Statistical Service of Greece-Hellas in Numbers.

3.2 Compulsory Schooling

Compulsory education begins at age 6 and lasts for nine years (since the 1978 educational reform). It is divided into primary school and Gymnasium (lower education school)

The primary school (Dimotiko) At the age of six, children enter primary school (Dimotiko) which lasts for six years and comprises 160 school days per year (five teaching hours per day).

The aim of the Primary school is the multi-faceted mental and physical development of the students within the framework set by the wider goals of Primary and Secondary education. More particularly, the aim of Primary School is to widen and rearrange the relations between children's creative activity and the things, situations and phenomena they study, to build up the mechanisms that contribute to the assimilation of knowledge, to improve their physical and mental health and cultivate their motor abilities. Furthermore the aim of Primary School is to allow children to acquire the content of the most important notions and gradually have the ability to move from the data of the senses to the region of the abstract

thought, to acquire the ability to use oral and written speech correctly. Finally, the aim of Primary School is for children to familiarise themselves slowly with moral, humanitarian and other values, to organise them into a system, to cultivate their aesthetic criteria so as to be able to appreciate works of art and express themselves accordingly through their own artistic creations.

Students who finish primary school receive a certificate of studies, which is used for enrolment in Secondary School.

Primary schools, depending on the school capacity, can have up to 12 positions for teachers but when the number of students, the classrooms available and the distance between schools so require, it is possible to have from 7 to 11 positions. The School capacity is based on the ratio of 25 students/teacher but a common decision by the Minister of Education and the Minister of Finance may reduce the number of students in each permanent one.

The establishment and improvement of primary schools and the proportional increase of their capacity is arranged by a Presidential Decree issued on the motion of the Ministers of Education and Finance. In some cases, where special local circumstances call for it, it is possible to establish a one-teacher school regardless of the number of students.

In 2001/02 there were 641,368 pupils attending primary schools, which is 14.9% lower than about ten years ago, given the decline in the birth rate. During the same period, the teacher/pupil ratio was 1/11 and the

	Pupils		Classrooms		% change of pupils	% change of of classrooms
	1992 /93	2001/02	1992 /93	2001/02		
Primary schools	753,401	641,368	37,418	39,823	- 14.9%	+ 6.4%

Table 3: Greece -Estimation of the Department for Corporate Research and Statistics of Ministry of Education

number of classrooms was 39,823 which is 6.4% higher than 1992/93.

Teaching in primary schools is done by one teacher and it is formally teacher-centred and textbook based.

The Ministry of Education has adopted a unique curriculum and for every grade textbook development is undertaken by individuals or groups following specific guidelines and instructions and finally selected by the Pedagogic Institute.

Primary education teachers must have a four-year degree from a department of education in order to be certified. However, the first departments of education within universities were cre-

ated in 1985 and the first teachers with university degrees graduated in 1989. The largest number of teachers has a degree from a two-year programme at a Teachers Academy and a large number of teachers, without university degree, are involved each year in a retraining process.

Once a year, the Ministry of Education appoints teachers according to the needs of the schools. According to the 1997 reform law, examinations were instituted for the appointment of teachers in primary and secondary education, regulated by an independent body, the Supreme Employee Selection Council (SESC) and the precedence list (epetiri-

da) was gradually abolished over a period of five years.

Lower Secondary Education. After completing primary education all children are automatically enrolled into *Gymnasium*, which consists of three years of schooling.

There are daytime and evening lower secondary schools (gymnasia).

during the same period was 351,302 (332,407 were enrolled in public and 18,895 in private schools) and the number of teachers was 36,894.

Teaching in Gymnasia is also formally teacher - centred and based on textbooks developed and selected by the Pedagogical Institute and the Ministry. Detailed guidelines suggest methods to

	Pupils		Schools		Teachers	
	1991/92	**2001/02**	**1991/92**	**2000/01**	**1991/92**	**2000/01**
Gymnasium	439,000	351,302	1,820	1,884	28,000	36,894

Table 4. Source: Ministry of National Education and Religious Affairs

Young working people are accepted into evening gymnasia, as long as they are at least 14 years of age.

As its general objective, Gymnasium aims to promote the integrated development of the students, in accordance with the possibilities and capabilities they have in this special age and the needs of life and society.

These schools offer general education, although some of them specialise in sports or music. Classroom capacity is not greater than 35 students and when there are more than 35 in a grade then it is divided into separate classes.

There are 165 days in every school period while every school day has six hours.

In 2000/01 there were 1,884 schools offering general education. The number of pupils that attended Gymnasium

teachers for conducting the lessons at every grade.

Teachers must have a university degree in order to be certified and teaching staff vacancies in secondary education are filled annually by appointments made after the positions are advertised in accordance with the law.

After completing the Gymnasium pupils receive the certificate (*apolytirio*), which allows enrolment to any type of upper - secondary education.

3.3 Upper Secondary Education

The aims of education system are fulfilled with Lyceum, which has as its main goal to help students to reach a better understanding of the social reality, to make the right choices for their professional careers and to develop their personalities.

After the 1997 reform law, two types of upper secondary education schools (Lyceum) were instituted. Unified *Lycea* (UL) and Technical Vocational Schools (TVS) that gradually replaced all the existing types of senior secondary schools. At this stage there are also many Technical - Vocational Schools, which provide two-year vocational training.

The ULs are general education schools, but they have different internal programmes, which include compulsory subjects or elective subjects. ULs that emerged from former musical and ecclesiastical schools have retained the additional hours of music and theological subjects respectively.

The first grade of Unified Lyceum is a grade of orientation, thus the student will come to acquaint herself/himself with various subjects of knowledge so as to help him/her to choose the course of studies that they want to follow in the second grade of Lyceum.

The Second Grade of Lyceum has three directions - Branches (Theoretical, Practical - Applied and Technological) while courses in these directions will direct students towards the studies that they have to attend in the 3rd grade.

In grade 3 there are 9 periods of studies, 4 of which are for the first 2 (two) directions and 5 for the Technological one, while examinations are to be written at the level of Lyceum and at the national level.

Pupils who graduate from a United Lyceum receive diploma from the Lyceum. These graduates have the following options. 1) They may seek admission to higher education. 2) They may study at a Vocational Training Institute (VTI) of their choice to acquire a specialisation. 3) They may participate in competitions for employment in the public or private sector. 4) They may enter the labour market without a specialisation.

The Technical Vocational Schools (TVS) aim to provide a combination of general knowledge with specialised technical and vocational knowledge, with a view to the pupils' absorption into the labour market.

These schools are classified as secondary non-compulsory education and offer both day and evening classes. They offer two levels. The first lasts for two years, the second for one year. For the evening classes, there is an additional

2000/01	Students	Schools	Teachers
Unified Lyceum UL)	241,081	1,282	22,980
Technical Vocational School (TVS)	124,105	492	16,545

Table 5. Source: Ministry of National Education and Religious Affairs

year added for the first level and six months for the second. These two levels are independent and a certificate is awarded for both.

Graduates of the first level of technical vocational educational schools (TVS) have the following options. 1) They may receive a certificate to practice a trade. 2) They may register in the corresponding specialisation in the second level. 3) They may register in the second grade of an UL.

Graduates of the second level of TVS have the following options. 1) They may receive a certificate to practice a trade. 2) They may register, in order of precedence, in a corresponding specialisation at a Vocational Training Institute (VTI). 3) They may seek admission to a Technological Educational Institute (TEI) after passing nation-wide examinations in two general knowledge subjects and a specialisation subject.

Just as in the Gymnasium, teachers of upper secondary education schools must have a university degree in order to be certified, and are appointed after examinations regulated by an independent body, the Supreme Employee Selection Council (SESC).

3.4 Post Secondary Education

The institutes of higher education in Greece belong to the state and they are made up of Universities and Technological Educational Institutes (TEI). The difference between them is that TEIs do not have University status. Furthermore, at the TEIs the studies last for 3 years, while at Universities last for 4 years or more. Studies at some faculties such as Medicine and Polytechnic Studies last more than four years.

The Higher Education Institutes are self-governing bodies, regulating their

own operations through elected bodies. Decisions regarding programmes and hiring policies are made at the departmental level, but decisions regarding resources and new teaching posts are made at the Senate and Rector level.

Today there are 20 Universities in Greece, with some 237 departments. In 2002 the total number of students that entered Greek Universities was 40,000. Respectively there are 14 Technological Educational Institutes (TEI), with some 170 departments and the total number of students that entered TEIs in the same period was 43,000.

The academic year begins on September 1st and ends on August 31st of the following year. Educational activity is divided into two semesters, each of them containing 13 weeks of teaching and two weeks of examinations. Students have a number of core courses and the right to choose a given number of those courses. The students are examined and graded by the professors who teach the courses. A student is awarded a University degree after passing all the examinations and after being enrolled for at least four years.

University teachers must have a Doctorate degree and are appointed by a committee consisting of department members of the same or higher rank. A Ministry of Education committee appoints TEI professors.

The general objective of the courses in the University departments is to provide a high level of theoretical and all-round training to the country's future

	1993	2002	% change
Universities			
Number of Institutions	18	20	
Number of departments	180	237	+31.7%
Number of entrants per year	22,000	40,000	+81.8%
Greek Open University			
Pre-graduate students		6,000	
TEI			
Number of Institutions	12	14	
Number of departments	121	170	+40.5%
Percentage of students aged between 18-21 in Universities - TEIs	27%	58%	+114.8%

Table 5. Source: Ministry of National Education and Religious Affairs. The Greek Educational System.

professionals, scientists and academics. University programmes place emphasis on the grounding, production, development and transmission of knowledge, science and technology, on pure and applied research and on the development of modern postgraduate studies.

The ultimate aim of University education is to equip graduates with the ability to adapt to the ever changing and constantly growing demands of financial and community life.

The Hellenic Open University (HOU) was established in 1997 and provides long distance learning in undergraduate and postgraduate education. In 2002 the HOU received 52,346 applications for the 5,000 positions it had to offer.

3.5 Postgraduate Studies

There are two levels of postgraduate studies, the Diploma of specialisation (which is equivalent to the Masters Degree) and the Doctorate Degree. Full postgraduate studies last at least 6 semesters and the Masters studies at least 4 semesters. Doctoral studies follow the Master degree and last at least a year in which a three months period of thesis preparation is included.

Candidates are admitted to postgraduate study programmes (Masters) either through a selection process or through written or oral examinations. The admission procedure is determined by the internal regulation of the postgraduate programme in question. A necessary condition is the knowledge of a foreign language for Greek candidates and of the Greek language for foreign candidates. The following factors are taken into account in the selection process: the mark received on the candidate's undergraduate degree; performance in undergraduate courses related to the

The National and Kapodistrian University of Athens

The Academy of Athens

postgraduate programme in question; the undergraduate thesis; and any research or writing activity on the part of the candidate. The necessary requirement for registration in a doctoral programme is for the candidate to hold a University level postgraduate specialisation degree (the equivalent of a master's degree). There are however, departments in Universities (for example in the polytechnic field) where it is possible to obtain a doctoral degree without having a first postgraduate degree (Masters). The general objective of doctoral degree studies is, on the one hand, to offer students specialisation in fields of strategic importance. On the other, the objective is to deepen and develop basic research in various disciplines leading to the simultaneous strengthening of the research work done in the country which will contribute to its economic development and to its cultural and social advancement.

Programmes for postgraduate studies are proposed either by groups of members of teaching staff of every University, and/or from University departments, but they must have the final approval of the Ministry of Education.

According to data from the Ministry of National Education and Religious Affairs, in 2002 there were 233 programmes of postgraduate studies, 356.9% higher than 1993. In 1999-00 there were in Greece 2,275 students holding a Masters Degree and 1,049 a Doctoral Degree.

3.6 Scholarships

The Policy of Scholarships is exercised by the National Institution of Scholarships. The Scholarship programmes are mainly distinguished according to the process by which they are granted.

Some scholarships are granted after examinations and are given to graduates of Universities or TEI for post Graduate Studies abroad and to university graduates for postgraduate studies in Greece. There are also scholarships, which are granted on the basis of performance or on the basis of evaluating the personal portfolio of each candidate. These are given to candidates who have excelled in the entrance exams or to students who have excelled in universities and TEI. There are also scholarships within the framework of Educational Exchange Programmes for foreign students.

3.7 Special Education

Until the 1970s special education in Greece was offered by private and more specifically by Philanthropic organisations, but in the mid 80's the Greek government undertook its responsibility towards people with special needs.

Today Special Education and Special Vocational Training for people with Special needs is offered:

1. In ordinary schools where these individuals are registered.

2. In Special classes, units, or groups which operate within regular schools or special classes or supervised groups which operate, and which aim to diagnose and deeper understanding of difficult cases by applying special programmes.

3. In special Kindergarden and autonomous special schools of Primary and Secondary education.

4. In special schools and special classes or units or groups that operate as departments in Neuro-psychiatric orthopaedic centres and other Hospitals or Clinics.

5. In Special Vocational Schools or in special units of Vocational Training education in regular schools.

In exceptional cases special education is offered at home.

According to statistics provided to date by the Special Education Directorate, there are 13,595 students in 1,172 Schools of Special Education, which operate under the auspices of The Ministry of Education. The number of pupils with

diagnosed special educational needs using facilities of Special Education is 3,125 in 1st grade of lower secondary education, 1,504 in 2nd grade of upper secondary education and 8,748 in Technical Vocational Schools (TVS).

3.8 Curriculum Development

According to a recently proposed educational Reform, an Integrated Framework of A Studies Programme will be established which will determine the teaching objectives from public school to Lyceum and will also define the framework within which the context of analytical programmes will be developed. The Uniform Curriculum Framework (EPPS) will be detailed after the Pedagogical Institute (PI) expresses its opinion but the final decision will be that of the Minister of National Education.

The texts are written on the basis of the analytical programmes and the Programmes of Studies. The writing of the texts is done either through a call for proposals or by assigning to one or more writers or to a legal institution after a call for expressing an interest. Alternatively it is done through directly assigning writers or legal institutions or groups of educators who are detached to PI merely for this engagement, without paying them a second salary. For the writing of the texts, educators the advisors or presidents of PI as well as other special scientists can participate in these groups.

The introduction of more than one textbook in the school for each student has been established in subjects where considered necessary. In this case the textbooks are either written by special writing groups who are put together for each book, after a decision of the Educational Council of PI or are drawn from the free market and appointed to the group.

The right to use and to take advantage of the books belongs solely to the Ministry of National Education and Religious Affairs unless there is a different agreement.

The subjects taught and the course content at the Universities are determined by the teaching staff and student representatives in the general assembly of each department.

3.9 The Pedagogical Institute

The Pedagogical Institute constitutes an independent public institution, based in Athens. It is directly associated to the Minister of National Education and Religious Affairs. According to its charter, the role of the Pedagogical Institute includes the following.

a) scientific research and study of issues concerning the primary and secondary sectors of education, **b)** the preparation and submission of proposals instrumental in setting new directions, and the designing and planning of educational policy, with the purpose of achieving the objectives of primary and secondary education, in parallel with the programme for economic, social and cultural development of the country, **c)**

close observation of the evolution of educational technology, study of its implementation within education and monitoring of the results of its application and **d)** the design and implementation of further education programmes for teachers.

In particular, the Pedagogical Institute:

a) studies and evaluates the results of education, **b)** assesses the necessity for educational research, organises, co-ordinates and provides directives for its optimal implementation by school counsellors and teaching personnel, and utilises the results appropriately, **c)** prepares and proposes schedules and curricula for lessons and laboratory exercises in primary and secondary schools, as well as the educational programmes for radio and television, **d)** recommends invitations to tender the authoring of school books, for both students and teachers, their procurement on the open market, their way they are written and their final approval, and formulates guidelines for their writing, **e)** recommends measures for improving didactic methods and educational work in general, **f)** offers its expertise on the needs, form and content of further education and the training of teachers, **g)** advises on the establishment, organisation and operation of laboratories, as well as the specifications and use of audio-visual and other educational resources in schools, **h)** conducts studies and implements research on issues of educational technolo-

gy, supervises their implementation and development and further recommends measures for the full and widespread use of technology, **i)** studies the organisation of school vocational counselling and supervises its implementation, **j)** collaborates with school counsellors and assists them in exercising their scientific and instructional role, **k)** offers its expertise on the content of Draft Bills, Presidential Decrees and Ministerial Decisions, which regulate educational issues, when these are referred to the Institute by the Minister of National Education and Religious Affairs and **l)** studies every educational issue which pertains to the structure, framework, operation and content of primary and secondary education and which is referred to the Institute by the Minister of National Education and Religions.

3.10 Educational Evaluation and Examinations

Education evaluation is divided into two categories

a) Assessment of the educational work in Primary and Secondary Education, and **b)** Student evaluations

Assessment of educational work:

Is characterised by external and internal assessment of the educational work in Primary and Secondary Education.

Internal Assessment:

Is exercised by the Directors of the School Units, the Supervisors of Departments and offices, School Advisors as well as the Assessment Committee of the School Unit.

External Assessment

Is done by Permanent Assessors.

During the assessment, the adequacy of the educators in Primary and Secondary Education is taken into consideration in addition to the efficiency of the school units and the general effectiveness of the Primary and Secondary Education system at the Regional and the National Levels.

Evaluation of the Students

Evaluation of students at both Primary and Secondary levels is undertaken in the classroom and is the responsibility of the teachers who assess individual student performance. Written examinations take place in the last two grades of primary school and in the lower Secondary schools, but normally students are automatically promoted from one grade to the other.

4. Vocational Training in Greece

Vocational Education and Training includes various forms of Education.

Basic Training includes:

1. Apprenticeship
2. Vocational Training Institutes for Post-Secondary Education

Continuous Vocational Training includes:

1. Training of Unemployed
2. Training of Employed and On the Job Training

3. Informal Continuous Vocational Training

4.1 Initial Vocational Training Learning Schools

The System of Apprenticeship was established internationally. It combines the education of the student in the Schools of Apprenticeship of the Greek Manpower Employment Organisation (MO) with practical experience in private and public Enterprises. In 1984 OAED established the dual system, which is continuously being improved with new programmes or through the improvement of existing ones (By introducing new technologies from the workplace and as a means of teaching).

In the first year the students take theoretical and practical courses 5 days per week in the educational units of the Organisation. In the second year they dedicate 1/5 of their time to the educational units and 4/5 of their time to the practical experience near the employer.

The students who are insured by IKA are provided with an allowance of practical experience and they also have the opportunity to stay in Student Dormitories provided that they fulfil the necessary requirements. At the same time the organisation examines the possibilities of placing the graduates in the same or other work positions.

Technical Vocational Schools

Apart from the general objectives of Primary and Secondary Education, the ultimate objective of the Technical - Vocational school is to transmit technical and vocational knowledge and the fostering of skills so that the graduate can successfully practice a specific vocation. Thus the graduate can contribute to the

quantitative and qualitative development of production. At the same time, the strengthening and the enrichment of the general knowledge of the students is sought. The Schools are divided into day and night schools. Attendance at the day schools lasts for up to two years and at the night schools it is prolonged by one year. If there is a need for practical experience in the vocation, attendance is prolonged to one more year whether the school is day or night.

Students register in the (II) Second year, without examinations, provided they have a degree from technical or Vocational schools. They register in the same department that they have graduated from but in a different course of studies.

Institutes of Vocational Training

In 1992, the National System of Vocational Education and Training (NSVET) was established by law to en-

hance the training of the middle-echelon work force in the context of competition within the single European market. The Organisation for Vocational Education and Training (OVET), a legal entity of public law created by the same law, was charged with the establishment, the organisation and the operation of the Vocational Training Institutes (VTIs). The report introducing the law refers to the incomplete technical and vocational training provided at the Technical Vocational Lycea (TVL), the Comprehensive Lyceum (CL) and the former Technical and Vocational Schools (FTVS) owing to lack of modernisation. No system of vocational training had been instituted apart from that of the MO apprenticeship schools, which operated to a very limited extent.

This lack was becoming especially obvious among the tens of thousands of graduates of General Lycea who did not go on to higher education and, lacking elementary job qualifications, were having a difficult time becoming satisfactorily integrated into the labour market.

Other reasons that prompted the foundation of the VTIs were the non-existence, in most cases, of recognised trade rights and the lack of a degree or diploma-granting system that would be recognised in the European Union.

On the basis of this necessity, the VTIs officially opened on 1 February 1993. Fourteen state or public VTIs had begun operating experimentally on 1 September 1992. Today there are a total of one hundred and thirty-six (136) state VTIs operating nation-wide. Of these, 114 are independent VTIs and 22 operate administratively as branches of independent ones. Parallel to the public VTIs, private VTIs began operation for the first time during the winter semester of 1993. Today there are ninety-three (93) private VTIs, whose programmes of study and specialisations are the same as those of the state VTIs. The corresponding operating regulations for private VTIs were drawn up in June of 1993.

Admission to state Vocational Training Institutes (VTIs) requires a leaving certificate from lower secondary school (gymnasium), from a technical vocational school, from the Manpower Employment Organisation (MO) apprenticeship school, or from any type of upper secondary school (lyceum). Also, adults with the minimum level lower secondary school certificate may be admitted. In practice, most students have been to date graduates from various types of gymnasia or Lycea and TVSs. The same is true of private VTIs.

The Vocational Training Institutes (VTIs) grant a vocational training diploma certifying post-secondary vocational training in a trade. Each Institute may have one or more course of studies and each direction offers a certain number of specialisations.

The training includes theoretical courses, workshops and mixed courses (i.e. theoretical classes undertaken while the student is in the process of acquiring of practical skills). The teaching hour for all these courses is 45 minutes. Workshop courses or the workshop section of mixed courses may continue uninterrupted for up to 3 hours. Attendance is compulsory for all subjects and all courses.

On completion of their training, students receive a Confirmation of Vocational Training. This Confirmation gives them the right to participate in certification examinations to acquire a Vocational Training Diploma. The examinations cover both the practical and theoretical part of the training, and graduates of public and private VTIs alike are examined by means of common statewide examinations. By a joint decision of the Minister of National Education and Religious Affairs as well as the Minister of Finance, a National System of Vocational Training Certification has been established. OVET, which is responsible for running the certification system, with the assistance of the Central Committee for the Certification of Vocational Training (CCCVT) in which the social partners participate, conducts examinations for certification of vocational training on a nation-wide level twice a year.

4.2 Adult Education / Continuing Education

Greece does not have a long tradition in adult learning. However, during the last decade there have been rapid developments in vocational training at both levels - initial and continuing - largely due to the impact of the structural policies of the European Union, in particular the European Social Fund support. Nevertheless the development of human resources in the country is still far behind actual need.

The General Secretariat for Adult Education (GSAE) is broadening its activities by addressing special programmes for partial target groups to all adults. The programmes to be launched in the year 2002 deal cover a number of fields. These include: language and arithmetic literacy; cultural and social literacy; strategies of learning, information, digital literacy; multi-modal document literacy; skills to develop information Business (Organisation -management of social activity, multiple skills in the workspace). Other fields covered by these programmes are: Greek for immigrants based on dual literacy (teaching the language of the host country in combi-

nation with the development of skills in the mother tongue of the adult immigrants); family planning; support programmes for special groups; volunteer programmes; programmes for senior citizens.

From 1998-2000, 50,000 adults who received this kind of education.

Since the academic year 1998-1999 there have been 21 Alternative Study Programmes (PSE) in operation. The fundamental purpose of these programmes is to promote lifelong learning and training within a higher education framework. The Hellenic Open University (HOU) has also begun operation. All upper secondary school graduates have access to the HOU, with precedence given to candidates between the ages of 23 and 45 years of age, who for any reason, were unable to achieve college or university education. It also provides long distance learning and teaching with, as a target population, employees whose work commitments prevent actual attendance at a university or a course, residents of remote regions and islands (especially relevant in Greece), housewives, disabled persons and so on.

The General Secretariat for Adult Education (GSAE) plans, co-ordinates and supports actions with three main objectives: to combat illiteracy and supplement basic education; to provide preparatory and non-formal vocational training, mainly to the unemployed; and to provide social and cultural enrichment. More generally, the aim of GSAE policy is to prevent and combat social exclusion.

Law 2525/97 provided for the possibility of establishing Second Chance Schools, in collaboration with the local authorities, for persons over 18 years of age who have not completed the compulsory nine-year schooling. Their aim is to give young people who have been excluded from the classical school system a new opportunity by means of appropriate educational methods, using in particular the new multi-media technologies. The Second Chance schools provide formal secondary education for adults. Graduates are awarded certificates of study within the framework of formal adult education, which are fully equivalent to those given in their day school counterparts.

Non-formal adult education is provided at the Adult Education Centres operating under the supervision of the Prefectural Adult Education Committees. It is also provided at the Vocational Training Centres run by the General Secretariat for Adult Education and in special areas (e.g. correctional institutions, institutions. Regarding participation in non-formal adult education, there are eligibility criteria according to each programme.

Basic skills programmes are addressed to a number of different groups. These include: adult immigrants; adults 18-30 years of age; unemployed adults 25-64 years of age that have either not completed or have ceased their education after having obtained compulsory education school leaving certificates; adults wishing to gain new basic skills; and special groups (gypsies, inmates, individuals endangered by social exclusion).

General Objectives:

Persons studying in formal adult education are seeking to improve their general educational level and to acquire the formal qualifications that can be expected to improve their employment prospects.

The participation of adults in non-formal adult education aims primarily at providing them with basic knowledge (language, culture, etc.) as well as some aspects of vocational training so that these adults can be integrated or re-integrated into working life and learn to deal with the constant social and occupational changes.

The new programmes promoted by the General Secretariat for Adult Education are in the context of supporting life long learning and aim at activating the public in all fields of their lives (work, family, society). A basic concept in adult education is the assumption that these fields are learning environments and that this very dimension should constantly be supported and fed back to the formal and non-formal educational system.

WOMEN AND POLITICS

By M. Pantelidou Maloutas

Greek political culture is a very complex and in some ways contradictory entity which combines in a particular way traditional elements with aspects of a modern culture. A structural element of Greek political culture refers to women's low visibility in politics and their under-representation in all political

elites, which accompanies the "equality of rights between the sexes" stipulated in the 1975 Constitution. In fact, in spite of the changes in the legal status of women that took place during the 80s as a result of feminist demands and reformist politics of the party in power (PASOK), women's social inferiority and political marginalisation are still evident. Greek society exhibits one of the lowest levels in the EU of women in positions of power and in socio-economic decision making, while today there are only four women in government and twenty-six in a parliament of three hundred (8.7%), which constitutes nevertheless a big improvement.

I. General overview

Late in obtaining full political rights (1952), Greek women followed until 1985 the "traditional" voting pattern, favouring the Right, and traditional styles of lack or with very low levels in all other types of formal political participation. Even though there

is a long tradition of informal participation by Greek women in national liberation and democratic struggles, the
political system's lack of interest about
the reality of gender discrimination
were repaid by women's very low levels of formal political activity. Party
membership, standing for public office
and entering the political elites was until recently almost exclusively male and
legitimised as such. What must be
stressed however, is that in Greek political culture women's political profiles
vary enormously (maybe more so than
in other European societies). This is due
to the large variation in women's patterns of personal life relative to the
rigidity of gender roles and the division
of labour within the family. In more traditional environments (i.e. in rural areas) women's social inferiority is much
more pronounced and much less challenged, while older cohorts, both in
rural and urban areas, largely accept
their lower social status as normal.
Younger women on the contrary,
proving the wide diffusion of feminist
ideas during the last decades, massively
reject the legitimacy of their social inferiority considering it "a problem that
must be solved". According to research
data of the National Centre for Social
Research (see I. Nicolacopoulos, M.
Pantelidou Maloutas, 1988, *Women's
political behaviour, Final report*,
Athens, National Centre of Social Research [in Greek]), one out of three
women over 60 absolutely agrees with

the idea that "politics must be men's
prerogative". However, less than 4% of
young women (18-29) share this point
of view.

The important social changes that
took place in the past decades, such as
the diminution of the agrarian population and the percentage of illiteracy,
the development in women's employment in the wage sector and a tendency
towards a decline in gender occupational segregation, in addition to
changes in the rigidity of gender roles
had an impact especially on young
women's political perception. In fact,
age presents itself as a variable of particular importance in Greek political
culture, where the differences in the
level of political participation in the
same age group according to gender,
can be smaller than in different age
groups of the same gender. There is a
greater similarity between young
women and men (18-29) than between
young and old women (60+), in the
frequency of reading of the press
(64.6% and 78.3% of young women
and men declare frequent reading of
newspapers against 34.8% and 68.2%
for the old). This also holds in the frequency of exchanging political opinions
(37.5% and 42.9% of young women
and men declare frequent exchange of
political opinions against 23.4% and
58.2% for the old). This is also so in the
absolute lack of political interest (15.9%
and 16.6% of young women and men
against 32.9% and 11.6% for the old)

and in the frequency of participation in electoral campaigns (15.6% and 19.8% of young women and men declare frequent implication in campaigns against 8.1% and 23.2% for the old). The same tendency is notable concerning the ideological orientation of the young. It appears that in the late 80's, it is young women that constitute the social group positioned more in favour of the Left: 42.2% of young women and 33.2% of young men declare belonging rather to the Left, against 19% and 27.2% for the old. (M. Pantelidou Maloutas, 1992, *Women and politics*, Athens, Gutenberg [in Greek])

In spite of the above trends in the political outlook of younger women, it is evident that Greek women in general continue to participate less in the formal political process. They also express lower levels of political interest and expect less from the political system, which is obviously less inclined to give voice to their experience and their perspectives. This is more so for older and less educated women, whose social inferiority translates itself into obvious political inequality, in spite of formal citizenship which they gained only fifty five years ago. It is in fact notable that the electorate in Greece still comprises voters that have had the unique experience of being adults without political rights: Women over 70

The 80s were a decade of great importance. The dynamic presence of the feminist movement, since the second half of the 70's, and the socialist party's (PASOK) - in government since 1981- both wish to "modernise" the country in order to harmonise its coexistence with other EEC members, and also to appeal to the "non-privileged" members of the electorate, brought important legal measures towards the equality of the sexes. Although incapable of abolishing women's deep-rooted social inferiority, these measures, as well as welfare provisions then instituted, did offer solutions to specific problems. Also they legitimised for the first time in Greek political culture the vision of a society not based on brutal gender discrimination and promoted "equality" of the sexes to the level of a widely accepted value. The fact that issues concerning women were no longer totally excluded from the political agenda had important and lasting effects on women's political attitudes and patterns of behaviour. The most interesting of these for *PASOK* was that women generously "repaid" the attention they received by voting massively in its favour in the 1985 general elections. Thus a "gender gap" was created for the first time in Greek electoral history.

II. Evolution of Voting Patterns

The convergence in the levels and patterns of participation noted above between women and men of the younger generation is also apparent as a tendency in the voting patterns according to gender. The fragmented, sometimes un-official and not always comparable data, concerning the evolution of women's vote, indicate that in 1956, when women participated for the first time in the electorate for general parliamentary elections, the gender divergence in favour of the main party of the Right (ERE) was in Athens +13.2 points for women (56.7% agaist 43.5% for men). (I. Nicolacoloulos, *Parties and Elections in Greece: 1946-1964*, Athens, National Centre of Social Research, 1985 p. 277 [in Greek]. Other data in this section derive from calculations of the author based on official data). This dispar-ity is noted while an important increase of the Left is sanctioned in the 1956 election, with women voting in Athens at 40.9%, against 53.8% for men in favour of a "Democratic Union" of the Left with centrist parties. It is evident that women largely contributed to the favourable results of the Right, repaying their dues to the party that gave them political rights.

The gender divergence in the per-centage of the vote for the Right was smaller in Athens in the next (1958) par-liamentary elections (+8.2 points for women), as well as for the Left (+8 points for men). During the sixties, in urban areas, a steady decrease is noted in the gender disparities in the vote for the Right: 3.8 points in 1961, 3.6 in 1963 and 2.6 in 1964, always in favour of women. These three general elec-tions marked on the national level in-significant gender divergence in the vote for the Centre, and as far as the two poles of the axis are concerned, a divergence lower or equal to 2.6 points. When the Greek electorate is called again to the polls ten years later in a completely different climate after a sev-en year dictatorship, the disparity of voting behaviour according to sex reap-pears accentuated. In the 1974 and 1977 elections, when the charismatic personality of the leader of the Right (K.

Karamanlis) secured electoral victory, the specific distribution of the vote by gender verified the existence of a conventional gender disparity in his favour of about 5 points. In 1974 the gender divergence in favour of New Democracy in the area of Athens went up to +5.9 points for women and at the national level up to +4.8 points, while in 1977 the relative figures rise at +6.6 and +5.2. An important aspect of these two elections of the 70s, both won by the ND, was the rapid growth of PASOK that almost doubled its vote in three years. Women voted both times a little less than men in favour of *PASOK*, (-2.3 points in 1974 and -3.8 points in 1977 in the area of Athens), something that they would "rectify" less than a decade later.

The 80s mark a new diminution in the gender disparity of the vote. In 1981 women vote at 3.1 points more than men in favour of the Right in urban areas, and only at 1.1 point in the 1985 elections. But, although the 1981 election was a turning point in Greek political history, putting an end to decades of almost continuous government by the Right, what is most important from the point of view of gender disparities was the 1985 election. Then women voted for the first time more than men in favour of a party that did not belong to the Right, claiming to be socialist: *PASOK*. Women generously repaid the attention they received from *PASOK*, which had incorporated "equality" in its

program of reforms wanting to appeal to yet another category of "non privileged" Greeks. It is interesting to note that this "gender gap" appeared for *PASOK* in all areas: urban (+1.5 points for women), semi-urban (+1.3) and rural (+0.7) in accordance with *PASOK's* policy (helped by *EGE*, the women's organisation that it had created) of addressing itself to women of all social environments. Thus while *PASOK* gained power in 1981 with more men's votes (48.8% against 47.2% for women), in 1985 when it had lost 5.8 points of its electoral force, losing many fewer women's votes contributed to its retaining power. 44.6% of men (-8.7) and 45.9% of women (-2.7) voted in its favour during difficult economic times, and while the campaign was polarised around the issue of the election of a new president of the Republic. *PASOK's* policy of gender "equality", which can be described as a point of intersection between its modernising and its populist discourse, had certainly secured benefits in terms of votes. Also this 1985 election marked another (symbolic) novelty. For the first time in Greek electoral history the vote in favour of the Right marked no real gender variation: 40.1% of men and 40.8% of women voted in 1985 for *ND*.

From June 1989 to April 1990 three general elections took place in a climate of uneasiness. After eight years in government *PASOK* had to face elections in a changing international atmo-sphere, but also, in the middle of internal political crisis and intense polarisation. In all three elections *PASOK* gained slightly more women's votes than men's, proving the stability of the gender gap in Greek political culture. Winner or looser, *PASOK* seemed to be able to count (slightly) more on women's support: 38.8% against 38.1% for men in June 1989, 40.4% against 39.7% in November of the same year, 38.6% against 37.8% in April 1990. Evidently, the difference in voting in favour of *PASOK* according to gender is minimal, but its importance is not, since it seems to have become a new constant feature in Greek political culture, present beyond the 1985 conjuncture. We must add that during the same three elections, women voted also slightly (insignificantly in fact) more than men (+0.6, +0.6 and +0.8 point) in favour of ND (the main party of the Right).

What is important to underline on the basis of the diminishing gender divergence in the voting is that if women and men differ on the level of attitudes and perceptions concerning the vote (and they definitely do, since i.e. in older cohorts 48.6% of women against 70% of men think that their vote can influence the solution of everyday problems), this difference does not materialise in their voting behaviour. In the October 1993 general election, the disparity of women's and men's vote was for all parties, Left and Right, smaller or

The Mayor of Athens, Dora Bakoyanni

equal to 1, *PASOK* being the only exception with +1.3 point for women (45,6% for men against 46,9% for women). In the September 1996 election, the relevant (inverse) disparity was even larger (39.4% of men and 42.1% of women voted in favour of *PASOK*). At the same time, gender was practically irrelevant for the vote in favour of the Right: 37.5% and 38% of men and women supported *ND* as well as 3% and 2.9% respectively, voted for *POLAN. DEKKI*, extracted from *PASOK*, obtained 5.1% and 4.1%. For the Left the gender disparity of the vote was traditional as far as the KKE was concerned (6.4% of men and 5.5% of women voted in its favour). An interesting novelty was displayed for Synaspismos, counting in the electorate in its favour 5.4% and 5.7% respectively of men and women. The gender gap that we may detect through the electoral data is more than confirmed if we take into account the variable of age. On the basis of exit poll data (Mega/BEVEA Opinion, I. Nicolacopoulos, Scientific Direction), in the 18-34 age group there is a disparity of 1-1.5 points in favour of men voting for a party belonging to the Right. Women of the same age group present + 2 points in the vote for the Left. The 2000 general election confirmed the above trend.

III. Women and parties

Although women do not demonstrate greater abstention than men, they are much less convinced of the importance of their vote and much less interested in parties and the party system. If 17.1% of men declared in the late 80s to be members of a party, only 6.6% of women had the same commitment. (Since membership cards do not exist, the relative declaration is more indicative of a sentimental attachment to a party than anything else). Furthermore there is a wide differentiation according the urban/rural divide: Today women represent around 30% of the members of *PASOK* in big cities, while the relative percentage for rural areas must be a lot smaller. Nevertheless 30% has been tar-

geted by *PASOK* as a quota in its legislative organs. Today, there are 44 women members of the Central Committee of 180 (24.4%) and 3 out of 11 in *PASOK's* Executive Bureau (27.3%).

The situation is worse in the relative picture of New Democracy, the main party of the Right, which has 5 women in its Executive Committee of 25 (20%) and 63 in the Central Committee of 495 members (12.7%). In the departmental Committees women amount also to 20% following the application of a quota decided in 1994 after the demand of the Secretariat for Women and stipulated in the party charter since then. As far as the March 1997 Congress is concerned, the press mentioned a gender composition of the participants, amounting to 3106 men and 498 women, 86.18% against 13.82% respectively.

Synaspismos, the Coalition of the Left, seems less "woman unfriendly" than any other Greek party. Its Central Committee comprises 39 women in a total of 111 members, a percentage (35.1%), that reflects the gender composition of the party membership. This analogous quota is applied to all legislative organs, but not to executive ones. Thus in the case of the Political Secretariat, out of 18 members 4 are women (22.2%).

KKE, the Communist Party of Greece, actually the only party with a woman at its head, seems to include women at 18% of its total members. It has 21% women in the Central Committee, 22% in the Secretariat of the Central Committee, 27% of the heads of the 41 departments of the CC, but only 11% in the Political Bureau. It seems that the party did apply a quota for women in decision-making organs between 1990 and 1996, but at the 1996 Congress it was decided that "the effectiveness of such an administrative measure was rather small".

Although there is no particularly "woman friendly" party in the Greek political system, it is interesting to note that in the spring of 1991 two women were elected as party leaders, for the first time in Greek political history, both by parties of the Left. (in the *KKE*, the Communist Party of Greece and *Synaspismos*, Coalition of the Left). If this novelty seemed to challenge the traditional patriarchal character of the party system, the way that the first woman Secretary General of the Communist Party of Greece was received by the press, with comments on her appearance, proved the profound sexism with which women politicians are judged and evaluated.

IV. Women in public office

If voting patterns are not significantly differentiated according to gender, on the contrary, Greek political culture is characterised by a massive disparity in the proportion of men and women in public office. It must be underlined that today Greece presents the lowest level of women Members of Parliament in the EU (8.7%).

The high hopes created by the election of the first woman member of the Greek parliament in 1953, when in a local by-election in Thessaloniki women participated in the electorate for the first time[1] were soon severely disappointed. During the first period of women's vote (1952 until the dictatorship of 1967) in five general elections (1956, 1958, 1961, 1963, 1964) plus several local by-elections only 13 times was a woman elected, with a maximum of four women coexisting in a Parliament of three hundred (during the 1958-1961 session). In total only 8 women succeeded during this period in becoming members of the Greek parliament, of which five belonged to the Left (all of them members of the, then illegal, Communist Party), two to the Right and one to the Centre.

The first elections after the fall of the dictatorship brought seven women into Parliament, of which four belonged to *ND* (Right) one to the Centre, one to *PASOK* and one to the Left. This meagre 2.6% comprised mostly women of polit-

---

[1] It must also be noted that the 1944 elections took place in the liberated part of Greece with the participation of women. It is noteworthy that five women were then, under extremely difficult conditions, elected "national councilors", one of whom was Maria Svolou, a well known feminist\suffragist of the interwar period, who became, in the 50s, one of the first women MPs.

ical families, a well-known actress and an important lady of the press, setting a very conventional pattern for women in politics. More women entered the Parliament in 1977, raising the percentage to 3.7%: Again four for the Right, but this time five from *PASOK* and two from the Left. Of the latter, one was a well known figure of the student's communist resistance against the dictatorship, who was to play a leading role in the affairs of the Left in the early 90s (party leader of *Synaspismos* in 1991).

1981 set a pattern for three consecutive elections with a standard of thirteen women in Parliament (4.3%). In 1981, the year of *PASOK's* victory, and again in 1985, the year of women's surpassing men in the socialist vote, eight women were elected under *PASOK's* banner, along with three from the Right (*ND*) and two from the Left in 1981, and four and one respectively, in 1985. But in June 1989 there were thirteen women MPs with only four from *PASOK*, against seven from *ND* and two from the Left. It seems that in a losing *PASOK* the first to go are its women representatives.

In November 1989, twenty women MPs were elected, but for a very short session, since in April of the next year new elections would take place. It is interesting to note, concerning the November 1989 elections, that for the first time the ecological movement is represented in the Greek Parliament and this happens via a woman MP. Al-

so, an important female political figure of the Right appears, for the first time, taking the seat of her late husband, just assassinated by terrorists. One of the ten women MPs under the *ND* banner, she managed to obtain more votes than her husband did in the past. While there is a long tradition of "political widows" in the Greek Parliament, she has been proved to be much more than that, and was to play a central role in Greek politics.

April 1990 election brought sixteen women into Parliament, a meagre 5.3% that grew to an equally meagre 6% in the 1993 elections when eighteen women were elected. The death of Melina Merkouri, MP since 1977 and Minister of Culture in every *PASOK* government, rendered the number of women MPs to seventeen, until in 1995 it became nineteen (after the winning of a disputed seat and of an evacuated one by two women). Eight were from the governing *PASOK*, eight from *ND*, two from *POLAN* (Right) and one from the traditional Left. It is interesting to note that these MPs included three university professors, all of them jurists, another four lawyers, two philologists, one architect and two other graduates of the Polytechnic, a political scientist, an economist and an actress. After the 1996 elections there were again 19 women out of 300 (6.3%): Seven belonged to *PASOK*, six to *ND*, three to Synaspismos, two to *KKE* and one to *DEKKI*. Five of them were elected for

Vaso Papandreou member of Parliament, ex-minister of PASOK government

the first time in the Greek Parliament.

An important increase in the number of women elected to Parliament was noted at the 2000 election, when thirty-one appeared to have gained seats. After the annulment of the election of five by the courts, finally twenty-six women are today MPs: twelve from *PASOK*, ten from *ND*, two from *KKE* (CPG) and two from Synaspismos (Left). Twelve were elected for the first time.

The general picture of women's "under-representation" in decision making is, as expected, evident also in the gender composition of Greek governmen-

ts. After the first (and only one before the dictatorship) woman appointed Minister in 1956, twenty-five years passed before the next appointment, of M. Merkouri in 1981 as Minister of culture. But seven other women had occupied positions of under-secretary of State or Minister alternate from 1974 to 1989. Thus against one woman member of government in the pre dictatorship period there are eight from 1974 to 1989, all, with only one exception, responsible for areas that are in perfect accordance with stereotypes of women's aptitudes and roles. Also it is of particular symbolic value that the *"ecumenical"* government of 1989, which was supposed to represent a very wide political and social spectrum of interests, did not include any woman, something that was strongly criticised both by women politicians and by feminist groups.

During the 90s, the general picture of women in government is one of a representation of no more than 12% at best. Women are responsible for or involved mostly in matters of Welfare (six women), Culture, Education and Justice, with the rare exception of only one, occupying a Ministry considered crucial (Ministry of Development) in the 1996 Simitis government in which there were 3 women in total. In the past (PASOK governments after 1985), the same politician, V. Papandreou, has been Minister Alternate of Industry and later of Commerce, while today she occupies the post of Minister for the Environment, Planning and Public Works. There is a total of four women in government today.

Women's participation in decision making in local government is also very poor, although in the relative electoral campaigns it is often stressed (even by women themselves) that women have "special abilities" considered very useful on the local level. After the 1998 local elections, that took place after the application of a plan for regrouping and reorganising municipalities, less than 2% of mayors were women (14/900), as well as less than 1% of presidents of communes (1/133). Only 1 out of 54 Departments had a woman at its head. In the 2002 local elections a 33% gender quota was applied for the first time on the lists. This had a small impact on the results given that there is a preferential vote. Thus today, there are 16 women out of 900 mayors and five out of 133 presidents of the communes. But, for the first time, Athens, as well as the wider departmental area that includes Athens, both have women at their heads.

On the other hand women in the Greek delegation to the European Parliament passed from 8.3% in the 1981-1989 period to 16% after the 1994 election, with four women in a delegation of twenty-five. This number increased to five after the occupation of an evacuated seat by A. Karamanou in February 1997, thus augmenting the relative percentage to 20%. The profiles of women members of the European Parliament indicate that most of them have been chosen either because they are well known from a different area of activity, or because there is a wish to recompense them (or both).

V. Epilogue

Greek society still exhibits a very low level, one of the lowest in the EU, of women in positions of power and in decision making, a feature in accordance with its undeniable androcentric character. Furthermore, this is a period of recession in feminist organisation and mobilisation, with almost no mechanisms for promoting women's interests independent of the state. For various reasons, both specific to Greek society as well as in common with many others, feminism is not expressed as a movement in Greece of the 2000s. This does not necessarily mean that feminist ideology is in crisis today in Greek society. On the contrary, if women's social inferiority is always apparent in Greek society, it functions today in a new climate of gender awareness and of legitimisation of gender "equality", created in previous decades by feminist political activity. Furthermore, scholarly thinking and writing is today influenced by feminist theory, while seminars, conferences, and courses in Universities and specialised journals in which gender is a central object of study, do exist. It seems as if a phase of feminist introspection is prevalent today, out of which new political interventions will eventually be born by, and in favour of women, beyond public measures taken in accordance with European decisions. It is apparent today that legal equality and welfare provisions, although necessary, are not sufficient as a remedy to the profoundly sexist character of the socio-political reality. Gender inequalities being far deeper than legal, what remains to be seen is how the maturing of younger cohorts with new values and priorities, fewer gender stereotypes and a greater awareness of gender as an unacceptable discriminating factor, plus the growing implication of women in politics, are going to influence the political process in Greece, and thus, the position of women in Greek society.

ENVIRONMENTAL PROTECTION

By N. Chlepas and E. Mertziou

In 1975, the Constitution of the new-born Third Republic embodied pioneering, detailed regulations for the protection of the "natural and cultural environment". Art. 24 underlines the obligation of the State to take all preventive and restrictive measures required to protect the environment, while forests and forest areas obtained a special protection status including restrictions of private property rights. Having in mind the extensive damage caused to the "urban landscape" by the uncontrolled building craze during the fifties and the sixties, the new Constitution introduced strict standards for physical and urban planning as well as for the safeguard of cultural heritage.

These new regulations enabled the development of a pioneer jurisprudence by the Greek *Conseil d' Etat (Symvoulion Epikratias)*. The Court has underlined that the Constitution accepts only sustainable development. So, it demands all-embracing environmental impact studies and affirms citizen's rights for access to environmental information. The Court's decisions forced the government to re-plan a major project and confirmed the reputation of the Greek *Conseil d'Etat* as an independent, steadfast guardian of the environment.

Environmental policy

Responsibility for environmental matters at the national level lies with the Ministry for the Environment, Physical Planning and Public Works. This Ministry, originally established in 1980 with the intention of concentrating all responsibilities within one body, has constantly been expanding its activities, as has no other Ministry during the past decade. Nevertheless, some important responsibilities remained in the domain of other Ministries, such as the Ministry for Agriculture (forestry, hunting etc.) and the Ministry for Industry, Research and Technology.

Recently (1995), a new Bureau was established in the Division of Environmental Planning, namely the "Bureau for a National Environmental Information Network and a European Environmental Agency" (hereinafter referred to as the Bureau). The Bureau has two major aims:

• to co-ordinate the National Environmental Network and its connection with the European Network (EIONET);

• to co-ordinate and operate the Greek Focal Point (NFP) of the European Environmental Agency (EEA).

The first aim is being supported by the National Environmental Information Network (EDPP) and is to be completed in four years. The pilot phase of EDPP has been completed, including five Prefectures and three Regions. Presently, the University of Athens, in co-operation with the Bureau is executing a feasibility study for the expansion of EDPP at the National scale.

The second aim was initially accomplished through administrative actions such as staffing and budget allocations. Recently the Ministry of the Environment, Physical Planning and Public Works began co-operating with the University of Athens, in order to be technically and scientifically supported in the activities of the National Focal Point.

The environmental Programme of Greece for the period 1994-2000 aims at addressing the major environmental problems of the country as well as cre-ating the infrastructures for the efficient management of the Greek environment in the 21st century. In addition, the Programme reflects the commitment as well as the efforts of the Greek Government to pursue a development policy for Greece, in a manner that will at the same time safeguard the environment and the physical resources.

Both national and community funding support the Operational Environmental Programme of Greece (hereafter referred to as OEP). National funding comes from the country's budget and is complemented by a special levy applied on gas. Income from the levy is invested on projects with potential to rectify environmental problems, or to allow the study of environmental problems. Community funding comes from the Structural Funds as well as from the

Cohesion Funds. The legal frame work of the OEP are the National Framework Law 1650/86 for the protection of the environment, the EC environmental regulations and directives and the obligations of Greece with respect to International environmental Agreements and Conventions. The recent law 3010/2002 harmonises the existing law 1650/86 according to the Directives 97/11/EC and 96/61/EC.

• The *OEP* is based upon:

• **the sustainability principle** aimed at improving or protecting environmental conditions in Greece, while preserving the developments efforts in the industrial, tourist and agricultural sectors;

• **the polluter pays principle** which recognises the responsibility of the major pollutants which need to be addressed;

• **the precautionary principle** which attempts to prevent, rather than to rectify an environmental problem, with technical interventions at the source rather than at the end of the pipe line;

• **the joint responsibility principle** which recognises the common obligations of the central, regional and local authorities as far as the environment is concerned.

These principles have been specified and complemented by a number of rules, which briefly are:

• Untangling economic growth from environmental degradation;

• Sectoral integration providing for environmental considerations to be included in the objectives and priorities of sectoral policies;

• Prioritisation of avoidance and non-management of environmental pressures aimed at minimising the risks and reducing the cost of end-of-pipe solutions;

• Problem solving at the source, recognising that local solutions are more efficient and are relatively less costly;

• Identification and management of carrying capacity as sustainable management prerequisites the identification of exploitation limits of natural resources and ecosystems.

OEP consists of seven sub-programs: six of the sub-programmes reflect respective environmental action areas, while the remaining programme aims at the provision of technical assistance in selected thematic areas. Each sub-programme is further divided in action programmes aimed at resolving specific environmental problems as depicted from a thorough assessment of the state of environment in Greece. Part of OEP aims at developing the *National Environmental Informatics Network*, the Greek contribution to the EIONET of the European Environment Agency (EEA).

Since the *Earth Summit* in 1992, Greece has been implementing a comprehensive policy towards sustainable development. Sustainability is introduced in the development policies of the country and sustainable practices are integrated in sectors such as energy, tourism, transport, agriculture and industry.

The *Ministry for the Environment, Physical Planning and Public Works* has developed a co-ordination mechanism for sustainable development and the implementation of Agenda 21, in order to mobilise the interest and involvement of all the competent ministries and other public sectors and to co-operate with all relevant groups. Under this mechanism, the Ministry undertook the preparation of the annual reports for submission to the *United Nations Commission on Sustainable Development* (CSD) in order to assess the progress towards the principles of Agenda 21.

The National Strategy for Sustainable Development (NSSD) establishes a framework for the development of an Action Programme capable of meeting the global challenges, compatible with the EU guiding principles and adaptable to national particularities.

Greece follows closely and contributes regularly to the development of international and EU environmental policy. It participates in all the relevant processes and submits national reports annually to the Committee for Sustainable Development of the UN (CSD) in relation to the implementation of Agenda 21. Sustainable Development is promoted at global, EU, regional (Mediterranean and Black Sea) and national lev-els supporting the initiatives of the international community for the success of the World Summit for the Environment in Johannesburg.

Recently, the Council of Ministers adopted a National Strategy for Sustainable Development aimed at a balanced approach of all parameters, which define social prosperity in harmony with natural environment:

• The economic parameter focuses on the support of entrepreneurship and competitiveness and the national use of natural and man made resources;

• The social parameter is focused on poverty alleviation and the support of social cohesion and solidarity;

• The environmental parameter is focused on the natural resources of Greece and on the confrontation of pressures from human activities.

The National Strategy for Sustainable Development aims at the co-ordination and integration of policies in a long term and effective framework.

Giving the necessary priority to the environmental dimension of Greece's Sustainable Development, the main targets are the following:

• Confrontation of climate change;

• Reduction of air pollutants;

• Reduction and rational management of solid waste;

• Rational water resources management;

• Confrontation of desertification;

• Protection of bio-diversity and ecosystems.

Management and protection of bio-diversity

In Greece, 5500 species of flora and 900 species of fauna have been recognised. Many of them are rare. Today 4% of flora and 22% of fauna in Greece are considered endangered.

There are also many protected areas, a significant number of which is of international interest, and Greece is committed to their protection through international conventions. There are 10 National parks, 11 Wetlands of international interest (Ramsar), 51 preserved natural monuments, 300 Corine biotopes, 113 important areas for the birds of Europe etc. There are also 265 areas that have been proposed for the Natura 2000 network, covering approximately 16.6% of Greece. Approximately 2.5% of Greece is covered by protected areas.

In the last decade, several measures have been taken. These include the ratification of international conventions, the incorporation of EU Directives in the National Legal Order, the constitution of a National Inventory of NATURA 2000 sites, the publication of Law 2742/99 "on physical planning and sustainable development" and the establishment of a new body for the management of the National Marine Park of Zakynthos.

The targets of the National Strategy to address the abatement of bio-diversity coincide with the targets of the UN Convention for Bio-diversity and con-cern the reversal of the existing trend of reduction in bio-diversity and the effective protection and restoration of natural ecosystems.

Based on the above targets, in 1999 the Ministry for Environment, Physical Planning and Public Works has prepared a Strategy for Wetland Resources and a National Plan for Natural Environment.

The basic sectors of action of the NSSD for Bio-diversity are:
• Conservation and restoration of natural ecosystems and species of wild fauna and flora;
• Management of water and soil resources;
• Promotion of horizontal environmental policies;
• Integration of bio-diversity in sectoral policies.

The above sectors also concern the unprotected zones between them so that these connect and not separate the protected areas. Especially in areas where primary sector activities are developed, the role of agriculture, husbandry and forestry on the management of landscapes and ecosystems and the protection of bio-diversity should be defined.

The main problems for Greek ecosystems are caused by some intensive human activities (tourism, mining, agriculture, animal grazing etc.) which have as a result the degradation of biotopes and the diminution of flora and fauna populations.

The lack of urban planning and National Cadastre (Land Registry) as well as of a general planning for the management of the natural environment and resources had, until recently, caused serious problems for the valuable ecosystems of Greece.

Since the Earth Summit in 1992, Greece has been implementing a comprehensive policy aimed at sustainable development. The main goal of actions taken on the management and protection of bio-diversity is to provide the knowledge and the facilities for monitoring, protecting and managing the flora and fauna species.

More specifically, the actions taken on the management and protection of bio-diversity, significant bio-topes and for sustainable development through the Operational Environmental Programme are:

• The action programme *"Management and protection of bio-diversity"* of OEP aims at providing the knowledge and the facilities for monitoring, protecting and managing the flora and fauna species. Specific actions of this programme are:

- Completion of national lists of flora and fauna species in danger.

- Development of specific programmes for the protection of endangered flora and fauna species.

- Definition of special management measures for selected fauna species, including the specification of the hunting code.

- Inventory of fish stocks in ecologically sensitive areas.

- Management schemes for fish stocks.

• Action programme *"Infrastructure for the management and protection of*

The Evros delta

important bio-topes at the National level" which aims at providing the facilities and technical means for the protection, guarding and management of the most important bio-topes in Greece. The programme will build upon existing knowledge of these areas as acquired from the assessment of the state of environment as well as from their mapping.

● The action programme for *Sustainable development applications* reflects a new spirit in the environmental programme of Greece, as it is the first time that significant amounts are being invested for the protection of natural sites. The programme is expected to support protection measures for 100 (25% of Greek bio-topes) Greek bio-topes which are included in the NATURA 2000 list. Specific actions of this programme are:

- Programme for the protection and management of wetlands.

- Programme for the protection and management of forest ecosystems.

- Programme for the protection of bio-topes though the development of eco-tourism activities.

- Anti-erosion measures at selected sites.

● The Action programme "*Cadastre for ecologically sensitive areas*" aims at developing a special Cadastre for ecologically sensitive areas which protect forested areas from destruction, as well as from land use modifications which usually take place at the expense of forests. The programme, which will build on the existing CORINE programme and include the Cadastre for archaeological monuments and sites, reflects 15,000 Km^2 of ecologically sensitive areas in the vicinities of Municipalities.

Greece is represented in the "*European Topic Centre on Nature Conservation*" by the Greek Bio-tope Wetland Centre, which has been designated the National Focal Point of Nature Conservation for Greece and Southeast Mediterranean.

A major problem for Greek forest ecosystems is that of forest fires. The lack of a Forest Cadastre encourages the process of illegal settling and building on the areas of forest, which have been burnt. A huge effort has been launched quite recently with the Cadastral survey of the country. According to the Greek Constitution, the reforestation of the burnt forests and forest areas is obligatory while any change in forestland use is prohibited. The completion of the Forest Cadastre is expected to protect forestland from illegal land grabbing. The forests of Greece are mainly natural, with a high bio-diversity, which is considered the richest in Europe, including thousands of species of fauna and flora. The most important functions of forests are the protection of soil from erosion and the enrichment of groundwater resources.

During the last decades, the forest ecosystems have been degraded due to large development plans, urban development and the lack of a binding physical planning framework. Furthermore, forest fires have increased during the last decade. Greek forests present a low production capacity but a high ecological value. As an economic activity, forestry is not sustainable in its present form. In addition, the management quality and the protection of forests are diminishing. The over-exploitation of woodcutting is the most characteristic example.

The targets of the National Strategy for the protection of forests are based on sustainable management and the protection of forests. These will balance the need for the multiple and combined production of goods and utilities with the requirements for the protection of wildlife and the protective-environmental function of forest ecosystems.

The basic sectors of action of the NSSD for Forests are:

• The integration of forest legislation;

• The development of a new national strategy for forests;

• The development of a national map for land use;

• The settlement of land-ownership problems in Greece;

• The development of a forest certification scheme.

Desertification in Greece is a gradually emerging danger. This is a result of the country's geological, topographical and climatic characteristics, which cause soil erosion, often leading to the final and almost total loss of productivity, as well as the drastic reduction of water resources.

Greece recently ratified the *United Nations Convention to Combat Desertification* and in close co-operation with the other European Mediterranean Countries is proceeding towards the formulation of the national and regional programmes to confront the danger. For this purpose, a National Committee was set up and various scientific and technical meetings have been organised. The targets of the National Strategy for the abatement of desertification are presented in the National Action Plan. They are concerned with the effective reversal of the desertification trend in the 35% of the Greek territory directly affected by desertification, and the prevention of the desertification process in 60% of the Greek territory.

The basic sectors of action of the NSSD for desertification are:

• Forest protection;

• Protection of water resources;

• Protection of agricultural land and grassland from intensive use;

• Reinforcement of research, exchange of information and training and organisation of monitoring mechanisms using appropriate indicators.

The Ministry of Agriculture has already started implementing the National Action Plan with the construction of small reservoirs for rainwater in threatened areas and by controlling and reducing irrational use of irrigation waters. The Ministry for the Environment, Physical Planning and Public Works and the Ministry of Development have also taken measures in the same direction. The total estimated funds for the abatement of desertification are approximately 450,000,000 Euros.

In October 1996, an International Congress on "Desertification in the Mediterranean Area - Research Results and Policies" was held in Crete, organised by the European Union and the Hellenic National Institution for Agricultural Research, in order to facilitate exchange of information and experience and to enhance international co-operation.

In May 1997, a "Pre-Congress" was organised in Athens on Forest Protection in preparation for the Earth Summit + 5. At this meeting Greece committed itself to the sustainable management of 10% of its forests, thus becoming the 18th country internationally, to support the 10% target for forests.

In co-operation with the OECD, Greece organised an International Workshop on "Sustainable Use of Water for Agricultural Purposes", which was held in Athens in November 1997.

Coastal zones -
Marine environment

Greece gives high priority to the protection of the marine environment and the sustainable development of coastal areas and islands. The country's coast-line of 15,021 km is the most extensive among all Mediterranean countries. This coastline is evenly distributed between the continental part of the country and the Greek islands, which number approximately 3,000. The coastal area contains diverse and productive ecosystems that house many rare species in need of protection (e.g. sea turtle Caretta - Caretta, monk seal Monachus - Monachus, etc.).

The high coastal concentration of population and economic activities generates pressure on coastal areas. Non-built up and natural conservation areas have decreased and the coastal landscape has been altered in the recent years. At the same time, pollution problems have emerged in enclosed seas and bays. All these call for the adoption of a special management policy that will ensure both the protection of marine and coastal eco-systems, and the future development of human activities in a sustainable manner.

An International Workshop of experts on Sustainable Development Policies for Mediterranean Coastal Areas was organised on the island of Santorini in April 1996. Following that workshop, the Greek Ministry for the Environment, Physical Planning and Public Works formed a Committee to address the problems of Greek coasts and islands in an integrated way, and launched the National Programme for the Sustainable Development of Greek Coastal Areas and Islands. This Programme is expected to determine the main policy targets and principles for coastal management, to establish principles delimiting coastal zones and to prepare the legal framework regarding the management of coastal areas.

Furthermore, actions are being taken within the framework of the *Greek Operational Environmental Programme for the Protection of Marine Environment*, aimed at the development of the necessary infrastructure for oil spill treatment and reception facilities for oil and chemical residues from ships. Cleaning and restoration projects have been carried out as well. These have covered the islands of Kos, Evia, Kefalonia, Corfu, N. Sporades, Cyclades, Samos, Chios, Lesvos and the Provinces of Rethymnon and Chania in Crete, as well as certain coastal areas in continental Greece, including Piraeus, Achaia, Ilia, Aitoloakarnania and Preveza.

The Greek Ministry of the Environment has established an integrated network for monitoring the quality of seawater.

● The *quality of swimming water* has been monitored in major swimming areas during the tourist period for six years. The results presented annually in a special report, show that over 97% of the areas examined meet the requirements of EEC Directive 76/160. Consequently, a great number of swimming beaches has been awarded the EU Blue Flag.

● The quality of seawater in general is monitored under the MED-POL pro-

gramme. This involves monitoring stations covering enclosed bays as well as the open sea. The results are presented annually in a special report, and show that in the open sea no pollution problem has been observed. In the bays, certain parameters show increased values.

● Greece pays special importance to, and is involved in the *Mediterranean Action Plan* (MAP), which operates in the framework of Barcelona Convention. The Co-ordinating Unit of MAP has been hosted in Athens since 1982. The UNEP programme MAP concerns the protection of the Mediterranean basin from pollution originating in land based activities. Furthermore, a Protocol is being prepared for the prevention of pollution in the Mediterranean from trans-boundary transportation and the disposal of hazardous waste. An action plan is also being promoted for the priority toxic substances.

The *Attica Coastline Protection and Management Programme* currently under study by the Organisation for Planning and Environmental Protection of

Athens, aims at the protection and rehabilitation of coastal ecosystems in Attica, and the establishment of a Coastline Management Organisation. A Programme for the Sustainable Development of Greek Coastal Zones and Islands providing for the guiding principles as well as the general and sectoral directions and approaches to zoning and integrate management is already under implementation. Within this context, a special Directive for the Sustainable Development of Coastal areas has also been developed. In this respect, the NSSD aims at the balanced integration of tourism activity in the natural environment according to its capacity. More specifically, the NSSD provides for effective management of mass tourism and reduction of pressures on local natural resources. In addition it provides for the diversification of tourism services and the promotion of alternative forms of tourism (e.g. eco-tourism, agro-tourism, conference tourism) as well as development of adequate infrastructure integrated into the natural and human environment, through participatory processes. To this end, the implementation of a series of specific projects and interventions is already underway, within the framework of the Operational Programme "Competitiveness" of the 3rd Community Support Framework.

Waste Management

One of the major environmental problems of Greece was, until recently, the lack of management (collection, treatment, disposal) of solid and toxic wastes. Therefore in many uncontrolled waste disposal areas, there are odours, pollution of surface and underground waters, air and soil pollution, fire danger and aesthetic pollution.

Over the last few years, Greece has been promoting the actions needed for a solution to the problem as a result of the country's national needs and responsibilities to the EU.

At the national level, technical specifications for the safe handing of waste are being determined. A system of permits was introduced for the collection and transport of solid waste. Legislation has been issued aimed at reducing air pollution from waste incineration plants. Threshold limits have been established for heavy metals in sewage sludge used in agriculture. In accordance with EU Directive 91/156 the establishment of an integrated network of waste disposal is being planned. Activities were initiated to promote waste prevention and recycling. Recycling programmes are being implemented for paper, glass and aluminium. Programmes are being introduced for the reduction of the weight and volume of packaging material. Awareness campaigns are being carried out. Responsibilities for waste management have been delegated to local authorities.

The management of liquid wastes is focused on the treatment of liquid wastes at the national scale with the construction of waste treatment facilities in settlements larger than 15,000 inhabitants. The problem of industrial pollution in Greece is not as significant as it is in the countries of northern Europe, because Greece has a little heavy industry.

Even so, there is problem of industrial pollution in some areas particularly in the large urban centres, i.e. the areas in which industry is concentrated in Greece. Industry today in Greece is characterised by improvement efforts at environmental protection.

Specific actions are:

- Development of a national management scheme for urban and industrial liquid wastes;

- Development of Support Centres for the Operation of Waste Treatment Facilities;

- Construction of waste treatment facilities (3rd phase) in sensitive regions;

- Implementation of innovative and adjusted technologies for the treatment of urban liquid wastes in selected areas, reuse of treated wastes;

- Construction of facilities for the treatment of industrial wastes;

- Programme for the integration of clean technologies in industrial practices;

- Programme for the recycling of industrial waste.

Greece is promoting the actions needed for the implementation of the new directive for landfills, and gives considerable weight to the cleaning up

The Psytalia wastewater biological treatment plant

of coastal areas and swimming sites. Specific actions are:

- Development of an integrated national programme for waste management;

- Rehabilitation of abandoned landfill sites;

- Construction of new landfills;

- Extended recycling programme;

- Construction of composting unit;

- Implementation of innovative techniques for the collection, treatment and disposal of waste;

- Coastal zone cleaning, with emphasis to tourist sites;

- Construction of waste transfer stations;

- Construction of sites for the disposal/treatment of agricultural waste, hazardous wastes and hospital wastes.

There is also a programme for the holistic, environmentally sound management of solid industrial and special (not municipal) waste produced in the wider Thessaloniki region.

The action programme "*Management of environmental hazards*" aims at protecting the human, man made and natural environments from industrial accidents. Upon its completion, the requirements of Directive SEVESO will be fully met. It should be mentioned that aim of the programme is to also increase the awareness of the residents in the nearby areas regarding the operational plans for the management of the environmental hazards once these occur.

The Basel Convention on the Control of Trans-boundary Movements of Hazardous Wastes and their Disposal was signed in 1989 ratified in 1994. National legislation provides for the planning of the management of toxic and dangerous waste, procedures for the transport of dangerous waste, special permits for the disposal and storage of dangerous wastes and measures for building facilities for toxic residues at ports. The *EU Eco-Label Award Scheme* has been implemented at the national level with a view to minimising certain waste products.

Activities producing dangerous waste and facilities for disposal of dangerous wastes require an environmental impact study and special permits. Controls are in place. Planning on the management of hospital waste has been completed. Regulations on the collection and disposal of batteries and accumulators are being established. Two facilities are under construction for the controlled storage of solid toxic waste and mud. EU legislation has been adopted concerning the supervision and monitoring of the trans-boundary movement of hazardous waste.

Joint Ministerial Resolution 72751/ 3054/85 on toxic and dangerous waste, issued in compliance with EU directive 78/319, provides measures for the prevention of said waste, recycling and reuse. Further Directives in this area being incorporated into national legislation.

The EU, with its 6th Environment Action Programme, sets as target the reduction of the total quantity of wastes directed for disposal by 20% and 50% until 2010 and 2050 respectively, compared to the levels of 2000. Furthermore, with the Directive 1994/62/EC, the EU gives priority to the production and management of packaging materials, aiming at maximising recycling. In Directive 1999/31/EC, strict specifications for the large landfill sites are set.

Within this framework, Greece has promoted measures for the expansion and organisation of related infrastructure, while passing on the responsibility for planning and management of wastes to the Regions. Finally, the National Plan for the Integrated and Alternative Management of Solid Waste has been completed and its implementation is under way.

The targets of the National Strategy for the management of solid wastes, as presented in the National Plan of Integrated Management, aim at safe disposal and maximisation of recycling. In parallel, long-term actions are mainly promoted for the reduction of the total quantity of produced solid wastes.

The basic sectors of action of the NSSD for Solid Wastes are:
- Safe disposal and recycling
- Exploitation of domestic wastes
- Management of industrial and hazardous solid wastes
- Reduction of the solid wastes quantity
- Institutional measures

The above directions will be accompanied by other actions, such as training the staff of the local authorities and raising the awareness of those responsible for decision making and the citizens in general.

Atmospheric Environment

Atmospheric pollution has been a problem for the last 25 years in Greece and is related to the urbanisation and the economic development of the country. The region of Attiki faces the most significant problems due to climatic features, heavy traffic and unfavourable topography for the dispersion of atmospheric pollution.

Measures for the solution of the problem have been applied since 1978. These measures were targeted to the reduction of SO_2 and Pb high emission rates.

The measures that have been taken for the reduction of SO_2 included the prohibition of crude oil utilisation to central heating and the continuous reduction of the S content in crude oil and diesel oil. The above measures had excellent results and therefore the problem of SO_2 is today under control.

As far as Pb is concerned, air pollution has been reduced due to the use of unleaded gasoline.

Parallel to the above measures, another action of the country is the continuous provision of the required infrastructure for better diagnosis of the problems and consequently for better interventions.

The Environmental Services have been also taken a series of measures which concern the industry, central heating, the improvement of fuel quality, the replacement of old cars, the improvement of traffic conditions (e.g. construction of metro), etc.

The noise zones in Greece are the urban areas and mainly Athens where 40% of Greek population, 35% of industrial and handicraft activities and 70% of Services have concentrated. Other noise zones are the main arterial roads, industries, ports, airports, tourist and construction activities.

The general aim of the Action Programme for Atmospheric environment and noise is the development of the infrastructure for the continuous monitoring of the atmospheric environment (including air emissions) of Greece, with emphasis on large urban centres and areas with significant energy production units. Specific actions are:

- National monitoring network of the atmospheric environment;

- An inspectorate for air pollution;

- An operational Centre for the monitoring of atmospheric pollution and the implementation of rectification measures in the wider Athens area;

- Development of a station for the monitoring of the meteorological parameters in the troposphere region of Athens;

- Development of a mobile station for the tele-detection of air pollutants with the use of lidars;

- On line connection of the Operational Centre and the National Network to the National Meteorological Centre;

- Development of an inventory system for VOC and other non-conventional pollutants (area of application - Athens);

- Development of an inventory for industrial emissions (area of application - country) and the assessment of the impact of greenhouse gases on Greek climatic conditions and the development of a network for the assessment of climatic variations;

- Installation of Global Atmosphere Watch (GAW) stations and stations for the monitoring of sea level;

- Programme for the compliance of Greece to the requirements of the Montreal Protocol (and subsequent amendments);

- Improvement of the calibration system of the automatic air pollution instruments;

- System for the monitoring of air pollution in museums;

- Monitoring network for urban noise;

- Assessment and mapping of noise pollution from traffic;

- Definition of noise zones for the wider Athens and Thessaloniki industrial areas.

Atmospheric pollution is a dynamic problem that evolves and changes over time. Further long-term efforts are necessary in order for it to be controlled.

The Noise abatement programme in major Greek cities attempts to reduce noise in major Greek cities through such actions as periodic inspections of motor vehicles/motorcycles and major industrial installations with respect to their noise levels. Other measures include the construction of noise protective barriers along major highways, the promotion of noise insulation materials in buildings, and the promotion of so-called "quiet products", that is products which are quieter and thus more favourable to the consumers.

The NSSD emphasises the reduction of air pollutants, since their increased concentrations are responsible for the phenomena of acid rain and eutrophication that threaten the equilibrium of ecosystems. Air pollutants have also proven to be related to problems of human health. In order to ensure a continuous reduction of air pollutants and to achieve the targets that have been set by the EU, much more progress must be made. More specifically, in 2001, the EU has adopted a multi - pollutant, multi - effective strategy for the effective lowering of atmospheric pollution. The pollutant concentration levels for Greece are lower than the respective levels for the whole of the EU, which reflects the level of development and the structure of the energy system of Greece. However, compliance with these measures requires the implementation of an Action Programme with specific measures per sector. Special attention will be paid to the releases on NMVOCs that show the greatest divergence from the target set for 2010.

The target of the National Strategy for the lowering of air pollution coincides with the targets resulting from the implementation of directive NECD for the period ending in 2010. In the long term, the Strategy will be readjusted within the framework of a common strategy and the decisions of the EU competent authorities.

The basic sectors of action of the NSSD for Air Pollution are:

• Reform and diversification of energy offer;

• Rational use and conservation of energy in the building sector;

• Measures for the transport sector;

• Measures for industry;

• Institutional and organisational measures.

The above measures will radically change the existing trends, achieving a substantial de-coupling of improved energy quality and other relative services from the increase of the negative effects on air quality.

According to its commitments, the Greek government has elaborated National Action Programme for Climate Change, in its desire to contribute to the world's effort to protect the natural environment. This Action Programme is to ensure the achievement of drastic reductions in the emissions of CO_2 and of the other greenhouse gases.

The first *Hellenic Programme for the Lowering of CO_2 and other Greenhouse Gas Emissions* was submitted to the UN-FCCC Secretariat in March 1995.

The programme aimed to achieve the lowering of CO_2 and other greenhouse gas emissions by:

a) the rationalisation of energy consumption, that is the achievement of energy conservation without any reduction in standards of living and

b) a diversification in the means used for satisfying energy demand, that is the substitution of conventional fuels, without causing any major disruption to the energy system's basic features.

The implementation of the measures is supported either by administrative policies focusing on the necessary regulations, or by economic policies aimed at modifying the behaviour of those involved. The interventions contained in the program are:

- supply-side interventions (modernisation of the existing power generation system, development of TIP generation system, the introduction of Natural Gas in the national energy and renewable energy sources exploitation)

- demand-side interventions (energy conservation in the domestic, commercial and public sectors, technological interventions in the industrial sector and for the transport sector interventions in the fuel types used, improvement of vehicles in circulation and rational management and modernisation of the entire transport system).

The programme aimed to stabilise - as a whole - its CO_2 emissions by the year 2000 at 1990 levels, as the Greek contribution to the EU obligation.

In May 1996, an inter-ministerial committee was set up under the co-ordination of the Ministry for the Environment, Physical Planning and Public Works, in order to provide the national co-ordination for the fulfilment of the Convention's obligations, the review of the 1st and the preparation of future Communications.

Estimates from the results from the National Greenhouse Gas Inventory and a preliminary review of the National Programme indicate that the emissions follow the realistic predictions of the National programme.

Greece participates regularly in meetings of the Ad Hoc Group on the Berlin Mandate and the other Subsidiary Bodies of the Convention.

In order to fulfil the obligations under the Convention, Educational Programmes have been organised on issues of Climate Change. Financial contributions have been made to the Trust Fund of the Convention for the participation of the developing countries, to the GEF and to Regional Development Banks. Technical assistance is also provided to developing countries.

Greece considers climate change one of the major environmental hazards, since the pressures of desertification, water scarcity and temperature rise are already clear in Greece. Furthermore, the restriction of climate change is one of the priority targets of the European Strategy for Sustainable Development. Greece ratified the Kyoto Protocol in May 2002.

The target of the National Strategy for the abatement of climate change coincides with the targets of the implementation of the Kyoto Protocol, with a time period of reference the years 2008 - 2012. Within the framework of the common policy of the EU, Greece is committed not to increase its releases of the 6 greenhouse gases more than 25% (mean of years 2008 - 2012) relative to its 1990 emissions.

Based on the above, the Council of Ministers has discussed and approved the main points of the new National Programme for the Reduction of Greenhouse Gas Emissions. This Programme is based on the analysis of the contribution of different sectors to total greenhouse gas emissions, taking into account the specific features and the perspectives of the country.

The basic sectors of action of the NSSD for Climate Change are:

• Reform and diversification of energy offer;

• Rational use and conservation of energy;

• Measures for the reduction of other greenhouse gases;

• Institutional measures.

Within this framework, it is considered important to prioritise the selected measures based on economic efficiency, as defined by the relation between cost and reduction potential, taking into account all other constraints.

It should be noted that many of the measures of the NSSD have already been integrated into the respective sectoral policies (e.g. energy sector, transport) and are being promoted through the implementation of the Operational Programmes of the 3rd Community Support Framework. Greenhouse gas policy simultaneously benefits the economy, society and the environment, while assisting the lowering of typical atmospheric pollution.

Water Resources

The uneven distribution of activities in the country has resulted in water demands that often cannot be covered by local water resources. Therefore rational water resource management at a national level is a high priority in Greece.

The management of the quality and the quantity of the waters in lakes and rivers Deltas, where there are important biotopes, is of high significance.

Water resource management in Greece has progressed significantly over the last few years, mainly after the creation of a new legal framework (L.1650/86-L.1739/87). However, the spreading of management responsibilities over a large number of Ministries and Public Services raises serious difficulties.

The development of a management plan is closely linked with the efforts of Greece to comply with the Water Framework Directive 2000/60/EC. The Hellenic Ministry for the Environment, Physical Planning and Public Works has already proceeded to the necessary actions for the implementation of the Directive and the related institutional framework is in the final stage of preparation.

The targets of the National Strategy for the management of water resources are set out in the National Action Plan for Water Resources. They concern the sustainable use of existing water reserves, the efficient protection of water ecosystems and the attainment of high quality standards for all surface and ground water bodies by the year 2015.

The basic sectors of action of the NSSD for the Water Resources are:

The Prespa wetland

• Integrated approach for water management;

• Decentralisation of water management authorities - bodies;

• Upgrading and expansion of infrastructure;

• Socio-economical consideration of water resources management;

• Protection from hazardous substances

The important rivers of Greece (Axios, Strymon, Nestos, Evros) have their springs in other countries while two of the main lakes (Doirani and Prespes) are international. For the above reasons, co-operation with the neighbouring countries in the management of fresh waters is very important for Greece.

Urban, industrial and agricultural liquid wastes are responsible for the pollution of fresh waters in Greece. The extent of pollution in the different regions of Greece depends on the local conditions and on the availability of wastewater treatment facilities.

The general aim of the Action Programme is to monitor the quality of inland waters through the development of a National network for surface, underground and coastal waters. The Programme is complemented by special actions for the monitoring of the pollution loads to the water environment. The specific actions are:

• Development of the National Monitoring Network (NMN) for the quality of waters consists of the monitoring networks for surface waters, underground waters, waters in trans-boundary rivers, drinking water, bathing waters, as well as of a central laboratory for the calibration and co-ordination of regional laboratories involved in the monitoring networks;

• National monitoring system for urban and industrial wastes

• Assessment of sensitive regions with respect to the treatment of liquid wastes

Land & Urban Planning / Aesthetic Pollution

Inadequate land and urban planning from 1950-80 resulted in the gradual degradation of the natural and urban environment in many areas of the country.

The *National Action Plan for Cities and Housing* (1996-2000), which

Greece has developed as part of its participation in the HABITAT II International Conference of the United Nations on Human Settlements (Instanbul 1996) has two main objectives. These are: *the creation of cities that provide safe, healthy, equal and sustainable living conditions and the guarantee of adequate housing for all.*

National actions taken with regard to human settlement development are:

1. *Urban Planning programme* for the definition of urban plans for cities which lack relevant plans, as well as for the improvement of existing urban plans in light of modifications in the urban structure and the operations in the city. Considerable emphasis is given to the development of urban plans for estates located in ecologically sensitive areas, coastal zones and islands.

2. Projects for the *protection of historical and traditional sites aimed* at the improvement of urban conditions in selected Greek cities, traditional settlements and tourist sites, in order to improve the quality of life and living and working conditions. Under this framework a special programme for the *"Urban restoration in cities and settlements"*, excluding Athens, Attica and Thessaloniki, is being implemented.

Special programmes are financed that include interventions at local and regional levels in such thematic areas as: air, water, waste, traffic, noise, land planning, urban development, environmental awareness and legislation.

Regarding urban development, the key objectives of the NSSD are: adoption of a "solid city" approach adapted to Greek particularities, reduction of urban sprawl with peri-urban settlements of low density and low integration potential and promotion of a new urban development model. Regarding the non-urban and rural areas, the key objectives are: regulation and containment of illegal and uncontrolled urban sprawl outside the existing town Master Plans as well as planning and clear definition of land use zoning. To this end, the establishment of organised sites for receiving and supporting trade, manufacturing and husbandry activities as well as reduction of diffused tourism activity will play a decisive role.

The new Operational Programme of Greece (2000 - 2006) - Programme 7.1 includes interventions in regional and town planning. It aims at the organisation of urban and regional areas based on new technologies, the development of plans at the national and regional level, the implementation of pilot and specific local interventions, the development of metropolitan areas plans (Attica and Thessaloniki).

Environmental Education

The Ministry of Education has as a target the reorientation of education towards sustainable development. In this context, eighteen Environmental Education Centres (EEC) have been established where students participate in special Environmental Education programmes. The EEC also organises special Environmental Education training programmes for employees, community organisations, teachers, etc.

Systematic co-operation has been established on special pedagogical Environmental Education pilot projects, with major environmental groups such as WWF, the Goulandri Museum of Natural History, Greenpeace, etc.

Two Greek Ministries and the USA have signed an intergovernmental Co-operation Agreement for the global network GLOBE concerned with the creation of environmental stations in schools.

In its effort to co-operate in such activities, Greece has organised in co-operation with UNESCO, an International Conference on "Environment and Society: Education and Public Awareness in view of Sustainable Development". The Conference took place in December 1997, in Thessaloniki.

The necessity for brevity does not allow a more extensive reference to be made to numerous other individual programmes, actions and decrees relevant to the protection, management and rehabilitation of the environment in Greece. Nevertheless, what is clear from the above is that Greece has adopted an environmentally friendly policy which it attempts to apply to all sectors through national legislation, the adoption of European environmental laws, and participation in international agreements concerning the protection of the environment.

A broad training programme for 10,000 teachers of primary and secondary schools in collaboration with Universities, EE Centres and Regional TT Centres has also been developed. There was also a pilot programme targeted to incorporate environmental issues into the curriculum of the Gymnasium (High School).

INFORMATION &TECHNOLOGY

SCIENTIFIC AND TECHNOLOGICAL RESEARCH

By Ioanna Kaftanzoglou

The scientific potential of Greece is remarkable and acknowledged worldwide. Considerable progress in developing the national scientific and technological research system has been made during the last decades. The R&D system has been expanded, successful participation in E.U. and international R&D programmes as well as the formulation of research excellence which meets international standards have been achieved.

Research and technology institutions

Research is mainly carried out by the research centres and the public universities. The latter play a most important role, not only in conducting basic research but also in "producing" scientists and researchers. The leading ones are: the Aristotelian University (Thessaloniki), the National and Capodistrian University as well as the National Technical University (Athens) and the Universities of Patras, Crete, Thrace and Ioannina. Research centres have developed either in cities with university infrastructure, or in collaboration with foreign institutes. The system was thus mainly oriented to basic research until recently, when several new research centres and programmes were created, in more direct relation to concrete needs. There is now a large number of research centres and institutes, of which

The National Hellenic Research Foundation Periodicals Library in Athens

the most outstanding ones are: the National Research Centre for Physical Sciences "Demokritos", the Foundation for Research and Technology and the National Hellenic Research Foundation. Several Technological Bodies and R&D Companies have been created (in textile technology, ceramics and refractories, aquaculture etc) which offer research and technological services and address specific production problems of small to medium size enterprises that form the largest proportion of the Greek productive sector. Four public technology parks have also been set up with the aim of providing high grade facilities, services and know-how to pioneering industrial units, so that these are in position to commercially exploit the results of scientific research; the parks are located in close proximity to research establishments in Attica, Thessaloniki, Heraklion and Patras. Another 4 private S & T incubators are operating in Athens and Thessaloniki since 2003.

The size of activities of the Greek R&D system is comparatively small: Gross Domestic Expenditure on R&D (GERD) as % of GDP, amounted to 0.46% in 1991 as compared to over 2% in more developed countries, but reached 0.68% in 1999, growing at a rate of 8.71% a year from 1995 to 1999, the highest growth rate in the E.U. . The average annual real growth of R&D investment, from 1995 to 1999 was 12%, one of the highest in the E.U.. Thus, Greece may be still below average in

The Bio-Medical Research Foundation of the Academy of Athens

terms of investment level but is catching up at a very rapid pace. The limited number of Scientific and Technological Research personnel can also be considered a draw-back, although there has been an evident increase: from 10,905 as FTE (Full Time Equivalents) in 1991, in a population of 10,000,000, i.e. 0.11%, to 26,382 as FTE in 1999, i.e. 0.26%. The ratio of personnel active in research (as FTE) was but 2.8 per thousand labour force in 1991, growing to 3.30 in 1999, an average annual growth of 11.03% from 1995 to 1999, the highest in the E.U. The Government budget allocated to R&D as a % of GDP has risen from 0.24% in 1992 to 0.35% in 2000, with a high annual growth rate of 7.3% from 1995 to 2000. The number of R&D institutions of the overall public sector (Research Centres, Sectoral Industrial Technology Development Companies, Technology Parks, etc) is still relatively small, but growing fast. Another noticeable fact is the steady increase of productive enterprises with research activities (217 in 1991, 317 in 1993 and 598 in 1997).

Research and technology policy

The first authority responsible for R&D administration was established in 1971, and became a Department for Scientific Research and Technology of the Ministry of Economic Coordination in 1977. It formed the nucleus of the Ministry for Research and Technology, created in 1982; later it became the General Secretariat for Research and Technology (GSRT) which merged into the Ministry of Industry in 1985 and now belongs to the Ministry of Development.

The GSRT is the central agency responsible for the planning, co-ordination and project-funding of research and technology. Through it's programmes, it supports the research activities of both the country's research institutions and those of it's productive industry, focusing on areas that are important for the national economy and for the improvement of the quality of life. It promotes the transfer and dissemination of advanced technologies throughout the country's productive sector, thus ensuring early utilisation of the results of research activity and contributes to the reenforcement of the country's research manpower. It represents Greece in relevant institutions of the EU, thus bringing the country's re-

Technology Science Center and Technology Museum: The exhibition area covers about 1.800 sq.m and is divided in various themes about science and technology

search and technology activities into line with the requirements of the international community and promotes cooperation with other countries and international orgaisations on research and technology issues. It establishes new institutes, technological centres and parks in support of sectors of high priority for the development of the Greek economy, supervises, underwrites the fixed costs of, and otherwise provides support for 20 of the country's best-known research and technological entities. It supports the dissemination of research and technology information throughout the country and internationally by means of advanced systems and networks and encourages activities aimed at raising awareness of the general public about research and technology issues.

In addition to the GSRT which is responsible for more than one third of Public Expenditure for Scientific and Technological Research, other ministries are also involved in funding of research, mainly those of Education, of Agriculture and of Health and Welfare Services. However, these ministries do not have specific responsibilities for the drafting and implementation of research policy, the only body to formulate a cohesive research and technology policy in Greece and to have the adequate structure and mechanisms to work out and implement operational progammes on research and technology, being the GSRT.

During the 80 'ties, two elements influenced the course of scientific and technological research: at the national level, research priorities were initiated by the GSRT and organised institutionally within a legal framework and at the level of the E.U., an overall policy for the development of research and technology was implemented, in addition to the adoption of structural policies directed to enhance -among other- each country's research and technology system (E.U. Support Framework and Structural Programmes). New opportunities were taken advantage of and not only did the funds allocated to research increase drastically but several important measures for the implementation of a research policy were adopted.

Since 1989, the national science and technology policy has been increasingly supported by an important flow of the E.U. structural funds for RTD (Structural funds plus Framework Programme). From then onwards, the Operational Programmes for Research and Technology (EPET I, II) and the Operational Programmes for Competitiveness (EPAN), under the respective Community Support Frameworks as well as the STRIDE HELLAS initiative have been the main instruments for the formulation and the implementation of science and technology policy in Greece.

The general principles of Greece's research policy are the development and optimisation of human potential, the training and mobility of researchers, the gearing of research and technological development to the country's specific needs, the maintaining of a proper balance between targeted and open-ended research. The means to implement this policy are international research programmes -especially the E.U.'s Framework programmes as well as national operational programmes co-financed by the EU and national programmes with local funding. Special measures are also taken to gear research to production and to co-ordinate research in universities, institutions and industries through networks.

The main policy guidelines are to enhance demand of the buisiness sector for new knowledge and research results; to increase cooperation between R&D organisations and production units; to encourage technology transfer from abroad; to support the innovative capacity of Greek firms, so as to integrate innovation; to introduce information and assessment mechanisms of the outcome of government funded scientific research; to assess and support the training needs of human capital, through training programmes in new technologies and techniques; to enhance the cultural assimilation of new communications, information and expression techniques resulting from technological innovation, thus supporting technological culture.

Nine priority axes have been set up: improving the business environment; supporting and encouraging business initiatives; promoting excellence in busi-ness activity; technological innovation and research; differentiation of the tourism product-provision of Greece as a tourist destination; securing the energy supply and promoting the liberalisation of the energy market; energy and sustainable development; human resources; technical aid.

The following thematic priorities have been identified: life sciences, genomics, biotechnology for health; information society technologies; nanotechnologies and nano-science, multi-functional materials, new production procedures; aeronautics and space; food quality and safety; sustainable development, global climatic change, ecosystems; citizens and governance in the Information Society.

The national R&D effort thus focuses in selected fields of high economic interest, such as environmental technology (environmental friendly methods of production, renewable sources of energy, energy saving), life sciences (health and agriculture, with emphasis on biotechnology applications), information technologies (applications in product manufacturing and supply of services), new or improved materials (new production and processing methods) as well as analysis of the social, economic, administrative and cultural features of development.

The promotion of the Information Society is also one of the main orientations of research and technology policy. Complementary actions are launched by

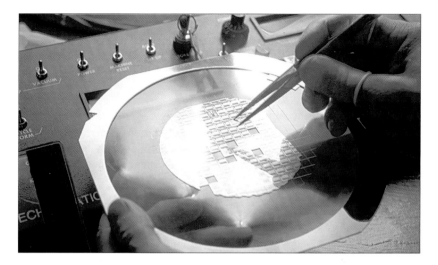

the GSRT to create the appropriate infrastructure and improve the efficient distribution and utilisation of knowledge in the Greek S&T system, namely the development of a Greek Research and Technology Network (GR-NET) and the implementation of the National Information System for Science and Technology. Networking and dissemination of S&T information are also enhanced in order to meet some negative aspects of of the S&T system, namely the small size of the national research community, the broad dispersion of research effort in multiple sectors and themes, the weak communication links between research laboratories and between the research and production systems.

Specific actions to meet the basic problems of the country's R&D system are directed to industrial research, technology transfer, innovation, intellectual property rights, benchmarking and foresight activities; the support and restructuring of the national research tissue; the upgrading and expansion of human capital.

In order to increase the links between science and industry, public programmes which support cooperative research between higher educational institutions, public research centres and enterprises, have been launched and intermediary organisations for the transfer of knowledge and information from producers to consumers (sectoral RTD companies, Science and Technology Parks) have been created.

Incentives and support for R&D include tax treatment and specific measures addressed directly to enterprises for them to establish and enhance their scientific, technological and innovative capacities and to promote public/private scientific research partnership. The target was to increase the contribution of the business sector in the formation of GERD to aproximately 30% by 1999: the share of Business enterprise expenditure on R&D (BERD) was indeed 28,5% in 1999, but is still low, reflecting a relatively weak business sector knowledge investment.

Specific measures to enhance human capital in R&D are also to be mentioned, mainly the "training through research" programmes of the GSRT.

It should be noted that the GSRT now takes part in the E.U.'s effort to mainstream it's policy regarding gender equality. The severe under-representation of women in science is a concern and calls for their mobilization (in 1999, female researchers in Greece were but 41% as a share of the total). Thus specific actions are undertaken in order to raise the awareness of the Greek scientific community concerning gender equal-

ity. A "National Report on Women and Science, 2002" has been drawn up and the guidelines of the GSRT's Operational Programme for Competitiveness include gender issues.

Special reference should be made of the Greek Technology Foresight Programme, which aims at looking into the future of Greek society by identifying the implications of emerging science and technology, the main challenge being the transition from a "knowledge economy" to a "knowledge society".

The divergence between certain figures reflecting Greece's scientific and technological development and the equivalent E.U. average (such as GERD as % of GDP: 0,68% as compared to 1,93% -2000 data or BERD as % of GERD: 28,5% as compared to 65,5% - 2001 data) illustrates the problems to be adressed and explains the formulation of the ensuing priorities. These can be listed as follows: increasing the demand

Clean room for the production of radiopharmaceutical kits in National Center for Scientific Research "Demokritos"

for new knowledge and research results, reorganizing the research system and provision of knowledge, "freeing-up" the research system and opening it further to the international field, developing the technological infrastructure in the context of a policy for S&T, defining thematic/sector priorities for a policy on S&T and quantifying goals.

International and bilateral collaboration

International scientific and technological cooperation is a must for all countries and especially for smaller ones, as it offers solutions to research and development problems which often exceed the possibilities of a single country, since they necessitate interdisciplinary efforts, require substantial technical and financial resources as well as numerous highly qualified and trained scientific personnel.

Greece has established an active collaboration with intergovernmental organisations which have a scientific or technological mission such as C.E.R.N. (European Nuclear Research Centre), E.M.B.L. (European Molecular Biology Laboratory), E.C.M.M.F. (European centre for Mid-range Meteorological Forecasting), NATO's political wing (Science for Partnership, etc), C.I.S.M. (International Centre for Engineering Studies), C.I.E.S.M. (International Scientific Committee for Mediterranean Exploration), W.I.P.O. (World Intellectual Property Organisation), E.P.O. (European Patent

Office), etc. Most recently, Greece has been participating in optional programmes of the European Space Agency (E.S.A.), with which negotiations for full membership are on the way. Greece also collaborates with international organisations which have a political mission and incorporate scientific and research activities, such as the organisations of the U.N. system (U.N.I.D.O., U.N.C.T.A.D., U.N.E.S.C.O., F.A.O., U.N.E.P., etc) and the O.E.C.D.. Multilateral cooperation with the Black Sea area has been launched within the framework of the Black Sea Cooperation initiative and Greece is also a participant of the Asia-Europe Meeting, of which a priority is the enhancement of cooperation in S&T. More recently, during her Presidency of the E.U., Greece elaborated an Action Plan of Cooperation between the E.U. and Balkan countries, which was approved by the Thessaloniki Summit in June 2003 and is now being implemented.

In addition to international cooperation through participation in the above-mentioned international organisations of which she is a member, Greece has set up a framework of bilateral cooperation in scientific and technological fields of mutual interest. The main objectives of bilateral cooperation are to transfer technological know-how (to and from Greece), to broaden basic scientific knowledge, to plan common research activities, to develop international R&D networks, to extend know-how to industry, to enhance industrial and commercial cooperation, open new markets and bring RTD added value to the Greek Research System.

Thus, the strengthening of relationships between scientists and research institutes in Greece and abroad and the promotion of partnerships in science and technology is well under way with several E. U. countries (France, Germany, Great Britain, Italy, Spain), with central and eastern european countries (Albania, Armenia, Bulgaria, the Czech Republic, Georgia, Hungary, Poland, Romania, Russia, Slovakia, Slovenia, Ukraine, the F.R. of Yugoslavia) and with other countries (China, Cyprus, Israel). The framework of cooperation through bilateral agreements has been extended so as to include countries such as Egypt, Ethiopia, F.Y.R.O.M., Morocco, South Africa and more recently, Cuba, Tunisia and Turkey. Finally, a new form of collaboration was set up in 2002- a pilot call for proposals, concerning cooperation of Greek R&T institutions with countries with stronger RTD systems (U.S.A., Canada, Japan, Australia, South Korea, etc). It is to be launched again in 2004.

The main fields of international and bilateral collaboration are informatics, micro-electronics, information technologies, new and composite materials, environment, geosciences, biology, biotechnology and agricultural sciences, health sciences, socio-economic and humanistic sciences, cultural heritage

The submarine neutrino telescope NESTOR

(especially with Balkan and Eastern European countries) food technology, astronomy and space research, industrial technologies, marine sciences.

Scientific research and technology development: a tentative assessment

Greece's average share of the E.U.'s research programmes budget (4th and 5th Framework Programmes) is 3.6 % whereas her population is only 2.8% of the E. U.'s. The total number of researchers employed (FTE) in Greece was 14,828 in 1999, i.e. 1.6% of the E.U.'s and GERD only 0.7% of the E.U's. These figures are eloquent and demonstrate the dynamic participation of Greek scientific teams and their high competitiveness. The areas in which Greek researchers are most successful are information and communication technologies, energy, industrial technology and materials, life sciences and biotechnology. In addition to domestically based research teams, the important number of researchers of the Greek Diaspora within and beyond the E.U. - approximately 8,000 - constitute a serious asset, as they contribute to the scientific effort undertaken domestically.

However, much still has to be done in order to reach a satisfying level of endogenous and sustainable development of the research system, as well as to implicate it in the economic and social development of the country and to enhance the role of the productive sector in relation to research. Obviously, a sustainable dynamic in research and technological development cannot easily be achieved by a small country alone. And in an era of integration and globalisation, the issues are further complicated.

The limited participation of the production sector (private and State enterprises) in research activities, which amounts only to 25% of total research activity, is a problem. The increase of R&D activities of the productive sector will push forward other sectors, boost the demand for R&D services, help to link production to research and gear the R&D system to the needs of the economy and strengthen the process of technology transfer to enterprises. There is a relative stagnation in the increase of the number of state-run research institutions, and this could have a negative impact on the dissemination of results and the support of enterprises in areas of

R&D. The concentration of the R&D tissue in the greater Athens metropolitan area, where more than 60% of the public R&D infrastructure are situated is also a problem, even though the distribution of Universities and Technical Educational Institutions is more evenly spread with 50% of them in the Athens area. All this leads to the relative isolation of other regions from R&D activities and a low interest of regional enterprises for R&D.

The E.U.'s Framework and specific RTD Programmes are an important channel of technology transfer. The involvement of Greek research teams has grown substantially over the years, with university and research centres accounting for most of it, but industrial participation remains below expectations.

Even though public funding of R&D in Greece remains low compared to the rest of the countries of the E.U., considerable progress has been made during the last two decades. Funds have increased significantly, the modernisation of the infrastructure has been achieved and R&D activities fostered. However, the need for a drastic increase in the public and private sector funding level remains urgent. The objectives are to increase GERD as % of GDP to 1.5% and the participation of enterprises to 40% of GERD in 2010, following the recommendations of the Lisbon and Barcelona Summits (3% and 67% respectively). A significant increase in funding is still necessary to ensure that

Bathyscaph "THETIS"

the efforts made are upheld and reap the most positive results: full long-term utilisation of the experience, the know-how and the infrastructure that has been developed as a result of the national boosting of R&D and the successful participation of Greek scientific teams in international and E.U. programmes will thus be achieved. The private sector still contributes poorly to research and technological development, while enterprises still question the abilities of local research teams in the Universities and the Research centres for full technological support, although relations between the productive sector and research are changing and attitudes concerning science and technology being transformed.

Ex -post policy evaluation of publicly funded R&D is of great importance in order to determine the quality and effec-

tiveness of specific research and operational programmes as well as the performance of the national research structure. The results of the evaluations undertaken such as the GSRT's "Evaluation of research institutes -2000", although of academic orientation, could be useful as a feedback for policy formulation as well as for a more efficient allocation of funds.

Notwithstanding the leading role of the GSRT as the basic policy-maker in the field, the fragmentation of research activities and the dispersion of relevant agencies are still a concern and are being addressed. Collaboration between Research Centres, Institutes and Universities as well as between the jointly responsible Ministries of Development, of Education, of Agriculture, of National Defence etc, is enhanced in order to ensure the best possible exploitation of existing human resources and infrastructure. Further mobilisation of the research establishments and enterprises towards participation in various international and E.U. programmes is sought in order that the Greek economy eventually reaps the benefits of increased competitiveness brought by technological development.

A most encouraging fact is that, although they are still below E.U. average, both of the composite indicators of investment and performance in the knowledge-based economy show a high rate of growth from 1995 to 1999. This seems to be the positive consequence of the strong efforts made during the 1990s.

Through the concerted actions of the government, the research community and the private sector, the impact of the E.U.'s scientific research and technologi- cal development policy as well as international and bilateral cooperation, substantial progress has been achieved in solving the problems of the national scientific and technological research system.

R/V "Aegeo"

TELECOMMUNICATIONS *

By V. G. Cassapoglou

The new Hellenic telecom era was inaugurated in the Summer of 1992 by the promulgation of the first Telecom Act (Law • 2075 of 31st July 1992) introducing the gradual opening of the telecom market to free competition. This fundamental institutional and legis-lative reform was not only the Greece's first step towards the implementation of the relevant legislation and policies of the European Union, but also the result of a substantial techno-logical and organisational development programme regarding the restructuring of the Hel-lenic telecom sector. This Programme was launched and has been abundantly financed by the European Commission since January 1991. It was successfully implemented by the Greek Government in almost six years.

Today, after the publication of the fourth consecutive Telecom Act (Law • 2867 of 19th December 2000) and the issuing of the related secondary legislation by which many of the pertinent EU Directives were transposed into the domestic legal order, the Telecom envi-ronment in Greece can be described as follows:

Legal regime

The legal (institutional and regulato-ry) regime governing the Hellenic Telecom sector by mid-1992 was based upon the strict separation between the functions of Regulator and Operator. The Regulator's competencies are firmly shared between the *Ministry of Transport & Communications* (MTC) and the *National Telecommunications & Posts Commission* (NTPC).

The MTC is exclusively responsible for national Telecom policy-making, legislative initiatives, assignment of radio frequencies, management of the earth satellite orbits, and the issuing of the National Regulation for the Assignment of Radio Frequencies Bands.

The NTPC, which is the National Regulatory Authority under European law, is an independent State entity with administrative and financial autonomy. It is composed of nine members appointed for five years by the Minister of Transport & Communications upon prior consent of the Parliament, and it enjoys individual and functional independence from the Government.

The main responsibilities of the NTPC include the adoption of all regulations gov-erning Telecom activities. These include tariffs, pricing and competition, the issuing of the National Num-

---

* When not otherwise mentioned, all quoted data are as of the 31-12-2002

bering Plan and the National Radio Regulation, the management of the radio spectrum including the allotment and the assignment of the radio frequencies (single and bands) to individual users. Other NTPC responsibilities include the regulation of the provi-sion of Internet services, data protection, the awarding of general and special operating licences, the monitoring and the sanctioning of all Telecom enterprises regarding their com-pliance with the legislation and the terms of their licenses. NTPC is also responsible for the determination of operators with significant power in the public (fixed and mobile) Telecom market. Finally, the NTPC is empowered to act as a permanent arbitrator in the

settlement of disputes either amongst the Telecom enterprises or between the latter and the State or the users, and also to maintain a database containing information on the Hellenic Telecom market.

Actually, in Greece, all categories of Telecom activities (equipment, infrastructure, and services) are fully liberalised. These activities may be freely undertaken by any Telecom entity operating either under a general or special license granted by the NTPC or after a relevant declaration submitted to the NTPC. As a result, an important number of new business and professions (e.g. operators, providers, dealers, distributors and retailers of telecom services) have enriched the market, and, thanks to that

The Hellenic Telecommunications Organisation headquarters in Athens

opening up, over 15,000 new jobs have been created from 1992 until today.

Traditional Services (Switched Public Network and Voice Telephony)

Among the Telecom enterprises operating today in the fully opened Telecom market, the dominant position is still occupied by the **Hellenic Telecommunications Organisation** (OTE). It is the national operator, which was incorporated in 1949 as a private law company (*societe anonyme*). It was wholly owned by the State until March 1996, when the company's issued shares were listed on the main market of the Athens Stock Exchange and 7.6% were sold to private investors. It was the first and largest privatisation operation ever undertaken in Greece.

Currently OTE's fully paid share capital totals 1.2 billion euros. Approximately 33% is owned by the State, the shareholding rights of which are overseen by the Minister of Na-tional Economy and Finance. The remaining stake of close to 67% is owned by a very large number of private, institutional and retail Greek investors as well as by international institutional investors and its shares are publicly traded on the Athens, New York, London and other foreign Stock Exchanges. In 2002, the total assets of OTE were 4.3 billion euros, whilst its investments during the same period were in the order of 1.08 billion euros.

OTE holds a Special License, awarded to it in December 1995, for a 25-year renew-able term. Under the terms of this license, OTE is obligated to provide, in line with the Open Network Provision (ONP) Directive provisions and other EU rules, access to, and use of the public network and services. It must also provide leased lines both to end-users and other Telecommunications Organisations (TOs,) as well as emergency call service and special fa-cilities to disabled persons. At the same time, OTE is entitled to develop, under clearly competitive conditions, mobile and other liberalised services, including satellite and cable TV. Within this framework, in addition to the traditional services, OTE also provides many new and value added services, such as data transmissions, ISDN, card phones, terminal equip-ment, third party and Infonet services. In the near future, it will also provide broadband services and message handling systems.

OTE acts through a widespread number of subsidiaries and affiliates established in Greece and abroad constituting the OTE Group of Companies, which deals, apart from tele-coms with a variety of other similar businesses. The OTE Group is fully Greek managed and retains directly about 27,500 employees. It operates through its 15 regional branch offices and about 400 sales points plus a wide range of re-sellers and dealers, covering the entirety of the national territory (mainland and islands) and of the country's population. By the end of 2001 the installed capacity of OTE was 5.415 million PSDN telephone lines (97% digital and 3% analogue) and 880 thousand ISDN connections (350 thousand of 2 channels and 6 thousand of 30 channels). The turnover of the OTE Group for the fiscal year 2002 was 4.3 billion euros and its net profits amounted to 482.4 million euros, while the EBITDA were 1.9 billion euros and the corresponding margins 43.7%, that is one of the highest amongst the European TOs.

With regard to the competitors of OTE in the market of voice telephony that was completely liberalised by the 1st January 2001, other operators have emerged. These include Forth-Net, Lanet, Q-Telecom, and Tellas (a subsidiary of the Greek Public Electricity Corporation), but as they began their commercial operation very recently, complete data about them are not presently available. On the other side, concerning the market of local access (broadband) services, apart from OTE which is not yet active, the companies Intra-Connect and Vivodi Telecoms are for the moment the sole players in the DSL business. However since they began business such a short time ago, all the relevant information is not currently available.

Mobile Radiotelephony Services

Three nation-wide operators function today in the local mobile cellular radioteleph-ony market, namely **Vodafon** (ex-Panafon), **Telestet** and **Cosmote**. The first two belong es-sentially to foreign investors and were established in early 1992. In September 1992 they acquired their special operating licenses to provide GSM-900 services for 20 years through an international public bidding procedure in consideration of ECU 116 million each, and they began their business in Summer 1993. On the other hand, the third operator is owned primarily by OTE and was established in October 1996. It was granted a special operating license directly by the Government to provide DCS-1,800 services for 20 years, and it com-menced its commercial operation in 1998. More specifically:

The first mobile operator is the company Vodafone (ex-Panafon) with fully paid share capital totalling 179.3 million euros, 75.6% of which is actually owned by the British cellular operator Vodafone Group (UK) Plc.. The latter is now going to acquire the remaining 24.4% through public trade in order to exit from the Athens Stock Exchange.

During its ten years of operation Vodafone-Panafon has invested 1.5 billion euros in infrastructure and licenses. In particular, the company recently acquired an LMDS license in the 23 GHz band and also extra spectrum in the 900 MHz and 1,800 MHz bands, as well as in the 3G. This capacity makes it the company with the highest radio frequency spectrum among national operators in Europe.

Vodafone-Panafon provides the entire range of mobile telephony services in to the GSM 900 system, including many value-added services. It is also connected by roaming agreements with 250 networks in 115 foreign countries, which is the largest number of such agreements ever signed in the Hellenic mobile telephony market. In addition, it is certified under the international quality standards: ISO-9001, ISO-14001 (Environmental Manage-ment), OHSAS-18001 (Occupational Health and Safety), BS-7799, and also recognised by EFQM "for Excellence in Europe".

The company is fully Greek managed and directly employs about 2,500 individuals. It operates primarily through its own retail chain of 190 Vodafone-Shops as well as inde-pendent dealers exploiting in total 1,500 sales points.

Vodafone-Panafon's turnover for the fiscal year 2001 was 990 million euros and its net profits amounted to 169.3 million euros. Also in 2002 it covered 98.2% of the country's population and its subscribers reached 3.2 million, bringing its market share to 35% of the local market.

The second mobile operator acting under the brand name **Telestet** is the company **STET Hellas** with fully paid share capital totalling nearly 126.5 million euros. Its sharehold-ers are the Dutch holding company TIM International N.V. with 80.257% (through its 100% subsidiary Telecom Italia Mobile S.p.A.) and the Greek companies Inter-

american Hellenic Life Insurance Company S.A. and DEMKO Investments and Commercial S.A., together holding 5.051%. The remaining stake of 14.692% is publicly traded on the NAS-DAQ National Market and the Euronext Amsterdam Stock Exchange.

During its ten years of operation, STET Hellas has invested more than 1.16 billion euros in infrastructure and licenses. In particular, the company has recently acquired an extra 2G (1,800 MHz) spectrum and also an extra 3G spectrum.

Telestet provides the entire range of mobile telephony services according to the GSM 900 system, including 36 value-added services, 14 of which are exclusive, and it is con-nected by roaming agreements with 246 networks in 111 foreign countries.

The company is mainly Greek managed and employs directly over 1,360 persons. It operates primarily through its own retail chain of 127 Telestet Centres and 11 independent master dealers and their relevant distributors.

Telestet's turnover for the fiscal year 2002 was 690.3 million euros and its net prof-its amounted to 76.4 million euros. In 2002 it covered 99.35% of the country's population and its subscribers exceeded 2.5 million, bringing its market share to 27% of the local mar-ket.

The third mobile operator is the company **Cosmote** with fully paid share capital totalling 155.2 million euros. Its major shareholder is OTE with 58.97% of its shares, fol-lowed by the Norwegian Telenor possessing 9.00%, while the remaining stake of 15.90% is publicly traded on the Stock Market.

During its five years of operation, Cosmote has invested 286.2 million euros in local infrastructure and licenses (UMTS and LMDS).

Cosmote provides all typical telecom services in the DCS-1,800 band, and as of October 2002, through the GSM-900 band it covers mainly the islands of the country. It holds the largest network operating in Greece, with over 2,600 base stations, and it is also connected by roaming agreements with 238 networks in 114 foreign countries.

The company is one of the leading mobile operators in Europe in terms of the plan-ning and implementation of new and innovative technologies. It was the first operator that introduced the "chat" services, as well as one of the first to roll out a GPRS network. Also, it has developed My-Cosmos, one of the most comprehensive mobile service portals in Europe, while it was the first company to introduce an artificial intelligence system, allowing access to a wide range of services through voice commands.

Cosmote is fully Greek managed and directly employs 1,744 individuals. It operates primarily through its own retail chain of 10 Cosmote-Shops, as well as the OTE-Shops and a number of independent dealers and distributors exploiting in total 3,000 sales points.

The company's turnover for the fiscal year 2002 was 1.2 million euros and its net profits amounted to 223.3 thousand euros. Even though Cosmote began its business five years ago following its two

From the official presentation of the first Greek satellite "Hellas Sat", 15-09-2003

other competitors, after only three years of operation, i.e. in June 2001, it became the dominant Greek mobile operator with 3.5 million subscribers and sharing almost 38% of the local market.

Satellite Services

Satellite services in Greece are mainly used for one-way transmissions of television programmes without any kind of connection to the public switched telephone or data net-works. However, this situation has changed since the launching and productive operation of the first Hellenic private commercial satellite Hellas-Sat I, which was effected from Cape Ca-naveral on 14 May 2003 by the U.S. company International Launch Services (ILS) with an Atlas V 401 booster made by Lockheed-Martin. The satellite, which was commercially opera-tional on 1st September 2003, belongs to the Hellas Sat System, which is owned by the Hel-las Sat Consortium (Cyprus) Ltd, a joint undertaking of Greek and Cypriot investors, the major (83.3%) shareholder of which is now OTE.

The Hellas-Sat I, is a Multi-Region Geostationary Satellite operating in the Ku-Band (uplink: 13.75-14.0/14.0-14.5 GHz; downlink: 10.95-11.2/11.45-11.70 GHz and 12.50-12.75 GHz) at the associated orbital position of 39° East on the GSO. It was provided by the French manufacturer Astrium SAS, designed for a fifteen-year lifetime. It is equipped with 30 x 36 MHz transpon-ders, onboard plus 8 x 36 MHz redundant. Its uplink/downlink foot-prints will be fixed over Europe and will be steerable over Southern Africa, Middle East, In-dian Subcontinent, South East Asia and Australia.

Internet Services

Despite the fact that the rates of accessibility and penetration of the Internet serv-ices in Greece do not actually surpass the 19.5%, many private companies are involved in the provision of Internet services. Amongst them the better known in the ISP market are the following (in alphabetical order): • CN, Algo-Net, Compulink, Forth-Net, Hellas-On-Line, Internet Hellas, OTE-Net, Tellas, and Vivodi Telecom.

Flat rate Internet charging is not currently available, but the tariffs charged by all ISPs are very low and thus Greece is ranked as the second in lowest tariffs in the EU for Internet access on a 20-hour provision per month.

Telecommunications Industry

The main manufacturer in the sector is the Hellenic Telecommunications and Elec-tronics Industry Intracom SA, incorporated in 1977. Its fully paid share capital is today 545.8 million euros, its total assets are 1.6 billion euros and its shares have been publicly traded on the Athens Stock Exchange since 1990. It provides its products and services to the public and private sectors both in Greece and abroad. Its turnover for the fiscal year 2002 was 798 million euros, its exports amount to 279 million euros and its net profits come to 101 million euros. Also, its total work force is close to 7,000 positions, 1,600 of which were created during the period 1997-2001. Finally, within the framework of its high-tech research programmes, Intracom founded the Athens Information Technology Centre, a Post-Graduate level institution affiliated to the Carnegie Mellon University of Pittsburgh, whose courses began in September 2002.

In conclusion, Greece has a dynamic telecoms sector. It is also emerging as a hub for the Balkans, the Black Sea and the Eastern Mediterranean regions.

"2001 Peace Odyssey", in Bucharest, Romania, 07-06-2001. An event organized by OTE International, Cosmorom and Roomtelecom

MASS MEDIA IN GREECE

By Stelios Papathanassopoulos

Greece is a small country with a plethora of media outlets. In fact, Greek media have been characterised by an excess of supply over demand since the foundation of the modern Greek state. In effect, this appears to be a sort of tradition in Greece, since there are more newspapers, more TV channels, more magazines and more radio stations than such a small market can support. Looking at Greek media history, one observes various explosions in the sector. The most recent ones took place in the mid 1980s and particularly in the late 1980s with the deregulation and privatisation of the broadcasting system. During that decade one observes chronologically a first explosion in mid 1980s in the newspaper market. A second took place in the broadcasting sector in the late 1980s due to the deregulation of the state monopoly of broadcasting frequencies, resulting in a plethora of private, national, and local TV channels and radio stations. In 2002 there were 160 private TV channels and 1,200 private radio stations in the country. In the mid-1990s, one also observes a new explosion in the magazine sector, which resulted in a new proliferation of magazines (from 400 to 900).

In addition, Greece has undergone commercialisation of the broadcasting sector, adopting a market-led approach resulting in more channels, more adver-

tising, more program imports and more politics. As in other countries, publishers and other business-oriented interests have entered the broadcasting landscape in large numbers. Since the mid 1990s, one notes various efforts by the state to regulate the sector (regarding radio and television licenses, advertising time, program quotas, protection of minors and media ownership).

Although developments in the Greek media sector may not entirely respond to the needs of the industry, the Greek media system has been surprisingly adaptable and flexible in the face of new developments. To understand this, one must remember that this system has functioned under Western democratic rule for only 26 years now, and it has had suddenly to face all the upheavals that other Western media systems have taken years to deal with.

The press
Newspapers

Traditionally, the press paid attention to all developments in political life and played an important role in the political arena. However, since the fall of the dictatorship in 1974, the press has been undergoing a process of modernisation. The development of advertising as one of its main sources of revenue in the 1960s has worked as a catalyst in relation to the newspapers' political choices, and in particular has neutralised the partisan division approach.

Moreover, the introduction of new printing technologies in the 1980s, the entry of entrepreneurs and businessmen into the media sector as well as tough competition from television has changed the field since the 1980s. As a result, the content of the press has become more objective and the traditional close association with particular parties or individuals has been superseded by a tendency to identify more with a political camp, right, left or centre. This has arisen in part out of a need to attract a broader spectrum of readers, to increase circulation in a period of economic difficulties and in part it reflects a drift within the political community itself towards larger block parties. However, the political stance of the newspapers is always present, especially in periods characterised by a politically intense climate and certainly during elections.

Regardless of the fact that the level of literacy in the population is high, newspaper readership is very low (with 63 out of 1,000 buying a daily paper in 2000). Since the arrival of private television and radio and the plethora of magazines, newspaper advertising and readership have come under pressure. By 2002 there were about 280 local, regional and national daily newspapers in Greece. However, the largest 23 nationally circulated daily titles in 2002 were located in Athens.

Another characteristic is that there is a strong Sunday press, again mainly originating in Athens, since almost all dailies have their Sunday edition. Most of the Sunday papers offer a supplement or they increase their number of pages in order to cater to the interests of a wider readership. By and large, due to the competition from the electronic media, the Greek press has tried to cope with the new conditions by re-designing their titles and/or publishing new

ones. In 1989 there were 13 dailies with a total average circulation of 1.27 million copies while in 2001 there were 23 titles with a total average daily circulation of 50,000 copies. On the other hand, the press share of advertising revenue has decreased in the last decade (from 18 percent in 1988 to 15 percent in 2002). Greek newspapers present two additional paradoxes:

Firstly, while the average circulation of newspapers in Greece is falling, the same cannot be said for the number of daily titles. Though a number of established newspapers suspended or ceased publication in the last ten years, new titles, or old ones under new ownership, seem to spring up all the time.

Secondly, since 1993 when the publishers saw that the sales of their newspapers were declining rapidly, all newspapers started offering gifts to their readers ranging from books to cars to houses etc. But, as relevant data reveals, the continuous 'priming' of printed media with 'offers' or gifts only temporarily halts the decline of circulation. It seems that gifts and special offers have become a constituent part of newspaper publication, resulting in significant drops in sales if the practice is abandoned.

Magazines

The Greek market is a very rich market in magazine titles, with more than 900 popular and special interest titles. However, there are about 50 consumer magazines - mostly monthlies - of real importance. While circulation of the general interest weekly magazines has declined, the special interest monthlies are gaining the upper hand. The TV listings market has expanded as well to reflect the increase in programming and now comprises nine titles. The highest circulation magazines are linked to TV game shows and offer cash prizes. During the 1995-1996 period, there was a another explosion of the magazine sector with new titles entering the field trying to attract the attention of Greek readers. This growth was also reflected in their advertising revenues. However, the Greek magazine sector has entered a period of re-shaping in terms of titles and publishers in order to

cope with the new and highly competitive media environment.

By and large, the major developments in the Greek magazine sector during the last five years have been the following: first, the 'old' weekly information-oriented magazines have perished. Some years ago, this category represented the bulk of the magazine sales. This also has to do with the entry in recent years of the Sunday newspapers into the magazine market, through supplements that may be considered magazines in their own right.

Second, there has been an increase since 1992 in the volume of specialised magazines, which have tried to attract the interest of younger Greek readers. Thus, one notes new titles in women's and men's interest magazines, music, computer magazines, sports, business and financial magazines, motorcar and motorcycle magazines, technology, history, home furnishing and decoration magazines etc.

Third, TV-guide magazines still attract the highest sales in the magazine sector but whether the market can support new titles is questionable. Fourth, there has been an increase in 'light entertainment' magazines, which present gossip about celebrities and their personal lives.

Fifth, in the period 1995-1999 there was a major increase in monthly general and specialist magazines, which combine the lifestyle of younger people with politics and societal issues.

In terms of sales, the TV-guide magazines come first and are followed by monthly women's magazines, monthly consumer, and life style magazines. The total volume of sales in the magazine sector has increased.

Broadcasting

Broadcasting was initiated and established during the dictatorships in modern Greek history. As in most European countries, Greek broadcasting was established as a state monopoly and this remained the case after the restoration of parliamentary rule in 1974. In fact, the state was the sole controller of the broadcast media and government manipulation of state TV news output was also a common practice.

The deregulation of Greek broadcasting, as in other European countries, represented more than the removal of certain rules and regulations. As in most countries, it was rather the outcome of the internationalisation of broadcasting in addition to pressure from domestic economic forces. As in most European countries, broadcasting deregulation commenced at the level of radio frequencies (in 1987) and then moved to television (1989). The entry of private TV channels was led by *Mega Channel* owned by *Teletypos*, a group of the most powerful publishers in Greece. It was quickly followed by *Antenna TV*, owned by a ship owner and owner of *Antenna Radio station*. In effect, transmitters sprang up all over Greece, most of them operating on a de facto and, technically speaking, illegal basis.

Private television

Both imported TV programs and domestic production have soared, thanks to massive increases in TV advertising revenue. While the regulatory structure of Greek TV had remained cloudy, the dominance of two of the private networks - *Mega Channel* and *Antenna TV* - was clear from very early on. Recent challenges from other private channels, including *Alpha* (previously Sky) *TV* and *Star Channel* have made a dent in *Mega* and *Antenna's* audiences. In the 1996/ 1997 TV season, for the first time since deregulation, the cumulative monthly shares of the two leading private television channels (*Mega* and *Antenna*) did not exceed 45 percent. In 2001-02, they attracted 42 percent of the TV market share, while *Alpha, Alter* and *Star* attracted 31 percent. During 2001-02, a new channel, Alter, increased its performance in the Greek television universe with new and attractive programming and well-known professionals.

Mega, Antenna, Alpha, Star and *Alter* channels are pitched at a mass-market audience. Sitcoms, satire shows, TV games, soap operas, movies and TV films as well as tabloid-style news and informational programs dominate their output. As the private channels. entertainment-dominated schedules have become stronger, there has been a parallel decrease in educational and documentary programs.

Private TV channels, though they initially relied to a high degree on cheap imports, swiftly built up the level of local and in-house production. The share of Greek-originated production is now larger than imports and this is mostly transmitted in primetime, while imported programs dominate the rest of the broadcasting time.

Public television

A major element in the Greek broadcasting scene is the decline in viewership of public service broadcasting. Few other public broadcasters in Europe have suffered as badly from the introduction of private TV. The Greek public broadcaster, *Hellenic Broadcasting Corporation (ERT)*, has sharply declined in ratings and advertising expenditure. Regarding television, ERT channels' viewership declined to 11 percent (*ET1* 5.6 percent and *NET*

Hellenic Broadcasting Corporation (ERT), the main building

4.5 percent) in 2001-02, which resulted in large advertising losses. (*ERT's* advertising market share for seven months in 2002 was about 4 percent of total TV advertising.) In effect, all three *ERT* channels have witnessed steady erosion of their market share since private commercial TV was launched in late 1989. *ERT* had also accumulated a debt of 45 billion drachmas. However, in 1999 *ERT* managed to pay off the main bulk of its debt. In fact, the 1999 and 2000 budgets were the first ones that found *ERT* profitable and in 2001, for the first time after a long period, *ERT* had no debts.

ERT's decline *stems* from the pub-

GREECE AT A GLANCE

Population:	11,500,000
Number of TV households:	3,710, 000
Overall movie admissions in 2000:	13.5 million

Audience reach (percentage of households) of:

Terrestrial TV:	98%
Terrestrial pay-TV:	10%
Satellite digital TV:	3%
Cable:	negligible
VCR penetration:	47.2%
Satellite receivers:	4%
DVD:	3%
% of households with digital TV reception:	3%
Internet use:	10-11%
Mobile phone ownership:	77%

lic broadcaster's one-time role as a mouthpiece of government propaganda. This led to the erosion of its credibility in the eyes of the Greek public and was, in effect, the entry-ticket for private television and the total deregulation of the TV sector. In effect, *ERT* had to pay for the democratisation and increased number of television channels, since it was unprepared to meet competition from private broadcasters.

The public broadcaster includes:

a) Two national-coverage channels – *Elliniki Teleorasi 1 (ET1) and NEA Elliniki Teleorasi (NET*, previously *ET2)* -- which are based in Athens.

b) A third channel *ET3*. This is based in Thessaloniki and has a stronger coverage of Northern Greece but can also be viewed in other parts of Greece. In effect, it is the regional channel of *ERT* and in its profile emphasis is on Northern Greece, arts and culture.

c) Hellenic radio (*ERA*) broadcasts on

Titles of daily newspapers & their average national circulation (2001 and 2000):

Newspapers	2001	2000
Ta Nea	84,586	86,149
Eleftherotypia	79,296	79,568
Ethnos	53,644	57,795
To Vima	50,357	30,555
Kathimerini	40,431	41,515
Eleftheros Typos	36,948	43,054
geymatini	31,707	32,423
	23,254	27,243

five national radio channels and originates from Athens through relay stations. The fifth channel, the 'Voice of Greece,' is aimed at Greeks abroad and includes regional programs. *NET 105.8* is the principal information radio station of the public broadcaster, *ERA2 presents mostly Greek music, Cosmos* mostly world music, while *ERA3* is a quality and classical music station, and ERA *4/Sports* is a sports and music radio station. There is also one more radio station, Filia, which broadcasts on AM frequencies (665) and presents a multilingual program (in 12 languages) for migrants who live and work in Greece.

d) It also publishes its weekly TV/radio listing magazine *Radioteleorasis*.

In recent years, the public broadcaster has tried to implement a long overdue reorganisation and positive results have started to appear, although there is still a long way to go. *ERT's* management has sought to turn a new page in the public broadcaster's troubled history. In October 1997, the first channel *ET1* became a general channel with more emphasis on entertainment. The second channel, previously named *ET2*, no longer exists. In fact, it has been re-launched under a new name as *NET (Nea Elliniki Teleorasi* - New Hellenic Television) and is mainly a round-the-clock information channel with news bulletins, information programs, talk shows and documentaries. It remains to be seen whether the ambitions of the *ERT*'s management will be fulfilled. On the other hand, *ERT* has had to reduce labour costs by applying a system of voluntary retirement for some of its personnel. In effect, through a new law and a redundancy plan, *ERT*'s management has sought to have over a thousand employees retire through 2002.

In terms of financing, ERT appears to be in better condition. All Greek households have to pay 12,000 to 14,000 drachmas (€39 to 42) per annum for the public broadcaster, which is collected through household electricity bills. In 1999, *ERT* collected 62 billion drachmas through the license fee plus 3.7 billion drachmas (€10,9 million) through TV advertising and sponsorship. Its programming costs in 1997 were 16 billion drachmas (€47 million), while in 1998/99 this went up to 27 billion

drachmas (€5,9 million). Moreover, labour costs accounted for 31 billion drachmas (€9,1 million).

ERT has ambitions for the future. Its first goal is to re-attract some of the Greek viewers and it seems to be achieving this gradually, at least in the perception of the Greek people. In effect, its public image seems to be better nowadays than some years ago. ET1 seeks to compete directly with the private channels, while NET has become a prestigious channel not only of the public broadcaster but also within the Greek television landscape. Moreover, ERT also has plans for the digital era, and particularly with regard to the Athens 2004 Olympic Games. According to Law 2644 of 1998, ERT already holds a license for a digital platform. ERT has established a subsidiary company called, *Nea Syndromitiki Tileorasi,*

International Broadcasting Center for the Olympic Games

S.A (New Subscription Television, S.A.). However, most of ERT's plans are on paper and its digital goals have not yet been met.

Pay-TV

While cable TV is virtually non-existent in Greece, pay-TV has found a niche on analogue terrestrial television. *Multichoice Hellas* dominates pay-TV. It buys premium programming from sister-company *NetMed Hellas*, which operates the channels *FilmNet, K-TV* and *Supersport*. These remain the first and only analogue pay-TV services in the country. The monthly subscription fee for *Filmnet* is 7,500 drachmas (€22), for *Supersport* 9,100 drachmas (€26,7), and for the three pay channels 11,200 drachmas (€33).

Filmnet was launched in October 1994, offering a diet of blockbuster movies and live league soccer games. In 2001, it pulled in 290,000 subscribers. In 1996, the network acquired the exclusive soccer rights for the Greek championship for the period 1997-2001 at 15 billion drachmas. In August 1996 *NetMed Hellas* launched two more pay-TV services, *Supersport* and *K-TV*, using a frequency leased from the state broadcaster, *ERT*. In summer 1998 *Supersport* won a new battle for the exclusive TV rights to televise the Greek Basketball League games in the period 1998-2002, offering an unprecedented 11.6 billion drachmas for the rights for the first two years.

In 2001-2002 *NetMed Hellas* dealt with individual basketball teams. In effect, by 2001 Supersport dominated the TV sports games of the Greek market since it had the exclusive rights to cover soccer and basketball, the most popular games in Greece. Currently, the company is negotiating the renewal of its con-

Private channels	TV viewership (%)*	TV viewership (%)**
Mega Channel	22.1	20.0
Antenna TV	21.9	22.5
Alpha TV	15.3	13.4
Star channel	13.4	11.0
Alter	2.2	7.4
Tempo	2.2	4.4
Public channels		
ET1	6.1	5.6
NET	4.2	4.5
OTHERS	12.6	11.6

Viewership of national terrestrial TV channels (market share %)

* 1 September 2000- 31 August 2001 ** 1 September 2001- 31 August 2002)
Source: AGB Hellas

tracts, while it has lost the most attractive soccer games to its competitor in digital television, *Alpha Digital*. *NetMed Hellas* has signed exclusive rights with all major Hollywood studios to broadcast new releases to Greek subscribers.

Digital television

Greeks have not paid much attention to satellite television, although the deregulation of the Greek television system started through the re-transmission of satellite channels via the UHF frequencies. But, as in most cases, digital satellite television entered the Greek television universe suddenly and with strong competition. In the beginning of 2000, there were two digital satellite platforms in operation (*Nova and Alpha Digital*).

In fact the story, if not the development, of Greek digital satellite television began in March 1998, when *Multichoice Hellas* announced its plans to go ahead with its digital satellite project *Nova*, ushering Greece into the digital age. *Alpha Digital* started operations in October 2001. But after a year of intense competition, especially on soccer TV rights, Alpha Digital, on September 9, 2002 announced the suspension of its operations due to its failure to meet economic obligations. Its collapse impacted very negatively on soccer television rights as in other European countries.

This outcome clearly shows that the Greek digital pay-TV market is still undergoing a state of development. More-

over, it demonstrates that the domestic market, due to its size and peculiarities, is not in a position to sustain two competitive digital platforms.

TV rights for Greek soccer games, which were erroneously considered the main engine of digital TV development, became too expensive. In 1996, Netmed (which owns digital platform Nova) had acquired the rights to televise the matches of the top three divisions for 5 billion drachmas (15 million euros). In 2001, thanks to a new law, individual professional sports clubs were made responsible for negotiating their own TV contracts. Alpha Digital was set up expressly for this purpose, offering large sums to teams and hoping to recoup the 90 million euros it had invested from advertising and subscribers' fees. However, there were no more than 35,000 subscribers willing to buy a second digital signal decoder to place on top of their Nova one, and pay yet another fee. Compared to the size of the population of subscribers, TV rights for Greek soccer had become the second most expensive in Europe, after the UK. What Europeans had learned six months earlier, involving the limits of soccer's attraction to the public, Greeks also learned. As a result, soccer and other sports are now considered an overvalued product.

Radio

As noted earlier, the radio sector was deregulated with the entry of municipal and private local stations. Nowadays,

Hellenic
Broadcasting
Corporation (ERT),
a radio studio

private stations dominate the radio sector (see statistics at end of chapter). Approximate 270 radio stations broadcast regularly throughout Greece. The most important ones are located in Athens and have networking arrangement with local stations. Generally, each of Greece's 52 administrative regions has two or three local commercial radio stations, with more in the largest cities.

However, most of them are without an official license to broadcast. The gov-

Main radio channels in Athens

Private radio stations	Audience (%)
Sky	13.5
Antenna	12.4
Sfera	12.1
Melodia	11.2
Village	9.4
Supersport	9.0
Love	8.6
Flash	8.6
Ciao	7.5
Public radio stations	
ERA Sport	3.5
NET	2.1
ERA	1

For the period December 2001- January 2002
Source: Alco

Division of advertising revenue (2001):

Medium	Percentage (%)
Television	43.50
Magazines	35.03
Newspapers	16.81
Radio	4.66

ernment in 1997 invited the radio stations operating in the Athens and Thessaloniki region to apply for a license. In March 2001, the government announced the 28 most desired radio licenses for the Attica region, generating anger among those stations not granted a license. Finally, the number of licensed radio stations in the Attica region increased to 35. Regarding the second largest city of the country, Thessaloniki, the government announced that it would allocate 27 radio licenses.

There are three categories of radio stations in Greece: state owned, municipal and private. The vast majority of them are privately owned and of a local character (transmitting via the FM frequencies). State owned and municipal radio stations have exhibited a sharply declining trend in audience figures and advertising revenue. Greeks listen to the radio for approximately 4 hours daily, while those between the ages of 25 to 54 are the most loyal to radio.

The effects of television deregulation

A) More choice and more TV consumption

Greek viewers have turned willingly to private channels since their inception. One also notes, according to the data of the TV research company AGB Hellas, that there is an increasing trend in both time consumed in front of a television and in the use of more than one television set per household. In 2001, over 43% of households used two or more television sets, a fact indicating more personal viewing patterns as television programming choices increase. The central position of television in the home is manifested by the fact that 87.4% of

Media Press Center for the Olympic Games

households placed the TV set in the living/dining room, where the family gathers. In a significant percentage of households (7.8%) the main TV set is located in the adults' bedroom, and only 6% of the main TV sets operate in other areas of the house. Moreover, secondary television sets are usually located in the adults' bedroom (61.8%) while their presence is also significant in the children's bedroom (22.5%). 8.7% of the secondary television sets are located in the kitchen and only 6% in the living room. The variety of locations of the secondary TV sets in the households confirms television habits of individuals within the family may vary considerably.

Furthermore, according to AGB Hellas, average daily figures reach a maximum during the winter months, approximating four hours per day. During the summer, daily viewing is limited to two and a half hours, while during the autumn and spring months it ranges around three and a half hours. Average daily viewing increased slightly during the 2001-02-television season due to the entry of new "reality" programs as well as some attractive programs in specific slots. The average daily viewing had increased to 239 minutes per day in the first six weeks of autumn 2002, while a year earlier it was 232 minutes.

B) On programming

Primetime television programming and ratings involve predominantly local products, mainly game and reality shows, news, and sitcoms. Current exceptions are imported TV movies, which air on networks around 10 p.m. or later as well as some TV series mainly on Star channel.

After eleven years of deregulation of Greek television, one observes the following in terms of programming:

a) A standardisation of main program genres on the private stations. With respect to television programming, reality shows/games were given significantly more airtime on Mega and Antenna. Other channels (Star) followed suit. In effect, 'event TV' seems to have become a fashionable program for the time being.

b) Particularly successful programs are renewed (e.g., the soap opera "Lampsi" [Reaching for the Light]) for the next TV seasons. However, this appears to be an exception to the rule, since most programs cannot continue after their second consecutive year, as they do not manage to maintain their high ratings of the previous year.

c) Television viewing remains stable, although in November and December 2001 there was a significant increase in TV viewing time due to the entry of the reality game "Big Brother."

d) An analysis of Greek television programming between 1994 and 2002 shows that information and news programs led television program output followed by films and series. On the two main channels (Mega and Antenna TV), news and information programs, films and series combined, comprised at least 75% of their total airtime. Additionally, Mega and Antenna devoted less airtime to films in 2001-02.

e) The bulk of Greek television production has increased considerably over the last four years. In the 2000-2001 TV season, Greek primetime series and serials faced strong competition from reality programs, but in 2002-2003 they seemed to come back.

As in most countries, Greek commercial television scheduling seems to seek, through a careful mixing of programs, to build a desirable venue for advertisers on their channel. When a particular program declines or is too costly for the channel, it is replaced.

Regarding the overall quality of television output, the picture is not very clear. First of all, one must acknowledge that there has been a democratisation of television output from political interference as well as improved presentation of information. For some TV critics however, the profile of private channels is akin to glorified versions of "tabloid newspapers."

Internet and online media

Greece has the lowest proportion of Internet users within the European Union. According to EU data, the PC penetration rate in Greece was 11 percent at the end of 2001, compared to an EU average of 36 percent. Not surprisingly, Greece lags behind other European countries on a wide range of Internet indicators. In 2001, according to a national survey conducted by the V-PRC Institute, 10 percent of the Greek pop-

TV Channels' programming mix by Typology 2001-02 (Market Share %)

Typologies	Mega	Antenna	Star	Alpha	Alter	NET	ET1
Total	100	100	100	100	11,5	100	100
Series	19.3	25.1	22.2	13.9	27.0	0.5	17.4
Films	18.0	19.9	27.2	17.4	6.7	7.6	10.1
Light entertainment	5.5	3.6	9.8	2.4	11.6	0.1	1.0
Arts/culture	2.0	1.0	0.1	1.3	25.9	13.6	9.3
News/ information	45.4	39.1	23.9	59.9	14.7	74.1	37.5
Children's programs	3.0	5.6	14.4	0.0	0.5	0.4	6.8
Sports	2.6	0.9	0.3	4.3	2.0	2.8	14.1
Other	3.5	2.8	2.0	0.8		0.9	3.9

Source: AGB Hellas 1996, the data refer to the period of October 2, 2001 to June 3, 2002

ulation was reported to have an Internet connection. By comparison, the average Internet connection rate throughout the EU was 18 percent in 2000. Moreover, the number of web-sites originating in Greece is roughly one-tenth of the number of German web-sites and one-fifteenth the number of UK sites. The number of secure servers is a rough indication of a country's e-commerce readiness. With only one-fifth the number of secure servers per capita in comparison to the EU as a whole, Greece remains relatively unequipped for online transactions. Corporate use of the Internet in Greece also trails behind the rest of Europe. Only 32 percent of all companies surveyed in Greece by the EU reported having Internet access by the end of 1999, compared to an EU average of 63 percent. A smaller percentage of Greeks state that they use banking on-line (17 percent) in comparison to other EU citizens (25 percent) (Eurobarometer, 2000).

Advertising

While in the 1990s advertising appeared to be one of the healthiest industries in Greece and achieved high levels of growth, especially with the advent of private television, in the beginning of the new century, signs of decline have appeared. However, many believe that this is due to the general global recession, which has affected the Greek market, too. On the eve of the Olympic Games, the Greek advertising market is expected to recover. About 45% of the advertising expenditure is directed to television, which occupies the lion's share. In the same period, the market share in ads of newspapers and magazines has declined, while radio exhibited a fluctuating trend.

Regulation and the media

Greece has a rather strict regulatory framework on almost all aspects of the media sector. Nevertheless, many of the regulations, whether too strict or out of date, cannot easily be implemented. For example, article 40 of Law 1086 of 1988 allows courts to scrutinise the finances of press and broadcast companies, but no related action has been taken. Moreover, Law 2328 of 1995 provides that TV companies have to pay a fee for the use of their frequency, which is still not the case. Additionally, the laws of 1989 and 1995 (2328) refer to the allocation of terrestrial TV licenses. But these licences have not been fully awarded. At the same time, a clause in Law 2644 of 1998 on pay TV and digital television notes that TV companies, which have applied for a terrestrial-licence, operate legally until the allocation procedure has been completed. As a result, market forces have created an overcrowded broadcasting environment with 160 national and local TV broadcasters operating alongside the public broadcaster's three national TV channels.

The new National Broadcasting Council (NBC), the regulatory body, is expected to award licenses within 2003. The NBC was established in 1989 to oversee the audio-visual sector and to act as a 'buffer' between the government and the broadcasters. In effect, under its first administration, the NBC remained inactive, if not virtually absent from the broadcasting affairs of the country. But, one has to admit that its role at the time was only advisory to the government. Nevertheless, the NBC under its first administration (1990-1993) prepared three codes on the operating conditions of radio and television stations: one on advertising, the second on journalistic ethics and the third on programming. During its second administration, the Socialist government introduced a new law in 1993, whereby the NBC board members were reduced from 19 to 9.

The nomination procedure for the election of NBC board members remained a contentious issue. Rules stipulate that four members should be nominated by the party in power, four by the opposition parties and its chairman by the Speaker of Parliament, thereby giving the government a controlling vote.

Under its second administration (1993-1997), the NBC adopted a more active role regarding a number of broadcasting-related issues. It imposed fines on national and local channels for various infractions: on national channels in relation to some of their 'reality' and news programs, while on local channels because they failed to pay copyright fees for programs broadcast.

During its third administration (1997-2001), the NBC had to examine the files of radio and television stations that applied for an official license to broadcast. The proposed licenses for radio stations in the Attica region provoked the anger of the excluded stations. Eventually, a compromise was apparently reached between the state and the radio stations resulting in a new era for Greek radio.

The NBC under its fourth administration (2002-2005) must examine the files and grant licenses to television stations with national, regional and local coverage. This is not an easy task, as any decision is bound to provoke the anger of the excluded channels, as happened earlier in the case of radio.

Moreover, Law 2325 does not allow publishers to own more than two daily political newspapers - that is, a morning and an evening daily, published either in Athens, Piraeus, or Thessaloniki. In August 1998, with Presidential Decree 214, the government introduced a regulation to oversee the "transparency of media ownership." In 2002 there was further regulation regarding the "basic shareholder," a principal provision of which was that a person or company involved as suppliers in connection with public works cannot be shareholders of a media company owning more than 5% of its shares.

What is equally interesting about the history of broadcasting deregulation in Greece is the entry of publishers and other entrepreneurs into the broadcasting scene as in most such cases in Europe. It has been noted that the media sector is dominated by a handful of companies. Needless to say, most of them have other business interests. This provides an answer to questions over the new media magnates' motives. Some politicians, including the Speaker of the Hellenic Parliament, are concerned about how easily and quickly the media sector could be concentrated in the hands of a few influential magnates. To a certain extent, the new television environment gives the impression that it has largely copied the situation in the printed press and there is a clear indication that there are too many stations for such a small market.

In effect, all TV stations face severe financial problems, while most of the Greek media are in the red. This has made analysts wonder about the real intentions of their owners. At the beginning of the new century, the Greek television landscape seems to be undergoing a new, though silent, deregulation, associated mostly with the economics of the sector, the development of new media, the reorganisation of smaller channels, and a new wave of competition. However, the biggest dilemma for the Greek media and its owners is whether it can withstand new and increased competition or whether the media outlets will have to change hands.

THE HELLENIC AUDIO-VISUAL INSTITUTE. IOM

I.O.M.
ΙΝΣΤΙΤΟΥΤΟ
ΟΠΤΙΚΟΑΚΟΥΣΤΙΚΩΝ
ΜΕΣΩΝ

The Hellenic Audio-visual Institute IOM is the national applied research organisation in the realm of audio-visual communication in Greece. It was established in 1994 as a legal entity of Private Law under the supervision of the Ministry of Press and Mass Media. Since then, IOM has been actively engaged in carrying out methodical research-projects concerning a variety of fields, namely *Radio, Television, Cinema, Multimedia and New Technologies*, keeping abreast of the latest nation and world-wide developments in the audio-visual industry. By distributing up to date and reliable data it accomplishes its primary goal, which is the encouragement of public and private institutions running in the national audio-visual sector.

The Institute's research work has so far covered a wide spectrum of subjects. These include the protection of minors in the broadcast media, financial trends in the Greek Media, political advertising campaigns during elections at both the national and the European level for the past decade, the available bibliography on the broader area of Communication and so on.

European procedures and programmes, whose objective is the strengthening and support of audio-visual production, hold a significant place in the scope of the Institute's activities. Hence, IOM constitutes the national representative and co-ordinator of Greece's stance vis-a-vis the EU initiatives of this kind. An example is the *MEDIA Programme*, which is already in its third five-year period and in fact its potential depends partly on the Greek Presidency of the EU. In addition, IOM represents our country in the pan-European organisation *European Audio-visual Observatory* (35 member-states and the European Commission) with headquarters in Strasbourg and accountable to the Council of Europe. The central EAO task is the supply of efficient data services to media professionals across Europe. The Institute is also involved in actions within the framework of the *Euro-Mediterranean Audiovisual Partnership*, which was in practice set up through the first "High Level Conference on Audiovisual and TV Cooperation", conducted in 1997 (Thessaloniki) under the presidency of IOM on behalf of Greece.

In an attempt to define the essence of the Hellenic Audio-visual Institute's involvement in matters of national representation, one must bear in mind that it concerns the promotion of issues in favour of *countries and regions with low audio-visual production capacity and restricted linguistic or geographical area.*

Additionally, the Institute, recognising the need for skills and expertise of people working in the audio-visual industry, contributes to media training, by carrying out seminars to familiarise the participants (new professionals, students, unemployed) with the New Information Technologies. Moreover, in order to provide a comprehensive career handbook to those wishing to work in the media sector, IOM has prepared the first *Guide to Media Education and Training in Greece.*

As for the need common to all European countries for preserving the audio-visual heritage, the Institute has suggested the implementation of a *Central Information System for the Hellenic Audio-visual Memory,* which could function as a useful guide within the internet environment. The project is put into practice under the auspices of *Information Society* and in collaboration with the appropriate national institutions and the respective organisations of other EU member-states.

Equally significant is the establishment of the first *Public Centre of Documentation and Library Services* for the disciplines of Communication and Information, which supports and ensures the total output of the Institute's research-projects. It should be stressed that this is a resource fully accessible to journalists, researchers, government officials, experts, students, and to anyone merely interested in learning about the Mass Media in the digital era.

In order to outline the mission of the Hellenic Audio-visual Institute, throughout its multifarious activities, one should understand that the IOM *methodically promotes joint action between political decision groups, academic and other research institutions, public and private agencies of audio-visual programmes and, last but not least, the industry's workforce in Greece.*

ARTS & CULTURE

LITERATURE

By Dr. Philip D. Dracodaidis

The fall of Constantinople in 1453 marks the collapse and the death of the Byzantine Empire a state that lasted for 1200 years and extended, in the period of its greater expansion, from Asia to the Atlantic and from the Russian south to the sands of Northern Africa. This event constitutes a historical milestone as it creates once and for all a clear separation between two totally opposed systems of social and political organisation, two different civilisations and cultures: Christendom in Western Europe on the one side, the Ottoman Turks, true believers of Mohammed and rulers of the Islamic world, on the other side. These two systems tend to move in the same direction: to the West. Columbus leaves the shores of the Iberian peninsula to reach the Indies navigating westwards; the Turkish sultans and armies move to the Northwest through the Balkans to the Hungarian open fields and to the outskirts of Vienna: the Ottoman Empire's dominions include the remote areas close to China, the infertile lands of Arabia, part of Africa, the Crimean peninsula, the Dalmatian cost south of Trieste.

Greece, due to its geographical position, is, as from the 12th century, a land of "passage", a thoroughfare that links Europe to Asia, the Aegean sea to the Mediterranean, the south of Europe to

the Holy Land and from there to the north of Africa. Influences from all parts converge in this land: Venice occupies the islands along the Ionian sea as well as Creta and brings its culture to them; many islands of the Aegean sea remain under the rule of Italian noblemen that had privileges on them dating back to the Byzantine emperors; Rhodes is governed by the Knights of Saint-John; the peninsula is under the Turks, while places like Mani in the south of the Peloponnese remain free and other areas live under a quasi-autonomous government headed by local Greek rulers. These disparities will wither away in the second half of 17th century as the Turkish Crescent dismantles the Venetian outposts in the Mediterranean and the European diplomacy recognises the supremacy of le Grand Turc .

These historical events and political changes leave layers of cultural marks in all areas inhabited by Greek populations. Some examples amongst a variety of others prove that these marks have been the seeds for the growing up of the Greek cultural identity: the theatre in the Ionian islands, in Zakynthos mainly, is an adaptation of the Italian comedia del' arte; poetry in Cyprus follows the stereotypes of the Renaissance poets, such as Petrarca, succeeding however to promote a genuine love poems tradition; in Creta, the Italian (and quite often the French) heritage is moulded within the local fabric giving birth to original literary works such as the tragedy of Erofili by Georgios Hortatzis (1637), the love, hate and war epic of Erotokritos by Vitsentzos Kornaros (written probably in 1646 and published in 1713), the comedies and dramas of anonymous masters whose identity is slowly emerging through arduous research that underlines the value of a "Cretan literary school" that goes strong well into the 18th century.

If the cultural influences are successfully adapted and reworked to fit the Greek vision of the world and of life as well as the aspirations of the people to shake off the Turkish rule, the Orthodox Church whose headquarters remain in Istanbul and the Patriarch of Constantinople is considered the spiritual leader of all orthodox laymen within and outside the Ottoman Empire, tries to fix the dogma, to make it flexible in order to avoid clashes with the authorities, to clarify points of the Holy Scriptures that refute the arguments of the Catholic Church, suspected to work for the conversion of the masses to the papal rule. If this standing strengthens the opposition between the two Churches, it promotes at the same time the conservatism of the Orthodox priests and their strong desire to educate the "enslaved brothers" so that by "science and knowledge" they serve their true faith. The longing for education will become a standard feature

during the whole period of the Ottoman rule: the Patriarch of Constantinople will invest in printing machines as early as the 17th century, an action that infuriated the Sultan who ordered his killing.

Printing moved to Venice and later on to Vienna and Paris. Religious books, historical memoirs, books of comments on Ancient Greek authors, propaganda material and pamphlets on social and political issues, manuals of conduct, works on the modern Greek grammar, vocabulary and even orthography, essays on philosophical concepts, translations of literary works mainly from Latin, Italian and French constitute an exceptionally rich production that allows ideas and innovative theories to circulate widely. This production relies on a broad basis of "wise" or "knowledgeable" persons, educated in Padova, Paris, Mount Athos and the Greek diaspora educational centres supported by the Orthodox Church providing teachers and curricula and by rich benefactors providing lavish financial contributions. As a consequence, this educated elite will develop and consolidate two main lines of thought, e.g. that Orthodox Greeks are the descendants of Ancient Greece and that this glorious heritage will be recovered and flourish once the Greek "nation" is liberated from the Turkish slavery.

In the second half of the 18th century the message for the liberation of the country will spread throughout Europe thanks to this elite. In the first quarter of the 19th century the "philhellenic" movement, spreading from France and England as far as the U. S. A will give political leverage to the aspiration for a liberation war against the Turkish domination. The main centres for the planning and the organisation of the national rebirth are the Balkan territories governed by Greeks under special status initiated and implemented by the Sultan. In these territories will be active Rigas Ferraios (1757-1798), preaching the revolt against the Turks, drawing up the map of Greece and inviting the Balkan brothers to unite and participate in the liberation cause for the creation of a multi-ethnic, multi-cultural state. Rigas will compose the famous Anthem asking "brave men not to live any longer under the oppression". The activity of Rigas, translator at the same time from Italian and French, will displease the Turkish and European establishment: he will be arrested in Vienna and given back to the Turkish authorities in Belgrade which preferred to strangle him together with some of his supporters.

Adamantios Korais (1748-1833) has been luckier: born in Smyrna from a family of merchants having their roots in the island of Chios, he lived in Amsterdam, studied in Montpellier, but established in Paris and has been the witness of the French Revolution. He was 73 when the War of Liberation of Greece started in 1821, a breakthrough he helped to shape, give it a coherent projection, a sense of conceptual continuity

and a realistic configuration. His contribution, always in the spirit of a pragmatic liberalism, is still apparent, whether one looks at the Modern Greek language development, the philological comments and explanations concerning the publication of Ancient Greek texts, the political priorities, the survival and expectations of a reborn Greek state. His prestige has been enormous all over Europe; he lived long enough to see the liberation of his beloved country (officially proclaimed independent in 1830), the "resurrection of the Nation" and the first uncertain steps of the modern Greek state whose territory included the Peloponnese and a part of the peninsula, the frontier traced 200 kilometres north of Athens.

These developments would have never materialise, if there were not a strong and recurrent moral support from the Greek minority living in Constantinople around the Patriarchate in the area of Fanari (presently Fener) and, at the same time, offering its services to the Ottoman Empire. Occupying diplomatic and government highly regarded posts, in close relation with Europe, eager to maintain and develop its privileges, this minority called "the Fanariots" has been in fact a mini-state within the Empire, a close collaborator of the authorities and simultaneously an independent group, open to ideals coming from Europe, adapting them to the reality of the Empire, giving them a Greek content that helped in putting them quickly into practice. By amalgamating these inputs, the Fanariots lived dangerously: from time to time, the Empire disgraced some them or decapitated others.

The Fanariots, many of them merchants established in Trieste, Livorno, Genova, Vienna, Marseille, even India, land owners in Bulgaria, Romania, Moldova and the south of Russia, shipowners sailing as far as Montevideo under British, French or Russian flags, capital providers to the Ottoman Empire have not been only the supporters, backers and bankers of the idea of the return to life of the fatherland. Adopting the bourgeois class life-style and priorities, they have been mainly the promoters of culture. Thanks to the proliferation of newspapers and magazines (some of them with a real feminist orientation), the development of amateur and later on professional theatrical groups, the spreading of social events related to art events, Constantinople and Smyrna became cultural centres of excellence. European literary movements and schools found disciples (or enemies) in these places. A "Fanariotic literary school" was born that introduced romanticism in prose and verses, in epics and feuilleton -story telling. If French influences are present, Byron (who died in Greece during the liberation war) is imitated more or less successfully. The names of Panayotis Soutzos (1806-1868), who is considered the first modern Greek romantic author, or of Alexander Rizos Rangavis (1809-1892), who develops an

intellectual -like neo-classical approach to poetry, are examples of the Fanariotic understanding of literature as a litterature de salon .

Romanticism will acquire a broader signification and will become a way of life as well as a school of aesthetics and social renewal in the Ionian islands so close to Italy, so long under Venetian rule, so fond of the ideals of the French Revolution (1789) and of social radicalism, so dazzled by Napoleon and the Napoleonian wars. After the occupation of Venice by Napoleon, the French

D. Solomos

army occupied the Ionian islands and stayed there for almost 20 years (1797-1815). However, romanticism was there before the French. A particular kind of romanticism blending symbolistic overtones long before Charles Baudelaire's concept of correspondances between sounds, colours, words linking in a mystical and quasi-transcendental way Nature to the aspiration for an out-of-this-world .

The leading figures of this romanticism are Dionysios Solomos (1798-1857) and Andreas Kalvos (1792-1869), both born in the island of Zakynthos. Solomos, the son of a rich old count and a poor young housemaid, was educated in Italy, a usual procedure for the children of the local aristocracy speaking Italian. There he will be initiated to the romantic principles and will compose his first poems. He will continue writing in Italian after his return to Zakynthos in 1818 and a good part of this production will be published in Corfu (Rime improvvisate, 1822). It seems that at that time he has started writing in Greek, a language he has hardly studied or spoken. His Hymn to Liberty, a long poem of 158 quatrains, is the first proof of his mastering the Greek language and the literary metier. Written in 1824, when the Liberation War was embracing the whole of the Greek peninsula and the Aegean islands, while the Ionian islands were, after the Vienna Congress in 1815 and the withdrawal of the French forces, a British protectorate, the Hymn was widely acclaimed and gave extra strength to the "philhellenic" movement. Soon, the composer Nicolaos Mantzaros (born in Corfu) put the poem into music and the Greek national anthem was born. Solomos moved to Corfu in 1828 and died there in 1857. No one knew then that Solomos did not stop to write poems (as well as finely elaborated proses) and work ceaselessly on vast lyrical compositions that modern scholars call "sketches", because they have never got a final touch, they have never been published during the poet's lifetime, but constitute a patchwork of brilliant inventiveness and the best sample of the Greek poetical language.

Andreas Kalvos is the poet of just 20 lyrical Odes, half of them published in Geneva in 1824, the rest in Paris two years later (1826). An introverted and sensitive person, he lived in Italy and Switzerland, worked as a university professor in Corfu and then left for England, where he married and managed a young girls' school with his new wife. His poems are a blend of romantic enthusiasm and melancholy, a real commitment to the struggle for the liberation of Greece, a call for a moral standing under difficult circumstances. Kalvos created his own poetical language and technique, a unique phenomenon that relates his inspiration to the ancient times, to an aristocratic standing, to the rejection of any ornamentation. The dryness of his lyrism has the monotony and the thrill of a Walkyrie-like cavalcade.

The independence of Greece and the choice of the city of Athens as the capital of the country drew the literary forces from the periphery (Constantinople or the Ionian islands) to this new centre so much burdened by its glorious past. There is an "Athenian literary school" which promoted a late romanticism, quarrelled about literary styles and, more important, about the language to be used in literature: a vocabulary close to the ancient Greek? A vocabulary based on the spoken language which had given anonymous folkloric songs (called "demotic poetry") of high value during the centuries of Turkish occupation? A language like the one produced by Korais, a "middle of the road path"? The so called "language problem" will plague the intellectual and political life of the country and it will be solved more than 150 years later by government decision in favour of the spoken language, the result of the evolution of Ancient Greek enriched by foreign vocables, Turkish and French, Slavic and English, German to a lesser degree.

An outstanding example of this osmosis is the work of Yannis Makriyannis (1797-1864), a general of the Liberation War, an illiterate soldier who, at the age of 32 learned how to write and decided to present his Memoirs, the text of an eye-witness that goes to the heart of the events, a kind of mise a nu where the best and the worse of human behaviour are given equal chances, the general

keeping the role of the story-teller and of honest commentator and judge. This text remained unknown up to 1907. Its publication did not arise the interest of the intellectuals or the scholars. It is Giorgos Seferis (poet and Nobel Pize laureate) that 60 years later, revealed the importance of Makryiannis, the "illiterate master" as he called him.

By 1880, a "new" Athenian literary school will emerge. Emmanuel Roidis (1836-1904) is its proeminent representative. Born in the island of Syros, educated in Genova and established in Athens after 1863, he is a unique figure in Greek letters as he combines a cosmopolitan spirit with a deep understanding of daily life in the small Greek kingdom. His Papess Johanna is the narration of a medieval story relating the life and adventures of Johanna, a young and pretty woman which succedes in occupying Saint Peter's throne in Rome, becoming a "papess". Alfred Jarry in France and Laurence Durell in England have been those who gave publicity to this novel outside Greece forgetting on the way to remind the name of the author. This work must not put aside the short stories written by Roidis, excellent samples of realism and social satire.

In the "new" Athenian literary school belongs Kostis Palamas (1859-1943), an extremely productive poet, fiction writer, critic and playwright. His inspiration is embracing national, personal and religious themes, his versatility allows him to pass from the one genre to the other

K. Palamas

studied philosophy and psychology in Germany is the representative of a new trend in Greek literature that gives consistence and physiological depth to the characters created by the author's imagination. He is known today for his fictions that have a real "modernistic" touch and they are written in a concise but staccato style that leaves romanticism aside privileging the meanders of the soul.

In the same context, Alexander Papadiamantis (1851-1911) is a true explorer of the provincial and Athenian life, a personality that suffers watching the human mediocrity but has enough stamina to describe it in all details, without forgetting that "the beast is not far from the angel" and that life is a kaleidoscope allowing bright images to form. In all his fictions and novels, Papadiamantis puts forward Freudian problems (before Freud) either concealed or exposed in full view, a psychoanalytic approach that makes acts and words seem natural, the light of the Greek climate not allowing things to settle in gloominess and rust in darkness. There is a thirst for life that revigorates the reader and a sense of unstable but manageable peace that gives a unique touch to the writer's art. Papadiamantis lived with little money writing for newspapers and magazines. His Complete Works in a critical edition appeared in 1981-1985. Since then, many scholars and authors (including Milan Kundera) tend to put Papadiamantis in the tradition of the great European romanciers.

in a kind of mystique that reminds Victor Hugo, in a melancholical sotto voce close to Lamartine, in a patriotic enthusiasm where Antiquity, the opposition to the Turkish occupation and the "Great Idea" of Greece pushed by its duty to reconquer the Byzantine glory and recover lost territories, are closely related. This outline must not hide the great contribution of Palamas to the foundation of a real national literary environment, away form a sterile and complacent romanticism, very close to the development of moral values and of the idea that the writer has a mission within society: to help it improve.

The same high value attributed to literature is visible in Georgios Vizyinos (1849-1896) prose. Vizyinos who

C. Cavafy

Poetry recovers a new start with Constantine Cavafy (1863-1933), a poet born in Alexandria (Egypt) where he lived making a living as a low level public servant. He used to work meticulously on his verses and print periodically at his own expenses the so-called "loose leaves" introducing some of his poems to an audience he selected himself. These publications form a kind of chronological (and sometimes thematic) units. Their reprints present notable changes as some poems are re-worked, others are eliminated and replaced by new ones. The canon of Cavafy's works includes 107 poems composed in the course of more than 35 years. Scholars divide them in three categories: philosophical, historical and sensual, where the homosexuality of the poet emerges in the middle of melancholy

overtones and a wording that reveals while it conceals. This parallel game of introverted-extroverted approach is a constant parameter in Cavafy's style. His poems bring in mind Fernando Pessoa's (a Cavafy's contemporary) works full of desasosiego (desillusionment). Cavafy belongs to a particular literary category that emerged in the first quarter of the 20th century and had no continuation: this is a "stand alone" category in which one could put Kafka and Joyce, Kavafy and Pessoa.

Kavafy's poetry is in full contrast with that of Angelos Sikelianos (1884-1951), another lyrical poet of the same period that succeeded in moving romanticism beyond traditional boundaries thanks to his recreation of ancient Greek myths and legends in elegies, long poetical

A. Sikelianos

compositions and theatrical plays that he liked to call "tragedies". A visionary that brought back to life the Delphic celebrations (1927), an effort that has been acclaimed but collapsed financially.

After the Paris Commune (1871) and the emergence of socialism, the vision of a just, moral and equalitarian society took a literary shape. This is the canvas for the poems and the fiction works of Kostas Varnalis (1884-1974) who faithful to the communist ideals has been rewarded with the Lenin Prize. Varnalis is the representative of a literary movement that brings to the forefront the social injustice, the bourgeois ideology decline, the expectations nourished by socialism and the revolution. In the same framework, Konstantinos Theotokis (1872-1923) born in Corfu in a wealthy and aristocratic family, an admirer of Nietzsche, is a true believer and a systematic promoter of socialism (and communism). His novels describe in a realistic way and in a vigorous style that reminds Tolstoi or Dostoievsky the ups and downs of exemplary characters whether they belong to the upper social strata or to a particular Greek proletariat living mainly in the country.

Nikos Kazantzakis (1883-1957), a prolific and versatile writer, traveller and poet, a follower of Henri Bergson's theories on the elan vital, is sensitive to the social problems and hails the Bolshevik Revolution, but turns soon to a metaphysical and existentialistic search of a spiritual apotheosis, the result of a contin-

N. Kazantzakis

uous struggle to overcome the "earthy" bonds. Although Kazantzakis tries to give a solid form to a philosophical system out of these ideas (his book Salvatores Dei published in 1927 encompasses his philosophy), he has been internationally recognised thanks to his novels, Zorba the Greek (1946) being the most widely known. However, all his novels (and in fact all his books) are supposed to be a by-work of a huge epic of 33,333 verses entitled Odyssey a "remake" of the Homeric epic, Ulysses being a desperado that leaves Ithaca after his return and continues his peregrinations that bring him to complete loneliness climaxing in his death in the South Pole.

Away from this kind of intellectual constructions, Kostas Karyotakis (1896-

1928), an obscure public servant who committed suicide in strict obedience to his pessimism and his visceral rejection of social rules that degrade the individual and lead him to despair, is the link between the declining romanticism and the modernistic trends. A genuine representative of intimism and decadence, a follower of Jean Moreas and Jules Laforgue, he created a poetic fashion that survived for a long time and is perceptible even in contemporary poets' works.

Greek literature enters modernism with the so-called "generation of 1930". The traumatic experiences of the First World War, of the defeat of the Greek army in the war with Turkey in 1922 that pushed more than 1,5 million refugees from Asia Minor into the Greek peninsula inhabited then by 6 million inhabitants, the emergence of a liberal bourgeois class influenced by Western Europe's cultural and civilisation developments, the formation of an urban proletariat, these are the main drivers that opened new horizons to literature. Giorgos Seferis (1900-1971) is the leading figure of this generation. A career diplomat, very demanding for himself, crafting with patience and accuracy his verses, he was awarded the Nobel Prize in 1963. Carefully studying and putting forward the Greek historical and literary heritage, he is aware of the contribution of high calibre authors of his time. An admirer and translator of T. S. Elliot and Pound, Valery and Michaux, he adapted and incorporated new literary trends in his poetry collections published in 1961 in a final edition under the simple title Poems. Seferis declared in an interview that his ultimate goal was to write simply and he kept this promise. If the first contact gives the impression that he is a difficult poet, his clarte pops up quickly. This is the reason why many of his poems put in music by leading song composers like Manos Hadjidakis, Mikis Theodorakis, Stavros Xarchakos and others have become and remain popular.

If in a way Seferis is close to the surrealists, Andreas Embirikos (1901-1975) is the emblematic figure of surrealism in Greece. Belonging to a wealthy family of ship-owners, he studied in France and introduced psychoanalysis in Greece. His first collection of poems Furnace appeared in 1935 (the same year Seferis published his first verses).

G. Seferis, Nobel prize 1963

A. Embirikos

at the same time the preacher of a dionysiac way of living, where everything leads to the light, to a particular joie de vivre that accepts death as a resurrection in this world we all live in, this world so small and simultaneously so glamorous. These ideas are carefully balanced in his Axion Esti (1960), a poetical composition in a style incantatoire, that gave him international fame and has been widely known thanks to the music of Mikis Theodorakis.

Yannis Ritsos (1909-1997), a gifted versificator, the second Greek Lenin Prize (1977) and a committed communist that lived long years in forced political exile, is the most prolific poet of modern Greek literature. Able to compose a whole collection of poems in few weeks, he plays with all forms, lets himself improvise on a single theme, reverts

The titles of his poems, like "Angels presence in a vapour machine" or "The vibrations of a tie", gave the chance to the literary establishment of that time to jeer and deride the poet. Embirikos continued "like a proud transatlantic vessel his voyage to the land of Beauty" and his work epitomises an idealistic belief in life and a sacred terror of death, both leading to a sensual and cathartic philosophy of being.

Odysseus Elytis (1911-1996), a friend of both Seferis and Embiricos, the second Nobel Prize laureate in 1979, close to the French poetical innovations of the 20th century such as surrealism, the ecriture automatique and the revelation of the subconscious, is an exuberant colourist of words he chooses from the rich tradition of the Greek language and,

Od. Elytis, Nobel Prize 1979

Y. Ritsos

to a rhetoric that sounds like a series of slogans. This lack of robustness (in comparison to Seferis for example) does not mask the fact that Ritsos reserves for himself the role of the bard, fighting for the dignity of the individual.

Looking at Seferis, Embirikos, Elytis, Ritsos, one is tempted to admit that poetry is the main genre in the Greek literature of most of the 20th century. Novels, short stories, theatre plays are there; however, at a distance, they do not have the punch neither the aura of poetry. Prose writing babbles, remains didactic and returns to the same themes: the lament on the death of a peaceful pastoral life, the wounds of the wars and internal political feuds, the uncomfortable sense of lost roots. Stratis Myrivilis (1892-1969), Ilias Venezis (1904-1973), Thanasis Petsalis (1904-1995) belong to this category. Kosmas Politis (1887-

1974) with his fiction Eroica, relating the impetus and dreams of adolescence, and Yannis Beratis (1904-1968) with his quasi-autobiographical novel The wide river that revives the day to day realities of the war in 1940-1941 in the Albanian front, introduce a palpable realism and tangible psychological insights. Michalis Karagatsis (1908-1960) goes a step further and makes carnal love the main driving force of his characters.

The second half of the 20th century is marked by a series of events that left deep wounds in the social fabric: the Second World War, the German Occupation (1941-1945), the Civil War (1945-1949) that came immediately after, the terror imposed by ruthless governments supported by the British and later on by the Americans, the dictatorship of the colonels in 1967, the permanent fight of the Right against the Left are the main characteristics that poisoned public life, resulted in a massive internal immigration from the countryside to the main urban areas and to a more important immigration to all parts of Europe (mainly Germany and Belgium), Australia, Canada and the U.S.A. Literature turned to a litterature engagee approach and style and offered its potential to the objectives of lofty ideals such as fraternity and to values that help humans to live in peace. These tendencies have been established by liberal minded authors (for this reason labelled "communists" and sent to exile, tortured or simply executed) so much so that one comes easily to the conclusion that the Greek literature after 1945 is best represented by the Left (a term that includes practically liberals, communists, anar-

M. Anagnostakis

chists and apolitical authors sympathetic to social questions). In poetry, Manolis Anagnostakis (1925) and Titos Patrikios (1928) represent those that fought for ideals, were disillusioned and preferred to remain on the sideway, alone but not morally defeated. Aris Alexandrou (1922-1978), in his novel The trunk, published in 1974, takes on the same theme: party companions transport a huge trunk and put big efforts to this mission understanding at the end of their odyssey that the trunk is empty. Dimitris Hadjis (1913-1978), a longtime refugee in Hungary and East Berlin, in his collection of short stories The end of our small town (1963) is the sharp witness of treasons and pettiness, a catastrophic mix that kills both innocent and criminal people. Stratis Tsirkas (1911-1975) in his trilogy Lost cities (1960-1965), better known under the title of the French translation Cites a la derive that has been awarded the "Best Foreign Book Prize", describes in detail the historical background in the Middle East (1941-1944), in which the Greek expeditionary army plays a secondary role. Many critics consider Tsirkas's trilogy as the first Greek novel, as the fiction part is in balance with the psychological portraits of the characters, the rhythm is sustained and the interest of the reader remains constant.

After the fall of the dictatorship of the colonels in 1974 and the re-establishment of a democratic regime, Greece becomes a more open (and permissive) society, joins the Common Market (the European Union of today) and struggles to modernise. Literature seems surprised by these changes and makes efforts to adapt. It will need a generation before a new group of authors appears. This group, composed by very young people, male and female, rejecting the traumas and wounds of the past tries to talk about the present. Although this trend has been visible in all literatures around the world, it acquires a particular significance in Greece as it coincides with consumerism that understands writing and book buying as a consumer move without any idealistic or political projection.

K. Dimoula

Literature explodes in this context: writing in itself becomes an opposition act in the sense of a revolt against an ill-defined "tradition" or "establishment" that seems to be an obstacle towards justice and happiness. Writers like Petros Tatsopoulos or Vanguelis Raptopoulos, in their early 20s by 1980, bring forward desoriented youngsters that remain available for "good causes" and live in their own world, away from the adults, supported by their own jargon that is a form of being and by their own codes of conduct that constitute the only viable alternative in a world they refuse to understand. Faidon Tamvakakis, belonging to the same age group and to the same literary trend that could be called "the small group of not very seriously angry young men but very seriously uneasy young men", a translator of Fowles and close to the British culture and literature, is a remarkable observer of a paralysed and stagnated society that does not allow adolescence to flourish.

If these are clear signs of a literary "search of the self" within a changing environment, writers that have been in the market by 1960 form the category of those that had a more or less direct experience of the political and social upheavals during the period that followed the Civil War (1945-1949). Kostas Taktsis with his novel The third wedding gives a wide gallery of characters that live in a purgatorio between the satanic innocence of angels and the heavenly corruption of the devils. Menis Koumandareas explores the petty bourgeois world and, like an entomologist, describes the small quakes that brought this world down. His novel The beautiful lieutenant is an exercise balancing style and the uncomfortable (almost erotic) relationship between two men. On the other hand, Thanasis Valtinos is a witness of war episodes, a memorialist of things forgotten (like large scale immigration or women emancipation timid steps in the 60s). Using a concise style, he outlines human characters of lost identities. In the same context, Yorgos Ioannou is the observer of a city, Thessaloniki, the second biggest urban centre in Greece: thanks to short stories, always written in "I" form, he builds a mosaic whose small pieces disappear in an ever expanding fresco, where the city becomes an ever demanding companion.

While prose redefines itself and finds out ways and means to proceed, wasting quite often time and stamina in unfortunate imitations of Kafka, Joyce or Proust, mixing internal monologue to surrealistic-like situations that seem des actes gratuits, poetry retreats in a kind of esoteric lament and, in the best cases of introverted melancholy, very rarely peppered by satire or irony. Scholars talk about the "generation of the 80s" that follows the "generation of the defeat",

meaning the generation of poets that somehow belonged to the Left and witnessed the Left's defeat after the Civil War. The poets of the 80s, bringing forward their voices in a kind of unisono, form a compact mass without leading figures.

From this mass have popped up young poets in the 90s that promise to rejuvenate poetry. Their task will not be easy as fiction is creaming (and pre-empting) the market. Young fiction writers obtain more and more often a thundering success with their first book and create ephemeral fashions that are translated into future best-selling expectations, normally not fulfilled. Literature seems a kind of short distance running competition, in which men and women, all having the same technique, attract the applause of the public. If many critics and dilettanti complain that this is a bad omen for the years to come, the reality is that Greek literature is geared to the present. The phenomenon is not specific to Greece. Supposing that it marks the coming of a new area, one has to be confident: as Andreas Embirikos said, "we are all within our future".

MUSIC

By A. Deffner

The global reputation of Modern Greek music rests largely on the work of Manos Hadjidakis and Mikis Theodorakis. Albums containing Byzantine music have also been released. However, the field in which Greece has made the most important international contribution is classical music.

Music is possibly the most popular cultural activity of the Greeks. It is connected to the historical importance of the song and to the popularity of musical expression through dancing. Although concerts are largely concentrated in the three largest cities (primarily Athens, secondarily Thessaloniki and Patras), in recent years there have been attempts at decentralisation, mainly through the policy of the National Cultural Network of Cities and of the Domain of Culture. Music has also continuously played a central role in rural Greek life, since in every region, dance and song are community activities.

Regional infrastructure. The 13 regions of Greece have their own musical institutions (notably choirs and town bands) most of which have a long tradition and still contribute to the active musical life at the local level. There are 81 town bands and their most intense concentration (i.e. the expression of the

The Athens Music Hall "Megaron"

connection of the absolute number with the population) is observed in the Ionian Islands. Some possible explanations lie in the musical history of the area (town bands have often produced creators and performers; and the "Ionian school" has exerted its influence on Greek music), isolation from the mainland, and the general cultural climate (largely attributed to foreign occupation). For example, between 1807 and 1814, Corfu was occupied by the French, and between 1814 and 1864, by the British. Greece's 158 choirs are most highly concentrated in the Northern Aegean (data from 1987).

Education. Music is taught in the 213 recognised music conservatories, of which only one is public. There are also 146 music schools. Of these conservatories and schools, 44.8 percent are located in provincial towns. A recent phenomenon is the growth of the teaching of traditional music.

Sales. Data concerning the number of albums sold between 1991 and 1994 show a decline in sales (7.9 compared to 6.3 million) and a greater percentage of Greek repertoire (48.8 percent compared to 59.1 percent). The distribution of premium CDs and cassettes by newspapers and periodicals is significant (4.7 million). The largest percentage is for CDs (92.4 percent) and for the Greek repertoire (56.3 percent). According to sales data for 1995, Greece has the highest proportion of indigenous music in Europe (56 percent). In the last five years, the main factor that has affected the decrease of sales is a combination of the growth of CD-Recorders (mainly incorporated in personal computers) with the possibility of downloading songs from the Internet.

Traditional music. The country is remarkable for both the abundance and the variety of its traditional music. Greek music has developed over many centuries and has been subject to numerous and varied historical and geographical influences. Ancient Greek music, Byzantine and church music, for example, provide a whole series of distinctive musical traditions.

There is also a long tradition of traditional rural music connected with the Greek War of Independence against the Turks (1821-1829). The type of folk songs is defined mainly according to the place of origin: Islands (Crete, Ionian Islands), Epirus (a region in the northwest), Mani and Kalamata (in southern Peloponnese), Macedonia and Thrace (in the north and north-east). The doyenne of folk music is Dora Stratou (who is also the director of a dance company), and in 1997 she released, with her musical ensemble Panegyris, the album "Greek folk favourites" on the "Tradition" label.

A form of urban traditional music with strong links to the refugees from the disaster of Asia Minor is the "rembetiko" song with the "bouzouki" as its characteristic instrument. The audience for "rembetika" gradually broadened after the Second World War and these songs were especially popular in the 1970s.

Since the Second World War many of the younger composers have sought inspiration in both rural and urban traditional music. One of the most prominent figures is Dionysis Savvopoulos who has made an original synthesis using elements from "rembetiko", rural music, and Western rock/pop music.

Folk dance groups are deeply rooted in regional culture. There exist 580 such groups, the largest concentration being in Epirus, with its long cultural tradition

Popular types of music. At present, the four most popular types of Greek music are: dance music with elements mainly from eastern music, "art" music, pop music with elements mainly from western music, and rock music. The rock scene is particularly strong in Thessaloniki and a general tradition continues going back to the 1960s and including groups known abroad (e.g. "Socrates"). Various rock clubs have played an important role in the spread of rock music in Greece. These are mainly located in Athens, although Thessaloniki has Mylos, an exciting venue in a converted mill.

The jazz tradition is also important. The group "Sphinx" released the first Greek jazz album in 1979. Certain musicians have released albums on foreign labels, the most prominent examples being the pianist Sakis Papadimitriou, the clarinettist/saxophonist Floros

Floridis (who composed the soundtrack for Jeanine Meerapfel's film "Anna's summer" in 2002), and the guitarist Nana Simopoulos. Many Greek musicians have also collaborated with musicians from other countries, either in concerts or in albums. The most recent trend has been ethnic jazz, i.e. the incorporation of elements of world music in jazz. An important role in the spread of jazz in Greece has been played by the very active, albeit limited in number jazz clubs, especially in Athens.

A recent development is the growing popularity of world music, something that is typically expressed in the holding of the prestigious WOMAD (World of Music, Arts and Dance) international festival in Athens both in 2001 and 2002. This was situated in the context of the Cultural Olympiad 2001-2004, an original idea that is combined with the mega-event of the Athens 2004 Olympics.

Popular Singers. The internationally most famous singers live and work abroad: Vicky Leandros, Nana Mouschouri (who is a UNICEF ambassador and was a member of the European parliament between 1994 and 1999), Demis Roussos (a member of the famous Greek group "Aphrodite's Child"). The mezzo-soprano Agnes Baltsa released in 1987 a popular music album containing songs composed by Hadjidakis, Theodorakis, Tsitsanis and Xarhakos (conducted by the latter, who is also the director of the State Orchestra of Greek Music).

In recent years two female singers who have successfully sold records and performed concerts abroad are Eleftheria Arvanitaki and Savina Yannatou. A crossover artist who has an international career, and has been compared to Andrea Bocelli, is Mario Frangoulis; his CD 'Sometimes I Dream was issued by Sony International in 2002 in Europe, America, Asia and Africa, and is considered an artistic and commercial success.

Many Greek singers have collaborated with musicians from other countries, either in concerts or in albums. The leading figure is Maria Farandouri who collaborated with the world famous guitarist John Williams (1971) as well as the Turkish musician Zulfu Livaneli (1982).

Two peculiar figures are the US blues-men Nick Gravenites and Johnny Otis, who are of Greek origin, as are also the Anglo-Cypriot composer/ singer George Michael and the US composer/ guitar player Nicky Skopelitis.

Classical music audience. Western classical music did not gain a foothold in Greece until after the foundation of the independent Greek kingdom (1832). The 19th century composers of the "Ionian school", such as Nikolaos Mantzaros, Spyridon Xyndas and Pavlos Carrer were influenced mainly by Italian music. The establishment of the Athens Conservatory in 1871 was a significant step towards the formation of a national school of music.

Classical music in Greece appeals to a growing minority served mainly by the Concert Halls in Athens (which opened in 1991) and Thessaloniki (which opened in 2002). There also exist various orchestras (State Orchestra of Athens, National Symphony Orchestra of Greek Radio and Television), as well as the National Lyrical Scene, which was founded in 1939 but has operated in the "Olympia" theatre since 1957. In the season 2002-2003 it operated with three stages and a repertoire combining established and relatively unknown works.

The role of the Athens Concert Hall expands beyond the field of music, since in its first five years of operation it has showcased 602 cultural works, organised 957 artistic events, 197 educational programmes, 24 exhibitions/ lectures, and 118 congresses. It has commissioned 59 Greek works and published 338 books. It also has its own orchestra ("Orchestra of the Friends of Music" or "Camerata"), with musicians from many countries and with Alexandre Myrat as its conductor.

In addition to the three largest cities (Athens, Thessaloniki and Patras) there are other cities which have either a long tradition of musical life (Ermoupolis in the island of Syros) or an active musical life (Larissa and Volos in Thessaly, Corfu, Kalamata).

The growth of the listening audience provides better conditions for the growth of the buying audience, such as the small increase of specialised shops in Athens and of the representation of classical music in music shops in general.

Conductors and soloists. There has been a long tradition of internationally renowned Greek soloists and conductors: Gina Bachauer, Vasso Devetzi and Rena Kyriakou (pianists), Irma Kolassi, Yannula Pappas, Elena Souliotis and Nicola Zaccaria (singers). The two figures that constitute landmarks in the international classical music scene are Maria Callas (soprano) and Dimitri Mitropoulos (conductor, pianist and composer).

This tradition has continued in recent years by many artists. They include: Nicholas Economou, Aris Garoufalis, Christodoulos Georgiades, Elena Mouzalas, Dimitri Sgouros and Yannis Vakarellis (piano), Tatsis Apostolides and Leonidas Kavakos (violin), Yannis Vatikiotis (viola), Evangelos Asimakopoulos, Kostas Kotsiolis, Eleftheria Kotzia and Liza Zoi (guitar), Agnes Baltsa, Aris Christofellis, Jenny Drivala, Daphne Evangelatos, Dimitri Kavrakos, John Modinos, Vasso Papantoniou, Kostas Paschalis, Jeannette Pilou, Spiros Sakkas, Teresa Stratas, and Sonia Theodoridou

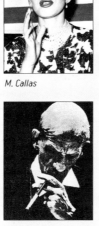

M. Callas

D. Mitropoulos

N. Skalkotas

(singing), Dimitri Agrafiotis, Nikos Athinaios, Miltiades Caridis, Dimitri Chorafas, Byron Fidetzis, John Georgiades and Alexandre Myrat (conducting). Certain performances of most of these artists have been released on LPs and/or CDs.

Composers in the 20th century. There are certain internationally renowned composers whose main work belongs to the 20th century: either to its first half (Manolis Kalomiris, Petros Petridis, Spiros Samaras and Nikos Skalkottas) or to its second half (Theodor Antoniou, George Aperghis, Jani Christou, Dimitri Dragatakis, Yannis Konstantinidis, Arghyris Kounadis, Yiorgos Kouroupos, Anestis Logothetis, Nikos Mamangakis, Yannis Papaioannou, Jean Prodromides, Yiorgos Sicilianos, Dimitri Terzakis, Iannis Xenakis. The majority of these composers (the most prominent being Skalkottas and Xenakis who was also an architect and collaborator of Le Corbusier) form the trend of the avant-garde, and certain of their works have been released on LPs and/or CDs.

Some of the avant-garde composers have shown an

eclectic mind and have written either popular songs-Konstantinidis, Kounadis, Kouroupos, Mamangakis- or music for films. Three examples at the international level are Antoniou for the British/ German film "The Girl from Mani" (1986), Mamangakis for "Heimat" (1985, a 15 hour German film shown also as a television series), Prodromides for the French/ Polish film "Danton" (1982). On the other hand, some composers who have been internationally famous mainly because of their film or television music have also written either classical music or popular songs. The most prominent are Manos Hadjidakis ("Sweet Movie", Yugoslavian/ French/ German film, 1974) who, till his death in 1994, managed and directed his own orchestra ("Orchestra of Colours" which was created in 1989 and still operates today), and Mikis Theodorakis ("Zorba the Greek", 1964, a film which made the "bouzouki" instrument world famous) who has also been occupied with politics. Other important composers, in-

cluding those internationally known mainly for their film music, are Stavros Xarhakos ("Rembetiko", 1983), Yannis Markopoulos ("Who Pays the Ferryman", BBC series, 1978), and Yiorgos Hadjinassios ("Shirley Valentine", British film, 1989). The composer who has been internationally successful lately is Eleni Karaindrou: her music for Theo Angelopoulos' most recent films has been released on the German label ECM.

In 1995 the British record company "Silva Screen" released an album titled "Classic Greek Film Music" which includes some of the most important themes composed by Greek composers for the cinema. A very successful composer, working in Hollywood, is Basil Poledouris. He has been active since 1971 and is of Greek origin.

Two internationally well established figures composing mainly "electronic" music are Yanni (one of his recent best-selling albums is "Live at the Acropolis", 1995, which is also available on DVD,

M. Hadjidakis
M. Theodorakis
E. Karaindrou

"Mythodea", by Vangelis

and he has also composed music for films), and, more importantly, Vangelis. The latter, another member of the group "Aphrodite's Child" has collaborated with Jon Anderson (the singer of the important rock group "Yes"). He has also composed classical music works ("Invisible Connections", 1985) and written music for many films winning a Best Music Oscar for the British film "Chariots of Fire" in 1981. His work 'Mythodea', which was performed live at the Temple of Zeus in Athens in 2001, is also available on DVD. Other awards won by Greek composers are: Best Song Oscar (Hadjidakis for "Ta Pedia tou Pirea" in "Never on Sunday" in 1960), British Academy Award for best music (Theodorakis for the French/ Algerian film "Z" in 1969).

[The composer Thanos Mikroutsikos, who was also the Minister of Culture from 1994 till 1996, released an album in 1995 in which the famous Italian singer Milva sang some of his best songs (in Italian and in Greek). The new age composers Chris Spheeris and Paul Voudouris are of Greek origin and have released many albums, which were sold overseas. The singer/ composer Demetrio Stratos was, till his death, the leader of the Italian avant-garde group Area.]

Foreign composers inspired by Greece. There are also three special cases of notable composers inspired by the music of the Greek Orthodox Church. The first is John Tavener, an English classical composer who has converted to Orthodoxy - one of his latest works released on CD in 1994 is the piece "Melina", composed in memory of Melina Mercouri. The second is the German new age composer and multi-instrumentalist Stephan Micus who released in 1994 an album titled "Athos". The third is Sister Marie Keyrouz who has released various albums in which she performs songs belonging to the Orthodox tradition of the Middle East.

Greek songs in foreign films. Greek songs have been heard lately in various films. In "Pulp Fiction" (1994) the direc-

V. Tsitsanis

tor Quentin Tarantino used "Misirlou" (composed by N. Roubanis in 1941 in the USA). In "Mighty Aphrodite" (1995, a film inspired by ancient Greek tragedy) the director Woody Allen used a song by Stavros Xarhakos and a song by Vassilis Tsitsanis. Hadjidakis's song "The Children of Piraeus" was used in Jonathan Nossiter's film "Sunday" (1997).

ARCHITECTURE

By G.A. Panetsos

Greece is universally known as the cradle of several architectural cultures. Besides the Classical (5th-4th c. B.C.) and the Byzantine (6th-16th c. A.D.), that acquired unprecedented and persisting dissemination westwards and eastwards respectively, one could mention a long succession of architectural traditions, that either emerged or flourished on Greek soil. Among the former one could mention the Minoan (~3000-1400 B.C.), the Cycladic (~1800-1400 B.C.), the Mycenean (~1400-1200 B.C.), the Archaic (8th-6th c. B.C.) and the Hellenistic (3rd-30th c. B.C.), among the latter the Roman (146 B.C. - 323 A.D.) and the Early Christian (4th-5th c. A.D.).

Due to the Ottoman Occupation (mid 15th c. A.D.), Greece knew architectural retreat and discontinuity. It missed the Renaissance and the subsequent evolution and did not profit from Ottoman architecture either, since this was only marginally spread in Greece, despite the fact that most Ottoman architects and craftsmen, - including Sinan (1490-1588), acknowledged as the greatest among them - were ethnic Greeks.

The appearance of a pluralistic and lively vernacular architecture in 18th

The Parthenon,
447-438 b.c.,
Athens

The new Museum of Acropolis projection, Athens

century, somehow re-established continuity. It was however soon superseded by the advent of neoclassicism, that was predictably adopted as the appropriate architectural language of the newly established independent Greek state, in the 1820s. Architects of the stature of K.F. Schinkel, Fr. Gaertner and L. von Klenze, were commissioned to design public building for Athens, as were Th. Hansen, later architect of imperial Vienna, S. Kleanthes (1802-1862), L. Kaftanzoglou (1811-1885) and others.

Early 20th century was marked by the rejection of classicism and historic styles. Vernacular architecture was reappraised by Greek "populist" intellectuals as embodying timeless principles, such as human scale, integration to the landscape, response to climate and lifestyle, correspondence between construction and form. Besides, it played a fundamental role in the evolution of world architecture through its influence on key figures, such as A. Loos and Le Corbusier, who were inspired their "Raumplan" and "Flat Roof/Roof Garden" principles respectively after they had visited the Greek islands.

This kinship of the modernist formal vocabulary to familiar domestic precedents, along with modernism's social agenda, functional priorities, hygienic approach and rejection of costly ornament, at a time of emergency after the influx of 1.5 million refugees from Asia Minor in 1922, may explain the unconditioned acceptance of the modern movement in the '20s and '30s. A group of talented young architects soon emerged: P.N. Djelepis (1894-1976), G.

Kondoleon (1896-1952), N. Mitsakis (1899-1941), K. Panayotakos (1902-1982), I. Despotopoulos (1909-1992), P. Karandinos (1903-1976), B. Douras (1904-1981), S. Papadakis (1906-1993), K. Biris (1907-1990), R. Koutsouris (1901-1997), P. Michailidis (1907-1960), T. Valentis (1908-1982), I. Saporta (1911-1998) and others. They even hosted the major architectural event of the time, the IV CIAM (International Congress of Modern Architecture) in Athens in 1933. They worked successfully for the cultured elite, and the state programmes of urban infrastructure, but failed to set some solid foundations for modernised practice of architecture. The unsettled issues of the time-antiquated building industry and professional rights distribution, flexible ethics, tolerance of illegal construction, lack of a tradition of planning - still remain unsettled.

World War II (1940-44) and the subsequent ferocious civil war (1946-1949) caused enormous human and material loss and crashed the social and productive infrastructure, particularly of the countryside. The proposals of K. Doxiadis to put priority in the reconstruction and the revitalisation of the provinces, were ignored and thus a major imbalance was established between Athens and the rest of the country. The emergence of the small building company that managed construction and development without own capital, personnel and apparatus, through the system of "antiparoche" - acquiring the right to develop a site in exchange for developed

The Erechteion, 421-405 b.c., Athens

Byzantine "Katholikon", 1300, Chilandari Monastery Mount Athos

property in the projected building - and the development of an aggressive "contractor's culture" that discouraged any search for quality and innovation beyond immediate profit, also defined the conditions of post-war reconstruction. It was against this unfavourable background that Greek architecture re-emerged.

The early '50s are marked by the dominant presence of D. Pikionis (1887-1968). Influenced by the "populist" intellectuals thought, Pikionis was attracted by an a-historical study of Greek and oriental artistic patterns which led him to the formulation of a theory of global unity in art. He had already produced two small but important buildings: a

subtle essay on the vernacular and the reconstruction of an antique house. He also experimented with modernism, producing the outstanding Pefkakia Elementary School (1932). Dissatisfied, he rejected modernism, in favour of a personal neo-vernacular idiom. This developed slowly. It was not until the '50s that it acquired full coherence. In the Philothei House (1954), we can speak of a highly original, processed representation, not a reproduction, of vernacular architecture.

In 1951, Pikionis was commissioned to design the landscaping of the Acropolis surroundings. Unbothered by issues of function, he concentrated on the visual and experiential aspects of architecture, so as to produce meaning out of an unprecedented collection of materials, objects, and forms, of emblematic nature and purposefully unidentified origin, wisely unfolding over the site in an expression of timelessness. Due to this work, probably the single most important one in 20th century Greek architecture, Pikionis was later recognised as a pioneer of architectural regionalism worldwide.

The late '50s and '60s were a period of unparalleled growth, coupled with a will for development and progress, after a long period of depression and conservatism. In architecture too, despite shortcomings, this also was an era of true achievement. It was then that the great majority of recent public buildings of merit were produced, along with quite a few private ones of importance. Greek architecture attracted international attention and a few Greek architects, based in Greece or abroad - like K. Doxiadis (1913-1970), I. Xenakis (1921-2001), later an avant-garde music composer, G. Kandylis (1913-1994), A. Provelenghios (1914-1999) - even acquired international reputation. Others - like S. Papadakis, I. Saporta and I. Despotopoulos - launched international careers.

A. Konstantinidis (1913-1993) confined his career within Greek territory, but equally acquired wide recognition. Reality, involving limited available technology and economic means, recognition of the sublime presence of the landscape and the celebration of frugal sincerity of popular lifestyle was a primary factor in his architecture. Konstantinidis also looked to the vernacular, not for patterns or forms, but for principles. He gradually distilled his design and building method into a coherent, rational system, that could be, and indeed was, applied unaltered to all building types,

Pikionis, Children's Playground, Philothei, Athens, 1961-64

Pikionis, paving details, Acropolis surroundings landscaping, 1951-57

Pikionis, Lombardiaris church and pavilion, Acropolis surroundings landscaping, 1952-57

*Th. Chansen,
The Academy of
Athens, 1859*

from workers housing to public build-ings, such as museums. He consistently worked within this system, involving a standard concrete-frame bearing struc-ture with non-bearing infill, or load-bearing stone walls, carrying a flat slab,

*Th. Chansen-Fl. Boulanger, The Zappeion Hall,
Athens, 1874-88*

in a straightforward and sincere manner, until he felt that the system had been perfected. In 1978 he willfully withdrew from practice maintaining however an acute and finally self-destructive critical activity.

Among Konstantinidis' outstanding works one should mention the Xenia Hotels (1958-64), workers housing in Athens, Thessaloniki and Herakleion (1955-57), private residences in Athens (1961), Philothei (1961), Vouliagmeni (1961), Anavyssos (1962) and Aegina (1974, 75), and the Museums of Ioanni-na (1965) and Komotini (1967).

Another version of the same reality, less critical but thoroughly progressive and optimistic, inspired the generation of architects that emerged in the '50s. It can be said that a cross-section of its ori-entations and achievements, at their

L. Kaftanzoglou, The Polytechneion
(Technical University), Athens, 1861

best, lies in the work of N. Valsamakis.

N. Valsamakis (1924-), subverted the commercial cliches of the period already in his Semitelous street apartment house (1951). The typical pierced outer wall receded behind an abstract gridded plane defining a continuous loggia. The plan was cleaned from any redundant complexities or concessions to pretentious formality. Materials, colours and textures, selected so as to enhance the buildings' articulation within the frame of a reserved plasticity, replaced the established uniformity of off-white plaster. After testing and expanding this vocabulary of sensuous warmth in a series of paradigmatic apartment houses Valsamakis focused on a search for spatial experience, which was fully achieved in his outstandingly elegant houses in Anavyssos (1961, 1961) and Philothei (1963). Under the influence of Mies van der Rohe's planar composition, structure is minimised and through the use of full height sliding glass doors of unusual dimensions, total continuity between interior space and cantilevered verandahs is obtained. By that time he had already developed a particular spatial scheme, which accommodated both functional and visual requirements, an architectural type of his own, that he would apply from then on, analtered to this day, to designs of widely ranging scales.

Beyond the '60s, constantly within this frame, the architecture of Valsamakis continued to evolve. A process of elimination of projections and variety of materials and textures led to a highly original minimalistic idiom that was applied in residences in Philothei (1971), Kefalari (1972), Sounion (1974) and elsewhere, as well as, in the Amalia Hotel at Olympia (1977).

The late '70s and '80s evolved as period of exploration of the possibilities of contextualism. Essentially along the path of the previous decade, but with an appropriately varied iconography, sometimes with post-modernist overtones, that only intensified the importance of the constant typological reference, Valsamakis experimented with versions of classicism and the vernacular with consistently successful results. This experience of discipline allowed a subsequent revisiting of previous achievements, which now acquire a new intensity, that only re-affirms Valsamakis's position as a protagonist, until well into the '2000s.

Among the numerous key-figures of this distinguished generation and within the inevitably reductive limits of a brief survey, one should also mention: T. Zenetos, (1926-1977) for his technological refinement, innovative design strategies, typological research and anticipation of a totally controlled environment, I. Liapis, (1922-1992) / E. Scroubelos (1921-) for the introduction of Le Corbusier's brutalist idiom and its

P. Michailides-Th. Valentis, Averof Residence, Kifissia, Athens, 1930's

original manipulation in evocative public buildings and places, like the Piraeus Port Passenger Terminal, the Zahariou Foundation and the Kalavryta Monument, K. Dekavallas, (1926-) for his rationally and meaningfully organised apartment buildings, residences and resorts, his distinguished bank interiors and his heading of the mature reconstruction of the Santorini settlements (1956), V. Grigoriadis (1932-), among others, for his innovative church buildings, P. Mylonas (1915-) and D. Fatouros (1928-) for their multifaceted activity that combined practice, teaching and innovative research, D. Zivas (1928-), among others, for the urban regeneration project of the Old City of Athens, A. Simeon/D. Kollaros/S. Kondaratos (1933-) for their architectural and urban designs and their insightful theoretical contributions, J. Koutsis (1933-), Th. Papayannis (1932-), G. and E. Manetas (1937- ,1939-) and others.

Two new generations emerged in the '60s. Quickly established through architectural competitions, their members shared the solid education offered at the school of Athens and enjoyed the last period of certainty about the authority of modernism. Corbusian brutalism was their preferred idiom. Among them one should mention K. Papaioannou/K. Fines, L. Kalivitis/G. Leonardos, K. Gartsos, K. Krokos, T. & D. Biris, E. Papayannopoulos and I. Vikelas (1931-) who was instrumental in the develop-

A. Konstantinidis, hotel Xenia, Mykonos, 1960

A. Konstantinidis, private residence, Athens, 1961

ment among others of high-rise buildings in Athens and later of high quality commercial office spaces.

However, the truly radical contribution was that of D. & S. Antonakaki (1933- , 1935-). Despite established values and expressive means D. & S. Antonakaki introduced a strong critical attitude as primary element of their discourse. Pikionis and Konstantinidis can be considered their predecessors, although both of them established their criticism on the premises of tradition. D. & S. Antonakaki seem to equally derive their critical apparatus from such disparate sources as Mies van der Rohe's modular ordering, Le Corbusier's irregular forms and brutalism and the Dutch structuralist mode of organisation, which they integrate into a highly original idiom.

D. & S. Antonakaki quickly proceeded from the "rational" and straight-forward layout of their early works - house at Haidari, Athens (1961) and Chios Archeological Museum (1965) to more complicated devices. The kind of functionally and structurally significant "zoning" that underlies their designs and the use of irregular modular grids in plan and section, allowed for an unprecedented variety and power in the interiors of their works, which holds together, thanks to the introduction of the "pathway", a promenade that unifies individual elements. It was upon this solid canvas, largely unchanged in concept for the last three decades, that the iconography was attached. Initially intentionally plain, textured and materially poor, it gradually accommodated contradiction, acquired richness and a density of elaboration that endowed each one of their projects with a particular intimacy. At the same time the dialectics of public and private are perpetuated within and beyond the building, further enhancing spatial qualities. The solidity of the canvas was also proven by the fact that it is equally operable in such extreme situations as the modest private bungalow and the university campus, particularly in a practice consciously organised on the principle of collectivity. The work of D. & S. Antonakaki domestically widely influential, has been internationally acclaimed as representative of critical regionalism.

Along a similarly thoroughly radical approach the work of N. Kalogeras/P. Koulermos/S. Amourgis addressed crucial issues at unexpected times long before they became shared discourse among architects.

A. Tombazis (1939-), also emerged in the '60s, he approached architecture and practice in a radically different way from that of most of his contemporaries: not as a cultural issue or a question of function and esthetics, but as a way of problem-solving in the sense of engineering, with a strong interest in construction. Probably influenced by his period of assistantship to C. Doxiadis, he opted for the internationally active large-scale practice, where interchange can take place in a generous way. Fascinated by technology, he used it as the principal theme of his works until, at least, the late '70s. In these works, largely consisting of internationally distinguished competition entries, he saw ar-

chitecture as a system and the building as potentially evolving and developing overtime. This approach is clear even in small- or medium-scale works, like private residences, the New Smyrne High School, the outstanding AGET offices, the Difros Apartment Tower, the Athens Law School and others.

In the '70s, following the energy crisis, Tombazis became increasingly interested in solar design. The first outcome of this interest was the house at Trapeza (1977), a pioneering work at an international level. Soon after he had the opportunity to design an entire "solar settlement", in the vicinity of Athens (1979). He gradually took a more integrated approach to the issue. Solar design was replaced by bio-climatic design, and this was established as a primary factor in his architectural practice, resulting even in strongly contextual approaches in Greek or international projects, that previously were out of its scope. He is currently established as one of the world's authorities in the field.

The year 1967 was that of the establishment of Architecture in Greece by O. Doumanis, still published and the leading greek architectural review, a remarkable achievement, particularly by greek standards. It was also the year of the establishment of a military dictatorship and a convenient point in time to signify the end of the '60s "spring". This however did not come until 1972-73, after the international energy crisis. At that time architecture was still widely per-

*N. Valsamakis, tourist complex,
Kos island, 1994*

ceived mainly as technique and not also as an ideological practice. It was too abstract to be censored and the regime too short-lived to produce any kind of official architecture. It did however have some long-term consequences: the paradoxical recession of architecture from the public to the private realm, a condition from which it has not yet recovered, the nourishment of speculation in the building sector through excessive land development and minimal control and, finally, the rise of political populism that persisted for at least two decades and hindered many attempts of progress and reform, among others in architecture.

The collapse of the military regime in 1974 was followed by conditions no favourable for architecture, particularly

when accompanied by a persistent economic crisis, as was the case in Greece. Within the architectural community, this change gave rise to maximalistic and radical political involvement, which largely discredited architecture as "elitist" from within, in favour of "democrat-

*N. Valsamakis, private residence,
Vouliagmeni, Athens, 1997*

T. Zenetos, private residence, Glyfada, Athens, 1961

ic" planning. Formal and typological research was rejected along with "designed" or "learned" architecture. Models were looked for in vernacular or,
even, recent illegal constructions. Despite this dreadful state of confusion, the
work of G. Pantopoulos, D. Diaman-
topoulos/M. Borne, A. Tripodakis, I. Li-
akatas/A. Pehlivanidou and others,
mainly competition entries, emerged as
visions with clarity and originality and
asserted their already independent position against the architecture of the '60s.

The '80s started with a major crisis
in the building sector and an unprecedented shock in the profession. The
total debasement of professional examinations, after the transfer of their responsibility from the University to the
Technical Chamber of Greece, made
possible the entrance of almost four
thousand of previously considered in-

competent graduates, coming mainly
from low-rank international universities. Soon after, due to political clientelism, many of them entered public administration. The number of architects,
already quite inflated, doubled within
three years, causing serious changes in
many aspects of the profession. The architect was no longer the imaginative
artist/engineer catering mostly to the
well-off, but the jobless relative catering to the broader family. Architectural
services became available to all segments of Greek society for the first time
and architecture was disseminated
widely - or was it not architecture any
more?

This series of subversions coincided
with a period of major revisions in architecture internationally. The rejection
of modernist dogmas, a new critical approach, a new meaningful attention to

form and memory, a new consciousness of the authority and the limitations of architecture were characteristic of the time. In Greece, where widespread conservative populism and facile regionalism of the '70s could not easily withstand the new progressive elitism coming mostly from architects active internationally, this evolution acquired the form of a major challenge. In the realm of theory, this took the form of two seminal papers by D. Porphyrios and A. Christofellis, published in Art and Design in Greece, an influential review also published by O. Doumanis, in 1979, and an unprecedented exhibition entitled "Trends in Contemporary Architecture" in the National Gallery of Athens, curated by M. Kaltsa, P. Nicolacopoulos and S. Rogan, that introduced major figures of international avant-garde of the time to the Greek public.

The publication of a thick volume on "Modern Greek Architecture (1830-1980)" by D. Filippides, following that by A. Antoniades (1979) and two critical historical essays, stirring issues of ideology (1987) and public architecture (1984) by H. Fessas-Emmanonil, among others, mainly in Architecture in Greece, adopted a more moderate but equally penetrating attitude.

Architectural education, conducted exclusively in the State Schools of Athens (established in 1917) and Thessaloniki (established in 1957) did not manage to respond creatively to the successive challenges. Trapped between radical rhetorics and conventional practice, within a social context that oscillates between practicality, ostentation and greediness, they took a defensive position that prevented absorbing new tendencies and accommodating innovative ideas and individuals, despite

J. Liapis-I.Scroubelos, sea passenger terminal, Pireus, 1964

increasing uneasiness, and some important - but isolated - efforts towards modernisation and openness.

Largely, beyond the world of academia, the shaky ground allowed for new expression and experimentation, which however remained outside mainstream Greek architecture. A. Christofellis (1946-1991), a professor in Milan, assumed a strongly intellectual approach, and based on history, aimed at an elaborate representation of tectonics as language and memory. S. Rogan (1950-)introduced the conceptual approach, as starting point of the design process (beyond function or construction), also in projects of urban scale, often using architecture itself as a theme. A, Altsitzoglou/I. Koukis developed a highly individual syntax that involved individualistic spatial exercises even in small-scale projects. A. Samaras (1949-) instilled formality and rigour to upper-scale residential and office building typology and sincerely promoted theoretical interchange. B. Ioannou/T. Sotiropoulos/A. Van Gilder proceeded to a refined and opulent minimalism after a period of post-modern classicism. The Alalitos group invested their competition entries, with a version of the purist vocabulary of Valsamakis and Italian Post-Modern Rationalism with recognizable but also innovative public character. N. Theodosiou, probably the only true post-modernist, adopted a particular version of eclecticism that he carried through with exceptional coherence.

The involvement of distinguished Greek architects, settled abroad, provided opportunities for synchronic evolution between Greek and the international discourse. E. Zenghelis (1937), an influential and established figure of the world avant-garde already since the '70s, founded a branch of OMA (Office for Metropolitan Architecture, Koolhaas/Zenghelis), his London firm, in Athens in 1981 (later took the form of Gigante/Zenghelis) and applied the multiple facets of his unsentimental contextualism and unrelenting modernism to innovative projects of various sizes and locations. D. Porphyrios (1949-), a central figure in architectural theory and a protagonist of the classical revival internationally, based in London, designed a house and an office building in Athens, and later a small settlement on the island of Spetses, in a plain and elegant version of neo-classicism, seen not as yet another style, but as a representation of building technique. P. Koulermos (1933-1999) already mentioned as a '60s emergent, active in California and Italy, designed several buildings for the newly established University of Crete and the series "Twelve House Versions in the Hellenic space" of strong poetic aim, all inspired by the genius loci, (the spirit of the place), history and memory, and appropriately rendered in an abstracted purist idiom. One should also mention D. Manikas of Vienna, S. Polyzoides of Los Angeles and Y. Tsiomis (1944-)of Paris, who provided new perspectives within the established tradition of Greek architecure. Last but not least, A. Tzonis, teaching at Harvard and later at Delft, contributed detailed discussions of the notion or regionalism and the classical architectural syntax, and the fundamental critical essay on the architecture of D & S. Antonakis, which, among others, established the - only recently challenged - lineage Pikionis-Konstandinidis-(Fatouros)-Antonakis in Greek regionalism.

Some off-springs of this lineage that emerged at this period, enhanced their reputation in the year that followed. D. Issaias/T. Papaioannou (1955 / 1953) absorbed the syntactic lessons of Konstandinidis and influences from the '60s brutalists into a well-balanced "realist" architecture, relying on shared typological experience and the sublimation of "low" technology, particularly in the case of public buildings. M. Souvatzides (1946-) gradually adapted the standard

C. Dekavalas-Th. Argyropoulos, Deinocratous street apartments, Athens, 1960-62

brutalist idiom - exposed concrete frame and textured infill - to the needs of individual expression and environmental responsibility, without concession to the anticipated power of his imagery. P. Babalou/A. Noukakis and G. Triantafyllou built their idioms as developments of that of D. & S. Antonakaki.

P. Mylonas, Mount Parnes Hotel, Athens 1963

Beyond the forementioned attempts at innovation and the dominance of N. Valsamakis, D & S Antonakis and A. Tombazis, the '80s, were the period of consolidation for the work of T. & D. Biris, and soon afterwards, probably in the early '90s, of K. Krokos.

T. & D. Biris (1942- , 1944-2002) emerged in the late '60s. Partners in the office of Prof. K. Biris, their father, they had a series of outstanding works to their credit already by the early '80s. In these works - the Livadia Court of Justice, the Konitsa Dormitories, the Nea Smyrna High School, the Zea Recreation Complex, the short, but significant sequence of houses in Ekali, Polydrosso and Politeia, all Athenian suburbs, and others - influences of the triumphant '50s brutalism of Le Corbusier and the positivism of J. Despotopoulos, were absorbed into a coherent and rigorous tectonic language of their own, that attracted quite a few followers, among which one could mention Christodoulou/Dimopoulou/ Saiti/ Stathopoulos.

The establishment of this language, along with challenges from their already long academic experience and the work, theory and moral attitude of A. Konstandinidis resulted in their exclusive focusing on the issue of public architecture, understood in its entire spectrum, from the permanent civic institution building to the temporary tensile tent. Their concept of the "central social nucleus" was consistently applied in a series of distinguished competition entries, during the '80s. Absolutely none of these was realised in a lamentable proof of the administration's neglect and ignorance. Several of these outstanding projects reach far beyond mere response to programme, budget and site. The celebration of the "spontaneous" sheet metal shed in the Olympic Covered Swimming Pool Complex (1984) or the monumental glazed pergola over the natural sloping rocky site that constitutes their New Acropolis Museum (1991) are powerful poetic references to the mythology of archetypal conditions of building and living, persisting in Greek architectural culture.

K. Krokos (1941-1998), followed a radically different track. An early assistant of I. Liapis, and influenced by artists and intellectuals, he soon rejected modernism as both a style and a cultural project, on the basis of its nurturing facility and even vulgarity, and discarding values of the past. In a manner reminiscent of Pikionis, he turned to vernacular architecture, not that of the countryside, but the urban vernacular neoclassicism, that had shaped the Greek towns he knew in his youth, and that he associated with a particular middle-class warmth and sincerity. He extended this tradition back to ancient Greek atrium houses, in which he looks less for models, precedents or even principles, than he does for spatial experience, as modulated by the sense of time, light and material, to be reproduced in an architecture of memory. This memory

D. & S. Antonakakis,
private residence,
Athens, 1983

D. & S. Antonakakis, Technical
University of Greece, Hania, 1987

A. Tombazis, solar energy village, Pefki,
Athens, 1978-79

Tombazis, office building, Athens 1997-98

even includes and sublimates undistinguished half-finished or abandoned recent buildings, particularly their structural composition, consisting in a regularly spaced concrete frame, filled with plain brickwork.

This combination, always superbly hand-finished, and accompanied by integrally colored and polished stucco surfaces, thick marble, colored glass, and bronze metalwork, is applied to private and public buildings alike. Among the latter, one should mention the museum of Byzantine Culture in Thessaloniki, where "beautiful" and "sublime" elements, coming respectively from the classical and byzantine tradition, are combined in a highly individualistic composition. Premiated in a 1977 architectural competition, its construction started only in 1990 and was not terminated until 1994, in a manner again indicative of public (lack of) effort for architecture.

The state of Greek architecture in the '90s was largely defined by the persisting and multifaceted crisis in the profession and the architectural education and the total absence of any policy in search or in support of architecture.

Despite this unfavourable background, thanks to the preparation of the '80s, the emergence of "an interesting group of youngsters, ..., whose mouthpiece is the journal Tefchos" has been noted by Vittorio Gregotti, a world-reputed critic, already since 1992. Product of post-modern liberality and inter-national interchange, often educated and/or active in major, mainly Anglo-Saxon schools, they felt free not to take sides with any of the established recent local traditions: vernacular, critical regionalist, brutalist or modernist, although a deep appreciation of the work of Valsamakis and Zenetos is clear. Mostly confined to private commissions of modest scale, they have developed new versions of the residential typology initiated by D. &. S. Antonaki, responsible to evolving family structures and lifestyles, and retail and office interiors in the manner of enclosed public spaces, working critically with architecture as discipline/continuity/ rupture or experience/instant/event.

Notable contributions to this pluralistic discourse have been made by P. Davlandi / C.W. Lo (also an internationally acknowledged furniture designer), the Anamorphosis team (N. Georgiadis, C. Kakogiannis, T. Mamalaki, V. Zitonoulis), C. Diakomidou/N. Haritos, G. Foucas/C. Matrakidou, E. Gigante, Th. Kanarellis, M. Kokkinou/A. Kourkoulas (architects of the significant Mechaniki office complex), P. Kokoris, C. Kontozoglou, N. Ktenas, Ch. Bougadelis, P. Nicolacopoulos, G. Panetsos, A. Patsouris/K. Vassilarou, Ch. Papoulias (also active in Slovenia), D & L Potiropoulou, Z. Samourka, A. Spanomaridis/G. Zachariades of Athens, M. Papanikolaou/R. Sakellaridou and K. Tsigarida of Thessaloniki, K. Tsakalakis, N. Skoutelis/F.

A. Tombazis, Difros appartments, Athens, 1973-75

Zanon of Crete and others, all born between 1953 and 1963.

Being essentially the first generation of Greek architects with serious theoretical interests and apparatus, they re-established public discourse among architects and beyond, through lectures, exhibitions, publications and film, in an effort of a new understanding of architecture not as technique, but as an aspect of culture. Among the important theoretical and critical contributions were those by Y. Simeoforidis (1955-2002) (responsible among others for the renewal of the journal of the Architects' Association and active internationally), J. Peponis and P. Tournikiotis (influential faculty in Athens), E. Constantopoulos (co-editor of the London review 9H and also a designer), G. Tzirtzilakis (also an art-critic, co-editor of Tefchos with Y. Simeoforidis, C. Papoulias and T. Koubis), V. Petridou, V. Colonas, K. Patestos and the somehow younger A. Antonas and Z. Kotionis.

Further along the same path, the emerging generation of the (20)'00s, is clearly and consciously estranged from all traditional and even humanistic precedents. Fascinated by the culture of the Metropolis, living in Greece, now a multinational/multicultural country, crossroads between Europe, the Balkans and the Near East, and well adapted to the possibilities of information (and other) technologies, they perceive the city and the undefined territory at its limits, as the only possible landscape for their perspective activity. Among the members of this generation, well-tuned with international novelties, one could mention Y. Aesopos (also a co-founder, with Y. Simeoforidis, of the review Metapolis), A. Angelidakis, , P. Charalambidou, A. Dallas, P. Dragonas/V.Christopoulou, Chr. Loukopoulou/ I. Bertaki/C. Panegyris, K. Manolidis, Th. Moutsopoulos (also a culture, art and architecture critic and writer), N. Nikodimos, M. Filippides (also a cultural critic), the editors of the review A3 E. Kostika, M. Papadimitriou and S. Spiropoulos, M. Papadomarkakis of the newspaper Architectoniki Antilipsi and the late C. Spyrides.

The restless climate of the early '90s has been instrumental in the foundation of the Hellenic Institute of Architecture (EIA) in 1995. An association gathering most of the significant actors of contemporary Greek stage, from Valsamakis to Davlandi, it is seriously active in the promotion and development of progressive architecture, with emphasis on international relations and communication. The invitation of distinguished international speakers, by Chairman N.

Kalogeras and the inauguration (2003) of the new architectural library, greatly enriched by the Doxiadis family bequest (1998) of the K. Doxiadis Library at the School of Architecture in Athens, the regular participation of Greece to the international architectural exhibitions of Venice and Milan, the organization of monographic exhibitions on greek architecturein Frankfurt (DAM), in Roterdam (NAI) and elsewhere, the important exhibitions and other events in Thessaloniki-Cultural Capital of Europe 1997, the multifaceted activity of the Center for Mediterranean Architecture (KAM) in Chania, Crete (founded 1997), under the direction of D. Antonakakis, focusing among others on the notion of "Mediterraneity" and the relation of architecture to the rest of cultural production, and the foundation (1999) and rapid growth of three Schools of Architecture in Pa-

K. Krokos, private residence, Halkidiki, 1993

T. & D. Biris, Company offices, Athens 1998

tras, Volos and Xanthi, testify to the new vitality of Greek Architecture.

With the exception of the Architecture Network, that was put forward by the Ministry of Culture in 2001, in order to coordinate and accelerate pace, this vitality, the "promise of the '90s", is totally ignored, if not opposed, by the administration, central and local, which has practically no interest beyond "getting the job done", which is "get it built anyhow" without any attention to environmental impact, quality of design, even of construction. All established processes related to quality, like architectural competitions, open or limited, or selection according to merit, have been practically abolished. The passing of a law introducing a design-build process "exclusively for specialised or urgent works" in 1986, which conveyed the authority of selecting architect and scheme to the contractor, resulted in the ridiculous labeling of all projects as "specialised or urgent", in expenditure beyond initially approved budgets, in strong suspicions of corruption and in low construction quality. It is indicative of the current state of affairs that even prestigious projects -like the Athens and Thessaloniki Concert Halls, the new Athens International Airport and the Athens Subway System- have not been objects of competitions, and that most public projects are allotted through processes in which architecture plays only a negligible role. As far as respect for recent architecture is con-

cerned, it is enough to say that the publicly owned Xenia hotels, by Aris Konstantinidis, are literally falling apart and that the National Bank of Greece, one of the very few patrons of architecture in Greece, oscillates between commissioning M.Botta and his team for its new headquarters and destroying or altering beyond recognition many of the most worthy branches it developed in the '60s and '70s. The failure to bring to realisation the new Museum of Modern Art in Athens, commissioned from an architect of the rank of I. M. Pei by the V. & E. Goulandris Foundation, several public projects by E. Zenghelis and a series of seaside pavillions by A. Van Eyck, A. Siza, M. Botta, R. Koolhaas and others in Thessaloniki is another facet of the same situation that prolongs a state of backwardness and inertia and sacrifices aspiration and possibilities to established interests and short-sighted prejudice. It is at least hoped that the New Acropolis Museum, by B.Tschumi (2001) will have a different fate.

The Olympic Games 2004, to be held in Athens, were seen by most as no less than the opportunity for a new beginning of architecture in Greece, that would bring it back to the public realm. New construction for athletics and beyond, new infrastructure, new landscapes were envisioned. New public buildings and spaces were being planned. Architectural and historic sites and protected settlements seemed to start being seen not only as objects of preservation, but also as elements of quality to be enhanced. Being a fact that Greece has entered a much needed process of modernization and achievement of quality being for the first time, if not promoted, at least set as a principal policy aim, it was innocently hoped that the heavy legacy of decades and the hardships of the recent past would be overturned. It was considered inevitable - despite resistance - that a new frame of mind would permeate the area of building activity, particularly the part concerning public construction and that the existing deficit in infrastructure, from health and care to transport, education and culture facilities, would be covered in a qualitative manner. It was soon discovered that what was supposed to be the initial planning was totally superficial and unfeasible. It is indicative that, in a city plagued by sprawl, the new Olympic Village was planned -and, sadly, finally built- on virgin, not recycled, land. A lot of time was spent on the necessary amendments which resulted, beyond infrastructure, into a rather modest general scheme of little or no distinction. It is true that extensive urban regeneration projets are in progress in the center of Athens, and that the main archeological area of the city, surrounding the Acropolis, has been largely re-landscaped. It is also true on the other hand

S. Calatrava, mockup of the Katehaki foot-bridge, Athens

that the architects that were involved in the projects have publicly complained that their designs have been abused by several strata of the administration, including the otherwise respected Archeological Council. It had been hoped that urban regeneration would spread to the less privileged areas of the city, which did not come true. Now it is feared that costly cosmetic interventions will only hastily take place. Olympic construction seems also to be lagging far behind expectations. Mostly mediocre design and low construction quality are evident so far. The emblematic additions to the existing Olympic Stadium (1977) by S. Calatrava are hoped to help reverse this image, but construction has yet (3/2003) to be started and the bid has resulted in-

to an unprecedented swelling of the initial budget.

Within this context the long anticipated leap of greek architecture seems to be postponed once again. This has caused a great uneasiness within the profession and has started being discussed more and more widely, last but not least in the serious newsparers. Increasing segments of city-dwellers seem to realize why the quality of their living environment is inadequate and to be interested in promoting ways to improve it. We now know better than ever before the conditions that prevent the mise en architecture of building construction and also their true reasons. It is hoped that this knowledge will be taken advantage of in the near future.

THE VISUAL ARTS

By M. Stephanidis

19th century: in search of a visual identity

The history of the visual arts in Greece has been similar to that of the modern state itself, and has experienced the given relationship between centre and periphery. No sooner had Greece become independent (in 1830) than it began to function as a satellite to specific political or artistic centres elsewhere. This caused its creative artists and their works to be permeated, from an early date, with the mentality of the pupil who wishes to ingratiate himself with the teacher whose authority he respects. When King Othon and his Bavarian entourage arrived to rule Greece, Greek art was subjected to a process of forcible Europeanisation and split in two. On the one hand was the vernacular, post-Byzantine tradition, which continued to be popular among the general public, and on the other was the new ruling class of Phanar Greeks* and scholars, who wished to see a process of "modernisation" and rationalisation of the forms employed. The new dominant idea was given the name "Hellenocentrism", and its ambition was to use the glories of the past to prettify a present that could only be described as miserable. *Neo-classicism*, with the blessing of the Othonian State, became the official interpretation of art and history. The same aesthetics were manifested in the archaising, the purist dialect of Greek called *katharevousa*, "historical" architecture, public statuary consisting of depictions of togaed dignitaries, a "heroic" school of painting which used a romantic style to illustrate the recent liberation from the Ottoman Empire. Other examples include the theatrical genre known as the "comedy idyll", and the first fiction on historical themes. It was seen as imperative that Athens, the new capital, should cease to be a hamlet of Albanian-speaking peasants and don a mantle of ancient glory - or rather, that it should bring itself into line with the image that the entire Western world had shaped of it. It can thus be seen that the ideological and aesthetic problems were largely of an imported nature, though this did not prevent them from affecting artistic creation.

During the Othonian period (1832-1862), classes in drawing and tracing were introduced into schools (1836). In 1840, a Department of Painting was set up in the National Technical University

---

* A small number of rich and well-educated families that served as official translators for the Sublime Porte and Admiralty and later as rulers in the Danubian principalities.

(founded in 1835), whose teaching staff, in 1853-1855, included the Bavarian Ludwig Thiersch, who served as "liaison officer" between Munich and Athens. It would be true to say that throughout the nineteenth century a fertile relationship developed between Greece and Bavaria. It was common for young students at the Technical University to make their way to "Athens on the Isar" - Munich, that is - for their postgraduate studies. There, they became completely assimilated into the prevailing Academic climate. They did however retain distinctive artistic virtues that were all their own. As an example, one might cite Nikolaos Ghizis (1842-1901), who was elected Professor in the *Kunstlerakademie* of Munich, a post in which he served to the time of his death. Ghizis and his fellow-islander (of Tinos) Nikiphoros Lytras (1832-1904) became the twin centres of a group of painters who combined Academic tendencies with advanced technical accomplishments (Constantinos Volonakis, Polychronis Lembesis, Symeon Savvidis, Georgios Iakovidis, and others) and gained the name of the "Munich School". When Iakovidis (1853-1932) returned to Greece he came to occupy a dominant position in the art world, being appointed Director of the newly-founded National Gallery (1900), Professor in the School of Fine Arts (to 1930), and Academician. It is characteristic of the situation that the National Gallery exis-

N. Lytras

ted as an institution from the beginning of the nineteenth century, but did not actually acquire a building in which to house its collections until 1970.

Theodoros Vryzakis (1817-1878), apologist of the Greek War of Independence, *is often seen as the first "art painter" of modern Greece.* Vryzakis' works are illustrations of the struggle for liberty rather than interpretations of it. Although they are moving in their naivete, their approach is entirely devoid of character. Vryzakis stayed on in Munich and was among the founders of the School based there. Yet Munich was not the only source from which this "fustanella painting" emanated. Recent evidence leads to the conclusion that much of this visual historiography can be ascribed to influences from Italy and France. Dionyios Tsokos of Zakynthos (1820-1862), another of the patriotic painters, studied in Venice under Ludovico Lipparini and returned to Greece in 1847.

The progress being made in painting led the Greek state to include works of the visual arts among the exhibits it sent to the World Fairs of Paris (1855) and London (1862), where, indeed, they won awards. At about this time, two associations whose aim was to promote the arts were founded: the Fine Arts Association, and the Hellenic Association of the Sciences and Arts. By the end of the nineteenth century, Greek society felt that it had become European enough to indulge in a little nostalgia for the East and its *mores*, following in the footsteps of the French Orientalists. Among the artists of this tendency were Theodoros Rallis (1852-1909), who had studied with J.L. Gerome, and Iakovos Rizos (1843-1916). Sculpture was evolving in parallel, with Yannoulis Halepas (1851-1938) and Dimitrios Philippotis (1839-1920) as its principal representatives. The biography of Halepas is the stuff of fiction. After studies in Munich, and still in extreme youth, he produced works which combined Neo-classical techniques with realistic observation, but he succumbed to mental illness and disappeared from the artistic scene

for almost half a century, fourteen years of which (1888-1902) he spent in the Corfu Mental Hospital. After 1920, he returned to sculpture, turning out works completely free of Academic influences while at the same time exuding profound spirituality.

20th century: in line with the Western artistic movements

• The first modern steps

Greek art came of age, and attempted to set the boundaries of a national school, in the early twentieth century. Exhibitions of works by both Greek and foreign artists became more common, and the flow of artistic information often went beyond the unambiguously scholarly level. 1901 saw the publication of the first periodical devoted exclusively to the arts. It was called *Pinakothekes* ("Art Galleries"), and its production was timed to coincide with the Olympia Festival at Zappeio Hall. In 1885, there was an exhibition of 400 works of painting, sculpture and icons by 115 different artists. Of equal importance was the exhibition that took place in 1896 on the occasion of the Olympic Games. In 1897, the "Society of the Friends of the Arts" was formed and embarked on the task of promoting a generation of artists whose educational background was European. In 1900, the Society organised an exhibition with participants which included two artists whose names were to become landmarks in twentieth-cen-

K. Parthenis

tury Greek painting: Constantinos Parthenis (1878-1967), exhibiting for the first time, and Georgios Bouzianis (1885-1959). Parthenis was later to become the patriarch of the "national" school of painting. His inquiries set out from the Jugendstil and brought him to Impressionism and Cezanne, in other words, he was the best-informed artist of his day, and he clashed with the Academic establishment of the School of Fine Arts, in which he taught from 1929 to 1948. Another progressive move was the formation, in 1917, of the "Art Group", headed by Nikolaos Lytras (1885-1927). In 1919, the Group held an exhibition in Paris, among whose participants was the important engraver Dimitris Galanis, a friend of Derain, Braque and Picasso and a member of the French Academy. The nineteenth-century painters Ioannis Altamouras and Periklis Pantazis (both of

G. Bouzianis

whom died young) could be seen as forerunners of this group.
- The 1930's: the quest for "Greekness"
The successes which Greece record-

ed during the two Balkan Wars and the First World War - with Eleftherios Venizelos as Prime Minister - created an atmosphere of elation and a spirit of optimism as far as artistic expression was concerned. The *Hellenocentrism* of the nineteenth century now seemed to have been vindicated. However, the Asia Minor Disaster which followed hard on the heels of the triumphs created new conditions of national self-awareness: Greece might have lost in terms of territory, but she had gained a profounder understanding of herself.

During the inter-War period, the Greek artist Georgios Bouzianis lived in Berlin and Paris and was part of the Expressionist movement (belonging to the *Neue Munchener Sezession*). Bouzianis was a leading representative of Expressionism, which explains the degree of incomprehension and rejection that greeted him in his homeland.

Photios Kontoglou (1895-1965) was an artist of equal stature. His purpose was to blend the Byzantine tradition through the requirement for Hellenocentric modernism. In that sense, Kontoglou had a decisive impact on what is often called the "generation of the Thirties".

The "generation of the Thirties" was the most cohesive group ever to appear in Greek art, and some of its representatives were active abroad as well as in Greece. Among its members were Nikos Ghikas (1906-1995), Yannis Tsarouchis (1910-1989), Diamantis Diamantopoulos (1914-1996), Nikos Engonopoulos (1910-1985), Yorgos Mavroidis (b. 1913), Yannis Moralis (b. 1914) and Nikos Nikolaou (1909-1986). This generation of artists - whose most characteristic representative was perhaps Yannis Tsarouchis - combined vernacular and "art" elemen-

N. Ghika

M. Oikonomou

Y. Moralis

Y. Tsarouchis

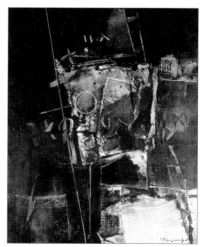

Y. Spyropoulos

S. Papaloukas

ts, the two-dimensional painting of Matisse, and the Karaghiozis shadow theatre and the world it represented. The "generation of the Thirties" was, in fact, most active after the Second World War; its teachers were Parthenis and Kontoglou, and also the vernacular painter Theophilos (1867-1934), the Greek equivalent of the naif painter Douanier Rousseau. The central concern of the generation of the Thirties was "Greekness": an inquiry similar to that being conducted at the same time by the Italians into *Italianita* and by the Spanish into *Hispanidad*. "Greekness" could be defined as a belated desire to exploit antiquity, a kind of localised, flaccid Renaissance, or a form of neo-classicism lingering on, in blissful ignorance, into the twentieth century.

The cultural policy of Greece took the form, in the visual arts, of a pavilion at the Venice *Biennale* and of uninterrupted participation in that institution after 1934. In 1938, while the dictatorships in Greece and Italy were at their height, Parthenis, Michalis Tombros and Angelos Theodoropoulos were sent to Venice to represent their country. In 1930, the School of Fine Arts was elevated to university level and reorganised under the directorship of the sculptor Constantinos Dimitriadis, creator of the popular *Discobulos* which stands outside the Panathenaic Stadium. Dimitriadis was also the first President of the new Association of Greek Artists, founded in 1937. This body enjoyed the favour of the official state and stood at the opposite end of the spectrum to the avant-garde Art Group.

• The post-war era.

In *1945*, with the assistance of the French government, a large group of young creative artists whose ideological orientation was progressive (K. Koulentianos, Ianis Xenakis and others) were able to leave *en masse* for Paris in order to avoid the consequences of the Civil War in Greece. Since that time, there has always been a Greek cultural community in Paris, and it has had an extremely positive impact on the artistic production of Greece itself.

The internationally famous sculptor Takis (born in 1925) soon followed the first members of the community. He created pioneering works called "Signals" and "Telemagnetic Sculptures". In 1959, he presented a series of works called *Antigravity* at the Paris gallery run by the Greek lady Iris Clair.

The Sixties were a period of intense turmoil in the visual arts. In 1960, the

Tassos

Greek representative at the Venice *Biennale* was Yannis Spyropoulos (1912-1990), whose *Oracle* was awarded the UNESCO prize. Thereafter, Spyropoulos exhibited at some of the world's greatest museums, establishing himself as the most eminent Greek representative of abstract sculpture. In 1964, three young artists presented their *Proposals for a New Greek Sculpture* at the La Fenice Theatre in Venice; they were Vlasis Kaniaris, Nikos Kessanlis and Daniil Panagopoulos. Kaniaris developed intense socio-political concerns which were reflected in his *Gastarbeiter-Fremdarbeiter* series, and in 1996-97 he was selected *honoris causa* for the "Face à l'histoire" exhibition at the Pompidou Centre in Paris. Kessanlis was an active member of the New Realism movement and of MecArt. Other artists studied in Berlin on DAAD scholarships (Costas Tsoclis, Alexandros Akrithakis, Jannis Psycho-

pedis, S. Logothetis) and in America as Fulbright Scholars (Costas Varotsos) or Ford Scholars (Thodoros, N. Theophylaktopoulos, D. Kokkinidis).

In the particular case of the United States, some of the leading members of the Modernist movement were artists of Greek descent: Loukas Samaras (b. 1936), Chryssa (b. 1933), Thodoros Stamos (1922-1997), and others.

The fall of the junta (1974), the restoration of democracy and Greek accession to the European Union (1981) established an atmosphere of communication and international exchange, which has promoted expression in the visual arts. As far back as the Seventies, the gallery-owner and collector Alexandros Iolas had built an artistic bridge between Athens, Milan, Paris and New York. In this role he was succeeded, during the 1990s, by the collector Dakis Ioannou, President of the DESTE Foundation and of the International Council

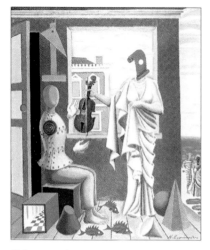

N. Engonopoulos

bitions such as Natural Geometry and Post Human. Since the Eighties, the island of Andros has been the home of the Goulandri Museum of Contemporary Art, which has held retrospective exhibitions of work by Kandinsky, Klee, Giacometti, etc. In 1985, Athens inaugurated the annual institution of the Cultural Capital of Europe, and was followed in 1997 by Thessaloniki. In that year, the Greek artist Alexandros Psychoulis (b. 1966) won the Benese Prize at the Venice Biennale for his work Black Box, which combines computer technology with the video wall. It is clear that despite the absence of any reliable institutions or an explicit cultural policy (Athens still lacks a Museum of Modern Art, while that in Thessaloniki is in serious financial trouble), Greece is making a positive contribution to international developments in the visual arts. It is laying claim to,

of the Guggenheim Foundation. The Ioannou collection, which concentrates on American art, has been exhibited - and enthusiastically received - at major museums around the world as well as providing the material for original exhi-

P. Tetsis

Chryssa

and is deserving of - at the very least - treatment on equal terms with other countries.

Costas Tsoclis (b. 1930) presented his Video-portraits at the Venice *Biennale* of 1986. In these which he combined the traditional painterly rendering with the technological movement. In 1990, at the same forum, the younger sculptors Yiorgos Lappas and Yiannis Bouteas took part. They were then invited by the Berlin Metropolis group show and by the Cultural Capital of Europe, at the time, Dublin. In 1993 the sculptor George Zongolopoulos (b. 1903), who first participated at the Venice *Biennale* was in 1946, installed an imposing hydraulic structure, 10 meters long, titled "Umbrellas", outside the Greek pavilion. The same artist had successfully participated in the 1995 and 1997 *Biennale*. In the 1995 *Biennale*,

the official representative of Greece was Takis, who introduced a trend in sculpture by using electromagnets, mobile elements and flushing bulbs and whose oeuvre was shown in a retrospective at the Musee Jeu de Paume of Paris.

In 1994, Yiannis Kounellis (b.1936) installed his most important pieces on board the ship IONION, docked at the port of Piraeus. This exhibition was a major artistic event that influenced the country's avant-garde. At the same time, painters who follow the figurative tradition and support themes based on local imagery, such as P. Tetsis, D. Mytaras, Alecos Fassianos, C. Carras are very active, showing in Europe and in U S (Mytaras shows even in Tokyo).

Since 1993, the Association of Owners of Greek Galleries organizes the annual *foir* ART-ATHINA in which all the Greek Galleries, as well as some

foreign, show contemporary visual art. This forum has proved its durability and prestige, justifying the replacement of the previous "Panellinies" *foir*.

The 1995-96 season saw the presentation, at the National Gallery in Athens, of the famous Costakis Collection, which contains some of the most important works of the Russian avant-garde

Finally throughout 1997, while Thessaloniki was the host of the "Cultural Capital of Europe", a number of impressive retrospective exhibitions of progressive representatives of the 60's, such as Nikos (Kessanlis), C. Xenakis, Pavlos, Daniil, etc. were arranged.

G. Zogolopoulos

Outlook exhibition

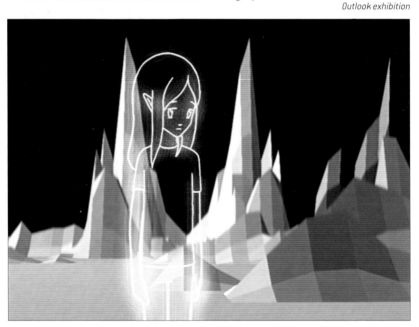

TRACING THE ARTISTIC AND CULTURAL MAP IN CONTEMPORARY GREECE:
Steps Towards a Globalised World

By Dr. Anna Athanasopoulou

Since the establishment of the Greek state in early 19th century, Greek visual arts have followed a slow and rather esoteric development over the long period leading up to the first decades after World War II. They have covered the ground between Western European and international art and local tradition, with a shifting emphasis from academic to avant-garde references.

Appropriation of the international has been more or less swiftly complemented with iconographic elements reflecting a local cultural tradition, fuelled with a different content under the influence of contemporary socio-political context (i.e. mid-19th century, late 19th century, beginning of 20th century, the 1930s, the 1950s-1960s). The broad scope of the local character, ranging from Classical Antiquity to post-Byzantine iconography and vernacular craftsmanship, points at the rich pool of visual elements available to Greek artists in their quest to shape a modern artistic identity. It further indicates the significant weight of cultural heritage in this case. Even more, since, in the first steps of the Greek state, culture rather than language was projected as the chief determinant of the modern Greek national identity. This

was later combined with a theory of the "indivisibility" and "unity" of "Greekness" over time and in space. The visual arts played a role in this discourse. First, they claimed a connection with the cultural heritage of Classical Greece. Later they reaffirmed a glorious and uninterrupted cultural past running from Classical Antiquity to the Post-Byzantine times through their solicitation of a solid link with the artistic establishment in Western European capitals, namely Munich, Vienna and Paris.

A number of elements fed into the deliberations on the "Greekness" of modern Greek visual arts in the course of 19th and 20th centuries. These included: the "East" and the "West", the Ottoman and the European, Ancient Greece and Post-Byzantine legacy, folk art and other vernacular forms of craftsmanship, cultural heritage, tradition and modernism are all notions - in most cases rather artificially shaped and sustained, if not somewhat distorted. The genres and landscapes of the major Greek painters of late 19th century known as "the Munich School" (i.e. N. Ghyzis, N. Lytras, N. Volanakis, G. Iakovides) were, on one hand, embedded in the academic tradition of European art. On the other

C. Tsoklis

hand, they reflected a certain locality on the thematic and ideological level. Breaking away from the academic doctrine at the beginning of the 20th century, artists like C. Parthenis, K. Maleas, M. Economou, N. Lytras, introduced visual elements into their iconography. They drew from *Jugendstill* and Symbolism as well as Expressionism and Cubism, while opening up to the visual wealth of post-Byzantine tradition and vernacular art. Theirs was a quest for a coherent visual language capable of integrating the modernist paradigm with the historical elements of Greek artistic tradition.

Modern Greek art slowly found its way to maturity in the period leading to World War II. It followed a long path starting from the European academic tradition and passed progressively through the movements of the historical avant-garde at the turn of 19th and 20th century (i.e. Impressionism, Post-impressionism, Fauvism, Cubism, Surrealism), while maintaining an undercurrent of locality. Instrumental in this process were the artists of the so-called "1930s Generation" (N. Hadjikyriacos-Ghikas, N. Egonopoulos, Y. Tsarouhis, Y. Moralis) who came of age shortly after World War II and the Greek Civil War, during the 1950s. Exhibiting new appreciation for local elements (naive painting, traditional shadow theatre - Karaghiozis) and a deep knowledge of the 20th-century avant-garde art movements, they developed an imagery that lingered creatively between European modernism and local tradition.

Coming of age with the "1930s Generation", modern Greek art had to wait until the 1950s and the 1960s to find itself in line with contemporary international avant-garde. In the post-war era, the interest of the younger generation of artists shifted largely from the affirmation of a modern Greek artistic identity to the quest for a place for Greek visual arts on the international avant-garde scene. Abstract painting, the avant-garde of the time, found solid representation in the work of a number of artists (Y. Spyropoulos, A. Kontopoulos, Y. Gaitis, early V. Kaniaris, D. Kontos, K. Xenakis,). Antiformalist references also surfaced in the work of artists of the mid- to late 1960s,

either through the medium of sculpture and installation (V. Kaniaris, N. Kessanlis, Daniel, and C. Tsoclis) or through a Pop-art lineage (Pavlos).

The 1960s led Greek art towards international paths, Greek society towards intensive urbanisation and the country towards a sad political adventure. Indeed, the establishment of the military regime (1967-1974) marked an abrupt interruption to artistic developments at a moment when contemporary Greek art was ridding itself of references of topical interest. The discourse on local tradition and national cultural identity, vested with nationalistic undertones, was revived by the new political authorities and ended up suffocating any alternative expressions in the cultural domain. A

P. Tetsis

significant number of Greek artists remained abroad (mostly in Paris) until the beginning of 1980s, when they returned to their country to be gradually integrated into the local artistic establishment (Kessanlis, Kaniaris, Tsoclis, C. Romanou, Y. Psychopaidis, Pavlos, and A. Fassianos). Others (J. Kounelis, Chryssa, Takis) have maintained a constant international presence since the 1960s, securing their own place in the post-war artistic scene.

Due to the ambivalent political climate until the mid 1970s and, possibly, influenced by the pervasive anthropomorphic tradition of visual arts in Greece, alternative avant-garde forms such as Body Art, Performance Art or Land Art, found minimal reception among Greek artists, with a few exceptions (i.e. S. Logothetis, A. Prodromides).

During the 1980s, painting emerged as a dominant practice, also under the influence of current international trends. Leaning either towards the abstract or the figurative, a number of Greek artists (i.e. H. Botsoglou, D. Mytaras, M. Theophylaktopoulos, Kalfayan, G. Rorris,) explored the specifics of the human figure, elaborating a somewhat introspective imagery or they experimented with the visual potential of landscape painting (i.e. P. Tetsis, D. Kokkinides). Sculpture also found some commendable representatives in the younger generation that matured artistically around the mid 1990s (i.e. G. Lappas, C. Varotsos).

At the same time that the country was pursuing its integration into the European Community, the local art scene presented signs of unparalleled openness and activity. Athens became the first Cultural Capital of Europe (1985), an institution proposed by the Greek Minister of Culture Melina Mercouri. Brussels presented a showcase of Greek art in the context of Europalia (1982) and Thessaloniki hosted the newly established Biennale of Young Artists from Europe and the Mediterranean (1986). Art galleries began to surface in the Greek capital, mostly presenting contemporary Greek art, a trend that would be only countered during the 1990s with the emergence of a new generation of art galleries in downtown Athens exhibiting international contemporary art.

Over the last decade, the visual arts scene in Greece has become more vivid, less isolated, more experimental and receptive to contemporary international developments, despite pervasive topical cultural references. The regular exposure of Greek artists to the dynamics of major contemporary art centres (i.e. London, Paris, Berlin, New York) has contributed a great deal to the opening up of the Greek visual arts scene.

Local references at visual or thematic level remain, but they are part of an integrated historical experience, often presented in a critical or satirical way, rather than a chapter of a polemic discourse on cultural identity. Access to new technologies and the Internet, as well as the new "globalised cultural situation", combined with an emerging multi-cultural urban environment in Athens, have helped Greek artists a great deal to by-pass questions of locality. Now their work more systematically experiments with forms other than the conventional forms of art, such as installation, mixed media, photography, new media (video, Internet), performance, exploring new territories of expression. (The Greek participation in the Venice Biennale over the last few years, the candidates for the DESTE Art Award for Young Greek Artists of 2001 and 2003, as well as the latest series of exhibitions organised by the National Museum of Contemporary Art are indicative.)

Furthermore, improved educational opportunities are offered for the study of both the visual arts and Art History, thereby allowing for a more coherent framework for the theory and the practice of art in Greece. At another level, private collections of Greek art are being opened up to the public (i.e. Emfiet-zoglou, Kouvoutsakis, Portalakis). Notable collections of contemporary art of international standard, such as the D. Joannou collection are still rare in Greece, as the patterns of major Greek collectors (most of them based abroad) bespeak a continuous preference for the modernist avant-garde (i.e. the impressionist and post-impressionists masters, Cubism, Surrealism).

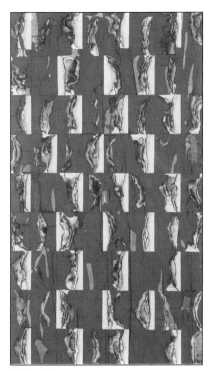

D. Xonoglou

Nevertheless, this newly acquired vitality is not unequivocally measurable by the usual parameters of a competitive newly emerging art scene such as coherent cultural policies and adequate funding at state level, international recognition of individual artists (i.e. art prizes, participation in established international exhibitions and art events). Others include emphasis on modern and contemporary art in the programming of museums and exhibition venues, artistic exchanges and participation in international networks, higher attendance of exhibitions and other art events, an active academic community (i.e. conferences, symposia, publications), and a dynamic art market. State cultural policies are predominantly focused on the protection of cultural heritage (also reflected in state funds allocated to cultural heritage programs). This is often at the expense of contemporary artistic expression; the local art market operates in a less transparent and rather unregulated mode[1]; women artists continue to be under-represented in official presentations of Greek art abroad as well as among the staff of Fine Arts Schools. Artistic activity remains largely centralised in Athens; and contemporary Greece is still in search of its own place on the international artistic and cultural map.

One should not fail, however, to trace a series of positive signs possibly bespeaking of an active present and an ever promising future for the visual arts in Greece.

In 1997, the Ministry of Culture introduced the appropriate legal framework for the establishment of the National Museum of Contemporary Art (Athens), the State Museum of Modern Art (Thessaloniki) which houses the Costakis collection of Russian avant-garde, the Centre of Contemporary Arts (Thessaloniki) and the Museum of Photography (Thessaloni-

ki). Despite their erratic beginnings, difficult financial situation and persistent housing problems, these venues have been slowly making their presence felt on the local cultural map while also undertaking earnest efforts to secure international collaboration.

At about the same time, the National Gallery of Art (Athens), established in 1900, started pursuing an exhibition programme inspired by the principle of block-buster shows. Due to a mainstream and somewhat conservative theoretical and museological approach and by virtue of concentrating on emblematic periods and figures of European art (Renaissance, El Greco), its exhibitions have attracted record numbers of visitors by Greek standards. The permanent collection of 19th and 20th century Greek art saw a new hanging in 2000. The National Gallery is currently undergoing a new period of expansion with the refurbishment plan of the main building and the construction of a new exhibition space in another venue, including a sculpture park (Goudi).

Regional contemporary art centres are encouraged at the municipal level, some of which have already shaped an international profile for themselves (i.e. the Rethymnon Centre of Contemporary Art, Skopelos Centre of Photography). Gem collections of 19th and 20th cen-

---

[1] It is worth noting that, due to the local orientation of the Greek art market, none of the international auction houses operates in Greece at present, with Sotheby's organising its Greek Sale in London and Christie's with a short-lived presence in Athens (1994-2001).

G. Vakalo

tury Greek art can be found in various places around Greece (Andros, Rhodes, Metsovo, Corfu, Larissa).

Complementing efforts at the state level are the creation of new exhibition venues (i.e. The Factory, Ghazi) and the expansion of existing museums (ie. Benaki Museum), the opening of private exhibition spaces (i.e. DESTE Foundation) and museums (i.e. the Fryssiras Museum). Multi-functional cultural spaces are also contributing to an appropriate institutional framework for the visual arts in demand for many decades.

Athens is far from a recognised international art centre, but it has gradually established its own annual art events. These range from the international art fair ARTAthina and the Vavel Festival of Comics to the Festival of Art and Technology-Medi@terra, the Art Festival for Human Rights and Trash Art: a Marathon of Creation and Recycling.

The beginning of 21st century finds the artistic and cultural scene in Greece at a critical juncture. The 2004 Athens Olympic Games offer a major occasion to bring not only the international audience closer to modern and contemporary Greek art, but also the Greek audience closer to renowned works of art as well as contemporary trends in international art. This can be accomplished through the presentation of unprecedented exhibitions organised under the auspices of the Cultural Olympiad 2001-2004 and Athens 2004. (Further information can be found at www.culture.gr, www.cultural-olympiad.gr, www.cultureguide.gr).

It is true that Greek visual arts witnessed a rather slow development and that they have exhibited a relative delay in the reception of contemporary or/and avant-garde international trends. Unquestionably, chronic under-funding, general introversion and lack of experimentation, conservative audiences lim-ited in numbers, the absence of a transparent and regulated art market and the lack of infrastructure in art education are some of the factors that hindered the evolution and further promotion of the visual arts in Greece. Nevertheless, in today's globalised world, where the notions of cultural centre and periphery are being reconsidered and cultural, regional and geographical differences are being renegotiated, contemporary Greek art has a golden opportunity to establish international confidence in itself by elaborating its distinctive qualities and projecting an encompassing cultural experience.

THE GREEK THEATRE TRADITION

By E. Georgoussopoulou

Theatre in Antiquity

Every year Greek people continue to admire, not only the new theatre productions, which almost always deal with everyday matters and characters, but also the oldest Greek plays - especially ancient Greek drama - presented today under a new prism, always trying however, to maintain the traditional and classical style.

The importance of theatre in the Antiquity cannot be neglected or underestimated. Tragedies, comedies and satirical plays were thought to be the centre of the Ancients' cultural life which often seemed empty without theatre presentations, *"agones"*. The audience participated in full during the performances (*"methexis"*) and the plays by Aeschylus, Sophocles, Euripides, Aristophanes and later Menander cultivated and succeeded in including all these people in the dramatic or comic situations their characters experienced.

The Evolution of Greek Theatre

Theatre never ceased to exist through the centuries and to influence the way of life and the thought of the Greeks. This was especially so during the monumental evolution of the Arts in the Middle Ages and the Renaissance. These two periods offered success and motivation to the European Theatre (William Shakespeare, Ben Jonson, Carlo Goldoni), but also to Greek Theatre as they contributed a great deal

The National Theatre in Athens

K. Paxinou

to the evolution of theatrical production in Crete and the Islands of the Ionian Sea (Eptanissa). Vitsentzos Cornaros, Georgios Hortatsis, Petros Katsaitis, Antonios Matessis, Dimitrios Gouzelis introduced new theatre types and patterns, mostly influenced by the Italian Theatre and sometimes imitating the ancient Greek texts and its myths

(Katsaitis, for instance, has written a play called "THYESTES", a tragedy of ancient Greek form and descent). The language used was original, mostly the Cretan or Ionian dialects that nowadays have almost totally disappeared.

19th Century

Greek Theatre flourish up to the end of the 19th century (approximately 1880), when the first professional theatre groups make their presence felt on the Greek stage, basically presenting plays of French origin *(vaudevilles or comic farces)*. At that time, new playwrights appear that represent and introduce new theatre forms, which will become strongly established in Greece and will open a new era towards the 20th century. Dimitrios Vernardakis, Dimitrios Koromilas, Angelos Vlachos, Spyridon Peressiadis and others are made popular through their tragic plays (especially Vernardakis) and the *comic*

The National Theatre

or dramatic idylls - descriptions of traditional family life in the provinces or in the old quarters of a different Athens.

In 1894, a new theatre type appears upon the Athenian stage, introducing a lurid spectacle that created a whole different atmosphere and a new type of theatre, totally unknown at that moment, but very promising and creative for the future: the *Athenian Cabaret (Athinaiki Epitheorissis)*. It included music, lyrics, songs, dance and mostly cheerfulness and liveliness. Basically, the scripts satirised the political, social, religious or moral situations of those times. The casts were made up of excellent actors who were experienced in those kinds of roles. The spectacles were mainly influenced by the cabaret shows in Europe (Paris, London) and found great success in Greek society. Nowadays, the *Epitheorissis* flourishes every winter or summer period in Athens, since the political and social situation often changes radically, offering the authors the spark for satire, critique, abuse or protest. The audience usually accepts the criticism and the laughter is often spontaneous.

D. Horn

20th Century

At the dawn of the 20th century, a new era begins for the Greek theatre, which is influenced by the theatre of North-western Europe (Norway, Sweden, Germany). Henrik Ibsen became one of the greatest ancestors of the so-called *Bourgeois Drama (Astiko Drama)*, represented in Greece by Grigorios Xenopoulos, Spyros Melas, Pandelis Horn and Dimitris Bogris. Up until 1950, there is also an evolution of *Poetic and Historical Theatre* that was usually written by dramatists very familiar with certain historical periods or with poetry, such as Angelos Sikelianos, Nikos Kazantzakis, Vassilis Rotas, and Angelos Terzakis.

The 1950s found *Farces and Comedies* at the peak of theatrical productions. They contained realistic descriptions of the comic characters' everyday life, the misunderstandings, the caustic satire of Greek customs and habits and tender love affairs. They had everything that would dominate the Greek stage - and the cinema - for many years. Generations and generations of Greek audiences were fascinated with their themes and continue to prefer them even today, as they are always powerful and contemporary.

Modern Greek Theatre

1957 is an important and critical point in the history of Modern Greek Theatre. It is the year that Iakovos Kambanellis - the "father of Modern

Greek Theatre", as he is called - presented his play "THE YARD OF MIRACLES" (*"AVLI TON THAVMATON"*) at the ART THEATRE of Karolos Koun. This marked the beginning of a new era of talented playwrights whose goal was to change the scenery and the atmosphere and to introduce new ideas and ideologies concerning the evolution and the maturity of the Greek theatre. The audience - then and now - always discovers something creative, tragic, dramatic, comic, satirical, even complicated or inconceivable under the themes and the characters of the new playwrights. These include: Vassilis Ziogas, Dimitris Kehaidis, Giorgos Skourtis, Marios Pontikas, Mitsos Efhimiadis, Pavlos Matessis, Giorgos Maniotis, Loula Anagnostaki, Kostas Mourselas, Giorgos Dialegmenos, Stratis Karras and Yannis Chryssoulis. All of them dominate the Greek stage and are daily renewing their repertory, imitating situations and characters of every day life and choosing to present nothing but REALITY.

Theatre Groups

It is worth noting that, besides the authors who led Greece and the Greeks towards a brand new theatrical era at the beginning of the century, there were also the directors and actors who put all those texts into action and gave them life and substance on the stage. The first professional groups were those of Dionissios Tavoularis, Eftihios Vonasseras, Dimosthenis Alexiadis,

Evangelos Pantopoulos and others (1880). Two great actresses, old-fashioned with performances well worth mentioning performances are Evangelia Paraskevopoulou and Ekaterini Veroni. After them there appeared a new generation of actors and directors who introduced more advanced propositions about the scenic presentation of certain texts and certain theatre currents such as Realism, Naturalism, Classicism and Romanticism.

In 1901, Konstantinos Christomanos, director, author, translator and mainly a well-educated scholar, created *NEA SKINI*. It abruptly ended its career in 1905 - due to financial problems. It had however presented plays by Euripides, Ibsen, Goldoni and made known how the currents of Realism and Naturalism

K. Koun

*Melina
Merkouri and
Yiannis Fertis*

can be combined in a single, well-organised performance.

Parallel to *NEA SKINI*, the German-educated great director Thomas Oikonomou founded the ROYAL THEATRE where, until 1908, he directed and kept the leading roles in excellent performances of monumental plays (Ibsen's, "THE GHOSTS", Strindberg's "THE FATHER"). Other great theatre teachers followed these two pioneering directors of the 20th century. They inculcated generations of actors and audiences with their sometimes revolutionary and radical ideology. They include: Fotos Politis, theoretician, scholar and director, founder of the NATIONAL THEATRE in 1932; Dimitrios Rondiris, successor of Fotos Politis' tradition at the NATIONAL THEATRE and the first to inaugurate the Epidaurus' Festival in

1954. Others who must be mentioned are: Karolos Koun, founder of the ART THEATRE in 1942; Sokratis Karadinos who created the STATE THEATRE OF NORTHERN GREECE in 1961; Takis Mouzenidis, Pelos Katselis, Kostis Michailidis, Alexis Solomos. The latter was the only director who introduced Aristophanes in the ancient theatres and presented 10 out of his 11 comedies. Others include: Spyros Evangelatos, Minos Volanakis, Giorgos Michailidis.

These directors have, over the decades, directed or, sometimes, kept up during their efforts with unique actors and actresses who left their indelible traces on the Athenian stages. These include: Marika Kotopouli, Kyveli, Katina Paxinou, Alexis Minotis, Emilios Veakis, Eleni Papadaki, Vasso Manolidou, Mary Aroni, Dimitris Horn, Elli Lambeti, Kate-

Representation of ancient Greek drama (Aristophanes), Epidaurus

rina Andreadi, Thanos Kotsopoulos, Giorgos Pappas, Christophoros Nezer and Kostas Moussouris. The people who had the chance to see all of them on the stage speak today with admiration about the miracles they have seen and about the unique and ineffable pleasure and joy they have experienced.

The role of Greek Theatre

The role of theatre in Greece has not changed since the Antiquity. Then it used to be amusing, recreational and instructional and, as we have already seen, the audience's participation was thought to be indispensable. This was because the tragic poets' success and establishment, in people's mind, as excellent authors and great representatives of the Greek culture and civilisation, always had to do with the positive or negative reaction of the audience.

Nowadays nothing has actually changed, especially during the summer Festivals of Athens or Epidaurus, where the ancient Greek drama always provides the spark, offers pleasure and arouses the interest of the participants. An important and quite encouraging aspect of the change in the spectators' participation is the entrance to the theatre world of more and more young people.

The introduction of the most important theatre currents into the Greek Theatre (Realism, Naturalism, and

Symbolism) has made acquaintance and the connection with the European and the American Theatre easier. The European and the American way of writing have, to a great extent, influenced their Greek colleagues as well as the views of the directors.

The combination of theory and action in a performance lies basically in the good co-operation between actor and director and in their mutual acceptance of certain "conventions", basic and indispensable aspects that constitute a good performance. The new generation of modern Greek playwrights quite often follow the patterns and the form of their European and American colleagues, but one should see this effort only as a slight imitation of those writers' "mould" and not as a complete conveyance of the foreigners' customs and habits to Greece. The Greek writers transform their characters and the events of the play by transporting and establishing them with the Greek facts and by describing realistic matters as close to the audience's experience as possible. In this way, they succeed in capturing their attention and in rendering their reaction as positive and approving as possible.

In our century, one could as well note that the spectators' reaction towards a performance can also be critical, if one decides to accept Brecht's view and ideology about a critical participation of the audience and a kind of alienation - "*Verfremdung*" - from what is going on the stage.

Critique

The evolution of Greek theatre and its regenerative ideas and influences have brought to the surface of Greek cultural life a number of notable critics - mainly since 1920 - who established the theatre critique as an important and indispensable factor of the theatrical reality and its creative representation. The majority of the first critics were scholars, theoreticians or even authors or directors (Fotos Politis, Emilios Hourmouzios, Spyros Melas, Angelos Terzakis, Vassos Varikas, Alkis Thrylos, Leon Koukoulas, Marios Ploritis and others). At the beginning they were restrained, literal and analytical towards the performances, mainly because some of the innovative ideas seemed to them strange or even provocative and outrageous. Some of them, old-fashioned and conservative, were often more demanding towards the new creations and they strictly criticised or even deplored them. One must point out, though, that their critiques were often very interesting, intriguing and with excellent analyses and theoretical views about the plays.

Nowadays, the new generation of critics is more open to suggestions, more tolerant, more approving and basically receptive. The plays that were recently written and added to the theatrical "market" (plays of Greek or universal descent) found the critics and the critiques more mature and forced them towards further reading in order to be

Representation of ancient Greek drama (Medea), Epidaurus

totally informed about current matters or radical texts.

Modern Theatre Groups

What strikes one today in Athens is the superabundance of theatre groups and buildings - old or modern - that house the efforts of actors and directors in order to present their work as perfectly as possible in front of a curious and, sometimes, voracious audience. At that moment there are more than 150 theatre groups only in Athens and the number increases if one adds the amateurs, the school or the University theatre groups that are making their presence more and more powerful and prominent into the theatre world.

From approximately 1900 -1960, there were basically 20 -25 theatre groups that presented many plays, even two or three every week (*NEA SKINI, ROYAL THEATRE, KYVELI'S* and *KOTOPOULI'S* groups, NATIONAL THEATRE, *LAIKI SKINI* of Karolos Koun (later the ART THEATRE), *PIRAIKO THEATRO* by Dimitrios Rondiris, KATERINA ANDREADIS' group, MOUSSOURIS' group, LAMBETI - HORN group, etc...).

Furthermore, one could watch performances of cabaret sketches or farces by groups that played in Athens or toured in the provinces where theatrical life has become very intense and also indispensable. Since 1981 in almost every town outside Athens MUNICIPAL THEATRES have created (over than 15, in almost in every major city of the province: Larissa, Patra, Volos, Veroia, Kavala, Kalamata, Kozani, Kerkyra, Chania, Komotini, Giannena, Agrinio, Serres, Lamia, Rhodes, Chios). They have very good directors and actors, some of them protagonists on the main Athenian stages. The increased interest in theatre in the provinces is very promising for the future and especially the participation of the younger generation. The plays presented oscillate between the classical and the more contemporary repertory, but all of them are received by the audiences with a very positive interest and often with enthusiasm.

The return to some form of modern Greek theatre and to farces demonstrates the increase of the audience's curiosity and interest in theatre which seems more and more to have surpassed the cinema and the other forms of present day amusement and relaxation.

Conclusion

The new theatre currents are now more arty and sophisticated and some

Lefteris Voyatzis, actor and scene - director, one of the leading figures of the contemporary Greek theatre

groups present their work based on more peculiar and experimental views that appear to be provocative and appealing to the audience. The pioneering ideas and versions of some plays seem basically to attract younger people (18-25 years old) who constitute today the majority of the Greek audience. They have begun to discover the motivations and the spark of the NEW.

Finally, one should mention that many years ago (and to larger extent today) co-operation has begun between theatre groups abroad and Greek theatre groups. The NATIONAL THEATRE, the ART THEATRE and some of the well-known Athenian groups have travelled to different cities or countries of the world to present their work and almost always receive an enthusiastic welcome.

The Greek audience had - and still has - the chance to see foreign groups coming to Greece, groups that have always something new, alluring or extreme to propose. The critique and the points of view differ, but the interest remains.

The conclusion of all the above shows clearly that Greek theatre is no longer a negligible part of Greek civilisation. Rather it now seems to hold a very high position in the Greeks' estimation and belief of a true, good, interesting, creative and respectable spectacle, a spectacle that could and should - belong exclusively to the Greeks.

CINEMA

By A. Deffner

The reputation of Greek cinema centres on the work of Theo Angelopoulos. Cinema was a very popular cultural activity in the 1950s and 1960s. Although its popularity later declined, it is now in a phase of recovery, mainly due to the building of new venues and the restoration of older ones. Most of them are in Athens and in Thessaloniki.

Education. Private cinema and television schools operate like Greek universities. Acting training is obtained in drama schools. Almost all of these schools are located in Athens.

Cinema clubs. Cinema clubs are a phenomenon in Greece. There are 61 throughout Greece, with the most intense concentration in the Ionian Islands. There is a similar trend with regard to town bands (see Section on Music, data from 1987).

Sites and admissions. According to the data for 1998, the number of cinema units is 319 (3 per 100 thousand inhabitants). Their distribution is the following: 84 one screen sites, 5 two screen sites and 8 multiplexes (more than eight screen sites) which are the latest fashion. Multiplexes have been built in Athens, Thessaloniki and Patras. One is being built in Larissa, and more are planned. Research shows that Athenians are the biggest cinema-goers. Individual cinemas (like the old outdoor variety) are in decline. The average number of screens per site is 1.1 and the total admissions are 12.4 million. Box office receipts were 61 million ECU (5.8 ECU per inhabitant).

History. The first full-length Greek feature ("Golfo", a bucolic melodrama) was produced in 1914. The country's major studio (Finos Film) was formed in 1943. The Greek film industry produced films that attracted growing audiences despite strict censorship, casualties suffered in the hostilities (the civil war

M. Cacoyannis

lasted from 1944 till 1949) and the acute poverty of the post-war years. By the late 1950s the film industry was at its most dynamic, experiencing explosive (and profitable) growth. The first two films which attracted significant international attention were "Stella" (1955), directed by Michael Cacoyannis and "The Ogre of Athens" (1956), directed by Nikos Koundouros.

Film production. Between 1955 and 1969 Greece was making the highest number of films per capita in the world. For several years it produced around a hundred feature films a year: peaking at 117 films in 1966. The number of Greek feature films has declined significantly since 1970. It has dropped from 90 films in 1971 to 10 films in 1990 and 1992. The trend is the opposite in short films. In 1990, 130 films were produced, compared to in 1971 and 1972 (31 films). This is a clear indication of the difficulty of making feature films, unless co-financing is achieved (e.g. by the EU).

Foreign films produced in Greece. Greece has been an ideal location for the production of many foreign films. These include "The Boy on a Dolphin" (filmed in Hydra) and "Ill Met by Moonlight" (filmed in Crete) in 1957, "The Guns of Navarone" in 1961 (the top grossing film of the year, filmed in Rhodes). Other examples are "It Happened in Athens" (referring to the 1896 Olympics) in 1962, "For Your Eyes Only" (a James Bond film with parts filmed in Meteora)

in 1981, "The Big Blue" (parts filmed in Amorgos) in 1988, "Shirley Valentine" (from Willy Russell's play, filmed in Mykonos) in 1989, "Signs and wonders" (filmed in Athens and directed by Jonathan Nossiter) in 2000. The Italian film "Mediterraneo", which won the Oscar for Best Foreign Language film in 1991 was filmed in Kastellorizo, Dodecanese. The film that received extensive coverage in the international media in 2001 was "Captain Corelli's Mandolin" (from Louis de Bernier's novel, filmed in Cephalonia). The most recent blockbuster with parts filmed in Greece (Santorini) is "Lara Croft and the Cradle of Life: Tomb Raider 2".

Directors. The most famous director is Theo Angelopoulos. According to David Thomson (a leading film critic), he is one of the four greatest living film practitioners. His latest film "An Eternity and a Day" won the Palm d'Or at the Cannes Festival in 1998. His film "The Travelling Players" (1975) is considered to be the best Greek film ever made and one of the few masterpieces of world cinema in the last twenty-five years. His films are popular among the Greek audience, and he has also won many awards in the three most important international film festivals (1971 and 1973 at Berlin, 1975, 1984 and 1995 at Cannes, 1980 and 1988 at Venice).

Angelopoulos has continued a tradition of important directors of the recent past (some of them continue to work, albeit sporadically). They include

T. Angelopoulos

Michalis Cacoyannis (two Oscars for "Zorba the Greek" in 1964), Alexis Damianos (Best Direction Award at the Hyeres Festival for "To the Ship" in 1967), Nikos Koundouros (Best Direction Award at the Berlin Festival for "Young Aphrodites" in 1963), and *Robiros Manthoulis* ("Face to Face", 1966) who made a comeback in 2002 with the film 'Lily's Story'.

Angelopoulos belongs to the "New Greek Cinema" which emerged during the military dictatorship (1967-1974). His film "Reconstruction" (1970) and Damianos' film *"Evdokia"* (1971) are typical examples. "New Greek Cinema" differs from the mainstream in three major respects. a) Thematically, it focused on Greek social issues and the shaping of Greek society. b) Aesthetically, it favoured forms influenced by militant and experimental cinemas. c) Most productions were made possible by the dedicated, often voluntary, contributions of filmmakers to each other's films. Audience response to the new approach was initially favourable, but the term "New Greek Cinema" faded in the mid-1980s.

Still active directors who belong to the New Greek Cinema include the following: Kostas Ferris (Silver Bear Award at the Berlin Festival for *"Rembetiko"* in 1984), Frieda Liappa

"Young Aphrodites", N. Koundouros

(Award SIGA at the San Sebastian Festival for "A Quiet Death" in 1986), Tonia Marketaki (First Award at the Festival of Mediterranean Civilisation for "The Price of Love" at Bastia, Corsica, in 1984). Other include: Nikos Panayotopoulos (two awards in two different festivals for "The Idlers of the Fertile Valley" in 1978), Nikos Papatakis, Nikos Perakis (also made films in Germany), and Pandelis Vulgaris (two awards at the Valencia Festival for "Stone Years" in 1986).

In recent years a new generation of promising directors has appeared. Here one should mention Sotiris Goritsas (three awards at two different festivals for the 1993 film "From the Snow"), Pericles Hoursoglou (Golden Dolphin at the Festroia - Troia International Film Festival for "The Man in Grey" in 1998). Antonis Kokkinos (Crystal Globe at the Karlovy Vary International Film Festival for "End of an Era" in 1995), Constantine Giannaris (three international awards for the 1998 film "From the Edge of the City") are also noteworthy.

Many important directors of Greek origin have been working abroad (mainly in the USA). They are John Cassavetes (Golden Lion for "Gloria" at the Venice Festival in 1980, and also a very talented actor), George Pan Cosmatos ("Tombstone", a box office hit in 1993) and Costa Gavras (Adapted Screenplay Oscar for "Missing" in 1982). In this group we also find Elia Kazan (Best Director Oscars for "A Gentleman's

"Evdokia", A. Damianos

Agreement" in 1947 and for "On the Waterfront" in 1954), George Miller (Mad Max 1, 2 and 3), Alexander Payne ("Citizen Ruth", 1996), Agnes Varda (Golden Lion for "Vagabonde" at the Venice Festival in 1985). Jules Dassin, Melina Mercouri's husband, was born in the US, but is a naturalised Greek and won two awards at the Cannes Festival (for "Rififi" in 1955 and for "He Who Must Die" in 1957). A surprising hit of 2002 in USA was the film 'My Big Fat Greek Wedding' (written and acted by Nia Vardalos, produced by Tom Hanks and his wife Rita Wilson, who is also of

"Loafing and Camouflage",
N. Perakis

Greek origin). A recent phenomenon is the strong presence, also related to the size of Greek community, of Greek directors working in Australia: Ana Kokkinos, Nadia Tass ("Amy", 1998), John Tatoulis ("Zone 39", 1997), and Aleksi Vellis ("Wog Boy", 2000).

Actors. There are many Greek actors (or of Greek origin) who have appeared in foreign films. These include Jennifer Aniston (has won Golden Globes, Golden Satellite, Emmy, American Comedy and Screen Actors Guild Awards for the TV series "Friends") and George Chakiris (Best Supporting Actor Oscar for "West Side Story" in 1961). Others include Olympia Dukakis (Best Supporting Actress Oscar for "Moonstruck" in 1987), Spiros Focas (he acted in many Italian films in the 1960s), Elias Koteas (he acted in most of Atom Egoyan's films), Alexis Minotis ("Notorius", directed by Alfred Hitchcock in 1946), Irene Papas (active

from 1954 till today). Still others to be noted are Katina Paxinou (wife of Minotis, Supporting Actress Oscar for "For Whom the Bell Tolls" in 1943), Telly and George Savalas (TV series "Kojak"), Titos Vandis (active from 1960 till 1989 mainly in the USA), Andreas Voutsinas ("Big Blue", 1988), Yorgo Voyagis (active from 1964 till 1992). An actor who was made internationally famous through the 2001 film "15 seconds" ('forcing' Robert De Niro to speak Greek) was Melina Kanakaredes. The most recent successes by an actor were the two awards (the Australian Film Institute and Film Critics Circle of Australia Awards) for best actress by Maria Theodorakis for the film "Walking on Water" (Australia, 2002).

The most charismatic personality was Melina Mercouri, actress, singer and politician. She acted in many of Dassin's films, and won the Best Actress Award for "Never on Sunday" at the Cannes

Festival in 1960. She was also the Minister of Culture in all the PASOK governments until her death (from 1981 till 1989, and from 1993 till 1994).

Popular types of film. The most popular film genres are comedy and melodrama. Popular Greek comedy developed after World War II, reaching its peak in 1955. It was influenced by numerous sources, such as theatre (revues, variety, farce, travelling troupes), cinema (Italian comedy), ancient Greek comedy (Aristophanes), circus, country fairs and shows, shadow puppet theatre, etc. The main format is stereotypes from the lower middle classes. An example belonging to this period is the film "The Counterfeit Coin" (1955, director Yiorgos Tzavellas).

From the early 1960s Greek comedies lost their farcical elements, and became musicals influenced by Hollywood musicals. There were sometimes more popular than the earlier farces. In the mid-1970s, Greek comedy virtually disappeared, along with commercial Greek cinema in general. This was due to television. However, these films are among the most popular programmes on TV. Comedies continue to be produced, such as the films directed by Nikos Perakis.

Melodrama forms the core of mainstream Greek cinema. The key theme is human relationships. Greek melodrama can be divided into three categories: "art", "high" and "melo". "Art" and "high" melodramas were less common but carried more critical prestige. "High" melodrama was influenced by Hollywood, "art" melodrama by Italian neo-realism ("The Magic City", 1954, directed by Nikos Koundouros), while the "melo" built on aspects of the Middle Eastern and Asian cinemas.

A genre that has not been very

"From the Edge of the City",
C. Giannaris

popular but has an important history is the documentary. The first ever film made in Greece was a newsreel of the interim Olympics of 1906. The documentary developed in the late 1950s and 1960s. The 1967 coup put an end to it. After the fall of the dictatorship in 1974, feature-length political documentaries were produced for the first time. By the 1980s, the production of documentary films had declined. The most important director who specialised in documentaries is Vassilis Maros. He has won awards at various Festivals. An unexpected recent artistic and commercial success was the film "Mourning Rock" (2000).

In the heyday of the commercial cinema, Greek films accounted for 16 percent of the total and a 25 percent share of the national box office; Hollywood provided 45 percent of the films and took about the same market share.

Greek films are not very popular nowadays: between September 2001 and May 2002, amongst the 40 most popular films shown in Greece there were only two Greek films: "One Day in August" (directed by Yannaris, Golden Berlin Bear at the Berlin International Film Festival in 2002) and "Silicon Tears". The latter one was in 5th position and was directed by Thanasis Papathanasiou and Michalis Reppas, who also directed the film that sold the most tickets in the history of Greek cinema, i.e. the 1999 comedy "Safe Sex" (around 1 million admissions).

Institutions. The Greek Film Centre (GFC) was set up in 1970 as a profit-making subsidiary of the Greek Industrial and Development Bank. In 1982 the Ministry of Culture offered to provide substantial aid to promote the quality of Greek films. In 1983, the GFC began to finance scriptwriting. In 1986, a special

"Mourning Rock",
Ph. Koutsaftis

department called "Hellas Film" was created to promote Greek films abroad. By 1988 the GFC was the only Greek film production company in existence. Almost all "New" Greek filmmakers had received funds from its co-production programme, and it remains today the main Greek producer of new films (some of them international co-produc-

tions). Funds are raised through a percentage of cinema receipts, under the administration of the Ministry of Culture. Another means of state involvement is the Annual State Cinema Awards.

[For the Thessaloniki Film Festival, which became international in 1992, see the Section on Festivals]

MUSEUMS IN GREECE

By R. Kaftantzoglou

The history and the range of museums in Greece reflect the early priority accorded to national cultural heritage as well as more recent social and cultural developments of Greek society. Earlier museums concentrated on highlighting the most prestigious period of national history, classical antiquity. They were closely followed by historical museums that were concerned with more recent times and by folk art museums. Over the last twenty years the scope of museological activity in Greece has been extended to include many and diverse fields. As a result, museums and galleries of contemporary art can be found alongside those focusing on science, technology, design, natural history, specific cities and regions, branches of economic activity and production, etc. The larger and best-known museums are concentrated in Athens and Thessaloniki. Countless smaller ones are distributed throughout the country, while most towns possess local archaeological and/or folk culture museums.

The first museums were founded in the 19th century, following the creation of the independent Hellenic state. It is significant, however, that a consciousness of the importance of the national cultural heritage predates the war of independence. Concern with preserving and protecting the nation's antiquities was first voiced in 1807 by the great scholar Adamantios Korais, who developed a series of proposals for the protection of manuscripts, books, coins, vessels, columns, and "many other elements of Greek art or history." The works were expected to be acquired by the Ecumenical Patriarchate or the Holy Synod, catalogued, and deposited in a safe building called "Hellenic Mouseion", whose financing was to be assured by wealthy Greeks.

A few years later, four Athenians founded an educational Association, the "Philomousos Etaireia." Alongside its other activities, the Association aimed at collecting and preserving "archaeological objects" that were to be deposited in a site called Mouseion. Although the actual museological part of the Association's program was not implemented, during the first years of the war of Independence its members actively contributed to the safeguarding of antiquities. It is noteworthy that throughout all the years of war, although conditions were far from favourable, special care was taken to protect antiquities in Athens and the rest of the country. After the creation of the Hellenic state, the governor I. Capodistrias instituted a series of measures destined to curtail the illegal exportation of antiquities and established the first National Archaeological Museum in 1829 on the island of Aegina.

King Otto's reign ushered in a period of intense interest in and care for the nation's classical heritage, laying the foundations for the creation of national museums. The Archaeological Service was founded in 1833 and under the supervision of its director Ludwig Ross, the first Central Public Museum was established in 1835 near Theseion. The first legislative measures and plans for the creation of the National Archaeological Museum in Athens date from this period. The Museum was completed in 1889 and, by the beginning of the 20th century, nearly all the antiquities from the first public collections had been transferred and housed there. Although today many other important archaeological museums exist in many parts of Greece, the National Archaeological Museum in Athens remains the country's foremost museum, offering a panorama of the evolution of Greek art from Prehistoric times to late Roman antiquity. Of special interest are the Mycenaean Hall, the Cycladic hall, and the galleries containing finds from the Geometric, Archaic, Classical, and Hellenistic periods, as well as the Minoan period frescoes from Thera. The National Archaeological Museum closed down for renovation in September 2002 and is scheduled to reopen in 2004.

The outstanding Museum of Cycladic and Ancient Greek Art in Athens was created in 1985 by Nicholas and Dolly Goulandris. Specially commended by

The Athens National Archeological Museum

*Museum
of Cycladic Art*

the European Museum of the Year Award in 1987, the Museum houses a collection of Cycladic statuettes and Ancient Greek art, offers educational programs for children of school age supported by advanced electronic equipment, organises conferences and

The Numismatic Museum

seminars, and hosts other exhibitions. Other central archaeological museums in the Athens area are the Numismatic Museum and those of the Kerameikos and the Agora. Specially commended by the 1988 European Museum of the Year Award, the Tactual Museum (sponsored by the 'Lighthouse for the Blind') allows sightless visitors to come into contact with antiquity through its models and copies of statuary, bas-reliefs, vases etc. from the plaster cast workshop of the National Archaeological Museum. The Tactual Museum also houses smaller sections concerned with Byzantium, architecture and natural history. On the site of the Acropolis, just below the Parthenon, the Museum of the Acropolis houses the stone sculptures from the monuments found on the site. Under the inspired and

The new Acropolis Museum, mockup

ceaseless efforts of Melina Mercouri, Greece's Minister of Culture from 1981 to 1989 and 1993-1994, preparations for the new Museum of the Acropolis have begun. The Museum of the Acropolis will hold all the finds from the site of the Acropolis and a great hall has been specially designed to house the Parthenon sculptures.

The Archaeological Museum of Thessaloniki, built in 1962, is another leading institution in the field, winner of the Bank of Ireland's Special Exhibitions Award in 1979. Its central section houses a collection of sculpture from the Archaic to the late Roman period, as well as special exhibits on the history of Thessaloniki from prehistory to Roman times. A new wing added in 1980 houses the spectacular findings from the Royal Tombs at Vergina. Other outstanding archaeological museums are those of Delphi, Olympia, Santorini and Heraklion (focused primarily on the Minoan Civilisation) and those of Volos, and of Lemnos, the latter of

which was nominated for the 1996 European Museum of the Year award. Countless smaller, but in no way less interesting archaeological museums, are to be found in many towns and archaeological sites of Greece.

The early academic and museological concern for the culture of classical antiquity was followed by an interest in more recent periods. In 1882, a group of scholars interested in preserving relics of the nation's more recent history founded the Historical and Ethnological Association in Athens. The Association aimed at collecting historical and ethnological material in order to cast light on the recent history, philology, customs, and language of the Hellenic people. Its Museum's collection of paintings, statues, armouries, relics, costumes, and furniture extends from post-Byzantine times to the mid-twentieth century and is housed in the building of the Old Parliament in central Athens. The Museum includes a specialised library, historical and photographic archives and a conservation workshop.

A number of museums in Greece combine an approach to recent historical times with various thematic focuses. For those concerned with the history of the city of Athens, is the Vouros-Eftaxias Museum, with its collection of paintings and engravings connected to the history of the capital from the 18th to the early 20th century. There is also the Museum of Post-Independence

Athens, focusing on the period from the War of Independence to the 1950s, with a collection of costumes, objects of everyday life, archival, and photographic material. In addition, there are the Museum of the University of Athens and the Museum and Study Centre of Greek Theatre in Athens.

The Centre of Historical Studies of Judaism in Thessaloniki commemorates the centuries-old history of Jewish communities in Greece with its exhibition of photographs from the life of the important Jewish community of the city, its museum and specialised library. The Jewish Museum of Greece in Athens, located in Syndagma, includes more than 7000 objects, testifying to the 2300 years of Jewish communities in Greece. The exhibits document the history of the Greek-speaking Romaniot Jews, whose presence in Greece goes back to the 3rd century BC and the arrival of the Spanish-speaking Sephardim Jews in the 15th century CE. It documents the daily life of Greek Jews through their costumes, jewellery, embroideries, military souvenirs, photographs and various documents, the rites of passage, which mark the lifecycle of Jews. The fourth floor is dedicated to the history of the Shoah and the decimation of 87% of Greece's Jewish population by the Nazis. Prisoners' clothing from the concentration camps, photographs, official documents and other items evoke the tragic fate of Greek Jews. The

museum contains a photographic archive and laboratory, a rich research library, which will soon be electronically recorded, and a study room open to the public during museum hours.

Illustrating the importance of the naval tradition in Greek history, a number of museums focus on the history of seafaring. In Piraeus, the Museum of the Merchant Marine houses exhibits from the seafaring societies of Galaxidi, Kymi, Syros, Spetsae, Chios, etc. Models of merchant ships from prehistoric times to the present, nautical books, ships' instruments and accessories,

Benaki Museum

New Benaki museum

documents related to the seafaring tradition of Greece are displayed together with a collection of lithographs. The Museum includes a library with Greek and foreign-language publications. The Nautical Museum of Crete in the city of Chania has classified its exhibits by historical periods, from the Bronze and Hellenistic Age to the post world war two period. Other Naval and Marine Museums are found in Galaxidi, Andros, Mykonos and elsewhere.

Created in 1931, the Benaki Museum offers a panoramic view of Greek history and material culture from Neolithic times to the 1920s. Founded and endowed by Andonis Benakis, a wealthy Greek of the Diaspora, the Museum houses a number of interesting, extensive and varied collections. These include ancient Greek art, Byzantine and post-Byzantine icons, manuscripts, relics of the War of Independence, paintings by early travellers to Greece, works of Greek popular craftsmanship, costumes and jewellery, Islamic and Coptic art. The museum

also houses an outstanding collection of Chinese ceramics, historical and photographic archives, a research library, and a store selling copies of its exhibits. It provides educational programs for children, and was one of the first museums to adopt contemporary technology. The Benaki Museum has undergone restoration and extension over the last years and is scheduled to reopen in 1998. The original building with its new wing in the centre of Athens now houses the Greek collection. The other collections and archives have been relocated in various buildings in Athens.

The Ilias Lalaounis Jewellery Museum in Athens, below the Acropolis, includes 40 permanent collections of jewellery inspired by the history of Greek art from antiquity to the Byzantine period as well as from other parts of the world. The Museum features a specialised library, an educational department and a children's workshop. Also in Athens, the New Museum of European and Eastern Art houses the Passa collection of Chinese, Indian and Japanese porcelain, works of art of ivory and semi-precious stones, carved wooden objects, statues, silks, period furniture, jewellery etc. Founded in 1886, the Anthropological Museum of the University of Athens is one of the oldest Museums of Mankind in Europe. Mainly focusing on Prehistoric Anthropology, its collection includes human remains, fossils and artefacts as well as a smaller ethnological exhibition of functional and decorative objects from the continents of Africa and Asia. The research activities of the Museum have resulted in the collection of over 30,000 classified and recorded finds. The Paleontological and Geological Museum of the University of Athens houses the collections of the Physiographic Society of the early 19th century. Its exhibits comprise thousands of plant and animal fossils some of which date from the Pleistocene, fossilised protozoa and other marine species of the upper Palaeozoic era, shells from the Mesozoic and Cainozoic eras, offering a panorama of the evolution of our planet before the appearance of Man.

Greece's leading Museum of Natural History however, is the Goulandris Museum in Kifissia, a north suburb of Athens. Founded in order to promote interest in the natural sciences and to raise public awareness of the importance of natural environment and wildlife, the Museum is included among the 40 "Museums of Influence" of the world. It was selected as such by museologist Kenneth Hudson and has been repeatedly specially commended and cited by international award-giving committees. Its collections include insects, mammals, birds, reptiles, shells, rocks, minerals, and fossils from Greek territory, over 200,000 species of plants, 145 of which have been newly discovered through research by the Museum's staff. Scientific studies in ecology, zoology, geology, palaeontology and biotechnology are carried out in its laboratories. The Museum functions as an educational institution on many levels. It organises seminars, lectures, publishes books and other material, and offers itinerant exhibitions on environmental issues in Greece and abroad.

The Museum of Byzantine and Christian Antiquities in Athens came

Goulandris Museum of Natural History

The Athens Museum of Byzantine and Christian Art

into being as an initiative of the Christian Archaeological Association, which was founded in 1884. It has recently been renovated and extended to cover a total area of 10,000 square meters. Besides its important collection of icons, it offers a multidimensional view of Byzantine society from early Christian to late Ottoman times. The Museum houses laboratories, workshops and spaces for lectures. Among its recent achievements, the exhibition "1884-1930: From the Christian Collection to the Byzantine Museum," that ran from spring to fall 2002, featured over 700 objects, including icons, sculptures, works in the minor arts, wall-paintings, manuscripts, textiles and pottery, the majority of which were displayed for the first time. Unpublished original photographic and archival material as well as multimedia installations accompanied the exhibits. Besides its technical and aesthetic excellence, this exhibition was unique in that it represented the first attempt on behalf of a national museum to adopt a reflexive attitude toward its own past, linking its origins to the prevailing social, political, intellectual and ideological climate of the times. The exhibition was intended to heighten public awareness of how the Byzantine and Christian Museum came into being, and the particular role of this museum in the context of modern Greek history.

In Thessaloniki, the Museum of Byzantine Culture, inaugurated in 1994, is involved in the preservation, study and research of Byzantine culture centred on Macedonia and the city of Thessaloniki. In 1977, the Museum hosted the "Treasures from Mount Athos" exhibition, an event of major

The Thessaloniki Museum of Byzantine Culture

significance, since this was the first time in history that exhibits had been allowed to leave the Holy Mountain sanctuary.

From the second half of the 19th century onwards there was a lively academic and museological interest in folk culture. Greek scholars recorded, documented and preserved the various forms of folk culture throughout the country, which resulted in the establishment and the important quantitative and qualitative development of folklore museums. The first museum for folk art, the Museum of Greek Folk Art, was created in 1918. Housed in Plaka, its fine collections contain weavings, ceramics, national and regional costumes, wood-carvings, metalworkings, gold and silver objects and jewellery. The museum also houses a photographic archive and a library. Of special interest are the wall

paintings of Theofilos, the popular painter from Lesbos. The Mosque in Monastiraki Square also houses a collection of ceramic objects crafted during the first half of the 20th century in Greece and Cyprus. Other major folklore museums in Athens are the Centre for Popular Art and Tradition, housed in the home of the great folklorist Angeliki Hatzimichali in Plaka. Built around her private collec-

Museum of Greek Folk Art

tion, the Museum comprises costumes, jewellery, instruments and tools of traditional craftsmanship, weavings, embroidery, a library, archives and spaces for research. Also in Plaka, the Spathareion Museum of the Shadow Theatre founded in 1965 houses a collection of shadow theatre figures and accessories from the nineteenth century to the present, posters, programmes, press cuttings, as well as published studies of this form of art.

Vorres Museum of Modern Greek Art

The Museum of Greek Musical Instruments, created in 1991 and located in a beautiful 19th century private home in Plaka, houses over a 1,000 musical instruments from the collection of Foivos Anoyeianakis, the Museum's inspired founder. The collection is divided into four levels, corresponding to the four major categories of instruments. An advanced acoustic system allows visitors to experience the sounds produced by the musical instruments and the techniques of their use. Particular care has been taken to present the organs in the context of their production and use, supported by drawings, photographs and videotapes. The Museum also features a specialised library, a centre of research, archives and a store. In the first eighteen months of its operation, over 10,000 people visited it.

The "Pyrghi" section of the Vorres Museum in Peania outside Athens, a complex of two old rural dwellings, a stable and a wine press, exhibits pottery, jars, rugs, furniture, troughs, millstones and other objects of everyday use in agricultural society.

In Thessaloniki the Museum of Ancient Greek, Byzantine and Post Byzantine Instruments, provides a 4000-year panorama of musical instruments. Models of musical instruments manufactured according to historical evidence are displayed together with a system that enables visitors to hear how they sound. The museum includes a library, electronic musical archives and a research laboratory. The Macedonian Folk Art and Ethnographic Museum of Thessaloniki, established in 1970, engages in the study of the material culture of Northern Greece over the last centuries as well as wide ranging educational activity. The Museum's collections of 15,000 objects are constantly enriched through purchases and donations.

A great number of smaller museums are found in towns and villages throughout the country. In the town of Serres in Northern Greece, the Museum of the Sarakatsani Transhumant Pastoralists, winner of the 1987 European Museum of the Year Award, offers a panorama of their culture and economy. In the town of Komotini in Thrace, the Museum of Rom Basket Weaving houses a collection of baskets manufactured by itinerant and settled Roma, Greeks from the Black Sea and the Pomaks of the Rhodope mountains. Another award-winner, the Historical and Ethnological Museum of Kappadocia in Nea Karvali near the town of Kavala was founded in 1981. Its collection includes historical documents, archival material, costumes icons, and objects of worship salvaged and brought to Greece by the refugees from Kappadocia.

In Epirus, the Municipal Ethnographic Museum of the Town of Ioannina, housed in the 17th century Aslan Pasha Mosque, exhibits material representative of the life of the Greek, Jewish and Turkish communities that lived there. Costumes, jewellery, eastern fabrics and carpets, furniture, objects of worship, silverwork, and weapons are exhibited by origin and chronology. Also in Epirus, the Ethnological Museum of the Pyrsogianni Stonemasons, housed in a typical stone building, exhibits documentary, material and photographic evidence of the Pyrsogianni masons' way of life and work. The Museum's activities include seminars and educational programmes.

In Volos, the house of folk historian K. Makris, houses works of the folk painter Theofilos, Byzantine icons, woodcarvings and pottery. More works by Theofilos are found at the Theofilos Museum at Anakasia, a village near Volos, and in the Theofilos Museum in the village of Varia in Lesbos, a donation of the art publisher Stratis Elefteriades (Teriade) together with 86 Theofilos paintings from Teriade's own collection.

Founded in 1974 and winner of the Museum of the Year Award in 1981, the Peloponnesian Folklore Foundation's Folk Art Museum in Nafplion, represents Greece's leading folklore establishment. The Museum is involved in the research, preservation, and presentation of the material culture of the Peloponnese and the whole of Greece. Its collection comprises more than 16,000 objects: costumes, textiles, utensils, furniture, a large number of audio-visual documents and reference material from almost every region of Greece. The foundation's activities include publications of books, records and the scientific review "Ethnographika", the financing of research, fieldwork and scholarships, the organisation of international museum specialists and scholars meetings, and educational programmes for schoolchildren. In the city of Patras, the Museum of Folk Art focuses on transportation, food production, pastoral economy, and textile production. The Museum also organis-

*Peloponnesian Folklore
Foundation's Folk Art
Museum*

es conferences and scientific meetings and provides educational programmes. Another museum of regional interest in the Peloponnese is the Historical and Ethnographical Museum of the Mani, housed in the 19th century Tzannetakis family tower. It features pictorial and printed material produced by travellers to Mani between the 15th and the 19th centuries and thematic units presenting the area's human settlements, their evolution through time, local economic production, social, religious and military organisation.

In Crete, the open-air museum Lychnostatis, located at Hersonissos offers a complete view of local traditional vernacular and religious architecture, workshops of weaving, pottery making, fragrance distilling, production of foodstuffs and beverages, textile making. Countless other smaller local and regional folklore museums are distributed throughout the country.

Another area of museological activity, which has developed over the last years in Greece producing impressive results, is that of technology and design. The Technical Museum of Thessaloniki was founded in 1978. Located in the city's industrial zone, it displays exhibits related to the historical development of technology and the natural sciences. Its collections cover the fields of electricity, telecommunications, computers, aviation, space, meteorology, navigation spinning, printing, medicine, photography, holography and the history of industrial development in the area of Thessaloniki. The Eureka technological park features 'participatory' exhibits, visitor-operated appliances and devices and a Planetarium. The Waterworks Museum of Thessaloniki was established in 1985 in the central water-pumping station built at the end of the 19th century. A monument of industrial archaeology, the Waterworks Museum also functions as a centre of research and documentation. The Museum of Design of Thessaloniki, founded in 1993, presents the development of design in connection with the progress in materials and technology and in the wider context of social movements, consumer needs and aesthetic trends and tendencies. Its collection of 20th century design features furniture, domestic appliances, toys, and packaging. Also in Thessaloniki, the Museums of Photography and Cinema comprise collections of the works of Greek and foreign artists, cinematographic and photographic equipment, archives, libraries, cinematographic music scores and recordings, posters, programmes and organise research and educational programmes.

The Railway Museum of Athens exhibits locomotives, tramways and wagons of the 19th and 20th centuries, models, photographic material, instruments and tools. Founded in 1990, the Telecommunications Museum of Athens focuses on the development of telecommunications, from the times predating electricity to the present. Its

exhibits feature reproductions of constructions and devices for sending messages from the 13th century BC on, through a network of fire-signals. Early versions of telecommunications units, Morse machines, electronic instruments, telegraphic systems of the 19th century, the first telephones and their evolution through time are displayed as well as the first television studio installed in Greece in 1964. In addition to its library and film archives, the Philatelic Museum in Athens houses a collection of post-boxes, postal stamping machines, postmen's bags and horns, and a wide range of items related to stamps and the process of their printing.

In co-operation with the municipality of the town of Soufli, the Culture and Technology Foundation of the Bank of Industrial Development that focuses on the research and study of pre-industrial and industrial techniques in modern Greece has created the

The Railway Museum of Athens

impressive Silk Museum of Soufli in Northern Greece. The Silk Museum's exhibits, grouped in four units offer a concise survey of the long history of silk. They constitute an analytical presentation of the phases and techniques involved in the cultivation and processing of silk, in the wider socio-economic context of the silk industry in Greece, up to the final phase of the local industry's decline. Another achievement is the Bank of Industrial Development's Culture and Technology foundation is the outdoor Hydrokinetic Museum of Dimitsana in the Peloponnese. It offers a view of the history of the region with its rich and varied installations of pre-industrial and industrial production focusing on the importance of water and the natural environment.

In the field of Modern and Contemporary Art, the private sector has contributed a great deal through the initiatives of wealthy citizens who have created important art collections, some of which have been donated to public museums and galleries. The Dimitri Pierides Museum of Contemporary art, founded in 1980 and located in Glyfada, a southern suburb of Athens, includes over a thousand works of Greek and Cypriot art created since world war two and a library of Modern Greek art. In the Vorres Museum in Peania, a Modern Greek art section houses paintings and sculptures by Greek artists from the second half of the 20th century. The Frysira museum, housed in two adjacent buildings in Plaka, also contains a collection of contemporary Greek art.

The Basil and Elise Goulandris Foundation's museum of Modern Art on the island of Andros was founded in 1979 and houses a collection of some of the most important Greek and foreign artists. The collection is constantly being enriched. The Museum has organised international summer exhibitions of works by Picasso, Matisse, Klee, Kandinsky, Giacometti and other outstanding twentieth-century artists.

In a stone building at the foot of the spectacular Meteora Rocks, the Beltsios Center for Contemporary Art in Kalambaka contains a collection of outstanding works of contemporary Greek and international artists and also offers educational programs. Inaugurated in the spring of 2002 with a show curated by art critic Denys Zacharopoulos, the centre has been warmly received by the local population.

A recent and important addition to contemporary art in Athens, the National Museum of Contemporary Art (NMCA), is housed in an industrial building of the 1960s on Syngrou Avenue. The NMCA has hosted exhibitions of major Greek and international artists, including Chen Zen, Yorgos Chatzimichalis and Yannis Tsoklis. Next to the Athens School of Fine Arts, 'The Factory', an old industrial building, houses temporary exhibitions of

Macedonian Museum of Modern Art

contemporary art that have included, among others, Gilbert and George and the collection of the Van Abbemuseum.

The Yannis Tsarouchis Museum in Maroussi, north of Athens was founded in 1981. It displays works by Tsarouchis and other artists, organises thematic exhibitions and produces art publications. On the island of Lesbos, the Teriade Museum and Library created by the leading art book publisher Stratis Eleftheriades-Teriade, houses works by Giacometti, Miro, Picasso, Leger, Le Corbusier, Chagall, and the Greek artists Tsarouchis, Kanellis, Rorris, Vakirtzis and others.

In Thessaloniki, the Macedonian Museum of Modern Art was founded in 1979. The nucleus of its collection was made possible through the donations of Alexandre Iolas, Franz Geierhaas and a number of Greek artists. The Museum features works by Oppenheim, Finotti, Warhol, Y. Moralis, Takis, Y. Tsoclis,

D. Alitheinos, G. Lazongas, A. Akrithakis, and others. During its 13 years of operation, it has organised over 30 shows of artists such as M. Ernst, S. and R. Delaunay, D. Hockney, K. Varotsos, I. Molfessis and retrospective exhibitions of N. Hadjikyriakos-Ghikas, Theofilos, F. Kontoglou. Also in Thessaloniki, the city's Municipal Gallery includes a collection of 20th century artists from Thessaloniki and Northern Greece, a collection of Greek engravings, a collection of icons from the 14th to the early 20th centuries, and a small collection of works representative of the history of modern Greek art.

In the village of Metsovo in Epirus, the Averoff Gallery, in operation since 1988, includes over 250 works by renowned 19th and 20th century Greek artists. Its collection is considered by specialists to be one of the most inclusive and representative of its kind. Another important collection of 19th and 20th century Greek artists is that of the National Bank of Greece, housed in the National Bank's building in Eolou Street, Athens. The core of the collection consists of works by the finest artists of the Munich school and their followers, and has been enriched by works from the early 20th century and by artists from the generation of the 30s.

The National Art Gallery and Alexander Soutzos Museum in Athens is the most important public institution devoted to the history of Greek and Western European art. The Art Gallery presents Greek art from the post War of Independence period onwards. The initial nucleus of its exhibits has been steadily growing, enriched by donations of Western European art from wealthy Greeks of the Diaspora and the collection of Alexander Soutzos, which included works by Caravaggio, A. Pavia, S.Tzangarolo, Greek artists Lytras, Ghyzis, Volanakis and others. All through its life, the Gallery has been offered works of art by Greek and foreign donors and has steadily worked to increase its collections. It has done so through the purchasing of works by artists such as Domenicos Theotocopoulos (El Greco), L.Veneziano, an exceptional collection of engravings from the 16th to the 20th centuries and others. The Koutlidis collection was incorporated into the National Art Gallery in 1977, contributing to a comprehensive view of 19th century Greek art. The National Art Gallery features a large specialised library, complete photographic and conservation workshops, a laboratory for wood and paper restoration and carpentry. A gallery on the ground floor houses 19th and 20th century sculptures. In recent years, the National Gallery has organised several exhibitions in collaboration with international centres of art. These included works of Greek painter Yannis Moralis, of Western Philhellene artists of the late eighteenth and

El Greco

National Gallery

nineteenth centuries, from the G. Kostakis collection of Russian avant-garde artists, fom the Whitney Museum's collection of contemporary art, Anthony Caro's "Trojan War", and many others.

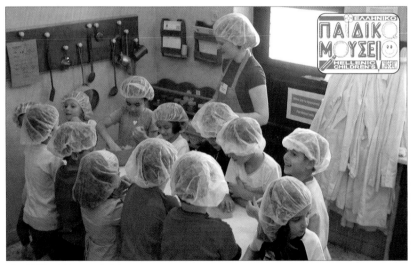

The Children's Museum in Athens

THE BOOK PUBLISHING MARKET

By S. Kabouropoulos

Book publishing has displayed a continuous upward trend over the past 25 years in Greece, that is, since the fall of the dictatorship (1976-1974). It was during and after this period that most of today's publishers were established. During the '90s however, this trend became sharper, changing the climate of fragility that had prevailed in the last half of the '80s. Between 1988 and 1999, Greek family spending rose ten times in current prices and three times in constant prices, according to research carried out by the National Statistical Service. There was also a marked increase in the number of new titles published each year from 1990 to 2001(from fewer than 3,000 to 7,000 titles). New businesses have emerged, media groups have penetrated the book sector and there has also been a gradual development of booksellers' chains.

Greek household spending on consumer goods increased by 22% in constant prices between 1994 and 1999. This, in combination with the expansion of expenditure on education, makes up the general framework in which the increase in book consumption has occurred. Other factors that have influenced this development are the improvement in educational levels, a growing readership (particularly among the youth), an improvement in the general income level, effective advertising campaigns and the 'impetus'

The 2003 Book Festival in Athens

given to the market by the development of new distribution channels and new, contemporary bookshops.

Nevertheless, the absolute value of the market remains relatively low, indicating that there are still substantial margins for further growth. According to a 1999 survey, only 38% of the adult population identify themselves as 'book readers'. In more recent data from an EU cultural survey *(Eurobarometer 2001)* Greece ranks low among the EU member states in book reading. The level of private consumption, based on household spending, is equivalent only to the price of two general trade books a year per citizen over 15.

What will the future of the Greek publishing market be? How realistic is the picture of a flourishing cultural industry, which emerges from the data? The consistently positive developments during the last decade provide a satisfactory framework and allow for some optimistic forecasts. Yet one must keep in mind the family structure of many of the companies and the range of organisational and technological restraints that result from this. Furthermore, the signs of a slight recession appeared in the market in the 2000s. These were affected by factors such as the persistent inflation rate of over 3%, the adjustment of the Greek economy to the Euro, the high level of credit borrowing by the households and the spectacular fall in the transaction index of the Athens Stock Market between 1999 and 2001.

This of course followed on the heels of another equally abrupt decline from 1998-1999. Nevertheless, as an independent commentator has said "this is a market which, over a period of 27-28 years has made achievements such as the setting up of structures for a "mature" book market and the cultivation of a more or less systematic readership. Other markets took much longer to achieve these goals".

Value of the book market

According to data from the *Family Budget Surveys* of the National Statistical Service, processed and presented by the Book Monitoring Unit of NBC, Greek household spending on books amounted to 399.4 million Euro in 1999. This value is in current prices, compared to 221.6 million Euro in 1994, 39 million Euro in 1988 and 3.1 million Euro in 1974. This means that in 1999, Greek households spent, on average, 129 times more in current prices, for the purchase of books, and 4 times more in constant prices, relative to 1974.

During the past five years, the mean annual increase in household spending was 12.5%, a percentage indicating that the growth in the book market is founded on a sound basis. Nevertheless, in comparison with the first half of the 1990s, a relative slowing of the market was observed, since in the period 1988-1994 the mean annual increase of household spending was 35%, due mainly to the increased demand for school books. The most important factor that affected the increase in expenditure between 1994-1999 was, by contrast, the demand for trade books. As a percentage share in an average household's spending, book consumption increased from 0.26% in 1988 to 0.71% in 1999, outpacing the preference for newspapers, magazines, cinema and public spectacles.

Public expenditure on books

We can calculate the total value of the book market, which amounts to 449.6 million Euro in 1999, if to the above figures, public expenditure on books is added. Book purchases by the State were estimated at 50.2 million Euro in 1999. Out of this 20 million Euro were spent on book purchasing by public libraries of all types and 5.8 million Euro by school libraries. In addition, 18.8 million Euro was spent on the outsourcing of the "free" academic textbook printing to commercial publishers and 5.6 million Euro on other book purchasing by various Ministries and Public Institutions. It should be noted that the total of the primary expenditure of the public sector on books recorded in the State Budget Accounts was 51.4 million Euro in 2000, relative to 49.9 million Euro in 1999, maintaining its share at the levels of 0.24%-0.25%.

Book production: new titles and reprints

Recent data on book production in Greece show that the 6,000-title barrier was surpassed in 1998. Thereafter increasing trends followed, according to data derived by the Greek books-in-print agency "Biblionet" (in 1998, 6,649 new book titles were registered[1], in 1999, 7,379 - an 11% increase, in 2000 7,590 - a 2.9% increase, and in 2001, 6,917 - an 8.9% decrease). 90% of these titles were new editions and 10% were revised editions. The first place in book production is held by adults' and children's literature, with 40.1% of the new book titles published in the three-year period 1998-2000, while non-fiction represents 59.9% (social sciences: 16.6%; history & geography: 7.6%). Within literature, children's literary fiction and novels showed an increase, in contrast to drama and poetry. 64.2% of the novels were translations, half of them from English, while the equivalent percentages for drama and poetry were 41% and 9% respectively. The trends noted in the international publishing market are putting "pressure" on the Greek market, since the total number of new titles published in Greece during the 80s and 90s amounted to only 70,000, a number equivalent to 2.8% of the English language books-in-print. The constant increase of the number of book

---

[1] Including revised editions and reprints which bear the new year of publication. Data updated on 14. 11.2002.

2.6% and 4.8% respectively, following the general trend of holding down prices and controlling the inflation rate. This is due to an restriction on the increase in the prices of all categories of books. Despite this, foreign language textbooks and Greek companion school-books have contributed, comparatively, to the rise in prices to a greater extent, in contrast with literary fiction which showed almost no increase at all. This was in a period that coincides chrono-logically with the implementation of the RPM *(Retail Price Maintenance)* Law for books. According to the most recent data, however, these trends were reversed in 2002.

Imports and exports

A glance at the country's export trade offers an equally positive impression. Book imports show an upward trend, since the value of imports increased by 5% between 1999-2000 (53.7 million Euro in 2000, compared to 50.9 million Euro in 1999 and 49.1 million Euro in 1998, in importers' prices). The largest import countries of origin are the United Kingdom (41%), Israel (16%), Germany (8%) and The Netherlands (8%). Book exports represent less than 1/3 of the value of imports; however, they show a continuous increase in recent years - 28% between 1999-2000, thus tending to reduce the difference between imports and exports. The greatest proportion of exports goes traditionally to Cyprus (53%), to the United Kingdom

titles published, however, constitutes a phenomenon of independent signifi-cance.

Prices of books

As far as the evolution of prices is concerned, according to data produced by the National Statistical Service, aver-age book prices increased by 3.5% between 2001-2002. This can be compared to 1.7% between 2000-2001, 0.98% between 1999-2000, 3.9% during the period 1998-99 and 8% during the period 1997-98. The increase in the price of books is lower than that of the General Price Index since 1999, which increased by 3.6%, 3.3%, 3.2%,

(9%), the USA (3%) and other countries with significant Greek communities, but also to new markets such as Poland (14%) and Turkey (6%), for Greek books in translation. The complicated procedures usually involved in the export of books to non-EU member states constitute an important obstacle to Greek exports, in combination with the waning demand for Greek language books in countries where 2nd and 3rd generation descendants of Greek immigrants live.

Reading behaviour

Are the books that are being bought actually being read? According to the Survey on Reading Behaviour carried out by the National Book Centre and the V-PRC Institute in 1999, there is a close interrelation between consumer behaviour and reading behaviour. All the same, only 37.8% of the population over 15 identified themselves as "book readers", and only 8.5% stated that they read more than 10 books a year. The proportion of medium to systematic readers represents a number of about 700,000, who, it is calculated, consume approximately 7 million books per year, while the 2.4 million "weak" readers are calculated to consume another 8 million books, according to conservative estimates. Among the remainder interviewed, 31.8% said that they only consult "practical", coffee table, do-it-yourself and/or professional training books, at undetermined intervals, while the remaining 30.4% said that they never read books at all.

In spite of the increased interest in books shown by the Greeks, the indices mentioned above are the lowest among the EU member states. According to various national statistics, the reading public corresponds to 85% of the adult population in Sweden, to 76% in the United Kingdom, to 75% in France, to 45% in Spain and to 42% in Italy. Taking into account the fact that publishing is flourishing and that the number of book titles published is still low, there are strong opportunities for the readership to increase in the near future.

The publishing industry

The Survey on Greek Publishers carried out by the National Book Centre in 1999, confirmed the profile of the Greek publisher as a traditional, family-based company, often under-capitalised and under-funded, facing distribution problems and lacking economies of scale, necessary if one is to take advantage of the new technologies. Nevertheless, the preservation of cultural diversity in the field of publishing, the survival of small publishing houses and the in-print maintenance of less popular books bears witness to the degree of pluralism and democracy in a country. The establishing of the Retail Price Maintenance Law for books in 1997 has assisted, by protecting the profit margins of small publishing houses against the large booksellers, who were excessively discounting their prices to the public.

The general increase in the market is considered to create favourable conditions for all categories of books, especially for non-fiction, knowledge and information and professional training books. At the same time, the publishing industry is in a process of restructuring, with a small number of larger companies modernising to become the absolute market leaders, and with some examples of small publishers' acquisitions by larger ones or by media groups. According to data from the books-in-print database of "Biblionet", there are more than 480 active publishing houses in Greece; 80 businesses publish more than 10 book titles yearly. The five largest publishers (*Patakis, Ellinika Grammata, Modern Times, Kastaniotis* and *A. Sakkoulas*) produce approximately 28% of the total number of book titles yearly. The ten largest (the above mentioned with the addition of *Kedros, Livanis, Ion, Minoas* and *G. & K. Dardanos*) are responsible for 38% of the book title production.

Distribution / retail

Greek books are distributed through 2,000 booksellers and another 1,500 "point-of-sale" outlets (press agencies, supermarkets, kiosks, etc, while there is a total of 11,000 press point-of-sale outlets). These figures determine the low degree of concentration in the retail sales channel, the two largest chains, *Papasotiriou* and *Eleftheroudakis* with no more than 20-22 branches. *Eleftheroudakis* is a third-generation family-owned bookseller, the second biggest chain in Greece, and (with *Hellenic*) the main importer of non-educational & non-academic foreign books. Their showcase eight-story bookstore on Panepistimiou Street in central Athens competes with Europe's best. A recent co-operative venture between *Eleftheroudakis* and the major foreign press distributor (Hellenic), amounts to approximately 45 branches nation-wide *(News Stand)*. Only two hundred and seventy six bookstores are "pure", selling exclusively books, according to the National Book Centre's data included in its web site. The types of books that rank higher in the sales of most mixed bookstores are companion and auxiliary school books, foreign language textbooks, children's books and mass market fiction, mainly in the form of best sellers. In contrast, the types of books that rank higher in the sales of pure bookstores include literary fiction, children's books, social and pure science books and textbooks.

Overseas providers and/or clients are putting pressure on the larger retailers to modernise by digitising their catalogues, adapting to electronic ordering systems and to the use of *Enterprise Resource Planning (ERP)*. This is often done by making use of the books-in-print catalogue of "Biblionet", an agency that was jointly founded by the National Book

Centre and 45 independent publishers in 1998. A number of online booksellers have appeared during the last years, providing Greek books to both local, distant or overseas customers (*protoporia.gr, ianos.gr, mathisis.com, papasotiriou.gr, paratiritis.gr, greekbooks.gr, malliaris.gr* - to name but a few), related, in most cases, to successful conventional bookstores.

• National Book Centre of Greece www.ekebi.gr
• The Greek books in print www.biblionet.gr, www.gbip.gr
• National Library www.gnl.gr
• European Translation Centre for Literature and Human Sciences www.ekemel.gr
• The Hellenic Literary and Historical Archives www.elia.org.gr
• Hellenic Authors Society www.dedalus.gr

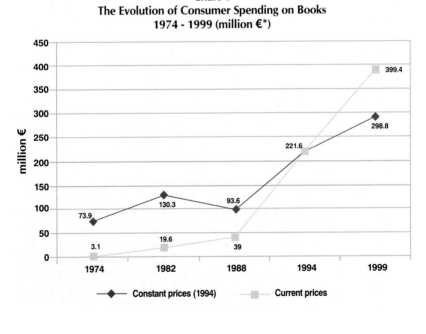

Chart 1
The Evolution of Consumer Spending on Books
1974 - 1999 (million €*)

Chart 2
Percentage of Spending on Books, Press / Magazines and Spectacles in Average Household Spending, 1988 - 1999

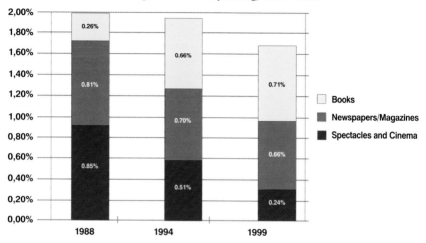

Table 1
Book Title Production 1998 - 2001 by Subject Category

	1998	1999	2000	2001
GENERAL BOOKS	238	313	358	305
PSYCHOLOGY	149	145	135	115
PHILOSOPHY	179	198	243	172
RELIGION	308	299	324	255
SOCIAL SCIENCES	1047	1237	1252	1198
LANGUAGE	316	367	463	423
PURE SCIENCES	382	458	372	364
APPLIED SCIENCES	433	471	499	448
FINE ARTS	460	517	414	405
ADULT LITERATURE	1648	1728	1703	1698
CHILDREN'S LITERATURE	942	1075	1243	1008
HISTORY	369	364	392	371
GEOGRAPHY	178	207	192	155
TOTAL	**6649**	**7379**	**7590**	**6917**

Source: BIBLIONET S.A, data updated on 14.11.2002

Chart 3
Book Title Production in 1998 - 2001
by Subject Category

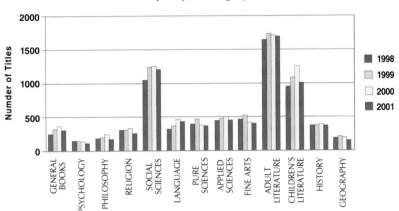

Source: BIBLIONET S.A, data updated on 14.11.2002

Chart 4
Book Price Index vs. General Price Index, 1996 - 2002

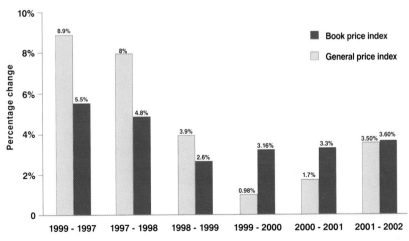

Source: National Statistical Service of Greece /Department for Economic Indicators, data processed and printed by the Book Monitoring Unit of the National Book Centre of Greece

Chart 5
Foreing Book Imports, 2000*

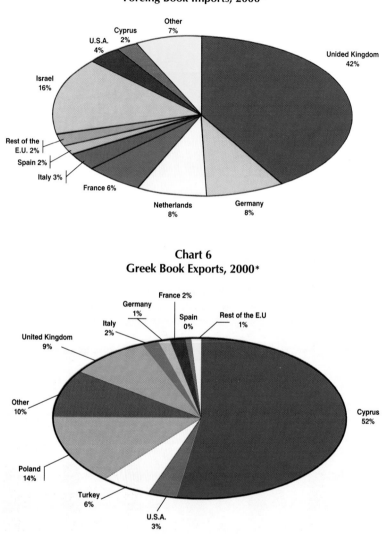

Chart 6
Greek Book Exports, 2000*

*Note: Temporary data of the National Statistical Service of Greece
Source: National Statistical Service of Greece/Department for Industry and Foreign Trade and EUROSTAT/
COMEXT database.
Data processed and printed by the Book Monitoring Unit of the National Book Centre of Greece

Chart 7
Readership Breakdown According to
the Number of Books Read within 12 Months

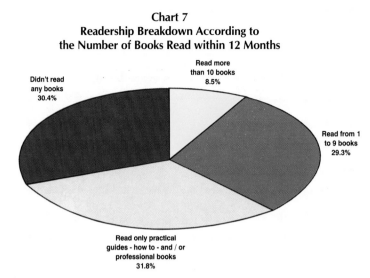

Read more
than 10 books
8.5%

Didn't read
any books
30.4%

Read from 1
to 9 books
29.3%

Read only practical
guides - how to - and / or
professional books
31.8%

Sample: 3,807 persons

Chart 8
Publishers' Share in Book Title Production*

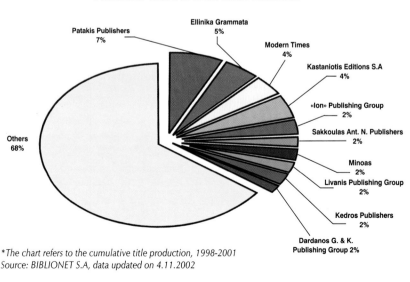

Patakis Publishers
7%

Ellinika Grammata
5%

Modern Times
4%

Kastaniotis Editions S.A
4%

«Ion» Publishing Group
2%

Sakkoulas Ant. N. Publishers
2%

Minoas
2%

Livanis Publishing Group
2%

Kedros Publishers
2%

Dardanos G. & K.
Publishing Group 2%

Others
68%

The chart refers to the cumulative title production, 1998-2001
Source: BIBLIONET S.A, data updated on 4.11.2002

THE HOLY MOUNTAIN OF ATHOS

By J. Konidaris

Historically proven facts have shown that by the 9th Century monks had settled in the peninsula of Athos. The introduction of the coenobitic system and the establishment of the first coenobitic monasteries were the work of Athanasius the Athonite, who with the help of Emperor Nikeforos Fokas founded the Monastery of Great Lavra in 963/964 AD. At that time, the first "Typika" (monastic rules) of the Holy Mountain, namely the "Typika" of Athanasius the Athonite (circa 970) and Emperor Ioannis Tsimiskis (972) were established.

Throughout the long and significant history of the Holy Mountain, there have been milestones such as the settlement of monks from abroad and the establishment of the Russian, Serbian, and later the Bulgarian monasteries. Other significant events include the conflict with the Ecumenical Patriarchate over the extent of the autonomy and self-rule of the monasteries and the Hesychast disputes in the 14th Century. Finally should note in the early 15th Century particularly in the 18th Century, the manifestation and lasting prevalence of "idiorrhythmism" (the system of self-regulation of monasteries). This constituted an outright violation of the principles of the communal life of the monks through the permitting of personal property, not sharing the common refectory and following an individual programme.

The Athonite Peninsula devolved to the Hellenic State through the treaties ending the wars of 1912-1922. By 1924, a five-member Committee had drafted a Constitutional Charter of the Holy Mountain (CCHM), which was approved of at the Extraordinary Double Assembly of the Twenty Monasteries in May 1924. In the short-lived Constitution of 1925/1926, provisions concerning *"the administration of the Holy Mountain"* were included for the first time. These same provisions were included in the Constitution of 1927 (articles 109-112) and they have been in effect ever since, almost in identical form. In the present Constitution these provisions come under the more appropriate heading, "the Regime of the Holy Mountain". According to article 105 of the Constitution, the peninsula of Athos, extending from Great Vigla and inwards, comprising the territory of the Holy Mountain, is, in accordance with its age-old preferential status quo, a self-ruled area of the Hellenic State, whose sovereignty remains intact.

There are twenty sovereign monasteries on the Holy Mountain, which are entities of public law. Other monastic establishments come under their jurisdiction as appendages, namely *scetes, cells, huts, hermitages and "kathismata"*

. . . *which have no separate legal status (monastic houses)*. It is forbidden to increase or decrease the number of the sovereign monasteries, nor can their administrative and hierarchical relations with the appendages be altered (Article 3, CCHM).

The Monasteries of the Holy Mountain are distinguished as coenobitic and idiorrhythmic. Coenobitic monasteries are not permitted to become idiorrhythmic but idiorrhythmic monasteries may become coenobitic, provided that the presuppositions of the Constitutional Charter are satisfied (Articles 84-85, CCHM). Following this procedure, the original nine idiorrhythmic monasteries became communal again and thus all twenty sovereign monasteries are now coenobitic.

Within the territory of the Holy Mountain no female persons are allowed accessibility - the so-called "avaton" (Article 186, CCHM). Violation of this prohibition results in imprisonment (Article 43b, Legislative Decree 10/16.9.1926).

The Monasteries of the Holy Mountain are directly under the jurisdiction of the Ecumenical Patriarchate of Constantinople, which exercises spiritual supervision. Surveillance of the Athonite territory is also exercised by the Hellenic State through its Governor, who along with the Vice-Governor, is appointed by Presidential Decree upon recommendation by the Ministry of Foreign Affairs. He has the rank and salary of a Regional General Secretary in accordance with the new Organisation of the Foreign

Ministry (Article 21, Law 2594/1998).

The preferential status of the Holy Mountain was not only left intact when Greece joined the European Community (now Union), but indeed it was secured specifically by Joint Declaration no 4. The plenipotentiaries of the contracting parties made this Declaration during the signing of the accession treaty, which was ratified by Law 945/1979. According to the Declaration, *"recognising that the special status granted to Mount Athos, as guaranteed by Article 105 of the Hellenic Constitution, is justified exclusively on*

grounds of a spiritual and religious nature, the Community will ensure that this status is taken into account in the application and subsequent preparation of provisions of Community Law, in particular in relation to customs franchise privileges, tax exemptions and the right of establishment". Greece ensured mention of this Declaration in the Treaty of Amsterdam (the Summit noted these Declarations in Article 8 as a sub-note), which was ratified by Law 2691/1999.

In the territory of the Holy Mountain the administration of the monastic polity is clearly distinct from the administration of each Monastery.

The administration of the Holy Mountain is exercised by the "Holy Community of the Holy Mountain Athos", which has twenty members. It is located in Karyes and made up of representatives from each of the twenty monasteries. The appointment of each representative is done in accordance with the by-laws of each Monastery and the appointments are for an annual term (Articles 11 and 14, CCHM).

The daily affairs are administered by the "Holy Superintendence", the representatives of four Monasteries each time, alternating annually under the chairmanship of the first in rank of each group of four monasteries, called the "First Superintendent" (Article 28 & sub. CCHM). Heading the five groups of four representatives are the Monasteries of Great Lavra, Vatopedi, Iveron, Chilandari and Dionyssiou respectively.

The supreme organ, which assembles only twice a year, is the Extraordinary Twenty-member Assembly, consisting of the Abbots of the twenty coenobitic monasteries. Besides this Biannual Assembly, there is also in the history of the Holy Mountain the Extraordinary Double Assembly, which consists of the Holy Community and one more representative of each monastery, making it forty members in all.

The Abbot, the Council of Elders and the Committee govern the coenobitic Monasteries of the Holy Mountain (Article 108, 111 & sub. CCHM). All the members of the monastic brotherhood, who have been such for at least six years elect the Abbot for life by secret vote. The members of the Council of Elders are also elected for life, in accordance with the provisions of the by-laws of each Monastery. Finally, the Committee consists of two or three members according to the by-law of each monastery. They are elected for a one-year term by the Council of Elders from among its members. When there were idiorrhythmic monasteries, they were ruled by a Governing Council and the Assembly of Heads (Article 123 & sub. CCHM). The Assembly of Heads corresponds to the Council of Elders in the coenobitic monasteries and its members are elected for life in accordance with the by-laws of each monastery. Among the appendages, the "Scetes" are the ones that have the more significant position and they are distinguished as either Coeno-

bitic or idiorrhythmic. The "Scetes" are administered by the "Dikaios" (Superior), from two to four Councillors and the Assembly of Elders.

A precondition for a male to be tonsured a monk on the Holy Mountain is that he must be 18 years old and have undergone a noviciate of between one and three years (Article 93, CCHM). All monks on the Holy Mountain, upon their tonsure, are exempt from military service from the moment they become either monks or novices. (Article 93, CCHM and 38 of L.D. 10/16.9.1926) and in the case of foreigners, they acquire ipso jure Hellenic citizenship (Article 105, § 1, verse iii of the Constitution, footnote and 6, CCHM). Both the monks and the novices are registered in special registers called "monachologia". Each monastery keeps its own sets and there is a general register for the entire Holy Mountain, which is kept at the Holy Community (Articles 94-95, CCHM).

A fundamental presupposition must be clarified in order to understand the provision referring to property rights of the monks (Article 101, CCHM). This concerns the distinction between the monks of a communal monastery and those of the idiorrhythmic monastery and between property acquired prior to or after the tonsure. Every Athonite monk is entitled, prior to his tonsure, to donate any of his property to the monastery of his penitence. Hence, any property not donated in the case of a monk from an idiorrhythmic monastery shall remain in his possession. In the case of a monk living in a communal monastery, his property shall pass on to his heirs since he is not permitted to have personal property after his tonsure, according to prevailing practice. A monastery is not permitted to acquire more than what a monk wished to donate prior to his tonsure.

Property acquired after the tonsure of a monk is bequeathed to the communal monastery in the case of a communal monk since it is specifically made clear that communal monks cannot have their own property (Article 101, CCHM). However, in the case of a monk of an idiorrhythmic monastery, said property remains in the possession and administration of the monk, who may dispose of it as he wishes as long as he is alive. However, in the event of his death and regardless of whether he belonged to a communal or an idiorrhythmic monastery, his property always and necessarily passes on to his monastery.

In the territory of the Holy Mountain, the right of owning property belongs only to its twenty monasteries, among which the whole peninsula is distributed and all its land is unalienated (Article 105 § 2 of the Constitution). Both movable and immovable property of the monasteries is managed by the Monastic Brotherhood, which is carried out by the Abbot and the Committee in the case of the coenobitic monasteries. In the case of idiorrhythmic monasteries, when they existed, only the Committee exercised management.

The legislation of the Holy Mountain and its special provisions arm the Holy Mountain with a number of customs and tax privileges (Article 12, CCHM and 2 Legislative Decree10/16.9.1926). Among these is the exemption from all customs tariffs on goods imported for the needs of the monasteries (Article 167, CCHM). Monasteries are exempted from land taxes of net revenue, transfer taxes, income taxes for real estate inside the Holy Mountain, VAT and stamp taxes, while the forestry legislation is not applied to the forests of the Holy Mountain since special regulatory provisions apply here. Finally, Law 1198/1981 established the "Centre for the Preservation of the Athonite Heritage" for the final planning of the programme and the execution of the works of infrastructure, preservation and restoration of the Holy Mountain.

THE EUROPEAN CULTURAL CENTRE OF DELPHI (ECCD)

The European Cultural Centre of Delphi (ECCD) was founded upon the initiative and inspiration of Konstantinos Karamanlis. Its main purpose was the revival of Delphi as a cultural and intellectual centre of Europe and the world.

In 1977, by Act of the Hellenic Parliament, the centre acquired its present legal status as a non-profit cultural organisation in the form of corporal body of private law, under the supervision of the Hellenic Ministry for Culture and the auspices of the Council of Europe. As mentioned in its founding law, the aim of the ECCD is the "promotion of international cultural interest" and "the development of common cultural elements, which unite the peoples of Europe, through the "publication of studies on European culture and civilisation, the organisation of cultural meetings and other artistic activities (....)".

The regular budget of the ECCD is subsidised by the Greek Ministry of Culture. The Administration Council of the ECCD consists of 11 members, of whom 7 are Greeks while the rest are from other countries of the Council of Europe. Ex officio members are the Secretary General of the Council of Europe, the President of the Commission for Cultural Co-operation of the Council of Europe and representatives of the Greek Ministries for Culture and of Foreign Affairs. The other members are outstanding personalities of Arts and Letters.

International Meetings on Ancient Greek Drama

The International Meetings on Ancient Greek Drama are held every two years, usually at the beginning of the summer and are the most important artistic events of the ECCD

The International Meetings on Ancient Greek Drama have a complex pro-

gramme which combines a theoretical approach, artistic creation and theatrical education aimed at recording new approaches and schools of thought in ancient drama and presenting new artistic concepts in staging tragedy.

The programme includes theatrical presentations - many of which are new productions and world premieres - symposia, workshops, exhibitions and other parallel artistic events.

The Ancient Hydraulis reconstructed

Other International Meetings

During the interim year, when the Meetings on Ancient Greek Drama are not held, the ECCD organises international meetings on various subjects such as the International Meetings on Music, the International Meeting "Apollo" etc. These meetings usually include a scholarly symposium and parallel artistic events.

The festivities held on the occasion of an anniversary constitute a special unit of the ECCD artistic programme. Examples of these are the *Homage to Delphic Festivals*, on the 70th anniversary of the first Delphic Festival in 1997 and the international symposium *"From the Enlightenment to the Revolutions"* held on the 200th anniversary of the death of Rigas Velestinlis.

Of particular importance was the great tribute to Socrates, on the occasion of the 2,400 years from the death of the great Athenian philosopher.

The International Programme on Fine Arts

The International programme on Fine Arts of the ECCD encompasses symposia, exhibitions, seminars and artists-in-residence at Delphi. Within the framework of this programme the ECCD has created a *Park of Sculpture* in the gardens of the conference venue in Delphi which numbers today 14 works of art, as well as a *Collection of Contemporary Works of Art* with more than 25 works by Greek and foreign artists. Both are being enriched yearly with new acquisitions.

Educational Programmes
Seminars on the Ancient Greek
Language and Civilisation

The Seminars on the Ancient Greek Language and Civilisation began in 1995. They are addressed to philologists and teachers of Classics of Secondary Education of the European countries.

The Seminars on the Ancient Greek Language and Civilisation are organised by the ECCD on an annual base. Approximately 60 teachers from a different country each time participate in addition to trainers who are university professors of classical studies and specialised research centres from Greece and the respective country of the trainees. This educational programme, which lasts two weeks, also includes teaching of the ancient Greek language by means of computer.

Within the framework of the Seminars on the Ancient Greek Language and Civilisation the *Network "АМФІ-KTYONIA" (AMPHICTYONY)* has been founded to promote the study of ancient Greek in the European countries. The Network has also established the European Student Contests *"Pythia"* addressed to third grade high school students of the European countries who attend courses in ancient Greek.

Conferences

Conferences, symposia, seminars and meetings are held on a wide range of subjects such as Hellenic Studies, Philosophy, Sociology, Economics, History, Archaeology, Architecture and Environ-ment, Mathematics, Computers, Technology etc.

They are organised either by the ECCD as the sole organiser or in co-operation with other institutions (universities, research centres, international foundations) in Greece or abroad.

Other Activities

- Ancient Hydraulis: Programme for the reconstruction of the first keyboard instrument in the history of music.

- Multimedia Encyclopaedia: The Encyclopaedia of the Olympic Games presenting the history of the Olympic Games from antiquity to the present.

The center's infrastructure
Delphi: Conference Premises and
Museum of Delphic Festivals

The conference premises of the European Cultural Centre of Delphi lie at the western side of the modern town of Delphi, in a landscape of rare natural beauty, overlooking the famous olive grove of Amphissa and the sea, the gulf of Itea. They spread over a treed area of 150,000 m^2. There is a Conference Venue and a Guesthouse. The ECCD also supervises the Museum of Delphic Festivals (House of Angelos and Eva Sikelianos).

Conference venue

The Conference Venue consists of main and auxiliary conference halls, library and rooms for the secretariat, technical and conference equipment.

More specifically:

Main Conference Halls

Apollo Hall (Amphitheatre): capacity of 250 persons, equipped with a simultaneous translation system of EU specifications.

Dionysos Hall: capacity of 90 persons, equipped with simultaneous translation system of EU specifications.

Auxiliary halls and other facilities:

- Two (2) conference halls of a capacity of 30 and 20 persons respectively
- Two (2) underground halls for workshops and exhibitions
- Exhibition hall
- Library
- Secretariat and Press Room
- Reception halls
- The Atrium

Guesthouse

The Guesthouse has a capacity of 46 rooms, 44 with twin beds and 2 suites, with the possibility of converting 4 twin-bed rooms into 2 extra suites. All the rooms overlook the olive grove of Amphissa and the gulf of Itea.

There are also 2 small separate independent buildings with 5 studios.

The dining-hall, overlooking the pine forest of the Centre of Delphi and the gulf of Itea, can accommodate 160-200 persons (for reception-buffet: 250 persons).

The distance between the Guesthouse and the Conference Venue is 2 minutes' walk through the gardens of the ECCD and the Sculpture Park.

Museum of Delphic Festivals (House of Sikelianos)

The Museum of the Delphic Festivals is located at the house of Angelos and Eva Sikelianos in Delphi. Its exhibits include photographs and brochures of the Delphic Festivals (1927 and 1930), costumes from performances of ancient Greek drama at the ancient theatre of Delphi, the loom and the piano of Eva Sikelianos, manuscripts of the poet etc.

Athens: Head Office

The Head Office of the European Cultural Centre of Delphi is housed in a neo-classical building in Plaka, the old city of Athens. The building, owned by the Centre, dates back to the 19th century (c.1890) and was for many years the home of an Athenian family.

The building was restored to serve as the ECCD Head Office in Athens. In a total area of 518 m^2, the offices are on the ground floor and on the first level of the building, while there is a hall on the basement level, which can host small artistic events, lectures, seminars etc.

ONASSIS FOUNDATION- HOUSE OF LETTERS AND ARTS

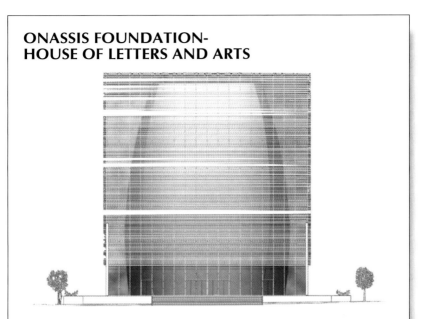

On Monday the 19th April 2004 the official laying of the foundation stone of the Onassis House of Letters and Arts took place. The building is being erected on a plot of land privately owned by the Foundation located at 109 Syngrou Avenue in Athens. The construction funded by the Foundation, is estimated to cost about 50 million euros, not including the price for the plot of land.

The major advantage of the building is its flexibility and adaptability. With an interior space covering 18.000 m², it will host symphonic orchestras, theatre, operas, cinematographic projections, exhibition halls for visual arts, a conference centre, a library, a professional recording studio, reception areas, and a roof-top restaurant with an open-air area for cultural events where the viewers will be able to enjoy the uninterrupted view of the Acropolis and the Parthenon.

The mission of the Foundation for this building is to promote the excellence of contemporary and ancient Greek culture, without ignoring the presence of the major international cultural currents.

The building is programmed to be substantially completed by the last quarter of the year 2006.

FESTIVALS AND CULTURAL EVENTS

By R. Kaftantzoglou

Linked to tourism and a warm climate that allows cultural events to take place in open air spaces, festivals in Greece have for many decades been an integral part of the country's culture and economy. In recent years, festivals have ceased to be the exclusive prerogative of Athens and the Greek National Tourism Office (GNTO). All over the country, municipal authorities, in collaboration with cultural centres and other agents, have established festive cultural events in countless smaller towns and villages. The majority of festivals in Greece are held during the summer months in open air spaces, ancient theatres or specially created facilities on sites of particular historic and aesthetic interest.

The oldest and best known Festival is the Athens Festival, organised by the cultural department of the GNTO and hosted in the theatres of Herod Atticus and Lycabettus in Athens as well as in Epidaurus. The Festival runs from June to the end of September. In Athens, the Festival held in the 5,000 seat Roman theatre of Herod Atticus below the Acropolis, has been an annual event since 1955. Initially planned to host ancient Greek drama and musical performances, over the years it has extended its programme to include modern and contemporary theatre, music and dance. The theatre of Herod Atticus, offering a breathtaking view of the lighted Parthenon, has hosted some of the great-

The theatre of Herod Atticus

The theatre of Epidaurus

est performers, orchestras, and artistic companies of the world. These include Maria Callas, Leonard Bernstein, Mtislav Rostropovich, David Oistrach, Yehudi Menuhin, Colin Davis, The Bolshoi Ballet companies, the Berliner Ensemble, the National Theatre of Great Britain, the Netherland Dance Theatre, the Dance Company of Pina Bausch and many others. Since 1996, the Acropolis has been open to the public on every summer evening with a full moon and visitors can listen to concerts on the site.

The Lycabettus Festival, operating since 1964 in a setting designed by the innovative architect T. Zenetos on the hill of Lycabettus, initially concentrated on performances of ancient Greek drama. The facility was renovated in 1977 and since then, as part of the Athens Festival, it hosts theatrical and dance events and music with more emphasis on rock,

pop, jazz, and ethnic music, from June to the end of September.

The first artist to appear at the 4th century BC theatre of Epidaurus which seats 14,000 and is internationally renowned for its beauty and excellent acoustics was the great conductor Dimitri Mitropoulos in 1935. Three years later the first performance of Greek drama was held there. Since 1954, the Epidaurus Theatre has hosted performances of ancient drama and musical events featuring internationally renowned artists such as Maria Callas, Monserrat Caballe, Mtislav Rostropovich, the Berlin Philarmonic Orchestra of Berlin conducted by Herbert Von Karajan, the Orchestra and Choir of the Scala of Milan conducted by Claudio Abado. Next to the theatre of Epidaurus is "Small Epidaurus" a smaller recently excavated ancient theatre that has been hosting musical performances organised by the Athens Concert Hall since 1995.

A number of festivals that take place in the vicinity of Athens during the summer are organised by cultural centres and municipal authorities. These include the "Krystalleia" named after the poet K. Krystallis, held at the 19th century mansion of the Duchess of Plaisance in Pendeli and offering performances of contemporary Greek and classical music. In addition there is the Festival at Vyronas, held in the Melina Mercouri Theatre in an abandoned quarry since 1987, whose programme includes performances of ancient drama, contemporary Greek music and dance. The Aechyleia in the city of Eleusis should also be mentioned, It hosts ancient drama, contemporary dance and theatre, art exhibitions and various musical events.

The Festival at the Byzantine Monastery of Kaisariani hosts concerts, the Festival of Chalandri focuses on theatre and music, the Veakeio Theatre in Piraeus is mainly dedicated to dance. On Philopappos Hill opposite the Acropolis, an open-air theatre hosts performances of Greek dance in traditional costume by the Dora Stratou singers and dancers from May to September. In autumn, a Panorama of European Cinema organised by the newspaper Eleftherotypia and a Cinema Festival organised by the periodical Cinema are held in Athens.

Thessaloniki is the seat of the International Film Festival, the major annual cinematic event in Greece, which made its debut in 1960 as a Greek Film Festival and established a separate international section in 1966. After a series of changes in its structure dictated by political and social factors, the Festival asserted its international profile in 1992. It is held every autumn. The Demetria Festival, also in Thessaloniki, hosts theatrical, musical, dance and operatic performances by Greek and foreign companies as well as lectures, exhibitions and symposia. The venues for these events are distributed throughout the city. In the town of Kalamata, the International Documentary Film festival is held every October

Many of the festivals in other parts and towns of Greece have gained great renown and popularity over the last years; some of them focus on particular forms of art while others offer a variety of performances. These include the Festival of Nafplion under the direction of the famous pianist Yannis Vakarellis, staged in historic sites of the city and concentrating on music. In addition, there are the Festival of Argos, the International Dance Festival organised by the International Centre of Dance in Kalamata and the Olympos Festival held in the ancient theatre at the site of Dion. The Festivals of Philippoi and Thasos at the ancient theatres at Philippoi and on the island of Thasos are also noteworthy. In addition, the Festival of Herakleion, held at the Manos Hadjidakis

Theatre and the Nikos Kazantzakis Garden Theatre offers one of the largest and more varied programmes, hosting theatrical performances, traditional music and dance events, opera, art exhibitions, lectures and symposia.

The International Festival at Patras includes performances of ancient drama, classical and modern theatre, opera, classical music art exhibitions, seminars, conferences, etc. The Dodoni Festival at the ancient theatre of Dodoni in Epirus is dedicated to historic drama, the Dionysia on the island of Naxos offers concerts, dance performances, folklore events, literary evenings and shadow puppet shows. In the town of Rethymno in Crete, the Renaissance Festival hosts drama, music, and dance events, cinema, and visual art performances. The Festival of Chania, hosted in the city's Venetian port and fortress, includes art exhibitions, music and dance performances and puppet theatre shows. In a medieval castle in the city of Rhodes, the Summertime Festival hosts music concerts, theatre and dance events, traditional and renaissance music concerts and recitals.

Special festival events dedicated to specific forms of artistic expression include the Hydra International Puppet Festival, featuring shadow theatre performances by Greek and foreign artists and the Ithaca Theatre Competition hosting new and innovative theatrical performances. In addition, there is the Hippocratic Oath Festival on the island of Kos that stages classical Greek drama performances as well as a re-enactment of the Hippocratic oath ritual. Finally, the Festival of Art and Speech in the island of Lefkada is dedicated to literature and hosts lectures, plays, concerts and exhibitions, the Santorini International Music Festival offers concerts of classical music.

Many more cultural events and festivities of shorter duration are hosted from springtime to fall by a multitude of towns and villages. These are usually celebrations of events and persons of local historical significance, local products and crafts, such as the wine festivals in Samos and Crete, the Ouzo festival in Mytilene, the Agonia Festival in Crete with dancing and singing contests, musical events and local handicraft exhibitions. Other examples are the Miaouleia Sailing week in Hydra, dedicated to Admiral Miaouli, which organises traditional dance performances, and re-enacts Miaouli's torching of the Turkish Armada during the War of Independence. There is also the 'Armata' in Spetses, a re-enactment of the Ottoman Navy's defeat in the island's harbour and the Mykonos' Grape Harvest celebration held at the Agrarian Museum that revives traditional production activities such as wine making.

LIFE - STYLE

YOUTH

By A. Deffner

According to population estimates for 1993, the age group 20-24 (young adults) constitutes the largest age group of the population: 7.6 percent, i.e. 788,656 out of 10,379,354 people. The age group 15-19 constitutes the third largest age group: 7.4 per cent (771,012 people) of the total population. The age group 10-14 constitutes the fifth largest age group: 7 per cent (726,586 people) of the total population. The female population is generally larger than the male, this holds true especially for people over 30. But in all of the three aforementioned age groups, males out number females.

Values and interpersonal relations

The main common elements of young people in general are believed to be dynamism, spontaneity, a tendency to revolt (these three factors are all based on instinct), novelty, change, and vitality. Greek youth does not always conform to these stereotypes, and it also has to cope with certain trends in society such as ethnocentrism. However, Greek youth are in a privileged position. On the one hand, their ethnocentrism does not strongly contrast with other western cultures, and, on the other hand, it is more open to influences from eastern cultures, since historically, Greece has

always been at the cross-roads of the east and the west.

As far as companionship is concerned, there is a general preference for being alone, which is directly related to the preference for being at home and is an expression of the individualistic tendencies observed in various studies about youth. This is also reflected in the rather small degree of participation in clubs and/or associations. The only cases in which there is a significant degree of participation are student clubs (especially for females) and sports clubs (for males). However, the preference for being alone is connected with the existence either of "pareas" (group of friends who meet regularly) or of groups related to cultural activities, e.g. music groups.

Leisure

Leisure constitutes a very significant component in the life-style of Greek youth. The leisure preferences of youth can only be established through research. The only thorough and scientific study on the time disposition of youth was conducted in 1983-1984 by the National Centre for Social Research (NCSR). Overall, the first preference was cafeterias/confectioneries, the second preference was discotheques, the third preference was cinema, and the fourth preference was spaces with food and/or music (restaurants/ taverns/ fast-foods/ pizzerias/ bars/ pubs/ "boites"/ "bouzoukia" etc.). Of course, there were differentiations according to: type of area (Greater Athens, Thessaloniki, remaining urban areas, semi-urban areas, rural areas); age group (15-19 and 20-24); and gender.

There seems to be a general dominance of passive leisure, since most young people are not the initiators but the spectators of activities. The differentiation between active and passive leisure is spread throughout the day, although public performances usually take place during the evenings. Greek youth follows the general trend in consumption, which is hedonistic consumption focusing on pleasure - a characteristic of postmodernism since it contradicts the work ethic. However, consumption does not coincide with passive leisure and production does not coincide with active leisure. Also consumption can be transformed into production, a characteristic example being the formation of musical groups.

The following three observations concerning the leisure of young people in Greater Athens can be made. First, they tend to emphasise the importance of block leisure, as most people do, but piece leisure is more important as far as cultural activities are concerned (bars and cinemas in weekdays). However, this is usually considered part of the daily routine. Second, they show a strong preference for out-of-home evening and/or night leisure. Third, their most popular activities relate primarily to music and secondarily to cinema.

A recent phenomenon is the use of PCs for leisure purposes (playing games, writing CDs and/or connecting to the Internet) at home or outside the home in cyber cafes (their number is growing relatively fast). According to 2000 data, the household penetration of PCs for students is 58.8 percent, with an Internet connection 32.4 percent (second after managers). As far as on-line activities are concerned, 46.1 percent of student users searched for sport or leisure information, 35.9 percent played games, and 30.4 percent made plans for a holiday.

Music

Young people in Greece constitute a large section of the music market (including concerts and records/ CDs/

cassettes/ DVDs) with the exception of classical music and opera. This role has a spatial dimension, since it is reflected in the peculiarity of the existence of venues for youth (e.g. bars, music clubs).

In the period after the fall of the military dictatorship in 1974, four phases in the development of musical tastes were observed. In the first years the domination of "antartika" (popular songs which were sung by supporters of the left during the civil war) and political songs expressed an increased politicisation of youth. In the subsequent years, the domination of rock music expressed the disillusionment of youth concerning the effect and role of political parties. An important dimension is the resistance to authority.

In the early eighties, the music preferences were established by the NCSR research on the time disposition of youth. The first preference was Greek light/ "light popular", the second dance music, the third rock/ pop/ new wave, the fourth "rembetika" (songs mainly introduced by the Minor Asia refugees, their popularity has decreased since), and the fifth Greek "art" music. Thus, a tendency to prefer Greek types of music existed.

At the end of the eighties and the beginning of the nineties new trends appeared mainly due to the expansion of the media, e.g. domination of CDs, satellite television stations, and the emergence of various commercial radio and television stations, some of which specialised in music. Three main tendencies were noticed. The polarisation between Greek and foreign had decreased. There was a growth of interest

in classical music (a type of "high" culture in differentiation from other types of "low" or popular culture) and there was a tendency to listen to a variety of types of music. A common element in all these phases is the impact of music on the cultural identity of young people. At the end of the nineties the new element that appeared is the diffusion of DVDs, something that is also valid for the case of cinema

An opposition which is continuously growing is that between eastern and western influences, although, in the last phase one cannot easily speak of one type of music dominating the other. Western influences on Greek music are seen mainly in elements of contemporary popular music, in the creation of a rock scene for the first time since the sixties, and in the major role of rock in the lifestyle of young people. The east-

ern influences are seen mainly in "rembetika", in "skiladika" (heavy songs which are mainly connected to the least cultivated social elements), and in elements of "art" music.

Cinema

Cinema audiences consist mainly of young people. Research done in 1990-1991 by the NCSR showed that 73 percent of the audience is under 34 year of age and that the majority are females. For 66 percent of these individuals, going to the cinema is an opportunity to socialise, usually on a Saturday evening, and is often combined with going to a bar afterwards. The most important criteria for going to the cinema are high quality viewing combined with an evening out.

As far as the youth cinema preferences are concerned, NCSR research reveals that the first preference was adventures/ war /westerns; the second comedies/ romances/ music; the third police/ thrillers/ horror; the fourth socio-political films; and the fifth science fiction.

LEISURE AND HOLIDAYS

By A. Deffner

Leisure is increasingly important as a sector of the economy. Private consumption expenditure for leisure/ entertainment/ education for the period 1970-1994 has grown at a rate greater than the average (5 percent compared to 3.1 percent in fixed prices). However, the highest growth is observed in the equipment sector (7.5 percent for television sets, musical instruments, films etc.) compared to leisure services (3.9 percent) and printed matter (1.6 percent). The data for 1995 displays more expenditure (5.6 percent). The importance of leisure is also reflected in employment. For example, the employment of artists was tenfold compared to that of the country as a whole (6.5 percent compared to 0.6 percent).

As far as the structure of consumption expenditure is concerned, 1999 data show that 4.5 percent of consumption expenditure per household is on recreation and culture, while 9 percent is on restaurants, hotels and package holidays. The price level indices for 1998 (EU-15 = 100) are 98 for recreational equipment and repairs, 75 for recreational and cultural services, 115 for books-newspapers-magazines, and 88 for restaurant-cafes-hotels.

No one can be certain if the amount of leisure time has increased over the years, even if certain studies point in

that direction. There are four main issues related to this subject. The first is the qualitative aspect of the use of time. A second issue is the definition of leisure time, i.e. does it coincide with non-working time? This is related to the different characteristics of the various types of leisure activities, for example watching television, which occupies much time in many people's lives, is not considered part of leisure time by many research respondents, but as a "necessary" component of everyday life. A third issue is the effect of new conditions such as second job, teleworking and the great amount of time spent in transportation. A fourth issue is the problem arising from the generalisations based on a wide variety of samples.

Popular activities.

The four main categories of leisure activities are cultural, tourist, sport and

entertainment (including social life) activities. Watching television is the most popular leisure activity overall. It belongs to the more general category of staying at home, which also includes sitting and resting, listening to music and radio, reading, taking care of children (the latter applies especially to females who show, in general, a greater emphasis on at-home leisure including sewing/ knitting/ embroidery). Going out for a walk or stroll is the most popular activity of out-of-home leisure. This also includes going out to drink or eat (in places such as restaurants, taverns, cafeterias, pubs/bars), visiting friends/ acquaintances/relatives, and going out for sports (the latter applies especially for males). The aforementioned activities belong mainly to the category of piece leisure (i.e. leisure distributed throughout the weekdays). Travel is considered to be the most popular block leisure (i.e. leisure concentrated on weekends, holidays and vacations) activity of the Greeks. [For sport, music and cinema see the respective Sections]

Time and space

Leisure options are obviously limited by time and opportunity. Some important differentiations are those between noon, afternoon and evening, as well as between the four seasons of the year. In the larger cities there is almost a complete concentration of musical and cinematic activities in the afternoons and evenings. Only recently have there been some lunchtime concerts at the Athens Concert Hall, for example. Space plays an important role in the determination of the type of activity, since it relates to the type of spatial structure. For example, the modern structure of the Lycabettus Theatre (in Athens) is translated into modern ballet performances, Greek music, rock, jazz, and world music concerts. In contrast, the traditional structure of Herodion (in Athens) is translated into classical music concerts, ancient Greek tragedy, opera and ballet performances. Also, in the large cities leisure is concentrated in the centre.

Habits

The behaviour of the Greek people is a result of the changes in the family (which is shrinking), an ageing population, and Greek participation in the EU. Changes in the political landscape, media influences, and the massive shift to urban areas are also responsible for social changes.

There is an emphasis on at-home leisure in comparison to out-of-home leisure, as well as on passive leisure in comparison to active leisure. This is connected with the invasion of new technologies into the home. However, at-home leisure does not coincide with passive leisure. Even if it usually takes the form of watching television, listening to music or reading, it can also imply active leisure. Examples are playing music, gardening and home improvements. The domination of passive leisure does not imply that there is lack of value judgements or lack of people's participation in an activity initiated by others. As the example of the mass concerts has shown, people are responding to the performances of artists who express their own desires.

There are three main out-of-home leisure pursuits. The first, and cheapest, is going to the cinema (in 2002 tickets cost between 5 and 7 euros), sometimes substituted by television and video. The second is going to the theatre. Prices range from 7 (for students) to 24 (musicals) euros. The third is going to musical concerts. Prices range from 5 (small clubs) to 60 euros (Athens Concert Hall and National Lyric Scene). In the case of working people, staying at home and drinking/eating out-of-home are followed by sports and theatre/cinema. A new phenomenon is the construction of multiplexes, i.e. buildings (or groups of buildings) combining restaurants, cinemas, music halls, and/or theatres.

In recent years, there has been a substantial increase in the amount spent on gambling. It is estimated that approximately 6,000,000 Greeks have gambled in recent years. Popular game include LOTTO (lottery), "Stoihima" (prediction of scores in games of sport) and "Xysto" (scratching hidden numbers).

New games are added from time to time, mainly as an effort to collect additional revenues for the state. There has also been a growth of casinos, especially after the operation of five private casinos in Loutraki, Xanthi, Chalkidiki, Patras and Thessaloniki. These casinos registered a total turnover of 256.7 billion drachmas.

Watching television

Watching television is the most popular activity for Greeks. It is characteristic that 99 percent of the households own a television set, while only 37 percent own a video recorder (data for 1998) and 0.7 percent own a DVD player (data for 2000). European data reveals that the 1999 average Greek daily television viewing time per individual is 227 minutes (third place), showing an increase on 1997 and 1998. TV viewing is on an upward trend, in line with the tightening of the economy: 55.5 percent of households in Greece now own two or more television sets.

The majority of TV programmes is news and chat shows followed by films and serials. The majority (79 percent) of the audience watches news regularly, so the political content in each channel is weighted accordingly. The national origin of programmes is mainly Greek, while most of the imported programmes are from the US. Greece is among the EU countries that have a larger percentage of European (including Greek) programmes, which has increased since 1993. The domination of Greek programmes is not due to strict policy, but relates more to audience preferences. A recent phenomenon is the appearance

of pay television (8.8 percent of the households in 1999), as well as satellite television.

Holiday Destinations

In 1998 there were 5,500,000 holiday trips (52.3 percent of the population) in Greece and 261,000 trips abroad (2.5 percent). Most of the trips in Greece were done by private and hired vehicles (3,279,000) followed by sea transport (1,331,000). As far as the favourite types of destinations are concerned, seaside destinations are clearly the most popular (78 percent). There is lack of official data providing a breakdown of particular destinations in Greece. However, it is likely that the favourite summer (or Easter) destinations are certain islands and especially Mykonos, Paros, Santorini and Sifnos (Cyclades), Rhodes and Patmos (Dodecanese), Corfu and Zante (Ionian), Skiathos (Sporades) and Crete. Another favourite destination is the Chalkidiki peninsula in Macedonia. The quality of the water at Greek beaches is the best among the EU countries: 99.9 percent of the sample of 1690 points checked has proven to meet the obligatory specifications for swimming, while 95.8 percent are characterised as "good quality".

Winter tourism is not well established, except for skiing (on Mount Parnassus) and weekend trips to ar-

CLUBS AND ASSOCIATIONS

Greece has a plethora of clubs and associations. However, of the estimated 15.000 in operation, very little data is available - except that in 1978 there were only 2,000 associations. One method of discovering the degree of participation of the population is through research. For example, it has been observed that Greek working people, as well as youth, demonstrate limited participation in clubs and associations.

Variety

The variety of clubs and associations ranges from wine lovers to friends of Wagner. Associations usually connect with certain professional, business, social or other groups with specific interests: workers, bank employees, journalists, industrialists, merchants, consumers. They can be attached to certain groups, such as youth and women, and they can reflect conflicting interests, e.g. house owners and tenants. They can also be affiliated to politics, which occurs either at the central level (e.g. youth organisations of parties) or at the regional level. The location of clubs and associations also varies, ranging from the capital to the villages, where local culture is the usual focus. A particular phenomenon in large cities is the existence of associations affiliated to people originating from various places, e.g. Cretans in Athens.

Sports and environment

Clubs and associations related to sports and the environment show the greatest increase in recent years. Typical examples of the former are soccer and basketball unions. Even though the majority are affiliated to the three teams of Greater Athens, i.e. the largest teams in terms both of financial infrastructure and the number of supporters, there are fan clubs of "smaller" teams (PAOK and Aris Thessaloniki, Panionios and Apollon Athens, OFI Heraklion, Larissa). Other examples are the motorcycle and car clubs: these are 75 spread throughout 41 cities, although there is a small concentration in Athens (21.3 percent, i.e. 16) and Thessaloniki (9.3 percent, i.e. 7).

There are many non-governmental ecological organisations. These can be roughly divided into two groups: the "interventionist", which are usually the largest and appear often in the media such as "Greenpeace" and the "recreational", which are usually small locally-oriented organisations such as naturalist clubs.

Greek Automobile
and Touring Club
2-4 Messoghion Avenue
Athens 115 27

eas such as Mount Pilion. It can be argued that the international growth of alternative tourism (e.g. eco-tourism, rural tourism) is reflected in Greece. In 1999 there were 14,840,000 overnight stays by domestic tourists. The most popular region of the country is Attica (Athens, Hydra, Spetses), followed, with a large difference, by Central Macedonia (Thessaloniki, Chalkidiki), Southern Aegean (Cyclades, Dodecanese), Thessaly (Pilion) and the Peloponnese.

As far as Greeks travelling overseas, the favourite destinations are Germany and France (1997 data). Other popular European destinations are Italy, United Kingdom, Spain, Cyprus, the Scandinavian countries, and Malta. The non-European destinations favoured are the USA, Egypt, Morocco, and Tunisia.

The choice of global destinations has grown enormously, and places that were previously considered of limited appeal can now be considered relatively popular. The reasons vary: from honeymoon trips to cheaper group travel. Exotic resorts are the first preference of Greek people. Jamaica (and the Caribbean), Bahamas (West Indies), Indonesia (especially Bali), Thailand (especially Phuket), Singapore, Hong Kong are also becoming relatively popular.

As far as Greek inbound tourism is concerned, the data for 1996 show

that most of them originate from Germany and, secondly, from the United Kingdom, followed by Italy, France, Holland and Sweden. The total number of arrivals was 9,497,338, including 508,352 cruise passengers. The majority of tourists (88 percent) come from European countries, and especially EU countries (68.6 percent of European countries and 60.3 percent of the total). The total number of overnight stays by foreign tourists was 36,268,524. The regional variation differs from that of the domestic tourists. In this case the most popular region (32.8 percent of stays) is the Southern Aegean, followed by Crete (25.5 percent), and, to a lesser degree, Attica, the Ionian Islands and Central Macedonia.

SPORTS

By A. Deffner

The Greeks preoccupation with sport has a long tradition that can be traced to Ancient Greece. In the post-war years it has been, especially for males, a very popular activity in Greece. In recent years it is also considered a profitable occupation, especially in cases like soccer or in cases in which sponsoring can be achieved (track and field). In recent years Greek athletes or teams have been particular successful in international competition. The most characteristic example is the 2000 Olympic Games in Sydney, which wee the most successful in the history of Greek athletics.

Soccer

Soccer has always been the most popular sport, although national teams have not been very successful inter-nationally. The most important distinctions earned by the Greek national soccer team were: their participation in the 1994 World Cup Finals in the USA; their participation in the 1980 European Championship Finals in Italy; and the winning of the Mediterranean Championship of 1951 in Alexandria (Egypt) and 1991 in Athens.

Panathinaikos (from Athens) has been the most successful team inter-nationally. It played in the 1971 European Championship Final against the Dutch team Ajax (it lost·0-2). It reached the semi-finals of the 1985 European Championship Cup as well as the quarterfinals of the 1988 UEFA Cup. Recently it reached the semi-finals of the 1996 and the quarter-finals of the 2002 Champions League.

The National Football Team

Other teams of international distinction are: AEK (Athens) which reached the semi-finals of the 1974 UEFA Cup; PAOK (Thessaloniki), Larissa (the team of the eponymous town in Thessaly); and Olympiakos (Piraeus) which reached the quarter-finals of the 1974, 1985 and 1993 European Cup Winners Cup respectively. The most successful team inside Greece is Olympiakos. What is characteristic of Greek soccer is the concentration of the three best teams in Greater Athens (Olympiakos, Panathinaikos, AEK), although Thessaloniki has two teams with some success (Aris, PAOK), and certain smaller teams have occasionally won the cup.

Many Greek players have played abroad. This phenomenon has diminished in recent years, but the relatively few players that still work abroad are quite successful. Current examples are: Nikos Dabizas (England), Angelos Charisteas, Ioannis Amanatidis, Dimitris Grammozis and Kostas Konstantinidis (Germany), Akis Zikos (France), Zisis Vrizas, Kostas Loumpoutis and Traianos Dellas (Italy), Demis Nikolaidis (Spain) and Alexandros Kaklamanos (Belgium). Mahlas has also played in the World Selection Team (in 1993), for which other Greek players have also been selected (e.g. Antonis Nikopolidis in 2002).

Basketball

Basketball is the sport in which national teams have achieved the most international success. It was established as the second most popular sport, particularly after Greece won the 1987 European Basketball (Eurobasket) Championship in Athens, only the second West European team to achieve that victory at the time. In the 1989 Eurobasket Championship in Zagreb, Greece won the Silver Medal, while it was fourth in three occasions: the 1993 Eurobasket Championship in Munich, the 1995 Eurobasket Championship in Athens, and the 1997 Eurobasket Championship in Barcelona.

The highest positions earned by Greek national teams in the World Basketball (Mundobasket) Championship have been fourth place both in 1998 in Greece and 1994 in Canada. The 1996 Olympics in Atlanta were the first in which the national team took part, and it was fifth. Very significant events Greek basketball were the winning of the 1995 World Junior Men Championship in Athens, and of the 2002 European Young Men Championship in Lithuania.

There have been many team distinctions in Europe. Panathinaikos has been the most successful European team in recent years since it won the European Championship in 1996, 2000 and 2002. Olympiakos won this Championship in 1997. PAOK won the European Cup in 1991 and the Korac Cup in 1994. Aris has also won both these Cups (in 1993 and 1997 respectively). AEK won the European Cup in 1969 and the Saporta Cup in 2000. Marousi won the Saporta Cup in 2001. The most successful team inside Greece is Panathinaikos. In the case of basketball, and in contrast with soccer, Aris has managed to break the domination of the three teams of Greater Athens, since it is the second most successful team, with Olympiakos in third place.

Women's basketball has also achieved international distinctions. The national team won the Bronze Medal in the 1991 Mediterranean Games in Athens, while Sporting (Athens) was third in the Final Four of the 1991 European championship in Barcelona and fourth in the 1992 Final Four in Bari.

The development of Greek basketball has been helped enormously by the presence of many players of Greek origin who came from abroad, mainly from the USA. The best, and the most widely known, was Nikos Gallis who came to play for Aris in 1979. The famous "Bosman Case" has opened the way, since 1996, not only for European Community players to participate in the Greek Championship, but also for Greek players to participate in European championships. Recent examples are E. Retzias (Turkey), Theodoros Papaloukas and Nikos Chantzivretas (Russia). A new development is Greeks playing in NBA - Efthimios Rentzias and Iakovos Tsakalidis.

Other less popular but successful sports

There are many sports which are not as popular as soccer and basketball, but which have been more successful especially in relation to the Olympic Games. Characteristic examples are water polo and weight lifting. The national water polo team took second place in the 1997 World Cup in Athens and sixth place in the 1996 Olympics. The most recent team distinction is the winning of

The National Basketball Team

*The Women's Ensemble
National Team*

the 2002 European Championship and the European Supercup by Olympiakos.

The national weight lifting team has been particularly successful in recent years under the leadership of coach Christos Iakovou. The most prominent figure is Pyrros Dimas. He won Gold Medals in the Olympic Games of 1992 (Barcelona), 1996, and 2000, as well as in the 1993, 1995 and 1998 World Championships (in Melbourne, Guangzhou and Lahti respectively).

Greek track athletes, especially females, have always gained distinctions and this is something which has grown in recent years in terms of numbers and stability. The sprinter (and later long-jumper) Voula Patoulidou, who won the Gold Medal in 100 meters hurdles in the 1992 Olympics, opened the way. Three of the greatest female athletes of European track and field also deserve mention. The sprinter (100m) Katerina Thanou won the Silver Medal in the 2000 Olympics, and the Gold Medal in the 2002 European Championship in Munich. The long-jumper Niki Xanthou won fourth place in the 1996 Olympics, the Silver Medal in the 1997 World Championship of Athletics and the Gold Medal in the 2002 European Championship of Closed Track in Vienna). The javelin thrower Mirella Maniani won the Silver Medal in the 2000 Olympics and the Gold medal in the 1999 World Championship and in the 2002 European Championship. The top male track athlete in recent years is the sprinter (200m) Konstantinos Kenteris with a Gold Medal in the 2000 Olympics, in the 2001 World Championship and in the 2002 European Championship). A number of other great athletes should be noted. The javelin thrower Kostas Gatsioudis was sixth in the 2000 Olympics and second in the 1999 World Championship. The long-jumper Kostas Koukodimos was sixth in the 1992 Olympics, first in the 1994 Bruno Jauli-European Cup and second in the 1997 and 2002 Bruno Jauli. The high-jumper Lambros Papakostas was sixth in the 1996 Olympics and first in the 1998 Bruno Jauli.

Many other sports have brought distinctions to Greece. As far as gymnastics is concerned, Ioannis Melissanidis, a man of many talents, won a Gold Medal in the 1996 Olympics (floor exercises). Dimosthenis Tampakos won a Silver Medal in the 2000 Olympics (rings). Vlassis Maras won Gold Medals in the 2001 World Championship in Ghent and in the 2002 European Championship in Patras (horizontal bar). The Women's Ensemble National Team won a bronze medal in the 2000 Olympics, and three medals in the 2002 World Championship.

Volleyball is the third most popular team sport among Greeks. The Greek volleyball team won the Bronze Medal in the 1987 European Championship in Belgium and was sixth in the 1994 World Championship. Olympiakos won the 1996 European Cup in Athens and came second in the 2002 European Cup, while Iraklis came third. The beach volley players Efi Sfiri and Vasso Karadassiou took second place in the tournament of the World Circuit in Rhodes in 2002 and are 14th on the world list. The tennis player Lena Danielidou won the Den Bosch tournament in 2002 and is 21st on the world list.

Special events

In recent years Greece has been very active in the organisation of special events, which are also important in terms of tourism. Athens organised the 1987 and 1995 Eurobasket Championships, the 1997 World Championship of Athletics, and the 1997 World Cup of water polo.

It organised the 1998 Mundobasket Championship, aimed at a return to the athletic ideals of Ancient Greece, combining sport with culture. The same aim will characterise the organisation of the most important athletic event of all times in Greece, the 2004 Olympic Games in Athens. This will be a unique opportunity for Greece to play a new role in the field of international (and especially European) competition

[For sports clubs and associations see the Section on Clubs and Associations]

THE ATHENS OLYMPICS

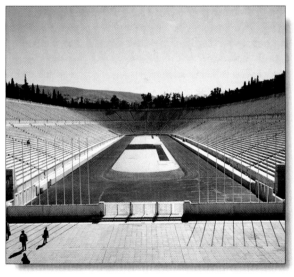

MESSAGE FROM THE PRESIDENT OF "ATHENS 2004"

The Olympic Games are returning to their ancient birthplace and the city of their revival. In 2004, athletes from all nations will unite in Greece to engage in noble competition. The Athens Olympic Games will combine History, Culture and Peace with Sport and Olympism. The people of Greece will host Unique Games on a Human Scale inspiring the world to celebrate the Olympic Values.

For Athens and Greece, this Unique Olympic Homecoming is of historic importance. It is a homecoming of the values and ideals of the Olympic movement, that were born in this country many centuries ago and have been embraced by the world ever since, turning the Olympic Games into a major international, cultural and sporting event.

Volunteerism is an integral part of the Olympic idea and the Games themselves. Volunteerism calls for everyone to participate in and enjoy the Olympic experience. Volunteers are the people who make the Games happen, supporting every athlete, spectator, and visitor in the most amazing event in the world. The greatest celebration of humanity is only possible through the will, the passion, the dedication and the professionalism of each and every volunteer.

Olympic Volunteerism links the Olympic Ideals and Values with contribution to society as a whole, and provides thousands of people with the opportunity to be part of a unique experience where people of all ages, races, creed and walks of life can participate.

Being an Olympic volunteer means, most of all, selfless contribution, giving your own precious personal time. It means becoming part of a team, part of the greater Olympic family.

Through the ATHENS 2004 Volunteer Program, and in view of the overwhelming response so far, the Volunteer Movement takes on a new dynamic dimension in the Greek society, creating a new potential for the post Olympic era, promoting the volunteer conscience in Greek society, creating positive attitudes, and enhancing post-Olympic volunteerism.

For everyone involved in the organization and hosting of the Games, for everyone living in this country, but also for every Greek in the world, the challenge of hosting the 2004 Games is great.

Thus, the Olympic Games become also an event with major economic and technological as well as social consequences for Greece.

Greece is invited to re-launch itself through the Olympic Games in the eyes of the world, showcasing not only its Olympic and cultural heritage, but also the image of the modern and vibrant country it has become. A country that is a full member of the European Union and the European Monetary Union, a people that works together as a team and accomplishes the task at hand.

The principal economic effects of the Olympic Games will be an increase in economic activity, employment, and productivity. Some basic sectors that are affected by the Games, and affect in turn the country's economy during the preparations period, are construction and equipment activities for the appropriate infrastructure necessary for holding the Games - works such as stadiums, the Olympic Village, the Media Villages, the Press and Broadcasting Centres, public transport, and others.

Other activities that are significantly influenced by the Games and affect economy, are those in the sectors of technology, textiles, sport products, food products, manufacturing and merchandising of furniture, electric products, and publishing.

Tourism is undeniably the sector of the economy, which, due to this great international sporting event, develops faster, most directly, and for a long period of time. The attraction of tourists begins from the moment the Games are assigned, it culminates

at Games-time and continues for a long period after the end of the Games.

The effect of the Olympic Games on Greek economy in 2002 was catalytic:

Development rate was maintained at 3.8%, despite the international recession. GNP increased (due to the Games) by 0.4%. 30,000 jobs were created.
The volume of retail trading went up by 5.2%.
The construction sector increased by 20%.

With regard to the overall positive effects of the Olympic Games on the country's economy, in the two years 2003-2004, it is estimated that a total of 95,000 new jobs will be created, 50,000 of which will continue beyond 2004. It is estimated that the effect on GNP will be an increase of 0.5%, while in 2004 it will fluctuate between 0.9 and 1.3%. Tourism is expected to increase by 0.5% in 2004 alone due to the Games.

The renewed civic pride, the massive surge in volunteerism, and the return of the Olympic Games to their ancient birthplace will all shape the Legacy of the ATHENS 2004 Olympic Games. When the last medal is awarded, and the Closing Ceremony of the Paralympic Games ends, the dynamism and spirit of the Games of ATHENS 2004 will remain.

Join us in this great celebration and take part in the challenge. Find out how you can participate in the Games and share the joy and excitement. Be part of the experience of a truly unique Olympic Homecoming.

Gianna Angelopoulos Daskalaki
President, ATHENS 2004

OLYMPIC PROJECTS

By M. Aivaliotou

2004 may be the year of the Olympic Games in Greece, the country where the Olympic Idea was born, but this year is critical for our country since it is when the Olympic projects will be completed.

Greece, as everyone knows, is the country that gave birth to the Olympic Games, making it essential to create venues worthy of its history. It is imperative that all goes well so mistakes must be avoided and should any be detected during the trials that are to take place this year then they must be rectified in early 2004 in order to ensure that the Olympic Games 2004 are flawlessly executed.

The aim of those in charge is to set up new infrastructures throughout the entire country. After all, the Olympiad is something that concerns all Greeks and not just Athenians, both with regard to the programme "Greece-2004" and the programme for the Cultural Olympiad. New athletic and cultural infrastructures, new brick and mortar infrastructures, new road works and new mass transport systems will all transform the features of public areas.

ATHENS 2004

Our country's Olympic heritage will also play a significant role, while post-Olympic use of this infrastructure will be impressive, since it will give the post-industrial development model for the country the opportunity it needs, offering many benefits. These benefits will be reflected in basic fields such as culture, sports and tourism.

At the same time, as far as the nation's economy is concerned, there

Unique Games on a Human Scale

In 2004, The Olympic Games are returning to their ancient birthplace and the city of their revival. Athletes from all nations will unite in Greece to engage in noble competition. The Athens Olympic Games will combine history, culture and peace, with sports and Olympism. The people of Greece shall host unique Games on a human scale, inspiring the world to celebrate Olympic values.

"Kallimarmaro" Stadium in Athens

will be positive effects on GDP as a result of investments in the country as well as in the creation of new jobs that are being created due to the Olympic Projects.

Preparations in the area of non-construction infrastructures are significant as well. These include telecommunications, promotion, marketing, tickets, human resources, volunteerism, education, culture and, of course, athletic preparation. The preparations are being made according to the practices used during the organisation of previous Games, especially after 1998, and irrespective of the historical advantages of our country.

Olympic Sports Projects

The first modern Olympic Games were held at the Panathinaiko Stadium, whose restoration and funding were undertaken by the great benefactor from Alexandria, George Averoff.

The events in the Olympic Games of 1896 were 15 in all. In the Olympic Games of 2004 there will be 37 events. These are aquatics, archery, artistic gymnastics, athletics, badminton, baseball, basketball, beach volleyball, boxing, canoe/kayak sprint, canoe/kayak slalom, diving, equestrian, fencing, football, gymnastics-trampoline, handball, hockey, judo, modern pentathlon, mountain biking, road cycling-time trial, rowing, sailing, shooting, softball, swimming, synchronised swimming, table tennis, tae-kwon-do, tennis, track cycling, triathlon, volleyball, water polo, weightlifting and wrestling

This great increase in the sports events from the first modern Olympic Games

Athens Olympic Sports Complex: the center of attraction for both the Olympic and Paraolympic Games

to the Games of 2004 makes it even more imperative to create new sports facilities as well as to upgrade the old ones.

A large project is the reconstruction of the Athens Olympic Sports Complex (OCO), which contains the Olympic Stadium. It could well be considered the heart of the Olympic Games of 2004. The stadium is situated in Maroussi and is part of the OCO. It can seat about 75,000 people and is expected to be overflowing with spectators from all over the world, who will assemble there to watch the athletics events and attend the Opening and Closing Ceremonies. Following the initiative taken by Athens 2004 in co-operation with the Ministry of Culture, the well-known architect, Santiago Calatrava was asked to re-design and upgrade the OCO in an innovative and creative way. The General Secretariat of Sports (GSS) is responsible

for the renovation and extension of the OCO.

The Olympic Tennis Centre is located in Maroussi and it also constitutes a part of the OCO. It includes the main tennis court, seating for 8,000, two courts for the semi-finals (seating 4,000 and 2000), and 13 courts seating 200 each. (The main court is completely new whereas the others will be renovated under the direction of the GSS).

The gymnastics event (trampoline and artistic) as well as the final phase of the basketball competition will be held in the OCO Indoor Arena. When the competitions are ready to be held, it will seat 15,000 spectators for basketball and 18,000 for gymnastics.

The Olympic Aquatic Centre at the OCO will be holding the swimming, water polo, synchronised swimming and diving competitions. The Centre consists of an outdoor swimming pool for water polo and swimming, seating 11,000 spectators, two more outdoor swimming pools and one more for synchronised swimming (seating 5000) and an indoor swimming pool, seating 6550 spectators, where the diving and water polo events are to be held. The GSS has undertaken to renovate the Centre and it will be ready by the end of 2003.

Track Cycling will be held at the Olympic Velodrome, which is expected to seat 5000 spectators, who will be able to watch the competition in the modern facilities of the Velodrome. The complete renovation is being done under the aegis of the GSS.

The Stadium of Peace and Friendship, in operation for the past two decades, is located on the Faliro shore and is indeed a fine model of modern architecture. It has acquired an enviable reputation due to the European and international championships held there as well as the professional and commercial exhibitions that draw large crowds of professionals and consumers. Its renovation is under the supervision of the GSS. The stadium seats 14,000 spectators and it will host the volleyball competitions.

The Faliro Olympic Sports Pavilion is another large-scale sports venue for the Olympic Games of 2004, the construction of which was initiated in early 2002 along the Faliro coastline. It will have two Indoor Arenas, seating 10,000 and 8,000 each. The Pavilion will host the boxing, tae-kwon-do and the hand-ball finals competitions. The Ministry of Public Works will have the project ready by early 2004.

The Olympic Beach Volleyball Centre in Faliro will consist of two brand new courts seating 10,000 and 4,000 each. All the beach volleyball games will be held there. The Olympic Games of 2004 will host this event for the first time.

The Helleniko Olympic Centre is expected to host Olympic events that are not particularly popular among Greeks, although the establishment of this Centre is especially important.

The Olympic Baseball Centre, which is part of the Helleniko Indoor Arena Centre, consists of two main fields, one seating 12,000 and the other 7,000, welcoming the international fans of this sport. The Ministry of Public Works will

have the project ready by January 2004.

The Olympic Softball Field will be constructed by the Ministry of Public Works and will seat 8500. This is a completely new construction, found right in the heart of the Olympic Complex of Helleniko and will be ready by early 2004.

The Olympic Hockey Centre is another new piece of construction, including a large rink, seating 15,000 and a smaller rink seating 5000. There will also be a training rink for the athletes participating in the hockey events. The Ministry of Public Works anticipates completing the project by January 2004.

Arenas 1 and 2 of the Helleniko Olympic Complex will host three world sports events - the basketball preliminaries and the handball finals will be held in Arena 1, which seats 15,000, whereas Arena 2 with two halls seating 3500 and 500 each) will host the fencing semi-finals and finals. The Ministry of Public Works will have completed the project by January 2004, after the additions and alterations to the existing facilities have been made according to Olympic specifications.

The Olympic Canoeing/Kayak Slalom Centre is also found at the Helleniko Olympic Complex where it will host 5000 fans of the Canoeing/kayak slalom. Its completion under the direction of the Ministry of Public Works is anticipated by January 2004. At the Olympic facilities at Marathonas, the sports event that has long been a tradition in Greece will begin. It is, of course, the Marathon Race, whose origins date back to Ancient Greece and is singularly significant to Greece, since it symbolises the revival of the Olympic Games. In the 1896 Olympic Games in the Marathon Race, Spyros Louis, a Greek, was the first Olympic Gold Medallist. From these facilities, the Marathon Race will begin, following, as in the 1896 Olympic Games, the same route that Pheidippides ran bearing the victory message that the Greeks had defeated the Persians in the Battle of Marathon. It covers a distance of 41 kilometres to Athens.

The Schinias Olympic Rowing and Canoeing Centre, near Marathonas will host the rowing and kayak races. It will accommodate 14,000 spectators. The lake being constructed there will be 2222 metres long and will be connected with an auxiliary lake for training.

Another important part of the programme is to be found at the Goudi Olympic Complex that is hosting the modern pentathlon and badminton events. The uniqueness of the modern pentathlon has made this project a challenge to construct. It will be able to accommodate 2000 swimming fans, 5000 equestrian and race fans as well as 4500 fencing and shooting fans.

The Panathinaiko Stadium, also known as the "Kallimarmaro" (made of fine marble) dominates the heart of Athens. It was this very stadium that hosted the first modern Olympic Games

Rowing race at the Schinias Olympic Rowing and Canoeing Centre

in 1896. It is a monument whose restoration begins "with the reshaping of the arena and the surrounding areas, new lighting and fire protection systems". Upon completion of the renovations, it will seat 45,000 spectators for the finish of the Marathon Race and 5500 fans for the archery competition.

The road cycling event will be held on the track of the Athens Olympic Complex. Its design and alterations have been undertaken by the GSS. The Athens 2004 committee will decide upon the final route in the centre of Athens by July 2004. Olympic specifications will be used during the alterations necessary for the route.

The Agios Kosmas Olympic Sailing Centre is located in the southern coastal area of Attiki. The construction is tempo-

rary and is to accommodate 3000 spectators. The Ministry of Public Works will complete it by January 2004. During the Olympic Games, the weather is expected to be favourable for the Sailing Competitions, both for the competitors and the spectators.

The Mountain Biking Events are to be held at the mountain biking facilities in Parnitha at Aharnes, near the centre of Athens and the Olympic Village. The GSS has undertaken to carry out the necessary works and will be ready by December 2003.

At the Vouliagmeni Olympic Centre the triathlon event (swimming, cycling and running) will be held. This centre is located on the southern coast of Attiki, in Vouliagmeni. 3000 temporary seats will be ready to accommodate the triathlon fans. The GSS has undertaken to carry out the necessary works and it will be ready by July 2004.

The Markopoulo Olympic Equestrian Centre is located in eastern Attiki and the GSS is responsible for its completion by December 2003. It covers an area of 21,000 square meters and is comprised of work areas, permanent and temporary stands, equestrian areas and stables for 300 horses. The public will have access to an internal transportation network and parking areas.

The Centre will have seating for 20,000 spectators for the hurdle jumping events, seating for 8000 for the equestrian skills event and 40,000 seats for the equestrian triathlon.

The Olympic Weightlifting Hall in Nikaia consists of a main arena seating 5000 and was one of the first projects of the GSS. This large project will have training and warm-up areas, hygiene and medical services, changing rooms and dormitories for the athletes, as well as areas for security, Press, services for the spectators and entertainment.

The wrestling and judo events will be held at the Ano Liosion Olympic Arena. The structure, covering an area of 35,000 square metres, will include warm-up and training areas, changing rooms, areas for medical and hygiene care, administration offices and National Federations Offices as well as Security Services, a Press Office, service areas for spectators, entertainment, etc. The GSS will have completed it by May 2003.

The Galatsi Olympic Arena will host the table tennis events (ping-pong) as

The Olympic Weightlifting Hall at Nikaia

well as rhythmic gymnastics. It will include a central building on an area of 32,000 square metres seating 6,000 with parking areas, access, etc. By August 2003 the GSS will have it finished.

In Markopoulo there is also the Olympic Shooting Centre on an area of about 12 hectares. It is comprised of four main buildings seating 8000 for the shooting events with moving and fixed targets. At the facilities there are restaurants, dormitories, indoor arenas for the finals, reception areas, Pressrooms, green areas and parking. The GSS is responsible for the completion by September 2003.

Athens may be the organising city for the Olympic Games of 2004, but there are other cities in Greece that will host events of the games. More specifically, there are football facilities in Patras (National Stadium), in Volos (Panthessaliko Stadium), in Thessaloniki (Kaftanzoglio Stadium), and in Iraklio (Pancretio Stadium).

At the National Stadium in Patras the world's favourite sport will be held, football. The Stadium will be upgraded under the auspices of the GSS according to Olympic specifications. It will be able to seat 17,000 spectators. Renovations are primarily being made to the electromechanical and electrical infrastructures and equipment. Parking facilities are to be included and the surrounding spaces are to be expanded. By the end of 2003 the stadium should be ready.

The Panthessaliko Stadium in Volos will host certain preliminary football events. The project entails the construction of two stadiums, the redesigning of the buildings and the stands into a new construction with 8 lanes of synthetic carpeting and is to seat 20,000 spectators. An auxiliary stadium of similar specifications is also to be built along with additional parking facilities. The GSS is supervising the project.

In Greece's second largest city, Thessaloniki some of the preliminary and semi-final football events are to be hosted. More specifically, these events will take place at the Kaftanzoglio Stadium that is very close to the centre of the city. The GSS will upgrade the existing facilities to seat 28,000 spectators and will upgrade the electrical infrastructure and equipment.

Finally, in Iraklio there is the Pancretio Stadium. It seats 27,000 and is to host football events in a renovated field that also includes other facilities (a swimming pool, a multi-purpose arena, administrative offices, etc) for post-Olympic use.

Technical Works

The designs of Calatrava highlight the main avenue of the OCO that leads from East to West and connects the Olympic Venues.

One of the more significant Olympic sights is a piece of sculpture, which symbolises the link between Ancient Greece and the Olympic Games and the Olympic Altar and is visible from all the OCO's venues.

The designs of S. Calatrava for the OCO

A new partial roof made from a nexus of beams will be added to the Olympic Stadium. The structure is of steel and welded sheets of glass supported by side arches and a central arch, while cross beams will hold it all together.

The Mall will consist of the Complex's pedestrian walkway that unites the various areas of the OCO. It will also be the central link of the various facilities, such as the Olympic Stadium, the tennis courts and Velodrome. The middle of the Mall and the tree grove will be altered into a central square in amphitheatre shape and will be used for amphitheatre-type and other events. In addition, spectators will be able to view the sports events from giant screens.

The Velodrome will be covered entirely by a steel and glass structure, which resembles that of the Olympic Stadium. As well, there will be a double arch linked by bowed arches covering the stadium completely.

On the Olympic Hill, which is next to the area of the Olympic Sponsors, the landscape is to be redesigned to offer a unique view of the whole Complex.

The Wall of Nations is a piece of sculpture, on which the names of all the participating nations are to be inscribed together with their flags. It will be constructed from steel and will be 340 metres long and 3 metres high. This sculpture was designed to make a wave-like movement, thus creating an impressive picture of light and light shades.

The first but also the last impressions visitors to the Complex will have are the domed entrances. These are steel structures supported by steel arches covered with welded sheets of glass.

The circulation lanes will be built next to the eastern and western entrances to the OCO to service the flow of traffic and the parking of public buses and the sponsors' buses as well as the vehicles of the Olympic family.

Calatrava's designs provide for pedestrian access from the Neratziotissa junction, the mobile steel structure of the Wall of Nations as well as outdoor facilities in the common areas of the OCO.

The Olympic and Paralympic Village

The Olympic and Paralympic Village is located at the foothills of Parnitha in Aharnes Municipality. It covers an area of 1240 square metres. The designs include ecological air conditioning to maintain an average temperature three degrees lower than the outside temperature and the building materials are all ecological.

16,000 athletes will be staying at the village throughout the Olympic Games of 2004 and 6000 athletes during the Paralympics.

With regard to security and accreditation, two areas have been set up:

- A residential Area
- An International Area

In the Village here will be outdoor athletic facilities (30,000 m^2), indoor arenas (3000 m^2), public utility facilities (80,000 m^2) including schools, day care centres for children, fire fighting services as well as 31,000 m^2 of paved roads for use of both areas.

After the end of the Olympic Games of 2004, the Workers Housing Organisation (OEK) which is responsible for the designing by "the Olympic Village AE" will use these residences for its beneficiaries.

The project is scheduled to be completed

Olympic village

and handed over to Athens 2004 in February 2004.

Basic Infrastructure Works

The road network in the region of Athens covers 16,000 kilometres. Of these, 2800 are basic arteries, which have been upgraded recently with these motorways:

Attiki Road with 31 junctions and is 64.6 km long. It links the two national roads and the new Eleftherios Venizelos Airport.

Poseidonos Avenue with the new measures in managing traffic will reduce traffic congestion between the centre of

Attiki Road, the Kathehaki junction

the city and the northern section of the coastal road of Athens, thus improving access to the Olympic Venues of Agios Kosmas and Helleniko.

Kifissos Avenue will be upgraded to become a proper motorway, and it will extend from Pireos Street to 'Attiki Road' as well as to Poseidonos Avenue on the coast. It will also be the principal transport route for the Olympic family and will link the Olympic Village, OCO and the other Olympic Venues located in the northern section of the city with the Faliro Olympic Sports Pavilion. It will be 15.2 kilometres long.

Vari-Koropi Avenue will be upgraded to a four-lane artery and will be extended by a by-pass road up to Attiki Road. It will also be the only link between the coastal zone and the area of Mesogia and the new international airport.

The suburban railway will be 32 kilometres long and will be the new public transport system to and from the airport. It will be the most reliable link between the airport and the areas surrounding the city of Athens. It will also be an alternative means of transport to many Olympic venues and will link with the OCO.

The tram has been designed in two phases. The first phase includes 23.6 kilometres servicing the coastal area from Glyfada to Neo Faliro connecting them to the centre of Athens. Both phases consist of 5 lines 41.6 kilometres long.

The Attiko Metro subway will be extended when Line 2 runs from Dafni

The new tramway

to Ilioupolis and from Sepolia to Agios Antonios and Line 3 runs from Ethniki Amyna to Stavros. The Stavros Station will link the suburban railway and the central bus area that will service the region of north-east Attiki.

Finally, the international Airport 'Elefterios Venizelos', which is located in Spata, opened officially on March 28, 2001, is expected to be the new southern gateway of Europe to the world. It is one of the largest infrastructure works ever built in Greece.

Environmental Principles and Environmental Programmes

1. Environmental Principles:

- The use of new technology and saving of energy: Reduction in energy consumption with compatible fuels, pollution control, maximisation of energy autonomy of the venues and reduction in operational expenditure of energy.

- Use of environment friendly materials and practices: Selection and use of environment friendly solutions and materials/ products to build the infrastructures and adaptations as well as the practices and activities of Athens 2004.

- Bio-diversity: enhancement and protection of bio-diversity by redesign-

ing the spaces or through interventions, especially in the Olympic Village, the Olympic Velodrome in Schinias as well as in the Faliro Sports Pavilion.

- The contribution in the enhancement of the environmental performance of the Sponsors and Licensees: Enhancement of the environmental performances of the Sponsors and Licensees before and during the Games, and after their completion.

- "Green Athens": Enhancement of the landscape of the greater area of Athens, protection and enhancement of natural resources and rational management of water resources by introducing a water management system and water recycling methods for irrigation.

- Use of public transport systems: the Olympic Village as well as all the competition and non-competition venues will benefit from the use of environment-friendly vehicles, public transport management and environment-friendly maintenance practices of the fleet of vehicles.

- Waste management: Development of a waste management policy by using specific recycling practices, minimisation of the use of materials with negative effects on the environment during their lives.

2. Environmental Programmes

- A Network of Sponsors for the Environment: assurance that the planning and protection of products conforms to the certification systems for the environment and wherever possible to include messages aiming at shaping environmental awareness.

- Programme for the Environmental Management of the Olympic Venues: Securing effective control and monitoring of environmental performances of all competition and non-competition venues.

- Creation of an Olympic Environmental Alliance: Establishment of co-operation between the agents of the public and private sector, Local Government Organisations, social groups, Academies and Industrial Societies and Non-Governmental Organisations to guarantee measures, equipment and assistance in environmental works.

- Agenda 21 of the Olympic Movement: a framework that was adopted by the IOC to promote environment-friendly athletic practices and environmental achievements of the International Athletic Federations and other Olympic Agencies.

- Environmental Education and awareness: it includes an intensive educational programme for all those connected with the Games, regardless of capabilities to safeguard their desire to incorporate elements that manifest the development of an environmental conscience in their everyday activities.

Dimitris Papaioannou was born in Athens in 1964. He studied painting next to Giannis Tsarouchis. He became a comic artist and a performance art artist. In 1986, he and Angeliki Stellatou founded Edafos Dance Theatre, directing all productions. Director of big-scale live concerts and operas. In 2002 he was appointed Creator of the Opening and Closing Ceremonies of the ATHENS 2004 Olympic Games.

The two mascots of the 2004 Olympic Games

Phevos and Athena are two children of modern times, brother and sister. Just like their creation came from an ancient Greek doll, their names are linked to ancient Greece.

The boy holds the name of the mythical Greek God Apollo-Phevos (Phoebus), God of Light and Music. The girl holds the name of Athena, sister of Phevos (Phoebus) and Goddess of Wisdom.

In this way, Phevos and Athena represent the link between Greek history and the modern Olympic Games.

At the same time Phevos and Athena represent the values that the Olympic Spirit stands for: Through the joy of play-the joy of the games - these two children will show the true value of participation regardless of victory.

A brother and a sister, as symbols of the Olympic Ideal: the brotherhood of all men and women around the world. A boy and a girl, ambassadors not only of co-operation and fair play, but also of equality.

And principally, two children that show the everlasting Greek value of human scale and remind us that the heart of the Olympic Games, is and will remain man himself.

THE OLYMPIC TRUCE:
An ancient concept for the new millennium

By S. Lamrinides

The international Olympic Truce initiative is based on the Greek concept of Olympic Truce, or *"Ekecheiria"*. In Ancient Greece, the King of Elis, addresses the oracle at Delphi, seeking a way to end the wars that at the time devastated the Peloponnese.

According to the myth, Apollo replies "Ifitos and the Elians should restore the sports contests" in Olympia, as a celebration of peace. Ifitos proceeds to establish the Olympic Games and signs, along with Lycourgos of Sparta and Cleosthenes of Pisa, the longest-standing peace accord in history, the Olympic Truce.

Thus the sacred Greek tradition of *"Ekecheiria"* was in the 8th century BC and served as a cornerstone of the Olympic Games. Throughout the duration of the Olympic Truce, from the seventh day prior to the opening of the Games to the seventh day following their closing, all conflicts ceased. This allowed athletes, artists and spectators to travel to Olympia, participate in the Games and return to their homelands in safety.

For twelve centuries, the Olympic Truce is observed. The Olympic Games develop into landmarks of human creativity and excellence. They become the

Λάβετε θέσεις, έτοιμοι... παύσατε πυρ!

www.olympictruce.org

Διεθνές Κέντρο **Ολυμπιακής Εκεχειρίας**
Ολυμπία Λωζάννη Αθήνα

stage for the universal celebration of mutual understanding and noble competition.

Making it happen

Today, there is a strong move underway to revive the Olympic Truce. Its aim is to encourage nations to observe the Olympic Truce and to cease hostilities during the Olympic Games and beyond. Its hope is to create a much-needed window of opportunity for the peaceful resolution of conflict. To promote this goal, in July 2000, the International Olympic Committee founded the International Olympic Truce Centre, in a joint initiative with Greece.

The symbolic seat of the Centre is in Olympia, the birthplace of Olympics. Athens, where the first Olympic Games of the Modern era took place in 1896, and host city of the 2004 Olympic Games, houses the Centre's administrative headquarters. The Centre's liaison office is in Lausanne, where the International Olympic Committee is based.

The Centre's mission is to help promote the Olympic Ideals, to serve peace, friendship and international understanding. Through a multitude of programs and activities, it aims to uphold the observance of the Olympic Truce, calling for all hostilities to cease during the Olympic Games and beyond and mobilising the youth of the world in the cause of peace. Initiatives in favour of the Olympic Truce are a partnership.

They gain momentum with the active support of the members of the Olympic Family, international and national organisations and non-governmental organisations that all contribute to the cause of peace.

The United Nations has supported this effort through numerous Resolutions since 1993 and calls on all countries of the world to co-operate in the observance of the Olympic Truce and to give peace a chance. In addition, by early 2003, over 200 personalities from the world of politics, culture and religion had expressed their support for the Olympic Truce. These include heads of State and Government from conflict and non-conflict regions, Foreign Ministers, Nobel Prize winners such as Nelson Mandela, the Ecumenical Patriarch and the Pope of Rome.

Conflict will not cease overnight. But if we can stop fighting for 16 days, maybe we can do it forever.

Milestones of the Olympic Truce

776 BC: The ancient Olympic Games establish the *Ekecheiria* (Olympic Truce)

1894: The International Olympic Committee is established, with the goal of contributing to the peaceful power of sport and the Olympic Ideal in the beginning of a new era. The International Olympic Committee calls upon the international community to observe the Olympic Truce.

1896: Athens organises the first Olympic Games of the modern era.

1994: The Olympic Winter Game in Lillehammer, Norway, revive hope in conflict-torn Sarajevo, host city of the 1984 Olympic Winter Games. After co-ordinated diplomatic efforts, an International Olympic Committee delegation headed by its president has the opportunity to visit the city and extend its solidarity to the population.

1995: The resolution of the 50th Session of the United Nations General Assembly supports the idea of building a peaceful and better world through sport and the Olympic Ideal.

1996: The "Athens 2004" bid committee makes a commitment to revive the Olympic Truce and to promote it in the world through the Olympic Flame Relay.

1992: The Olympic Movement activates the peaceful power of sport and the Olympic Ideal in the beginning of a new era. The International Olympic Committee calls upon the International community to observe the Olympic Truce.

1993: During its 48th Session, the United Nations General Assembly urges its Member States to observe the Olympic Truce.

1997: The 52nd Session of the United Nations General Assembly adopts a resolution on the observance of the Olympic Truce during the Olympic Winter Games in Nagano in 1998.

1998: Greek Minister for Foreign Affairs George Papandreou presents the proposal of Greece for the institutional consolidation of the Olympic Truce in the new millennium to the members of the International Olympic Committee.

1998: During the Nagano Winter

Games, tensions in the Persian Gulf region are high. The observance of the Olympic Truce according to United Nations resolutions offers an opportunity to United Nations Secretary General Kofi Annan to intervene and seek a diplomatic resolution to the crisis in Iraq.

1999: 180 United Nations Member-States, a record number, co-sponsor a resolution to support the observance of the Olympic Truce during the Games of the XDVII Olympiad in Sydney Australia.

2000: The International Olympic Truce Foundation and the International Truce Centre are founded.

2000: World leaders include a special paragraph in the United Nations Millennium Summit Report in support of the Olympic Truce.

2000: North and South Korea march together under one flag during the Opening Ceremony of the games of the XXVII Olympiad in Sydney, Australia.

2001: The 56th Session of the UN General Assembly adopts a resolution on the Olympic truce in preparation for the Olympic Winter Games in Salt Lake City.

2002: The collection of signatures by international personalities in support of the Olympic Truce is launched in Ancient Olympia. Within a few months, over 200 Heads of State and Government and numerous political, religious and civic leaders support this call.

2004: The Olympic Games return to Greece, their birthplace. The symbolic Olympic Truce appeal is once again launched world-wide for the Athens games and for all future Olympic Games.

THE CULTURAL OLYMPIAD

By Eug. Giannakopoulos

In 1997 Athens was selected to host the 2004 Olympic Games. While undertaking the organisation of the upcoming Olympics, Greece also took on the responsibility of forming a new Olympic architecture to be bequeathed to the generations to come and to become a landmark in the history of the Olympic Ideal and the Olympic Movement.

As part of the organisation of the 2004 Olympics, Greece also designed and set up the Cultural Olympiad.

In addition to the close co-operation with the International Olympics Committee and Athens 2004, the Cultural Olympiad is also linked to UNESCO, the UN and all the countries of the world. Within this framework the International Foundation of the Cultural Olympiad was founded in 1998 by the Greek Minister of Culture Professor Evangelos Venizelos, the former President of the International Olympic Committee Juan Antonio Samarang and Federico Mayor, former Director-General of UNESCO. The headquarters are in ancient Olympia and its aim is to promote the institution of the Cultural Olympiad world-wide as a dynamic and integral part of the Olympic Games.

The Cultural Olympiad focuses on the creative coexistence of the timeless ideals of democracy, humanism, universality, harmony and moderation. At the same time it stresses the obvious interdependence between the universal ideals of state and democracy, religion and equality, science and progress, and art and creativity. Incorporating all the above, the Cultural Olympiad creates its particular environment and system of principles that both honour and are honoured by timeless Greek and world-wide values and ideals.

The Structure of the Cultural Olympiad

The Cultural Olympiad consists of three branches: its programme of events, its symbolic initiatives and its role as an international institution.

The programme of events includes a variety of expressions of cultural creativity. These events take place both in Greece and in other countries, underscoring both the elements that world cultures share but also the particularities of each national culture.

The symbolic initiatives have to do with the culture of everyday life under the conditions we experience today. These initiatives are taken in fields concerning major problems and critical deficiencies in today's societies and their main aim is to point towards these problems and crises and set an example for future action.

The Cultural Olympiad's symbolic initiatives convey the message of civilisation, solidarity, peace and social cohesion. They take place both on the national and international level and attempt, taking advantage of the excellent opportunity offered by the scope of an international organisation, to spark lasting human values. The initiatives include original actions whose practical effect may be limited, yet contain a developmental dynamic for the country and institution concerned. Consequently, the Cultural Olympiad 2001-2004 has planned and will carry out ten such initiatives mainly in fields concerning human survival, quality of life and international cultural and environmental heritage. One of these initiatives includes co-operating with UNICEF, a collaboration that has already been officially announced by both parties. The Cultural Olympiad will allocate the sum of $7m for the vaccination of 1,400,000 children from underdeveloped countries plagued by childhood mortality.

The Cultural Olympiad's Function as an International Institution

This branch of the Cultural Olympiad consists of a number of actions that illustrate and establish the institution on an international level. The actions are the main line that links the activities of the institution with the international community, allowing for world-wide appeal.

These actions are organised by the guardian of the institution, which is the International Foundation of the Cultural Olympiad. It includes the International Kotinos and Kouros-Kore Awards, the International Committee that oversees and organises the award procedure, and the National Committees of the countries that attend, which are linked to and participate in the Cultural Olympiad.

The Hellenic Culture Organisation SA has undertaken the planning, the implementation and the promotion of the Cultural Olympiad 2001-2004.

Report for 2001-2002

In the two-year span from 2001-2002 the Cultural Olympiad organised the following actions:

1. The programme framework was put together and publicised;

2. The organisational body (Hellenic Culture Organisation SA) was organised, staffed and set into motion;

3. Proposals submitted for the programme of events were processed;

4. 48 programmes of events were carried out and attended by approximately 600,000 people;

5. The cost of the 2001-2004 programme totalled €23m;

6. The first communication campaign

was planned and implemented;

7. The design of the format of the Cultural Olympiad international institution was revised and finalised;

8. The International Committee carrying out the awards procedure and the National Committees for the Cultural Olympiad were set up.

Cultural Olympiad Programme of Events for 2003-2004

The following exhibitions have been scheduled:

1. THE TAURUS IN THE MEDITERRANEAN - MYTHS AND CULTS (BARCELONA, History Museum, 14/11/02 - 06/03/03 and ATHENS, Benaki Museum, 19/03/03 - 07/06/03)

2. MINOAN AND MYCENAEAN FLAVORS (STOCKHOLM, Mediterranean Museum, 07/02/03 - 29/06/03)

3. THE COSTUMES OF THE GREEK NATIONAL THEATRE (ATHENS, National Gallery, February - May 2003)

4. SEA ROUTES: FROM SIDON TO HUELVA (ATHENS, Museum of Cycladic Art, May - September 2003)

5. ALEXANDER THE GREAT (TOKYO, National Museum, 02/08/03 - 05/10/03 and KOBE, Hyogo Prefectural Museum of Modern Art, 18/10/03 - 03/12/03)

6. UNDER THE LIGHT OF APOLLO (ATHENS, National Gallery, 22/10/03 - 29/02/04)

7. OUTLOOK (ATHENS, Benaki Museum on Piraios Street, Gazi, Athens School of Fine Arts "The Factory", 24/10/03 - 25/01/04)

8. PERIPLES, PHOTOGRAPHIC ITINERARIES INTO CONTEMPORARY GREECE (ATHENS and THESSALONIKI, October - November 2003 and on tour in four cities abroad, 2004)

9. THE ART OF THE OTHER (ATHENS, December 2003 - March 2004)

10. ARCO (MADRID, 11 - 17/02/04)

11. PICASSO: GREEK INFLUENCES (ANDROS, The V. & E. Goulandri Museum of Modern Art, June - September 2004)

12. PLEATS: FROM ANCIENT GREEK CLOTHING TO 21ST CENTURY FASHION (ATHENS, Benaki Museum in Piraios Street, June - September 2004)

13. AUSTRALIA: INDIGENOUS AUSTRALIA NOW (ATHENS, Benaki

Picasso: Greek Influences

Museum on Piraeos Street,
June - September 2004)

14. THE ATHLETIC SPIRIT IN AN-
CIENT GREECE (ATHENS, National
Archaeological Museum,
June - September 2004)

15. SIX EUROPEAN SCULPTORS
CONVERSE WITH MAN
(ATHENS, National Gallery,
June - September 2004)

16. HENRY MOORE RETROSPEC-
TIVE (GOUDI, National Gallery premises, June - September 2004)

17. NEW MUSEUM OF ISLAMIC
ART: THE EXHIBITION (ATHENS,
Benaki Museum in Piraeos Street,
June 2004)

The following music events have
been scheduled:

1. TWO CENTURIES OF ART
MUSIC (May 2003)

2. SACRED MUSIC (ATHENS,
THESSALONIKI and 40 SACRED
PLACES AROUND GREECE,
05 - 11/07/03 and OLYMPIA, 13/07/03)

3. DELOS 2003 (DELOS, 13/09/03)

4. OPERA OF THE EARTH
(ATHENS, Athens Concert Hall,
December 2003)

5. MOTHER COURAGE (ATHENS,
Athens Concert Hall, Spring, 2004)

6. PHILIP GLASS (ATHENS and
THESSALONIKI, June 2004)

7. A CELEBRATION OF THE WORK
OF MANOS HADJIDAKIS
(ATHENS, June 2004)

The following theatrical performances have been scheduled:

1. TROJAN WOMEN - HECUBA
(ROME, Tor Vergata University,
26/06/03)

2. GREEK THEATRICAL
MONOLOGUES (ATHENS and
THESSALONIKI, September 2003)

3. GREEK SHADOW PUPPET
THEATRE, FIGURES MADE OF LIGHT
AND HISTORY (ATHENS,
15/03 - 09/05/04)

4. INTERNATIONAL THEATRICAL
MONOLOGUES (MIKRI EPIDAUROS,
May - June 2004)

5. OEDIPUS REX (ATHENS,
Herod Atticus Odeon, 01- 03/07/04)

6. GREEK ART THEATRE -
KAROLOS KOUN: ARISTOPHANES

From an event on sacred music

(EPIDAURUS, June 2004)

The following dance performances have been scheduled:

1. AMERICAN BALLET THEATER (NEW YORK, Metropolitan Opera House, 20/05/03, ATHENS - Herod Atticus Odeon, 06 - 07/07/03 and THESSALONIKI, 10-11/07/03)

2. ROYAL ACADEMY OF DANCE: THE COMPETITION (ATHENS, Herod Atticus Odeon, 29 - 30/05/04)

3. NETHERLANDS DANCE THEATER (ATHENS, Herod Atticus Odeon, 24 - 25/06/04, THESSALONIKI, 28 - 29/06/04)

In the field of literature, the Cultural Olympiad has scheduled the following:

1. CAVAFY 1863 - 1933 (THESSALONIKI, ATHENS, ALEXANDRIA, ISTANBUL, April-June 2003, October 2003)

2. THE GLOBAL NOVEL (ATHENS, 2003)

3. KAZANTZAKIS (CRETE, March - May 2004)

In the field of architecture, the Cultural Olympiad has scheduled the INTERNATIONAL ARCHITECTURE COMPETITION "EPHEMERAL STRUCTURES IN THE CITY OF ATHENS" (ATHENS, Byzantine Museum, 31/01/03 - 28/02/03)

The following audio-visual events have been scheduled:

1. PARTHENON (NEW YORK, May 2003)

2. THE PANORAMA OF EUROPEAN CINEMA (ATHENS, 10 - 16/10/03)

3. THE GREEK MYTHS IN THE MOVIES (ATHENS, THESSALONIKI, PATRAS, VOLOS, HERAKLEION, Autumn, 2003, and BERLIN, PARIS,

The Netherlands Dance Theater group

*The Greek Myths
in the Movies*

LONDON, BOLOGNA, Winter-Spring 2004)

Concerning contemporary digital culture, the event ART ON THE NET: AN INTERNATIONAL COMPETITION (Autumn, 2003) has been programmed.

The following meetings have been scheduled:

1. GLOBALISATION AND CULTURE - THE ROADS OF PEACE (NICOSIA, KYKKOS MONASTERY, 02 - 05/05/03)

2. MEETING ON BIOETHICS (ATHENS, October 2003)

Finally, as part of the major events, the following have been scheduled:

1. THE LABOURS OF HERCULES (MOSCOW, September 2003)

2. AGORA (IN 68 CITIES AND TOWNS AROUND GREECE and the BALKANS, 17/07/03 - 06/06/04)

PHOTO AND PICTURE CREDITS

Special Thanks to:

- The Presidency of the Hellenic Republic
- Hellenic Parliament's Museum
- Prime Minister's Office
- Ministry of Culture
- Ministry of the Environment, Urban Planning and Public Works
- Ministry of Interior, Public Administration and Decentralisation
- Ministry of Development: Secratariat General for Research and Technology
- Ministry of Labor and Social Affairs
- Ministry of Health and Welfare
- Ministry of Transport and Communications
- Ministry of Merchant Marine
- General Secretariat of Sports
- Ministry of Culture: General Secretariat for the Olympic Games
- New Democracy Party
- Organizing Committee for the Olympic Games "Athens 2004"
- Cultural Olympiad
- International Olympic Truce Center
- The Athens News Agency (ANA)
- Municipality of Athens
- Municipality of Thessaloniki
- Greek Ombudsman
- General Confederation of Greek Labour (G.S.E.E)
- Research Center for Gender Equality (KETHI)
- National Hellenic Research Foundation
- Hellenic Tourist Organization
- Social Insurance Foundation (IKA)
- Agricultural Insurance Agency
- National Bank of Greece
- Greek Telecommunication Organization (OTE)
- Piraeus Port Authority
- Unification of the Archeological Sites of Athens S.A.
- Public Gas Corporation
- Athens Airport "Eleftherios Venizelos"
- Attiko Metro S.A.
- Egnatia Odos S.A.
- Tram S.A.
- Gefyra S.A.
- Athena Kazolea, photographer, for L. Voyiatzis' photo

- G. Ventouris, photographer, for the photo of Idravlis
- S. Psiroukis, photographer for the photo of the National Gallery
- Thessaloniki's International Fair (HELEXPO)
- National Book Center
- The European Cultural Center at Delphi
- Greek Cinema Center
- Athens Concert Hall
- National Gallery of Athens
- National Theatre of Athens
- Acropolis Museum
- Athens Museum of Byzantine and Christian Art
- Thessaloniki's Museum of Byzantine Culture
- Goulandris Museum of Natural History
- Athens National Archaeological Museum
- Museum of Cycladic Art
- Vorres Museum of Modern Greek Art
- Benakis Museum
- Athens Numismatic Museum
- Museum of Greek Folk Art
- Theatre Museum
- Peloponnesian Folklore Foundation
- Children's Museum
- Railway Museum
- The National Broadcasting Corporation (Hellenic Radio Television - E.R.T.)
- MEGA Channel • ANT1 TV • ALPHA TV • STAR Channel • ALTER Channel

Photos reproduced from Books:
- "The Acropolis Restoration". Academy Editions. London 1994.
- "To Agion Oros". Ekdotiki Athinon Editions. Athens 1979
- "Neoelliniki Architectoniki" by D. Philippidis. Melissa Editions. Athens 1984
- "Architecture in Greece". Annual review. Athens 1998
- "1926-1977, Architecture in Creece Press" by T. C. Zenetos. Athens 1978
- "Public Architecture in Modern Greece, 1827-1942". Papasotiriou Editions. Athens 1993
- "Landscapes of modernnisation" by Y. Aesopos, Y. Simeoforidis. Metapolis Press Editions. Athens 1999.
- "The Nature of Postwar Art in Greece" by Eleni Vakalo. Kedros Editions. Athens 1982.
- "The Greek Painters". Melissa Editions. Athens 1976
  Assistance received from other government departments and organizations
  is gratefully acknowledged.

LIST OF CONTRIBUTORS

- **Petmezas, S.**, Assistant Professor, University of Crete.
- **Chryssanthakis, C.**, Professor, University of Athens
- **Lyrintzis, Ch.**, Professor, University of Athens.
- **Nikolakopoulos, El.**, Professor, University of Athens.
- **Metaxas, An.-J.**. Professor, University of Athens.
- **Spanou, C.**, Associate Professor, University of Athens.
- **Hlepas, N.-K.**, Assistant Professor, University of Athens.
- **Tassopoulos, J.**, Assistant Professor, University of Athens.
- **Stephanou, C.**, Professor, Panteion University, Athens.
- **Tsinisizelis, M.**, Professor, University of Athens.
- **Ifantis, K.**, Associate Professor, University of Athens.
- **Chryssochoou, D.**, Associate Professor, University of Crete.
- **Dollis, D.**, Secretary General for International Economic Relations and Development Cooperation, Ministry of Foreign Affaires.
- **Kazakos, P.**, Professor, University of Athens.
- **Liargovas, P.**, Associate Professor, University of Peloponnese.
- **Samiotis, G.**, University of Piraeus.
- **Vlachos, G. P.**, University of Piraeus.
- **Tselentis, B., S.**, University of Piraeus.
- **Komnenides, N.**, Director of Special Service for Planning and Evaluation of Regional Policy and programmes, Ministry of Finance.
- **Dr Kostopoulou M.**, Head of Strategic Planning and Analysis Unit, Ministry of Finance.
- **Yfantopoulos, Y.**, Professor, University of Athens.
- **Koukoules, G.**, Professor, Panteion University, Athens.
- **Dr Aranitou V.**, Economist. Advisor to the National Confederation of Helenic Commerce.

- **Dr Yannakourou, M.**, Attorney-at-Law. Advisor to the Economic and Social Council of Greece.

- **Adam, Chr.**, Senior Investigator at the Greek Ombudsman

- **Diamantouros, N.**, Professor, University of Athens, European Ombudsman

- **Dr Defigou, M.**, Educational Sociologist. Director of "Ergon" Vocational Training.

- **Pantelidou-Maloutas M.**, Professor, University of Athens.

- **Mertziou, E.**, Forester and Environmentalist.

- **Kaftanzoglou, J.**, Assistant Professor, University of Athens.

- **Cassapoglou, V. G.**, Lawyer, Executive Director, Greek Centre of Space, Science and Technology.

- **Papathanassopoulos, S.** , Associate Professor, University of Athens

- **Dr Drakondaidis, Phil. D.**, Author.

- **Deffner, Al.**, Assistant Professor, University of Thessaly.

- **Panetsos, G.**, Professor, University of Patras.

- **Dr Stephanidis, M.**, Curator, National Gallery.

- **Dr Athanassopoulou, An.**, Art Historian, Council of the European Union, Geneva Liaison Office.

- **Georgoussopoulou, Ev.**, Archivist at the Theatre Museum of Arhens.

- **Dr Kaftantzoglou, R.**, Social Anthropologist, Researcher, National Centre of Social Research.

- **Kabouropoulos, S.**, Senior Officer, National Book Centre of Greece.

- **Konidaris, J.**, Professor, University of Athens.

- **Daskalaki-Angelopoulos, G.**, President, Athens 2004.

- **Aivaliotou, M.**, General Director of Urban Planning.

- **Lambrinides, S.**, Ambassador; Director, International Centre of Olympic Truce.

- **Giannakopoulos, Eug.**, President of Cultural Olympiad